Asian/Oceanian Historical Dictionaries
Edited by Jon Woronoff

Asia

1. *Vietnam,* by William J. Duiker. 1989
2. *Bangladesh,* by Craig Baxter and Syedur Rahman, second edition. 1996
3. *Pakistan,* by Shahid Javed Burki. 1991
4. *Jordan,* by Peter Gubser. 1991
5. *Afghanistan,* by Ludwig W. Adamec. 1991
6. *Laos,* by Martin Stuart-Fox and Mary Kooyman. 1992
7. *Singapore,* by K. Mulliner and Lian The-Mulliner. 1991
8. *Israel,* by Bernard Reich. 1992
9. *Indonesia,* by Robert Cribb. 1992
10. *Hong Kong and Macau,* by Elfed Vaughan Roberts, Sum Ngai Ling, and Peter Bradshaw. 1992
11. *Korea,* by Andrew C. Nahm. 1993
12. *Taiwan,* by John F. Copper. 1993
13. *Malaysia,* by Amarjit Kaur. 1993
14. *Saudi Arabia,* by J. E. Peterson. 1993
15. *Myanmar,* by Jan Becka. 1995
16. *Iran,* by John H. Lorentz. 1995
17. *Yemen,* by Robert D. Burrowes. 1995
18. *Thailand,* by May Kyi Win and Harold Smith. 1995
19. *Mongolia,* by Alan J. K. Sanders. 1996
20. *India,* by Surjit Mansingh. 1996
21. *Gulf Arab States,* by Malcolm C. Peck. 1996
22. *Syria,* by David Commins. 1996
23. *Palestine,* by Nafez Y. Nazzal and Laila A. Nazzal. 1997
24. *Philippines,* by Artemio R. Guillermo and May Kyi Win. 1997

Oceania

1. *Austrialia,* by James C. Docherty. 1992
2. *Polynesia,* by Robert D. Craig. 1993
3. *Guam and Micronesia,* by William Wuerch and Dirk Ballendorf. 1994

4. *Papua New Guinea,* by Ann Turner. 1994
5. *New Zealand,* by Keith Jackson and Alan McRobie. 1996

New Combined Series (July 1996)

25. *Historical Dictionary of Brunei Darussalam,* by D. S. Ranjit Singh and Jatswan S. Sidhu. 1997
26. *Historical Dictionary of Sri Lanka,* by S. W. R. de A. Samarsinghe and Vidyamali Samarsinghe. 1997

Historical Dictionary of Palestine

Nafez Y. Nazzal
and
Laila A. Nazzal

Asian/Oceanian Historical Dictionaries, No. 23

The Scarecrow Press, Inc.
Lanham, MD. & London
1997

SCARECROW PRESS, INC.

Published in the United States of America
by Scarecrow Press, Inc.
4720 Boston Way
Lanham, Maryland 20706

4 Pleydell Gardens, Folkestone
Kent CT20 2DN, England

British Cataloguing in Publication Information Available

Library of Congress Cataloging-in-Publication Data

Nazzal, Nafez.
Historical dictionary of Palestine / by Nafez Y. Nazzal and Laila A. Nazzal.
p. cm.—(Asian historical dictionaries ; no. 22)
Includes bibliographical references.
ISBN 0-8108-3239-9
1. Palestine—History—Dictionaries. 2. Jewish-Arab relations—Dictionaries. 3. Israel-Arab conflicts—Dictionaries. I. Nazzal, Laila A., 1952– . II. Title. III. Series.
DS102.8.N397 1997
956.94′003—dc20 96-30594
CIP

ISBN 0-8108-3239-9

∞ ™ The paper used in this publication meets the minimum requirements of American National Standard for Information Sciences—Permanence of Paper for Printed Library Materials, ANSI Z39.48—1984.
Manufactured in the United States of America.

To Yousef and Rami

Contents

Editor's Foreword

It is not as frequent nowadays that a new state is born. But Palestine is an exception. And it always has been. Its very birth was exceptional. For decades consisting of a people, living on various bits of land and abroad, long without international recognition, it has faced one hardship after another. Now that it is a state, it will face many more. Still, its people have shown uncommon fortitude in the struggle for independence, and should be able to face the challenges of maintaining peace, developing the economy, running a government and getting along with their neighbors and the rest of the international community.

Appearing so soon after statehood, this *Historical Dictionary of Palestine* should be one of the most useful in the series. It provides information on significant persons, places, parties, and movements, institutions and aspects of the economy and culture. It also traces the historical background and shows initial efforts of the new state. The maze of acronyms is sorted out in a special list, and the shifting boundaries are tracked in several maps. Particularly important, for those who want to know more, there is a comprehensive bibliography classified according to essential topics.

This book was written by two Palestinian academics, Nafez and Laila Nazzal. Both were born in Palestine, studied locally and then abroad, later taught in various institutions, including Birzeit University and presently, the Jerusalem Center for Near Eastern Studies of Brigham Young University. Both have lectured and written widely, Nafez Nazzal being the author of *The Palestinian Exodus from the Galilee*, 1948. Together they have produced an accessible and insightful guide to one of the youngest states in one of the most historic regions.

Jon Woronoff
Series Editor

User's Notes

We have concentrated on individuals, events, factions, and institutions that have a historical, political, and social significance in the shaping of the nascent Palestinian State. Omitting the Palestinians in Israel and those in exile is not to slight them in any way, but we have primarily focused our attention on the Palestinians in the Occupied Territories and the autonomous areas.

Persons are entered in this dictionary under the last or family names, with the exception of those whose first names are common: Abdallah, King, for example. Titles, such as *Sheikh* or *Mufti*, are not considered part of a person's name, and names have not been alphabetized in accordance to titles. For example, Sheikh Mohammad Al-Ja'bari is entered as Al-Ja'bari, Mohammad Ali, Sheikh. Definite articles that are part of a name are not taken into account in the alphabetization of the entries. Hence, al-Husseini, Faisal is entered under the "H". Definite articles within the entry itself are sometimes used; other times are not. Definite articles also are usually capitalized, as in the heading of the entry, but may appear in lower case in the entry itself. Moreover, the Arabic definite article "al" or "el" is used interchangeably. The alphabetization of entries are word-by-word, as in:

General Union of Palestinian Students
General Union of Palestinian Women's Committees
General Union of Women's Struggle Committees

It is customary in Arab society to publicly call a man and a woman by the name of their firstborn son, by using the honorific Abu or Um, meaning father of, or mother of, followed by the name of the son. Hence, Abu 'Ali is the father of 'Ali, and Um 'Ali is the mother of Ali. This naming system is also used by members of the Palestinian factions as their pseudonyms. In the entries, the nom de guerre is placed after the individual's name when it functions as the alias. If the Abu is part of the name, then it is considered a single word in the alphabetization order. For example:

Abu Ghazaleh, Hatem
Abu Hilal, Ali
Abu Lughod, Ibrahim

Furthermore, to facilitate matters for the reader, "Palestine" is used after a city or a village if the date refers to pre-1948. There is no exact transliteration of Arabic names and terms, and names of persons, places, or events are often spelled differently. Every attempt has been made to check the spelling, and entries are entered under the general and most widely accepted spellings. Wherever possible, persons have been asked for the preferred spelling of their names.

Moreover, to simplify matters, we have not used diacritical marks. Common names (Arafat, for instance), terms, and events also have been transliterated without the guttural aspirate (ayn), often represented by an apostrophe, if they regularly appear in the press, and people are familiar with them. However, where it is considered necessary for an uncommon name or term, it is placed at the beginning or between two vowels or consonants; hence, Shak'a. Most Arabic terms have been italicized. We have not, however, italicized Arabic terms that appear as key entries, nor Arabic terms that are part of a person's name, i.e. Sheikh Ahmad Yassin.

The duplication of information is inevitable in a work of this type. To reduce repetition as much as possible, and to help the reader locate information, we have employed extensive cross-references. We have used "q.v." and the plural "qq.v." following names, places, and events.

We are grateful to PASSIA for allowing the use of the maps in this dictionary.

Maps

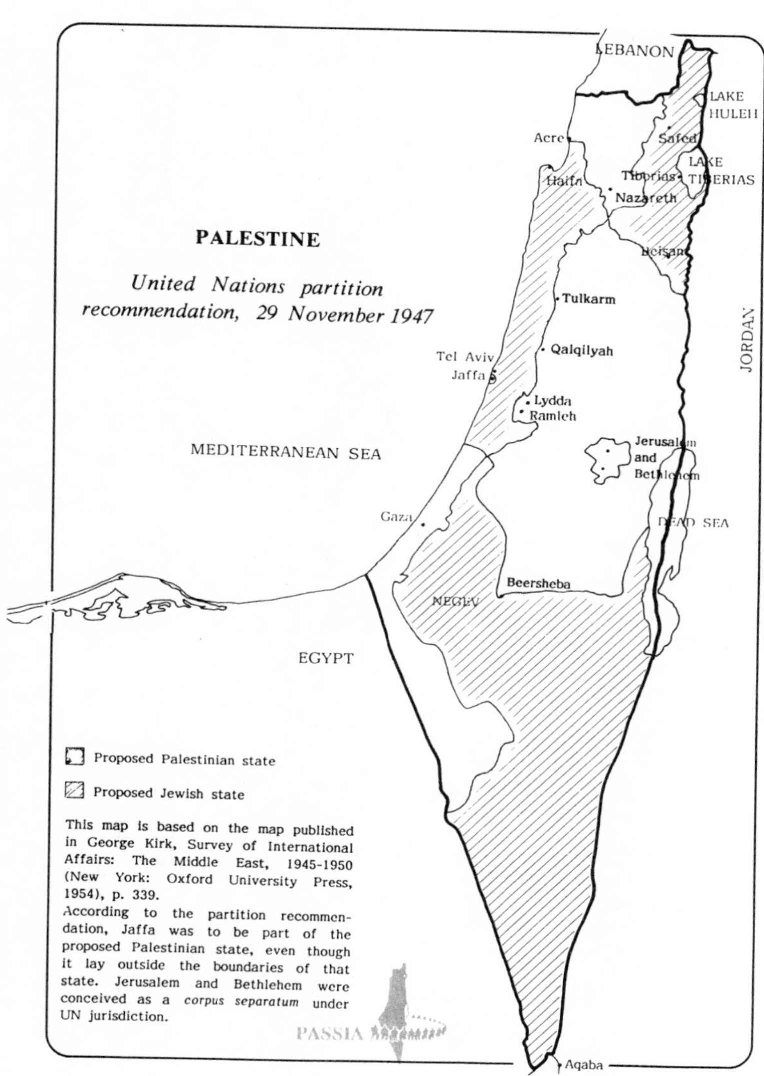

This map is based on the map published in George Kirk, Survey of International Affairs: The Middle East, 1945-1950 (New York: Oxford University Press, 1954), p. 339.

According to the partition recommendation, Jaffa was to be part of the proposed Palestinian state, even though it lay outside the boundaries of that state. Jerusalem and Bethlehem were conceived as a *corpus separatum* under UN jurisdiction.

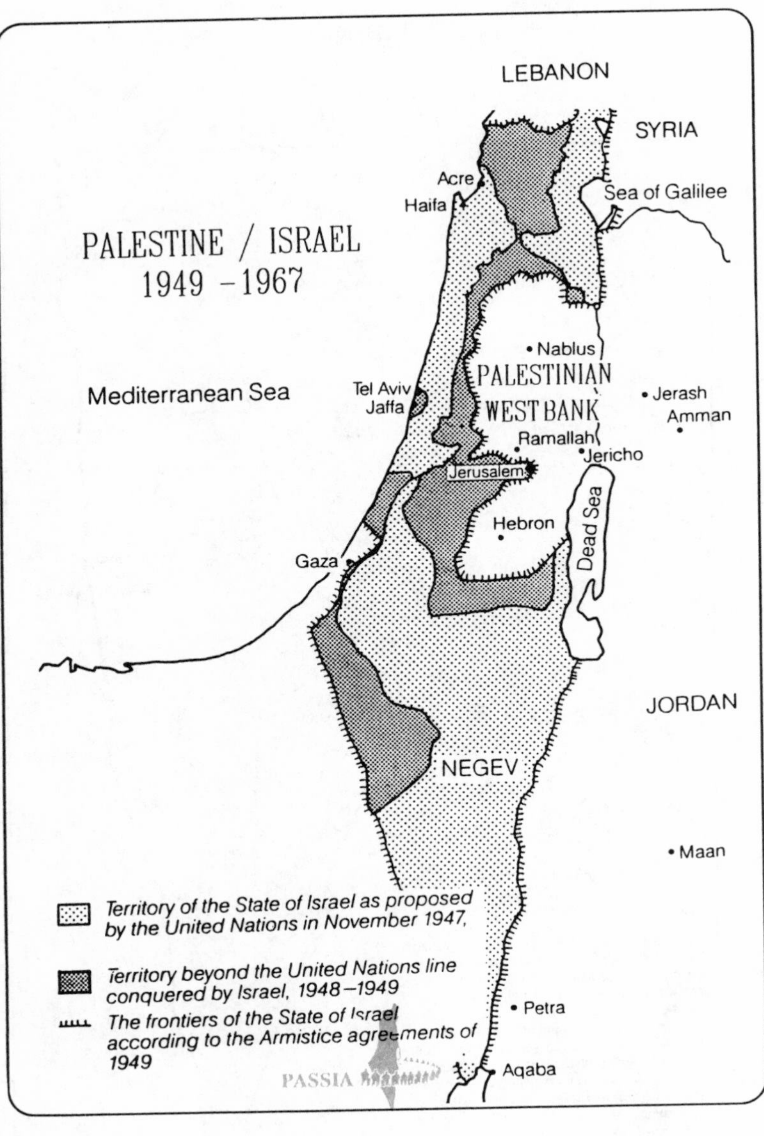
PALESTINE / ISRAEL
1949 -1967
LEBANON
SYRIA
Acre
Haifa
Sea of Galilee
Nablus
PALESTINIAN
WEST BANK
Mediterranean Sea
Tel Aviv
Jaffa
Jerash
Amman
Ramallah
Jericho
Jerusalem
Hebron
Dead Sea
Gaza
JORDAN
NEGEV
Maan
Territory of the State of Israel as proposed by the United Nations in November 1947,
Territory beyond the United Nations line conquered by Israel, 1948–1949
The frontiers of the State of Israel according to the Armistice agreements of 1949
Petra
Aqaba
PASSIA

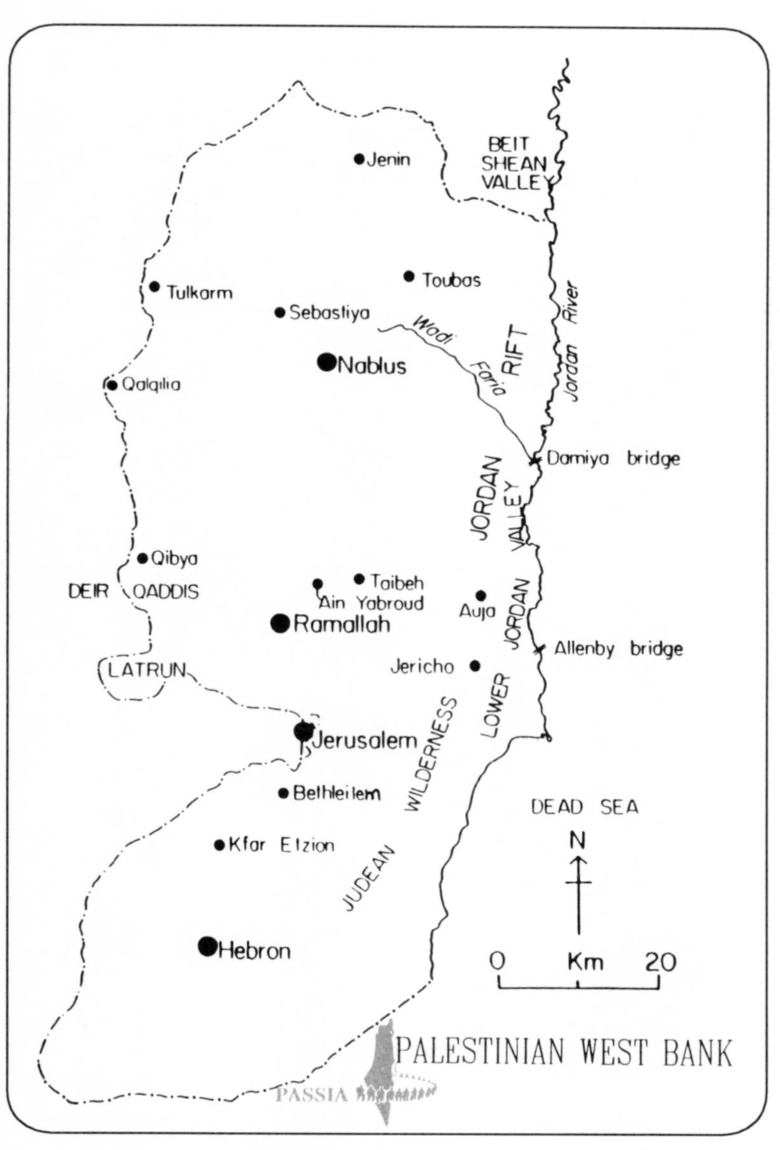
BEIT
SHEAN
VALLEY
Jenin
Toubas
Tulkarm
Sebastiya
Wadi
Faria
RIFT
Jordan River
Nablus
Qalqilia
Damiya bridge
JORDAN
VALLEY
Qibya
DEIR QADDIS
Taibeh
Ain Yabroud
Auja
JORDAN
Ramallah
Allenby bridge
LATRUN
Jericho
LOWER
WILDERNESS
Jerusalem
Bethleilem
DEAD SEA
N
Kfar Etzion
JUDEAN
Hebron
0
Km
20
PALESTINIAN WEST BANK

Beit Lahiya
Jabaliya
& Nazla
Beit
Hanoun
Gaza
MEDITERRANEAN SEA
Nuseirat
El Breij
Zaweida
Mughazi
Deir el Balah
Bani
Suheila
Abasan es Saghirah
Khan Yunis
Abasan el Kabirah
Ikhzaa
Rafah
PALESTINIAN GAZA STRIP
EGYPT
PASSIA

Abbreviations and Acronyms

AHC	Arab Higher Committee
ALF	Arab Liberation Front
ANM	Arab Nationalist Movement
ASS	Arab Studies Society
BSO	Black September Organization
CNG	Committee For National Guidance
CHE	Council for Higher Education
DFLP	Democratic Front for the Liberation of Palestine
DOP	Declaration of Principles
ECCP	European Coordinating Committee of NGOs on the Question of Palestine
EDG	Economic Development Group
FATAH	The Palestine National Liberation Movement
FIDA	The Palestine Democratic Union
GFPTU	General Federation of Palestinian Trade Unions
GUPS	General Union of Palestinian Students
GUPW	General Union of Palestinian Workers
GUPWC	General Union of Palestinian Women's Committees
GUPWSC	General Union of Palestinian Women's Struggle Committee-Gaza
HAMAS	Islamic Resistance Movement
HIC	Higher Islamic Council
MCA	Muslim-Christian Association
NENGOOT	Network of European Non-Government Organizations in the Occupied Territories
PA	Palestinian Authority
PASSIA	Palestinian Academic Society for the Study of International Affairs
PCC	Palestine Conciliation Commission
PDFLP	Popular Democratic Front for the Liberation of Palestine
PEC	Palestine Executive Committee
PECDAR	Palestine Economic Council for Development and Reconstruction

PFWAC	Palestinian Federation of Women's Action Committees
PISGA	Palestinian Interim Self-Governing Authority
PLA	Palestine Liberation Army
PLC	Palestinian Legislative Council
PLF	Palestine Liberation Front
PLFP-GC	Popular Front for the Liberation of Palestine-General Command
PLO	Palestine Liberation Organization
PNA	Palestine National Authority
PNC (Mithaq)	Palestine National Charter
PNC	Palestine National Council
PNF	Palestine National Front
PN (Fund)	Palestine National Fund
PNGO	Palestine Non-Government Organizations
PNSF	Palestine National Salvation Front
PPP	Palestinian People's Party
PPS	Palestine Press Service
PPSF	Palestine Popular Struggle Front
PRCS/Hilal	Palestinian Red Crescent Society
PFLP	Popular Front for the Liberation of Palestine
PSF	Popular Struggle Front
PTS	Palestinian Theological Society
PUWWC	Palestinian Union of Women Works Committee
PWU	Palestinian Women's Union-Gaza
SAMED	Society of the Sons of Palestinian Martyrs
SHMC	Supreme Higher Muslim Council
SMC	Supreme Muslim Council
UNLU	Unified National Leadership of the Uprising
UNRWA	United Nations Relief and Works Agency for Palestinian Refugees
UPMRC	Union of Palestinian Medical Relief Committees
UPWWC	Union of Palestinian Women's Works Committee
UWCUW	Union of Women's Committees for Unified Work
VOP	Voice of Palestine
WAFA	Palestinian-Arab News Agency
WBPNF	West Bank Palestine National Front

Chronology

638	Omar Ibn al-Khattab, the second Rashidun Caliphate (634–644) leads an expedition to Jerusalem. Palestine becomes an Arab-Islamic military district
661	Mu'awiya Ibn Sufyan of the Umayyad Caliphates proclaims himself Caliph in Jerusalem, Palestine
685–691	The Umayyad Caliph Abdul Malik Ibn Marwan (685–705) builds *Qubbat Al- Sakhra* (the Dome of the Rock) in Jerusalem
705	Al-Walid Ibn Abdul Malik (705–715) of the Umayyads builds *Al-Aqsa* Mosque in Jerusalem
715–717	The Umayyad Caliph Suleiman builds the Palestinian town of Ramleh
771	The Abbasid Caliph Ibn Ja'fer al Mansur (754–775) renovates *Al-Aqsa* Mosque in Jerusalem
969	The Fatimid Caliphates capture Jerusalem
1077	The Seljuk Turks seize Palestine, including the city of Jerusalem
1099–1187	The Crusaders invade Palestine and establish the Latin Kingdom of Jerusalem
1187	Salah al-Din Yusuf Ibn-Ayyub of the Ayyubid Caliphates captures Jerusalem and restores Islamic rule over *Al-Haram Al-Sharif*, which includes the Dome of the Rock and *Al-Aqsa* Mosques in Jerusalem
1260–1515	Palestine is ruled by the Mamluks of Egypt after they defeated the Mongols in 1260
1516–1917	Palestine becomes part of the Ottoman Turkish Empire
1537–1541	The Ottoman leader Suleiman the Magnificent (1520–1566) rebuilds the wall around Jerusalem
1799	Ahmad al-Jazzar, governor of Acre, prevents the French from occupying Palestine
1830	Ibrahim Pasha, the son of Muhammad Ali, conquers Palestine and makes it part of Egypt
1834	The Arabs in Palestine revolt against the Egyptian policy of conscripting them into the army (May 19); Ibrahim

	Pasha crushes the Palestinian Revolt in Jerusalem, Hebron, and Nablus, Palestine (July 4–August 4)
1863	The first Palestinian deputies from Jerusalem are elected during the first meeting of the Ottoman Parliament in Constantinople.
1878	Petah Tikva, the first Jewish settlement, is built in Palestine
1882–1904	First Aliya, or wave, of Jewish settlers arrives in Palestine
1897	First Zionist Congress meets in Basel, Switzerland. The Basel Program is launched to settle Jews in Palestine
1899–1902	Arab-Jewish relations are strained following Jewish land purchases in the Tiberias region, Palestine
1904–1914	Second Aliya, or wave, of Jewish settlers arrives in Palestine
1908	The first Palestinian newspaper, *Al-Karmil*, is published in Haifa, Palestine
1911	*Filistine* (Palestine) newspaper is founded in Jaffa by 'Isa al-'Isa. The newspaper addresses the Arabs in Palestine as "Palestinians," and warns them of the consequences of the Zionist colonization of their country
1914	The Ottoman Turks enter World War I. They side with Germany against the Allies
1915–1916	Sharif Hussein of Mecca and Henry McMahon, the British high commissioner in Egypt, exchange letters attesting to an agreement that guarantees Arab independence and unity after the war, in return for an Arab military revolt against the Ottoman Turks (July 1915–January 1916)
1916	Britain, France, and Russia sign the Sykes-Picot Agreement, which divides the Ottoman Middle East provinces among them (May 16)
1917	Lord Arthur James Balfour, British foreign secretary, sends a letter (Balfour Declaration) to Edmond de Rothschild in which he pledges British support for the establishment of a Jewish national home in Palestine (November 2)
1918	British forces occupy Palestine (December 9)
1919	Amir Faisal, son of Sharif Hussein of Mecca, welcomes Jewish immigration to Palestine, as long as the British fulfill their wartime promises to the Arabs (January 4); at an Arab-Palestinian Conference held in Jerusalem under the auspices of the Jerusalem and Jaffa Muslim-Christian Associations, Arif al-Dajani of Jerusalem proposes a Palestinian autonomy under the British. The majority of Palestinians attending the conference reject the plan, and

demand an independent Palestine united with Syria under the leadership of Faisal, son of Sharif Hussein, King of the Hejaz (January 27–February 10)

1920 The British Government removes Mussa Qassem al-Husseini, the mayor of Jerusalem, and appoints Ragheb al-Nashashibi in his place (April)

1921 Arab disturbances break out in Jaffa protesting the incorporation of the Balfour Declaration into the British Mandate System (May 1); upon the death of the *Mufti* of Jerusalem, Kamil al-Husseini, the British Mandate Government appoints Hajj Amin al-Husseini as the Grand *Mufti* of Jerusalem (May 8)

1922 The Supreme Muslim Council is established under the leadership of Hajj Amin al-Husseini (January); the British Government issues the Churchill White Paper to affirm that its policies in Palestine are not designed to undermine the Arab population, language, or culture (June 2); Palestine, east of the River Jordan, becomes Transjordan and is excluded from the scope of the Balfour Declaration (July 1)

1923 The League of Nations approves the British Mandate for Palestine (December 22)

1929 Palestinian riots erupt in Hebron and Jerusalem to protest the continuing Jewish immigration to Palestine, Jewish land purchases and rumors of Jewish intentions to control *Al-Burak* (the Western Wall) in Jerusalem (August 28–29)

1930 Lord Passfield, the British colonial secretary, issues a statement to reaffirm Sir Walter Shaw's Commission and Sir John Hope-Simpson's Inquiry Committee, which criticize Jewish "independent and separatist" practices, and calls on the Arabs to accept the Jews who are living in Palestine (October 21)

1931 British census shows that the total population of Palestine is 1,035,154, distributed as follows: Arabs 83.10 percent and Jews 16.90 percent (November 18); at the Pan-Islamic Congress meeting in Jerusalem, 145 representatives from the Muslim world support Hajj Amin al-Husseini as the Muslim leader in Palestine (December 16); four Palestinian parties are founded—the Independence Party, the Palestine Arab Party of the Husseinis, the National Defense Party of the Nashashibis, and the Reform Party of the Khalidis (August 2)

1933 The Arab Executive Committee declares a general strike in Palestine to protest British policies and Jewish immigration, and to demand the formation of a government in Palestine based on proportional representation (October 8–13)

1935 British forces kill Sheikh Izz al-Din al Qassam, a Syrian Muslim preacher who organized a commando group to fight the British in Palestine (November 19)

1936 The Arab Higher Committee is established (April 25); an Arab Revolt breaks out in Palestine (May 8)

1937 The Peel Commission Report recommends the partition of Palestine into a Jewish State and an Arab State incorporated into Transjordan, and that Jerusalem and Bethlehem be placed under the British Mandate with access to the sea (July 7); the British outlaws the Arab Higher Committee. Hajj Amin al-Husseini escapes to Lebanon, and is placed under house arrest by the French (September)

1939 The British Government issues the MacDonald White Paper, to limit and restrict Jewish immigration and land purchases in Palestine (May 17)

1942 The Zionists attending the Biltmore Conference advocate the establishment of a "Jewish Commonwealth" in Palestine (May 11)

1945 The Anglo-American Committee of Inquiry recommends the admission of 100,000 Jews from Europe into Palestine (May 1)

1947 The U.N. Special Committee on Palestine recommends the Partition of Palestine into an Arab state and a Jewish state, and that Jerusalem and its environs be internationalized (November 29)

1948 The Arab Higher Committee rejects the partition of Palestine (February 6); Jewish forces kill Abd al-Qader al-Husseini, leader of the Palestinian resistance (April 8); Jewish underground forces, the Irgun and Stern Gangs, massacre 245 Palestinian men, women, and children in the village of Deir Yassin near Jerusalem (April 9); Jewish forces capture the Arab quarters in West Jerusalem, and the Arab villages in the coastal plain, as well as the cities of Haifa, Tiberias, Safad, and Jaffa. The majority of the Palestinians in these areas flee their cities and villages (April 30); the Mandate over Palestine officially comes to an end, and the Zionists proclaim the establishment of the State of Israel. The United States extends full diplomatic recognition to Israel (May 14); the Arab states of Egypt, Iraq, Transjordan, Syria, and Lebanon (Saudi Arabia and Yemen send token forces) dispatch troops to Palestine to prevent the establishment of Israel (May 15); the Soviet Union recognizes Israel (May 17); during the first U.N. truce of the 1948 Arab-Israeli War, both Arabs and Israelis consolidate their position and seek arms from abroad. Israel airlifts arms from Czechoslovakia (May 19); the United Nations imposes a second truce, and both Arabs and Israelis reinforce their manpower and equipment (August 19); the Palestinian National Conference meets in Gaza and the All-Palestine Government is established under the leadership of Hajj Amin al-Husseini (September 1); Israelis begin capturing positions beyond the truce lines (September 8); Hajj Amin al-Husseini heads the meeting of the Palestinian National Council in Gaza. The first Palestinian Congress convenes in Amman, Jordan, and takes an oath of allegiance to the Hashemite monarch (September 30); Egypt, Syria, Lebanon, and Saudi Arabia recognize the All-Palestine Government (October 15); Israel lays claim to the entire Neqab (October 17); the U.N. enforces a third truce (October 28); Palestinian notables from the West Bank meet in Jericho and advocate a temporary union with Transjordan (December 1); the U.N. General Assembly adopts Resolution 194 (II), which recognizes the right of Palestinians who left during the 1948 war to return to their homes and live in peace with their neighbors (December 11); Sheikh Hussam al-Din Jarallah replaces Hajj Amin al-Husseini as the new *mufti* of Jerusalem (December 20); Amin Abd al-Hadi is appointed the head of the Supreme Muslim Council in Jerusalem (December 20); Israeli troops move into parts of the Sinai. Anglo-American pressure brings about Israeli withdrawal from the Sinai (December 28)

1949 Armistice agreements are concluded between Israel and Egypt (February 24), Israel and Lebanon (March 23), Israel and Transjordan (April 3), and Israel and Syria (July 20). At the end of the War of 1948, Israel extends its holdings of Palestine, and now controls 77 percent of it, instead of the 56 percent allotted by the United Nations Partition Plan of 1947

1950 U.N. General Assembly announces the establishment of the United Nations Relief and Works Agency (UNRWA) to assist Palestinian refugees in the West Bank, Gaza Strip, Jordan, Syria, and Lebanon (December 2); the West Bank officially becomes part of the Hashemite Kingdom of Jordan (April 24)

1951 Ragheb al-Nashashibi, former mayor of Jerusalem, is appointed by King Abdallah of Jordan as the custodian of the Holy Places in Jerusalem (January 2); Mustafa Shukri Usho, a Palestinian, kills King Abdallah at *Al-Aqsa* Mosque in Jerusalem (July 20)

1952 Hussein Ibn Talal is declared King of Jordan after his father abdicates the throne (August 11)

1953 Israel launches a large-scale assault on the Gaza Strip (February 28); U.N. Security Council unanimously condemns the Israeli attack (March 29); Israel attacks the West Bank village of Qibia and kills 53 people (October 14)

1956 President Nasser of Egypt nationalizes the Suez Canal (July 26); Israel occupies the Gaza Strip and the Sinai Peninsula in preparation for a British-French invasion of Egypt, to reinstate western control of the Suez (October 28–29)

1957 U.N. Emergency Forces move into the Gaza Strip and the Sinai after the evacuation of Israeli troops (March 8)

1959 Hajj Amin al-Husseini leaves Egypt and takes up residence in Lebanon (January)

1960 President Nasser challenges the Arabs to preserve the Palestinian entity and to support the Palestinian problem (April 26); the Voice of the Arabs, an Egyptian radio station broadcasting from Cairo, expands its program and establishes the "Voice of Palestine" (October 29)

1961 The Egyptian daily newspaper *Akhbar al-Youm* (Today's News) begins a weekly newspaper, *Akhbar Filastine* (Palestine's News) (March); the U.N. Conciliation Commission recruits Dr. Joseph E. Johnson, president of the Carnegie Endowment for International Peace, to explore with the Arab countries and Israel practical means of implementing U.N. Resolution 194 of 1948, which calls for the reintegration of the Palestinian refugees by repatriation or settlement (August 21)

1964 FATAH leaders Yasser Arafat and Khalil al-Wazir travel to China to meet Premier Chou-En-Lai (March 17); Ahmad Shuqeiri, the Palestinian representative to the Arab League heads the Palestinian National Council meeting in Jerusalem, where the First PLO National Covenant is drafted. At the PNC meeting, he is appointed the first chairman of the PLO (May 28); the Palestine Liberation Organization is formed (June 2); during the second meeting of the Arab Summit in Cairo, the PLO is recognized as the symbol of the Palestinian struggle for the liberation of Palestine (September 5–11)

1965 Arafat's organization, FATAH, carries out its first military operation against Israel (January 1); President Habib Bourguiba of Tunisia urges the Arabs to accept Israel according to the terms of the 1947 U.N. Partition Plan, as well as the repatriation of Palestinian refugees (March 6)

1967 The Six Day War breaks out (June 5); Israel captures East Jerusalem and the West Bank from Jordan, the Gaza Strip, and the Sinai from Egypt, and the Golan Heights from Syria (June 5–11); cease-fire agreements are concluded on the Jordanian (June 7), Egyptian (June 8), and Syrian fronts (June 9); George Habash establishes the Popular Front for the Liberation of Palestine (December); Israel annexes East Jerusalem and begins construction of Jewish settlements in East Jerusalem and the West Bank (June 28); Palestinian religious and political leaders set up the Higher Islamic Council in East Jerusalem to administer Muslim affairs in the West Bank and East Jerusalem (July 24); the Israeli authorities deport Sheikh Abd al-Hamid al-Sayyeh, the head of the Higher Islamic Council, to Jordan (September 23); the representatives of Arab states meeting in Khartoum, Sudan, announce there will be no recognition, no negotiation, and no peace with Israel (August 29); the U. N. Security Council adopts Resolution 242, which recommends Israeli withdrawal from territories occupied during the Six Days War of 1967 in return for peace and secure borders (November 22)

1968 Palestinian commandos and the Jordanian army repel an Israeli attack on the village of Karameh, in the Jordan River Valley (March 21); the PNC moves to Cairo and modifies the PLO Charter (July 17–18); the PFLP hijacks an Israeli airliner (EL AL) and lands in Algeria (July 22); Ahmad Jibril splits from the PFLP and establishes his own Popular Front for the Liberation of Palestine-General Command (December)

1969 Palestinian commandos, particularly FATAH members, dominate the PLO; Yasser Arafat is nominated chairman of the PLO Executive Committee (February); Nayef Hawatmeh splits from the PFLP and establishes the Democratic Front for the Liberation of Palestine (February 12); PFLP commandos hijack an American airliner, TWA, to Damascus, Syria. The hijackers evacuate the passengers and destroy the aircraft (August 29); Israeli embassies in the Hague and Bonn, as well as EL AL offices in Athens and Brussels, are bombed (September 8); part of the *Al-Aqsa* Mosque in Jerusalem is set on fire by an Australian tourist (August 21); the PLO and Lebanon sign the Cairo Agreement. The PLO establishes Fatahland in Southern Lebanon to target Israel (November 3)

1970 Rashad al-Shawwa becomes the mayor of the city of Gaza (September); PFLP members hijack three international airliners, Pan American, Swissair, and TWA, to Jordan and blow them up (September 6); King Hussein of Jordan attempts to restrict PLO activities in Jordan. Fighting breaks out between the Jordanian army and the PLO commandos (September 9)

1971 Jordanian army evicts the PLO from Jordan and dismantles its infrastructure (July 9); Israeli security forces led by Arik Sharon destroy the PLO military presence in the Gaza Strip (July); Black September, a Palestinian organization formed after the war between the PLO and Jordan in September 1970, claims responsibility for the assassination of Wasfi al-Tal, Jordan's prime minister (November 28)

1972 Palestinians in the West Bank are allowed to hold municipal elections in accordance with the 1955 Jordanian Municipal Law (March 28 and May 2); Black September holds 11 Israeli athletes hostage at the Munich Olympics. Most of the hostages and the Palestinian commandos are killed during the rescue operation (September 5); King Hussein of Jordan proposes the "United Kingdom Plan," a confederation between the West Bank and Jordan (March 15); Ghassan Kanafani, editor of *Al-Hadaf* (The Target) Magazine and member of the Political Bureau of the Popular Front for the Liberation of Palestine, is killed in Beirut when a bomb explodes in his car (July 8)

1973 Wail Zu'aiter, the PLO representative in Rome, is killed by a member of a PLO rejectionist organization (October 16); the October/Yom Kippur/Ramadan War breaks out (October 6); U.N. Security Council adopts Resolution 338, recommending negotiations between Israel and its Arab neighbors (October 22); Israeli commandos raid FATAH headquarters in Beirut and kill Palestinian leaders Kamal Nasser, Kamal Udwan, and Muhammad al-Najjar (April 10); the Palestinian National Front is set up in the West Bank to coordinate activities with the PLO (August)

1974 The Palestinian National Council accepts the establishment of a Palestinian state in any liberated part(s) of Palestine and discards the option of establishing a secular democratic state in all of Palestine (February 19); the United Nations General Assembly passes Resolution 3236, which accepts the PLO as the representative of the Palestinian people (October 14); meeting in Rabat, Morocco, the heads of the Arab states recognize the PLO as the sole, legitimate representative of the Palestinian people (October 28); Israel deports Hanna Nasser, president of Birzeit University in the West Bank (November 21); George Habash, head of the PFLP, resigns from the PLO Executive Committee and, together with the Popular Front for the Liberation of Palestine-General Command and the Arab Liberation Front, establishes the PLO Rejectionist Front to oppose possible Palestinian participation in a Geneva Peace Conference (September 26)

1976 Palestinian leaders Bassam al-Shak'a of Nablus, Hilmi Hanun of Tulkarm, Karim Khalaf of Ramallah, Ibrahim al-Tawil of al-Bireh, Fahd al-Qawasmi of Hebron, and Muhammad Milhem of Halhul are elected mayors of their respective towns on pro-PLO platforms (April 12); six Israeli Arabs are killed during the Land Day general strike in Galilee, held to protest Israeli expropriation of Arab land in Israel (March 30); Lebanese Christian forces demolish Tel al-Za'tar Refugee Camp in Beirut, Lebanon, killing 3,000 Palestinians (August 12); Palestine, represented by the PLO, becomes a full member of the Arab League Organization (September)

1977 President Anwar al-Sadat of Egypt arrives in Israel and addresses the Knesset in Jerusalem (November 20); Palestinian rejectionist organizations establish a "Steadfastness and Confrontation Front" to oppose Sadat's peace initiative (October 1); A Council for Higher Education is established to supervise higher education in the Occupied Territories (June 16)

1978 Said Hammami, the PLO representative in London and an early pioneer of Israeli-Palestinian contacts, is assassinated (January 4); eight FATAH seaborne commandos led by a Palestinian woman, Dalal Mughrabi, embark on Israel's Coastal Highway, hijack a bus, and kill 37 Israelis. Six of the hijackers are killed, and two others are arrested (March 11); in retaliation, the Israeli army invades South Lebanon, demolishes a number of villages and kills some 700 Lebanese and Palestinians (March 14); U.N. Security

Council adopts Resolution 425, which demands the immediate withdrawal of Israeli troops from South Lebanon (March 19); after meeting with Arafat, U.N. Secretary General Kurt Waldheim announces Arafat's acceptance of a cease-fire in South Lebanon and willingness to cooperate with UNIFIL (March 28); UNIFIL units move into positions vacated by Israel in South Lebanon (April 6); the Lebanese army redeploys in South Lebanon (July 31); President Jimmy Carter, President Anwar Sadat, and Prime Minister Menachem Begin sign the Camp David Accords. Israel agrees to withdraw from the Sinai in exchange for peace with Egypt, and to grant the Palestinians "full autonomy" in the Occupied Territories, after a transitional period of five years (September 17); Palestinians in the West Bank and Gaza Strip organize the Committee for National Guidance (CNG) to coordinate resistance against the Camp David Accords and the Israeli occupation in the West Bank and Gaza Strip (October); at the ninth summit meeting in Baghdad, Iraq, representatives of the Arab states form a joint committee, composed of Jordanian and PLO representatives, to channel $150 million to the Occupied Territories to support Palestinian steadfastness (November 15)

1979 The PNC convenes for the first time in Damascus, Syria. The PLO leaders reject the Camp David Accords, and recommend the continuation of Jordanian-Palestinian rapprochement (January 15); Arafat travels to Iran to meet the new leaders of the Iranian Revolution. During his visit, Arafat dedicates a PLO embassy in the building where the Israelis formerly had their diplomatic mission (February 17–18); the United Nations Security Council adopts Resolution 446, which demands that Israel dismantle the settlements in the Occupied Territories (March 22); Egypt and Israel sign the peace treaty in Washington (March 26)

1980 Mayors Fahd al-Qawasmi of Hebron and Muhammad Milhem of Halhul are deported to Lebanon (May 2); Mayors Bassam al-Shak'a of Nablus and Karim Khalaf of Ramallah are maimed by bombs, placed in their cars by members of Jewish underground organizations (June 2); the Israeli Knesset "officially" adopts the Jerusalem Law, which annexes East Jerusalem to Israel (June 30); Palestinian leaders—Ibrahim al-Tawil, mayor of al-Bireh, Walid Hamdallah, mayor of 'Anabta, Ibrahim Dakkak, chairperson of the West Bank Engineers Union and secretary of the Committee for National Guidance (CNG), Ma'mun al-Sayyad, editor of *Al-Fajr* (The Dawn) Arabic daily newspaper, Akram Haniyya, editor of *Al-Sha'b* (The Masses) Arabic daily newspaper, Bashir al-Barghouthi, editor of *Al-Tali'a* (The Vanguard) Arabic weekly, and Samiha Khalil, chairperson of *In'ash al-Usra* (Family Rehabilitation Society)—are all confined to their homes by an Israeli military order (August 10–16); Mayor Amin al-Nasir of Qalqilya is arrested for publishing a leaflet in which he condemns the "burden of the Israeli occupation" (September 22)

1981 Israel creates the Civil Administration in the Occupied Territories and appoints Professor Menahem Milson of the Hebrew University as its head (November 2); Israeli authorities close Bethlehem University (November 12); acting president of Birzeit University, Dr. Gabi Baramki, is placed under house arrest (November 12); Israeli military authorities arrest Akram Haniyya, editor of *Al-Sha'b* (The Masses) (November12); the PLO claims responsibility for the killing of Yusuf al-Khatib, the head of the Ramallah Village League Association, and his son (November 18)

1982 Elias Freij, the mayor of Bethlehem, advocates mutual recognition between Israel and the PLO (January 22); the PLO condemns Mayors Freij of Bethlehem and al-Shawwa of Gaza for supporting recognition of Israel (January 27); the government of Jordan orders the Village League Association to dissolve itself within 30 days, otherwise they will be charged under Jordanian Law with high treason, which includes the death penalty and the confiscation of their property (March 9); Israeli authorities outlaw the CNG (March 11); Israel dismisses Mayor Ibrahim al-Tawil of al-Bireh, Mayor Rashad al-Shawwa of Gaza, Mayor Karim Khalaf of Ramallah, and Mayor Bassam al-Shak'a of Nablus for refusing to cooperate with the Israeli Civil Administration. Israeli army officers are appointed to administer the municipalities in the Occupied Territories (March 19–25); Israel imposes restrictions on the transfer of money exceeding 1,000 Jordanian dinars into the Occupied Territories (April 2); Birzeit University re-opens after a two-month closure (April 10); Alan Harry Goodman, an American-Israeli, opens fire inside the Dome of the Rock Mosque in Jerusalem, killing two Palestinian guards and wounding 30 Muslim worshipers (April 11); the Higher Muslim Council in East Jerusalem calls for a one-week strike to protest the shooting inside the mosque (April 13);

Israeli authorities dismiss Walid Hamdallah, mayor of Anabta, a town on the West Bank (May 1); mayors in the Occupied Territories agree to halt municipal services until the dismissed Palestinian mayors are reinstated (May 6); two Village League Associations are established in the towns of Jenin and Tulkarm (May 18); Jordan blacklists 19 West Bank Palestinians for cooperating with the Israeli-sponsored Village League Association (May 27); the Israeli army invades Lebanon to evict PLO commandos in Southern Lebanon (June 4); the Municipal Councils of Nablus and Dura, on the West Bank, are dismissed for refusing to cooperate with the Israeli Civil Administration (June 16); Crown Prince Fahd of Saudi Arabia announces a new Middle East Peace Plan that consists of eight points: Israeli withdrawal from the territories it occupied during the war of 1967, the removal of Israeli settlements from the Occupied Territories, freedom of worship for all in Jerusalem, recognition of Palestinian rights to return, and monetary compensation for those who do not wish to return, the supervision and administration of the West Bank and the Gaza Strip by U.N. officials for several months, the establishment of a Palestinian state with Jerusalem as its capital, a guarantee of the right of Palestinians and all the states in the region to live in peace (August 8); members of the Phalange and Haddad militia massacre about 2,000 Palestinian refugees at Sabra and Shatilla refugee camps in Beirut, Lebanon, in anger over the death of Lebanese President-elect Bashir Gemayel (September 16–18); Jordan stops its economic assistance to West Bank municipalities (October 21); Israeli military authorities close Birzeit University for the second time in three months (November 10)

1983 The PNC meets in Algiers and approves the concept of a confederation between an independent Palestine and Jordan (February 14–21); PLO leader Issam Sartawi, Arafat's advisor in Europe, is assassinated in Lisbon, Portugal (April 10); Israeli authorities close An-Najah National University for the academic year following student protests marking the first anniversary of the invasion of Lebanon (June 4); Syria expels Arafat and Khalil al-Wazir, and announces that they are "persona non grata" in Syria, and in the Syrian-controlled areas of Lebanon (June 24); in response to Syrian President Hafez al-Assad's decision to bar Arafat from entering Syria, Sheikh Sa'd al-Din al-

Alami issues a *fatwa* (Islamic decree) promising martyr status to any Muslim who kills President Hafez al-Assad (June 27); Israeli authorities dismiss the mayor of Hebron, Mustafa Abd al-Nabi al-Natshe (July 7); the government of Israel approves the restoration of the Old Jewish Quarter in central Hebron (July 10); a group of masked gunmen open fire on students at Hebron Islamic College, killing three people and wounding 33 (July 26); Mustafa Dudin resigns as the head of the West Bank Village League Associations (September 4); Jawdat Su'allah, head of the Nablus Village League Association replaces Dudin (September 7); Israeli authorities close Bethlehem University for two months after two days of clashes between students and Israeli soldiers (November 20); Israel releases 4,500 Palestinian prisoners in exchange for six Israeli prisoners held by the PLO in Lebanon (November 24); Arafat, together with an estimated 4,000 PLO commandos, leaves Lebanon on Greek ships and under the protection of French warships (December 20)

1984 Israeli police discover explosives on the platform surrounding *Al-Aqsa* Mosque in East Jerusalem. The Jewish group "Terror Against Terror" is held responsible for placing the bombs (January 28); Israeli military authorities close Birzeit University for three months following students' protest against the attempt to destroy *Al-Aqsa* Mosque (February 2); fighting breaks out between pro-Communist and Muslim fundamentalist students at An-Najah National University (February 19); Israeli military authorities close An-Najah National University (February 24); Arafat meets Hussein to discuss the coordination of their positions regarding the peace process (February 26); Israeli authorities warn Palestinians from the Occupied Territories not to meet with Arafat during his visit to Jordan (February 27); Palestinians from the Occupied Territories meet Arafat in Amman, Jordan, and urge him to accept a joint PLO-Jordanian strategy, based on U.N. Security Council Resolution 242 and 338 (February 28); West Bank Palestinian prisoners end their 10 day hunger strike (October 4); the 17th meeting of the Palestine National Council opens in Amman, Jordan. PNC speaker Khalid Fahum is replaced by Sheikh Abd al-Hamid al-Sayyeh (November 22–29); deported mayor Fahd al-Qawasmi of Hebron is assassinated in Amman, Jordan (December 29)

1985 Arafat and Hussein agree on a formula for a joint Jordanian-Palestinain peace strategy (February 11); Jordan makes public the text of the agreement, including the Israeli withdrawal from territories occupied during the War of 1967, in accordance with U.N. Resolutions 242 and 338, Palestinians right to self-determination within the context of a confederation between Jordan and Palestine, resolution of the Palestine problem in accordance with U.N. Resolutions, a joint Jordanian-Palestinian delegation to negotiate peace in the Middle East in an international conference (February 22); the Israeli army raids Birzeit University and closes its new campus for two months (March 1); the PFLP, PFLP-GC, Sa'iqa, Popular Struggle Front, Palestine National Front, and Abu Musa's FATAH dissidents form the "Palestine National Salvation Front" to obstruct the Arafat-Hussein agreement (March 25); deposed mayor of Ramallah, Karim Khalaf, dies of a heart attack in Jericho (March 30); Israeli army raids Bethlehem University and orders it closed (April 18); Israel agrees to release 1,150 Palestinian prisoners in exchange for three Israeli soldiers captured during the Israeli invasion of Lebanon in 1982 (May 20); four armed members of the Palestine Liberation Front hijack an Italian cruise ship, the *Achille Lauro*, off the shores of Egypt and demand the release of 50 Palestinian prisoners in Israeli jails. The hijackers kill Leon Klinghoffer, an American confined to a wheelchair (October 7); Israel closes the last Arab Hospital (Hospice) in the Old City of Jerusalem (July 29); *Al-Sha'b* daily newspaper in East Jerusalem is ordered closed for three days for sneaking two censored reports into the obituaries (August 1); Israeli military authorities close An-Najah National University for three months (August 2); *Al-Bayadir Al-Siyyasi*, a Palestinian weekly magazine, is ordered closed for two weeks for publishing censored materials (October 17); the PLO Executive Committee meets in Baghdad, Iraq, and reaffirms the PLO's rejection of U.N. Resolutions 242 and 338 (November 19); Israeli authorities appoint Palestinian businessman Zafer al-Masri as mayor of Nablus (November 26); Aziz Shehadeh, a Palestinian attorney, is stabbed to death outside his home in Ramallah (December 2)

1986 Jordan extends recognition and support to Zafer al-Masri, the newly appointed mayor of Nablus (January 30); the Israeli Civil Administration appoints Ibrahim Hamad as mayor of Yatta, a town near Hebron on the West Bank

(February 17); King Hussein ends joint peace efforts with the PLO (February 19); Hussein asks West Bank Palestinians to decide quickly who should lead them, before Israel usurps all of the land (February 22); Israeli Defense Minister Yitzhak Rabin meets Palestinians from the West Bank and announces that a joint Jordanian-Palestinian delegation could include anyone from the Occupied Territories, although, Palestinians from the diaspora who join the delegation must not be members of the PLO (February 25); Zafer al-Masri, the mayor of Nablus, is murdered by a member of the PFLP rejectionist faction (March 2); more than 50,000 Palestinians attend the funeral of al-Masri in Nablus, where he is buried (March 3); in the wake of al-Masri's assassination, Nadim Zaru of Ramallah and Walid Mustafa Hamad of al-Bireh withdraw their candidacies for mayor (March 2); Palestinians in the Occupied Territories begin to use tactics of non-violent resistance against the Israeli occupation (March 17); Rashad al-Shawwa, the mayor of Gaza, suggests that Egypt supervise a plan of self-rule for the Gaza Strip, before the status of the West Bank is settled (May 31); Israeli authorities ban the sale of *Al-Fajr* (The Dawn) daily newspaper in the Occupied Territories for three days (June 20); *Al-Mithaq* (The Covenant) newspaper is closed because of its support for the PFLP (July 6); Israeli authorities appoint Abd al-Majid al-Zir mayor of Hebron, Khalil Musa Khalil mayor of Ramallah, and Hassan al-Tawil mayor of al-Bireh (September 28); *Al-Fajr* (The Dawn) daily newspaper is banned for seven days by the Israeli authorities for "censorship violations" (October 1); following students' demonstrations at Bethlehem University, Israeli military authorities close the university for one week (October 30); Israel allows the Cairo-Amman Bank, which has been closed since 1967, to re-open in Nablus (November 3); Jordan deports PLO leader Khalil al-Wazir and closes the PLO offices in Amman, Jordan (July 7–10)

1987 Israeli military authorities close An-Najah National University for one week because of leaks of "planned students' disturbances" (January 4); in a meeting with five West Bank university officials, Defense Minister Rabin revokes the order that has closed An-Najah National University since January 4. However, Rabin threatens to close all Palestinian universities permanently if unrest continues (January 20); the first open-heart surgery in the Occupied

Territories is performed by Dr. Shawki Harb at Ramallah Hospital (January 24); Jordan announces that PLO leader Khalil al-Wazir will be allowed to attend the meeting of the Joint Jordanian-Palestinian Committee in Amman, Jordan (February 2); following students' demonstrations at Islamic University, Israeli authorities close the university for three days (February 16); the PLO moves the office of the Palestine National Fund from Amman to Abu Dhabi. Israeli authorities close Hebron University for three days because of students' demonstrations (February 23); Samiha Khalil, head of the Family Rehabilitation Society, is denied permission to leave the West Bank (March 24); Israeli military authorities close Bethlehem University until April 4, and An-Najah National University until April 12 because of students' protests (March 26); *Al-Sha'b* (The Masses) daily newspaper is not allowed to be distributed in the Occupied Territories (April 28); PFLP supporters in the Occupied Territories burn two cars belonging to Hanna Siniora, editor of *Al-Fajr* (The Dawn), a daily newspaper, because of his plans to run for the Jerusalem City Council (June 21); Israel releases PLO official in Jerusalem Faisal al-Husseini after three months in jail (July 9); an Israeli military court finds Saeb 'Erekat, a professor of political science at An-Najah National University, guilty of incitement for writing an article in *Al-Quds* (Jerusalem) daily newspaper encouraging Palestinians to resist the occupation (July 16); Israel detains prominent PLO leader Faisal al-Husseini for six months (September 13); in the wake of clashes between students at Bethlehem University and the Israeli army, the university is closed for three months (October 29); Radwan Abu-Ayyash, editor of *Al-Awdah* (The Return) Magazine, is accused of being a member of FATAH and is placed in administrative detention. The Palestinian Intifada (Uprising) begins in the Gaza Strip and spreads to the West Bank (December 9); Palestinians in Jerusalem strike to protest Israeli Agricultural Minister Arik Sharon's move to Market Street in the Muslim Quarter of the Old City of Jerusalem (December 15); Israeli authorities close Hebron University for one month (December 20); the distribution of *Al-Quds* (Jerusalem) daily newspaper is prohibited in the Occupied Territories for one month because of censorship violations (December 22)

1988 Israeli Defense Minister Yitzhak Rabin stops shipments of food to refugee camps in the Gaza Strip and the West Bank until Palestinian merchants end their strike; Rabin announces a new policy of "might, power, and beating" to stop the Intifada (January 19); *Al-Quds* (Jerusalem) daily newspaper is banned from the Occupied Territories for 25 days because of censorship violations (January 22); Palestinians in Israel demonstrate in Nazareth in support of the Palestinians in the Occupied Territories. During the demonstration, Abd al-Wahhab Darawsheh, an Arab Knesset member, announces his resignation from the Israeli Labor Party (January 23); Jamil al-Amlah resigns as head of the Hebron Village League Association (February 6); the PLO indefinitely postpones the voyage of the *Boat of Return* to Palestine after a bomb explodes on the boat while it is docked in Limassol, Cyprus (February 14); following a 25-day ban on the distribution of *Al-Quds* (Jerusalem) daily newspaper, Israeli authorities extend the ban for an additional 20 days (February 16); Abd al-Wahab Darawsheh establishes the Arab Democratic Party (March 1); in the Gaza Strip, Palestinian employees of the Income and Property Tax Division of the Israeli Civil Administration submit their resignations (March 6); the Israeli authorities extend the administrative detention of PLO leader Faisal al-Husseini for an additional three months (March 10); upon the request of the Unified National Leadership of the Uprising (UNLU), an estimated 625 Palestinian policemen resign from the Israeli police force (March 10–12); Dr. Nabil al-Ja'bari, president of the Board of Trustees of Hebron University, is placed under administrative detention for six months (March 13); Israeli authorities stipulate that Palestinian exit permits to Jordan are contingent on the payment of all taxes, including the value-added tax (March 14); in anticipation of Land Day, Israeli military authorities place the Gaza Strip under curfew and ban all Palestinians in the Occupied Territories from entering Jerusalem and Israel until April 1 (March 29); Khalil al-Wazir, PLO military leader partially responsible for coordinating the Intifada in the Occupied Territories, is killed in his Tunis home (April 16); Israeli authorities place 15 Palestinian refugee camps in the Occupied Territories, as well as the city of Nablus and the town of Anabta, under curfew (April 17); *Al-Fajr* (The Dawn) and *Al-Nahar* (The Day) dailies, as well as *Al-Awdah* (The Return) weekly, are ordered closed (April 18); after closing schools for four months as collective punishment for the disturbances in the Occupied Territories, Israel allows some 20,000 Palestinian elementary school students and 70,000 junior high school students to return to their schools in the West Bank (May 23); UNLU adopts a policy of national disobedience (May 11); West Bank high schools are allowed to re-open after being closed for five months, because of demonstrations by students (June 6); Israeli military authorities deport Raghida al-Masri, widow of the late Nablus mayor Zafer al-Masri, after she is accused of smuggling money from Jordan to support the Intifada (June 9); King Hussein dissolves the 60-seat lower house of parliament, half of which is composed of Palestinians from the West Bank (July 30); in another move, King Hussein officially breaks Jordan's administrative and legal ties with the West Bank, and announces that he is relinquishing control of the West Bank to the PLO (July 31); in the wake of King Hussein's disassociation from the West Bank, the PLO declares its acceptance of the responsibilities for the affairs of the West Bank and the Gaza Strip (August 3); the PLO Executive Committee renames the West Bank the "Palestinian Bank" (August 26); Sheikh Ahmad Yassin, head of HAMAS in the Gaza Strip, announces that Islam must be the constitution of the Palestinian state (September 13); Rashad al-Shawwa, the twice-deposed mayor of Gaza, dies (September 28); the Palestine National Council (PNC) opens its 19th session in Algiers, and 57 council members boycott the meeting; the PNC proclaims an independent Palestinian state in the West Bank and the Gaza Strip and, for the first time, implicitly recognizes Israel's existence and accepts U.N. Resolutions 242 and 338, linking them with the "National Rights" of the Palestinians (November 12–15); a total of 55 countries, including China and the Soviet Union, recognize the Palestinian State (November 24); the Unified National Leadership of the Intifada approves the PNC resolutions and the Declaration of Independence. The Palestine National Salvation Front (PNSF) denounces the PNC resolutions (November 19); Arafat declares in Stockholm that the PLO accepts Israel's right to exist and denounces terrorism (December 7); speaking to the U.N. General Assembly in Geneva, Arafat challenges Israel to make peace with the Palestinians (December 13); during the first year of the Intifada, the Israeli army kills 366 Palestinians and wounds more than 20,000. Thirteen Palestinians are murdered by fellow Palestinians for suspected collaboration with Israel. Reports also state that more than 15,000 Palestinians have been arrested, 12,000 Palestinians are jailed (1,200 are in administrative detention) and 36 Palestinians are deported. Israel also has demolished a total of 54 Palestinian houses (December 5); the United States authorizes its ambassador to Tunis, Robert Pelletreau, to open a diplomatic dialogue with the PLO (December 14); FATAH announces the establishment of a popular army in the Occupied Territories (December 30)

1989 Yasser Arafat raises the Palestinian flag on the Palestinian embassy in Amman, Jordan (January 7); the U.N. Security Council grants the PLO the right to speak directly to the Council as "Palestine," and with the same status as any U.N. member nation (January 12); Israeli authorities close all West Bank schools to prevent disturbances (January 20); the UNLU rejects Yitzhak Rabin's proposal to hold elections in the Occupied Territories in return for a lull in the Intifada (January 22); the deposed mayor of Anabta, Walid Hamdallah, is placed under house arrest (January 22); Israel releases PLO leader Faisal al-Husseini from prison (January 29); Palestinians in East Jerusalem are told by the PLO to boycott the Israeli municipal elections in Jerusalem (February 27); Palestinian lawyers end their two-month boycott of Israeli military courts (March 12); for the second year, Roman Catholic bishops cancel the Palm Sunday procession in East Jerusalem in support of the Intifada (March 19); the PLO Central Council appoints Arafat the first President of Palestine (April 2); the UNLU rejects Israeli Prime Minister Shamir's plan for elections in the Occupied Territories, because it ignores Palestinian political aspirations (April 11); Israeli military authorities arrest HAMAS leaders Sheikh Ahmad Yassin and Sheikh Mahmoud al-Zahhar (April 19); the U.N. General Assembly condemns Israeli practices in the Occupied Territories and calls on the U.N. Security Council to protect Palestinian civilians (April 20); the Israeli government approves Shamir's plan for elections in the Occupied Territories, which will enable the Palestinians to elect a self-governing authority to negotiate an interim and a permanent settlement with Israel (May 14); Israel declares that HAMAS and Islamic Jihad are illegal organizations, and membership in these organizations would carry a penalty of up to 10 years in prison (June 18); in a letter to the Israeli attorney general, Defense Minister Rabin asks the government's permission to enact the following measures: to allow the Israeli army to deport Palestinian suspects within seven days of their arrest, to extend administrative detention to one year instead of six months, and to demolish Palestinian activists' homes without any prior notification (June 20); Christopher George, director of Save the Children in the Gaza Strip, is released after 29 hours in captivity. The kidnappers give him a letter for President Bush in which they demand the following: President Bush is to hold a meeting with Arafat, the deportations of Palestinians is to end, and Palestinian prisoners are to be released (June 23); a leaflet distributed in Nablus and signed by the Palestinian Popular Army Command attacks Sari Nuseibeh and prominent FATAH supporters in the Occupied Territories (July 17); a total of 200,000 Palestinian elementary and high school students return to their schools, which have been closed since January 1989 (July 22); Arafat opens a new office for the Palestine National Fund in Amman, Jordan (August 22); Israel bans PLO leader Faisal al-Husseini from entering the West Bank and the Gaza Strip for three months (December 6); demanding peace, some 30,000 Palestinians, Israelis, Americans, and Europeans form a human chain around the Old City of Jerusalem. About 70 people are wounded and 50 are arrested when the Israeli police attempt to break up the gathering (December 30)

1990 HAMAS supporters win five of the nine seats in the elections for the Gaza Engineering Association. The other four are won by PLO members (January 26); the Palestine Press Service resumes operation after Israeli authorities had closed it in March 1988 (March 28); Arafat rejects HAMAS's condition to join the PLO, which controls 40 percent of the PNC's seats (April 9); Jewish settlers occupy St. John's Hospice, a Greek Orthodox building in the Christian Quarter of Jerusalem's Old City. Christian shrines in the Holy Land, including the Church of the Holy Sepulcher, are closed to protest the settlers' occupation of St. John's Hospice. In a show of solidarity with the Christian Community, the Islamic *Waqf* (Islamic endowment) closes *Al-Haram Al-Sharif* to visitors (April 12); Ami Popper, an Israeli, kills seven Palestinian workers at Rishon Le Zion while they are waiting to be picked up and taken to work. As news of the attack spreads in the Occupied Territories, violence erupts and seven Palestinians are killed and hundreds are wounded in a confrontation with the Israeli army (May 20); an unsuccessful seaborne attack on Israeli beaches is carried out by the Palestine Liberation Front, headed by Abu al-Abbas (May 30); the United States suspends its diplomatic dialogue with the PLO because Arafat refuses to condemn the PLF aborted attack on Israel (June 20); Palestinian leaders in the Occupied Territories begin a hunger strike at the Red Cross headquarters in Jerusalem to protest the killing of the seven Palestinian workers at Rishon Le Zion near Tel Aviv; Palestinian leaders in the Occupied Territories announce that they will no longer meet with U.S. officials and demand U.N. protection (June 1); Israel extends the closure of the Arab Studies Society in East Jerusalem for another year (July 29); the UNLU urges Palestinian factions to unite, and condemns the fatal beatings and torture of suspected Palestinian collaborators under interrogation by Palestinians (July 31); the Israeli High Court of Justice upholds the Israeli army's order imposing a permanent night curfew in the Gaza Strip. The night curfew already has been in effect for two years (August 19); Palestinians in the Occupied Territories demonstrate in support of Iraq's President Saddam Hussein. HAMAS issues a statement demanding Iraqi withdrawal from Kuwait and the "restoration of Kuwait's self-determination" (August 16); Palestinians crossing the bridges into Israel from Jordan are allowed to bring with them the equivalent of 500 Jordanian dinars, an increase from the previous regulation of 300 dinars (August 22); Elias Freij, the mayor of Bethlehem, announces that, because of the lost subsidies from Kuwait and other Arab states, the municipality would soon have difficulty paying the salaries of its employees (August 29); the UNLU distributes a special leaflet bearing the headline "U.S. Invasion of Arab Land," expressing unequivocal support for Iraq, and calling on foreign troops to withdraw from Saudi Arabia. The UNLC declares September 26 a strike day in solidarity with the Iraqi people (August 29); Israeli military authorities allow Bethlehem University to re-open after a closure of two and a half years (August 31); Birzeit University, Hebron University, and An-Najah National University are ordered closed for another three months (September 3); the Israeli Broadcasting Authority orders Israeli radio and television networks to use the Biblical Hebrew names, not the Arabic, when referring to Palestinian towns and villages in the Occupied Territories (September 4); Israeli border police kill 17 Palestinians and wound nearly 200 at *Al-Haram Al-Sharif* during a protest against members of the Temple Mount Faithful, who want to place a cornerstone at the *Al-Aqsa* Mosque area for the construction of the "Jewish Third Temple" (October 8); Israeli officials close *Al-Haram Al-Sharif* for the first time since 1967. Palestinians in Jerusalem and the Occupied Territories are not allowed to enter the entire area of *Al-Haram Al-Sharif* (October 9); the U.N. Security Council unanimously adopts Resolution 672 condemning the October 8 killing of Palestinians, and indirectly criticizes Palestinian actions on that day (October 12); the U.N. appoints a commission to investigate the *Al-Haram Al-Sharif* incident. Israel announces it will not cooperate with the U.N. Commission (October 14); in response to the Israeli refusal to receive and cooperate with the U.N. Investigative Mission, the United Nations issues Resolution 673 attacking Israel's position (October 24); Israeli military authorities arrest for "subversive activities" Radwan Abu Ayyash, head of the Arab Journalist Association, and Ziad Abu Zayyad, editor of *Gesher* (Bridge), a bi-monthly Hebrew paper published by Palestinians (November 13); Yasser Abed-Rabbo leaves the Democratic Front for the Liberation of Palestine and forms the Democratic Union Party (Fida) in the Occupied Territories (December 1)

1991 Salah Khalaf (Abu Iyyad), the PLO second-in-command, together with Hayel Abdel Hamid (Abu al-Hawl), the PLO security chief, and Fakhri al-Omari, an aide to Khalaf, are assassinated in Tunis by Hamza Abu Zayd, Khalaf's bodyguard (January 14); the Israeli High Court orders the Defense Ministry to begin distributing gas masks and chemical warfare defense kits to Palestinians living in the Occupied Territories (January 15); in response to the outbreak of the Gulf War, a state of emergency is declared in Israel. East Jerusalem and the Occupied Territories are placed under curfew (January 16); Israeli military authorities lift the curfew imposed on East Jerusalem, and allow the Palestinians in the Occupied Territories to leave their homes for a few hours to shop for necessities (January 22); Israeli authorities detain Sari Nuseibeh, a professor at Birzeit University, for allegedly spying for Iraq (January 29); a Jerusalem court sentences Nuseibeh to three months in prison (February 3); Israeli military authorities lift the curfew imposed on the Occupied Territories since January 16. Palestinians in the Occupied Territories are not allowed to travel to East Jerusalem and Israel (February 4); only 1,400 of the usual 120,000 Palestinian workers are allowed to return to their work in Israel (February 10); Israel permits only 400 Palestinians per day, instead of the usual 1,000, to cross the bridges into Israel from Jordan. Palestinians who are unable to enter from Jordan lose their residency permits (February 20); in the wake of the Allied ground offensive against Iraq, Israeli military authorities re-impose the curfew on the Occupied Territories (February 24); the Israeli Defense Cabinet demands that all Palestinians from the Occupied Territories working in Israel must have a permit from the Israeli military administration (March 31); Hebron University is allowed to re-open after a closure of three years (April 30); the first Chamber of Commerce elections since 1964 are held in Hebron; six seats are won by HAMAS, four by the PLO, and one by an independent candidate (June 19); U.S. Secretary of State James Baker informs Palestinian personalities led by PLO leader Faisal al-Husseini that the American initiative envisions the creation of "less than a state, and more than an autonomy." Baker tells the Palestinian delegation that the PLO cannot have direct relations with the peace delegation, nor can the Palestinians from East Jerusalem participate during the initial stages of the peace talks (July 21); An-Najah National University is allowed to re-open after three and a half years of closure (August 21); the PLO agrees to participate in the Middle East Peace Conference provided the following conditions are met: the Palestinians' right to self-determination is recognized, the Palestinian delegation is appointed by the PLO, East Jerusalem Palestinians are allowed to participate, and settlement activities in the Occupied Territories are halted (August 28); prominent U.S. university professors Edward Said and Ibrahim Abu Lughod resign from the Palestine National Council (September 18); during its meeting in Algiers, the PNC agrees to participate in the Middle East Peace Conference. Members of the PNSF boycott the meeting (September 23); Abu Abbas of the PLF resigns from the PNC (September 28); Israel imposes a ban on Palestinians from the Occupied Territories entering East Jerusalem (October 7); hundreds of Jewish settlers invade the village of Silwan, on the outskirts of Jerusalem, and occupy eight Arab homes (October 9); HAMAS, the Islamic Jihad, the PFLP-GC, FATAH Uprising, FATAH Revolutionary Council, and Sa'iqa denounce the PNC meeting in Algiers, and describe it as a "conference to sell out Palestine" (October 11); an Israeli military court sentences HAMAS leader, Sheikh Ahmad Yassin to life in prison (October 16); the PLO and Jordan agree to form a joint Jordanian-Palestinian delegation to attend the forthcoming Middle East Peace Conference in Madrid (October 16); PLO leader Faisal al-Husseini announces the names of the 14 Palestinian delegates to the Middle East Peace Conference. They are Samir Abdallah, Zakaria al-Agha, Mamduh 'Aker, Elias Freij, Abd al-Rahman Hamad, Saeb 'Erekat, Nabil al-Ja'bari, Sami Kilani, Freih Abu Middeyan, Mustafa al-Natsheh, and Haider Abd al-Shafi. An advisory council is created under the leadership of Faisal al-Husseini. It includes Hanan Ashrawi, Rashid Khalidi, Kamil Mansur, Sari Nuseibeh, and Anis al-Qassem (October 22); the Middle East Peace Conference sponsored by Russia and the United States begins in Madrid. Representatives from Israel, Egypt, Syria, Lebanon, Jordan, and Palestine attend the conference (October 30); Israeli, Jordanian, and Palestinian delegates agree in Madrid to work toward self-rule for the Palestinians in the Occupied Territories, in accordance with U.N. Resolutions 242 and 338. The Israeli-Jordanian-Palestinian delegation reaches a consensus that future talks would be conducted on "two tracks." Elections for the Chamber of Commerce are held in the city of Gaza for the first time since 1964. The PLO wins 13 seats, HAMAS two seats, and an independent candidate wins one seat (November 4); the PFLP suspends its membership in the PLO Executive Committee to protest the PLO's endorsement of the peace process (November 6); thousands of cheering Palestinians wait in Jericho to welcome the return of the Palestinian delegation from Madrid. During a news conference in Jerusalem, the delegates announce the establishment of "political committees" in the Occupied Territories to form the basis of the future Palestinian self-government (November 10); B'Tselem, the Israeli human rights organization, announces that since the Intifada began in December 9, 1987, the Israeli army has killed 806 Palestinians. The Palestinians themselves killed 484 fellow Palestinians for collaboration and 31 Israelis. Israel has deported 66 Palestinians, demolished 425 houses, and sealed 279 others (December 8); three sets of bilateral talks begin in Washington: Israeli-Syrian, Israeli-Lebanese and Israeli-Jordanian-Palestinian (December 10); about 30 Jewish settlers escorted by the Israeli police raid Silwan, south of Jerusalem, and evict Palestinian families from six houses (December 12); the two-week curfew imposed on Ramallah and al-Bireh is lifted during the daytime, but remains in effect at night. Israeli military authorities issue a regulation requiring Palestinians in the Occupied Territories to maintain a distance of 150 yards from the sides of the roads, between sunset and sunrise, to prevent attacks on Israeli settlers driving at night in the Occupied Territories (December 15); the U.N. General Assembly revokes Resolution 3379 of November 10, 1975, which states that "Zionism is a form of racism and racial discrimination" (December 16)

1992 Following the Israeli decision to deport 12 Palestinians from the Occupied Territories, Palestinian and Arab delegates delay their attendance at the third round of the bilateral peace talks in Washington (January 4); Palestinian and Jordanian negotiators arrive in Washington to begin the peace talks (January 9); the heads of the Israeli and Jordanian-Palestinian delegations to the peace talks agree on the "two tracks" approach, on condition that two Jordanians will be present with the Palestinian delegation, and two Palestinians will attend with the Jordanian delegation. The Palestinian delegation to the peace talks presents the Israeli delegation with a self-rule plan (January 14–16); leaders of the main Christian churches in the Holy Land threaten to request international assistance if Israel does not protect the Christian archaeological sites in Jerusalem. The Christian leaders also condemn the confiscation of Palestinian homes in the village of Silwan, near Jerusalem (January 14); the United States and Russia refuse to allow the Palestinian delegation to participate in the multilateral talks in Moscow, because the delegation includes Palestinians from the diaspora and East Jerusalem (January 26–27); for the first time since 1967, the Israeli High Court of Justice asks military authorities to lift the night curfew imposed on Ramallah and al-Bireh for the last two months (January 28); representatives from Jordan, Israel, Egypt, Saudi Arabia, Kuwait, Oman, Qatar, Bahrain, United Arab Emirates, Tunisia, Morocco, Mauritania, Turkey, China, Japan, Canada, the European Community, the European

Free Trade Association, the United States, and Russia attend the Multilateral Peace Conference in Moscow. Algeria, Lebanon, Syria, Yemen and the Palestinians boycott the meeting. The conference establishes five working groups: economic development, environment, arms control and security, refugees, and water resources. Hanan Ashrawi, the Palestinian spokeswoman, announces that the Palestinians will participate in these working groups. Ashrawi suggests the establishment of two additional working groups, one on Jerusalem and the other on human rights (January 28–29); Israeli authorities arrest two Palestinian delegates to the peace process, Muhammad Abd al-Fattal al-Hawrani and Jamal al-Shawbaki. Hanan Ashrawi protests and announces that the Palestinian delegation will not participate in the forthcoming peace talks (February 18); following discussions with the U.S. State Department, the Palestinian delegation agrees to attend the fourth round of the bilateral peace talks (February 19); the Israeli delegation submits its own version of a self-government plan to the Palestinian delegation. It would allow the Palestinians in the Occupied Territories control and administration of 12 areas, among them taxation, education, and health. The Palestinian delegation rejects the plan, and instead gives the Israeli delegation a proposal to elect a 180-seat parliament to manage the Occupied Territories during the interim period of self-rule (February 27–March 8); Israeli military authorities close Birzeit University for another three months. The university is the only one in the West Bank to remain closed (February 28); HAMAS supporters win 10 of the 11 seats in the Chamber of Commerce elections in Ramallah (March 4); a total of 117 members of the Palestine National Council sign a petition and send it to PLO leaders expressing reservations about the peace talks, demanding Israeli recognition of the PLO, and a freeze on Israeli settlement activities in the Occupied Territories (March 14); the EC "troika" representatives meet with Palestinian leaders in Jerusalem to discuss the peace process and economic assistance to the Occupied Territories (March 28); the PFLP, DFLP faction, Palestine Liberation Front, and the Palestinian Popular Struggle Front declare in Damascus, Syria, their support of a confederation between Jordan and Palestine in accordance with the PNC resolutions of 1988 (March 30); Arafat's plane crashes in a desert sandstorm near al-Sarra in southern Libya. The plane is found 12 hours after the crash. Three of Arafat's crewmen die, while Arafat and nine others survive (April 7); Birzeit University is allowed to re-open the Science and Engineering colleges; the rest of the colleges in the University are to remain closed (April 20); the fifth round of the bilateral peace talks starts in Washington. The Israeli negotiators propose municipal elections and Palestinian administration of hospitals in the West Bank and the Gaza Strip. The Palestinian negotiators reject the Israeli proposal and ask that elections be held for a Palestinian Legislative Assembly (April 27–30); HAMAS, the PFLP, and the DFLP support the Israeli proposal of holding municipal elections in the Occupied Territories, if the elections are held under international supervision. FATAH rejects the municipal elections proposal (April 28); King Fahd of Saudi Arabia expresses willingness to restore the Dome of the Rock in Jerusalem. His announcement angers King Hussein of Jordan, who has traditionally been responsible for *Al-Haram Al-Sharif*, which includes *Al-Aqsa* and the Dome of the Rock Mosques (April 29); the Jordanian cabinet announces that Jordan will pay all the expenses of renovating the Dome of the Rock. Hussein declares that he will personally contribute $8.25 million to the restoration of the two mosques (May 5); FATAH supporters win all the seats in the elections to the Staff Union at An-Najah National University. FATAH supporters also defeat HAMAS in the elections for the Workers' Union at Augusta Victoria Hospital in Jerusalem (May 11); PLO supporters running on a "Nationalist Muslim List" win nine of the 12 seats in the election for the Chamber of Commerce and Industry in Nablus. HAMAS wins the remaining three seats (May 21); the UNLU condemns the killing of Palestinian collaborators by fellow Palestinians (May 30); student demonstrations break out at An-Najah National University. Israeli military authorities close the university for one month (June 2); Radwan Abu Ayyash, a member of the Palestinian Advisory Council to the Palestinian delegation, establishes the Social Solidarity Society, a new socio-political organization composed of 178 members (June 17); the Palestinian delegation to the peace talks holds its first public meeting with PLO Chairman Arafat in Amman, Jordan (June 18); Israel detains 17 Palestinian delegates for questioning, after their meeting with Arafat (June 29); an agreement to end the violence between PLO and HAMAS supporters is arranged by Haider Abd al-Shafi, a Palestinian-Israeli delegation led by MK Abd al-Wahhab Darawsheh and Sheikh Raid Salah, the mayor of Um al-Fahm, (July 10); a four-day siege of An-Najah National University ends. Four Palestinian activists inside the campus agree to surrender to Israeli military authorities, and to accept "voluntary exile" to Jordan for three years (July 17); Israel prevents four delegates to the peace talks from crossing the bridge into Jordan. In protest, the entire Palestinian delegation returns to the Occupied Territories (August 21); the Palestinian delegation leaves for Washington to attend the sixth round of the bilateral peace talks. As a gesture of goodwill to the Palestinians, Israel's new Prime Minister Yitzhak Rabin orders the release of 800 Palestinian prisoners who have not committed violent activities resulting in Israeli casualties, and who have already served more than two-thirds of their terms. He also orders the opening of some homes and streets that have been sealed by the Israeli army, and allows Palestinians more than 50 years of age to enter Jerusalem without a permit. Rabin retracts the January expulsion order to deport 12 Palestinians. Instead, they are placed in administrative detention for six months (August 23–24); Haider Abd al-Shafi, head of the Palestinian delegation to the peace talks, calls for a referendum on whether or not the Palestinians in the Occupied Territories wish the delegates to continue with the peace process (September 19); more than 5,000 Palestinian prisoners start a hunger strike to protest conditions in Israeli jails (September 27); Israel expresses willingness to investigate the demands of the Palestinian prisoners. The prisoners end their hunger strike (October 11); 85 PLO Central Council members out of the total 105 meet in Tunis, and give the "green light" to the Palestinian delegation to pursue the peace talks with Israel (October 17); at the seventh round of the bilateral peace talks, the Palestinian delegates agree that UNSCR 242 will be applied in the final stages of the talks, and not in the transitional period. Palestinian working groups are established to formulate a plan for Palestinian self-rule, and the nature of its authority (October 23–29); in response to the killing of an Israeli soldier, Shmuel Geresh, Israeli military authorities place a curfew on Hebron (October 25); in a winner-take-all election at Birzeit University, five seats are taken by FATAH, three by the PFLP, and one by the DFLP.

Supporters of these three groups create a pro-PLO United Front at Birzeit University. The front defeats HAMAS supporters in the student council elections (November 12); to protest the lack of progress in the peace process, the PLO leadership meets in Tunis and decides to send only four delegates, not the usual 14, to the eighth round of the bilateral peace talks (December 6); Arab and Palestinian delegates to the peace talks in Washington suspend their participation for one day to mark the fifth anniversary of the Intifada (December 9); HAMAS activists kidnap an Israeli border policeman, Nissim Toledano, and threaten to kill him unless Israel releases their leader, Sheikh Ahmad Yassin (December 13); the Israeli delegation at the eighth round of the bilateral peace talks gives the Palestinian delegation documents dealing with the following issues: interim self-rule, confirming UNSCR 242 and 338 as the basis for negotiations; a tripartite land management proposal for the interim period, which gives the Palestinians in the Occupied Territories autonomy to manage their lands, while the Israelis would manage lands in the Occupied Territories used by the Israeli army and settlers; a joint Israeli-Palestinian team to administer public lands (December 14); the kidnapped Israeli border policeman, Nissim Toledano, is found dead outside Jerusalem (December 15); in response to the murder of Toledano, Israeli authorities deport to Lebanon 415 Palestinians who allegedly are members of Islamic organizations from the Occupied Territories. The PLO suspends the peace talks until the deportees are allowed to return to their homes. The delegates of the Arab states boycott the negotiations to protest the deportations. HAMAS denounces the deportations and declares war on "every Zionist in Palestine." HAMAS and the UNLU issue the first-ever joint statement in the Occupied Territories, in which they demand the return of the Palestinian deportees and agree to coordinate their strike days (December 17); U.N. Security Council unanimously condemns the deportation of Palestinians and adopts Resolution 799, which calls on Israel to immediately return the deportees to their homes (December 18); the Jerusalem district attorney issues a brief that the Israeli Custodian of Abandoned Properties had improperly transferred six Arab houses in the village of Silwan, south of Jerusalem, in October and December 1991 to the Jewish Settlers Housing Association, and that the evicted Palestinian families are entitled to compensation or reclamation of their homes (December 22); the Palestinian deportees decide to stay in the no-mans land, Marj al-Zuhur, between Israel and Lebanon, until the U.N. enforces Resolution 799, and orders Israel to return them to the Occupied Territories (December 29); Nabil Sha'ath, the PLO advisor and head of the Palestinian Delegation Steering Committee, declares that the peace process and the Palestinian deportees are "two battles which have to be fought separately" (December 31)

1993 Rabin states that Israel would allow the return of 415 Palestinian deportees in exchange for a suspension of the Intifada for nine-months (January 1); at a meeting in Khartoum, Sudan, HAMAS and FATAH leaders create three committees to supervise the continuation of their dialogue and the return of the Palestinian deportees (January 4); the International Red Cross (IRC) airlifts two Palestinian deportees to Israel. One is suffering from kidney problems, and the other is a teenager deported by mistake. The IRC is unable to bring nine others who were inadvertently deported, because Lebanon refuses to allow more airlifts (January 9); Israel permits the IRC to deliver medicine to the Palestinian deportees and allows the return of 15 deportees who were mistakenly expelled (January 13–14); in a vote of 39 to 20, the Israeli Knesset rescinds the 1986 law legalizing contacts with the PLO (January 19); U.N. envoy Chinmaya Gharekhan asks Israel to implement U.N. Resolution 799, and allow the return of the Palestinian deportees (January 20); in an interview with Israeli televison, Arafat invites Rabin to meet with PLO leaders. Rabin rejects the invitation and reiterates that his government will not negotiate directly with the PLO (January 21–22); Israel permits the IRC to return 17 Palestinian deportees. Four are taken to a hospital, two return home, and 11 are imprisoned. A total of 396 Palestinian deportees remain in Lebanon (January 23); the Palestine National Salvation Front denounces Israel's decision to lift the ban on contacts with the PLO (January 27); the Palestinian deportees begin a hunger strike to protest Israel's brutal policies against the Palestinians in the Occupied Territories (January 28); Israel declares that it will allow the immediate return of 100 Palestinian deportees, while the rest will be allowed to return in one year. The deportees reject the offer and demand the return of all deportees at the same time, in accordance with U.N. Resolution 799. The PLO and HAMAS reject the Israeli "100" offer and insist upon the return of all Palestinian deportees (February 1); U.S. Secretary of State Christopher declares that Israel's offer is a "sufficient solution" to the Palestinian deportees stranded in South Lebanon (February 2); Yasser Abed-Rabbo confirms his split from the DFLP, and declares the establishment of the Palestinian Democratic Union (Fida) in the Occupied Territories (February 5); Sheikh Sa'd al-Din al-Alami, the *Mufti* of Jerusalem and the head of the Higher Muslim Council, dies in Jerusalem (February 6); the former mayor of East Jerusalem, Anwar al-Khatib, dies in Jerusalem (February 7); Jordan appoints Sheikh Suleiman al-Ja'bari, the *Mufti* of Jerusalem (February 17); Palestinian negotiators declare that their participation in the next round of peace talks is conditional on the Israeli commitment to "never again deport more Palestinians," and a timetable for the return of the Palestinian deportees (February 22); after their meeting with Christopher, the Palestinain delegates state that they will not return to the peace talks until the Palestinian deportees are allowed back to the Occupied Territories (February 23); to encourage the Palestinians to resume the peace talks, Christopher gives the Palestinian delegates a six-point plan: Palestinian deportation to Lebanon is illegal. U.N. Security Council Resolution 242 and 338 (land for peace) are the bases of the peace talks, a binding Israeli commitment against future expulsions; the return of the Palestinian deportees from Lebanon, an end to human rights violations in the Occupied Territories, and the return of many post-1967 deportees (February 24); in response to demonstrations by armed and masked youth in Gaza, Israeli military authorities close the Islamic and al-Azhar universities in the city of Gaza (February 24); Israel declares that the expulsion of the Palestinians to Lebanon on December 17, 1992, is not a government policy, and pledges to allow the return of many Palestinians who were expelled after the war of 1967, if the Palestinians agree to resume the peace talks in April (February 25); the Palestinian delegates refuse to participate in the ninth round because Israel has not resolved the problem of the Palestinian deportees (March 10); Israeli authorities close the Occupied Territories indefinitely, barring Palestinians from entering East Jerusalem and Israel (March 30); Israel allows Jerusalem resident and PLO leader Faisal al-Husseini to head the Palestinian delegation to the peace talks (April 9); Palestinian Christians in the Occupied Territories demand that they be allowed to enter East Jerusalem on Easter (April 15); in a meeting held in Damascus, Syria, Palestinian and Arab delegates agree to participate in the ninth round of the bilateral peace talks (April 21); Ghassan al-Khatib, a delegate to the talks, announces that he and fellow PPP member Samir Abdallah will boycott the ninth round of talks (April 21); Israel declares that 35 to 50 of the estimated 1,200 Palestinians who were expelled from the Occupied Territories between 1967 and 1987 will be allowed to return (April 23); the head of the Palestinian negotiating team, Dr. Haider Abd al-Shafi, resigns because of disagreement with the PLO's decision to resume the peace talks. Palestinian delegates and Gaza supporters pressure Abd al-Shafi to withdraw his resignation and to resume heading the Palestinian delegation (April 24); during the first day of the ninth round of the bilateral peace talks, Abd al-Aziz al-Rantisi, spokesperson for the Palestinian deportees, declares that the deportees will not accept any agreement signed by the Palestinian delegation (April 27); the Israeli delegation agrees to the return of 30 post-1967 deportees, from a list of 55 names that the Palestinian delegation submitted. Israel allows about 5,000 Palestinian expatriates visiting their families to remain permanently in the Occupied Territories. The Israeli and Palestinian delegations agree to establish three subcommittees to discuss Palestinian autonomy, land, water, and human rights issues (April 28–29); another 15 post-1967 deportees return to the Occupied Territories. Among them is Dr. Hanna Nasser, President of Birzeit University, who was deported in 1974, as well as the former mayor of al-Bireh, Abd al-Jawad Saleh, who was expelled in 1986. The Palestinian deportees in Lebanon describe the return of the post-1967 deportees as a "stab in the back," because the spotlight has been transferred to them and away from the recent deportees in Lebanon (April 30); an additional 14 post-1967 deportees return to the Occupied Territories. Among them is Rawhi al-Khatib, the former mayor of East Jerusalem (May 3); after the ninth round of the peace talks, Haider Abd al-Shafi calls for suspension of the Palestinian participation in the peace talks. He writes an open letter in *Al-Quds* (Jerusalem), the Arabic daily newspaper, asking the

PLO to "adopt the principle of collective leadership on a democratic basis" (May 19); in protest against the peace talks, Sheikh Abd al-Hamid al-Sayyeh announces his resignation as the speaker of the Palestine National Council (May 22); the Palestinian delegation accepts the U.S. invitation to attend the 10th round of the peace talks in Washington (May 27); Israel and the PLO send only a symbolic number of delegates to the peace talks. The Palestinian and Israeli delegations agree to establish a subcommittee to formulate the basic principles governing the structure of Palestinian autonomy (June 15); Hassan Tahboub becomes the new chairman of the Supreme Muslim Council in Jerusalem (June 17); to rescue the peace talks, the United States gives the Israeli and Palestinian delegations an informal working paper, suggesting the transfer of such responsibilities as budget, health, and education to the Palestinians in the Occupied Territories. The Israeli and Palestinian delegations reject the proposal (June 30); Faisal al-Husseini, the Palestinian delegation coordinator, Hanan Ashrawi, the Palestinian spokesperson, and Saeb 'Erekat, the deputy delegation head, travel to Tunis to submit their resignation over the PLO's new concessions and compromises on the issue of the five-year self-rule interim period (August 8); meeting in Tunis, the PLO Executive Committee rejects their resignations, and appoints them to the PLO Steering Committee (August 12); due to widespread sickness, the Palestinian deportees in Marj al-Zuhur, Lebanon, accept the Israeli proposal to allow the return of 187 persons to the Occupied Territories by mid-September and the remaining 208 persons by the end of the year (August 15); PLO Executive Committee member, Mahmoud Darwish, submits his resignation to protest the peace talks (August 20); Shafiq al-Hout, PLO representative in Lebanon, suspends his membership in the PLO Executive Committee to protest the peace talks (August 22); the Israeli cabinet approves the Palestinian Self-Rule Agreement reached with the PLO in Oslo. The plan includes the withdrawal of Israeli forces from the Gaza Strip and Jericho, and within two or three years, negotiations are to begin on the permanent status of the West Bank, Jerusalem, refugees, and Jewish settlements. The Norwegian government confirms that 14 secret rounds of talks were held in Norway between Israeli and Palestinian negotiators (August 30); the 11th round of the bilateral peace talks commences in Washington, and ends with no progress (August 31); Israel and the PLO mutually recognize each other; the United States resumes its dialogue with the PLO (September 10); to protest the PLO-Israel agreement, Taysir Khalid of the PFLP, Abd al-Rahman Mallul of the DFLP, and Abdallah Hourani resign from the PLO Executive Committee (September 10); Mahmoud Abbas, spokesperson for the PLO Foreign Affairs Department and member of the PLO Executive Committee, and Israeli Foreign Minister Shimon Peres sign the "Declaration of Principles" (DOP). Arafat and Rabin shake hands (September 13); the DFLP and PFLP encourage the Palestinians in the Occupied Territories to continue with the Intifada. The United States promises the Palestinians $250 million in assistance over a two-year period to support the agreement (September 19); the Israeli Knesset votes 61 to 50 in favor of the DOP agreement (September 23); meeting in Tunis, the PLO Central Council approves the Gaza-Jericho First Accord. The PLO establishes the Palestine National Authority (PNA) and appoints Arafat its head (October 12); Israeli and Palestinian negotiators meet simultaneously in Taba and Cairo to implement the DOP agreement (October 13–14); Israel agrees to release 700 of the estimated 12,500 Palestinian prisoners. As'ad Saftawi, headmaster of UNRWA school in the Buraij Refugee Camp in Gaza and a supporter of the peace process, is killed by two masked gunmen. Representatives from 43 countries pledge $2 billion, including $100 million from Saudi Arabia, over the next five years to support the implementation of the Israeli-Palestinian Accord (October 21); Israeli authorities allow women and men over 40 years of age, as well as children under 16 years, physicians, attorneys, and students, to enter East Jerusalem without a permit from Israeli military authorities (October 23); HAMAS, PFLP, and DFLP supporters unite against FATAH and win all nine seats of the Birzeit University Student Council; HAMAS supporters win all nine seats of the student council at Gaza Islamic College. The Palestine National authority asks Mansur al-Shawwa to form a municipal council for the city of Gaza. Hanan Ashrawi resigns her post as spokewoman for the Palestinian delegation, and forms the Palestinian Independent Commission for Human Rights (December 10); the remaining 197 Palestinian deportees return from Lebanon at the end of their one-year exile (December 15)

1994 Haider Abd al-Shafi travels to Tunis with a Palestinian delegation carrying a petition signed by 118 PLO members, asking Arafat to set up a collective Palestinian leadership (January 2); Israel releases another 101 Palestinian prisoners. A total of 700 Palestinians have been released during the past three months (January 7); Farouq al-Qaddumi, chief of PLO Foreign Affairs Department, signs an accord with Jordanian officials, granting the Jordanian Central Bank financial authority in the Occupied Territories (January 7); Faisal al-Husseini asks Saudi Arabia to resume its financial assistance to the PLO. It had been suspended because of Arafat's pro-Iraqi position during the 1991 Gulf crisis (January 7); B'Tselem reports that 770 to 942 Palestinians suspected of collaboration with the Israelis have been killed by Palestinians since the beginning of the Intifada in December 1987 (January 9); the Palestinian Development Bank, with initial capital of $250 million, is established to help develop the Palestinian autonomous areas (January 13); Dr. Baruch Goldstein, a U.S.-born Israeli living in the settlement of Kiryat Arba, in Hebron, kills 29 Palestinian Muslim worshipers at *Al-Haram Al-Ibrahimi* Mosque (Cave of the Patriarchs) in Hebron (February 25); Israel releases about 1,000 Palestinian prisoners, and establishes a Commission of Inquiry to investigate the massacre in Hebron (March 1–2); to protect the Palestinians, the PLO demands the disarming of Jewish settlers, and the deployment of an international force in the Occupied Territories (March 2); the Israeli Commission of Inquiry of the Hebron massacre opens hearings in Jerusalem (March 8); a total of 400 Palestinians, including 135 PNC members and 50 PLO Executive Committee members, demand the suspension of the negotiations with Israel until protection is provided for the Palestinians in the Occupied Territories (March 9); B'Tselem reports that 62 Palestinians were killed by Jewish settlers between 1988 and 1994, but that only one settler had been convicted of murder, and in only seven cases had the lives of settlers been sufficiently threatened to warrant shooting (March 15); the PLO agrees to the Temporary International Presence (TIPH) in Hebron, which is composed of 160 lightly armed observers from Denmark (35), Italy (35), and Norway (90) (March 31); Mustafa al-Natsheh, the deposed mayor of Hebron, is reinstated by the PLO as mayor. The Bank of Jordan opens its first branch in Ramallah, the West

Bank (April 1); Israel allows the return of 50 post-1967 Palestinian deportees. Twenty seven deportees return to the Gaza Strip and the rest to the West Bank (April 4); Israel begins to redeploy its army in Jericho and the Gaza Strip (April 4); Israel agrees to release 2,500 Palestinian prisoners after the signing of the Gaza-Jericho Accord, and an additional 2,500 prisoners when the Palestinians take over the autonomous areas. The PLO and Israel agree that the Palestinian police force would consist of 9,000 persons, including 2,000 from the Occupied Territories and 7,000 from the outside, who will be armed with automatic rifles and handguns (April 12); the renovation of the Dome of the Rock in Jerusalem, financed by King Hussein of Jordan, is completed (April 18); the former head of the Palestinian negotiating team, Haider Abd al-Shafi, and delegate member Ghassan al-Khatib, together with 21 prominent Palestinians, sign a petition urging Israel to end its settlement activities in the Occupied Territories. They warn that any agreement between the PLO and Israel that does not end such activities would not be binding, and the Palestinians would continue with their struggle against Israel (April 25); Arafat and Rabin sign the "Cairo Agreement" in Cairo, which deals with the control of border crossings and the principle of self-rule. The agreement allows Israel and the PLO to share responsibilities at border crossings, and to jointly control the roads leading from the Jewish settlements in the Gaza Strip to Israel. The Palestine National Authority will issue passports to the Palestinians in the autonomous area, print their own stamps, and obtain an international code. Israel agrees to release 200 Palestinian prisoners and allows 15 post-1967 deportees to return to the Occupied Territories (May 4); HAMAS, the PFLP, and the DFLP denounce the Gaza-Jericho Accord, but state that their organizations will not clash with the Palestinian police (May 5); Israel and the PLO sign an agreement in Cairo finalizing plans for Israel to hand over the administration of the Gaza Strip and Jericho to a Palestinian autonomous authority. About 117 members of the Temporary International Observers (TIPH) arrive in Hebron to promote stability and provide safety for the Palestinians in the city (May 8); the Israeli Knesset, by a vote of 52–0, approves the Gaza-Jericho agreement (May 11); 157 members of the Palestinian police enter the Gaza Strip from Egypt (May 13); *Al-Aqsa* Brigade of the Palestine

Liberation Army takes up its duties in Jericho (May 13); the IDF evacuates its Gaza City headquarters and the Gaza Central Prison. The Israeli occupation of Jericho and the Gaza Strip ends (May 17); Arafat revokes the Israeli military orders in the autonomous areas (May 24); the PLO names the members of the Palestine National Authority (May 28); Israel releases 500 Palestinian political prisoners, bringing to 4,200 of 5,000 prisoners Israel has promised to release (June 9); Jericho Mayor Jamil Khalaf resigns, and a transitional municipal committee is appointed (June 6); PNA pays the salaries of the 7,600 Palestinian civil administration employees, as well as the 9,000 Palestinian police officers (June 8); the Israeli Cabinet allows the entry of 10,000 Palestinians to work in Israel (June 19); the PNA holds its first meeting in Gaza City (June 26); the Israeli Commission of Inquiry on the *Al-Ibrahimi* Mosque massacre reports that Goldstein acted alone. It recommends that Jewish worshipers not be allowed to carry weapons inside the mosque, and that Muslim and Jewish worshipers be separated. The commission also reports that 29 people were killed and 125 were wounded inside the mosque (June 26); members of the PNA meet in Gaza City under the leadership of Nabil Sha'ath, the minister of Planning and International Coordination (June 26); Arafat enters Gaza (July 1); Palestinian deportees in Jordan demand that they be allowed to return to the Occupied Territories. The PLO estimates that there are 1,260 deportees, only 110 of whom have been allowed to return since the signing of the accord (July 4); Arafat arrives in Jericho and 12 of the 24 members of the PNA are sworn in. Arafat becomes the head of the PNA (July 5); Israeli Prime Minister Rabin, Foreign Minister Peres, and PLO Chairman Arafat are awarded the UNESCO Felix Houphouet-Boigny Peace Award (July 6); with the approval of the PLO, the Israeli Civil Administration appoints Ghassan al-Shak'a as mayor of Nablus (July 10); the PNA forbids the distribution of the pro-Jordanian *An-Nahar* (The Day), an Arabic daily, and *Akbar Al-Balad* (Town News), a weekly, in the autonomous areas. The PNA accuses the two newspapers of taking a stand contradictory to the national interests of the Palestinian people (July 28); the Temporary International Observers leave Hebron after their three-month mandate ends (August 8); HAMAS, Islamic Jihad, PFLP, and DFLP accuse Arafat of forcing the

Palestinians into a civil war (August 17); the PNA imposes a curfew in Gaza to stop the unrest following the death of a Palestinian at the hands of Palestinian police (August 20–21); HAMAS demands that executive positions in the Gaza City Council be given to the Palestinian opposition (August 21); 171 Palestinians, including members of the PNC, PLO Central Council, and PLO Executive Committee reject Arafat's call for a PNC meeting in Gaza to consider amending the Palestinian Charter (August 22); Danny Rothschild, the Israeli negotiator, and PNA's Minister of Planning, Nabil Sha'ath, agree in Cairo on early empowerment, which will give the PNA control over education, tourism, health, social welfare, and taxation in the West Bank (August 29); Morocco establishes official ties with Israel and opens a liaison office in Gaza (September 1); *An-Nahar* (The Day), a daily newspaper, resumes publication and distribution in the autonomous areas (September 5); meeting with HAMAS leaders, Arafat offers financial assistance to the Islamic University in Gaza, a HAMAS stronghold (September 8); Mahmoud Abbas, the negotiator of the Oslo Agreement, visits Jericho, Gaza, and the Occupied Territories for the first time in 25 years (September 9); the PNA receives $90 million of the $2 billion allocated by the donor countries. The PNA will need $11.2 billion to finance the autonomous areas until the year 2000 (September 16); to protest Arafat's authoritarian approach, PNA Economic Minister Ahmad Qre'i resigns. Arafat rejects the resignation (September 16); the PNA announces the establishment of a new *Waqf* Ministry to be headed by Sheikh Hassan Tahboub. The new ministry will assume charge of all Islamic sites in East Jerusalem. King Hussein of Jordan sidesteps the new ministry and reaffirms his responsibility for the holy places in Jerusalem (September 17–22); Ahmad Qre'i resolves his differences with Arafat and withdraws his resignation (September 22); the Jordan government declares that it is no longer responsible for administering *Waqf* (Islamic endowment) activities in the West Bank. However, Jordan insists on maintaining control of the *Waqf* in East Jerusalem (October 1); the Palestinian delegation gives the government of Israel a draft of the election laws for the Palestinian Council. The electoral regions are divided into 12 areas: three in the Gaza Strip, eight in the West Bank, and one in East Jerusalem (October 3); Khalid al-Hassan, founding member of the PLO and senior advisor to Arafat, dies of cancer in Rabat, Morocco (October 8); members of HAMAS kidnap Israeli soldier Nahshon Wachsman. The kidnappers demand the release of 200 Palestinian prisoners, including Shiekh Ahmad Yassin, Sheikh Salah Shehadeh, Sheikh Abd al-Karim Obeid, and Mustafa al-Dirani, in return for Wachsman's release. Israel holds Arafat responsible for Wachsman's safety, seals off the Gaza Strip, and suspends all negotiations with the PLO. The Israeli army raids a house in the village of Bir Nabala, north of Jerusalem, where Wachsman is being held. The two kidnappers and Wachsman are killed. Two other soldiers also are killed, and 12 are wounded (October 11–14); the *Mufti* of Jerusalem, Sheikh Suleiman al-Ja'bari, dies. Jordan appoints Sheikh Abd al Qader Abdeen in his place (October 11); Jordan and the PNA agree that the Jordanian dinar will continue to serve as an official currency in the Occupied Territories (October 12); HAMAS supporters demonstrate outside Gaza's Central Prison, demanding the release of Palestinians who were arrested by the PNA's police during the search for the kidnapped Israeli soldier (October 15); the PNA appoints Sheikh Ekrameh Sabri as the *Mufti* of Jerusalem (October 16); the PNA authorizes the publication of *Al-Istiqlal* (Independence) weekly newspaper, which is affiliated with the Islamic Jihad (October 21); to balance its ties, the Vatican establishes official relations with the PLO (October 25); Israel and Jordan sign a peace treaty ending years of hostilities between them (October 26); a car bomb kills Hani Abed, leader of the Islamic Jihad, in the Gaza Strip (November 2); DFLP leader Nayef Hawatmeh declares that his organization will not participate in the Palestinian National Council nor the PNA's institutions (November 5); Arafat appoints HAMAS members Hamid Bitawi and Muhammad Salameh as deputy justices to the Supreme Religious Courts (November 13); Israel hands over responsibilities for social welfare and tourism in the West Bank to the PNA (November 15); fighting breaks out between the Palestinian police and supporters of HAMAS and Islamic Jihad at the end of the noon prayer at Gaza City Mosque. Sixteen Palestinians are killed and more than 200 wounded (November 20); Israel hands over the responsibilities for health and taxes in the West Bank to the PNA, thus completing the early transfer of five areas (education, health, taxation, social welfare, and tourism) (December 1); Arafat, Rabin and Peres accept the 1994 Nobel Peace Prize in Oslo (December 10); a Palestinian cyclist carrying explosives on his body detonates himself and kills three Israelis and wounds many others near the Israeli settlement of Natzarim in the Gaza Strip. The Palestinian police arrest more than 100 Islamic Jihad activists in the Gaza Strip soon after Islamic Jihad claims responsibility for the attack (December 11); violent clashes between Palestinian police and the Islamists in the Gaza Strip leave 13 people dead and more than 200 injured (December 18); FATAH supporters win all the seats on the student council at al-Azhar University in Gaza (December 20); to prevent the PNA from laying claim to East Jerusalem, Israeli authorities prevent the Palestinian Economic Council for Development and Reconstruction (PECDAR) from convening a workshop in East Jerusalem (December 21); Israeli Peace Now activists and Palestinians gather at the village of al-Khader, near Hebron, to protest the extension of the settlement of Efrat on Arab-owned land (December 22)

1995 Israeli Prime Minister Rabin stops Efrat settlers from extending the borders of their settlement, but allows them to build 500 apartment units at a site near the settlement. FATAH Higher Committee in the West Bank, together with HAMAS, calls on the PNA to suspend all current negotiations with Israel for the implementation of the second part of the Palestinian-Israeli Declaration of Principles until Israel halts its settlement activities in the West Bank and East Jerusalem. Four Palestinian police officers are shot dead by Israeli soldiers in a gun battle near the village of Hanun, north of the Gaza Strip (January 2); PNA minister of Planning and International Coordination, Nabil Sha'ath, threatens to quit as chief negotiator unless Israel releases Palestinian prisoners (January 3); Palestinians meet at al-Bireh Municipality to protest the Israeli expropriation of 5,000 dunums (1,250 acres) for the construction of new "settler" roads designed to bypass Palestinian areas. Among the demonstrators are Suleiman al-Najjab, head of the Palestinian People's Party and a member of the PLO Executive Committee (January 4); the Israeli government allows entry of vehicles with Palestinian license plates into Israel. However, individuals must have a permit that allows them to leave the Palestinian autonomous areas and to enter East Jerusalem and Israel (January 8); Arafat and

Rabin meet at the Israel-Gaza border and agree on the following: the routes linking the autonomous areas of Gaza and Jericho, use of these routes by Palestinian men more than 50 years of age and women more than 35 years old, recognition of the Palestinian passport and the release of Palestinian prisoners, the resumption in Cairo of Israeli-Palestinian talks on election procedures and the expansion of self-rule in the West Bank (January 9); HAMAS urges the PNA to cooperate in escalating attacks and sabotage activities against Jewish settlers, to force them out of the Occupied Territories. PNA Minister Nabil Sha'ath announces that the PNA has committed itself to peaceful resistance (January 13); to increase transparency in its spending, the PNA forms a ministerial committee to list economic priorities and supervise the expenditure of millions of dollars in foreign aid to the autonomous areas. The committee is headed by Arafat, and includes Ahmad Qre'i, Nabil Sha'ath, Zuhdi Nashashibi, and Farouq al-Qaddumi (January 14); alleging that the offices of *Al-Quds* (Jerusalem), Arabic daily in East Jerusalem, are bases for HAMAS, Israeli police raid the offices and confiscate papers and equipment (January 16); meeting at the Erez checkpoint, between Israel and Gaza, Rabin assures Arafat that Israel will halt the construction of new settlements in the Occupied Territories (January 19); two Palestinian suicide bombers explode themselves at a bus stop at the Beit Liot junction in Israel, killing 19 people and wounding 62, mostly soldiers returning from home leave. Islamic Jihad claims responsibility for the explosion, and states that it is in retaliation for the murder of Hani Abed of Gaza and the continuous settlement activities in the Occupied Territories. Israel seals off the autonomous areas and the Occupied Territories, and prevents Palestinians from entering East Jerusalem and Israel. Israel's President Ezer Weizman calls on the government to stop negotiating with the PNA. Israel delays the release of Palestinian prisoners and the opening of the safe-passage route between Israel and the autonomous areas of the Gaza Strip and Jericho (January 22); Jordan and the PNA agree to settle their differences over East Jerusalem. The PNA recognizes Jordan's custody over the Muslim holy places, while Jordan supports Palestinian sovereignty over East Jerusalem. The Israeli army, equipped with welding machines, seals off the offices of the Islamic League of Palestinian Ulama (religious scholars) in the West Bank towns of Hebron, al-Bireh and Jenin on suspicion that the league has links with HAMAS (January 23); the PNA in the Gaza Strip disarms 60 Palestinian policemen accused of being members of HAMAS and Islamic Jihad, and gives them office positions. Israeli soldiers raid *Al-Quds* University's College of Science and Technology at Abu Dis, near Jerusalem and arrest 30 students and one lecturer for allegedly being members of HAMAS and Islamic Jihad. Four female students are taken to a hospital and treated for trauma and bone fractures (January 27); the Israeli cabinet approves the entry of 6,000 foreign workers to replace Palestinian workers, and extends the closure of the autonomous areas and the Occupied Territories (January 29); the PNA opens two comptrollers offices in Gaza and Ramallah to oversee the Palestinian authority's ministers, municipal and rural councils, and general associations. The National Movement for Change, a new Palestinian group, is formed. The group accepts the DOP, demands the removal of Israeli settlements and security forces in the Occupied Territories, rejects the linkage of the Palestinian and Israeli economies, and calls on the Arab countries to reject normalization with Israel (January 30); the donor countries give the PNA $179 million to initiate projects that will provide work for Palestinians in the Gaza Strip. Five hundred million (which was supposed to be paid in 1994) also is transferred to the PNA for infrastructure, health, and educational projects. The Israeli army raids HAMAS and the Islamic Jihad's charitable institutions in the Occupied Territories (February 1); Palestinian police in Gaza disperse demonstrators outside Arafat's office protesting the demolition of houses allegedly built on state land (February 2); Israeli authorities prevent Palestinians from leaving the autonomous areas of Jericho. The Israeli cabinet extends the closure of the Occupied Territories and bans all Palestinians, except doctors, and teachers, and agricultural goods, from entering East Jerusalem and Israel (February 4); an Israeli is killed and another is wounded in an ambush on an Israeli oil tanker at Nahal 'Oz junction in the Gaza Strip. Israel suspends fuel deliveries by Israeli trucks to the Gaza Strip in retaliation for the attack (February 6); Palestinian police close the offices of *Al-Istiqlal* (Independence) newspaper, which is affiliated with the Islamic Jihad, and arrest 63 DFLP activists and 20 Islamic Jihad members after the attack on the Israeli gas truck in the Gaza Strip (February 7); Palestinian police raid a communication center in Gaza and arrest Ali al-Saftawi, editor of *Al-Istiqlal* (Independence), and seven of his workers. Arafat announces the establishment of the Preventive Security Courts in the autonomous areas to try suspects of security violations (February 8); Israel declares that it intends to close the following PNA institutions in East Jerusalem: Orient House, the Islamic *Waqf*, the Palestine Economic Council for Development and Reconstruction, the Palestinian Industrial, Health, and Housing councils, the Palestinian Statistics and Energy centers, the Palestinian Land and Water Institute, the Palestinian Broadcasting Company, the Palestinian Commission for Citizens' Rights, Al-Quds University, and Al-Quds Open University's branch in East Jerusalem (February 10); to provide jobs for the Palestinians in the autonomous areas and the Occupied Territories, Israel and the PNA agree to establish industrial zones along the borders between Israel and Palestine. U.S. President Bill Clinton announces that he will ask Congress to consider the industrial zones as free trade areas to encourage investment (February 12); Israel and the PNA agree that Palestinians will vote separately for the Palestinian Council and the council's president. Israel begins to lay pipelines near the settlement of Nahal 'Oz and the Rafah checkpoint for fuel deliveries to the Gaza Strip, eliminating the need for Israeli trucks (February 13); Palestinian police detain the leading human rights lawyer in the Gaza Strip, Raji al-Sourani, for criticizing Arafat's decision to establish the Preventive Security Courts in the autonomous areas (February 15); HAMAS distributes a leaflet attacking the PNA's Preventive Security Courts and threatens to start a civil war if the Palestinian police continue to arrest HAMAS supporters and prevent them from carrying out attacks against Israel (February 18); the PNA declares that East Jerusalem is an integral part of the Occupied Territories, and that the custody of the holy places in the city is the responsibility of the PLO (February 19); the founder and spiritual leader of HAMAS, Sheikh Ahmad Yassin announces that co-existence between the PNA and HAMAS is possible if the PNA halts its hostile activities against HAMAS supporters, and does not plan on establishing a one-party system in Palestine. Sheikh Yassin confirms that HAMAS will not participate in the forthcoming self-rule elections because it rejects the principle of administering Palestine for Israel (February 20); Bassam al-Shak'a, the former mayor of Nablus, announces the establishment of Al-Tajamo'u Al-Filastini (the Palestinian Aggregate), a new Palestinian political group in the Occupied Territories that includes HAMAS, Islamic Jihad, PFLP, DFLP, and several independent members. The group opposes the Oslo Agreement, and its platform calls for the establishment of a Palestinian state, Jerusalem as the eternal capital of Palestine, the right of all Palestinians to return to their homes, and the dismantling of Jewish settlements in the Occupied Territories (February 22); Nabil Sha'ath, the PNA minister of Planning and International Coordination, meets in Amman, Jordan, with the foreign ministers of Egypt, Israel, and Jordan to discuss the fate of the Palestinian refugees of the 1967 war (March 7); meeting at the Erez junction, located at the Israeli-Gaza border, Arafat and Foreign Minister Peres agree to conclude the negotiations on extending Palestinian self-rule in the Occupied Territories by July 1, 1995. Israel agrees to open the safe-passage routes between the Gaza Strip and Jericho, to expedite the passage through the Erez checkpoint from Gaza into Israel, to increase the number of permits for Palestinian workers from 18,000 to 21,000, and to establish a joint Security and Civilian Committee (March 9); meeting Arafat in Gaza, U.S. Secretary of State Warren Christopher promises to supply the Palestinian police with 200 trucks and spare parts, and to continue supporting the PNA (March 10); a new Palestinian political group, the Palestinian Unionist Group, is formed in the Occupied Territories to support Arafat and the Oslo Agreement (March 12); the Israeli army raids the *Waqf* (Islamic endowment) offices in the town of Jenin, in the West Bank, and confiscates files concerning land, religious endowments, mosques and *zakat* (tithing) (March 13); Israel permits the entry into Israel of 3,600 Palestinian workers who are married and over the age of 30 to work in the building sector, agriculture, and services. Meeting in East Jerusalem with a Palestinian delegation led by Faisal al-Husseini, British Prime Minister John Major confirms that East Jerusalem is part of the territories occupied by Israel in 1967. Major meets Arafat in Gaza and declares that the British government will donate 50 military vehicles to the Palestinian police. Israeli authorities place Hebron and the surrounding areas under curfew after a member of HAMAS attacks an Israeli bus near the settlement of Kiryat 'Arba, near Hebron, killing two settlers and wounding five others (March 19); at a news conference in East Jerusalem, the Higher Islamic Council appeals to the international community to halt the Israeli construction of a tunnel, which already has destroyed a part of Al-Omari School in the Muslim Quarter, in order to build a northern entrance to the Western Wall at the Via Dolorosa (Way of the Cross) (March 22); PNA Minister of Post and Telecommunication Dr. Abd al-Hafiz al-Ashhab announces that the PNA has commenced using Palestinian postage stamps in the autonomous areas. The Palestinian police ban a human rights seminar to discuss the establishment of the PNA's Preventive Security Courts in the autonomous areas. Raji Sourani, head of the Gaza Center for Human Rights and Law, describes the ban as a "violation of the right of expression, free assembly, and academic-legal discussion" (March 23); U.S. Vice President Al Gore meets Arafat in Jericho and signs a U.S. aid package totalling $73 million for development and public works projects in the autonomous areas. The money will be channeled through UNRWA and UNDP (March 24); a new Islamist group in the Gaza Strip, the Islamic Front for the Salvation of Palestine, is formed. The group, modeling itself on Algeria's Islamic Salvation Front, declares war on the influences of the West, which include cinemas, alcohol, gambling, and prostitution, in its first leaflet, and threatens every Jew on the land of Palestine (March 25); the PNA allows the re-opening of *Al-Abrar* Press offices, which were closed for two weeks by the Palestinian police. *Al-Abrar* Press publishes the Islamic Jihad weekly newspaper, *Al-Istiqlal* (Independence), in the Gaza Strip. The Palestinian police close down *Al-Rasid* (The Monitor), a bulletin published in Gaza, for attacking King Hussein of Jordan (March 26); to protest the Israeli closure of the autonomous areas and the Occupied Territories, the PNA announces that all Israeli merchandise, with the exception of medicine, flour, milk, and fodder, will not be allowed into the autonomous areas (March 28); the Israeli occupation authorities prevent the former mayor of Nablus, Bassam al-Shak'a, from leaving the Occupied Territories to travel to Jordan and Sudan (March 29); the PNA issues passports to Palestinians in the autonomous areas. The green passport is in Arabic and English, and is called a passport/

travel document (March 31); Russian Foreign Minister Andrei Kozyrev gives Arafat a letter from Russian President Boris Yeltsin expressing understanding for the Palestinian difficulties in implementing self-rule in Gaza (April 1); an explosion in an apartment in Gaza's Sheikh Radwan district, allegedly a HAMAS bomb factory, kills eight Palestinians and wounds 30 others. The Palestinian police announce that 150 unexploded grenades and a large quantity of chemicals and pistols are found in the ruins after the explosion. Among the victims is Kamal Kheil, a leader of the Izz al-Din al-Qassam Brigade, who is wanted by both Israel and the PNA; HAMAS holds the PNA and Israel responsible for the explosion and the massacre. The PNA cancels the performance of a Palestinian children's choir in a peace concert with Israeli children, because the political situation is not conducive to joint celebrations of peace (April 2); Raji Sourani, a leading human rights activist, is fired from his position at the Gaza Center for Human Rights and Law after accusing the PNA of violating the law and civil rights. B'tzedek, an Israeli right-wing legal organization petitions the Israeli High Court of Justice to close all the PNA institutions in East Jerusalem. They are: the offices of the Palestinian *Mufti,* the *Waqf* Institution, the PNA Ministry of Religion, the Palestinian Broadcasting Authority, the Palestinian Health Council, the Palestinian Statistics Center, the Palestinian Energy Center, and the Palestinian Housing Council (April 4); Palestinian police arrests Sheikh Ahmad Baher, a senior HAMAS leader in the Gaza Strip. The PNA accuses HAMAS of initiating suicide operations against Israel from the autonomous areas to delay the Israeli withdrawal from the Occupied Territories, to embarrass the PNA and to stop the peace process (April 8); to commemorate the anniversary of the April 9, 1948 massacre at Deir Yassin, and in retaliation for the apartment-building explosion in Gaza on April 2, 1995, HAMAS and Islamic Jihad carry out two suicide car bombings in the Gaza Strip, killing eight Israelis and an American tourist. One car packed with explosives, bumps into an Israeli bus, and the second car crashes into an Israeli convoy near the settlement of Natzarim (April 9); in an unprecedented step against Islamic groups in the autonomous areas, the Palestinian police arrest 200 Islamists and begin a campaign to confiscate all weapons from members of HAMAS and Islamic Jihad. The PNA's Preventive Security Court sentences two Islamic Jihad activists to two-year prison terms for attacking Israelis (April 11); the Palestinian police arrest *Al-Watan's* (The Nation) senior editors, Dr. Ghazi Hamad and Sayed Abu Musameh, raid the offices of the HAMAS weekly, and confiscate computers and fax machines after the publication of an article in which the newspaper accuses the Palestinian police of torturing prisoners (April 13); Arafat appoints Radwan Abu Ayyash, the former head of the Arab Journalist Association, as director-general of the Palestinian Broadcasting Corporation (April 18); the PNA and Jordan agree to restrict HAMAS activities in Jordan that target the Palestinian authority. Jordan's deputy prime minister declares that there is no place in Jordan for Palestinian opposition groups. Israeli occupation authorities lift the daytime curfew on Hebron that was imposed a week ago, following the killing of three HAMAS members by an Israeli border police undercover unit. The nighttime curfew, from 6 p.m. to 5:30 a.m., remains in effect (April 19); the Jerusalem Municipality confiscates 500 dunums (135 acres) of Arab land near Beit Hanina in the north and Sur Bahr in the south for the construction of 7,000 new apartments in the Jewish settlements of Pisgat Ze'ev and Gilo. Meeting in Paris, the donor countries agree to give the PNA $60 million of the $136 million budget deficit to cover the PNA expenses. Israel agrees to give the PNA an additional $6.5 million, in addition to the $4 million it already has contributed from taxes collected from Palestinians; the PNA minister of Planning and International Coordination, Nabil Sha'ath, states that the donor countries agreed to "earmark 25 percent of the $1 million they pledged for 1994 and 1995 for the salaries for teachers, doctors, and police force" (April 27); the PNA asks the Arab League, the United States, Russia, Norway, and the U.N. Security Council to pressure Israel to reverse its decision to expropriate Arab land in East Jerusalem (April 29); the PNA passes its first death sentence against a Palestinian policeman who killed a fellow policeman. Following several incidents, Israel and the PNA agree not to allow Israelis to fly their flag in the Palestinian autonomous areas, and not to permit Palestinians to fly their flag in Israel. Arafat inaugurates the first electoral office in Gaza. A total of eight electoral offices are opened in the West Bank in preparation for the elections of the Palestinian

Council (May 2); to mark the Muslim's *Id al-Adha* holiday (the Feast of the Sacrifice), Israel releases 250 Palestinian prisoners, ends the night curfew in Hebron, simplifies procedures for cargo entering the autonomous areas, allows the construction of a heliport in Gaza, and increases the number of Palestinian workers entering Israel from 27,000 to 31,000 (May 8); *Waqf* (Islamic endowment) Director, Adnan al-Husseini asserts that the 40 dunum (10 acres) plot earmarked for the new American Embassy in Jerusalem belongs to Mohammad al-Khalili, who 200 years ago donated it to the Islamic *Waqf*. Palestinian police release 40 prisoners who are members of the opposition (HAMAS and Islamic Jihad) to mark the Muslim holiday of *Id al-Adha* (May 9); the PNA minister of Justice announces that any Palestinian caught with weapons that have not been registered will face a prison sentence of more than two years (May 11); hoping to encourage dialogue with Islamic Jihad and to reach an agreement with its supporters to suspend their attacks against Israel, the PNA releases Abdallah Shami, an Islamic Jihad leader, after three and a half months in detention (May 13); the Palestinian police close down HAMAS' *Al-Watan* (The Nation) weekly for three months. The PNA's Preventive Security Court sentences Sayed Abu Musameh, the general manager of *Al-Watan*, to two years in jail for incitement against the PNA (May 14); the United States vetoes a U.N. Security Resolution condemning Israel for the confiscation of Arab land in East Jerusalem. The Arab League in Cairo describes the vote as "illogical and biased" (May 15); in an Israeli radio interview, Faisal al-Husseini states that the Intifada could resume because of Israel's decision to expropriate Arab land in East Jerusalem (May 21); to prevent the fall of the Israeli government, in a no-confidence motion tabled by the two Israeli Arab parties, Hadash and the Arab Democrats in the Knesset, the government freezes its decision to confiscate Arab land in East Jerusalem (May 22); under a system of proportional representation instead of "winner takes all" elections for the student council are held at Birzeit and Bethlehem universities. At Birzeit, FATAH supporters win 21 seats of 51, HAMAS takes 18 seats, the PFLP eight seats, the PPP three seats, and the DFLP one seat. At Bethlehem University, FATAH supporters win five seats out of nine, and decide to form a coalition with supporters of the PPP (two seats), the PFLP (one seat), and

HAMAS supporters, who also won one seat (May 24); Israel agrees to give the PNA 75 percent of all income taxes, Value Added Taxes (VAT), and other taxes paid by West Bank Palestinian workers employed in Israel. A similar agreement exists between Israel and the PNA regarding the Palestinian workers from the autonomous areas. The Palestine National Authority declares that it is ready to release HAMAS and Islamic Jihad prisoners, as well as all those who have been convicted by the Palestinian Preventive Security Court, if the two opposition movements agree to halt attacks emanating from the autonomous areas against Israel (June 1); meeting in Tunis, the PLO Executive Committee gives Arafat the mandate to continue negotiations with Israel (June 4); the Israeli Security Service arrests 45 Palestinians from East Jerusalem and the surrounding villages of al-Tur, Abu Dis, Ras al-Amud, Azariya, and Sur Bahr for allegedly being HAMAS members (June 4); the Israeli army prevents Palestinians from returning to the Latrun region villages of Beit Nuba, Umwas, and Yalu, which were destroyed during the War of 1967 (June 5); former head of the Palestinian negotiating team, Dr. Haidar Abd al-Shafi, announces the establishment of the Palestinian Democratic Construction Movement to promote Palestinian democracy and human rights. The PNA inaugurates Palestinian television, which can be viewed in Jericho, Bethlehem, Jerusalem, and Ramallah (June 8); meeting with Arafat in Jericho, U.S. Secretary of State Warren Christopher urges the PNA to hold Palestinian elections after a partial, rather than complete, Israeli withdrawal from the Occupied Territories. The PNA decides to revive the former 12-member East Jerusalem Municipal Council, which was dismissed by Israel after the occupation of the city during the War of 1967. Palestinians demonstrate at the Israeli roadblock at al-Ram, north of Jerusalem, to protest the closure of East Jerusalem to Palestinians from the Occupied Territories. While dispersing the demonstrators, Israeli border police shoot a leading member of FATAH and arrest four FATAH leaders, including Marwan al-Barghouthi, FATAH's general secretary in the Occupied Territories (June 12); the PNA announces it will implement the prevailing Jordanian law in the Occupied Territories which considers anyone who sells land to an Israeli a traitor who should be killed (June 15); an estimated 5,500 Palestinian prisoners in Israeli jails begin a hunger strike to protest Israel's refusal to free them after the signing of the Oslo Agreement. The prisoners call on Palestinians to boycott the elections, unless Israel agrees to a timetable to release all Palestinian prisoners. All Palestinian political factions in the Occupied Territories, including the PNA, support the strike (June 18); Irish Foreign Minister Dick Spring meets with a Palestinian delegation led by Faisal al-Husseini at the Orient House in East Jerusalem, despite Israeli objections (June 19); HAMAS and FATAH supporters win 39 of 81 seats, and supporters of the PFLP win three seats in the student election at An-Najah National University in Nablus. Forty-one seats are needed to form the student council (June 20); to express support for the Palestinian prisoners' hunger strike in Israeli jails, Palestinians in the Occupied Territories hold strikes at the offices of the International Red Cross, and demonstrate in their villages and towns against the Israeli Occupation. The Israeli army opens fire to disperse Palestinian demonstrators near Juneid prison in Nablus, killing two people (June 25); Israeli Arab council leaders and thousands of Arab municipal workers stage a 24-hour hunger strike in solidarity with the Palestinian security prisoners (July 3); Palestinian security prisoners from seven Israeli jails suspend their hunger strike in order to give the PNA-Israeli negotiations a chance to succeed (July 5); using a new system of proportional representation, supporters of HAMAS, which won 39 seats (equal to the number won by FATAH) reach an agreement with supporters of the PFLP, which won three seats and holds the balance, to form the student council at An-Najah National University in Nablus, the West Bank. During a meeting in Gaza with Haim Ramon, chairman of the Israeli labor union, the Histadrut, Arafat asks that Palestinian laborers from the autonomous areas and the West Bank be granted priority over foreign workers for jobs in Israel, as long as the economy of the Occupied Territories remains underdeveloped (July 11); influential Israeli rabbis announce that there is a Torah prohibition against evacuating Israeli army sites in the Occupied Territories and transferring them to gentiles, since this would endanger Jewish life and the existence of the state. Israel's Prime Minister Yitzhak Rabin declares that such interference by the rabbis is "grave, unprecedented and inconceivable" (July 12); Mahmoud Abbas (Abu Mazen), who signed the Oslo Accords for the PLO and is considered second to Arafat in the Palestinian hierarchy, arrives in Gaza to take up residence in Ramallah, the West Bank. The Israeli Civil Administration announces that Palestinian students from the Occupied Territories will not be allowed to attend Palestinian universities in East Jerusalem (July 13); Israeli officials agree to the release in two stages of 1,500 to 2,000 Palestinian prisoners who are not guilty of serious crimes and are not members of HAMAS and Islamic Jihad. A group of prisoners will be released when the second stage of the interim agreement is signed with the PNA. The release would continue a few months later, but would be completed before the elections for the council. Figures differ, but there are currently some 6,500 Palestinians in Israeli jails, about 2,000 of whom were imprisoned before the Oslo Accords of September 1993, and 2,800 of whom were imprisoned afterward (July 14); Austrian Secretary of State Benita Waldner, together with PNA Minister Without Portfolio Faisal al-Husseini and Minister of Tourism Elias Freij, inaugurates the Austrian-Arab Community Clinic in the Old City of Jerusalem, which will provide health care for Palestinians and develop social programs (July 15); the first electoral pact between HAMAS and FATAH is signed in Hebron for the administrative board of the Patients' Friends Society. The coalition agreement states that the Islamic Movement and FATAH each will have three members, while the seventh member, an independent, will be chosen mutually; the PNA Deputy Minister Munzer Sharif announces that, as of August 1, 1995, the Palestinian health insurance system will be applicable in the autonomous areas and the West Bank. The PNA reduces the fees for health insurance for families from $38 to $25 a month. Israel and the PNA begin talks on the implementation of the second stage of the Oslo Accords. The crucial issues to be negotiated are: the redeployment of the Israeli army in the Occupied Territories, the elections for the council and the extent of the council's legislative powers, the transfer of the remaining 34 civil administration spheres of authority in the Occupied Territories to the PNA. Arafat announces that the Preventive Security Courts established in the autonomous areas will continue to try security offenders even after the Palestinian elections are held. PNA ministers Nabil Sha'ath and Saeb Erekat disagree, and declare that such courts are not consistent with democratic practices (July 16); PNA-Israeli negotiations on water rights in the Occupied Territories break down on the first day of talks when the Palestinians demand control of water sources in land administered by the PNA. The Palestinian team maintains that the 80–20 division of water in favor of Israel is unfair, given the fact that only 20 percent of the water flows under Israel (July 18); the Palestinian Housing Council, the Arab Bank, the Cooperative Housing Foundation, and the U.S. Agency for International Development sign an Agreement of Understanding on Home Improvement Loan Programs for Gaza. The Arab Bank is to supervise the program, which would provide loans of up to $10,000 for 15 years to individuals in the Gaza Strip for home improvements (July 20); PFLP activists in the Gaza Strip announce that they will no longer honor the agreement with FATAH to unite during the council elections against HAMAS and Islamic Jihad. The PFLP distributes a leaflet calling on the PNA to release PFLP members from Palestinian jails, and describes the PNA as the "servant of the Zionist enemy, Israel." The leaflet also assures Palestinians that the PFLP did not acquiesce to the PNA's demand not to attack Israeli targets outside the Gaza Strip (July 21); the PNA releases seven PFLP detainees who were arrested after the slaying of two Israelis in Wadi Kelt, near Jericho, on July 18. Six other PFLP members remain in jail (July 22); a Palestinian suicide bus bombing at Ramat Gan leaves six people dead and 33 wounded; Israeli authorities call off the talks with the Palestinians, seal off the autonomous areas and the Occupied Territories, and prohibit Palestinian workers from entering Israel until futher notice. Three Yeshiva students fire more than 20 shots in the air outside the home of PNA's Minister Without Portfolio Faisal al-Husseini in East Jerusalem (July 24); representatives of major U.S. firms meet with Palestinian officials and industrialists in Gaza to discuss the potential of investing $50 million U.S. federally guaranteed funds for construction, tourism, and medical equipment in the autonomous areas and the West Bank. The Knesset, by a vote of 53–51, defeats a bill proposing the inclusion of several Jewish settlements near Jerusalem into the city's municipal borders (July 26); the U.S. government gives the PNA $11 million to fund the first stage of the four-year wastewater processing project, which will cost $40 million to complete (July 27); to protest the presence of the Orient House in East Jerusalem, which they consider the PLO headquarters in East Jerusalem, right-wing Israeli demonstrators destroy Arab vehicles and property (July 29); three Palestinian residents of al-Khader village, near Hebron in the West Bank, petition the Israeli High Court of Justice against the settlers of Efrat, who have erected tents and prefabs on their land in order to expand the settlement of Efrat and to forestall the possibility of returning the West Bank to the Palestinians as part of the Israeli redeployment plan. Israel lifts the closure imposed on the autonomous areas and the West Bank after the Ramat Gan suicide bus boming a week ago. As many as 11,000 Palestinian workers from Gaza and the West Bank enter Israel to work. Israel and the PNA begin talks in Eilat, Israel, to complete the interim autonomy accord. The major issues to be negotiated are: water allocations, the size of the Palestinian Council, the size of the Jordan Valley area that will be under Israeli control, the size of the Palestinian police force to be deployed in West Bank villages, and the redeployment of the Israeli army from the West Bank towns of Ramallah, Bethlehem, and Hebron (July 30); Israeli border police evacuate and arrest hundreds of Jewish settlers on Arab land that they have seized in an attempt to expand the settlements of Efrat in the Occupied Territories and to prevent their return to the Palestinians (August 1); the *Waqf* (Islamic endowment) authorities in Jerusalem dismiss the decision by the Israeli High Court of Justice to allow members of the Jewish Temple Mount Faithful to enter the area of *Al-Haram Al-Sharif* to pray and to commemorate the event of the destruction of the second Temple (August 3); after the visit of 250 Israeli Arab school children to the Orient House where they meet Faisal al-Husseini and chant "one land, one people" to him, MK Yehoshua Mats calls on Prime Minister Rabin to close the Orient House, because it has become "Arafat's incitement mosque." The Palestinian police arrest Imad Faluji, editor of *Al-Watan* (The Nation), a HAMAS weekly published in Gaza, after he expressed support for the Ramat Gan suicide bus bomber (August 5). The Israeli police close down *Al-Haram Al-Sharif* to prevent a confrontation between Muslim worshipers and members of the Jewish Temple Mount Faithful, who plan to enter and worship at the site; the Palestine National Authority closes down the two weekly newspapers, *Al-Istiqlal*

(Independence) and *Al-Watan* (The Nation) for censorship violations (August 6). In a show of solidarity and support with Jewish settlers in the Occupied Territories, thousands of Israelis block forty intersections all over Israel and seize 15 sites in the Occupied Territories, to focus attention on the need for security on the roads (August 8). To avoid any disruption of Israeli-Palestinian negotiations on expanding the PNA self-rule in the Occupied Territories, the Palestinian police arrest 11 suspected HAMAS activists in the Gaza Strip; Israel seals off the Gaza Strip to prevent attacks in Israel by HAMAS and/or Islamic Jihad members to foil progress in the negotiations with the PNA (August 10); Arafat and Foreign Minister Shimon Peres agree on a "joint statement" to expand Palestinian self-rule authority in the Occupied Territories: Israel will withdraw from six Palestinian cities (except Hebron) and redeploy its army in three stages, each six months apart, from the 420 of the estimated 450 villages in the West Bank. The PNA will establish 25 Palestinian police stations. Palestinian police will coordinate their activities with the Israeli army in inter-city roads and villages, and will share responsibilities; Palestinian police will be responsible for public order among the Palestinians, and the Israeli army will protect Jewish settlers and be responsible for "overriding security" in the Occupied Territories. The release of Palestinian prisoners also will be carried out in three stages: the first group will be released after the agreement is signed, the second group will be released before the Palestinian elections, and the date for the last group will be decided later. Arafat agrees to amend the Palestinian Covenant and remove statements that call for the destruction of Israel two months after the Palestinian elections take place. Meeting in Jerusalem, the presidents of major American Jewish organizations call on Arafat to renounce publicly and in Arabic his *jihad* (holy war) appeal against Israel made at Gaza University on June 9 (August 12); Jewish settlers from Beit El open fire at Palestinian demonstrators from the village of Dura al-Kara' and kill one person. The villagers march to a hill near the settlement of Beit El to protest the expropriation of their land by the settlers. Ambassadors of Spain, France, and Italy, who currently constitute the rotating leadership of the European Union, announce that the EU will boycott all Jerusalem 3000 events because the Israeli festivities ignore the Christian and Muslim attachments to Jerusalem and focus only on the city's Jewish history (August 13); a number of PNA Preventive Security agents close *Al-Quds* (Jerusalem) Arabic daily newspaper for one day for publishing material critical of the PNA (August 19); Abd al-Sattar Qassem, a professor at An-Najah National University in Nablus, is shot four times in the arms and legs near his home. Professor Qassem, who opposes the DOP, published an article in *Al-Watan* (The Nation) newspaper on July 20 entitled "Democracy Under the President" in which he stated that Arafat is controlled by Western money and media and is authoritarian. The Bank of Israel issues licenses to a Jordanian mortgage bank to open a branch in Ramallah and to the Jordan-Kuwait Bank to open a branch in Nablus (August 20); a Palestinian suicide bomber, allegedly a member of HAMAS, explodes himself on a crowded bus in Jerusalem, killing six passengers and wounding more than 100. HAMAS releases a statement from Damascus, Syria, stating that the attack is a retaliation for Rabin's "open war" against HAMAS. The attack coincides with the arson attack on *Al-Aqsa* Mosque in Jerusalem in 1969 (August 21); the Israeli cabinet agrees to transfer eight more functional services to the Palestinians: commerce, industry, agriculture, local government, fuel and gasoline, postal services, labor, insurance, and statistics (August 27); as a result of increasing pressure from the Israeli public against the PNA institutions in East Jerusalem, the Israeli police issue closure orders for the Palestinian Statistics Center, the Palestinian Health Council, and the Palestinian Broadcasting Authority in East Jerusalem (August 28); to avoid closure, the three entities sign a declaration affirming that they will not carry out PNA activities in Jerusalem, unless it is agreed upon by Israel and the PNA. Palestinian leaders announce that the Palestinians will boycott Israeli festivities marking Jerusalem's 3,000-year anniversary (September 2); *Waqf* (Islamic endowment) officials and the *Shari'a* Religious Courts are moved back into the old city of Hebron as a symbolic first step in the Palestinians' reclamation of their city (September 6); Japanese Prime Minister Tomiieh Murayama, during a meeting with Yasser Arafat, pledges to donate $200 million in direct assistance to the PNA. A committee composed of representatives from FATAH and other Palestinian political factions assumes control of municipal affairs in Jenin following the resignation of the Israeli-appointed municipal council. According to the Oslo Two Agreement, Jenin is the first city in the West Bank in which the Israeli army will redeploy (September 18); after weeks of intense negotiations, Israel and the Palestinians initial the Oslo Two Agreement in Taba, Egypt, to expand Palestinian self-rule in the Occupied Territories (September 22); the PNA meets in Gaza and approves the Oslo Two Agreement (September 25); meeting in Tunis, the PLO Executive Committee endorses the Oslo Two Agreement (September 26); the Israeli cabinet, by a vote of 18–2 endorses the agreement (September 27); in a ceremony at the White House in Washington, D.C., Yasser Arafat and Yitzhak Rabin sign the Oslo Two Agreement, which represents the second phase of the Declaration of Principles. Israel agrees to redeploy its forces from heavily populated areas in the Occupied Territories, to facilitate elections for the 82-member Palestinian Legislative Council (PLC) in March 1996 and to release the approximately 5,000 Palestinian prisoners in three stages (September 28); nine PLO Executive Committee Members, Farouq Al-Qaddumi, Mahmoud Darwish, Shafiq al-Hout, Iliya Khouri, Abd al-Rahman Malluh, Taysir Khalid, Suleiman al-Najjab, Abdallah Hourani, and Muhammad Ismail release a joint statement rejecting the Oslo Two Agreement (October 4); the Israeli Knesset, by a 61–59 majority, approves the Oslo Two Agreement (October 5); Haidar Abd al-Shafi, the former head of the Palestinian negotiating team and founder of the National Democratic Coalition announces his intention to participate in the PLC (October 9); Israel releases 1,000 Palestinian prisoner as stipulated in the Oslo Two Agreement. President Ezer Weizman of Israel refuses to pardon four Palestinian women prisoners who have been convicted of murdering Israelis (October 10); Israel dismantles its civil administration offices in the West Bank villages of Salfit, Qabatiyya, Yatta, and Kharbata (October 11); Suleiman al-Najjab, head of the PPP announces that his party will participate in the elections for the PLC (October 13); Israeli Prime Minister, Yitzhak Rabin, is murdered after addressing a peace rally in Tel Aviv by Bar Ilan University law student Yigal Amir (November 4); Arafat flies to Tel Aviv for the first time to offer his condolences to Leah Rabin, the widow of Israeli Prime Minister Rabin. Shimon Peres becomes the new prime minister of Israel (November 9); Palestinians in the West

Bank and the Gaza Strip register for the elections to be held on January 20, 1996 (November 12); the IDF redeploys from Jenin and its environs and transfers authority to the PNA. The first joint IDF-PNA patrol begin in Jenin. The PFLP and the DFLP announce that they will boycott the elections for the PLC (November 13); Arafat holds a rally in Jenin to celebrate Israeli withdrawal from the city (November 19); the PNA assumes control of Tulkarm after Israeli redeployment from the city (December 10); Israel completes its redeployment from Nablus and hands it to the PNA (December 12); Arafat addresses a mass rally in Nablus and announces his candidacy for president (December 15); the Israeli army redeploys from Qalqilya (December 16); HAMAS declares that it will not participate in the elections for the PLC (December 19); the Israeli army hands Bethlehem to the PNA after completing redeployment (December 21); the Israeli army evacuates from Ramallah. The PNA assumes control of six West Bank Cities: Jenin, Tulkarm, Nablus, Qalqilya, Bethlehem and Ramallah (December 27)

1996 The European Election Unit criticizes Arafat for shortening the election campaign period from 22 days to 14 days and for increasing the number of PLC members from 82 to 88 seats (January 1); election campaigns for the PLC begin (January 2); Yahya Ayyash, allegedly behind many of HAMAS' attacks against Israelis is killed in Gaza. Arafat offers his condolences to HAMAS leaders in Gaza. Registration for the PLC elections ends (January 5); to prevent violence during Ayyash's funeral, Israel seals off the West Bank and the Gaza Strip to prevent Palestinians from entering its borders (January 6); Israel releases 812 Palestinian prisoners in accordance with the Oslo Two Agreement (January 10); the European Election Unit and the PNA criticize Israel for obstructing PLC election campaigns in East Jerusalem. Israel releases 230 Palestinian prisoners and lifts the closure on the West Bank and the Gaza Strip (January 11); the Palestinian Central Election Commission gives released prisoners an opportunity to register for the PLC elections. Israeli police prevent Hanan Ashrawi, the former PLO negotiator and spokesperson, from campaigning in East Jerusalem (January 14); the Israeli Knesset passes, by a majority of 48–44, the second and third reading of the bill on the implementation of the Oslo Two Agreement. U.S. Vice President Albert Gore meets Arafat in Jericho (January 16); by a vote of 48–42, the Israeli Knesset rejects expanding the border of Jerusalem to include the Jewish settlements of Beitar, Givat Ze'ev, Gush Etzion and Ma'ale Adumim. Campaigns for the PLC elections officially end. Israel assures Palestinians in East Jerusalem that they will not lose their Israeli identity cards if they participate in the elections for the PLC (January 18); Israel seals off the West Bank and the Gaza Strip on the eve of the Palestinian elections. The PLO agrees to finance a U.S.-Peace Studies Center as part of the settlement of a lawsuit brought by the daughters of Leon Klinghoffer, who was killed by members of a PLO faction that hijacked the Achille Lauro cruise ship in 1985 (January 19); Palestinian elections for the presidency of the PNA and the PLC are held (January 20); Arafat wins the presidency with 88.1 percent of the vote. Israel lifts the closure on the West Bank and the Gaza Strip. Israel's Labor Party nominates Prime Minister Shimon Peres as its candidate for prime minister in the upcoming elections (January 21); Palestinian security forces arrest attorney Hussein Shuoukhi of Hebron for "spreading false information", and claiming that 49 ballot boxes were lost for 36 hours, before they were discovered unattended in various places in Hebron. Bassam Abu-Sharif, a former Arafat confidant, returns to the West Bank after 28 years in exile (January 23); because of disputes over the initial results of the Palestinian elections, the Palestinian Central Election Commission allows a re-vote in two voting districts in north Gaza (January 24); as a gesture of good will, the PNA releases Sheikh Ahmad Nimr of HAMAS, who was arrested in March 1995 for preaching an anti-Arafat sermon in Gaza (January 28); meeting in Cairo, members of the PLO Executive Committee agree to amend the PLO charter calling for the destruction of Israel (February 7); in a dispute with Israel concerning access to Rachel's Tomb in Bethlehem, the PNA prevents Israelis from traveling through Bethlehem (February 11); Arafat is sworn in as president of the PNA (February 12); Israel allows the entry of 154 of 450 members of the PNC who live abroad, to attend a meeting in Gaza, convened to amend the PLO Charter (February 19); a bomb explodes in West Jerusalem killing 23 people including the bomber. HAMAS assumes responsibilty for the bombing and claims that it is in response to the killing of Yahya Ayyash, a HAMAS member accused of planning the bombings. Israel stops all negotiations with the PNA and closes it borders, preventing Palestinians from entering Israel (February 25); Palestinian police arrest 90 members of HAMAS in the West Bank and the Gaza Strip in connection with the bombing in Jerusalem (February 26); HAMAS offers to stop its attacks on Israelis, if Israel ends its attacks on HAMAS and releases its members (February 29); HAMAS claims responsibility for the explosion on a bus in West Jerusalem that killed 19 people (March 3); A HAMAS suicide-bomber detonates himself and kills 12 people and injures 126 others in a Tel Aviv shopping center. Israel closes the West Bank and the Gaza Strip and prevents Palestinians from entering Israel and traveling between the West Bank areas (March 4); Palestinian and Israeli security forces raid HAMAS strongholds in the West Bank and Gaza Strip, arresting more than 100 HAMAS activists (March 6); the Israeli army destroys three houses in Burqa, near Nablus, belonging to the family of Raid Sharnubi, who killed himself and 18 others in the March 3 bombing in West Jerusalem (March 7); U.S. President Bill Clinton grants a $100 million aid package of technical assistance and training to Israel to combat terrorism. Israel destroys the family home of Yahya Ayyash, the HAMAS member who allegedly planned the suicide bombings (March 14); Israel lifts the ban on travel between West Bank areas, except for al-Fawwar and Burqa refugee camps (March 15); Palestinian police clash with women demonstrators in Nablus, protesting raids on HAMAS strongholds (March 20); Israeli security forces raid Birzeit University and arrest 370 Palestinians, allegedly members of HAMAS and Islamic Jihad (March 28); Palestinian police open fire and shoot teargas in the air to disperse a student rally at An-Najah University protesting the arrest of HAMAS activists by the PNA (March 31); Arafat announces that Israel, by refusing to redeploy from Hebron and enforcing collective punishment policies, has declared war on the Palestinians. Japan donates $21 million to the PNA (April 1); at the PLC meeting held in Ramallah, Arafat agrees to demands that Nablus police commander Ali Hosni be recalled to Gaza, and that guards be stationed at university gates to prevent future violence on campuses (April 3); Jordan and the PNA sign a memorandum of understanding for exchanging information and for the free movement of publications

(April 4); HAMAS rejects any agreement with the PNA to end attacks on Israel. Arafat declares that he doubts whether HAMAS leaders have any control over its military unit (April 5); in exchange for releasing a number of HAMAS and Islamic Jihad activists, Arafat asks HAMAS to suspend its military operations against Israeli targets, until after the elections. Hundreds of Palestinians in Bethlehem, together with Israelis and European tourists demonstrate, in protest of the Israeli closure preventing Palestinian Christians from entering East Jerusalem during Easter (April 6); the council of Jewish settlements in the West Bank and the Gaza Strip protest the secret talks held between settlement representatives and the PNA (April 8); Arafat announces that HAMAS leaders in Jordan have instructed members in the West Bank and the Gaza Strip to attack Israeli targets to sabotage negotiations with the PNA (April 10); Israeli police prevent a rally supporting Palestinian Prisoners Day in East Jerusalem, because they believe that the PNA is behind it (April 17); HAMAS promises to drown Israel "in a sea of blood", if Israel continues its attacks against Islamists in southern Lebanon. Laila Khaled, who participated in the hijacking of two passenger plans in 1969 and 1970, arrives in Jericho. Palestinian police fire in the air to disperse a group of Jewish National Religious Party activists demonstrating on the outskirts of Jericho, protesting the return of Laila Khalid (April 18); Palestinian police discover the identity of six members of a "secret wing" of HAMAS in Gaza, who are suspected of plotting to kill Arafat, on orders from HAMAS activists in Jordan (April 21); the 21st session of the PNC convenes in Gaza to amend the articles in the Palestinian charter, which contradict the letters of exchange between the PLO and Israel. The PFLP-GC boycotts the PNC meeting in Gaza, and declares that any PNC meeting held in the Occupied Territories is illegal. HAMAS warns PNC members not to attend the PNC session held in Gaza, until all political prisoners in the PNA jails are released (April 22); the PLC unanimously elects Salim al-Za'noun, the speaker of the Council and Bishop Iliya Khouri and Taysir Qub'ah as deputy speakers (April 23); by a majority of 504–54, with 14 abstentions, the PNC amends the articles in the PLO charter calling for the destruction of Israel (April 24); the PNC, meeting for the first time with members from the West Bank and the Gaza

Strip, elects Arafat as president of the new PLO Executive Committee, (April 25); the Labor Party convention approves the removal of clauses banning the establishment of a Palestinian state, from its platform. The Palestinian General Security arrest HAMAS activist Adnan Ghoul, allegedly responsible for the Islamic Jihad bombing at Beit Lid in January 1995, which killed 20 soldiers and civilians, and the Kfar Darom bombing in April 1995, which killed six people (April 26); speaking at a press conference, Israel's Foreign Minister Ehud Barak announces that redeployment in Hebron will be postponed until after the Israeli elections (April 30); Arafat holds talks with U.S. President Bill Clinton at the White House, which are characterized as historical and successful (May 1); Israeli negotiations with the PNA on the final status of Jerusalem, the refugees, the borders, and Jewish settlements start in Taba (May 4); responding to a demand from Yossi Sarid, the Environment minister, Shimon Peres, the Prime Minister of Israel declares that new settlements will not be established in Hebron. The Arabs in East Jerusalem reject the municipality's plan to set up neighborhood councils in their parts of the city (May 6); at a meeting in Jerusalem, the Israeli government coordinator Oren Shahor informs Nabil Sha'ath, the PNA Planning minister, that the Palestinians must stop building the airport at Rafah, in Gaza, until security arrangements have been worked out with the Israeli Government (May 8); Nabil Sha'ath, the PNA minister of Planning, confirms that Israel has released all the equipment it has held up at Ben Gurion Airport and the Rafah Crossing in the Gaza Strip, and that work on the Gaza port has started (May 9); the Islamic list wins 43 percent of the votes-23 of the 51 seats at Birzeit University, near Ramallah (May 10); the World Bank approves a $65 million loan to the PNA, to build the infrastructure in the West Bank and the Gaza Strip and provide badly-needed jobs for the Palestinians (May 12); commenting on King Hussein's remarks that the holy places in East Jerusalem should not belong to any country, PNC Speaker, Salim Za'noun calls on all Arab and Islamic states to support the Palestinian claim to East Jerusalem, which is part of the West Bank (May 14); Faisal al-Husseini, member of the PLO Executive Committee and chief Jerusalem negotiator, urges the Arabs of East Jerusalem not to apply for Israeli citizenship and not to vote in the Israeli elections

(May 16); the Israeli authorities suspend the VIP pass of PNA minister, Intisar al-Wazir, for allegedly taking two students from Gaza in her car to the West Bank, and prevent her from attending the PLC meeting in Bethlehem (May 16); Israeli soldiers in Hebron, capture Hassan Salame, a top HAMAS fugitive, who is allegedly behind the bombing of bus number 18, in Jerusalem (May 19); PA Justice Minister Freih Abu Middeyan states that the Israeli closure of the West Bank and the Gaza Strip is costing the PNA $5 million a day, because 100,000 Palestinian workers cannot work in Israel and farmers are unable to export their produce. The PA police arrest Dr. Iyyad Sarraj, the director of the independent Palestinian Commission for Citizens' Rights in Gaza, for slandering the PNA (May 20); Palestinian journalists boycott the opening session of the PLC, to protest the beating of photographer Fayez Nurredin, by Palestinian police. The Palestinian Energy Authority signs a memorandum of understanding with Delma Power Company, a California-based firm that will build a $170 million power-plant in Gaza (May 22); a group of right-wing Jewish extremists attack Arab bystanders, smash shop windows, damage merchandise, and throw stones at Arab cars in East Jerusalem (May 26); the PLO Executive Committee elects Mahmoud Abbas, one of the founders of FATAH and an architect of the Oslo Agreement, as Arafat's deputy. Israel and the PLO reach an agreement on the establishment of an airport near Rafah, in the Gaza Strip. Israel is to retain exclusive authority over security in the airport area. Palestinian journalists boycott for two hours the PLC meeting, in protest of the intimidation, mistreatment and bureaucratic red-tape they face in reporting news in the Palestinian autonomous areas (May 23); Arafat states that he is not concerned about a right-wing Likud victory in the Israeli elections, because the 1993 PLO-Israeli agreement is guaranteed by the international community (May 29); HAMAS describes Netanyahu's victory in the Israeli elections as a declaration of war against the Palestinians and Arabs. HAMAS leaders deny that an agreement has been reached with the PNA, and confirm that HAMAS will not be transformed into a political party (May 31); by a majority of 50.4 percent, Binyamin Netanyahu wins the Israeli elections and becomes the prime minister of Israel. The PLO Executive Committee and PNA ministers meet to discuss Netanyahu's victory. After meeting for seven hours, Arafat appeals to the international community to continue supporting the peace process (June 2); the PFLP and the DFLP, two radical Palestinian groups, encourage Palestinians to renew their armed struggle against Israel after Netanyahu's victory in the elections (June 3); speaking in Aqaba, at King Hussein's winter palace, Arafat announces that the Palestinian people want to establish an independent state, with East Jerusalem as its capital. Israel eases the closure on the West Bank and the Gaza Strip, and allows 32,000 Palestinian workers to enter Israel (June 6); PNA ministers declare that the Likud platform is a complete rejection of the peace process and a declaration of war on the Palestinians. Jordan blames Israel for restricting its exports to the Palestinain self-rule areas. Trade between Jordan, the West Bank and the Gaza Strip, between January and May 1996, is $25 million. This is below the $300 million a year agreed upon in 1995 between Jordan and Israel (June 9); the PLC cancels its meeting in Nablus in support of the 22 PLC members from the Gaza Strip, who were unable to attend because they refused to be searched by Israeli soldiers at the Erez checkpoint (June 13); Sheikh Ekrameh Sabri, PNA *Mufti* of Jerusalem, warns that he would not stop suicide bombers, and encourages Palestinains to resist the Israeli occupation (June 14); the *Wakf* Religious Affairs Ministry condemns Israels' decision to grant permission to Jews to pray at *Al-Aqsa* Mosque (June 18); Amnesty International Report for 1995 censures Israel for holding Palestinians in administrative detention and for mistreating Palestinian prisoners. The PNA is also censured for holding unfair trials and torturing prisoners (June 19); HAMAS offers the new Israeli government a deal, in which it will stop attacks on Israelis, if the government agrees to lift the closure of the West Bank and the Gaza Strip, release HAMAS prisoners, and stop arresting HAMAS activists (June 21); during the Arab summit meeting in Cairo, the Arab states urge the new government of Israel to uphold the Oslo Agreement, but simultaneously reject the Syrian demand to link the process of normalization with Israel to progress in the peace process (June 23); speaking to the Jewish Agency assembly in Kiryat Gat in Israel, Netanyahu attacks the Arab leaders for setting preconditions to the peace talks and declares that "threats to security are incompatible with negotiations." (June 24); Palestinian police release human rights activists Dr. Iyyad Sarraj, after detaining him twice in one month for criticizing the PNA. The PNA High Court of Appeals in Ramallah, orders Arafat to explain why the PNA police is detaining 10 Birzeit University students in jail without charges or a trial (June 27); the PLC meeting in Gaza, approves the new cabinet (June 28); Israel's Foreign Minister David Levy, urges the PNA to uphold its commitments to the Oslo Agreement and stop its activities in East Jerusalem (July 1); the PFLP declares that it will cancel its membership in the PLO if Arafat does not void the agreements with Israel (July 2); the PNA cancels a multilateral conference in Bethlehem, after Israeli authorities refuse to allow the PNA delegation to host a reception for the participants in East Jerusalem (July 3); Israeli Internal Security Minister, Avigdor Kahalani states that Palestinian officials at the Orient House are violating the ban on PNA activities in the city (July 4); Arafat allows the family of Yahya Ayyash, HAMAS master bombmaker, to rebuild their home, which Israel destroyed in March 1996. Ayyash's home is located in Rafaat, near Tulkarm—area B, where the PNA has control of civil affairs, and Israel oversees security. Israeli officials prevent the Ayyash family from rebuilding their home (July 5); HAMAS calls on Palestinians to renew the Intifada in Hebron and East Jerusalem, and expel the Israeli occupiers from all of Palestine (July 7); Imad al-Faluji, the PNA minister of Communications leaves for Tehran, Iran to promote relations and to attend a conference of Islamic ministers for communication (July 8); Jerusalem police summon a number of PLC members in East Jerusalem to warn them against violating the ban on PNA activities in the city (July 9); Israel's Agriculture Ministry approves import of 10,500 sheep from Saudi Arabia. The sheep were slaughtered in April during the Muslim Feast of the Sacrifice, and they are a gift for the poor (July 10); Qatar slows down plans to open a trade office in Israel until a clearer Israeli position of the peace process emerges. Arafat warns that Israel has no right to close Palestinian offices in East Jerusalem (July 14); the foreign ministers of Egypt, Syria, Saudi Arabia, Qatar, Kuwait, Bahrain, and the United Arab Emirates reject Netanyahu's call for unconditional negotiations. The eight Arab countries warn that they would reconsider normalization ties with Israel, if the new Israeli government distances itself from the principles of the peace process. The PNA reacts angrily to the plan by the Council of Jewish Settlements Communities to increase the Jewish population in the West Bank and the Gaza Strip. Palestinian Finance Minister Mohammed Nashashibi condemns the plan and declares that settlements and peace are conflicting ideas (July 15); the International Olympic Committee rejects an Israeli demand to prevent Palestinian athletes representing the PNA from marching behind a banner reading "Palestine" (July 16); during a press conference with Arafat in Nablus, U.S. consul-general in Jerusalem, Edward Abington announces that the United States is granting the PNA $46 million to develop water resources in the West Bank. The European Union gives the PNA $23 million to improve public infrastructure, another $19 million to upgrade roads, the water system, sewers, and maintenance equipment in West Bank cities, and $4 million to encourage private businesses (July 18); Israeli Foreign Minister David Levy meets Arafat for 90-minutes at the Erez Junction. Arafat promises to write a letter to Netanyahu stating that the PNC has abolished the articles in the PLO charter calling for the destruction of Israel. Arafats meets in Gaza with France's Foreign Minister Harve de Charettee to discuss the peace process (July 24); the Israeli High Court of Justice upholds President Ezer Weizman's decision to pardon In'am Ja'bari and May Ghoussein, who were convicted of attacks against Israelis (July 25); Israel demands that Arafat closes the Youth and Sport Center and the Cartography office that are located in East Jerusalem (July 28); Arafat orders an inquiry in the death of Mahmoud Jumayal, a FATAH activist, in a Nablus prison. Three Palestinian officers from the coastal police are arrested (August 1); Israel demands that the PNA closes the office of councilman Hatem Abd al-Khader in East Jerusalem, in accordance with the Oslo Agreement which prohibits PNA activities in East Jerusalem. Thousands of Palestinians attend the funeral of Mahmoud Jumayal in Nablus. During the funeral procession, Palestinian youths throw stones, burn tires and shout abuses at the Palestinian police, but the police act with restraint (August 2); the Israeli cabinet lifts a four-year ban on settlement construction in the West Bank and the Gaza Strip; the chairman of the Council of Jewish Settlements welcomes the government decision and considers it a cause for celebration; the PNA considers the construction of settlements in the West Bank and the Gaza Strip a de-facto cancellation of the peace process. After one of its activists is killed in Tulkarm, HAMAS calls Arafat a "col-laborator", and encourages the Palestinians to start an Intifada against the PNA. In an open court in Jericho, Palestinian officers Omar Kadumi and Ahmad Biddo are sentenced to 15 years and hard labor, and Abdul Hakim Hijja is sentenced to 10 years plus hard labor for torturing to death Mahmoud Jumayal (August 4); Israeli police order East Jerusalem PLC member, Hatem Abdel Khader to close his office, which is a room in his home, within 24-hours (August 5); Israeli Internal Security Minister Avigdor Kahalani allows PLC member Abdel Khader to open his office. The Israeli National Religious Party demands that it be consulted before any Israeli redeployment takes place in Hebron (August 8); Netanyahu warns that the peace talks with the PNA will not move forward unless the PNA closes down its offices in East Jerusalem (August 11); U.S. undersecretary for Trade, Stuart Eizenstadt, appeals to Israel to expel the 100,000 illegal workers in Israel and hire Palestinians. The PNA denies that the Youth and Sports Center, the Map and Geography Deparment, and the Vocational Studies Institute in East Jerusalem are affiliated with the PNA (August 12); in a letter to U.S. President Bill Clinton, Arafat complains about Israel's new settlements in the West Bank, Israel's refusal to redeploy from Hebron and to open a safe passage between the Gaza Strip and the West Bank (August 15); Amnesty International demands that the PNA police stop torturing and detaining prisoners without charges. Arafat declares: "I will not tolerate torture." (August 18); the Palestinian High Court orders the PNA to release 10 Birzeit University students jailed since March 1996 since no charges have been brought against them. Jordan appoints Izzat Duffash as its new director of *Al-Aqsa* Mosque. The present director Sheikh Mohammad Hussein is being kept by the PNA as the director of *Al-Aqsa* (August 19); reacting angrily to a statement made by Arnestein Overkil, head of the Temporary International Presence (TIPH) in Hebron, that Jewish settlers in Hebron are provocative, spokesman of the Jewish Community in Hebron, Noam Arnon, demands the removal of the TIPH. Arafat reveals to Israeli journalists that the closure of the West Bank and the Gaza Strip is costing the PNA $6 million a day. The PNA bans for one-day, the entry of Israeli goods to the Gaza Strip to protest Israel's refusal to allow Palestinian goods into Israel. The Palestinian Development Company, funded by rich Palestinians living abroad, signs a contract with the PNA to build an industrial park in the Gaza Strip, entirely on the PNA-controlled side of the border (August 20); U.N. special coordinator Terje Larsen, calls on Israel to lift the closure of the West Bank and the Gaza Strip to prevent the financial collapse of the PNA. According to PECDAR, unemployment is 51 percent in the Gaza Strip and 40 percent in the West Bank. Minister of Local Government Saeb Erekat, is appointed head of the Palestinian steering committee to the talks with Israel. Demolition crews from the Israeli Interior Ministry destroy two Arab houses in East Jerusalem, allegedly built without permits (August 21); Arafat rejects any linkage between Israeli redeployment in Hebron and the PNA activities in East Jerusalem. Israeli security forces close down two Palestinian security service offices operating in East Jerusalem. Israel grants Arafat a one-time permit to fly in his helicopter from the Gaza Strip to the West Bank. Arafat will be escorted by an Israeli Defense Force helicopter and will fly along the Mediterranean coast to Hadera and then east, to Ramallah. Nehama Ronen, the director-general of the Israeli Environment Ministry, meets with PNA representatives to discuss the construction of the Palestinian airport, the building of a flour mill in the Gaza Strip, and the handling of solid waste and sewage in the West Bank (August 22); the PNA confiscates a book by Professor Edward Said of Columbia University, which is critical of Arafat's policies and of the Oslo Agreement. Mahmoud Abbas, member of the PLO Executive Committee and an architect of the Oslo Agreement reveals that Iran is plotting with Palestinian militant groups to assassinate Arafat. The PNA establishes a security unit to maintain peace and order at universities in the West Bank and the Gaza Strip (August 23); at a meeting with foreign diplomats, Arafat expresses his concern over Israel's destruction of a Palestinian center for the disabled, administered by the Bourges Luc Society, a non-government organization in the Old City of Jerusalem; Israel claims that the center allegedly was built without a permit from the Jerusalem municipality; PLC members Hanan Ashrawi, Hattem Abdel Khader, Ahmad Batsh, Hassan Tahboub and Ahmad Qrei' lead a march to the demolition site to protest Israel's action. Meeting with Israeli finance Minister Dan Meridor, PNA Minister of Economy, Trade, and Industry, Maher Al-Masri demands more economic measures for the Palestinians and lifting the closure of the West Bank and the Gaza Strip. Jerusalem Mayor Ehud Olmert boycotts the fifth World Conference of Historical Cities to be held in Xi'an, China because Faisal Husseini, the PLO official in East Jerusalem also is invited as a representative of the city (August 28); at a special session of the PLC in Ramallah, Arafat announces that Israel's Likud government has declared war on the Palestinians; Arafat orders a one-day general strike in the West Bank and the Gaza Strip, appeals to all Muslims to pray at *Al-Aqsa* Mosque on Friday, and Christians to pray at the Church of the Holy Sepulcher on Sunday. Gunmen open fire at an Israeli bus traveling on the bypass road to Hebron and injure two passengers (August 29); Jordan Prime Minister Abdel Karim Kabariti flies to Ramallah to meet with Arafat. This is the first time an official from an Arab country flies directly to the West Bank, since the war of 1967. Kabariti agrees with Arafat that the expansion of settlements in the West Bank and the closure of the territories are obstacles to peace. Faisal Husseini, PLO official in East Jerusalem, warns that Palestinians who support the peace process are in danger and likely to be killed by those who are angry with the stalled peace process (August 30); speaking at Balata Refugee Camp in Nablus, Arafat warns that the Intifada will be renewed if there is no progress in the peace process (September 1); in an attempt to prevent Arab residents of East Jerusalem from leaving the city because of high rents, Palestinian leaders call on Palestinian landlords to stop increasing rents for the next three years. At a news conference with Arafat in Gaza, Chancellor Franz Vranitzky of Austria declares that his country has offered the PNA $30 million in aid for development projects. The PNA reports that Arafat has released 120 HAMAS and Islamic Jihad activists from Palestinian jails in the West Bank and the Gaza Strip during the month of August 1995. Jerusalem Mayor Ehud Olmert cautions the PNA not to intervene in East Jerusalem's school system (September 3); Prime Minister Binyamin Netanyahu meets Arafat for the first time at the Erez checkpoint; National Infrastruture Minister Ariel Sharon denounces the meeting between Netanyahu and Arafat; Israeli Science Minister Ze'ev

Begin, and MK Uzi Landau declare that the meeting between Arafat and Netanyahu "contradicts the Likud Party platform and the government's guidelines." Israeli settlers in the West Bank and the Gaza Strip attack Netanyahu for meeting with Arafat, and describe the meeting as a black day for all Israelis who oppose the Oslo Agreement. Arafat dismisses the President of the Palestinian Supreme Court, Amin Abdel Salam, for demanding the release of 10 Birzeit University students, who are detained by the PNA without any charges being brought against them. Netanyahu pledges before the Likud Central Committee that there will never be a Palestinian state between the Mediterranean Sea and the Jordan River. David Levy, Israel's Foreign Minister, warns Ireland, the current European Union (EU) president not to send a fact-finding delegation to the Orient House in East Jerusalem (September 6); Israel agrees to give 18,000 permits to Palestinians seeking work in Israel, and allows 300 trucks from the West Bank and the Gaza Strip to enter Israel (September 8); members of the Knesset Interior Committee meet with Faisal al-Husseini at the Orient House in East Jerusalem, to hear about problems facing the Arabs living in East Jerusalem (September 9); the Israeli-Palestinian steering committee meets in Jericho for the first time and agree to renew negotiations of the civil, economic, and security sub-committees. Officials from the Jerusalem *Wakf* refuse the order from the Jerusalem Municipality to stop the renovations in the Al-Marwani Mosque, located in the southwest corner of *Al-Haram Al-Sharif.* Saudi Arabia contributes $2 million for the renovation of old Arab homes in the Old City of Jerusalem (September 10): Arab foreign ministers meeting in Cairo, warn that the Arab states will cancel their ties with Israel, if progress is not made in the peace process. The Arab League calls on Qatar, Oman, Tunisia, and Morocco to re-evaluate their relations with Israel (September 16); Israeli soldiers prevent Hebron residents from reopening 20 shops and the wholesale market, closed since 1994, after Baruch Golstein shot and killed 29 Arab worshipers at *Al-Ibrahimi* Mosque (September 17); Israeli Defense Minister Yitzhak Mordechi meets with Arafat for the first time, for nearly four hours on the Palestinian side of the Erez checkpoint. Arafat declares that Mordechi's approval of the construction of 1,800 units in the settlement of Mattityahu in the West Bank, is a breach of the Oslo Agreement (September 19); the Israeli Civil Administration approves the construction of 3,000 homes in the West Bank—1,400 in the settlement of Alfei Menashe; 1,160 in the settlement of Emmanual; over 200 homes in settlements in the Jordan Valley; 122 units in the settlement of Kedumim; and 16 homes, in the settlement of Otniel. Israeli leader Yossi Sarid of MERETZ appeals to parents not to send their children on tours to Hebron, which are sponsored by the Israeli Education Ministry, saying that these tours are "politically motivated and foster support for Jewish extremists" (September 20); Egyptian President Hosni Mubarak states that Netanyahu has not kept his promises to honor the agreements signed between Israel and the PNA. Mubarak predicts a repeat of the Intifada, if Netanyahu's government ignores the peace agreements, and continues to build settlements in the West Bank. He states that the next uprising "won't be limited to throwing stones." Arafat, speaking to journalists after a one-hour meeting with Ignatz Bubis, chairman of the Central Council of Jews in Germany, says he has "taken to heart" Bubis's advice to be patient with Netanyahu's new government. During his visit to Germany, Arafat invites German industrialists to invest in the West Bank and the Gaza Strip to help Palestinians prepare for the 2,000 anniversary of the birth of Jesus Christ. Palestinian youths destroy a plaque at the entrance of the Dome of the Rock Mosque, that lauds King Hussein of Jordan for his contributions to the cost of renovating the mosque (September 22); Israel's Prime Minister Netanyahu approves the opening of the Hasmonean Tunnel linking the Western Wall with the Via Dolorosa (the Way of the Cross) in the Old City of Jerusalem. Muslim leaders in Jerusalem blast the opening of the tunnel saying that it will damage *Al-Aqsa* Mosque. Palestinian youths demonstrate in East Jerusalem to protest the opening of the tunnel (September 25); thousands of Palestinian youths clash with Israeli soldiers at the roadblock south of Ramallah leading to the killing of five and wounding 240 Palestinians. PNA asks the U.N. Security Council to take the necessary steps to force Israel to stop the violence and close the tunnel. King Hussein of Jordan condemns the opening of the Hasmonean Tunnel and asserts that it undermines the structure of *Al-Aqsa* Mosque. Hussein calls on Israel to close the tunnel and adhere to international agreements. Thousands of Palestinians in the

West Bank and the Gaza Strip clash with Israeli soldiers, 49 are killed and more than 1,000 Palestinians are wounded in the cities of Ramallah, Bethlehem, Nablus, Hebron, and Gaza. Hundreds of angry Palestinians storm Joseph's Tomb in Nablus killing six Israelis and wounding eight. Another four Israeli soldiers are killed in Gaza and 30 are wounded. Israel seals off the West Bank and the Gaza Strip and prevents Palestinians from entering East Jerusalem and Israel. U.S. President Bill Clinton urges Israelis and Palestinians to end the violence and resume final-status negotiations. King Hussein of Jordan urges Israel to close the tunnel and recommends the formation of an international committee to deal with the issue. Meeting in Cairo, the permanent delegates to the Arab League Organization praise the Palestinian uprising. The Arab League issues a statement stating that the opening of the tunnel in East Jerusalem is part of Israel's conspiracy to destroy *Al-Aqsa* Mosque, obliterate Arab-Islamic landmarks, and create additional facts which harm the legal status of the city (September 26); in breaking up the demonstration at *Al-Aqsa* Mosque after the Friday prayers, the Israeli police kill three Palestinians and wound more than 100 people (September 27); the Supreme Muslim Council temporarily closes *Al-Haram Al-Sharif* to everyone but Muslim worshipers (September 28); Netanyahu agrees to meet with U.S. President Bill Clinton in an attempt to bring an end to the clashes between the Palestinians and Israelis and to resume peace negotiations (September 30); meeting in Washington with U.S. President Bill Clinton, Arafat and Netanyahu agree to hold non-stop talks on Israeli redeployment from Hebron starting October 6 (October 3); Israel allows Palestinians to travel between Area A and Area B in Bethlehem District. Palestinians are not permitted to travel to East Jerusalem and Israel. Arafat meets King Hassan of Morocco, the chairman of the Jerusalem Committee associated with the Muslim Organization, to discuss Israel's activities in East Jerusalem. PNA Minister of Agriculture Abd al-Jawad Saleh announces that the continued Israeli closure of the autonomous areas is costing the PNA a loss of $1.5 to $2 million a day, in the agricultural sector (October 4); Israel lifts the closure in Jenin and allows Palestinians to travel between Areas A and B in the Jenin District. Arafat urges Europeans to participate in the talks between Israel and the PNA. Hebron has been under curfew for ten days (October 5); negotiations between Israel and the PNA on redeployment in Hebron, resumes today at the Erez crossing between Israel and the Gaza Strip. Israel's Defense Minister Yitzhak Mordechai lifts the curfew in Hebron for four hours to enable residents to shop for food. Qatar decides to postpone the opening of a trade office in Israel pending the resolution of all Arab-Israeli problems (October 6); after meeting with U.S. Secretary of State Warren Christopher, Arafat states that he is not interested in changing the agreement with Israel regarding redeployment in Hebron. He reiterates that the PNA wants precise implementation of the Oslo Two Agreement. Israel allows 2,000 Palestinian laborers from the Gaza Strip to work in the Erez Industrial Zone, which is located between Israel and Gaza. U.S. President Bill Clinton hails the resumption of talks between Israel and the PNA. Irish Foreign Minister Dick Spring, whose country holds the current European Union presidency, arrives in Israel/Palestine to secure a role for the European Union in the peace process and to see that the Middle East Peace Process continues (October 7); Israel's President Ezer Weizman meets Arafat at his Caesarea villa in northern Israel. This is Arafat's second trip to Israel. In November 1995, Arafat secretly visited Leah Rabin to express his condolences after Yitzhak Rabin's assassination. U.S. Secretary of State Warren Christopher meets David Levy, Israel's Foreign Minister, and urges him to facilitate trade and export between the West Bank and the Gaza Strip to demonstrate that Israel is sincere about the peace process (October 8); Israel eases the closure of the territories and allows 35,000 Palestinians to work in Israel. Only married men and those over the age of 29 are permitted entry to Israel (October 10); the Supreme Muslim Council agrees to open *Al-Haram Al-Sharif.* Israel lifts the closure between Area A and Area B in the West Bank, with the exception of the city of Nablus (October 13); Arafat meets King Hussein of Jordan in Jericho. This is the first official visit by an Arab leader to the West Bank since 1967 (October 15)

Introduction

The land area of Palestine, 26,320 square kilometers, is located on the western side of the continent of Asia. It is bounded by Lebanon and Syria on the north, Egypt's Sinai Peninsula and Jordan's Gulf of Aqaba on the south and southwest, the Jordan River and the Hashemite Kingdom of Jordan on the east, and the Mediterranean Sea on the west. Geographically, Palestine is divided into four distinct regions. One is the highly developed and fertile coastal plains, which extend along the Mediterranean from Lebanon on the north to the Gaza Strip in the south. This area is known for its citrus fruits. The dry hilly mountains, known also by the biblical name Judea and Samaria, are planted with olive, fig, plum, almond, and apricot trees, as well as agricultural produce of wheat, barley, lentils, vegetables, grapes, cucumbers, and tomatoes. The Jordan Valley, rich in citrus and tropical fruits, lies about 1,300 feet below sea level, and is irrigated by the Jordan River, which flows through the valley, linking the Sea of Galilee to the north with the Dead Sea to the south. The Negen Desert region comprises almost half the land of Palestine. The northern part of the Negen is relatively fertile, and is used for agricultural purposes, while the southern half is barren, uninhabited desert.

Palestine, synonymous to many people with the holy land, is the home of the three monotheistic religions of Judaism, Christianity, and Islam. Historically, Palestine and/or the Land of Canaan was controlled by many peoples. During the 20th century B.C., the Canaanites, who were ruled periodically by the Egyptians, settled in the Land of Canaan. In the 12th century B.C., the Israelites invaded Palestine, and established the kingdom of Israel, which lasted for two centuries before it was divided into the kingdom of Israel in the north and the kingdom of Judah in the south. Palestine, thereafter, was ruled in turn by the Assyrians, the Babylonians, the Persians, the Greeks, the Hasmoneans, the Romans, and the Byzantines or Greek Christians, who controlled Palestine from Constantinople. Between 638 A.D. until World War I (the exception being 1099–1187, when the Crusaders were in control), Palestine was ruled by Arab and Muslim Caliphates: the Rashidun, the Umayyads, the Abbasids, the Suljuks, the Tater and Moguls, the Mamluks, and the Ottoman Turks. Prior to World War I, Palestine consisted of several parts of the former Ottoman province of Beirut and Jerusalem.

The inhabitants of Palestine supported Sharif Hussein's revolt against the Turks, and backed the Allies during World War I in return for their independence. Unbeknownst to them, however, Britain, France, and Russia had secretly reached consensus in the Sykes-Picot Agreement of 1916 to place Palestine and the holy places under an "international administration." Moreover, the British secretary of state for Foreign Affairs, Lord Arthur Balfour, had sent a letter to Edmond de Rothschild on November 2, 1917, known as the Balfour Declaration. It stated:

> His Majesty's Government views with favor the establishment in Palestine of a national home for the Jewish people, and will use their best endeavours to facilitate the achievement of this objective, it being clearly understood that nothing shall be done which may prejudice the civil and religious rights of existing non-Jewish communities in Palestine, or the rights and political status enjoyed by Jews in any other country.[1]

The Allies repudiated their promises to the Arabs, and after World War I, the League of Nations designated Britain as the mandatory power over Palestine. The Palestinians denounced Great Britain's decision to integrate the Balfour Declaration into the mandate system, and throughout the first half of the 20th century, they waged an armed revolt against both the British policies and the Zionists' plan to transform Palestine into a Jewish state.

Britain decided on February 14, 1947, to refer the Palestine question to the United Nations. After a long debate, the U.N. General Assembly recommended the partition of Palestine into an Arab state and a Jewish state, and for Jerusalem and its environs to be administered by the United Nations. The majority of Jews in Palestine accepted the U.N. partition plan, whereas the Palestinians rejected it because they viewed it as a violation of their self-determination and an infringement on their rights. The Palestinians in 1947 owned 90 percent of the land in Palestine, and constituted the majority of the population.

Fighting between Palestinian and Jewish military forces intensified after the U.N. partition plan, as each side attempted to strengthen its position before the British mandate ended on May 15, 1948. Jewish military forces, during March and April, 1948, occupied many Arab villages along the coast, and the cities of Haifa, Jaffa, Tiberias, and Safad. Their objectives for doing so were clear:

> . . . to gain control of the area allotted to the Jewish state and defend its borders and those of the blocs of Jewish settlements and such Jewish

> population as were outside those borders, against a regular or pararegular enemy operating from bases outside or inside the area of the Jewish State.[2]

Thousands of Palestinian civilians fled their homes into the neighboring countries before the Arab-Israeli War officially started on May 15, 1948. At the end of the war, Israel controlled 77 percent of Palestine, nearly 25 percent more land than they were granted by the U.N. Partition Plan of 1947. Palestine was dismembered, and about 700,000 Palestinians fled their homes and became refugees.[3] The parts of Palestine that remained under Arab control were later designated the West Bank, including East Jerusalem and the Gaza Strip.

The West Bank and the Gaza Strip: A Brief Profile

The land of the West Bank and the Gaza Strip is about 6,000 square kilometers. The West Bank is divided into four geographical areas. The northern area is composed of the Nablus mountains and the coastal plain areas that include the towns of Jenin, Tulkarm, Qalqilya, and Nablus. This is a fertile region famous for it citrus fruits, melons, and a wide array of vegetables. The city of Nablus is the largest commercial and industrial center in this region, where soap, oils, matches, sweets, and building materials are produced. The central region, which includes the towns of Ramallah, al-Bireh, Birzeit, and East Jerusalem, is a fertile agricultural area that receives sufficient rainfall. The southern region includes the towns of Bethlehem, Hebron, Halhul, Dura, and Yatta. The city of Hebron is also the largest commercial and industrial center. Moreover, it is the location of *Al-Haram Al-Ibrahimi* Mosque (the Cave of Machpela), where the patriarchs are entombed.

The Gaza Strip region lies in the southern part of the coastal plain. It is about 45 kilometers long and eight kilometers wide, comprising an area of 363 square kilometers. The Gaza Strip's main exports are citrus fruits, vegetables and an abundant supply of cheap labor.

After the war of 1948, the West Bank was severed from Palestine and became an isolated area, boxed in between Israel and Transjordan. It was formally annexed into Transjordan on April 24, 1950, and became the western region of the Hashemite kingdom of Jordan. The government of Jordan listed the population of the West Bank in 1952 as 742,289, distributed as follows: 301,402 persons resided in the district of Jerusalem; 315,236 lived in the district of Nablus; and 125,651 persons inhabited the district of Hebron.[4]

The union between the West Bank and Jordan from 1950 until 1967 rendered the West Bank economy subservient to the Jordanian economy, and mainly dependent on agriculture, tourism, services, the exports of fruits, stone, olive oil, and remittances from Palestinian relatives working in the Arab Gulf countries. There was, however, a modest growth in industry that involved the manufacture of consumer goods in the major towns of the West Bank. East Jerusalem, Hebron, Bethlehem, Ramallah and Nablus became important trade centers, and were notable for their important craft industries, such as glasswork, embroidery, and mother-of-pearl artifacts. Some light industries produced matches, textiles, shoes, beverages, tobacco, furniture, soap, and processed olive oil.

The Gaza Strip, prior to 1948, was an important port and commercial center for Palestine. It was part of the province of Gaza, an area comprising the districts of Gaza and Beer al-Sab'e. The population of the Gaza district in 1946 was estimated at 75,000. After the Arab-Israeli War of 1948, the population increased to 225,000 people due to the influx of about 150,000 Palestinians who fled their homes in Palestine to settle in the Gaza Strip.

After the war of 1948, the Gaza Strip was detached from Palestine and the West Bank, and was ruled by Egypt, pending the final settlement of the Palestine problem. From 1948 to 1967, the Egyptian administration neglected the Gaza Strip and treated it as a separate economic unit. The largest economic activity in the Gaza Strip was agriculture, which provided 30 percent to 40 percent of the employment opportunities. Agricultural products, such as citrus fruits, dates, barley, wheat, melons, vegetables, livestock, meat, milk, fish, and eggs, accounted for 90 percent of all exports. Industry in the Gaza Strip was underdeveloped and limited to citrus packing, citrus products, bottling and small traditional crafts workshops, such as pottery and the weaving of carpets and textiles.[5]

Worldwide, the Palestinian population in 1995 is estimated to be about 6.5 million, distributed as follows: the West Bank, including East Jerusalem, has 1.25 million; the Gaza Strip 880,000; Israel 810,000; Jordan 2.17 million; Lebanon 395,000; Syria 360,000; the Arab States 517,000; and 500,000 Palestinians dispersed in the rest of the world. The Palestinians who live in the West Bank and the Gaza Strip constitute about 31 percent of the Palestinian population: 19 percent in the West Bank and East Jerusalem, and 12 percent in the Gaza Strip. Another 31 percent live in Jordan; 20 percent in the Arab countries; 13 percent in Israel; and the remainder are scattered throughout the world.[6]

The Palestinians in the West Bank and the Gaza Strip are relatively young. In the West Bank, more than 50 percent of the population is under the age of 15, while in the Gaza Strip, about 73 percent of the population is under 15. It is estimated that 97 percent of the population residing in the Occupied Territories and the autonomous areas are Muslims, and 3 percent are Christians, who belong to more than 15 different denominations. The largest Christian communities are the Greek Orthodox, the Latins, and the Greek Catholics. A Samaritan community of approximately 400 persons live in Nablus.

The West Bank has approximately 450 villages, and the majority of the population is peasants engaged in agriculture. In the Gaza Strip, there are only nine villages, and the majority of the population resides in cities and refugee camps. It is estimated that 62 percent of the Palestinians in the West Bank reside in rural areas, and one-third of the total population lives in refugee camps, while 75 percent to 80 percent of the population in the Gaza Strip is urban dwellers, and two-thirds live in refugee camps.[7]

The Israeli Occupation of the West Bank and the Gaza Strip

After the war of 1967, Israel introduced policies and military orders which enabled it to assume total control of the West Bank, East Jerusalem, and the Gaza Strip.

Apart from the process to unify Jerusalem which was officially declared the capital of Israel, the government embarked on establishing exclusive Jewish settlements in all of the Occupied Territories. On June 28, 1967, three weeks after the war, the Israeli Government, expropriated 30 percent of the total land area of East Jerusalem in order to restore and develop the Jewish Quarter in the Old City. They also built high-rise Jewish residential communities in East Jerusalem to ensure permanent Israeli control over both the east and the west parts of the city. Currently, there are 160,000 Jews residing in and around East Jerusalem, while the Palestinian population in East Jerusalem is 156,000. Moreover, the Israeli government adopted a provision of a 19th-century Turkish land law; declaring itself the successor of the Turkish-Ottoman Empire, the government decreed that between 55 percent and 65 percent of the land in the West Bank and the Gaza Strip was "state domain," or public land, and was to be available for Jewish settlements. Since 1967, the Israelis have built 194 Jewish settlements in the West Bank (including East Jerusalem), and the Gaza Strip, and have seized approximately 40 percent of the land in the former and 30 percent of the later.[8]

The Palestinians recognize that settlements are the most threatening consequence of the Israeli occupation. Whereas the occupation intended to govern and rule, the settlements seek to transform. Regardless of their location, size, or purpose, the settlements are perceived as illegal, provocative and in violation of the Fourth Geneva Convention.[9] Palestinian sentiment toward the settlements has been expressed through numerous demonstrations and protests, creating an atmosphere of frustration and anxiety among the people in the Occupied Territories.

Israeli economic policies since 1967 have included the expropriation of cultivatable Arab land for military and settlement purposes; the control of scarce underground water resources; stringent measures imposed on the import of raw materials and on the export of products from the West Bank and the Gaza Strip; and as a by product, the absorption of the Palestinian labor force into the Israeli economy. Under the Israeli occupation, Palestinian agricultural productivity declined, and the Palestinian peasant was transformed into a wage laborer. The contributing factors to this were the inability of the Palestinian peasant to compete with Israeli agricultural produce, which the government subsidized, the scarcity of capital for mechanization, and Israeli and Jordanian measures against the produce of the Occupied Territories.[10]

Industry in the Occupied Territories also remained minimal and underdeveloped. This is attributed to the saving practices of the Palestinians, the lack of investment in the industrial infrastructure, the lack of protection from Israeli imports that flooded the market, the heavy taxation that Israel imposed on equipment, the lack of credit facilities (all Arab and international banks were closed after the war of 1967), and Israel's unwillingness to extend credit to the Palestinians. Consequently, many Palestinians from the West Bank and the Gaza Strip were forced to seek employment in Israel and/or to emigrate to Jordan and the Arab countries. Thus, the industrial base of the Occupied Territories has been restricted to the processing of olive oil, stone quarrying, the manufacturing of cigarettes, plastics, chocolates, candy, shoes, clothes, and pharmaceuticals. The Occupied Territories became an important and protected export market for Israeli goods.[11] Israeli capitalists were encouraged to exploit the Occupied Territories by subcontracting to small Palestinian factories and workshops. This, however, has not been as extensive as was expected, due to the political instability of the area.

The legal status and autonomy of the institutions of higher education also changed under the Israeli occupation. In July 1980, the military government issued military order No. 845, which brought the universities in the Occupied Territories under its direct supervision, and placed them in the same category as schools. This law increased the power of the Israeli officer of education to include control over who could be a student, a teacher, or a staff member at a university. The Israeli educational officer also had the power to censor all textbooks and scientific and social periodicals, prevent publications from reaching the universities, and cancel teaching certificates issued to anyone convicted of a security offense.[12] Moreover, universities and institutions of higher education were required to obtain an operating permit, valid for one year, from the Israeli authorities.

In November 1981, Professor Menahem Milson was appointed the head of the Israeli Civil Administration to provide a facade of nonmilitary rule in the Occupied Territories. However, the Civil Administration proceeded to issue military orders requiring prior approval on every activity undertaken by the Palestinian municipal councils, and placing the day-to-day civilian municipal responsibilities under the direct control of Israeli authorities. Municipal committees headed by Israeli army officials were appointed in the West Bank cities of Ramallah, al-Bireh, and Hebron after the pro-PLO mayors, who were elected in 1976, refused to cooperate and were dismissed. The Israeli Administration also encouraged the establishment of the Village League Associations as political opposition to the PLO in rural areas.

Palestinian-Jordanian Relations: Post 1967

The occupation of the West Bank and the Gaza Strip by Israel in 1967 ended the Jordanian, as well as the Egyptian, rule over these territories. Jordan, however, through its "open bridge" policy, provided most Palestinians with the lifeline so desperately needed to the Arab world. For example, funds from the Arab countries to support Palestinian steadfastness in the Occupied Territories were channeled through the Jordanian government, until the Arab League in 1974 officially recognized the PLO as the sole representative of the Palestinian people and entrusted it with Palestinian affairs. Jordan also maintained a close relationship with the Palestinians in the Occupied Territories, particularly the West Bank, through its own financial support. It contributed 25 percent to the budgets of the West Bank municipalities, and paid the salaries of approximately 9,000 Palestinian officials, including *Waqf* employees, teachers, lawyers, and *Shari'a* court judges. Many West Bank public institutions, such as clinics, hospitals, schools, charitable organizations, and *Shari'a* courts also were subsidized by the government of Jordan.

Changes in Jordanian-Palestinian relations occurred when a pro-PLO leadership was elected in 1976, to the municipal councils in the Occupied Territories. The newly elected Palestinian mayors represented a major change from the traditional pro-Jordanian leadership that had dominated Palestinian politics. They epitomized youth and struggle, and were all pro-PLO supporters. The similarities that prevailed among the mayors encouraged a consensus among the Palestinians who demanded an end to the Israeli occupation and the establishment of a Palestinian state in the West Bank and the Gaza Strip under the leadership of the PLO.

Jordan continued to support the Palestinians despite the wave of anti-Jordanian sentiments that swept the Occupied Territories immediately after the suspension of political coordination between Hussein and Arafat in February 1986. The rift between the PLO and Jordan widened on March 27, 1986, when the Jordanian House of Representatives approved a plan to enlarge the 60-member body of the Jordanian parliament. According to the plan, Jordan would have 65 representatives, the West Bank 56 representatives, and the Palestinian refugee camps in Jordan nine. The reason for this change was to enable Jordan to claim that its parliament represented the Palestinians. Consequently, Hussein could rely on these Palestinian representatives in his parliament to substitute for the PLO in any future peace talks.

Relations between the PLO and Jordan deteriorated in July 1986, when Jordan ordered the closure of 25 PLO offices in Amman, and expelled Arafat's deputy, Khalil al-Wazir from Jordan. In early August 1986, Jordan announced a five-year economic and social development plan to support Palestinian steadfastness in the Occupied Territories. The plan had a budget of $1.3 billion, which Jordan hoped to receive from the United States, European countries, Japan, and possibly some Arab countries. The objectives of the plan were to limit Palestinian emigration and to strengthen the Palestinian attachment to the land by promoting health, housing construction, agriculture, industry, education, and social development in the Occupied Territories.

PLO supporters rejected the Jordanian development plan for the Occupied Territories. They regarded Hussein's initiative as a scheme, coordinated with Israel, to erode the influence of the PLO as the sole representative of the Palestinian people, and to create de facto recognition of Jordan's right to administer the affairs of the Palestinians, while Israel maintained its military installations and Jewish settlements in the Occupied Territories. However, PLO sympathizers avoided an open confrontation with Jordan and its supporters, in the hope that political coordination between Hussein and Arafat would eventually be restored. They also knew many Palestinians in the Occupied Territories believed that, in the absence of a negotiated settlement, a major plan to develop the Occupied Territories would be beneficial. Moreover, PLO supporters knew Jordan remained the only geographical bridge the Palestinians under occupation had to the Arab world.

After the outbreak of the Intifada, King Hussein decided on July 31, 1988, to sever his country's legal and administrative ties with the West Bank. He dissolved the Jordanian Lower House of Parliament, half of which was made up of West Bank Palestinians; canceled the $1.3 billion five-year development plan; canceled the payments of all salaries given to West Bank Palestinian officials, with the exception of the *Waqf* (religious endowments); and terminated Jordanian citizenship for all Palestinians living in the Occupied Territories, allowing them only a temporary Jordanian passport valid for two years. This break meant that the Jordanian option was no longer a feasible alternative to a Palestinian state, and that Jordan was no longer a viable partner to any negotiations with Israel regarding the future of the West Bank and the Gaza Strip.

The Palestinian Uprising: The Intifada

The start of the Intifada or uprising has been linked to a spontaneous chain of incidents in the West Bank and the Gaza Strip between October and December 1987: the death of seven Palestinians in the Gaza Strip in early October; the shooting of a student at Bethlehem University on November 1; the glider air-raid attack by Palestinian commandos from Lebanon on Qiryat Shmoneh in Israel; the Arab states apathy toward the PLO and the Palestinian problem during the Amman Summit of November 8–11, 1987; and the road accident in the Gaza Strip on December 9, when an Israeli truck driver ran into a car, killing four Palestinians. All these factors played an important role in igniting the Intifada. However, it is simplistic to try to analyze the causes, the political direction, and the magnitude of the consequences of the Intifada on the basis of these events.

The causes of the Intifada are deeply rooted in the social, demographic, economic, and political policies and practices of the Israeli occupation. It represents the cumulative effects of an occupation that began in 1967, and led to the humiliation of the Palestinians on a daily basis: the incessant identity card checks and body searches by border police and soldiers at roadblocks and city streets; the house searches; the arrests of relatives; the refusal to grant family reunification permits to relatives stranded in the Arab world; collective punishment manifested in such acts as the demolition of houses and the sealing-off of rooms; the confiscation of land; deportations; the closure of schools and universities for three to six months at a time; the squalor of the refugee camps, particularly in the Gaza Strip. From these conditions and violations of an occupied people emerged the frustrations and humiliations, that opened up Pandora's box and began the Intifada.

The Palestinian uprising is a historic development, but it is not without precedent in the Palestinian struggle for nation-building. Since 1948, the Palestinians in the Occupied Territories, Lebanon, Syria, Jordan, Kuwait, and elsewhere have been struggling for the liberation of Palestine. The Intifada, however, epitomized the crux of the Palestinian-Israeli conflict and shifted the center of gravity of Palestinian politics from the Arab countries to the Occupied Territories.

The Intifada crystalized the significance of Palestinian unity. An ethos of national service and self-reliance developed and new communal organizations evolved. Moreover, all sectors of Palestinian society in the Occupied Territories adhered to the commands and strategies of the Unified National Leadership of the Uprising (UNLU), the Palestinian underground leadership that organized and directed the Intifada. For example, merchants closed their shops during strike days; landlords reduced rents by 25 percent, and some tenants were allowed to live rent-free for a number of months because of the poor economic conditions; contributions were also collected by youths and distributed anonymously to impoverished families; and neighborhood support committees for education were organized when the Israelis closed down the schools. It soon became apparent that a young and determined leadership that had grown up under the occupation was assuming control of the Occupied Territories. The UNLU, through the establishment of popular committees, challenged the authority of the Israeli occupational forces, and marginalized the power and control of the traditional leaders and the Village League Associations.

The Palestinian struggle during the Intifada also became economic. The UNLU ordered the Palestinians to stop paying taxes to the Israelis, and reiterated "no taxation without representation." Israeli authorities retaliated: In order for a Palestinian to receive a license or permit of any kind, such as a driver's license, a construction permit, or an import or export license, the individual had to present a document showing he had paid his taxes. Israeli taxmen raided the shops and homes of merchants to force them to pay their taxes, which increasingly were used to support the escalating cost of the occupation. At roadblocks the army often would impound vehicles belonging to tax dodgers and confiscate their identity cards. Moreover, villages and towns in which residents refused to pay taxes were subjected to economic sanctions. For example, the town of Beit Sahur, near Bethlehem, was closed off, isolated, and its residents prevented from working and cultivating their fields. They also were prevented from exporting their produce to Jordan.

The UNLU encouraged the Palestinians in the Occupied Territories to develop a domestic economy. Palestinian workers, employed by Israeli businesses and farms, were encouraged to cultivate their own land to raise chickens and rabbits, and to increase their home sewing and knitting. They were urged to restrict their purchases of consumer and luxury items, such as cars and electrical equipment, and instead to buy more basic foodstuffs such as rice, sugar, flour, canned food, and powdered milk in huge quantities at wholesale prices. This foray in self-sufficiency grew in conjunction with a boycott of Israeli products. Israeli-made goods were banned from shops, and in lieu of these products, the Palestinians encouraged their own small-scale enterprises, which began to work overtime and nights to produce enough for the local market.

The "Green Line," or the physical boundary of pre-1967 that separated the Israelis and Palestinians, also became a social-psychological barrier. Israelis avoided the Occupied Territories, and no longer frequented Palestinian vegetable markets and shops. Most significantly, the Intifada illustrated the fact that East Jerusalem could not be separated from the West Bank. Israel had officially annexed East Jerusalem and had consistently publicized the peaceful co-existence between the city's

Palestinian and Israeli residents. The uprising effectively destroyed this co-existence myth, and proved beyond doubt that East Jerusalem was part of the Occupied Territories and inseparable from it.

The Palestinians, who were citizens of Israel, supported the Intifada by observing strike days, demonstrating, and collecting contributions for West Bank and Gaza Strip hospitals. This show of solidarity by the Arab minority in Israel, with their Palestinian brothers and sisters in the Occupied Territories, astonished many Israelis. They feared that the Arab minority would emerge as an organized national entity that would jeopardize the internal security of Israel. Likud Knesset member Haim Kaufman went so far as to suggest reimposing the military government of the 1950s and early 1960s on the Arab population in northern Israel.

The Peace Process

The historic concessions made by the PLO in November and December of 1988—when it accepted U.N. Resolutions 242 and 338, which recognized Israel's right to exist within secure borders, and rejected terrorism—would not have been possible without the Intifada and the UNLU's political pragmatism.

This landmark change in policy by the PLO was ignored by Israel. Nevertheless, more than 100 nations recognized the November 15, 1988, declaration of Palestinian statehood, and the PLO acceptance of the principle of a two-states solution—an Arab and Jewish state within Palestine. Israel became increasingly isolated after U.S. officials in Tunis held talks with PLO representatives, ending a 14-year boycott. Pressure at home and abroad forced Prime Minister Yitzhak Shamir to respond to the Palestinian peace initiative.

On May 14, 1989, the Israeli cabinet approved the Shamir-Rabin plan, which offered the Palestinians in the Occupied Territories "free and democratic" elections. The elected Palestinian delegation would negotiate with Israel a five-year transitional period to restructure the administration of the Occupied Territories and, at a later stage, beginning no later than the third year, to negotiate a "permanent" solution to the Palestinian-Israeli conflict. The Palestinians categorically rejected the plan because it excluded the PLO, the Palestinians from East Jerusalem, and the establishment of a Palestinian state. Palestinians expressed indignation at Israel's threat that there would be no elections before the end of the Intifada and that Jewish settlements would continue to be built, and that stricter measures would be used if the Palestinians did not accept the Shamir-Rabin plan.

The Palestinians and Israelis were locked in a stalemate. President Hosni Mubarak of Egypt proposed on September 15, 1989, a 10-point peace initiative to persuade Israel and the Palestinians to begin direct negotiations of the Shamir-Rabin plan. Mubarak urged Israel to accept international supervision of the proposed elections and Israeli Defense Forces withdrawal from the balloting areas. He also encouraged Israel to stop settlement activities, accept the participation of Palestinians from East Jerusalem, and implement the exchange of territory for peace. The Israeli government denounced Mubarak's initiative and dismissed it as another attempt to bluff Israel into recognizing the PLO.

President George Bush seized the opportunity after the Allies' victory over Iraq in the Gulf War, and committed the United States on March 6, 1991, to a settlement of the Arab-Israeli conflict based on U.N. Resolutions 242 and 338. It took Secretary of State James Baker eight trips to the Middle East in seven months to organize, together with Russia, an international peace conference on the Middle East to be held in Madrid on October 30, 1991.

History was made when Israel, Syria, Lebanon, Egypt, Jordan, and the Palestinians attended the Madrid Middle East Peace Conference. At the conference, the Palestinian delegation was treated equally. Although there was no Palestinian flag at the table, Dr. Haider Abd al-Shafi, head of the Palestinian delegation was given equal time to present the Palestinian position. He openly accepted Israel's offer of autonomy, supported a confederation between Jordan and an independent Palestine, and called on the United States and Russia, co-sponsors of the conference, to directly or through the offices of the United Nations place the Occupied Territories under their trusteeship, pending a final settlement to the Palestinian-Israeli dispute.

The Madrid Peace Conference was followed by direct bilateral talks between Israel and the Palestinians on November 3, 1991. During the first round of talks in Madrid, the Israeli delegation agreed that negotiations would be conducted along two tracks: Palestinian-Israeli and Jordanian-Israeli. Furthermore, the delegates agreed that all future negotiations would be based on U.N. Resolutions 242 and 338.

The second round of bilateral talks was held in Washington on December 10–17, 1991. The heads of the Palestinian, Jordanian, and Israeli delegations disagreed on the principle of two-track negotiations, and held the talks in the corridors of the State Department.

The Palestinian and Arab delegations delayed their participation in the third round of the peace talks, to protest the deportation of 12 Palestinians by Israel, and the Jewish settlers' occupation of Arab homes in the village of Silwan, near Jerusalem. Nevertheless, the round began on January 13, and ended on January 16, 1992. In this round, the Palestinian delegation submitted to the Israelis a model for a Palestinian Interim Self-Governing Authority (PISGA), based on free elections under international supervision. The Israelis dismissed the concept of the PISGA.

However, an agreement was reached on the principle of two-track negotiations. Accordingly, the Palestinian track would consist of nine Palestinians and two Jordanians, and the Jordanian track would comprise nine Jordanians and two Palestinians. Under the terms of the agreement, each round would open and close with a general meeting of 13 Israelis, 11 Jordanians, and eight Palestinian delegates.

The Palestinian delegation was prevented from participating in the Multilateral Conference held in Moscow on January 28, 1992, because the delegation included representatives from East Jerusalem and the diaspora. However, the co-sponsors of the conference agreed that, in the future, Palestinian delegations to the economic development and refugee working groups could include Palestinians from the diaspora.

During the fourth round of the bilateral peace talks, the Israeli and Palestinian negotiators exchanged documents. The Israeli document emphasized that the Palestinian interim self-government would deal with the people, not with the status of the Occupied Territories. The document stated that the Israeli army would continue to be responsible for security, and that settlement activities would continue in the Occupied Territories. The Palestinian document maintained that representatives of the PISGA, as a transitional phase to Palestinian self-determination, would be elected by the Palestinians, and that the PISGA would have legislative, executive, and judiciary powers.

At the fifth round of bilateral talks held in Washington between April 27–30, 1992, the Israelis proposed municipal elections in the Occupied Territories "as a pilot stage," and also suggested their willingness to hand over the administration of health services to the Palestinians. The Israeli proposal was rejected, and the Palestinians insisted that elections for the PISGA members be held before anything else. After the talks, the Palestinian negotiating team met with Chairman Arafat in Amman, Jordan, and the relationship between the Palestinian delegation and the PLO became increasingly open and public.

The Israeli delegation, under the auspices of a Labor government headed by Yitzhak Rabin, attended the sixth round of the bilateral peace talks in Washington between August 24 and September 24, 1992. The delegates presented the Palestinians with a document dated August 20, 1992, entitled "The Administrative Council of the Interim Self-Government Arrangements: An Outline." In this document, Israel proposed the election of 15 Palestinian Administrative Council members, who would be responsible for administrative and functional duties in the Occupied Territories. The Palestinian delegation, however, insisted on the application of U.N. Resolution 242 to the entire peace process, and on September 1, 1992, handed the Israeli delegation a document called "Draft Proposal: Framework Agreements for Palestinian Interim Self-Government." In this document, the Palestinians demanded international protection during the proposed interim period, and insisted that the PISGA have authority over all the Palestinians, including those in East Jerusalem, and control over all economic activities and movements to and from the Occupied Territories.

Two weeks prior to the U.S. presidential elections, the seventh round of bilateral talks were held in Washington. At this round, the Israeli delegation demanded that all negotiations with the Palestinians be limited to the details of the proposed self-government arrangements. The Palestinians, in turn, rejected the Israeli model of self-government because it would lead to the establishment of a "dual judicial system" in the Occupied Territories. The Palestinians demanded assurances from the Israeli delegation that U.N. Resolution 242 would be applicable to both the interim period and the permanent status of the negotiations.

Frustrations intensified as Israel continued its oppressive policies in the Occupied Territories, and both the bilateral and the multilateral peace talks failed to move forward. The PLO decided to send only four delegates to attend the eighth round of the bilateral peace talks. At this round, held in Washington between December 7–17, 1992, the Israeli delegation presented the Palestinians with a document dated December 14, 1992, entitled: "Informal Compilation of Israeli Ideas on the Concept of the Interim Self-Government Arrangements." The document divided the Occupied Territories into five parts: East Jerusalem, Israeli settlements, and Israeli military encampments would be under Israeli jurisdiction; Palestinian localities would be under Palestinian control; and state land would be jointly administered by both Israelis and Palestinians.

Palestinian and Arab negotiators delayed their arrival in Washington for the ninth round of the bilateral peace talks to protest the deportation of 415 Palestinians by Israel to Lebanon on December 16, 1992. The deportees were accused of being members of HAMAS and other Islamic organizations, and were thought to be responsible for the killing of an Israeli soldier. The Palestinian delegation finally agreed to attend the ninth round, which began on April 27, 1993, following Prime Minister Yitzhak Rabin's statement that "massive deportations were not governmental policy", and the United States showed a willingness to assume the role of full partner in the peace talks. Moreover, Israel announced that it was willing to accept Faisal al-Husseini (PLO member from East Jerusalem) as the official leader of the Palestinian delegation, and to allow the return of 30 Palestinians deported from the Occupied Territories between 1967 and 1987. During this round, which also took place in Washington, the Israelis submitted to the Palestinian delegation on May 6 an interim proposal for self-rule. The Palestinian negotiators rejected the document because it did not contain anything new. Consequently, Arafat decided to protest what he perceived as unfulfilled promises, and did not send the Palestinian delegates to the three working committees on Palestinan self-rule, land and water, and human rights. He also reduced the number of Palestinian delegates to the 10th and 11th rounds of the bilateral peace talks, which ended in late August without any progress. However, Arafat did not want to be blamed for the collapse of the peace talks, and on June 11, 1993, agreed to meet with a journalist from *Ha'aretz*, the Israeli newspaper, and announced that, if Israel gave up the Gaza Strip and part of the West Bank to the PLO, it would prove that Israel was implementing U.N. Resolution 242.

The Palestine National Authority

The Israeli cabinet approved the draft proposal for establishing Palestinian autonomy in the Gaza Strip and Jericho on August 30, 1993. It had been agreed upon during secret negotiations with the PLO in Oslo, Norway. Israel and the PLO mutually recognized each other, and on September 13, 1993, they signed the Declaration of Principles (DOP) in Washington, ending two years of deadlocked negotiations that had begun in October 1991 at the Madrid Middle East Peace Conference.

The DOP agreement consisted of a timetable for negotiations on a Palestinian Self-Governing Authority in Jericho and the Gaza Strip that was later to be extended to the entire West Bank. Israel and the PLO agreed on the following: within two months of the signing of the accord, Israel would redeploy its army in Jericho, and in the Gaza Strip within four months; PLO security forces would enter the autonomous areas from Egypt and Jordan to form the Palestinian police, who would be responsible for internal security; Israel would remain responsible for external and foreign affairs; the Israeli Civil Administration would transfer its responsibilites in the West Bank to the Palestine National Authority; elections for a Palestinian Legislative Council to assume responsibility for all services in the Occupied Territories, except defense and foreign affairs, would be held after nine months; negotiations on the permanent status of the Occupied Territories, the refugee problem, Jerusalem, Jewish settlements, and borders would commence no later than May 1996, and full agreement should be reached by May 1999.

Following the signing of the DOP, the PLO Central Council met in Tunis, and approved the Gaza-Jericho Accord and the establishment of the Palestine National Authority (PNA), and elected Yasser Arafat the president. The PNA included the following ministries: Agriculture, *Waqf* and Religious Affairs, Culture and Information, Economy, Education, Finance, Health, Housing, Interior, Jerusalem Portfolio, Justice, Labor, Local Government, Planning and International Coordination, Post and Telecommunications, Social Affairs, Sport and Youth, Tourism and Antiquities, and Transport. The PLO also drafted the "Provisional Basic Law," which outlined the Palestinian administration and the role of the PLO during the five-year interim phase. The new provisions granted the head of the PNA, who is also the chairman of the PLO Executive Committee and the commander-in-chief of the Palestinian forces, control over the Legislative Council and government administration. Moreover, the "Provisional Basic Law" included a section on "Rights and General Liberties," which guaranteed individual, cultural, economic, and social rights, as well as civil liberties. Article 81 of the "Provisional Basic Law" also affirmed that "no one shall be expelled from his homeland, stripped of his citizenship, or prevented from leaving or returning to his country." Finally, article 65 stipulated that "every citizen has the right to participate in public life and to be nominated to public office in accordance with the law."

The implementation of the five-year transitional period, which was to begin first in Jericho and the Gaza Strip on December 1993 in accordance with the DOP, did not occur until Prime Minister Rabin and Arafat signed the Cairo Agreement on May 4, 1994. The agreement dealt with the principle of Palestinian self-rule, the redeployment of the Israeli army from Jericho and Gaza, and the entry of the Palestine Liberation Army into Jericho and the Gaza Strip. The agreement also stipulated shared responsibilities at border crossings and joint control of roads leading from the Jewish settlements in the Gaza Strip to Israel. Moreover, the PNA would issue passports to Palestinians in the autonomous areas, print stamps, and obtain an international code. Israel transferred political power to the PNA in Jericho on May 13, 1994, and in the Gaza Strip on May 17, 1994. Arafat crossed Rafah to the Gaza Strip on July 1, 1994. Four days later, he flew aboard an Egyptian helicopter to Jericho, where he swore in 12 of the 24 members of the PNA.

The PNA, during its short term in office, has been confronted with many challenges. The degree of economic cooperation between Israel and the PNA will remain uncertain as long as the DOP is not implemented and the issues of sovereignty, land, water, and borders are unresolved. Economic relations between the PNA, Israel, and other countries are based on the economic provisions of the DOP of September 13, 1993 and the Paris Protocol of April 29,1994. The PNA has no official currency. The legal tenders in both the autonomous areas and the Occupied Territories are the Jordanian dinar and the Israeli shekel. The absence of an official currency and a Palestinian central bank in the autonomous areas has deprived the PNA from making monetary policy, and has forced it to link its economy with Jordan and Israel.

After the convening of the donors' conference in Washington on October 1, 1993, where $2.4 billion were pledged in assistance to the Palestinians, the PLO established the Palestine Economic Council for Development and Reconstruction (PECDAR) to formulate economic policies, to select investment and technical projects, and coordinate financial assistance. According to the PNA's Economic Minister Ahmed Qre'i, the failure to implement major infrastructure projects in the autonomous areas, planned by the World Bank for the first year of the five-year interim phase, is because the donor countries paid the PNA only $240 million of the $700 million pledged for 1994. Also, the PNA, lacks an efficient tax-collection mechanism, and in 1994 spent more than $145 million of the $240 million on operating costs and salaries for an estimated 17,500 police and 27,000 civil servants. Israel's frequent closure and sealing-off of the autonomous areas and the West Bank have led to a high rate of unemployment, and have cost the PNA about $600 million a year. Palestinian businessmen in the diaspora also have been reluctant to invest in the autonomous areas and the Occupied Territories, and have made their investments conditional on the establishment of both a "Guidance Council" to share the responsibility of decision-making with Arafat, and a "Development and Construction Council" to assist the PNA's financial institutions.

Palestinian opposition to the PNA is led by the Islamists (HAMAS and Islamic Jihad), the Secularists (PFLP and DFLP), and Palestinians in the diaspora, who rejected the DOP and constantly question the legitimacy of the PNA. Moreover, the Islamists have engaged in militant activities against Israel leading to an open conflict between the PNA and the Islamists, and the arrest of Islamist leaders in the autonomous areas. Arafat has tried to rein in the Islamists by both conciliation and a show of force. For example, he announced that the Palestinian police would release HAMAS and Islamic Jihad prisoners if the opposition agreed to halt their attacks against Israel. However, after the clashes between the police and supporters of the Islamists on November 20, 1994, which left 16 people dead and over 200 wounded, Arafat established the Preventive Security Court to bring to trial offenders of security violations. The PNA also has closed Islamists newspapers, banned all their political meetings, and threatened that any Palestinian caught with unlicensed weapons would face a prison sentence of more than two years. The PNA has accused the Islamists of initiating suicide attacks against Israel from the autonomous areas in order to embarrass Arafat, delay Israeli redeployment from the Occupied Territories, and kill the peace process. HAMAS's spiritual leader and founder, Sheikh Ahmad Yassin, has stated that HAMAS refuses to join the PLO, rejects the DOP, and would not participate in elections for the Palestinian Legislative Council (PLC) because it rejects the principle of administering the Occupied Territories for Israel. He denounced the PNA's attacks against the Islamists, and announced that coexistence between the PNA and

HAMAS is possible only if the PNA ends its hostility against Islamists, and does not plan to establish a one-party (FATAH) system in Palestine.

The Palestinians in the diaspora, living in Jordan, Syria, Lebanon, Kuwait, and other countries, who have carried the burden of the Palestinian struggle since 1948, also are disenchanted. The DOP does not take into consideration U.N. Resolution 194 (III) of December 11, 1948, which recognizes their right to return to their homes, to live in peace, or to be compensated for the property they left behind if they decide not to return.

Israel was slow in implementing the terms of the DOP, which was signed on September 13, 1993. It was reluctant to redeploy its army in the Occupied Territories because of its fear for the safety of the 140,000 Jewish settlers, and because of its assessment that the PNA has not been competent in combating terrorism. Israel also did not expedite the transfer of services to the PNA. In early 1995, only five of 38 services were administered by the PNA: education, health, social welfare, tourism and taxation. Furthermore, Israel refuses to release all Palestinian prisoners, has banned PNA activities in East Jerusalem, closes the Occupied Territories at whim and has prevented Palestinian laborers from working in Israel. It also has been busy establishing facts on the ground to influence the outcome of the negotiations with the Palestinians regarding the "permanent status" of the Occupied Territories, which were to commence in May 1996. It continues with its settlement activities and the expropriation of Palestinian land.

The Oslo Two Agreement

Israel and the PNA met in Taba on July 16, 1995, to negotiate the implementation of the second phase of the DOP. The principal issues that were discussed include: the redeployment of the Israeli army from the Occupied Territories, the expansion of Palestinian self-rule, the elections of a Palestinian council, water resources and allocations, electricity, security, economy, law enforcement, and authority over state land.

After weeks of intense negotiations, Israel and the PNA signed the Oslo Two Agreement in Washington, D.C. on September 28, 1995. According to this agreement, the West Bank was divided into three areas. Area A comprising 3 percent of the West Bank was placed under Palestinian control. This area includes the heavily populated cities of Jenin, Tulkarm, Qalqilya, Nablus, Ramallah, Bethlehem and Hebron. However, Israel maintained control of 15 percent of the city of Hebron to protect the 400 Israeli settlers, who live in the city. Area B representing 27 percent and includes more than 450 small towns and villages was placed under Palestinian civil administration and Israeli security. Area C the remaining 70 percent is to be under Israeli control because it includes settlements and Israeli military bases. Moreover, elections for the 82 member PLC and a president would be held in 1996, after Israel has completed redeployment and the construction of 110 kilometers of new settlement roads, designed to bypass the heavily populated Palestinian areas. Israel also agreed to a second phase of redeployment in the Occupied Territories, to be carried out in three stages, each six months apart. It also agreed to release Palestinian prisoners in three stages. The first group would be released after the agreement was signed on September 28, 1995, the second group after the Palestinian elections, and the last group at a later date. Arafat agreed to revoke all statements calling for the destruction of Israel from the Palestinian Charter, two months after the inauguration of the Palestinian Legislative Council.

On January 20, 1996 elections for a president and the PLC were held in the West Bank (including East Jerusalem) and the Gaza Strip. The elections showed that most Palestinians supported the peace process, paricularly after the Israeli redeployment from the major cities (with the exception of Hebron) of the West Bank (Area A).

Between November 12 and December 12, 1995, approximately 7,000 specially trained Palestinian teachers registered voters. In late November, the laws governing the entire election process were endorsed by the PNA after being subjected to an intense public debate. By December 30, 1995, out of a population of 2 million, 1,013,235 had registered to vote. Two persons competed for the office of president, Yasser Arafat and Samiha Khalil of al-Bireh, and altogether 676 candidates ran for the 88 seats in the PLC.

The West Bank, East Jerusalem and the Gaza Strip were divided into 16 electoral districts, five districts in Gaza and 11 in the West Bank. There were 1,697 polling stations monitored by 300 persons from the European Union Election unit and 350 international observers from 32 countries and non-government organizations. In addition, former U.S. President Jimmy Carter headed an international group of 20 persons. The PNA deployed 6,000 police in the area.

The election campaign started on January 2 and ended on January 19. The Palestinian election laws did not specify the amount that a candidate could spend on his campaign. The majority of candidates financed their own campaigns and spent an estimated $30 million.

Participation in the elections (750,000 out of a potential electorate of 1,013,235—estimated at 74% in the West Bank; 86% in the Gaza Strip and 40% in East Jerusalem) was high despite calls by HAMAS, the Popular Front for the Liberation of Palestine, the Democratic Front for the Liberation of Palestine, Islamic Jihad, Islamic Liberation Party, and the Arab Socialist Party to boycott the elections. The nonpresence of candidates from the opposition led to the absence of clear and well-defined platforms in the election campaigns. Consequently, the selection of the candidates on election day were based on personal considerations, i.e. religion, family ties and political affiliations, and not on the candidates' political programs.

The election of Arafat as president and of the PLC members on January 20, 1996 signalled a new era for the Palestinians and an important step toward the process of state-building.

Notes

1. For the text of the "Balfour Declaration," see J.C. Hurewitz, *Diplomacy in the Near and Middle East, 1914–1965,* vol. II (New York: W. Van Nostrand, 1966), p. 26.

2. Netanel Lorch, *Israel's War of Independence, 1947–1948* (Hartford, Conn.: Hartmore House, Inc., 1968), p. 89.

3. See Nafez Nazzel, *Palestinian Exodus from the Galilee, 1948* (Beirut: The Institute for Palestine Studies, 1978).

4. Don Peretz, *The West Bank: History, Politics, Society, and Economy* (Boulder, Colo.: Westview Press, 1986), p. 31.

5. Sara Roy, *The Gaza Strip: A Demographic, Economic, Social and Legal Survey* (Jerusalem: The West Bank Data Base Project, 1986), pp. 20–21.

6. Muhammad Hallaj, "Palestinian Refugees and the Peace Process," *Middle East International* (November 1993): 462, 16–17.

7. Institute for Applied Social Science, *Palestinian Society in Gaza, West Bank and Arab Jerusalem* (Norway: FAFO, Center for International Studies, 1992), pp. 5–9.

8. See Meron Benvenisti, *The West Bank and Gaza Strip* (Jerusalem: The West Bank Data Base, 1982).

9. W.T. and S.V. Mallison, "International Law and the Palestine-Israel Dispute," *Journal of Palestine Studies* (Spring 1974): 11, 81; and Janet Abu-Lughod, "Israeli Settlement in Occupied Arab Land," *Journal of Palestine Studies* (Winter 1982): 42, 16–54.

10. See Hisham Awartani, *West Bank Agriculture* (Nablus, West Bank: Al-Najah National University, 1978).

11. Emile Sahliyeh, "West Bank Industrial and Agricultural Development: The Basic Problems," *Journal of Palestine Studies* (Winter 1982): 42, 55–69.

12. See Jonathan Kuttab, *Analysis of Military Order No. 854 and Related Orders Concerning Educational Institutions in the Occupied Territories.* (Ramallah, West Bank: Law in the Service of Man, 1981).

The Dictionary

A

ABBAS, MAHMOUD. Pseudonym, Abu Mazen. A top FATAH (q.v.) official, second to Arafat (q.v.) in the Palestine Liberation Organization (q.v.) hierarchy, and a member of the PLO Executive Committee (q.v.). Abbas, who is 60 years old, was born in Safad, Palestine, and fled with his family during the war of 1948 (q.v.). A pioneer in the FATAH movement, he was responsible for establishing FATAH offices in Saudi Arabia (q.v.) and Qatar. He was involved in the secret PLO-Israel negotiations that took place in Oslo, Norway, and negotiated the Oslo Accords (q.v.). On September 13, 1993, he signed the Declaration of Principles (q.v.) in Washington on behalf of the Palestinians. Abu Mazen later distanced himself from the Palestine National Authority (q.v.), asserting that the PNA had conceded too much to Israel. However, on March 20, 1995, he replaced Nabil Sha'ath (q.v.), the minister of Planning and International Coordination who had led the negotiations since July 1994, as the overall supervisor of negotiations with Israel. In 1996, Abbas was appointed Arafat's deputy.

In his memoirs, *The Road to Oslo* (Arabic, 1994), Abu Mazen created an uproar in Israel when he maintained that the PLO, through Sa'ed Kan'an (q.v.), a Nablus businessman, held 20 sessions of high-level talks with Ephraim Sneh—a prominent Labor Party official, who at the time was Yitzhak Rabin's (q.v.) representative and the chairman of the Labor Party election campaign, and later became the Israeli Health Minister—before it was legal for Israelis to meet with the PLO (q.v). They discussed ways of winning Arab votes for the Labor Party in the 1992 Israeli elections.

ABBAS, MUHAMMAD. Nom de guerre, Abu Abbas. Secretary-General of the Palestine Liberation Front (q.v.) . He also was a member of the PLO Executive Committee (q.v.) and served as the head of the PLO Department of Refugees. He is alleged to have master-minded the *Achille Lauro* hijacking (q.v.), and the unsuccessful attack on the beach in Tel Aviv, Israel, on May 30, 1990.

ABED-RABBO, YASSER. Nom de guerre, Abu Bashir. He was born in Jaffa, Palestine. He and Nayef Hawatmeh (q.v.) established the Democratic Front for the Liberation of Palestine (q.v.), and Abu Bashir became the assistant secretary-general of that organization. Internal feuding caused him to sever his relations with the DFLP in 1990. Abed-Rabbo became the director of the Information Department of the PLO (q.v) and a member of the PLO Executive Committee (q.v.). He founded FIDA (q.v.), the Palestinian Democratic Union Party, in February 1993. He is a close confidant of Yasser Arafat (q.v.), who appointed him minister of Culture and Information in the Palestine National Authority (q.v.) on July 5, 1994 and again, in June 1996. He strongly opposes the continued Israeli confiscation of Arab land and the construction of Israeli settlements (q.v.) taking place irrespective of the DOP (q.v.), and has stated on several occasions that the peace agreement should be suspended until Israel (q.v.) stops building and enlarging settlements (q.v.).

ABD AL-HADI, AWNI. A prominent lawyer and an active member in the early Arab National Movement (q.v.). He was born in Nablus (q.v.) in 1889, received his higher education in Istanbul, Turkey, and later went to Paris to study law. Abd al-Hadi helped co-found *Al-Fatat* (Youth) Nationalist Society (q.v.) in 1911, and two years later assisted in the organization of the Arab Nationalist Congress (q.v.) of Paris. He also was employed by both Amir Faisal (q.v.) in Damascus, Syria, and by Amir Abdallah (q.v.) of Transjordan. In 1930, he was appointed a member of the Palestinian delegation that went to England to discuss British policy in Palestine (q.v.). Abd al-Hadi and others formed the *Istiqlal* (Independence) Party (q.v.) on August 2, 1932, with a platform based on Arab unity. He also was a member of the Arab Higher Committee (q.v.), and was active in organizing the resistance against British policy and Jewish immigration. Like so many other Palestinian nationalists at the time, he was imprisoned by the British Mandate (q.v) authorities for his activities and later exiled. For a brief period in 1948, he was appointed Minister of Social Affairs in the All-Palestine Government established in Gaza (qq.v.). Afterward, he went to Jordan and held a number of government posts. From 1951 until 1955, he was Jordan's ambassador to Egypt (q.v.); in 1956, he was the minister of Foreign Affairs and Justice; and in 1958, he served on the Federal Council of the Jordan-Iraq Arab Federation. He died on March 15, 1970 in Cairo, Egypt (q.v.).

ABDALLAH, KING. A descendant of the Hashemite clan (the Prophet Muhammad's lineage), former ruler of Transjordan, and grandfather of King Hussein I of Jordan (qq.v.). He was born in 1882, the son of Sharif Hussein ibn Ali, the leader of the Arab revolt against the Ottoman Turks (q.v.).

After the dismantlement of the Ottoman Empire at the end of World War I, Transjordan was created in the Palestine territory east of the River Jordan. After 1920, Transjordan came under the control of the British Mandate (q.v.). In 1921, the British gave Abdallah control of this area, and he was assured that his country would never be made accessible to Jewish immigration. During the war of 1948 (q.v.), Abdallah joined the forces of the Arab League (q.v.) and fought against Israel. However, before the war started, he had made a secret treaty with Zionist leaders, in which he promised he would not fight the Jews on land that had already been given to them by the United Nations Partition Plan (q.v.). That secret agreement, however, did not include the city of Jerusalem (q.v.). Afterward, Abdallah changed the name of Transjordan to the Hashemite Kingdom of Jordan, and in 1950, the West Bank including East Jerusalem (qq.v.), became Jordanian territory. King Abdallah was assassinated on July 20, 1951, as he was entering the *Al-Aqsa* Mosque at the *Haram Al-Sharif* (q.v.) in East Jerusalem. His son Talal became king for a year, but abdicated because of illness in favor of his son Hussein, who became King Hussein I, the current monarch of Jordan.

ABD AL-LATIF, SALAH. Born in Nablus (q.v.), he trained as a lawyer. In 1920, he established a political party, *Hizb Al-Ahli* (the Clan Party). In 1922, he served as a member of the Supreme Muslim Council (q.v.), representing the district of Nablus (q.v.). He also founded the National Bloc in October 1935, a party which advocated the independence of Palestine. He later became the party's representative to the Arab Higher Committee (q.v.).

ABDEEN, ABD AL QADER, SHEIKH. The new *mufti* (q.v.) of Jerusalem (q.v.), appointed by Jordan to succeed the deceased *mufti*, Suleiman al-Ja'bari (q.v.), who died on October 11, 1994. Sheikh Abdeen had previously served as the chief judge and head of the Islamic Appeals Court in the West Bank (q.v). His appointment drew sharp criticisim from the PNA (q.v.), which maintained that Muslim affairs in East Jerusalem (q.v.) were the sole responsiblity of the PNA, not Jordan. The PNA then appointed Sheikh Ekrameh Sabri (q.v.) to the same position, and today there are two *muftis* in Jerusalem.

ABDUL HADI, MAHDI. Director and founding member of the Palestinian Academic Society for the Study of International Relations (q.v), a Palestinian think-tank established in 1987. He was born in Nablus (q.v.) in 1944, and later attended the School of Law at Damascus University, graduating in 1970. When he returned to Jerusalem, he edited the Arabic daily, *Al-Fajr* (q.v.), from 1972 until 1974, and in 1977 he became the public relations director of Birzeit University (q.v.). From 1977 until 1980, he served as the secretary-general of the Council for Higher Education and the president of the Arab Thought Forum (qq.v.). He then left for England to continue his education and received his Ph.D. from the School of Peace Studies at Bradford University in 1984. In 1985, he was appointed special advisor to the Ministry of the Occupied Palestine Land Affairs in Amman, Jordan. Currently, he is a member of the Council of Jerusalem, which was established by Arafat (q.v.) to oversee the affairs of East Jerusalem (q.v.). He has written several books on the Palestinian problem in Arabic and English, and is politically active.

ABED, HANI. A member of Islamic Jihad (q.v.), born on December 29, 1963. He died on November 2, 1994, when a bomb placed in his car exploded in the Gaza Strip. It is presumed that the bomb was placed by the Israeli secret service in retaliation for the killing of two Israelis, Sgt. Moshe Bukra and Cpl. Erez Ben-Baruch, on May 20, 1994, near the Erez checkpoint, on the border between the Gaza Strip and Israel (qq.v.).

Abed was married and had four children. He was a chemistry lecturer at the Khan Younis College of Technology, and co-editor of the Islamic Jihad weekly *Istiqlal* (Independence), the publication and licensing of which had been authorized by Arafat (q.v.) in 1994. Abed was arrested and detained for six months in 1991 by the Israelis for harboring a wanted relative. On May 24, 1994, he was held for 17 days by the Palestinian police after the May attack, just one day after the Israelis left the Gaza Strip and the Palestinian Authority (q.v) took over. It was the first political arrest made by the PNA, which, at that time, had warned Abed that the Israeli General Security Services were after him. At his funeral, held at the Omari Mosque in Gaza, Arafat (q.v) arrived to attend the funeral ceremony, but was quickly whisked away as an angry crowd mobbed him, because they thought that he had conceded a great deal to Israel and received too little in return.

ABSENTEE PROPERTY. Property once owned by Palestinians who fled their homes during the wars of 1948 and 1967 (qq.v.), or were absent when the wars took place. Consequently, they cannot claim the property as theirs, because they no longer reside in Palestine and the Occupied Territories (qq.v.). An official, the custodian of abandoned properties, disposes of these properties for Israeli purposes.

ABU AYYASH, RADWAN IBRAHIM. Former head of the Arab Journalists Association, and officially appointed by Arafat (q.v.) in April 1995 as the director-general of the Palestine Broadcasting Corporation. Abu Ayyash was born in 1950 in the Askar Refugee Camp in Nablus (q.v). He studied at the Men's Training Center in Ramallah (q.v.), and in 1982 received a B.A. degree in English from Birzeit University (q.v.). He taught school in Ramallah (q.v.), and worked as a journalist for *Al-Sha'b* (q.v) newspaper, a pro-PLO daily. He became active in FATAH (q.v.), and organized groups for the *shabibah* (q.v.), the pro-FATAH youth groups. He was blacklisted by Jordan and banned from traveling there because of his hostile rhetoric against that country. In 1979, he became a full-time journalist and worked as the chief editor for the Palestine Press Service (q.v.). From 1982 to 1986, he was the managing editor for *Al-Awdah* (q.v.) magazine. In 1984, he was placed under town arrest (q.v.) for six months, and on December 10, 1987, he was detained for six months after the Israelis accused him of channeling money from Tunis and Europe to support the Intifada (q.v.). From 1985 to 1991, he served as the head of the Arab Journalists Association, while continuing to direct the Arab Media Center. He was appointed in 1991 as the coordinator of the Palestinian Non-Governmental Organizations (q.v.). In 1992, he established the Social Solidarity Society, a new socio-political organization, that had 178 prominent Palestinian members. He also was appointed a member of the advisory council to the Palestinian delegation to the peace talks.

ABU GHARBIYEH, BAHJAT. Born and raised in Jerusalem, he became a schoolteacher and taught in Hebron (q.v.). He later fought and was wounded in the war of 1948 (q.v.). He established al-Ibrahimiyeh College, a high school in East Jerusalem (q.v.), which continues to serve Palestinian youths to this day. He was a member of the 1964 PLO (q.v.) Congress, and co-founder of the Popular Struggle Front (q.v.).

ABU GHAZALEH, HATEM KHALIL. Physician, political activist, and founder of the Society for the Care of Handicapped Children in Gaza. He was born in Jerusalem (q.v.) in 1935. His family originally came from Jaffa, Palestine, where his father served as a medical officer in the British Mandate (q.v.). Hatem, who is trained as a surgeon, received his B.S. in medicine in 1960 and an M.S. in surgery in 1962 from Kings College at the University of Cambridge in England. He worked at the Baptist Hospital in Gaza from 1961 until 1974. He also served as the vice-chairman of the Bank of Palestine from 1967 to 1984, and was one of the founding members of the Gaza Citrus Producers Union. His greatest contribution, however, has been the establishment in 1975 of the Society for the Care of Handicapped Children in Gaza. The organization serves 4,000 handicapped children, has 315 employees, and runs 14 different programs. It has an up-to-date speech therapy clinic and a program with the University of Calgary in Canada. Students can receive bachelor degrees in audiology, speech pathology therapy, and deaf education while attending classes in Gaza, conducted by professors on leave from the University of Calgary.

ABU GHAZALEH, HATEM SIDDIQ ABDEL-KHALIQ. Doctor, human rights activist, and author. He was born in Nablus (q.v.) on February 3, 1932. After studying medicine and surgery in Damascus, Syria, and receiving his degree in 1956, he worked in Jerusalem, Jordan (q.v.), and Algeria. He served for six months in the Jordanian parliament in 1962, but soon after was imprisoned for a year because of his political activities. He returned to the West Bank (q.v.) in 1967, and was detained by the Israelis. In 1970, he was placed under house arrest (q.v.) for three years. Abu Ghazaleh wanted to run for mayor of Nablus in the 1976 elections, but was discouraged from doing so because of the popularity of Bassam al-Shak'a (q.v.), who eventually became the mayor. Nevertheless, he continued to be politically active, and in 1978 helped establish the Society for Friends of Prisoners in Nazareth. In 1982, he founded the Franco-Palestinian Friendship Society and served as its president until 1991. He also was president of the An-Najah National University (q.v.) Friends Society. He has written several books in Arabic on the Arab-Israeli conflict.

ABU HILAL, ALI ABDALLAH MOHAMMAD. Trade union activist and one of the leaders of the Democratic Front for the Liberation of Palestine (q.v.) and a member of its political bureau. He was born in 1955 in Abu Dis, a village near Jerusalem (q.v.). In 1974, while still in high school, he was accused of being a member of the Palestine National Front (q.v.), and was detained and imprisoned by the Israelis. He began to study law in Cairo, Egypt (q.v.), but shortly after was expelled for his political activities. In 1978, he returned to the West Bank (q.v.) and began to work with the Public Works Union in Abu Dis. Once again, he was detained by the Israelis and placed in administrative detention (q.v.). From 1980 to 1985, he was placed under house arrest (q.v.), whenever he was not in jail. In 1982, he became an executive member of the General Federation of the Palestinian Trade Unions (q.v.) in the West Bank. He was arrested on December 5, 1982 and released in November 1983, but was subsequently placed under town arrest (q.v.) in Abu Dis. In 1983, he served as secretary of the Workers Unity Block Union in the West Bank and Gaza (qq.v). On January 30, 1986, Abu Hilal was accused of being one of the leaders of the DFLP, and subsequently imprisoned for three months. Afterward, he was deported to Jordan. He spent six years in Jordan working with the PLO (q.v.) in Amman. He also was a member of the Supporting Committee for the Intifada (q.v.), and became a member of the PNC (q.v.) in 1989. On September 13, 1991, he was permitted to return to the West Bank, in exchange for the remains of an Israeli soldier held by the DFLP. Following his return, he became the director of the Freedoms Defense Institute, and continues to serve as advisor to the Labor Unity Block.

ABU LUGHOD, IBRAHIM. Prominent professor and political activist born in Jaffa, Palestine. He studied in the United States, receiving a B.A. in 1953, an M.A. in political science from the University of Illinois, and a Ph.D. from Princeton University in 1962. He has taught at several U.S. universities, including Northwestern University. A member of the Palestine National Council (q.v.) for many years, he often was mentioned in the '80s as a possible Palestinian negotiator to the peace talks with Israel. In 1993, he was appointed vice president of academic affairs at Birzeit University (q.v.). He also is the leader of the Palestinian Independent Group for Elections in the Occupied Territories, a group that advocates democracy and respect for human rights. In 1995, he was given the task of updating and developing the curriculum in the Palestinian schools.

ABU MAYZAR, ABD AL-MUHSIN. A longtime member of the Palestine national movement, he was a founding leader of the Palestine National Front (q.v.). He also served as the PLO (q.v.) spokesman, a member of the PNC (q.v.) from 1973 to 1978, and a member of the PLO Central Council (q.v.) from 1974 to 1987.

ABU MIDDEYAN, FREIH. Appointed by Arafat (q.v.) in July 1994 and June 1996 as the Minister of Justice in the Palestine National Authority (q.v.). Abu Middeyan was born in 1944 to a bedouin family originally from Beer al-Sabe', Palestine. He studied law at Alexandria University in Egypt (q.v.), and received his degree in 1971. Afterward, he returned to Gaza and practiced law. He also became an active member of the Palestinian Red Crescent Society (q.v.) in 1973. The following year, he was imprisoned by the Israelis. After his release, he continued to provide legal aid for political detainees. In 1989, he became chairman of the Gaza Bar Association, and in 1991 a member of the Council of Law. Concerned with the deteriorating standard of education under the Israeli military occupation, he became a member of the Council for Higher Education (q.v.) and of the Board of Trustees of the Khan Younis College of Science and Technology. He also is a former member of the Palestinian delegation to the peace talks.

ABU RAHMAH, FAYIEZ SHA'BAN. Prominent lawyer born in Gaza (q.v.) on December 23, 1929. He attended the Arab College of Jerusalem, and went on to study at the Faculty of Law at Cairo University in Egypt (q.v.). He interrupted his studies in 1953, and joined the attorney general's office in Gaza. In 1957, he was selected to represent the Pro-Asian Solidarity Conference that convened in Cairo, Egypt. He was appointed a member of the Higher Committee of the Palestine National Union of Gaza from 1961 to 1967. He helped establish the Gaza Bar Association in 1976, and served two terms as its chairman—from 1976 to 1985 and from 1987 to 1989. Since 1979, he has been vice chairman of the Palestinian Red Crescent Society (q.v.), and a member of the Board of Trustees of An-Najah National University in Nablus (q.v.). Active in politics, he participated in the peace talks initiated by then-Secretary of State George Schultz. At that time, he was one of two Palestinians nominated to negotiate with Jordan and Israel (q.q.v.) in the event that peace talks were convened. He also was mentioned again in 1989 as a possible negotiator.

ABU SHARAR, MAJID. Palestinian author and former member of FATAH's (q.v.) Central Committee. He also was in charge of the PLO (q.v.) Information Office. He was born in Dura, in the Hebron (q.v.) area, in 1936, and he completed part of his schooling there before moving to Egypt (q.v.). He taught school in Jordan (q.v.), then Saudi Arabia (q.v.), where in 1966 he joined FATAH. He was assassinated in Rome on October 9, 1991, and is buried in Beirut, Lebanon (q.v.).

ABU SHARIF, BASSAM. Nom de guerre, Abu Sharar. A former member and spokesman of the Popular Front for the Liberation of Palestine (q.v.), and an editor of *Al-Hadaf* (The Target), the PFLP's paper. Switching ranks, he joined FATAH (q.v.) in 1987, and became Arafat's advisor, spokesman and troubleshooter in Tunis. However, a rift developed between them over policy issues, and Abu Sharif did not make the move to the Gaza Strip (q.v.) in July 1994, when the Gaza Strip and Jericho (q.v.) became autonomous, and the Palestine National Authority (q.v.) was established. He co-authored a book with Uzi Mahnaimi entitled *Tried by Fire* (Little, Brown, 1995).

ABU ZAYYAD, ZIYAD ALI. Lawyer, journalist, political activist, and PLC (q.v.) member for the East Jerusalem (q.v.) district. He was born in 1940 in Bethany, a village near Jerusalem (q.v.), attended local schools and received his law degree from Damascus University in Syria (q.v.) in 1964. Afterward, he worked as supervisor in the personnel communication department for the Jordanian government. He taught school and wrote a daily column for *Al-Quds* (q.v.) newspaper. Later, he moved to *Al-Fajr* (q.v.) newspaper, where he edited the Israeli news. From 1983 to 1986, he practiced law in Ramallah (q.v.). He then founded a bi-monthly in Hebrew called *Gesher* (bridge), which encourages dialogue with Israelis, and brings Palestinian views to the Israeli public. In 1990, he was placed under house arrest (q.v.) for six months. After his release, he participated in talks with then-U.S. Secretary of State James Baker. He served as a member of the Palestinian delegation of the Strategic and Political Committee to the peace talks, and has been responsible for drawing the security plans for the Palestinian entity in accordance with the Declaration of Principles (q.v.). He also is co-founder and co-editor of the *Palestine-Israel Journal*, which is devoted to encouraging coexistence between Palestinians and Israelis.

ABU ZULUF, MAHMOUD QASSIM. Born in 1924 in Jaffa, Palestine, he received his primary and secondary education at local schools there. He attended the American University of Beirut, Lebanon (q.v.), and majored in journalism. He then returned to Jaffa and co-founded *Al-Dif'a* (q.v.) newspaper. In 1951, he established *Al-Jihad* (The Struggle, or Holy War) newspaper with two partners during the Jordanian rule. After the Israeli occupation in 1967, the newspaper was reopened with the *Al-Quds* (Jerusalem) name, and has seen numerous technological advances as well as changes in editorial policy. The paper in 1985 changed political position, from a pro-Jordanian stance to pro-PLO mainstream. The paper is popular and widely read, and Abu Zuluf maintains relations with politicians from the entire political spectrum. He also is a successful businessman.

ACHILLE LAURO. The Italian cruise ship with 400 passengers that was hijacked on October 7, 1985, off the shores of Egypt (q.v.) by four members of the Palestine Liberation Front (q.v.). The hijackers threatened to blow up the ship if Israel did not release 50 Palestinian prisoners held in Israeli jails. An American-Jewish passenger, Leon Klinghoffer, confined to a wheelchair, was thrown overboard, and is thought to have suffered a heart attack and died. The Palestinian commandos eventually gave themselves up to the Egyptian authorities. On January 19, 1996, the PLO (q.v.) agreed to finance a U.S. Peace Studies Center as part of the settlement of a lawsuit brought by Klinghoffer's daughters.

ADMINISTERED AREAS. The term used by Israeli officials to denote the Occupied Territories (q.v.). It is based on the premise that the West Bank and the Gaza Strip (qq.v.) were not seized from sovereign rulers, but are part of Eretz Israel (the land of Israel) and, therefore, are not occupied, but liberated.

ADMINISTRATIVE DETENTION. Emergency regulations that were first imposed by the British in 1945 to quell both Palestinian and Jewish protests and demonstrations. The regulations also included deportations (q.v.) and house demolitions. In 1967, Israel reintroduced the regulations in the Occupied Territories (q.v.), together with more than 1,365 other Israeli military orders.

Administrative detention is when an individual is placed in jail without having access to a lawyer and without any knowledge as to the reason(s) for his arrest. According to international law, administrative detention is legal if the detained person is permitted an appeal (although the reason(s) for the individual's arrest does not have to be revealed, if it endangers the security of the state), and if he is brought before a judge within four days of his arrest. The order for imprisonment also must be examined every six months, if the period of detention is extended. Al-Haq (q.v.) estimates that from 1985 to 1987, about 316 Palestinians were placed in administrative detention. After the Intifada (q.v.) commenced in 1987, there were 3,000 to 4,000 Palestinians in administrative detention. Moreover, Israeli officials not only used administrative detention more often during the Intifada, but they extended the period of detention from six to 12 months. At times, detainees were released after serving two six-month terms, and jailed again a few days later. Faisal al-Husseini (q.v.), Sari Nuseibeh (q.v.), Nabil al-Ja'bari (q.v.), and Abd al-Aziz Rantisi (q.v.) are among the prominent Palestinians who have been placed in administrative detention.

ADWAN, KAMAL. Leader of the Black September Organization (q.v). An engineer by profession, he worked in the Persian Gulf countries. He joined FATAH (q.v.), became a member of its Central Committee, and was placed in charge of operations in the Occupied Territories (q.v.). He was killed in Beirut, Lebanon (q.v.), by Israeli commandos on April 10, 1973.

AL-AGHA, ZAKARIA IBRAHIM. Appointed Minister of Housing and Public Works in the Palestine National Authority (q.v.) in July 1994. He was born in 1942 in Khan Younis, Gaza (q.v.). He received his M.D. in medicine in 1971 from Cairo University in Egypt (q.v.). After completing his training, he was appointed as head of the medical section at the Khan Younis Government Hospital. He worked there until 1987, when he was dismissed by the Israelis for "political and security reasons." In 1989, he was hired by *Al-Ahli* Private Arab Hospital as part of the team that administered the hospital, and also as chief of internal medicine.

Al-Agha has been actively involved in the health and educational sectors of Palestinian society. He served on the executive committee of the Arab Medical Association from 1977 until 1985, and was chairman from 1985 until 1992. Since 1990, he has been the chairman of the Council of Health Services. He was treasurer of the General Assembly of the Council for Higher Education (q.v.) from 1986 to 1992. At the beginning of the Intifada (q.v.), he was placed in administrative detention (q.v.) for six months. He was a member of the Palestinian delegation to the peace talks.

AGRICULTURE. Palestinian agricultural productivity is dependent on land, water, labor, crops, and markets. All these components have been affected by the 1967 Israeli occupation of the area.

The Occupied Territories and the autonomous areas (qq.v.) have approximately 100–700 milimeters of rainfall annually. There are about 6.16 million dunums (1.54 million acres) of land in the Occupied Territories and the autonomous areas. Of these, only one quarter is cultivatable land, which must be sufficiently irrigated to produce crops. However, since the war of 1967 (q.v.), Israel (q.v.) has severely restricted land usage by various measures. These include the zoning of land for military use, the construction of settlements, converting land for nature reserves, and the expansion of municipalities.

In addition to land, water (q.v.) is an important component of agricultural output. Palestinians in the West Bank (q.v.) are allowed to use only 15 percent to 20 percent of the water available from the aquifers. Israel uses the rest. From the quantity allocated, more than 70 percent is used for agricultural purposes in the West Bank, and a little less than 60 percent is used in Gaza (q.v.) for agriculture. Moreover, according to the Palestinian Water Authority, the Palestinians pay more for their water than the Israelis do. Water costs about 17 cents per cubic meter; while the Israelis pay 14 cents and less when government subsidies are available. Palestinians also have been prohibited from digging new water wells.

Palestinian farmers grow the traditional crops, such as olives, grapes, wheat, barley, almonds, citrus, and a sundry of vegetables. One-third of the agricultural output has been based on livestock and poultry. Fishing also is a source of income in the Gaza Strip, which is closely supervised by Israel.

The number of Palestinian laborers involved in agriculture has been high. The Statistical Abstract of Israel (1992) states, that of 189,700 Palestinians employed in the Israeli labor force, a quarter of these are in the agricultural sector. In the years following the war of 1967 (q.v.), the Israeli market absorbed many Palestinian laborers (q.v.), who found lucrative employment in construction and services sectors. Since 1992, Israel has begun to restrict their numbers following militant, violent activities, and has increasingly turned to importing foreign labor from Rumania, Turkey, and Thailand. This has encouraged the Palestinians to return to cultivating their land. Moreover, the agricultural sector in the area has recently experienced a resurgence because of the border closures between Israel and Jordan, the Intifada (q.v.), and the return of Palestinians from Kuwait following the Gulf War (qq.v.).

AHMAD, ABD EL-AZIZ HAJ. Appointed minister of Transportation in the Palestine National Authority (q.v.) by Arafat (q.v.) in July 1994. He was born in 1942 in Jerusalem, and studied at Al-Ibrahimiyeh College. After studying dentistry at Alexandria University in Egypt (q.v.), he opened a private practice in al-Bireh (q.v.) in 1966. He was elected chairman of the West Bank (q.v.) Dentist Association in 1974. On March 26, 1976, Israel deported him to South Lebanon (q.v.). He became a member of the PNC (q.v.) in 1977, and the following year joined the Palestine National Fund (q.v.). Ahmad has also been a member of the Palestine Central Council (q.v.) since 1984. He returned from exile on April 30, 1993.

AHMAD, ABD AL-RAHMAN. Secretary-General of the ALF (q.v.). He was the head of the Popular Organization Department and a member of the PLO Executive Committee (q.v.). At one time, he also was the editor of *Filastine Al-Thawra* (Palestine, the Revolution) (q.v.), a PLO-sponsored magazine. He was appointed secretary-general of the PNA (q.v.) cabinet in 1996.

AKEL, EMAD. Founder of Izzedin al-Qassam (q.v.), the special military unit of HAMAS (q.v.) in the West Bank (q.v.). Akel was born in 1969 in the Jabalya Refugee Camp in the Gaza Strip (q.v.). He was on Israel's most wanted list for three years, because Israel alleges that he was responsible for the murder of three Israeli soldiers on December 7, 1992 and three others on September 13,1993. Akel was killed in a shoot-out with Israeli undercover security forces in Gaza City on November 24, 1993. He was 24 years old.

AL-AKER, MAMDUH. Physician and former member of the Palestinian delegation to the bilateral peace talks with Israel. He was born on

October 17, 1943 in Nablus (q.v.), where he finished high school. Afterward, he went to Cairo University in Egypt (q.v.), where he received a B.S. in medicine in 1968. Taking time off before specializing, he worked in government hospitals in Kuwait (q.v.) from 1969 to 1974. He then attended the Royal College of Surgeons in Edinburgh, Scotland, and King's College in London, where he specialized in disorders of the kidney and urinary tract. He returned to Jerusalem (q.v.) in 1981, and worked at al-Makassed Islamic Charitable Hospital. He left that position in 1986 after a disagreement over policy with hospital administrators. He joined the medical staff of St. Luke's and the Women's Union Hospitals in Nablus, and opened a private clinic in Ramallah (q.v.).

Aker is a member of the Doctors' Union of Jerusalem, the Society for Medical Care in Ramallah and the British Society of Kidney and Urinary Infections. He is on the Board of Trustees of al-HAKAWATI (the Arab Center for Culture and Arts), and a member of the Friends Schools in Ramallah and the Arab Studies Society (q.v.). He also is a founding member of the Mandela Institute for Palestinian Political Prisoners (q.v.).

Aker is highly regarded in political circles, and was affiliated in the past with the Popular Front for the Liberation of Palestine (q.v.). He was imprisoned in February 1991, and kept in solitary confinement for five weeks. He has published articles in the Arab press criticizing the Palestinian leadership for not having accepted the U.N. Partition Plan (q.v.) in 1947; he was especially pleased when the Palestine National Council (q.v.) accepted the two-state solution during its meeting in Algiers in 1988. He served as a member of the Palestinian delegation to the peace talks.

ALAMI, MUSSA. Founder of the Palestinian Information Offices in London, Jerusalem (q.v.), Beirut, and Washington. Their purpose was to disseminate accurate information about the Arabs. Alami was born in 1897 in Jerusalem, and studied law at the American University of Beirut in Lebanon (q.v.). After graduating, he returned to Jerusalem and worked as an official in the bureaucracy of the British Mandate (q.v.). He was later accused of inciting the Palestinians during the Arab revolt (q.v.) of 1936, and was dismissed from his job. He left for Syria (q.v.), and later moved to Iraq (q.v.). In 1941, he returned to Palestine and continued with his political activities, and for a brief period became involved with the Arab Higher Committee (q.v). However, he did not join any political faction, remaining an independent. He advocated the development of rural areas to make them productive, and proposed a plan that would restrict the sale of land to Jews. He established a farm for young men outside of Jericho (q.v.), which to this day continues to operate and carries his name. He has chronicled his experiences in a book, *The Lesson of Palestine*. He died in Amman, Jordan (q.v.), on June 8, 1984.

Al-ALAMI, SA'D AL-DIN, MUFTI. A member of a prominent Palestinian family, he was appointed the *Mufti* (q.v.) of Jerusalem by Jordan (qq.v.) in 1953, and held that position until his death on February 6, 1993. He also was the head of the Supreme Muslim Council (q.v.). He was born in 1911 in Jerusalem, and completed his high-school education there. He studied at al-Azhar University in Egypt (q.v.), and graduated in 1932. After returning to Jerusalem, he taught at the Islamic Orphans School, then in the school system in Jaffa. He was later appointed a clerk in the Jerusalem Court. In 1944, he became a *qadi* (judge) in the *Shari'a* (q.v.) Court in Acre, and later in Tiberias, Palestine. After 1948, he went to Jordan for a brief period, but returned to the West Bank (q.v.) and was once again appointed a *qadi* in Ramallah (q.v.).

AL-ALI, NAJI. Famed cartoonist and artist. He was born in 1937 in the Galilee village of Ash-Shajara in Palestine. In 1948, he fled with his family to Lebanon (q.v.), and settled in Ein al-Hilwe Refugee Camp. He enrolled at the White Sisters in Tripoli, Lebanon, and afterward worked in a small factory. Al-Ali then left for Saudi Arabia in 1957, and stayed there for three years. His work was first published in Kuwait (q.v.) in *As-Siyaseh* (Politics) newspaper. In 1977, he returned to Lebanon and worked as a cartoonist for the Lebanese newspapers, among them *Al-Muharar* (The Liberated). He then went to Kuwait and worked for *Al-Watan* (The Nation) newspaper for a few years, and in 1982 switched to *Al-Qabas* newspaper. In 1985, *Al-Qabas* transferred him to its London office. Closely affiliated with the PFLP (q.v.), his art explored the Palestinian condition and life under Israeli occupation. He also delved into the corruption and the misuse of funds in Palestinian society. He was shot in London on July 22, 1987, and died from his wounds on August 29, 1987. Exhibits of his work have been held all over the world and in the Occupied Territories (q.v.). He published three books of his cartoons.

ALL-PALESTINE GOVERNMENT. The Palestinian government established by a proposal made at the Palestine National Conference that convened in Gaza (q.v.) on September 1, 1948. The Arab Higher Committee (q.v.), on September 22, 1948, officially announced the formation of the government, which was to be the foundation of an independent Palestinian state. On that same day, the Palestinian Declaration of Independence (q.v.) was issued. The government replaced the "Administrative Council for Palestine," which had been appointed by the the Arab League (q.v.) in July 1948. Hajj Amin al-Husseini (q.v.), though absent from the country at the time, was chosen to be president of the All-Palestine Government, and his cabinet included Ahmad Hilmi (q.v.), who was elected acting president, Jamal al-Husseini (q.v.), Awni Abd al-Hadi and Hussein al-Khalidi (qq.v.). A General Assembly composed of 86 members also was elected. The government was adamantly opposed by King Abdallah (q.v.) because he had plans to annex the territory. Egypt (q.v.), Syria (q.v.), and Saudi Arabia (q.v.) however, recognized the government on October 15, 1948. In 1952, the Arab League announced the demise of the All-Palestine Government, and the affairs of the Palestinians were placed under the aegis of the Arab states.

AMERICAN COLONY HOTEL. The hotel, located in East Jerusalem, was originally the home of a rich Arab landlord, Rabbah Daoud Amin Effendi al-Husseini, who built it like a Turkish fortress, with a central courtyard and high vaulted ceilings. It was one of the first buildings outside the Old City of Jerusalem (q.v.), north of Damascus Gate. A small group of Americans and Swedes, led by Anna and Horatio Spafford, first rented, then bought the premises after al-Husseini died in 1895 without an heir. The building then became known as the American Colony. It was first used as a hostel in 1902, and became very popular under the management of the Spafford's daughters and their husbands. The American Colony Hotel has survived Turkish, British, Jordanian, and Israeli rule of the city. The running of the hotel was handed over to a Swiss firm in 1980, but it is still owned by the descendants of the Spafford's daughters. It continues to be a meeting place for journalists and prominent individuals, and was particularly popular during the Intifada (q.v.).

AMIRY, SU'AD MOHAMMED ADIB. Professor, author, and director general of the Palestine National Authority's (q.v.) Ministry of Culture, Art and Information. She also served as a member of the Palestinian delegation to the peace talks in Washington, a member of PECDAR's (q.v.) Committee on Regional Planning, and on the executive committee of the Palestine Housing Council.

Amiry was born in 1951 in Damascus, Syria (q.v.). She studied at the American University of Beirut, and went on for further study at the University of Michigan and the University of Edinburgh, Scotland, where she received a Ph.D. in architecture. Amiry has taught at the University of Jordan and Birzeit University (q.v.). She co-authored with Vera Tamari (q.v.) *The Palestinian Village House* (London, 1989).

AMRO, YASSER HASSAN. Appointed by Arafat (q.v.) as the Minister of Education in the Palestine National Authority (q.v.) in 1994 and 1996. He was born in Dura, Hebron, on January 12, 1930, and completed his high-school education in 1948. After teaching for several years, he went on to study law at Damascus University in Syria (q.v.), where he graduated in 1960. He practiced law in Hebron until 1962, when he was elected to the Jordanian parliament, representing the district (q.v.) of Hebron. In 1963, he was exiled by the Jordanian government to al-Jafer (a Jordanian desert prison), for carrying out a coup against the government. After his release, he joined the PLO (q.v.) and remained in the West Bank (q.v.) until Israel (q.v.) deported him in September 1968. In exile, he joined the PLO Central Committee (q.v.), the PNC (q.v.), and the PLO Executive Committee (q.v.). When the PNA moved to the autonomous areas (q.v.), Amro returned from exile.

ANANI, NABIL. An artist born in Halhul, a city on the West Bank (q.v.) in 1943. Anani studied at the College of Fine Arts in Alexandria, Egypt (q.v.). He has presented one-person shows in Jerusalem (q.v.) and Ramallah (q.v.) in 1974 and 1985, respectively. His work has also been part of group exhibitions in Jordan (q.v.), Syria (q.v.), Lebanon (q.v.), Egypt (q.v.), England, the United States, Japan, and Cyprus. Anani also has participated in "New Visions," an exhibition featuring four other Palestinian artists from the Occupied Territories (q.v.) that has been seen in Jerusalem, Jordan, Italy, and Germany.

Anani currently teaches art at the Vocational Colleges in Ramallah. He is a member of the Palestinian Research and Folklore Committee that is affiliated with In'ash al-Usra (q.v.), and co-produced *Palestinian Folk Dress* and *A Directory of the Art of Palestinian Embroidery.* He served as the head of the Palestinian Artists' League in 1985.

Themes in Anani's work reflect his surroundings. He focuses on the Palestinian condition and daily life, and portrays women prominently in his work.

AL-ANSAR. Arabic for "victors". The name given to the Israeli prison located in the Neqab Desert where Palestinians are incarcerated. It became infamous during the Intifada (q.v.).

AL-AQSA MOSQUE. see AL-HARAM AL-SHARIF.

ARAB CLUB. An organization established in Jerusalem (q.v.) by the Husseinis (q.v.) in 1918. It laid the foundation for the Palestine national movement. Its president was Hajj Amin al-Husseini (q.v), and its objectives were Palestinian unity with Syria (q.v.) and stopping the Zionist influx into the country. The club disappeared in 1921.

ARAB EXECUTIVE. A committee led by Mussa al-Husseini (q.v.) that was established in Haifa, Palestine, in December 1920 during the meeting of the third Palestine National Congress (q.v.). The purposes of the committee were to unite the various Palestinian organizations and associations, to champion the Palestinian cause, and to organize protests against Jewish immigration to the country. The Palestinians also wanted the British to recognize the committee, considering they had already endorsed the Jewish Agency for the Jews. However, the British insisted that the Palestinians first recognize British control over Palestine, which was not forthcoming. The committee was active for a time, holding discussions and sending delegations to the London conferences (q.v.). However, it was not successful, and it disappeared when Husseini died in 1934.

ARAB HIGHER COMMITTEE (AHC). Also known as the Fourth Higher Committee of the Arab League (q.v.). The committee was formed on April 25, 1936, by Hajj Amin al-Husseini (q.v.). It was successful in uniting religious and political leaders, as well as the different political parties. It included the following representatives: Ya'qub Ghussein, who had formed the Youth Congress Party in 1932; Dr. Hussein al-Khalidi (q.v.), mayor of Jerusalem and head of the Reform Party in 1935; Abd al-Latif Saleh of Nablus (qq.v.), who represented the National Bloc; Awni Abd al-Hadi of the *Istiqlal* (Independence) Party (q.v); Ahmad Hilmi, an independent member affiliated with the *Istiqlal* Party; and Ragheb Nashashibi (q.v.), head of the National Defense Party.

The committee organized the general strike and rebellions of 1936 that lasted for six months, and later evolved into an open revolt against British policies and the influx of Jewish immigrants into the country. The British accused the committee of directing the Arab revolt of 1936 (q.v.), and banned it in October 1937. Khalidi, Hilmi, and Ghussein were arrested and deported to the Seychelles Islands. Nevertheless, the rebellions continued. The committee eventually split into the Arab Higher Committee under Husseini and the new Arab Higher Front. The Arab committee did not take part in the London Conference (q.v.) because Husseini was not invited. It did, however, send a delegation to the United Nations (q.v.), and rejected the U.N. Partition Plan (q.v.). See ARAB-PALESTINIAN REVOLTS.

ARAB LEAGUE. A voluntary association of independent Arab states, the objectives of which were to coordinate policies and strengthen relations with each other. Originally, it was the brainchild of Nuri al-Said, then Iraqi prime minister, who championed inter-Arab cooperation in 1942. Egypt (q.v.) adopted the idea, and on March 23, 1945, an official agreement to cooperate and coordinate efforts and resources was signed by seven Arab states: Egypt, Saudi Arabia (q.v.), Iraq (q.v.), Syria (q.v.), Lebanon (q.v.), Yemen, and Transjordan. Today, all Arab states are members, as are a few African countries: Dijibouti, Mauritania, Somalia and Sudan.

The league has many specialized councils to oversee and administer its affairs. It has blacklisted foreign companies that do business with Israel (q.v.). In 1979, Egypt was ousted from the League because of the peace treaty it signed with Israel. It was re-admitted in 1982.

ARAB LIBERATION FRONT (ALF). A militant, leftist PLO (q.v.) faction established in 1969 by Zeid Haidar and Munif al-Razzaz. It is supported by Iraq (q.v.), and its ideology is closely affiliated with the Iraqi Ba'th (q.v.) party. It remained loyal to Arafat (q.v.) during the 1983 coup against him in Lebanon (q.v.).

ARAB NATIONALIST CONGRESS. The first congress of its kind, it took place in Paris in 1913 and was attended by Arab representatives. The purpose of the congress was to lobby for the autonomy of the Arab provinces under the rule of the Ottoman Turks (q.v.).

ARAB NATIONALIST MOVEMENT (ANM). In Arabic, *Harakat al-Qawmiyyin al-Arab.* A leftist movement that began in the 1950s at the American University of Beirut in Lebanon (q.v.), because of the general discontent with conditions in the Arab countries and dissatisfaction with the established political parties. The movement's objectives, influenced at the time by western ideas and philosophy, centered on Arab national unity and anti-communism. It appealed to the bourgeoisie and upper-class intellectuals. Later, the movement was affected by Nasser (q.v.) and his success in abolishing the monarchy in Egypt (q.v) during the 1952 revolution, and its ideology became anti-Western. In the early 1960s, the movement splintered into two groups: the progressive, radical group that favored absorption into Nasserism, led by Muhsin Ibrahim, Mohammad Kishly, and Nayef Hawatmeh (q.v.), and the more right-wing group that wanted to remain independent, led by George Habash (q.v.), Ahmad al-Khatib, Hani al-Hindi, and Wadi' Haddad (q.v.). After the war of 1967 (q.v.), both groups adopted a Marxist-Leninist ideology, and have since splintered into many leftist groups and parties. The Arab Nationalist Movement itself became obsolete. See POPULAR FRONT FOR THE LIBERATION OF PALESTINE, POPULAR DEMOCRATIC

FRONT FOR THE LIBERATION OF PALESTINE and the BA'TH SOCIALIST PARTY.

ARAB-PALESTINIAN REVOLTS. A series of revolts and rebellions carried out by Palestinians against the various occupiers of their country. In 1916, a revolt by nationalists demanding independence and greater interaction with other Arabs took place against the Ottoman-Turks (q.v.). In 1920, Palestinians held demonstrations against Jewish immigration near Jericho (q.v.). The following year, two demonstrations took place—one in Jaffa and the other in Jerusalem (q.v.)—to protest Jewish activities in both cities. In 1929, another conflict occurred, this time, over Jewish rights to pray at the Western Wall (q.v.), which is part of the Muslim shrine of *Al-Haram Al-Sharif* (q.v.). Palestinians rioted in Jerusalem and Hebron (q.v). On July 13, 1931, the city of Nablus (q.v.) called for a general strike during the month of August to protest British policies. In October 1933, Palestinians held demonstrations in Jerusalem and Jaffa. The Jaffa Massacre took place when 12 demonstrators and a policeman were killed. Between 1936 and 1938, the Palestinians carried out resistance activities to protest British policies supporting Zionism (q.v.) and Jewish immigration to Palestine. In 1936, the Palestinians coordinated their efforts in the major cities in Palestine, and set up national committees to organize the general strike, which lasted six months. The events leading to the Great Rebellion of 1936 were the deaths of two Arabs and two Jews, who were killed on April 15, 1936.

ARAB REBELLIONS. see ARAB-PALESTINIAN REVOLTS.

ARAB SOCIALIST BA'TH PARTY. see BA'TH PARTY.

ARAB STUDIES SOCIETY (ASS). An independent organization established in 1979 in East Jerusalem (q.v.) by Faisal al-Husseini (q.v.) and others. The objective of the society is to conduct research on social, economic, and political issues of concern to Palestinians. It runs a number of specialized centers and departments: it has a research center that encourages joint research between Palestinians and Israelis, a specialized library, a document and press archive, the Palestinian Geography Center, which has a map division, and a Documentation and Information Center. The society also runs the Palestinian Human Rights Information Center, and the Early Childhood Center, which establishes nurseries in the West Bank and conducts research on early childhood development. Israeli authorities closed the society in 1987, and prevented it from operating for two years.

ARAB THOUGHT FORUM. In Arabic, *Al-Multaqa Al-Arabi*. An independent Palestinian institution established in Jerusalem in 1977 by a group of Palestinian professionals and intellectuals. At the outset, it was an intellectual forum for the discussion of literary and cultural topics. However, it has evolved into a research and educational institution that studies developmental issues in Palestinian society.

ARAFAT, ABD AL-RAHMAN ABD AL-RAUF, also uses YASSER. Popularly known as Abu Ammar, chairman of the PLO (q.v.) since 1969. He is the founding member of FATAH (q.v.), the chairman of the FATAH Central Committee, the commander-in-chief of the Palestine Liberation Army (q.v.), and a member of the Palestine National Council (q.v.). The PLO Central Council (q.v.) named him the first president of Palestine on April 2, 1989, and he became the chairman of the PNA (q.v.) after the signing of the DOP (q.v.). On January 20, 1996, he was elected president of the PNA.

Arafat was born in Cairo, Egypt (q.v.), on August 4, 1929, and spent his childhood between Cairo and Jerusalem (q.v.). During the war of 1948 (q.v.), he recruited students at Cairo University and later fought under Abd al-Qader al-Husseini (q.v.) in Jerusalem. After the war, Arafat returned to Cairo and became the head of the Palestinian Student League. In 1954, while still a student in the engineering department of Cairo University, he co-founded FATAH (q.v.) with Khalil al-Wazir and Salah Khalaf (qq.v.). He also attended the Egyptian Military Academy, where he became an active member in the *Jihad al-Muqaddas* (Holy War) squad. Consequently, he was deported from Egypt in 1957, because of his affiliation with the Muslim Brotherhood (q.v.), which was declared illegal. Arafat continued his education at Stuttgart University in West Germany, where he majored in civil engineering.

Between 1956 and 1965, Arafat spent a great deal of time recruiting and organizing Palestinian refugees (q.v.) in the diaspora. Together with Khalil al-Wazir, he organized in 1957 the first FATAH group in Jordan and Lebanon (qq.v.). In the early 1960s, he organized al-'Assifa (q.v.), the military unit of FATAH, and became the leader of FATAH. In 1963, he and Khalil al-Wazir visited China to gain support, recognition, and military assistance. In 1964, he went to Algeria, where he received commando training by Algerian revolutionaries. In 1965, Arafat publicly declared the establishment of FATAH. The Battle of Karameh (q.v.) in 1968 enhanced the prestige of the Palestinian commandos. Moreover, the different Palestinian political factions were united under the Palestine Liberation Organization (q.v.). Arafat became the chairman of the PLO Executive Committee and the leader of the PLO in February 1969. Arafat visited Russia in

1969 and received support and arms from that country. Moreover, he established Fatahland in South Lebanon, with the assistance of President Nasser (q.v.) of Egypt, in accordance with the Cairo Agreement (q.v.). In 1970, he was appointed as commander-in-chief of the Palestinian forces.

The year 1974 was pivotal for Arafat. He gave a speech on November 22, 1974, at the United Nations during which he waved an olive branch in one hand and a gun in the other. During the Arab Summit meeting in Rabat, the PLO was granted recognition as the sole legitimate representative of the Palestinians, with Arafat as its leader. After the signing of the Camp David Accords (q.v.) between Egypt and Israel (qq.v.), Arafat encouraged his representatives in Europe to conduct dialogue with members of the Jewish communtiy. Soon after, a number of assassinations took place. Issam Sartawi (q.v.), the PLO representative in France, and Sa'id Hammami (q.v.), the PLO representative in London, were killed by unknown assailants. On June 13, 1980, Arafat's stature was enhanced when a U.S. representative at the United Nations met with the PLO observer at the United Nations, and the European Economic Community issued the Venice Declaration (q.v.), which confirmed Palestinians' right to self-determination.

Arafat's popularity waned when Israel invaded Lebanon (q.v.) on June 4, 1982, and the PLO commandos were forced to leave Southern Lebanon. Three months later, approximately 2,000 Palestinians were killed in the Sabra and Shatilla refugee camps in Lebanon by Israeli and South Lebanese forces. In December 1983, Arafat's forces, with the assistance of the international community, were evacuated from Lebanon. Arafat was able to establish headquarters in Tunis, but without his forces. To salvage his political role, Arafat engaged in a reconciliation attempt with Jordan; in 1985, they reached an agreement on a Jordanian-Palestinian confederation. This plan was rejected in 1987 by the PLO factions, who also pressured Arafat to stop talks with the Egyptians on a peace process. Arafat, in 1985, escaped an assassination attempt on his life in Tunis.

In December 1987, the Intifada (q.v.) erupted and enhanced Arafat's position. But in August 1988, Arafat lost his close confidant, Khalil al-Wazir, who was assassinated by Israeli commandos in Tunis. On November 15, 1988, the Palestine National Council declared an independent Palestinian state, and passed a resolution approving the establishment of such a state in any part of Palestine. On December 13, 1988, while in Geneva, Arafat recognized the state of Israel and rejected the use of violence in the struggle. In a press conference on December 14, 1988, he stated, "As for terrorism, I announced it yesterday in no uncertain terms, and yet, I repeat it for the record that we totally and absolutely renounce all forms of terrorism, including individual, group, and state terrorism."

There soon followed a series of personal and political setbacks for Arafat. When the Gulf War (q.v.) broke out, Arafat supported the Iraqi position and saw his finances dry up and the Palestinians expelled from Kuwait. He also escaped another assassination attempt on his life, on the Baghdad-Amman Highway. Two more of Arafat's close friends, Salah Khalaf and Hayel Abd al-Hameed, were assassinated in Tunis in January 1991. In September 1991, Arafat, under tremendous pressure, approved the peace plan proposed by U.S. President George Bush, and agreed to the participation of Palestinians from the Occupied Territories (q.v.) in a joint delegation with Jordan to the Madrid Peace Conference (q.v.), which was to be held in October 1991. In 1992, Arafat also approved secret negotiations in Oslo, Norway, with the Israelis, despite the fact that a Palestinian team was conducting public negotiations simultaneously in Washington at the time.

The secret negotiations in Oslo culminated in Israel's official recognition of the PLO on September 9, 1993. On September 13 Arafat and Rabin (q.v.) signed the Declaration of Principles (q.v.), and on May 4, 1994, they signed the Cairo Agreement (q.v.) for Palestinian autonomy in Jericho and the Gaza Strip (qq.v.). The Israeli army withdrew from these areas by the end of May, and Arafat entered Gaza on July 1, 1994, set up the Palestinian National Authority (q.v.), and became its president. He appointed his ministers, but kept the Interior Ministry portfolio for himself. On January 20, 1996, elections for the PLC (q.v.) and the presidency of the PNA (q.v.) were held in the autonomous areas (q.v.). Arafat was elected president by the Palestinian people.

Known for his moderation, flexibility, organizational tactics, and ability to preserve the unity of the PLO, Arafat now faces the biggest challenge of his career—the establishment of a Palestinian state. While in exile, Arafat lived a life of secrecy, moving about frequently to conceal his whereabouts and escaping many attempts on his life. At the age of 63, Arafat married Suha al-Tawil, a journalist and the daughter of Raymonda al-Tawil (q.v.), herself a prominent journalist and Palestinian activist.

ARAFAT, FATHI. Brother of Yasser Arafat (q.v.) and president of the Palestinian Red Crescent Society (q.v.). He studied medicine at Cairo University in Egypt (q.v.), graduated in 1957, and worked for 10 years as a pediatrician in Kuwait (q.v.). In 1968, he moved to Jordan (q.v.), where he established the Palestinian branch of the Red Crescent Society. He has received many awards for his work, the latest from the Greek Red Cross in May 1995. Arafat currently is formulating a national health plan for the autonomous areas (q.v.).

AL-ARD (1). Arabic for "the land". A movement established by Palestinian intellectuals and journalists in Israel, in the town of Umm al-Fahm in the Galilee. In 1958, Israeli-Arabs (q.v.) affiliated with the Israeli Communist Party, together with some nationalists, formed the Popular Front. Differences broke out between the two over policy, and the nationalists formed their own group, which they called *Al-Ard*. The movement's objectives were to support the Arabs in Israel; formulate a solution to the Arab-Israeli conflict; support the implementation of U.N. Resolutions (q.v.) of 1947–48; and to reclaim all the Arab lands that Israel occupied, particularly those taken in 1948. Al-Ard was declared a subversive organization and banned by Israel in 1964. It affiliates itself with FATAH and the PLO (qq.v.).

AL-ARD (2). A newsmagazine published in the West Bank (q.v.) that was forced to close in 1986.

AL-AREF, AREF. Born in 1892, he was educated in Jerusalem (q.v.) and Istanbul, Turkey, where he completed his Ph.D. in politics and economics. During World War I, he enlisted in the Turkish army, and was consequently incarcerated by the Russians for three years. He later escaped and returned to Palestine, where he published *Suriyya Al-Janubiyya* (Southern Syria), a newspaper that encouraged greater Palestinian affiliation with the Arab world. Later, Aref was accused by British Mandate (q.v.) authorities of inciting the Arab revolts (q.v.) of 1920–1921. He was tried and sentenced to death, but the sentence was never carried out. Instead, he was deported to Transjordan, and later became King Abdallah's (q.v.) secretary. Aref later returned to Palestine, where he became active in the British government bureaucracy from 1921 to 1948. He served as a district officer in the Palestinian cities of Jenin (q.v.), Bisan, Jaffa, Beer al-Sabe', Gaza, and Ramallah (qq.v.). The Jordanian government appointed him as mayor of East Jerusalem (q.v.) in 1950, and in 1955, he served for a short period as the minister of Public Works. In 1976, he became the director of the Palestinian Archeological Museum in Jerusalem. Al-Aref then retired to dedicate himself entirely to his writing. He was a prolific writer, and wrote histories on Jerusalem, Beer al-Sabe', Gaza, *Al-Aqsa* Mosque, *Al-Haram Al-Sharif* (q.v.), and the Palestinian-Israeli conflict. One of his most interesting books is *The Jerusalem Holocaust and Paradise Lost*. He died in Jerusalem on July 30, 1973.

ART. Like other aspects of Palestinian culture (q.v.), art has been affected by the political circumstances of the Palestinians. The art movement has been hampered by a stagnant, repressive atmosphere that has not encouraged creativity and freedom of expression. Artists have been forced to deal with the social and political reality that dominates their lives. This has included the exodus of artists from their homeland (Kamal Boullata and Vladimir Tamari, among others) and the lack of art schools, museums, and galleries. Artists have been imprisoned, their artwork confiscated, and their exhibitions never seen because of curfews and the closures of the Occupied Territories by Israel (qq.v.).

Despite numerous obstacles, Palestinian artists have managed to develop their art, which emphasizes the themes of Palestinian heritage and folklore, the longing for the homeland, a return to the past, the struggle for statehood, and tragic events in Palestinian history. Moreover, they have used such local resources as henna (a red dye), saffron, cobalt blue (used to whiten wash), stone, wood, leather, and clay and the techniques of the past to transmit their messages.

Artists such as Naji al-Ali (q.v.), Suleiman Mansour (q.v.), Vera Tamari (q.v.), Nabil Anani (q.v.), Khalil Rabah (q.v.), and Tayseer Barakat (q.v.) have fine-tuned their art and contributed to the culture of resistance. They and other artists have established the League of Palestinian Artists and the Al-Wasiti Art and Culture Center in East Jerusalem (q.v.). The Palestinian Ministry of Culture and Information has been active since its inception in promoting the artists and their work.

ASHAB, ABDUL HAFEZ ABDUL SALAM. Appointed Minister of Post and Telecommunication in the Palestine National Authority (q.v.) in July 1994. Ashab was born in 1927 in Hebron (q.v.). He received his Ph.D. from the University of Damascus, Syria (q.v.). He then became active in a number of NGOs (q.v.). In 1969, he became a member of the Family Planning Association; in 1976, he was a founding member of the Co-Operative Housing Association; and in 1977, he founded the Patients Friends Society.

ASHRAWI, HANAN MIKHAIL. Commissioner general and founding member of the Palestinian Independent Commission for Citizens' Rights, which was established in 1993, after she resigned as the PLO (q.v.) spokesperson. Ashrawi was born in Ramallah (q.v.) in 1946, and attended the Quakers Friends Girls School. She then went to the American University of Beirut in Lebanon (q.v.), where she received a B.A. (1968) and an M.A. (1970) in English Literature. Ashrawi continued her education at the University of Virginia, where she received her Ph.D. in 1981. She taught English at Birzeit University (q.v.), and from 1986 to 1990 served as the dean of the College of Arts.

Politically active in her student days, she was a member of the General Union of Palestinian Students (q.v.), and the General Union of Palestinian Women (q.v.), and worked as a volunteer in the Palestinian Information Office in Lebanon. While studying in the United States, she helped establish the American Friends of Free Palestine.

Ashrawi was appointed the spokesperson for the Palestinian delegation to the Israeli-Palestinian peace talks, and quickly became a media favorite. In August 1993, together with Saeb 'Erakat and Faisal al-Husseini (qq.v.), she was appointed to the Higher Committee for the Peace Talks at the PLO headquarters in Tunis. When the PNA (q.v.) was first formed, she refused a ministerial appointment. In 1996, she was elected a member of the PLC (q.v.), and she accepted the appointment as minister of Higher Education. She has written a book about her experiences, entitled *This Side of Peace: A Personal Account* (Simon and Schuster, 1995).

AL-'ASSIFA (1). In Arabic "storm". The military wing of FATAH (q.v.) that carried out sabotage activities against Israeli targets, and was active during the Intifada (q.v.). Its members in the Occupied Territories (q.v.) are known as FATAH Hawks (q.v.) and Black Panthers.

AL-'ASSIFA (2). FATAH's radio station, which broadcasted from Syria (q.v.) until 1982.

ATRASH, FARAJ SABA HANNA. Born in Beit Jala, a town adjacent to Bethlehem (q.v.), in 1915 and educated in Jerusalem (q.v.), he became active very early. In 1936, he was imprisoned by the British for resistance activities and for organizing a battalion of the National League in Beit Jala. In 1954, Atrash became the deputy mayor of Beit Jala. After he was elected mayor in 1959, however, the Jordanian government vetoed his appointment. Furious, he left for Latin America. Atrash eventually returned, and ran successfully for a seat in the municipal council elections in 1972. He was not, however, successful in the 1976 municipal elections; his bloc lost to the strong PLO (q.v) nationalist bloc. Nevertheless, he was appointed mayor by the Israeli authorities after they deposed the elected mayor, who, along with others, protested the Camp David Accords and refused to cooperate with the Israeli Civil Administration (qq.v.). During the Intifada (q.v.), he came under fire from the Unified National Leadership of the Uprising (q.v.), particularly when he refused to acquiesce to their demand that the entire municipal council resign to protest the

Israeli expropriation of land from Beit Jala and the village of Khader to build Highway 60.

AUTONOMOUS AREAS. The areas of the Gaza Strip and Jericho (qq.v) that were regained by the Palestinians in the aftermath of the signing of the Declaration of Principles (q.v.). They include 219 square kilometers or 60 percent of the Gaza Strip and 54 of a total 354 square kilometers in the Jericho district. According to the DOP, any additional extensions to the autonomous areas (q.v.) are subject to negotiations. In the autonomous areas, which are not sovereign, the Palestinians have self-rule over such matters as education, health, economy, tourism, and taxation.

After the signing of the Oslo Two Agreement (q.v.), the Palestinians assumed authority in the major cities of the West Bank (q.v.), excluding Hebron (q.v.).

AUTONOMY. see CAMP DAVID ACCORDS.

AWAD, MUHAMMAD HASSAN, SHEIKH. Founder and president of the Islamic University (q.v.), which was established in Gaza (q.v) in 1977. Born in 1914, he received his degree in religious studies from Al-Azhar University in Cairo, Egypt (q.v.). From 1932 to 1934, he worked as a journalist. In 1938, he was elected mayor of Al Faluja, but a year later the British imprisoned him for four years. After 1948, he and his family left for Hebron, and then to Egypt (qq.v.). When he returned to Gaza, the Egyptians appointed him to the High Islamic Court, where he remains the chief justice to this day. In 1954, he founded the Islamic Institute of Palestine in Gaza, which continues to operate. He also is a member of the Islamic Research Institute in Cairo.

Awad has received several awards. King Farouk of Egypt awarded him the Medal of Palestine in 1948; Gamal Abd al-Nasser (q.v), the former president of Egypt, recognized him with the Hero of Peace Medal; and in 1992, he received the Star of Palestine from Hosni Mubarak (q.v.), the president of Egypt.

AL-AWDAH (1). Arabic for "the return". A pro-PLO (q.v.) weekly newsmagazine published in East Jerusalem by the Palestine Press Services (q.v.).

AWDAH (2). The name of the ship that was damaged in Limasol, Cyprus, in February 1987. The Palestine Liberation Organization had chartered the ship and planned to send it to Haifa, Israel, with 131 Palestinians who had been deported by Israel (q.v.), to publicize the plight of deportees. Responsibility for the ship's damage was claimed by the Jewish Defense League.

AL-AYYAM. Arabic for "the days". An independent Palestinian daily newspaper founded by Akram Haniyeh (q.v.) in 1995.

AYYASH, YAHYA. The "engineer" was born on March 22, 1966 in Rafaat, a village near Tulkarm (q.v.). He received his education at Bidya High School, where he graduated with honors. He majored in electrical engineering at Birzeit University (q.v.). Ayyash was accused by Israel (q.v.) of being a member of Izzedin Al-Qassam (q.v.), the special military wing of HAMAS (q.v.), and of masterminding several suicide-bomb incidents as well as making the explosives used in the bombs. The bombing incidents include the Affula operation on April 6, 1993, the Khadayrah explosion on April 13, 1993, the Beit Lid bombing in January 1995, the Tel Aviv bombing on March 4, 1996, the Jerusalem bus bombings in 1996, and three suicide-bombings in the Gaza Strip (q.v.). Members of his family were arrested by the Israeli secret service, and his mother was placed under house arrest (q.v.), to prevent her from having any contact with him. He escaped arrest for many years and remained a fugitive, until Israeli secret agents planted a bomb in his mobile phone and killed him on January 5, 1996.

B

BALFOUR DECLARATION. A letter written by Arthur Balfour, the British foreign secretary, on November 2, 1917, to the Jewish leader, Lord Edmond de Rothschild, in which he pledged British support for Zionism (q.v.) and the establishment of a Jewish national home in Palestine, provided that the rights of the Arab communities in Palestine were not violated. The letter states: "His Majesty's government views with favor the establishment in Palestine of a national home for the Jewish people, and will use their best endeavor to facilitate the achievement of this objective, it being clearly understood that nothing shall be done which may prejudice the civil and religious rights of existing non-Jewish communities in Palestine, or the rights and political status enjoyed by Jews in any other country."

The Arabs felt that the Balfour Declaration contradicted the promise made to them by the British of becoming independent after the war in return for their revolt against the Ottoman-Turks (q.v.).

AL-BANNA, SABRI KHALIL. Nom de guerre, Abu Nidal. One of the former leaders of FATAH's Revolutionary Council (q.v.), and the head of Black June, a branch of the Black September Organization (q.v.), considered the most militant in all of the Middle East. It is alleged to have been responsible for the assassinations of many Arab and Palestinian leaders. Abu Nidal provoked and angered the PLO (q.v.), which dismissed him from the PLO Executive Committee (q.v.) for launching unauthorized militant activities in October 1974 that embarrassed the PLO. He was tried in absentia by a FATAH Revolutionary Court and sentenced to death. However, because of his close association with the Iraqis, he was given protection by the Iraqi government, and FATAH (q.v.) was unable to carry out the sentence. He also was supported by Libya. Al-Banna died of a heart attack in Baghdad, Iraq (q.v.), on November 6, 1984.

BARAKAT, FAI'EQ ABD AL BARI. Born in Jerusalem (q.v.) on November 1, 1924, to a family originally from Hebron (q.v.), he attended Al-Rashidiya High School in Jerusalem, and received a B.A. in Commerce from Baghdad University in Iraq (q.v.). From 1946 until 1948, he worked in the Department of Light Industry for the British Mandate (q.v.). After the war of 1948 (q.v.), he began his own business, and opened the Strand Hotel in Jerusalem. Barakat served three terms as a council member in the East Jerusalem Municipal Council. Since 1964, he has been the director of the East Jerusalem (q.v.) Chamber of Commerce, which has 2,400 members. When the East Jerusalem municipality was made obsolete by the Israelis in 1967, the Palestinians in the city refused to cooperate with the Israeli-run municipality, because that would imply a de facto recognition of the city's annexation by the Israelis. Barakat continues to serve as treasurer of both the Arab Orphans' Committee and the National Arab Hospital. He also is a member of the executive committee of the Higher Muslim Council (q.v.).

BARAKAT, TAYSEER. An artist born in Jabalya Refugee Camp in Gaza (q.v.) in 1959. He studied at the College of Fine Arts in Alexandria, Egypt (q.v.). He has held exhibitions of his work in the Occupied Territories (q.v.) and Italy. Barakat also participated in "New Visions," an exhibition with four other Palestinian artists that has appeared in Jerusalem (q.v.), Amman, Italy, and Germany.

BARAMKI, GABRIEL ANDONI. Former acting president of Birzeit University (q.v.), and currently a consultant to the Palestine National Authority's (q.v.) Ministry of Education. He was born in Jerusalem (q.v.) in 1929. Baramki's father was a prominent architect in Jerusalem (q.v.), whose home was confiscated by the Israelis after the 1948 war (q.v.) and converted into a museum. Baramki studied in Jerusalem, then went to the American University of Beirut, Lebanon (q.v.), in 1953, where he majored in chemistry. He returned to Jerusalem and taught at Birzeit High School, in the town of Birzeit north of Ramallah (q.v.). Afterward, Baramki decided to continue his education at McGill University in Canada, where he received a Ph.D. in physical organic chemistry in 1959. He then returned to the West Bank and helped develop Birzeit High School into a junior college. In 1974, he became the vice president of Birzeit University. When Hanna Nasser (q.v.), the president of the university, was deported by the Israelis in November 1974, Baramki became the acting president. He saw the university through the turmoil of 28 years of Israeli occupation, as he was repeatedly summoned by the Israelis and given closure orders for the university.

Since 1964, Baramki, has served as a member, then chairman, of the Department for Services to Palestinian Refugees for the Middle East Council of Churches. He also was a member of the executive committee of the Council for Higher Education (q.v.), and the Palestinian Planning and Development Board in the Occupied Territories (q.v.), and served on the steering committee for the peace talks.

AL-BARBARY, YUSRA IBRAHIM. Founding member and president since 1964 of the Palestinian Women's Federation. Born in Gaza (q.v.) in 1923, she attended Cairo University in Egypt (q.v.), and received a B.A. in 1949 and an M.A. in 1952. She returned to Gaza and became the principal of al-Zahra Secondary Girls School, and was later appointed supervisor in the Gaza school system. Politically active, she was a member of the Palestinian delegation to the United Nations in 1963, and a non-participating member of the Palestine National Council (q.v.). Barbary is involved in charitable activities, particularly the treatment of Palestinian prisoners in Israeli jails. Since 1973, she has served as the executive secretary of the Palestine Red Crescent Society (q.v.), and is active in the National Rehabilitation Committee for the Mentally Retarded and Handicapped. She was denied the right to travel by the Israelis in 1974.

BARGHOUTHI, BASHIR ABDELKARIM. The secretary-general of the Palestine Communist Party (later re-named the Palestine People's Party) (q.v.), which he established on February 10, 1982. He was appointed minister of Industry by Arafat (q.v.) in June 1996. Barghouthi was born in Deir Ghassane, a village near Ramallah (q.v.), in 1931. He studied economics at the American University of Cairo, and graduated in 1956. While he was a student in Egypt (q.v.), he became a member of the General Union of Palestinian Students when Arafat (qq.v.) was the president. In 1956, he was granted a license by the

Jordanian government to publish a newspaper, which had a short life span. Four issues were published, two issues were distributed, and the other two were confiscated by Jordanian authorities. Eventually, his political activities led to his incarceration by the Jordanians for eight years. After his release, he returned to the West Bank, and from 1975 to 1977 served as the editor-in-chief of *Al-Fajr* (q.v.) newspaper. He was placed under house arrest (q.v.) several times by the Israelis, who accused him of being a leader of the Palestine National Guidance Committee and the West Bank Palestine National Front (qq.v.). He has been a member, since 1978, of the Council for World Peace, and a member of the Board of Trustees of the Arab Thought Forum (q.v.). Barghouthi is currently the chief editor of *Al-Tali'a* (The Vanguard), a news weekly issued as the mouthpiece of the Palestine People's Party.

BARGHOUTHI, MUSTAFA KAMIL. Co-founder in 1983 and chairman of the Union of Palestinian Relief Committees (q.v.), an organization that provides a wide array of primary health-care services and health education. He was born in Jerusalem (q.v.) in 1954, but his family is originally from the village of Deir Ghassane, near Ramallah (q.v.). After the war of 1948 (q.v.), his family moved to Ramallah, and Mustafa attended the local schools. He then left to study medicine at Moscow University, and graduated in 1978. It was at Moscow University that he became active in the Palestinian Students' Union. Upon his return to the Occupied Territories (q.v.), he worked at al-Maqassed Islamic Charitable Hospital in East Jerusalem (q.v.), where he became involved in primary health-care. Barghouthi is the director of the Health Development Information Project, which disseminates health-related information to other organizations to prevent duplication of services. He also is a member of the steering committee for the Palestinian delegation to the multilateral peace talks.

BARGHOUTHI, SIHAM. One of the founders of the Palestinian Woman Works Committee (q.v.), established in 1978 as a grassroots organization to encourage women to take an active role in the decision-making process. That organization later became a member of the Union of Palestinian Woman Works Committees (q.v.).

Siham was born in 1948, the ninth girl in her family. She was studying mathematics in Egypt (q.v.) when the war of 1967 (q.v.) erupted. When she wanted to return to her home in 1968, she was refused entry by the Israelis on the premise that she was not in the West Bank (q.v.) when the Israelis conducted the census in 1967. In 1971 she was allowed to return and was granted a permanent residency permit to enable her to live in the West Bank (q.v.). Barghouthi was placed under town arrest (q.v.), and when caught breaking that order, she was imprisoned for two and a half years.

BARGHOUTHI, MARWAN. Member of the FATAH Revoultionary Council, chairman of the Higher Committee of FATAH in the West Bank (qq.v.), and a member of the PLC for the district of Ramallah (qq.v.). Barghouthi was born in 1959 in Ramallah (qq.v.). He attended Birzeit University (q.v.), where he was elected president of the student council for three consecutive years. Barghouthi was arrested several times by the Israelis for his political activities, and finally deported to Jordan just before the Intifada (q.v.) started. He returned to the West Bank (q.v.) after the signing of the Declaration of Principles (q.v.).

BA'TH SOCIALIST PARTY. Ba'th in Arabic is "resurrection". An independent Arab and national political party established in the 1940s at the University of Syria by Michel 'Aflaq. Its ideology is a blend of ideas from Arab culture and Western thought. Ba'th socialism emphasizes the value of man to society, justice, cooperation, and an equitable social order. Thus, liberation and the social transformation of society have top priority on its agenda. Its objectives include eliminating obstacles that prevent the unity of the Arab nations and their freedom, and the removal of corrupt, reactionary leaders and regimes in the area. The Ba'th party views Palestine as part of the Arab nation, and the liberation of Palestine, as a cause that all Arabs should struggle for and defend. The Ba'th is the ruling party in Iraq and Syria (qq.v). See also PALESTINIAN-ARAB SOCIALIST BA'TH PARTY.

AL-BAYADER AS-SIYASIYA. A weekly newsmagazine published in 1981 by Jack Khazmo (q.v.). It was the first Palestinian publication to hire an Israeli correspondent. The Israeli authorities in 1984 banned the distribution of the magazine in the Occupied Territories (q.v.) for three years for publishing censored materials. Israeli censors also sued the magazine; after a five year battle in the courts, the magazine was acquitted of all charges. Khazmo also established a literary magazine, *Al-Bayader*, in 1976, and the *Al-Bayader* publishing house and research center, which has specialized in conducting public opinion polls since 1982.

BEGIN, MENACHEM. Israeli Knesset member, prime minister of Israel (q.v.), and Nobel Peace Prize winner. He was born in 1913 in Russia, studied at the University of Warsaw, and worked actively to establish a national home for the Jews. Begin later became a member of the Irgun, the Zionist underground organization that carried out subversive activities against the British Mandate (q.v.) authorities. In 1948, he co-founded the Herut Party. As minister without portfolio in the National Unity government, he encouraged the Israeli army in the war of 1967 (q.v.) to take Jerusalem (q.v.). In 1977, Begin became Israel's prime minister, and in November of that year welcomed Anwar al-Sadat (q.v.) to Jerusalem (q.v.) and negotiated the Camp David Accords (q.v.) with him. On December 10, 1979, Begin and Sadat won the Nobel Peace Prize. After the invasion of Lebanon (q.v.) in 1982 and the massacre of the Palestinians in Sabra and Shatilla by the Phalangists, Begin was overwhelmed with problems. He resigned on September 15, 1983. Begin died in March 1992.

BEL'AWI, HAKAM. One of the first to join the ranks of FATAH (q.v.) and work in its Information and Political Education Department. He was born in the village of Bal'a, near Nablus (q.v.), in 1935. For many years, he directed the publication of the PLO (q.v.) magazine *Filastine Al-Thawra* (Palestine, the Revolution) (q.v.). In the 1970s, he was appointed the PLO (q.v.) representative to Tunis and Libya. He was a member of the first PLO team that began dialogue with the United States in Tunis. Bel'awi was assured in the early 1990s by Arafat (q.v.) that he would become the head of security services in the PNA (q.v.). That promise never materialized. Bel'awi was elected a PNC (q.v.) member from Tulkarm (q.v.) on January 20, 1996.

BETHLEHEM. A major tourist city in the West Bank (q.v.) and the birthplace of Christ, it also contains the largest concentration of Christians (the other Christian-dominated areas are Ramallah and Jerusalem) (qq.v.). Places of significance in Bethlehem are the Church of the Nativity (where Jesus was born) and Shepherd's Fields, where the three kings, on their way to visit Christ, are said to have seen the star that guided them to the manger. Bethlehem is famed for its skilled artisans and craftsmen, whose beautiful work in olivewood and mother-of-pearl is treasured by many. In 1968, the mayor of Bethlehem, Elias Freij (q.v.), asked the Israelis to grant the same status and privileges to the city as they did to Jerusalem (q.v.). This, however, never happened. The population of Bethlehem is 32,921. See also DISTRICTS.

BETHLEHEM UNIVERSITY. A co-educational institution that was officially opened in October 1973. The idea for establishing a university in Bethlehem was supported by the Vatican, which asked the De La Salle Order of Brothers of the Christian Schools to help set up and admininster the new institution in order to meet the higher educational needs of the Palestinians. It is a small liberal arts university, with about 2,089 students (39% male, 61% female) and 240 staff and faculty members. Located in the heart of Bethlehem (q.v.), it serves students of all faiths and offers undergraduate and associate degrees in the arts and sciences, nursing and hotel management.

AL-BILAD. Arabic for "the country". An independent Palestinian daily newspaper established on December 13, 1995. Its editor-in-chief is Hafeth al-Barghouthi.

AL-BIREH. A Canaanite city, originally called Ba-irut, probably built in 3500 B.C. Tradition has it that Abraham passed through it on his way to Egypt (q.v.). In the 17th century, a tribe called Haddadin moved to the area and split into two groups, one settling in adjacent Ramallah (q.v.), the other in al-Bireh.

Today, al-Bireh is a rapidly growing city due to the construction boom that the area is experiencing as a result of the signing of the Declaration Of Principles (q.v.). Land prices in general have escalated, particularly in al-Bireh and Ramallah as a result of the Israeli ban on the Palestine National Authority (q.v.) establishment of offices in Jerusalem (q.v.). A dunum (a quarter of an acre) of land ranges from $150,000 to $200,000 in residential areas, and $500,000 to $900,000 in commercial centers. More than 40 percent of al-Bireh's original inhabitants are American citizens because family members emigrated in the early 1900s to the United States to work. Al-Bireh's population is about 40,000.

BIRZEIT UNIVERSITY. The oldest of the universities in the West Bank (q.v.), it began offering a four-year higher-education program in 1972. The university is located in the village of Birzeit, north of Ramallah (q.v.). It has often been referred to by the Israelis as a "hotbed of Palestinian nationalism." Several students have been killed, teachers and students imprisoned, and many deported. In January 1988, as the Intifada (q.v.) was gathering steam, the university was closed by the Israelis for several years. Makeshift classes to help graduating students were set up in private residences, mosques, and churches. The university has a student body of 3,500 and approximately 500 faculty and staff members. It offers bachelor of arts and science degrees in the humanities, sciences, engineering, and commerce, and master of arts degrees in education and international relations. It recently established a women's research center and a law center.

AL-BITAWI, HAMID, SHEIKH. The head of the Palestine Theological Society (q.v.), the highest decision-making body of HAMAS (q.v.). He also is the vice president of the Islamic Charitable Society, a member of the *Sulha* (q.v.) Committee, and a member of the Mosques' Building Committee. Al-Bitawi was born in Beta, near Tulkarm (q.v.), in 1944. He studied *Shari'a* (q.v.) at the University of Jordan in Amman and graduated in 1968. He then worked in the *Shari'a* Courts in Nablus (q.v.), and studied *Shari'a* Law at An-Najah National University (q.v.). He was arrested and placed in administrative detention (q.v.) in December 1990. He was one of the 415 members of Islamic organizations who were deported by Israel in 1992 to Marj al-Zuhur, in Lebanon (q.v.).

Al-Bitawi has written several books about Islam. He believes that an Islamic Palestine stretching from the Jordan River to the Mediterranean Sea is the best solution to the Palestinian problem. He also supports a confederation with Jordan (q.v.) until the Islamic state is established.

Al-Bitawi and Mahmoud Salamah of Gaza (q.v.) were the first members of HAMAS to be appointed by Arafat (q.v.) in November 1994 as deputy justices to the Supreme Religious Courts.

BLACK SEPTEMBER ORGANIZATION (BSO). An offshoot of FATAH (q.v.). It was established and named after the September 1970 civil war between the Palestinians and Jordan (q.v.). During that confrontation, which took place because of King Hussein's (q.v.) fear that the PLO (q.v.) would take over Jordan, several thousand Palestinians died at the hands of the Jordanian army. It was after that confrontation that Jordan forced the PLO out of its territory.

Black September is loosely organized, and employs militant tactics. Its first operation took place in November 1971, when it claimed responsibility for assassinating Jordanian Prime Minister and Minister of Defense Wasfi al-Tal. In 1972, it claimed responsibility for the kidnapping of nine Israeli athletes during the Olympic Games in Munich. The athletes were killed during the rescue attempt carried out by German police. The faction is supported by Libya, Syria (q.v.), and Iraq (q.v.), and its main base is said to be located in Iraq (q.v.).

There are two Black September groups: one is a unit of FATAH that was led by Salah Khalaf (q.v.), which is believed to have stopped its violent activities in 1973; the other is the Black June faction led by Sabri al-Banna (q.v.), who was expelled from the PLO for the unauthorized terror acts that the faction carried out.

BRITISH MANDATE SYSTEM. The League of Nations gave Britain a mandate to administer and assist Palestine with the development of an infrastructure and to prepare the Palestinians for independence. The British incorporated the Balfour Declaration (q.v.) of 1917 into the mandate. The British Mandate System went into effect in Palestine in 1923 and lasted until May 14, 1948.

BRITISH WHITE PAPER. A series of statements issued by the British government that dealt with British policy on Palestine (q.v.).

(1) The Churchill White Paper of 1922 was issued to refute the Arab claim that the British wanted Palestine to be an exclusively Jewish state. The British reaffirmed their commitment to the Arabs in Palestine.

(2) The White Paper of 1939 was issued by Britain on May 17, 1939, to rally Arab support for the Allies during World War II. The British felt threatened by the Italian invasion of Ethiopia in 1935, the German absorption of Czechoslavakia in 1939, and the creation of a German-Italian military alliance on May 7, 1939. The proposal restricted Jewish immigration to Palestine between 1939 and 1944 to 15,000 annually. It also curtailed Jewish land acquisitions in Palestine.

C

CAIRO AGREEMENT (1). The agreement was signed in Cairo, Egypt (q.v.), on November 3, 1969, by the Palestine Liberation Organization (q.v.) and the Lebanese government. The agreement established an area in Southern Lebanon (q.v.) called Fatahland that PLO commandos could use as a base to target Israel. Moreover, the Lebanese (q.v.) gave the Palestinians permission to carry arms, conduct and administer their affairs, and oversee matters in the Palestinian refugee (q.v.) camps in Lebanon. In fact, this agreement, which was concluded with the support of President Gamal Abed al-Nasser of Egypt (qq.v.), laid the basis for the establishment of the state-within-a-state infrastructure. As a result of this agreement, Lebanon's sovereignty was challenged by the PLO because it could not control them, and, eventually, chaos spread throughout Lebanon. The Lebanese government attempted many times to restore order to the country, but to no avail. As a result of the Israeli invasion of Lebanon in 1982, the PLO was forced out of the country.

Cairo Agreement (2). Yasser Arafat and Yitzhak Rabin (qq.v.) signed the Cairo Agreement in Cairo on May 4, 1994. The agreement is based on the implementation of U.N. Resolutions 242 and 338 (qq.v.). It dealt with the timetable for the transfer of authority, the redeployment of Israeli forces, and the establishment of autonomy in Jericho and the Gaza Strip (qq.v.). It also specified that the redeployment in Gaza and Jericho would be completed within a three-week period, after which the Palestinian police force would assume responsibility. In addition, it stipulated that the Palestine National Authority (q.v.) was to restrict its offices to the Gaza Strip and Jericho (qq.v.) until elections were held in the Occupied Territories (q.v.) on July 1, 1995. (The elections were held on January 20, 1996). The agreement also stated that the Palestine National Authority could issue laws, but these laws could not contradict the agreements signed between Israel (q.v.) and the Palestinians. Israeli laws were to remain in effect until repealed. Moreover, the two parties agreed to set up a joint committee to oversee civil affairs in the Gaza Strip and Jericho, and both parties were to respect human rights.

CAMP DAVID ACCORDS. The agreement signed on September 17, 1978, at Camp David, the presidential retreat in Maryland, by the late Menachem Begin (q.v.), prime minister of Israel (q.v.) at the time, and the late Egyptian President Anwar Sadat (q.v.) under the auspices of former U.S. President Jimmy Carter. According to the agreement, Israel was to dismantle the settlements and withdraw from the Sinai Peninsula (q.v) in return for peace with Egypt. The treaty also led to the stationing of American troops in the Sinai. The terms of the treaty also stipulated that Egypt was not to join in any aggression against Israel, and Israel was granted the right to use the Suez Canal and the Straits of Tiran. The Camp David Accords culminated in the signing of a treaty between Egypt and Israel on March 26, 1979. It also provided a framework for peace in the Middle East.

Egypt was ostracized by the Arabs for signing the peace treaty with Israel, and consequently was dismissed from the Arab League (q.v.). Furthermore, the oil-rich Arab Gulf countries stopped the flow of financial assistance to Egypt.

The agreement also outlined the establishment of autonomy or self-rule for the Palestinians in the West Bank and the Gaza Strip (qq.v.). Israel was to withdraw its military and civilian authority, and a strong police force composed of Palestinians was to take its place. Israel and Jordan were to carry out joint security patrols and man security posts. This transitional phase would last for five years, after which Jordan (q.v.), Israel, and the Palestinians would negotiate the final status of the Occupied Territories (q.v.). The proposed Palestinian autonomy in the Occupied Territories was rejected by the Palestinians, because the process excluded the PLO (q.v.). Moreover, the Israeli interpretation of autonomy was self-rule for the people, but not jurisdiction over the land. Israel was to maintain its military apparatus in the Occupied Territories, while the Palestinians would run their own civil affairs, such as education, health, and social services.

CIVIL ADMINISTRATION. The Israeli Civil Administration was established by military order No. 947 in November 1981 to deal with civilian matters, such as the collection of taxes, the issuance of permits and licenses for business ventures, and the administration of health, social welfare, education, and development in the Occupied Territories (q.v.). The head of the Civil Administration was to report directly to the Israeli military commanders, who would continue to oversee the affairs of the Occupied Territories. The Palestinians believed the creation of an Israeli civil authority was a plan to fool them into cooperating with the Israeli military forces that would permanently impose their rule in the territories.

The Palestinian municipalities strongly protested the establishment of this authority, and adamantly refused to cooperate with the head of the Civil Administration, who at the time was Professor Menahem Milson. The Israeli Civil Administration went to work quickly, and in 1982 dimissed nine elected Palestinian mayors, and appointed Israeli military officers to run the affairs of the municipalities. Also, the Civil Administration began to cultivate the Village League Associations (q. v.) in order to weaken PLO support in the Occupied Territories (q.v.), and to create an alternative Palestinian leadership.

CLIMATE. A Mediterranean climate characterizes the West Bank and the Gaza Strip (qq.v.). The winters are short and cold, with brief periods of precipitation. The summers are hot and dry during the day, but cool at night. Occasionally, snow falls in the northern areas and in Jerusalem (q.v.). The four climate regions are the Jordan Valley, the Hills, the Coastal Plains, and the Neqab Desert. The amount of rainfall and the temperatures of the areas vary. In the Jordan Valley, for instance, daytime summer temperature reaches 32 degrees Celsius, or 90 degrees Fahrenheit. Temperatures in winter can drop to below freezing. The temperature in the Neqab Desert is extreme, with very little rainfall.

COMMANDOS. see FEDA'YEEN.

COMMITTEE FOR NATIONAL GUIDANCE (CNG). The committee was established by Palestinians at a meeting in Beit Hanina, a suburb of East Jerusalem (q.v.), in October 1978. It replaced the West Bank Palestinian National Front (q.v.), which had been declared illegal by Israel (q.v.) in 1978. At the beginning, the Committee was composed of 22 to 23 members, many of whom were closely affiliated with the PLO (q.v.). The CNG opposed the Camp David Accords (q.v.) and the autonomy plan, which was viewed as another act by Israel to maintain control of the Occupied Territories (q.v.), while divesting itself of the stigma of the occupation. The objectives of the committee were to affirm the Palestinians' right to establish a Palestinian state, and Palestinians' "right of return" to their home and country. On March 11, 1982, the committee was declared illegal and banned by Ariel Sharon (q.v.), Israel's defense minister at the time.

COUNCIL FOR HIGHER EDUCATION (CHE). An organization established on June 16, 1977, by 55 representatives of Palestinian educational institutions in the Occupied Territories (q.v.), because of the absence of a national government to coordinate policies for higher education. The council was responsible for overseeing educational affairs, improving the quality of education in universities and institutions of higher learning, and assisting in the professional development of faculty and staff. On August 28, 1994, the council was co-opted into the Palestine National Authority's (q.v.) Ministry of General and Higher Education.

CULTURE. Palestinian culture, whether art (q.v.), literature, theater, or music, has been overwhelmed by political circumstances.

The themes in literature—from the resistance poetry of Mahmoud Darwish (q.v.), Mitwakel Taha and Fadwa Touqan (q.v.), to the novella of Ghassan Kanafani (q.v.), or the letters from prison in Izzat Ghazzawi's *Point of Departure*—revolve around nationalism, the struggle for liberation, and the establishment of a homeland. They reflect the trials and tribulations of Palestinians in the diaspora or under occupation. Ghazzawi's experiences, for instance, emanate from personal tragedy and years in Israeli prisons in Ashkelon and the Neqab.

CURFEWS. A collective punishment that Israel (q.v.) uses to prohibit Palestinians in a town, refugee camp, or community from leaving their homes. Curfews are imposed following incidents of shootings, demonstrations, and disturbances. The duration of the curfew may last for days or several weeks. In fact, it also may continue for an indefinite period, as the permanent night curfew that was imposed on the Gaza Strip (q.v.) at the outset of the Intifada (q.v.) in 1987, and continued until May 1994, when the Israelis evacuated Gaza. Al-Haq (q.v.) estimates that in 1988, following the outbreak of the Intifada (q.v.), Israel ordered 1,600 curfews for the West Bank (q.v.) and the Gaza Strip, 400 of these were for periods ranging from three to forty days. See FOURTH GENEVA CONVENTION.

CURRENCY. When Israel occupied the West Bank and the Gaza Strip (qq.v.) in the aftermath of the war of 1967 (q.v.), the Jordanian dinar

(1995 exchange rate: 1 JD is equal to $1.50) remained in use with the new Israeli shekel (1995 exchange rate: 1 NIS is equal to 33 cents). All Arab banks that were operating in what became the Occupied Territories (q.v.) were closed, and Israel (q.v.) assumed control of all financial matters. Israeli banks opened branches in major West Bank cities, although it was extremely difficult for Palestinians to receive credit and loans from these banks. Also, Palestinians in general were reluctant to deposit their savings in Israeli banks due to feelings of insecurity in dealing with their occupier's banks and the fluctuating value of the shekel. Palestinian money-changers were allowed to operate, and handled financial matters such as the exchange of currency. People hoarded their savings at home in dollars, dinars, or gold (but never shekels), because of the stability of these currencies and/or because they received remittances from relatives in these currencies.

During the Intifada (q.v.), Israel introduced new regulations to restrict the flow of capital into the Occupied Territories. For instance, it limited the amount of money people brought from abroad; an individual could only bring in 400 Jordanian dinar ($600). Israeli banks soon became the target of Intifada activists; many were firebombed and subsequently closed.

After the signing of the DOP (q.v.), the Palestine National Authority (q.v.) established the Palestine Monetary Authority to manage official reserves, bank licensing and regulation, and the settlement of foreign exchange accounts with Israel and Jordan (qq.v.). Banks were allowed to reopen (including the Cairo-Amman Bank, the Housing Bank, the Arab Bank) in the West Bank. On January 7, 1994, Farouq al-Qaddumi (q.v.) signed an agreement with Jordan granting the Jordanian Central Bank financial authority in the area. The Bank of Jordan, closed since 1967, opened its first branch in Ramallah (q.v.) on April 1, 1994, and has since established 26 other branches in the Occupied Territories, all under the supervision of Jordan's Central Bank. In the autonomous area of the Gaza Strip (qq.v.), the Bank of Palestine has begun operating. According to a survey of 10 banks (41 branches) carried out by the Palestine Institute for Economic Policies in March 1995, Palestinians have now deposited $828 million dollars in these banks.

The Israelis insist that the Palestinians do not have the right to introduce their own currency because that would enable them to legislate monetary policy, a sign of sovereignty. Hence, the Palestinians remain dependent on the monetary policies of Jordan and Israel. The legal tender remains the Jordanian dinar, the dollar and the shekel.

D

AL-DAJANI, AHMAD SIDQI. Born in Jaffa, Palestine, in 1936, and moved to Syria (q.v.) with his family in 1948. He received a B.A. in history from Damascus University in 1958, and an M.A. and Ph.D. from Cairo University in 1963 and 1970, respectively. He has been an independent member of the Palestine National Council (q.v.) since 1963, and a member of the PLO Central Committee (q.v.) since 1973. He also served two terms as a member of the PLO Executive Committee (q.v.); from 1966 to 1967 and from 1977 to 1984. During his second term in the PLO Executive Committee, he also was the director of the Arab-European Dialogue. In 1977, he became president of the PLO Higher Council of Education, Culture, and Science. Al-Dajani has lectured at many Arab universities and published widely on Arab and Palestinian history.

DAJANI, HASSAN SIDQI. A prominent Palestinian, born in Jerusalem and trained as a lawyer. He established the *Muntada Al-Adabi* (the Literary Club) (q.v.) in 1919. He was one of the founders of *Hizb Al-Ahrar* (the Liberal Party), which was organized in 1930, and also served at one time as the secretary of the National Defense Party. He tacitly accepted the Balfour Declaration (q.v.), but demanded placing a quota on Jewish immigration to Palestine. He supported the 1936 Arab Revolt (q.v.), and encouraged the Palestinians to continue with their resistance activities. He died in 1937.

DAKKAK, IBRAHIM. One of the founding members of the Council for Higher Education and the National Guidance Committee (qq.v.). He was born in Jerusalem in March 1929. He received a B.S. from the American University of Cairo in 1952 in mathematics and science, and in 1961 a B.S. in civil engineering from Roberts College in Istanbul, Turkey. After teaching in Kuwait (q.v.) for a few years, Dakkak returned to Jerusalem, and became very active in Palestinian social and political life. From 1967 to 1987, he was the head of the West Bank Engineering Union and director of the Federation of Professional Unions. He served as the chief engineer of the *Al-Aqsa* (q.v.) Restoration Project from 1969 to 1977. He also was the founding director of Al-Maqassed Islamic Charitable Hospital in East Jerusalem in 1967. He is a member of the board of trustees of Birzeit University (q.v.), the College of Science and Technology of Abu Dis, and the Institute of Palestine Studies (q.v.). From 1977 to 1991, he was the chairman of the Arab Thought Forum (q.v.), a Palestinian think tank that arranges conferences and conducts research on development. He also has been a member of the Islamic Committee since 1985. A Marxist, Dakkak has written extensively. Among his works are *The Transformation of Jerusalem: Juridical and Physical Changes* (London, 1984); *Development Within: A Strategy of Survival* (London, 1988); *Back to Square One: A Study of the Re-Emer-*

gence of Palestinian Identity in the West Bank, 1967–1980 (London, 1983).

DARWAZZA, IZZAT MUHAMMAD. Born in Nablus (q.v.) in 1885, he co-founded *al-Jamiyyah Al-Filastiniyya* (the Palestinian Society) (q.v.), and was chosen in 1919 to represent Nablus in the Congress that was held in Damascus to proclaim Faisal (q.v.), the King of United Syria. In 1921, he became the principal, and member of the board of trustees, of An-Najah National College in Nablus. He was the secretary of the Arab Club (q.v), and also served two terms as the Nablus representative to the Palestine National Congress (q.v.). In 1928, he was appointed the director of the Islamic *Waqf* (q.v.). Darwazza became increasingly active in the Palestinian resistance, and staunchly opposed Jewish immigration and British presence in Palestine. In 1937, he was accused of assisting Palestinian commandos during the 1936 Arab-Palestinian revolt (q.v.), which led to his incarceration by the British. However, he was released after serving a year of his sentence, and promptly left for Syria (q.v.). During World War II, when the British occupied Syria, he escaped to Turkey. In 1947, Darwazza became a member of the new Arab Higher Committee for Palestine, which was formed by the Arab League (q.v.). Soon after, he resigned to write full-time.

DARWISH, MAHMOUD. National poet of Palestine (q.v.), former member of the PLO Executive Committee (q.v.), and chairman of the Supreme Council for Education, Propaganda and Heritage. He wrote the Declaration of Palestinian Independence (q.v.), which was announced by the Palestine National Council (q.v.) in Algiers on November 15, 1988.

Darwish was born in al-Birwah, near Nazareth, Palestine, in 1942. He lived and studied in Deir al-Assad and Kufur Yasif, Arab villages now in Israel (q.v.). After joining the Communist Party in Israel, he became a member of the editorial board of *Al-Itihad* (The Union) newspaper. In 1970, he left Israel to study in Moscow, and decided not to return. Instead, he went to Egypt (q.v.), and worked as a journalist for *Al-Ahram* (the Pyramid) newspaper. A few years later, he left for Beirut, where he managed *Palestinian Affairs*, a PLO magazine. Darwish has won many awards for his writings, among them the International Lotus Prize for Poetry. Among his works are *The Music of Human Flesh and Selected Poems of Mahmoud Darwish* (London, 1980) and *Memory for Forgetfulness: August, Beirut, 1982* (University of California Press, 1995).

DECLARATION OF PALESTINIAN INDEPENDENCE (1). The first declaration was also called the Proclamation of Independence and was announced on October 1, 1948, by the Arab Higher Committee (q.v.). It proclaimed the independence of Palestine (q.v.) as a free, democratic, and sovereign state.

DECLARATION OF PALESTINIAN INDEPENDENCE (2). This Declaration was written by Mahmoud Darwish (q.v.) and issued by the Palestine National Council (q.v.) on November 15, 1988. It declared the establishment of the state of Palestine, on Palestinian territory and with Jerusalem (q.v.) as the capital. Note: For the complete text of the Declaration of Independence, see Appendix No. 1.

DECLARATION OF PRINCIPLES (DOP). An interim agreement secretly negotiated in Oslo, Norway, and signed in Washington, D.C. on September 13, 1993, by Israel (q.v.), represented by its Foreign Minister Shimon Peres (q.v.), and the Palestinians, represented by Mahmoud Abbas (q.v.) under the auspices of the United States and the Russian Federation. The DOP immediately gave the Palestinians autonomous rule in Jericho and Gaza (qq.v.). It allowed for an interim period of three years, after which Israeli and Palestinian delegations would commence negotiations on final status matters regarding refugees (q.v.), settlements, (q.v.) and Jerusalem (q.v.). A Palestinian Interim Self-Government Authority composed of an elected council, which would serve for a transitional period not to exceed five years, also was to be negotiated. During the transitional period, the Palestinian Authority would administer and assume responsibility for various spheres of authority, such as education, health, culture, social welfare, direct taxation, and tourism. The main objective of the DOP is to establish a permanent settlement between the Israelis and the Palestinians, based on U.N. Security Council Resolutions 242 and 338 (qq.v.). Note: For the complete text of the Declaration of Principles, see Appendix No. 2.

DEIR YASSIN. A destroyed Palestinian village that once overlooked the Jerusalem-Tel Aviv road. It was attacked and occupied on April 9, 1948, by Jewish underground groups (a unit of the Irgun and Stern Gangs) led by Menachem Begin (q.v.), who later became Israel's prime minister. In the village, Jewish forces killed 245 Palestinian men, women, and children, and dumped their bodies in the village well. The massacre, which was covered in the press and broadcast on the radio, caused panic among the Palestinians, and forced them to flee their homes.

DEMOCRATIC ALLIANCE. A group of anti-Arafat PLO (qq.v.) factions that was formed in May 1984. It was composed of the Popular

Front for the Liberation of Palestine (q.v.), the Popular Democratic Front for the Liberation of Palestine (q.v.), the Palestine Liberation Front (q.v.), and the Communists. These factions had earlier boycotted a Palestine National Council (q.v.) meeting in Amman, Jordan. They were united by their outright rejection of Arafat's policies, and were furious with the PLO's forced evacuation from Lebanon (q.v.). However, they remained open to negotiations with Arafat, and in 1987 reconciled with him.

DEMOCRATIC FRONT FOR THE LIBERATION OF PALESTINE (DFLP). Nayef Hawatmeh (q.v.) seceded from George Habash's PFLP (qq.v.) in 1969, and established the DFLP in February of that year. Although the DFLP adheres to a Marxist ideology, it is more dogmatic than the PFLP. Many of its followers are intellectuals with leftist tendencies who support the establishment of a secular, democratic state in all of Palestine. The faction's headquarters is in Syria (q.v.). During the Intifada (q.v.), it was a member of the Unified National Leadership of the Uprising (q.v.). In December 1990, a new organization called the Democratic Union Party (Fida) (q.v.), led by Yasser Abed-Rabbo (q.v.) split from the DFLP. The DFLP is not opposed to the Palestine National Authority (q.v.). It, however, did not participate in the elections for the PLC (q.v.) that were held on January 20, 1996 in the West Bank and the Gaza Strip (qq.v.).

DEPORTATIONS. The practice of expelling unwanted persons from a country. This measure was introduced by the British in Palestine during the British Mandate (q.v.) as a method to curtail Arab resistance against Jewish immigration and British policies. Israeli authorities employed it to expel Palestinian political activists from their homes and country, on the basis that they endangered the security of the state of Israel (q.v.). It also was used to prevent the emergence of a Palestinian leadership that Israel did not approve. Immediately after the occupation of the West Bank and the Gaza Strip (qq.v.), Israeli authorities deported pro-Jordanian Palestinian leaders to undermine Jordan's influence among the Palestinians. In the 1970s and 1980s, the Israelis deported many Palestinian leaders who allegedly were supporters of the PLO (q.v.).

It is estimated that 1,200 Palestinians have been deported from the Occupied Territories (q.v.) since 1967. Article 49, Paragraph I of the Fourth Geneva Convention (q.v.) states: "Individual or mass forcible transfer, as well as deportations of protected persons from occupied territory to the territory of the Occupying Power or to that of any other country, occupied or not, are prohibited, regardless of motive."

Under Israeli rule, individuals or an entire group may be deported as a form of collective punishment, as was the case with the 415 Palestinians alleged by Israel to be members of Islamic organizations. They were deported to Lebanon in 1992. Israel considers deportations a military-security issue. A deportee may appeal to a military board and to the High Court of Justice, but rarely has a deportation been reversed. Deals have been negotiated whereby, instead of permanent exile, a person agrees to voluntarily leave the country for a specific time (three to five years), but is then free to return.

The United Nations and the world community have censored Israel for violations of the Geneva Convention.

DESERT STORM. see GULF WAR.

AL-DIF 'A. A daily newspaper established in 1934 by the Shanti (q.v) brothers during the British Mandate (q.v.). For five years, it was the mouthpiece of the *Istiqlal* (Independent Party) in Palestine (qq.v). After the war of 1948 (q.v.), the paper was relocated to Jerusalem (q.v.), where it merged with another newspaper, *Al-Jihad* (Holy War/ Struggle), under the name of *Al-Quds* (Jerusalem) (q.v.). It continued to be published there until the war of 1967 (q.v.). After the war, Ibrahim al-Shanti (q.v.) relocated *Al-Dif'a* for the third time to Jordan (q.v.), and published it there until 1971. *Al-Quds* resumed publication in Jerusalem in November 1968 under a new management.

DISTRICTS (1). Since 1967, the West Bank and the Gaza Strip (qq.v.) have been divided into districts: Each district includes the major city that the district is named after and surrounding towns and villages (see individual entries of major cities where indicated. Population figures for the districts are based on 1992 statistics).

Ramallah District includes the city of Ramallah (q.v.) and 96 villages and towns that surround it. Its size is 68,605 square kilometers and the population is 229,694.

Bethlehem District includes the city of Bethlehem (q.v.) and 34 nearby villages and towns, with a total population of 138,919.

Jericho District includes the city of Jericho (q.v.) and the 12 villages and towns that lie in its environs. The population is 25,957.

Nablus District includes the city of Nablus (q.v.) and 53 villages and towns. It is 159,107 square kilometers, and it has a population of 230,998.

Jenin District includes the city of Jenin (q.v.) and 63 towns and villages. Its size is 83,502 square kilometers , and it has a population of 197,211.

Tulkarm District includes the city of Tulkarm (q.v.) and 82 villages and towns. The population of the district is 202,432, and its size is 83,503 square kilometers.

Hebron District includes the city of Hebron (q.v.) and 64 villages and towns. Its population is 259,565, and it is composed of 2,076 square kilometers.

The Gaza District includes Gaza City and 17 towns and villages. The population of the major areas is as follows:

Gaza City, 292,999
Gaza North, 116,915
Khan Younis, 160,462
Rafah, 101,962
Gaza Middle, 116,600

DISTRICTS (2). The PNA (q.v.) designated the following 16 districts and the number of seats for the PLC (q.v.) elections that were held on January 20, 1996.

Jerusalem (7 seats)
Nablus (8 seats)
Jericho (1seat)
Salfit (1 seat)
Gaza (12 seats)
Jabaliya (7 seats)
Khan Younis (8 seats)
Deir Balah (5 seats)
Tulkarm (4 seats)
Hebron (10 seats)
Qalqilya (2 seats)
Ramallah (7 seats)
Jenin (6 seats)
Bethlehem (4 seats)
Toubas (1 seat)
Rafah (5 seats)

DOME OF THE ROCK. see AL-HARAM AL-SHARIF.

DUDIN, MUSTAFA. A politician who formed the first Village League Association (q.v.) in the village of Dura, near Hebron (q.v.), in 1978. For 20 years after the war of 1948 (q.v.), Dudin worked for the Egyptians who administered Gaza (q.v.). In 1968, he decided to leave for Jordan (q.v.), and his loyalty to King Hussein was rewarded with an appointment to the Jordanian parliament, a cabinet seat, and, eventually, an ambassadorial post. When he returned to the West Bank (q.v.) in 1975, he became interested in the modernization of rural areas. When Israeli authorities encouraged him to set up a village league, Dudin jumped at the opportunity to play a role in West Bank (q.v.) politics. Moreover, Dudin strongly supported the Camp David Accords (q.v.), because it gave Jordan a prominent role in West Bank affairs. In 1982, six representatives of the West Bank Village Leagues met and established the Federation of Palestinian Leagues. They then formed a party, which they called the Democratic Front for Peace. The idea for the village league was short-lived, because the Palestinians viewed anyone associated with the league as an Israeli collaborator. Jordan made membership in the league a crime equal to treason. Dudin resigned from the Village League Association on September 7, 1983.

E

EAST JERUSALEM. The Arab section of the city of Jerusalem (q.v.), which was occupied by Israel (q.v.) after the war of 1967 (q.v.) and annexed on June 30, 1980. East Jerusalem consists of the following areas: The Old City, Wadi al-Jouz, Sheikh Jarah, Raas al-'Amoud, Siwaneh, Mount of Olives, Silwan, Sur Baher, Jabal al-Mukaber, 'Essaweyeh, Shu'fat, and Beit Hanina. See JERUSALEM.

ECONOMIC DEVELOPMENT GROUP (EDG). A Palestinian NGO (q.v.) that was established in the West Bank and the Gaza Strip (qq.v.) in 1985. It was the first credit and loan institution to cater to the needs of the Palestinians. Financial support for the EDG is provided by the international community and the Arab countries.

ECONOMY. Immediately after the war of 1967 (q.v.), Israel subordinated and co-opted the economy of the Occupied Territories (qq.v.), and made it totally dependent on its own. In the agricultural sector, Israel placed heavy tariffs and taxes on Palestinian farmers, while simultaneously subsidizing its own farmers. Moreover, Israel confiscated large tracts of land, placed limits (by putting meters on existing wells) on how much water the Palestinians could use, and prohibited the digging of new wells. Palestinian farmers often were stranded with truckloads of produce because of curfews (q.v.), or because trucks carrying their produce could not cross the bridge into Jordan, both due to Israeli and Jordanian bureaucracy. Jordan also did not want competition for its farmers. The Palestinian peasants could not compete, and were forced off their land and into the Israeli labor market. Hence, the agricultural labor force in the Occupied Territories decreased significantly.

The proletarianization of the Palestinians contributed to the decline in agricultural productivity. More than a third of the Palestinian labor force was employed in Israel. Palestinian laborers built Israeli settlements (q.v.) on Palestinian-confiscated land. The Occupied Territories became a cheap labor market for Israel. Many Palestinians also emigrated to seek employment in the Arab countries, particularly in Saudi Arabia and Kuwait (q.v.). Remittances became an important source of income for families and relatives in the Occupied Territories.

As Palestinians increased their military attacks against Israel in the last few years, the Israeli government responded by closing its borders to Palestinian workers from the Occupied Territories and the autonomous areas (q.v.). It also imported approximately 60,000 foreign workers from Thailand and Turkey, primarily for construction work. Consequently, the unemployment rate in both the Occupied Territories and the autonomous areas increased dramatically; it is estimated that the unemployment rate in the West Bank is 30 percent, and more than 50 percent in the Gaza Strip.

Industrial productivity during the last 28 years of Israeli occupation has been limited to olive oil, limestone quarrying, textiles and clothing, metal processing, and food and beverages. There also has been some subcontracting for Israeli industries, particularly in small workshops employing less than 10 workers. Women also work at home for such subcontractors, who pay them by the piece. In sum, there has been little industrial development due to limited natural resources, limited markets, and heavy Israeli tariffs, customs, and taxes.

During the Intifada (q.v.), the Palestinians were encouraged by the Unified National Leadership of the Uprising (q.v.) to boycott Israeli goods, and to rely on themselves by re-establishing a domestic economy. Small business enterprises, food-production organizations, agricultural cooperatives, and household economic ventures mushroomed all over the Occupied Territories.

After the signing of the Declaration of Principles (q.v.) in September 1993, the international community pledged to help develop the infrastructure and economy of the Occupied Territories and the autonomous areas. Since then, the donor countries have not been forthcoming with the amounts they pledged, because they insist that the PNA (q.v.) must first establish a clear financial accounting system to outline the projects for which the money is targeted. See AGRICULTURE and INDUSTRY.

EDUCATION. The standard of education in the Occupied Territories (q.v.) deteriorated during the Israeli military occupation, particularly during the Intifada (q.v.), because of curfews (qq.v.), prolonged closures of schools and universities, and the imprisonment of students and teachers.

Education is compulsory from grade 1 to 9. Secondary education is not compulsory. At the end of grade 12, students sit for a matriculation exam, the *Tawjihi*; whatever score they attain determines both their entry into a university and their major. There are three types of schools in the Palestinian territories: public schools, private-religious schools (Muslim, Christian, or foreign missionary—the Quakers School, for example), and schools that are run by UNRWA (q.v.) for Palestinian refugee children. During the Israeli occupation, the Jordanian curriculum was used for schools in the West Bank (q.v.), and the schools in the Gaza Strip (q.v.) use the Egyptian curriculum. This is because students in these two areas continue their higher education at universities in Jordan and Egypt, respectively.

There are eight universities in the Occupied Territories. These universities are privately funded and grant Bachelor of Arts and Science degrees. The eight universities are (see individual entry where indicated): An-Najah National University (q.v.), Hebron University (q.v.), Birzeit University (q.v.), the Islamic University (q.v.), Al-Azhar University (Gaza), Al-Quds University (q.v.), Bethlehem University (q.v.), and an Open University. According to the Council of Higher Education (q.v.), there are 16,368 registered university students and 1,000 faculty members. In addition to the universities, there are 20 community and teacher-training colleges. These colleges provide technical training and know-how in engineering, agriculture, commerce (business administration), and social services. The universities and colleges are under the auspices of the Council for Higher Education.

In accordance with the Declaration of Principles (DOP) (q.v.), the Palestinian National Authority's (q.v.) Ministry of Education assumed responsibility for education in the Occupied Territories on August 28, 1994. Special task forces have been assigned to completely revamp the Palestinian curriculum in high schools and study the problems of the institutions of higher learning.

EGYPT, THE ARAB REPUBLIC OF. An Arab-Muslim country that has an area of 1,002,000 square kilometers (386,900 square miles) and a population of 60 million. It is located at the northeast corner of Africa, but the territory known as Sinai Peninsula (q.v.) is in Asia. On the north, it is bounded by the Mediterranean Sea; on the east by Israel, the Red Sea, and the Gulf of Suez; on the south by Sudan; and on the west by Libya. The country is barren desert, except for the Nile Delta region. Egypt was a British protectorate until 1922, when it was declared a republic. In 1923, it became a constitutional monarchy with a king. In July 1952, a group of army officers ("the Free Officers") staged a coup, and forced King Farouq, who had ruled since 1936, to abdicate and sent him out of the country.

Egypt has been involved in the Israeli-Palestinian conflict since 1939. At that time, Britain had asked Egypt to send a representative to the London Conference (q.v.). Egypt, as a member of the Arab League (q.v.), also participated in the war of 1948 (q.v.). At the end of the war, Egypt was placed in charge of administering the Gaza Strip (q.v.), but lost it and the Sinai Peninsula during the 1967 war (q.v.). In 1956, President Gamal Abd al-Nasser (q.v.) decided to nationalize the Suez Canal. Britain, France, and Israel immediately retaliated. Israel occupied the Gaza Strip and the Sinai. Britian and France attacked Egypt and occupied the Suez. However, the United States and the Soviet Union forced them to withdraw from the Egyptian territory, and a U.N. emergency force was placed in the Sinai Peninsula. In 1964, Egypt supported the formation of the Palestine Liberation Organization (q.v.). Tensions increased between Egypt and Israel in May 1967. President Nasser blocked the Straits of Tiran to Israeli ships and requested the withdrawal of the U.N. emergency force. On June 5, 1967 Israel, attacked, defeated the Arabs, and occupied Egyptian, Jordanian, and Syrian territories. After Nasser died on September 28, 1970, Anwar al-Sadat (q.v.) became the president of Egypt. On October 6, 1973, Egypt attacked Israel, and through the Disengagement Agreement of January 1974, regained the eastern part of the Suez Canal that had been under Israeli occupation since 1967. The Suez Canal was opened in June 1975, and Israeli cargo was allowed to be carried on non-Israeli ships. In an agreement mediated by Henry Kissinger on September 1, 1975, Egyptian and U.N. forces were permitted to increase their numbers in the Sinai, and Israel returned the Egyptian oil installations located on the Gulf of Suez. On November 20, 1975, Sadat made his historic trip to Jerusalem (q.v.). On September 17, 1978, Egypt and Israel, with the assistance of the United States, signed the Camp David Accords (q.v.), which culminated with the signing of the Israeli-Egyptian peace treaty on March 26, 1979. Israel completely withdrew from the Sinai Peninsula by April 1982. The Arab countries, angry with Sadat for making peace with Israel, broke off all relations with Egypt until 1983.

'ERAKAT, SAEB MOHAMMED. Appointed in July 1994, and again in 1996 by Arafat (q.v.) as the minister of Local Government and Municipal Affairs. He also is a PLC (q.v.) member representing Jericho (q.v.).

'Erakat was born on April 28, 1955, in Jerusalem (q.v.) and grew up in Jericho (q.v.). He finished his high school education and went to the United States to study, where he received a B.A. and an M.A. in international relations from San Francisco State University. When he returned, he taught at An-Najah National University (q.v.). A year later, he decided to continue his studies in Britain, where he received his Ph.D. in conflict resolution and peace studies from Bradford University in 1983. He returned to An-Najah National University and taught in the political science department, and served as director of public relations until 1986. He also worked on the editorial staff of *Al-Quds* (q.v.) newspaper and wrote weekly editorials. From 1985 until 1990, 'Erakat was arrested several times by the Israelis and prohibited from traveling abroad because of his political activities. Since 1992, he has served as secretary general of the Arab Studies Society (q.v.), and as a member of the board of trustees of the College of Science and Technology in Abu Dis near Jerusalem. He also was a member of the board of trustees of the Palestinian Cultural Council, a member of the Palestinian Writers Association, and a member of the Palestinian delegation to the Madrid Peace Conference (q.v.). He was elected along with Hanan Ashrawi and Faisal al-Husseini (qq.v.) to the Higher Committee for the Peace Talks at the PLO (q.v.) headquarters in Tunis, an indication of his status and prestige in the central PLO leadership.

ERSHAD, ZEEB MUSTAFA AL-HAJ. Prominent businessman and lawyer, he was born in the village of al-Kafir in the Jenin (q.v.) district. He studied at An-Najah National College in Nablus (q.v.) and at the American University of Beirut in Lebanon (q.v.). He practiced law in Jaffa, Nablus, and Jenin (q.v.). He also was a successful farmer, and established the Administrative Board of Vegetable Oils in Nablus and co-founded the Arab Sons of Jerusalem Association. From 1954 until 1956, he served as a member of the Jordanian parliament, and was elected the third president of the Syrian Socialist Nationalist Party. Ershad also owned and edited the *Kifah* (The Struggle) newspaper, published in Jaffa, Palestine, from 1935 to 1936.

EUROPEAN COORDINATING COMMITTEE OF NGOS ON THE QUESTION OF PALESTINE (ECCP). A committee based in Brussels, Belgium, the objectives of which include publicizing the conditions of Palestinians living under the Israeli military occupation; exposing Israeli violations and infringements on Palestinian human rights; promoting a just and durable peace in the Middle East on the basis of U.N. Security Council Resolutions 242 and 338 (qq.v.); and supporting the work of the European Commission and governments.

F

FAHD PLAN. A proposal for a Middle East Peace Plan submitted by King Fahd of Saudi Arabia (q.v.) and accepted at the Fez Arab Summit in September 1982. It called for the establishment of a Palestinian state in parts of Palestine, and for coexistence between Israel (q.v.) and the Palestinians. The plan consists of eight points: Israeli withdrawal from Arab territories occupied in 1967; the dismantlement of Israeli settlements; guaranteeing freedom of worship for all faiths in

Jerusalem; recognition of Palestinians' right of return, and compensation for those who do not wish to return; a U.N. mandate for several months over the West Bank and the Gaza Strip (qq.v.); the establishment of a Palestinian state with East Jerusalem (q.v.) as its capital; and ensuring the right of Palestinians and the states in the region to live in peace.

AL-FAHUM, KHALID. An independent member of the Palestine National Council (q.v.) since 1964. He was the speaker of the PNC from 1971 until 1984, and a member of the PLO Central Committee (q.v.) from 1973 until 1984. He served two terms as a member of the PLO Executive Committee (q.v.), from 1964 to 1965 and 1967 to 1969. Al-Fahum was ousted as the speaker of the PNC, because he helped to organize the National Salvation Front (q.v.), an anti-Arafat (q.v.) alliance.

FAISAL I, AMIR (Prince). Son of Sharif Hussein, the King of Hijaz, brother of King Abdallah (q.v.) and self-proclaimed ruler of the Syrian kingdom in 1919, who all had ingratiated themselves with the British by joining forces with them against the Ottoman-Turks (q.v.). After the Turks were defeated at the end of World War I, Britain approved Faisal becoming king of Syria (q.v.). However, the French forced him out in 1920, and proceeded to occupy Syria and Lebanon (qq.v.). The British then appointed him as the king of Iraq (q.v.), and his brother, Abdallah (q.v.), was given the territory of Transjordan.

Faisal had also been invoved in a series of meetings with Zionist representatives in Paris. Between 1918 and 1919, Faisal met several times with Chaim Weizmann, the leader of the Zionist Movement. On January 3, 1919, they reached an agreement whereby Faisal acknowledged the Balfour Declaration (q.v.) and accepted Jewish immigration to Palestine, as long as Arab rights were protected. Weizmann, for his part, agreed to Faisal's dream of ruling an Arab kingdom and even offered to assist in the development of its infrastructure. The agreement caused an uproar among the Arabs, and Faisal was attacked for the concessions he had made to the Zionists.

AL-FAJR. Arabic for "the dawn". A weekly paper started in 1972 by Yousef Nasser. It became a daily newspaper in 1974, and was supportive of the PLO (q.v.). It was published seven days a week and had a circulation of 20,000. An English language weekly, under the *Al-Fajr* name, also was published in 1980 and its circulation reached 10,000. Hanna Siniora (q.v.) served as editor-in-chief. The paper ceased publication in August 1993, but reappeared as *Biladi Jerusalem Times* (q.v.) in February 1994.

FARHAN, KHADIJAH SALIM. A founding member and currently the president of the Kalandiya Cooperative Society. The society was founded in 1958 to help women to become economically independent in the Kalandiya Refugee Camp and surrounding rural areas. It is located in the Kalandiya Refugee Camp, just outside of Ramallah (q.v.), and has 158 members and a nine-member executive board. The cooperative employs 580 part-time employees, and runs a sewing training center, a nursery school, a kindergarten, a literacy program and a cosmetology/beautician course for young women. It has established a University Student Fund, which distributes grants to needy and deserving students.

Farhan was born in Jerusalem in 1940 and finished her schooling there. In addition to the Kalandiya Society, she is very active in other organizations. Since 1973, she has served as a member of the Al-Bireh (q.v.) branch of the Palestinian Red Crescent Society (q.v.); in 1980, she became a member of the al-Maqassed Islamic Charitable Hospital Organization; and in 1982, she joined the board of the Friends of the Sick Society in Ramallah (q.v.).

FATAH. Arabic for "conquest" and the acronym for *Harakat Al-Tahrir Al-Filastiniyya* (The Palestine National Liberation Movement). FATAH, the backbone of the Palestine national movement, is the largest, most active, and the most influential of factions that make up the PLO (q.v.). Since its formation, FATAH's ideology and program have undergone many changes. During the 1960s and 1970s, it advocated guerilla-style tactics and armed struggle. In the 1980s and 1990s, pragmatism, moderation, and peace became part of the faction's agenda. Arafat (q.v.) is the head of FATAH, and the faction constitutes his power base. He is assisted by the Central Committee of FATAH, a governing body composed of 18 members that administers the affairs of the faction.

FATAH was first envisioned by Yasser Arafat and Khalil al-Wazir (q.v.) in the late 1950s in the Gaza Strip (q.v.), when it was under Egyptian administration. Among its other leaders are Salah Khalaf (q.v.), Farouq al-Qaddumi (q.v.), and Hani and Khalid al-Hassan (qq.v.). From 1957 to 1965, the organization was composed of a network of secret underground cells. Its objectives were the destruction of Israel (q.v.), political independence from the Arab countries, and the establishment of a democratic secular state.

FATAH started sabotage activities against Israel on January 1, 1965. It tried to establish bases in Syria (q.v.) in 1967, but failed. It did, however, use Jordan as a base to launch attacks against Israel. On March 21, 1968, at Karameh (q.v.), a village east of the River Jordan where FATAH had a base, a battle took place between Jordan (q.v.), PLO (q.v.) forces, and Israel. This battle was seen as a victory for the Palestinians, because Israel was not successful in evicting the Palestinian commandos (q.v.) from their base in the Jordan Valley. In February 1969, Arafat became the chairman of the PLO Executive Committee (q.v.), and FATAH became the leading PLO faction. However, FATAH suffered a serious setback in September 1970, when it clashed with Jordanian forces, and several thousand Palestinians were killed. The PLO was forced out of Jordan, and moved to Beirut, Lebanon (q.v.). During the Arab Summit Conference in Algeria in November 1973, the PLO was declared "the legitimate representative of the Palestinian people." In October 1974, the Arab Summit Conference in Rabat, Morocco issued a memorandum stating that the PLO is the "sole representative of the Palestinian people." The U.N. General Assembly passed Resolutions 3236 and 3237 (qq.v.) in November 1974, declaring that the PLO is the representative of the Palestinian people, and the Palestinians have the right to self-determination and statehood.

Between 1974 and 1975, FATAH carried out attacks against Israel. Among them were the March 1975 attack in Tel Aviv, the Savoy Operation, and the large bomb explosion in July 1975, which caused the loss of many civilian lives. In 1983, FATAH suffered from internal strife when Sa'id Mussa Muragha (q.v.), with Syrian support, rebelled against Arafat's leadership and established another faction, which he called FATAH Uprising (q.v.). The FATAH Revolutionary Council and The Revolutionary Council-Emergency Command (qq.v) seceded from FATAH because of disagreements over policy.

During the Intifada (q.v.), FATAH, together with other political factions, such as the Popular Front for the Liberation of Palestine and the Democratic Front for the Liberation of Palestine (qq.v.), formed the Unified National Leadership of the Uprising (q.v.). FATAH played a prominent role in the organization. FATAH Hawks (q.v.) were especially active during the Intifada. Many FATAH leaders consequently were deported from the Occupied Territories (q.v).

In 1989 and 1990, FATAH suffered several serious setbacks and was weakened by the assassinations of its leaders, Khalil Al-Wazir and Salah Khalaf (qq.v.). The movement also was strained by dissent and disillusionment, and members were dissatisfied with the decision-making process.

The Oslo Accords (q.v.) were approved by the 18-member FATAH Central Committee, except for a few of its leading founders: Farouq al-Qaddumi (q.v.), Khalid and Hani al-Hassan (qq.v.), Abbas Zaki, Muhammad Jihad, and Shakir Habash. These men remained Arafat loyalists and did not join the opposition; FATAH suffered from internal strife however as a result of the signing of the accords. Feuding within FATAH disturbed many Palestinians, who view it as a needless waste of resources and energy. Following the signing of the Declaration of Principles (q.v.), a group calling itself Black September 13th (a reference to the date of the signing of the DOP) joined ranks with the FATAH Uprising (q.v.) and engineered a power struggle within FATAH. Furthermore, half the members of the FATAH Revolutionary Committee boycotted the meeting in Tunis in November 1993 to protest Arafat and the signing of the DOP.

After the Palestinian National Authority (q.v.) moved to the autonomous areas (q.v.), FATAH emerged as the ruling faction, and the most active organization in terms of activities and recruitment in both the autonomous areas and the Occupied Territories (q.v.). FATAH offices opened in many cities in the West Bank and the Gaza Strip (qq.v.) in April 1994. However, divisions within FATAH surfaced, both inside the autonomous areas and in the diaspora. FATAH Hawks have challenged the decisions made by mainstream FATAH, and have continued to use violence against Israel (q.v.). The Hawks were so furious with FATAH leaders that they disrupted elections for the Gaza Strip Medical Association on February 5, 1994. On November 4, 1994, the first FATAH elections were held in Ramallah (q.v.), but the discord was so evident that Arafat quickly postponed elections in other cities. FATAH leaders have begun efforts to unite the splintered groups and to centralize authority within the faction.

A significant crossroad has been reached. Should FATAH restructure and become a political party, or should it continue as a revolutionary movement? Democratization reforms within FATAH in the West Bank have been called for by Marwan Barghouthi (q.v.), who has submitted new bylaws. The objective of these bylaws is to transform FATAH into a political party composed of many units. Each unit would in turn be made up of 40 or more members. Leadership positions are to be based on elections, rather than by appointment. Arafat and many of his close followers have insisted that the structural organization of both FATAH and the PLO (q.v.) should remain intact to represent the Palestinians in the diaspora. It is for this reason that FATAH's foreign affairs and mobilization departments have not moved to the autonomous areas.

Prior to the January 1996 elections for the PLC (q.v.), FATAH held primaries throughout the West Bank and the Gaza Strip to select a list of candidates. When the list was finalized by FATAH leaders, some members were dissatisfied with the results, because they felt that close Arafat loyalists had been given priority over other candidates. Not to be outdone, these FATAH rebels decided to run independent of their faction. FATAH won a resounding victory in the elections (52 seats or 61 percent of the votes), and FATAH rebels also were successful in capturing 12 seats in the PLC elections.

FATAH also has been challenged by HAMAS (q.v.). The confrontation between HAMAS and FATAH is not new. On November 18, 1994, a clash known as "Black Friday", between HAMAS and FATAH leaders in the Palestine Mosque in Gaza, resulted in the death of many Palestinians. On November 20, 1994, FATAH emerged in the streets of Gaza to confront HAMAS. FATAH has consequently been transformed into a quasi-army for the PNA (q.v.). Some members also have joined the Preventive Security Services (q.v.).

An "honor pact" was signed on April 24, 1994, between HAMAS and FATAH to prevent a civil war from escalating among the Palestinians. According to the terms of the agreement, both factions are to resolve their differences only through dialogue. But hurdles still remain for the two factions, and HAMAS did not join the PNA or take part in the PLC elections held in January 1996.

FATAH HAWKS. The military wing of FATAH in the Occupied Territories (qq.v.), now the auxiliary police in the autonomous areas (qq.v.). After the November 1994 clash between Palestinian police and HAMAS (q.v.) in Gaza, FATAH Hawks resurfaced as a show of force in support of Yasser Arafat (q.v.).

FATAH HIGHER COMMITTEE IN THE WEST BANK. A committee composed of 48 members under the chairmanship of Marwan al-Barghouthi (q.v.). It oversees the affairs of FATAH (q.v.) in the West Bank (q.v.).

FATAH REVOLUTIONARY COUNCIL. A faction that was formed by Sabri al-Banna (q.v.), a critic of Arafat (q.v.) in 1973. In the 1990s, some members led by Atef Abu Bakr and Abd al-Rahman Isa split off and formed The Revolutionary Council-Emergency Command.

FATAH UPRISING. A Palestinian faction organized in 1983 by a military commander, Sa'id Mussa Muragha (q.v.), alias Abu Mussa. He opposed Arafat (q.v.) and plotted to overthrow him after the Palestine Liberation Organization was forced out of Lebanon (qq.v.). The faction is based in Syria (q.v.), and adamantly rejects any settlement with Israel (q.v.).

FATAH PROVISIONAL COMMAND see FATAH UPRISING

AL-FATAT NATIONALIST SOCIETY. Al-Fatat is Arabic for youth. An organization established in 1911 by Awni Abd al-Hadi (q.v.) to encourage Arab unity.

FATWA. An Islamic legal opinion or decree that is issued by a *mufti* (q.v.) concerning social, economic, or political matters in Muslim society. It could deal with such diverse matters as abortion, land reform, taxes, nationalization, and foreign policy. The *fatwa* functions to provide an Islamic rationalization for an issue.

FEDAYEEN. Arabic for commandos or freedom fighters. See FEDAYEEN ORGANIZATIONS

FEDAYEEN ORGANIZATIONS. Resistance or commando organizations that were formed between 1936 and 1939, when the Arab Palestinian Revolts (q.v.) broke out. Between 1947 and 1950, these groups carried out sabotage activities against Israel (q.v.), but they were unorganized and often acted independently. The situation was remedied in the late 1950s and the 1960s under the leadership of the PLO (q.v.), which united the different factions and organizations. Moreover, most of the commando groups were permitted to set up bases in the Arab countries. They, therefore, had different loyalties and various sources of support.

FIDA see PALESTINE DEMOCRATIC UNION

FILASTINE. (1) Arabic for Palestine (q.v.).

FILASTINE. (2) This is also the name of a semi-weekly newspaper established in Jaffa, Palestine in 1911 by two Christian brothers, Yousef and Isa al-Isa (q.v.). It later evolved into a popular daily, and a weekly literary supplement was added in 1920. By 1946, it had a circulation of nine thousand. Its political stance fluctuated and reflected the changing times. At the beginning, it advocated support and loyalty for the Ottoman-Turks (q.v.). In the 1930s, it adopted an independent line, based on Palestinian nationalism and referred to the Arabs of Palestine as "Palestinians". Moreover, it cautioned against Zionist immigration into Palestine and encouraged resistance; from 1940–47, it supported the Nashashibis (q.v.); from 1943–46, the *Istiqlal* (Independence) Party (q.v.), and in the late 1940s, it opposed the Husseinis (q.v.). After the war of 1948 (q.v.), the newspaper was re-established in East Jerusalem (q.v.) and published as a daily until 1967.

FILASTINE AL-THAWRA. Arabic for "Palestine (q.v.), the revolution". A daily, and at times published as a weekly. It was founded in 1972 as the mouthpiece of the Palestine Liberation Organization (q.v.). Abd al-Rahman Ahmad (q.v.) served as an editor-in-chief.

FILASTINUO. Arabic for the "Palestinians". A paper that first appeared in 1959. It supported Arab unity as the only way to liberate Palestine. Khalil al-Wazir (q.v.) served as its first editor.

FLAG. The first Palestinian flag was approved by the All-Palestine government (q.v.) on October 1, 1948. It was modeled on the flag carried in the 1916 Arab Revolt (q.v.). It had white, green, and black stripes, with a red triangle on the right side. Today, the national flag of Palestine has black, white, and green stripes, with a red triangle on the left side. Prior to the signing of the Declaration of Principles (q.v.), it was illegal to fly the Palestinian flag in the Occupied Territories (q.v.). Anyone caught doing so would be imprisoned for six months. Nevertheless, the flag was virtually everywhere, flying from pylons and painted on walls, particularly during the Intifada (q.v.).

HAMAS (q.v.) has its own flag. It is green with a line in Arabic written in the middle: "There is no God, but God." This is the *shahadeh*, or the Islamic declaration of faith.

FORCE 17. A FATAH (q.v.) faction organized in the 1970s to provide personal security for Arafat (q.v.) and other leaders. It is a component of the security apparatus of the PNA (q.v.) and provides security for Arafat in the Palestinian autonomous areas (q.v.).

FOREIGN AID. The Palestine Liberation Organization (q.v.) has continuously received financial support from the Arab countries, particularly the rich oil countries of Saudi Arabia (q.v.), Kuwait (q.v.), and Iraq (q.v.). It also has received lump-sum transfers deducted from the salaries of Palestinians working in these countries. The money has not only been used for its institutions and activities, but also for education, health, and social services for the Palestinian refugees (q.v.) and those living under occupation.

Palestinians in the Occupied Territories (q.v.), in turn, receive support from the PLO, from Palestinian and non-Palestinian NGOs (q.v.), and from governments and international assistance agencies. On November 15, 1978, at the ninth Arab Summit in Baghdad, Iraq, a joint committee of Jordanian and PLO representatives was formed to channel $150 million dollars to the Occupied Territories to support Palestinian steadfastness. Remittances from relatives working abroad also have contributed to the financial stability of the Occupied Territories (q.v.) over the years.

After the signing of the Declaration of Principles (q.v.), an impressive array of countries and donors met at the "conference to support Middle East Peace" on October 1, 1993, under the auspices of the Russian Federation and the United States, to show their support politically and financially for the peace process. Donors representing 42 countries were confident that the $2.4 billion estimated by the World Bank to be the amount the Palestinians needed to develop their social, political, and economic infrastructure over the next five years could be found. Of the $2.4 billion, $1.6 billion was to be in the form of grants and $800 million was to be in the form of loans and guarantees.

The donor countries have been slow in transferring the funds, as they continue to insist on a system of accountability and transparency. Less than $300 million in foreign aid to the Palestinian Authority (q.v.) from the donor countries after the signing of the DOP has been received, far below that which had been promised for the first year. For 1995 alone, $500 millon was promised. Altogether, in the past two years, the Palestinians have received $600 million, or 37 percent of the $1.6 billion earmarked as grants, and only $10 million in loans or guarantees. The funds that are received from the donor countries are channeled through the U.N. programs for the Palestinians, the Holst Fund (named after the deceased Norwegian prime minister who helped negotiate the DOP in Oslo) and other agencies. Moreover, money received has been earmarked for the salaries of the Palestinian police and other PNA officials.

On January 14, 1995, the PNA formed a committee to outline economic priorities and supervise the expenditures of all funds received. Shortly afterward, on January 27, the PNA received $11 million (out of an estimated $40 million) from the United States for a four-year waste-water project. On January 30, 1995, the donor countries gave the PNA $179 million to initiate projects that would provide work for the people in Gaza, and transferred several hundred million dollars. Israel (q.v.), in accordance with the DOP, also has transferred money from taxes withheld from the salaries of Palestinian workers. On January 1, 1995, Israel and the PNA agreed that the PNA would receive 75 percent of all income taxes, VAT, and other taxes from the salaries of Palestinian workers. Israel transferred $11.5 million in two installments. On March 24, 1995, U.S. Vice President Al Gore, visiting Jericho, signed an aid package of $73 million for development and public works, which is to be channeled through UNRWA (q.v.) and other U.N. programs for the Palestinians. On April 27, 1995, the donor countries gave the PNA $60 million of the $136 million budget deficit to cover their expenses. In September 1995, Japan agreed to channel $200 million directly to the PNA. This was in addition to the $200 million it had contributed in 1994 and 1995, and which had been administered by the U.N. Development Program.

FOREIGN RELATIONS. The Palestine Liberation Organization (q.v.) began contacts with the outside world on March 17, 1964, when Yasser Arafat and Khalil al-Wazir (qq.v.) traveled to China and met with Premier Chow En-Lai to lobby support for their cause. A PLO office was opened in Beijing, China, and Mao Zedong officially recognized the PLO on June 18, 1965. After the PLO was officially formed on June 2, 1964, the Arab states attending the second Arab Summit in Cairo, Egypt (q.v.), on September 5, 1964, recognized the PLO as the symbol of the struggle for the liberation of Palestine. In 1974, the Arab countries, ignoring Jordan's (q.v.) claims, named the PLO as the sole, legitimate representative of the Palestinians. The United Nations that same year extended observer status to the PLO. On June 22, 1976, the PLO opened an office in Moscow. Austrian Chancellor Bruno Kreisky and Socialist International Chairman Willy Brandt held talks with Arafat in Vienna, Austria, to discuss the convening of an international conference on behalf of the Palestinians. The United Nations declared an "International Day of Solidarity" with the Palestinian people on November 29, 1979. The United States representative to the United Nations met with the PLO representative, and the European Community issued the Venice Declaration (q.v.) on June 3, 1980. Furthermore, the U.N. General Assembly called for the establishment of an independent Palestinian state on July 29, 1980. After the PLO declared Palestinian statehood on November 15, 1988, during the 19th session of the PNC (q.v.) meeting in Algiers, 100 nations recognized the new state. Arafat inaugurated his peace initiative on December 13, 1988, in front of the U.N. General Assembly in Geneva. The following day, U.S. officials held talks with PLO representatives in Tunis, ending a 14-year boycott of the organization. On January 12, 1989, the U.N. Council granted the PLO the right to address the council as "Palestine," and with the same status as any nation that was a member of the United Nations. On September 13, 1993, the entire world watched as the Palestinians signed the DOP (q.v.) with Israel and laid claim to international legitimacy. As the Palestinian National Authority (q.v.) moved into Gaza and Jericho (qq.v.), nations moved to establish representational offices in these areas. In 1995, Holland, Finland, Bulgaria, and more than 50 other states recognized the Palestinian passport.

FOURTH GENEVA CONVENTION. A set of international laws approved August 12, 1949, regulating military occupations and stipulating the humane treatment of prisoners and protection of civilian populations, property, and territory. These laws are applicable to the Occupied Territories (q.v.), which Israel (q.v.) has controlled since June 1967.

For example: On curfews (q.v.) and the sealing of rooms, Article 33 states: "No protected person may be punished for an offense he or she has not personally committed. Collective penalties and likewise all measures of intimidation or terrorism are prohibited."

On deportations (q.v.), Article 49, paragraph 1, states: "Individual or mass forcible transfers, as well as deportations of protected persons from occupied territory to the territory of the Occupying Power or that of any other country, occupied or not, are prohibited, regardless of motive."

On labor, Article 52 states: "The local workforce is to be protected, and the occupying force is prohibited from creating situations of unemployment, to induce the local labor force to work for the occupying powers."

On house demolitions, Article 53 states: "Any destruction by the Occupying Power of real or personal property belonging individually or collectively to private persons, or to other public authorities, or to social or cooperative associations, is prohibited, except where such destruction is rendered absolutely necessary by military operations."

On settlements (q.v.), Article 49, paragraph 6, states: "The Occupying Power shall not deport or transfer parts of its own civilian population into the territory it occupies."

Israel (q.v.) contends that the Fourth Geneva Convention is not applicable to the Occupied Territories, because they were not sovereign territories. It maintains that only Britain and Pakistan had recognized the Jordanian annexation of the West Bank (q.v.), and the Gaza Strip (q.v.) had not been annexed by Egypt (q.v.).

FREIJ, ELIAS. Prominent businessman, mayor of Bethlehem (q.v.) and minister of Tourism in the Palestine National Authority (q.v.) in 1994 and 1996. Freij was born in 1920 in Bethlehem. Elected to the Bethlehem Municipal Council, he served from 1960 to 1968. In 1972, he was elected mayor, and continues to hold that office. He has been a member of the Bethlehem Chamber of Commerce and Industry since 1954 and its president since 1970. He worked closely with the Vatican to establish Bethlehem University (q.v.) in 1973. Actively involved in politics, he is considered a moderate. In 1982, he opposed both the mass dismissal of the nine nationalist mayors and the protest strike by the other mayors in the Occupied Territories (q.v.) after the establishment of the Israeli Civil Administration (q.v.). He did not go on strike, nor was he dismissed. He was invited to meet with Sadat (q.v.) in Jerusalem in 1977, a visit that proceeded the Camp David Accords (qq.v.). As the minister of Tourism, he is active in promoting tourism in the Occupied Territories and encouraging investors to help develop the infrastructure necessary to accomodate tourists.

AL-FUTUWWA. Arabic for "youth". A paramilitary unit specifically for young men organized by Jamal al-Husseini (q.v.) and others.

G

GAZA STRIP. A narrow area composed of coastal plains and sand dunes, with limited rainfall (150–250 milimeters a year) and bordered by the Mediterranean Sea. The Strip is 363 square kilometers, 45 kilometers long and 8 kilometers wide. In accordance with the Declaration of Principles (q.v.) of 1993, about 219 square kilometers of the Gaza Strip has become part of the Palestinian autonomous areas (q.v). It also is the seat of government for Arafat and the Palestine National Authority (qq.v.).

During the war of 1948 (q.v.), approximately 150,000 to 200,000 Palestinian refugees moved into the Gaza Strip, and it became a recruiting ground for commando organizations, particularly between 1952 and 1956. Also, the Gaza Strip often was used as a base to attack Israel (q.v.). After the war of 1948 (q.v.), an armistice agreement was signed between Israel and Egypt (q.v.) on February 24, 1948, and the Gaza Strip was placed under Egyptian control; it was not, however, annexed to Egypt. Instead, an Egyptian governor was appointed to administer the area, which was called the "Palestine National Union." Gaza remained under Egyptian control until the war of 1967 (q.v.), when Israel occupied it.

Under the Egyptians, Gaza made some progress, particularly in education (q.v.), which was made compulsory. Egyptian universities accepted students from the Gaza Strip. However, Egypt, unlike Jordan, did not give the Palestinians passports, but instead issued them travel documents.

During the Israeli occupation, the Gaza Strip, with a population of approximately 850,000 Palestinians, became a most troublesome and unstable area, because of its high population density, poverty, and unemployment, and its dependence on the Israeli labor market.

GENERAL FEDERATION OF PALESTINIAN TRADE UNIONS (GFPTU). The federation was established to unite the various unions in the Occupied Territories (q.v.) and to organize their activities more efficiently. Professional and labor unions operate in the Gaza Strip and the West Bank (qq.v.). The unions have different political affiliations. For this reason, Israel kept close surveillance on union activities, and has waged a battle of wills against trade unions and union activists.

GENERAL UNION OF PALESTINIAN STUDENTS (GUPS). An organization formed in Cairo, Egypt (q.v.), in 1959 by Arafat (q.v.) and others to organize and unite Palestinian students for collective political action. The union provided recruits for FATAH (q.v.) and other political factions. Branches of the union have been established in Europe, the Middle East, and the United States.

GENERAL UNION OF PALESTINIAN WOMEN'S COMMITTEES (GUPWC). The union was established in 1980 to unite women's committees and to develop a greater role for women in the social, political, and economic spheres of their society. The union also represents the women's committees in national and international forums, and organizes workshops to train women to become economically and politically independent. It also coordinates projects in towns and villages, and assists women in setting up business ventures, such as carpet-weaving, food and pastry production, embroidery, and nursery schools. The union holds seminars and lectures to help women understand and deal with oppression and violence that is directed against them.

GENERAL UNION OF PALESTINIAN WOMEN'S STRUGGLE COMMITTEES/GAZA (GUPWSC). The union was established in Gaza in 1987 to unite the women's committees for collective action to effectively play a greater role in the institution-building in Palestinian society. The union also lobbies to improve conditions for Palestinian women, and to encourage their involvement in the development of their society.

GENERAL UNION OF PALESTINIAN WORKERS (GUPW). This union represents Palestinian workers in the diaspora. Prior to the Oslo Accords (q.v.), the GUPW headquarters were in Tunis, but were later moved to the autonomous areas (q.v.).

GENEVA CONVENTION. See Fourth Geneva Convention

GHOSHEH, SAMIR. Appointed minister of Labor in the Palestine National Authority (q.v.) in July 1994 and June 1996. Born in 1949, Ghosheh is a dentist by profession. In the 1960s, he joined the Arab Nationalist Movement (q.v.), and was imprisoned by Jordan (q.v.) in 1966 and again in 1971. He has been the secretary-general of the Popular Struggle Front (q.v.) since 1971, and a member of the PLO Executive Committee (q.v.).

GOLAN HEIGHTS. A strip of land (64 kilometers) that lies between Jordan and Lebanon (qq.v.). It is about 48 kilometers (30 miles) from Damascus, Syria (q.v.). Israel (q.v.) occupied the Golan Heights in the war of 1967 (q.v). On December 14, 1981, the Israeli Knesset passed the Golan Heights Law, which officially formalized the annexation of the area. Israel then proceeded to build 35 settlements (q.v.) and an urban center there.

Syria and Israel are currently engaged in peace talks. One of the conditions made by Syria, in order to establish peace, is the total Israeli withdrawal from the Golan Heights, and its return to Syrian sovereignty.

GREEN LINE. The border of Israel (q.v.) prior to the war of 1967 (q.v.) that was delineated following the war of 1948 (q.v.), designating the areas under Jewish control in Palestine. It is called the green line because it was drawn on maps at the time with a green marker.

GULF WAR. On August 2, 1990, Iraqi forces invaded Kuwait (q.v.) because of a territorial dispute over two small oil-rich islands (Warba and Bubiyan). Amassing an impressive U.N.-led coalition, the United States and its allies attacked Iraq (q.v.) on January 17, 1991, forced it to withdraw from the Kuwaiti territory that it had occupied, destroyed its military arsenal, and imposed a total economic embargo. Iraqi Scud missiles were fired on Saudi Arabia and Israel (qq.v.), but the latter stayed out of the war at the request of the United States, which wanted to preserve the alliance (which included many Arab countries) it had formed. However, apprehensive that demonstrations and disturbances would break out, Israel moved swiftly and clamped a total curfew on the Occupied Territories (qq.v.). The Palestinians and Jordanians who supported the Iraqi position subjected themselves not only to world criticism, but also put themselves in a financial straitjacket. Of an estimated 400,000 Palestinians in Kuwait, 350,000 were forced out. Also, burdened with the expense of the war and the burning of its oil fields, Kuwait stopped financially supporting Palestinian institutions in the Occupied Territories and the PLO (q.v.). See KUWAIT.

H

HABASH, ASIA. An activist who co-founded with Faisal al-Husseini (q.v.) and others the Arab Studies Society (q.v.). She was born in Jerusalem (q.v.) in 1936, and later attended the American University of Beirut in 1954 and received her B.A. and M.A. in educational psychology. After completing her studies, she taught psychology at the Men's Teacher Training Center in Ramallah (q.v.). In 1975, Habash became the director of UNRWA's (q.v.) Women Training Center in al-Tireh, Ramallah. Forced to resign from the center in 1983 because of policy differences, she became interested in early childhood development and left to study in England. After returning to Jerusalem in 1985, she directed the Early Childhood Resource Center, which is affiliated with the Arab Studies Society. She also is a founding member of the Arab Thought Forum (q.v.) and the Community Psychological Health Center in Bethlehem (q.v.).

HABASH, GEORGE. Nom de guerre, al-Hakim. Co-founder and secretary-general of the Popular Front for the Liberation of Palestine (q.v.). He was born in Lydda, Palestine, in 1925 to a Christian family. After studying at the Greek Orthodox College in Jerusalem (q.v.), he attended the American University of Beirut in Lebanon (q.v.), where he studied medicine. In 1946, he cut short his studies and went back to Lydd. Upset with the defeat of the Arabs in the war of 1948 (q.v.), he formed the *Kataeb Al-Fedaiyeh* (the Commando Battalions) and the Committee for Resisting Peace with Israel, whose objective was the political organization of refugee camps in Lebanon, Syria, and Jordan (qq.v.). A periodical, *Al-Thar* (the Revenge), was published under his direction from 1952 to 1954. Habash helped establish the Arab Nationalist Movement (q.v.), in Beirut. He settled in Jordan, but was forced to leave because of his political activities. He maintained his affiliation with the Arab Nationalist Movement (q.v.) until 1967, when he and a few others formed the Popular Front for the Liberation of Palestine. The faction has been socially and politically active on the West Bank and the Gaza Strip (qq.v.). It has established free clinics for people who are unable to afford medical care. Habash strongly opposes the Declaration of Principles (q.v.) signed by the Palestinians and Israel, and advocates the establishment of a secular democratic state in Palestine. The PFLP did not participate in the PLC (q.v.) elections held in the Palestinian territories on January 20, 1996.

AL-HADAF. Arabic for "the target". A newspaper published by the Popular Front for the Liberation of Palestine (q.v.).

HADDAD, WADI' ELIAS. Born in Safad, Palestine, in 1929, he was educated at St. Luke School in Haifa, Palestine, where his father was the principal. After completing high school, he left to study at the American University of Beirut in Lebanon (q.v.), where he became a member of the Arab Nationalist Movement (q.v.). Together with George Habash (q.v.) and others, he left the ANM to form the Popular Front for the Liberation of Palestine (q.v.), and eventually became its chief military strategist. He is alleged to have masterminded the PFLP's skyjackings in July 1968 and September 1970, and other attacks worldwide.

HAJJ (1). The honorific title given to a person after he has performed the pilgrimage to Mecca, Saudi Arabia (q.v.). It usually precedes an individual's name. Hence, Hajj Amin al-Husseini (q.v.).

HAJJ (2). Arabic for pilgrimage. One of the five rituals of Islam.

AL-HALLAK, OSMAN. Prominent businessman and publisher of *An-Nahar* (The Day) (q.v.). He was born May 5, 1935, in Jerusalem (q.v.), but his family originally came from Turkey. At the age of 15, he left to study in the United States. He received his B.S. in chemical engineering from Ohio State University in 1958 and an M.S. from the University of Southern California in the same major.

Hallak returned to Jerusalem and became a successful business entrepreneur. He started the first pharmaceutical company in 1970 and the first feed mill in the West Bank (q.v.). A salt factory and a refinery to produce industrial and table salt soon followed. In 1973, together with other businessmen, he established a large detergent factory in Ramallah (q.v.) and became vice chairman of AIC Star. He also opened a factory to produce automobile batteries, and is involved in the construction of housing projects for Arabs in East Jerusalem. He also co-owns and edits the daily *An-Nahar*, which he began publishing in 1985. Hallak, who holds pro-Jordanian sentiments, believes that a Palestinian solution must include a federation or a confederation with Jordan, particularly because of the large Palestinian population living there.

HAMAS. The Arabic acronym for *Harakat Al-Muqawama Al-Islamiyeh,* the Islamic Resistance Movement, which is an Islamic political movement that believes all the land of Palestine is an Islamic *Waqf* (qq.v.), consecrated for Muslims until judgment day. It advocates the spread of Islam, and supports extreme militant activities that will lead to the establishment of an Islamic state in Palestine (q.v.), where Islamic laws will be implemented. Furthermore, HAMAS totally opposes any peace initiative with Israel (q.v.), because this would involve renunciation of parts of the land of Palestine, which is *Waqf* (religious endowment) property and is not negotiable.

HAMAS is a highly organized institution. It has a security branch, which is responsible for maintaining order and punishing Palestinians who deviate from the norms of the society. There is a military section that carries out resistance activities against the Israeli occupational forces. A special unit, called Izzedin al-Qassam (q.v.), carries out extreme militant activities against Israel. The unit is organized into cells consisting of two to three members, who work together, independent of others, and whose identities are unknown to each other. The political branch oversees the overall decision-making process.

HAMAS also supports traditional charitable and philanthropic activities, which makes it popular to the masses. In the 1980s, the Muslim Brotherhood in the Gaza Strip (q.v.) held cultural activities, established schools and nurseries, and initiated sports activities. The Israelis, ever eager to establish an alternative to the PLO (q.v.) leadership, nurtured and encouraged HAMAS, which is a wing of the Muslim Brotherhood. When the Intifada erupted at the end of 1987, the Muslim Brotherhood wanted to be included and to garner its share of potential recruits. At this time, the leader of the brotherhood in Gaza, Sheikh Ahmad Yassin (q.v.), a paraplegic confined to a wheelchair and imprisoned by Israel, encouraged the formation of HAMAS, permitted the use of nationalist slogans, and approved the use of violence. HAMAS encouraged its members to participate in the Intifada (q.v.), but not to join the Unified National Leadership of the Uprising (q.v.). HAMAS published and distributed leaflets (q.v.) similar to those distributed by the UNLU. Its activities during the Intifada included: molotov-cocktail throwing, graffiti-writing, stone-throwing, demonstrations, ordering strikes, and violent confrontations. Consequently, HAMAS has emerged as the second-largest political faction in the Occupied Territories after FATAH (qq.v.), and has received a large majority of votes in student, professional, and chamber-of-commerce elections held in the Gaza Strip and the West Bank (qq.v.). On June 18, 1989, Israeli authorities declared HAMAS and Islamic Jihad (q.v.) illegal organizations, and membership in these organizations carried a penalty of up to 10 years in jail.

Today, HAMAS poses a serious challenge to Arafat (q.v.), and questions the legitimacy of the PNA (q.v.). It rejected the Oslo Accords (q.v.), and opposes any compromise with Israel. HAMAS boycotted the elections for the PLC (q.v.) in January 1996, and has demanded total legislative authority for the elected Palestinian council, if it is to participate in any future Palestinian elections and government.

On May 16, 1995, HAMAS issued a leaflet describing the Palestinian Authority (q.v.) as traitors, kowtowing to Israel. It also stated that the Palestinian masses realize this and that "the people will bring the Palestinian Authority to trial . . . ," and "*Jihad* (holy war) will continue to reach every place there is a Zionist." HAMAS is furious about the establishment of the PA security courts (q.v.), designed to bring members of the opposition, primarily HAMAS and Islamic Jihad (q.v.), to trial. HAMAS also refuses to negotiate with the PNA in Gaza for a ceasefire, and rejects the moratorium on attacks that the PNA is pressuring it to accept. Israel claims that HAMAS members train in Gaza, and has exerted pressure on the Palestinian National Auhority (q.v.) to curtail the activities of HAMAS and to collect all weapons in their possession. Consequently, the PNA imposed a May 11, 1995 deadline (later extended to May 15) on the registration of all weapons.

The following are some of the HAMAS activities that have antagonized Israel: In 1992, Nissim Toledano, a border policeman, was abducted and murdered. The Israeli government promptly expelled 415 alleged members of HAMAS and Islamic Jihad to Marj-al-Zuhur, in South Lebanon, because of the organization's suspected involvement in the killing of Toledano. The deportees were doctors, engineers, lawyers, and students, who lived in tents during their exile. However, due to international pressure, Israel was forced to return them after a year. HAMAS is alleged to have carried out the October 9, 1994 kidnapping of Cpl. Nahshon Wachsman, to barter his exchange for the release of Sheikh Yassin from prison. Wachsman was killed in the failed Israeli rescue operation in Beer Nabala, a village adjacent to Jerusalem. During the kidnapping, the Israelis maintained that Wachsman was in Gaza, suspended negotiations with the Palestinians, and pressured Arafat to arrest HAMAS leaders in order to find out Wachsman's whereabouts. Separately, HAMAS members attacked Jerusalem's Nahalt Shiva cafe district killing two people—Mayan Levy, a 19-year old soldier, and Samir Mughrabi, a 35-year-old Palestinian from Qufr 'Aqab—on the night of October 9, 1994. A kamikaze attack was carried out by Salah Abdel Rahim Nazal Souwi on October 26, 1994. He strapped 10 kilograms of TNT on his body, and blew himself up in Dizengoff Square in Tel Aviv. Twenty-two people were killed that day.

HAMAS is said to receive funding from Iran, Saudi Arabia (q.v.), Sudan, and Muslims worldwide. Hamas leaders are based in the West Bank, Gaza, Jordan (q.v.), Syria (q.v.), Iran, and Sudan.

HAMMAMI, JAMIL ABDUL RAHIM. Leader of HAMAS in the Occupied Territories (qq.v.) and the associate director of the College of Islamic Sciences in Abu Dis, Jerusalem. He was born in Ma'an, Jordan (q.v.), in 1952, and later studied at Al-Azhar University in Egypt (q.v.). In 1983, he was appointed the director of *Al-Aqsa* Mosque (q.v.). After two years in that position, he became the director of the *Waqf* (religious endowment) (q.v.) in the West Bank (q.v.), and was assigned to the Bethlehem *Waqf* in 1986.

HAMMAMI, SA'ID. Former PLO (q.v.) representative to London. He was born and raised in Jaffa, Palestine. However, when he was 7 years old, his family fled the city during the war of 1948 (q.v.). He became politically active, and in 1972 was appointed to the PLO post in London. An outspoken moderate, he called for an end to all violent activities against Israel in order to encourage the gradual development of peace. On March 20, 1975, he declared his support for a Palestinian state alongside Israel (q.v.) and peaceful coexistence between the two states. On January 4, 1978, Hammami was assassinated for his support of a negotiated settlement between the PLO and Israel.

HANANIA, GHAZI. Dentist, political activist, and PLC (q.v.) member from the district of Ramallah (q.v.). He was born in Ramallah (q.v.) on September 3, 1945. In 1972, he received an M.S. in dental surgery from the University of Frankfurt, Germany. While at the university, he served as secretary and secretary-general of the Union of Palestinian Students. He founded a branch of the Palestinian Red Crescent Society (q.v.) in 1968 in Germany and Western Europe, and became its president in 1969. Since 1976, he has served as a board member, then chairman, of the Ramallah Library Board. In 1978, he was cofounder, secretary, and later president of the Ramallah Patients' Friends Society. The society provides free medical care to people who cannot afford it, and has also opened clinics in villages that did not have medical facilities. Hanania, with the assistance of Sweden, established the $4 million Abu Rayya Physical Rehabilitation Center in Ramallah for Intifada (q.v.) victims. Hanania also has published works on health under occupation and the political situation in Germany.

HANIYEH, AKRAM. Member of the PLO Higher Committee for the Occupied Territories (q.v.) and a trusted advisor to Arafat (q.v.). He was born in Ramallah (q.v.) in 1953, and attended local schools there. After a short stint as a public-relations officer at Birzeit University (q.v.), he became the editor of *Al-Sha'b* (q.v.) newspaper until 1981. He also was elected chairman of the Arab Journalists Association in 1983. Israel deported him in 1986 for "security reasons." While in exile, he became a close friend and personal assistant to Arafat, advising him on West Bank (q.v.) affairs. He returned from exile after the signing of the Declaration of Principles (q.v.) to assist the Palestine National Authority in the autonomous areas (qq.v.). In 1995, Haniyeh established and is the editor-in-chief of *Al-Ayyam* (The Days), an independent daily newspaper.

HANNOUN, HILMI YOUSUF. The current mayor of Tulkarm (q.v.). He was born in Jaffa, Palestine, in 1913, then moved to Tulkarm (q.v.) with his family during the war of 1948 (q.v.). In 1936, he received a diploma in commerce from the American University of Beirut in Lebanon (q.v.). From 1942 to 1948, he was a member of the joint Arab-Jewish Council responsible for marketing citrus fruits. He served as a member of the Palestinian delegation that traveled to Europe under the auspices of the British Mandate (q.v.) to negotiate marketing citrus fruits. During the Mandate period, he also served as a member of the Jaffa Chamber of Commerce. After the 1948 war, he left for Lebanon, but returned to Tulkarm two years later. In 1959, he was elected a councilman for the Tulkarm municipality. In 1963, when he ran on Jordan's radical National Front Party ticket, he was elected mayor of Tulkarm. When elections were held in the West Bank (q.v.) in 1976, he was re-elected. Hannoun also was a member of the Committee for National Guidance (q.v.), until it was banned by the Israelis in 1982. When Israel fired several municipal councils in 1982, the Tulkarm municipality, in a show of solidarity with the dismissed municipalities, went on strike. But after nine months, the members of the council resumed their work. Hannoun also is active in many charitable societies, including the Palestinian Red Crescent Society (q.v.), and is President of the Islamic Funds Committee.

AL-HAQ. Arabic for "justice". Also known as Law in the Service of Man. The Palestinian human and civil rights organization, and the West Bank affiliate of the International Commission of Jurists in Geneva, was founded in 1979 by Raja Shehadeh (q.v.) and Jonathan Kuttab in the city of Ramallah (q.v.) to monitor Israeli violations of Palestinian human rights. On December 9, 1989, Al-Haq was awarded the Carter-Menile Human Rights Award, together with B'Tselem, the Israeli organization that also monitors human rights violations in the Occupied Territories (q.v.). Al-Haq also gives public lectures and publishes monographs on human rights and laws.

AL-HARAM AL-SHARIF. The Noble Sanctuary, as it is also referred to, includes the *Al-Aqsa* and the Dome of the Rock Mosques, an area comprising 35 acres in the Old City of Jerusalem (q.v.). For the one billion Muslims in the world, the site has been sacred from the time of Muhammad's prophetic call, and subordinate in importance only to the two holy mosques in Mecca and Medina, in Saudi Arabia (q.v.).

In 638 A.D., the Muslims, led by the second Caliph, Omar ibn al-Khattab, conquered Jerusalem. During his stay in the city, Omar discovered the site of *Al-Haram al-Sharif.* He ordered his followers to clean it and use it for prayer, but only "after three sets of rain have fallen on it." It was the Umayyad Caliphate, which ruled the Arab-Islamic empire from Damascus, Syria, between 661 and 750 A.D., that initiated the development of the site as an Islamic center of pilgrimage. The Caliph, Abd al-Malik ibn Marwan, built the Dome of the Rock Mosque on the site, where Muhammad is said to have prayed before he ascended to heaven during the Night Journey. The Koran in Sura 17:1 reads: "Glory be to Him, Who carried His servant by night, from the Sacred Mosque to the Furthest Mosque the precincts of which We have blessed, that We might show him some of our Signs, Surely, He is All-Hearing, All-Seeing." The *Aqsa* Mosque was built in 704 A.D. by al-Walid ibn Abd al-Malik.

According to Jewish tradition, it is also the site of Mount Morieh, where Abraham intended to offer his son Isaac as a sacrifice in accordance with God's command. Later, when the ordeal was over, Abraham called the site "Johovah Tireh" (God will be seen). During the time of King David, the site became a threshing floor belonging to a Jebusite named Ornan. The First and Second Temples, which were destroyed, are believed to have been constructed on parts of the site.

After 1967, an Israeli group known as the "Temple Mount Faithful" challenged the status of the site, which has been under Muslim control since 638 A.D., (the exception being 1099—1187 when it was controlled by the Crusaders) and aspired to destroy the Dome of the Rock and *Al-Aqsa* Mosques, and to build the Jewish Temple there.

Consequently, there has been a great deal of violence and bloodshed at the site. In 1951, King Abdallah (q.v.) of Jordan was murdered at *Al-Aqsa.* On October 8, 1990, Israeli police killed 17 Palestinians and wounded nearly 200 during the protest by Muslims to prevent the followers of the Temple Mount Faithful from placing a cornerstone at the site for the construction of the Third Jewish Temple. On September 27, 1996, three Palestinians were killed by Israeli soldiers and more than 100 injured when clashes broke out over the opening of the Hasmonean Tunnel, that connects the Western Wall (q.v.) with the Via Dolorosa.

HARB, SHAWKI KHALIL. Heart specialist and director of Ramallah Government Hospital. Born in Ramallah (q.v.) on December 13, 1938, he attended the Friends Boys Schools. He studied medicine in Heidelberg, Germany, then went on for surgical training at the University of Florida in 1967. Afterward, he spent a year at Baylor College of Medicine in Texas specializing in thoracic and cardiac surgery. He worked for many years in the United States, and in 1971 founded a branch of the Palestinian Red Crescent Society (q.v.). When he returned to the West Bank (q.v.) in 1975, he was instrumental in setting up heart and chest departments at Ramallah Hospital, and Maqassed and Saint Joseph Hospitals in East Jerusalem (q.v.). In 1976, he became chief of cardiovascular surgery at Ramallah Hospital, and was the first Palestinian doctor to perform open heart surgey in the West Bank. In 1986, he founded and chaired the West Bank

Society of Surgeons, joined the Union of Doctors, and was elected the vice chairman of the Ramallah Hospital Foundation. Between 1976 and 1980, he co-founded the Patients' Friends Society, an organizaton that provides medical care for the needy. Since 1991, Harb has served as a member of the board of trustees of the Friends Schools in Ramallah. He has spoken and written extensively on health conditions under occupation.

AL-HASSAN, HANI. Alias, Abu Tareq. He studied engineering in Munich, Germany, during the 1950s and 1960s, and was active in student politics. He became the leader of the Union of Palestinian Students in Europe, and was elected President of the General Union of Palestinian Students (q.v.). He organized his own guerrila group in Germany, joined FATAH (q.v.) in 1963, and became a close confidant and political advisor to Arafat (q.v.), particularly during times of crisis.

AL-HASSAN, KHALED. Nom de guerre, Abu al-Sa'id. He was born in Haifa, Palestine, in 1928, and completed his secondary education there before fleeing with his family in 1948 to Lebanon (q.v.), then to Syria (q.v.). While teaching school in Damascus, Syria, he tried to organize resistance cells. He was one of the co-founders of FATAH (q.v.), and among the first members of the Central Committee when it was founded in Kuwait (q.v.) in 1965. He also was a close advisor to Arafat, a member of the FATAH Central Council, head of the PNC's (q.v.) Committee for External Affairs, and a member of the PLO Executive Committee (q.v.) from 1968 to 1974. He became the head of the political department of the PLO (q.v.) when FATAH took over leadership in 1969.

Al-Hassan also cultivated relations with Arab and European leaders. He was appointed the head of the External Relations Committee, and guided Palestinian diplomacy in Europe. He spent most of his time in Kuwait (q.v.), where he became a successful businessman and maintained warm relations with its leaders. Al-Hassan was considered the foremost candidate for prime minister of the Palestinian government-in-exile when the state of Palestine (q.v.) was declared in Algiers on November 15, 1988. He disagreed with PLO policy during the Gulf War (q.v.), and opposed Palestinian support of the Iraqi position. Consequently, he withdrew from the inner circle of the PLO and suspended all of his activities with the organization. He also was particularly upset with the secret manner in which the Palestinian-Israeli peace talks took place, and criticized the Declaration of Principles (q.v.). Soon after, he considered forming a new faction that would demand the return of all 1948 refugees (q.v.) to Palestine.

Al-Hassan, a moderate, believed that politics should be the art of the possible. He believed in democracy and the rule of the collectivity, and opposed armed struggle and violence. He envisioned a "Swiss Cantons" solution to the Palestinian-Israeli conflict, rather than an autonomy of the territories, even if the latter would eventually lead to a Palestinian state. Al-Hassan envisioned freedom of movement and residency for both Israelis and Palestinians within a proposed confederacy that would guarantee each individual the right to vote in his own canton. Each canton would have a government, and the representative of each government would be a member of the Central Confederacy Government. A rotation system would guarantee that each representative had a turn as head of the confederacy. Israel would have as its border the 1948 green line (q.v.), and the Palestinian cantons would have the pre-1967 border. Jerusalem (q.v.) would be a separate canton and the capital of the Union of Confederacy. Al-Hassan spent his last years in Morocco. He died of cancer on October 7, 1994 and is buried in the Martyrs Cemetery in Rabat, Morocco.

HAWATMEH, NAYEF. Nom de guerre, Abu Al-Nouf. Secretary-general of the Democratic Front for the Liberation of Palestine (q.v.). He was born in Salt, Jordan (q.v.), in 1934 to a Christian family, and studied in Amman, Jordan. He continued his higher education at Cairo University in Egypt (q.v.) and at the American University of Beirut, where he majored in philosophy and psychology. Hawatmeh was a member of the Arab Nationalist Movement (q.v.) between 1954 and 1969, then joined Habash's Popular Front for the Liberation of Palestine (qq.v.). He was imprisoned in Jordan and Iraq (q.v.) because of his political involvement. He formed his own group in 1969, the Popular Democratic Front for the Liberation of Palestine, which is known today as the Democratic Front for the Liberation of Palestine (q.v.). Hawatmeh is the representative of his faction to the Palestine National Council (q.v.), and serves on the PLO Executive Committee (q.v.). He has suspended his participation in the committee since the Madrid Peace Conference (q.v), however, because of his opposition to the peace process with Israel (q.v.).

HAZBOUN, GEORGE YOUSEF. Born to a Catholic family in Bethlehem (q.v.) in 1943, he received his education at the Terra Sancta School in Bethlehem. After completing his studies in 1960, he went to work in Kuwait (q.v.). Hazboun returned a year later, and became involved with union activities. He co-founded the Union Rights Center, and in 1967 became its secretary. In 1973, he participated in the Conference of Union Movements in the West Bank, where it was publicly declared for the first time that the PLO (q.v.) was the sole legitimate representative of the Palestinian people. Hazboun was elected in 1976 to the Bethlehem municipality, and served as deputy mayor for eight years. In 1983, he was singled out and fired by the Israelis because of his political activtiy. Moreover, he was banned from traveling until 1989. He was a member of the Committee for National Guidance, and is an active member of the Palestine People's Party (qq.v.). Since 1987, he has served as the general-secretary of the Association of the Workers' Unions in the West Bank (q.v.), one of four groups that split from the Palestine People's Party because of disagreements over the distribution of positions and membership in the executive committee. In 1989, the Trade Union Movement resolved its internal problems, and Hazboun was placed in charge of international relations.

HEALTH. Palestinian health conditions have severely declined since the Israeli military occupation began in 1967. The Palestinian health-care system has not evolved to meet the needs of the people, who suffer from stress and anxiety—due to problems of under-development and the Israeli presence—in addition to "modern" sickness such as coronary heart disease, hypertension, diabetes, and cancer. The infant mortality rate is as high as 45 per 1,000. Life expectancy is 66 years.

According to the Union of Medical Relief Committees (q.v.), the Israeli Civil Administration (q.v.) since the early 1990s has spent only about $18.30 per capita on health for the Palestinians, while Israel spends $600 per capita on its citizens. The current hospital bed-to-population ratio for the Palestinians in the West Bank and Gaza (qq.v.) is 1.1 bed per 1,000 persons, while for the Israelis it is 6.1 beds per 1,000 persons. In 1994, the Israeli government's share for health services in the Occupied Territories (q.v.) was less than 28 percent for primary health care and 50 percent for hospital care.

To make up the shortage in health care, and in the absence of a national government, various health-care providers have emerged in the Occupied Territories. They include UNRWA (q.v.)—which caters to Palestinian refugees—charitable societies and clinics established by Palestinian Non-Government Organizations (q.v.), and private medical care. During the Intifada (q.v.), the number of medical facilities and physical rehabilitation centers increased dramatically to serve the many Palestinians who were injured in confrontations with the Israelis.

A National Health Plan was formulated in 1991, the objectives of which include the improvement of health, reducing socioeconomic disparities between the people, and the establishment of an insurance plan for all Palestinians. On December 1, 1994, the Palestine National Authority (q.v.), in accordance with the Declaration of Principles (q.v.), assumed responsibility for the health sector in the Occupied

Territories. The Palestinian National Health Insurance System became operative in the West Bank and Gaza on August 1, 1995. According to figures released from the Gaza Strip, 70,000 Palestinians have already enrolled in the insurance plan, which costs $25 a year; students pay $6.60, and those under 18 pay $15.

HEBRON. One of the most ancient and holy cities in the West Bank (q.v.), Hebron is located south of Jerusalem (q.v.), and has a population of more than 100,000. It is both an important urban community and an agricultural center. It is famous for its grapes, candy-making, and glass-blowing, which has been practiced in Hebron since 4000 B.C. Today, dairy, stone-quarrying, shoe-making, and textile industries also have been established. A conservative Muslim center, it is the location of the *Al-Ibrahimi* Mosque (q.v), built in the seventh century over the Cave of the Machpela, the site of the burial place of the patriarchs and their wives that is venerated by Muslims and Jews.

According to the Oslo Two Agreement (q.v.), the Israelis are to redeploy from the major cities in the West Bank. In 1995, redeployment took place in Ramallah (q.v.), Bethlehem (q.v.), Jenin (q.v.), Tulkarm (q.v.), Qalqilya (q.v.), but not Hebron. The Israelis argued that they did not want to undermine the security of the 450 Jews living in the center of the city. Israeli prime minister, Shimon Peres (q.v.) did not want to jeopardize his chances of winning the May 29, 1996 elections and procrastinated on the issue. When Netanyahu (q.v.) won the elections, he appointed a committee to investigate the matter. See DISTRICTS and Al-IBRAHIMI MOSQUE.

HEBRON UNIVERSITY. The university was established in 1971 by Sheikh Mohammad Al-Ja'bari in Hebron (q.v.). It was the first university to offer a four-year program in the West Bank (q.v.). It began as an Islamic Studies College, and has now expanded to include four colleges: *Al-Shari'a* College, the School of Arts, the School of Sciences, and the School of Agriculture. In 1983, the university was attacked by settlers from Kiryat Arb'a, a settlement (q.v.) in Hebron. Four students were killed and 50 others injured. During the Intifada (q.v.), the university closed from December 1987 until May 1991 by order of Israeli military authorities.

HIGHER COMMITTEE FOR THE OCCUPIED TERRITORIES. A PLO (q.v.) committee responsible for administering the affairs of the Occupied Territories (q.v.). It provided financial and other forms of assistance to Palestinians in the West Bank and the Gaza Strip (qq.v.).

HIGHER ISLAMIC COUNCIL (HIC). A committee established in East Jerusalem (q.v.) in 1967 by a group of religious and political leaders to administer Muslim affairs after the Israeli occupation of the city. It was headed by Sheikh Abd al-Hamid al-Sayyeh (q.v.), until he was deported on September 23, 1967.

HILMI, AHMAD ABD AL-BAQI. Born in 1878 in Sidon, Lebanon (q.v.), he worked for the Ottoman Turks (q.v.) for some years and was appointed the director-general of the Ottoman Agricultural Bank in 1908. A Husseini (q.v.) supporter, he also was appointed the head of the *Waqf* (Islamic endowment) (q.v.). In 1930, he formed the Arab National Bank, and later (1936) served as the treasurer of the Arab Higher Committee (q.v.). After helping to establish the Arab National Fund in 1943, he diverted financial support to the *Istiqlal* Party (q.v.). Hilmi was elected prime minister of the All-Palestine Government (q.v.). Afterward, he was appointed a governor in the Jordanian bureaucracy and a representative of the Arab League (q.v.). He passed away in Egypt (q.v.) in 1963.

AL-HOURANI, ABD-ALLAH. Hourani was born in 1936 in the village of Masmiyeh in Palestine. He fled with his family during the war of 1948 (q.v.) to the Aqabat Jaber Refugee Camp in Jericho (q.v.). Afterward, his family settled in Gaza (q.v.), and he completed his secondary school education in Khan Younis in the Gaza Strip. He left for Syria (q.v.) in 1965, and became the director of the Voice of Palestine (q.v.), which was broadcasting from Syria. In 1967, he joined the PLO and rose in its ranks. He became a member of the PNC (q.v.) in 1969, and the following year was elected to the PLO Central Council (q.v.). In 1973, Hourani was appointed the director-general of the PLO's Information and National Guidance Department. He was imprisoned for six months by the Syrians in 1974. A member of the PLO Executive Committee (q.v.) since 1987, he suspended his membership and boycotted the meetings of the Committee on September 9, 1993, when a vote was to be taken on the Oslo Accords (q.v.), which he strongly opposed. He accepted an appointment as Refugee Affairs advisor to the PNA (q.v.) cabinet in 1996.

HOUSE ARREST. A measure used by Israel to keep a Palestinian confined to his house under the pretext that, by leaving it, he endangers the security of the state. Often, a guard is stationed at the entrance of the house. There are varieties of house arrest, such as prohibiting an individual from leaving his house from sunset to sunrise. It also may be imposed in conjunction with town arrest (q.v.).

HOUSING. Traditionally, Palestinians have built single-family homes around courtyards, and the extended family shared the premise.

Today, because of the scarcity of land and escalating prices, Palestinians have begun to build apartment-style buildings.

Houses are built of stone, and range in price from $100,000 to $1 million. During the Israeli military occupation, mortgages were not available from banks, and family members usually pooled their resources to build a home.

The Palestinian Housing Council now builds housing units and grants long-term loans to Palestinians to allow them to purchase individual apartments—cheaper than building a house and favorable to paying rent.

HULEILEH, SAMIR. Appointed by the PNA (q.v.) in 1994 as director-general in the Department of Trade of the Ministry of Economy and Trade. He was born in Jericho (q.v.) in 1957, and was educated at local schools. He enrolled at Birzeit University (q.v.), where he received a B.A. in economics, in 1982. The following year, he received an M.A. in the same field from the American University of Beirut in Lebanon (q.v.). In 1993, Huleileh was a member of the steering committee and the Palestinian delegate to the multilateral peace talks on regional economic cooperation. He became a member of PECDAR (q.v.) in 1994, and served as the coordinator for the NGOs (q.v.) and the U. N. agencies.

AL-HURRIYAH. Arabic for "freedom". A newsweekly issued by the Palestinian Democratic Front for the Liberation of Palestine (q.v.).

HUSSEIN IBN TALAL, KING OF THE HASHEMITE KINGDOM OF JORDAN. Grandson of Abdallah (q.v.) and son of Talal, who abdicated because of illness on August 11, 1952, in favor of his son. Hussein took up his duties as king in May 1953, at the age of 17. He was born in 1935, and educated at Harrow and Sandhurst Military Academy in England.

An apt statesman and politician and deeply loved by his people, he has transformed Jordan (q.v.) into a modern country, and has seen it through many national and international crises. In the aftermath of the war of 1967 (q.v.), Palestinian refugees (q.v.) fleeing from their homes took up residence in Jordan. In 1970, a confrontation took place between Palestinian commandos (q.v.) and Jordanian forces that resulted in the defeat and expulsion of the PLO (q.v.). Rapprochement efforts with Arafat (q.v.) failed in 1986, and Hussein finalized the separation of the West and East Banks on July 31, 1988, finally giving up his family's claim to the territories. During the Gulf War (q.v.) in 1991, Jordan supported Iraq (q.v.), which angered the United States and the allies, and subjected the king to severe criticism. However, the king later won praise when he approved a joint Jordanian non-PLO Palestinian delegation to the U.S.-sponsored peace talks, and when he signed a peace treaty with Israel (q.v.), in October 24, 1994. King Hussein has appointed his brother, Prince Hassan, as his successor.

AL-HUSSEINI. A prominent Jerusalem clan that championed Palestinian nationalism, and whose members have served as the religious, political, social, and military leaders in Palestinian society. See individaul entries AL-HUSSEINI.

AL-HUSSEINI, ABD AL-QADER. A prominent Palestinian leader, ardent nationalist, the son of Qassem al-Husseini (q.v.), and the father of Faisal al-Husseini (q.v.). He was born in Jerusalem (q.v.) in 1907, and received his higher education at the American University in Cairo, Egypt (q.v.). After he returned to Palestine (q.v.), he founded *Al-Jihad al-Muqaddas* (The Sacred or Holy War), and led the commandos, who were popularly called *Jaish al-Jihad al-Muqaddas* (The Sacred War Army). He also led the Arab Palestinian Revolt (q.v.), and in 1938 was expelled from Palestine by the British. After the 1947 U.N. Partition Plan (q.v.), he became the leader of the military wing of the Palestine Arab Party. When he learned that the underground Hagana fighters had attacked the headquarters of Hassan Salameh (q.v.), a Palestinian commander, and captured Kastel, a village on the outskirts of Jerusalem, he swiftly moved his fighters into the area. The Jewish forces soon began to retreat, and Abd al-Qader mistakenly thought no one remained behind. Consequently, Abd al-Qader and two of his men were killed on April 8, 1948, and Jewish forces were able to recapture the village of Kastel and assume control of Jerusalem.

AL-HUSSEINI, ADNAN. Chairman of the Islamic *Waqf* (religious endowment) in Jerusalem (qq.v.) since 1989. Husseini was born in Jerusalem in 1947, and graduated from al-Ibrahimiyeh High School. He continued his education at 'Ain Shams University in Cairo, Egypt (q.v.), graduating in 1970 with a degree in architecture and civil engineering. When he returned to Jerusalem, he was hired as an engineer by the *Waqf* (q.v.). From 1971 to 1989, he was the director of engineers, and eventually became the chairman. Husseini also is a member of the Reconstruction Committee of *Al-Aqsa* Mosque and on the board of trustees of Al-Quds University (q.v.).

AL-HUSSEINI, FAISAL ABD AL-QADER. The son of Abd al-Qader al-Husseini (q.v.), who led the Palestinian resistance against the British in Palestine (q.v.) from 1936 to 1939, while Abd al-Qader's uncle, Hajj Amin (q.v.), the grand *Mufti* (q.v.) of Jerusalem (q.v.), organized strikes and riots. Faisal was born in Iraq (q.v.) in 1940, where his father, Abd al-Qader al-Husseini, was involved in the Iraqi revolution led by Rashid Ali al-Kilani. When his father was arrested in 1941, he returned with his mother and brother to Jerusalem. In 1942, his father was expelled to Saudi Arabia (q.v.), where his family later joined him. On January 1, 1946, the family left for Egypt (q.v.), and Faisal was able to graduate from a Cairo high school in 1958.

Faisal began his studies in the Science College at the University of Baghdad in Iraq, where his father had earlier received his education. A year later, he moved to Egypt and attended the University of Cairo. He was politically active, and in 1960 was a founding member of the General Union of Palestinian Students (q.v.). It was during this time that he became involved with FATAH (q.v.). In 1964, he returned to Jerusalem and became the deputy manager of the Public Organization Department of the PLO (q.v.). Faisal went to Syria (q.v.) in 1966, and attended the Military College in Aleppo. In 1967, he received a B.A. in military science.

After joining the Palestine Liberation Army (q.v.), he infiltrated into the West Bank (q.v.), where he met with Arafat (q.v.), whose headquarters were then located at the Casbah of the old city of Nablus (q.v.). In October 1967, he was imprisoned for a year by the Israelis and charged with possession of firearms. From 1969 to 1977, he worked as an X-ray technician in Jerusalem and was able to obtain permanent residency there. In 1977, he attended the University of Beirut as a history major. But this was cut short by the Israelis, who imposed travel restrictions upon him. In 1979, Faisal founded the Arab Studies Society (q.v.), which is housed in the new Orient House (q.v.), and he continues to serve as the society's chairman of the board. From 1982 to 1987, he was placed under house arrest (q.v.) after sunset, and town arrest (q.v.) during the day. During this time, Faisal developed numerous contacts with Israelis, particularly members of the peace camp. Between 1987 and 1989, he was placed in administrative detention (q.v.) for a total of 15 months. In October 1991, Faisal was chosen to head the Palestinian delegation to the Madrid Peace Conference (q.v). In 1993, he was appointed to the steering committee of the PLO, along with Saeb 'Erakat (q.v.) and Hanan Ashrawi (q.v.). Faisal currently holds the Jerusalem portfolio in the Palestine National Authority (q.v.).

AL-HUSSEINI, HATEM. Born in Jerusalem (q.v.) in 1941, he left the city in 1948, and began his exile first in Syria, then Lebanon (qq.v.). Studying at the American University of Cairo, he majored in economics and graduated in 1962. He received his M.A. in business administration from Rhode Island University in 1963, and a Ph.D. in political science from the University of Massachusetts in 1969. Afterward, he taught at several American universities: Smith College in 1970, the University of Maryland in 1974, and Shaw University in North Carolina from 1983 to 1989. During that time, he also was politically active. Husseini has been a member of the Palestine National Council (q.v.) since 1977. He also worked as the director of the Palestinian Information Center in Washington from 1978 to 1982, and served as the deputy director of the Palestinian delegation to the United Nations in 1983. He has written extensively. Among his books are *Toward Peace in Palestine* (Washington, 1980), *In Solidarity with the Palestinian People* (Washington, 1980) and *An Annotated Bibliography of the Palestinian Problem* (Washington, 1978).

When his father, Ishaq, who was the president of Al-Quds University (q.v.), died in 1990, Hatem was appointed to replace him. Hatem passed away in Jerusalem on December 27, 1994, at the age of 53.

AL-HUSSEINI, HIND. Founder of *Dar Al-Tifel* (The House of the Child) Society, a refuge for orphans and socially disadvantaged children in East Jerusalem (q.v.) that provides them with a home and an education. She was born in Jerusalem on April 25, 1916. Her father, a judge, died when she was two. Hind finished high school in Jerusalem in 1937, and spent the following year studying Arabic and English. She then taught for a year at the Islamic Girls School. When World War II broke out, her plans of attending a university were put on hold. Al-Husseini became a volunteer social worker in the Women's Social Solidarity Organization in Jerusalem. This organization soon expanded and 22 branches were opened all over Palestine (q.v.). The massacre of Deir Yassin (q.v.) and the war of 1948 (q.v.) left a number of orphaned children. This encouraged Hind to establish *Dar al-Tifel* in Jerusalem. By 1961, the institution ran classes from kindergarten to high school. In 1971, it expanded to include a Center for Education and Social Work, and granted students a diploma after three years of study. The Girl's Art College and the Islamic Research Center were accredited in 1982, and began to grant B.A. degrees. In 1992, a master's program in anthropology and an Islamic Civilization Center were added, and ultimately incorporated into Al-Quds University (q.v.) in East Jerusalem.

Hind al-Husseini was a member of many organizations. She dedicated her entire life to her institution, and bequeathed all her assests to the *Dar Al-Tifel* Society, which has since been renamed after her. She died in 1994.

AL-HUSSEINI, ISHAQ MUSA. Former president of Al-Quds University and father of Hatem al-Husseini (qq.v.). He was born in Jerusalem (q.v.) in 1904, and studied at the American University of Beirut, Lebanon (q.v.). When he returned to Jerusalem in 1926, he taught for a number of years, then left for London. After several years, he returned to Jerusalem, and in 1946 became the director of Education in Jerusalem. During the war of 1948 (q.v.), he left for Lebanon, and taught at the American University of Beirut until 1954, when he was appointed director of the Institute of Arab Studies in Beirut. When he returned to Jerusalem in 1974, he was elected a member of the board of trustees of Al-Quds University's College of Science and Technology. In 1982, he became president of the university's College of Arts. He received numerous awards for his contributions to education; among them, an award for science and arts from Egypt (q.v.) in 1983, and in 1990, the Jerusalem medal of Culture and Arts. He died in December 1990.

AL-HUSSEINI, JAMAL. Palestinian leader, political activist, and author of two books, *Higaz Highway* and *Thurayya.* He was born in Jerusalem (q.v.) in 1892, and attended the American University of Beirut. However, he left before graduating and joined the Turkish army. From 1918 until 1920, he worked for the Ottoman-Turks (q.v.) as secretary in the Department of Health. He also was active in both the Arab Club and the Literary Club (qq.v.). From 1927 to 1930, he served as secretary to the Supreme Muslim Council (q.v.). In 1935, he helped establish, organize, and lead the Palestine Arab Party, and also published the party's paper, *Al-Liwa* (The District). He represented the party at the Arab Higher Committee (q.v.), and became the deputy to the head of the Committee. Husseini also headed the Palestine-Arab delegation to the London Conference (q.v.) of 1939. British authorities soon tired of his political activities and deported him to Rhodesia in 1941. He returned to Palestine in 1946, and became the acting chairman of the Arab Higher Committee (q.v.).

Husseini encouraged armed resistance against Jewish immigrants, and organized *Al-Futuwwa* (q.v.). He also was elected to the All-Palestine Government (q.v.) as the minister of Foreign Affairs. However, shortly after the government collapsed, he left for Saudi Arabia (q.v.), where he became involved in business ventures. He died in Beirut, Lebanon (q.v.), on July 3, 1982.

AL-HUSSEINI, MUSSA QASSEM PASHA (honorable). An important leader in the Palestine national movement, he served as mayor of Jerusalem (q.v.), president of the Palestine Executive Committee, and co-organizer of the Muslim-Christian Association (qq.v.). He also was the father of Abd al-Qader al-Husseini (q.v.). Born in Jerusalem in 1853, he studied in Istanbul and later worked for the Ottoman-Turks (q.v.). In March 1918, he was appointed the mayor of Jerusalem by the British authorities to replace his deceased brother, Hussein. The British however, dismissed him in 1920, when they suspected Husseini of organizing the Palestinian resistance. He became the head of the Arab Executive (q.v.) in December 1920, and held that position until his death. He also was the head of several delegations, trying to negotiate with the British to have the Balfour Declaration (q.v.) revoked, and lobbying extensively against the establishment of a national home for Jews. Moreover, he rejected the British proposal for a legislative council that would over-see the establishment of Palestinian institutions. Husseini suffered injuries during a demonstration he was leading, and died in Jerusalem on March 23, 1934.

AL-HUSSEINI, MUHAMMAD AMIN, HAJJ. The spiritual leader of Palestinian nationalism was born in Jerusalem (q.v.) in 1896. After studying at al-Azhar University in Egypt (q.v.) and in Istanbul, he joined the Ottoman-Turkish army during World War I. On May 8, 1921, the British appointed him the grand *Mufti* (q.v.) of Jerusalem, and two years later he was elected president of the Supreme Muslim Council (q.v.) in charge of administering the Islamic *Waqf* (religious endowment) and *Shari'a* (qq.v.) courts. He held that position until 1937. As the president of the Arab Higher Committee (q.v.), he led several Palestinian delegations to the London conferences (q.v.), where he protested British policies, particularly the Balfour Declaration (q.v.). When the Peel Commission (q.v.) was issued in 1937, the British blamed the Arab Higher Committee (q.v.) for the demonstrations that followed, and arrested many of the members. The Arab Higher Committee was then declared illegal, and Hajj Amin was dismissed as the head of the Supreme Muslim Council. He was forced to leave the country and went to Lebanon (q.v.).

For several years, Husseini ran the resistance from abroad. In 1939, he went to Iraq (q.v.) and assisted in the revolt of 1941. When the revolt failed, he went to Italy and West Germany, where he met with Hitler. Hajj Amin thought that by doing so he would be able to stop the Jews from coming to Palestine. In 1946, he was detained by the French, but escaped to Egypt. He was appointed president of the Arab Executive (q.v.) while in exile. Husseini finally managed to return to Jerusalem, where he discovered that his cousin, Abd-al Qader al-Husseini (q.v.) had been appointed in his place. His spirit broken, he went to Beirut, Lebanon in January 1959. Husseini passed away on July 5, 1974.

I

AL-IBRAHIMI MOSQUE. The Cave of Machpela, or the Cave of the Patriarchs, as it is also called by the Jews, represents a microcosm of the Palestinian-Israeli conflict, and is an example of the difficulties of coexistence that the two peoples face. Located in Hebron (q.v.), it is the burial place of the patriarchs, and considered sacred by both Muslims and Jews. A high structure built by Herod 2,000 years ago encloses the tombs of Abraham, Sarah, Issac, Rebecca, Jacob, and Leah. Some remnants of that structure still remain. The Byzantines built a church at the location in the fourth century, and in the seventh century the Muslims built a mosque. In the 13th century, Jews and Christians were prohibited from entering the area of the mosque.

In the early 1920s, a small Jewish community lived in Hebron, and was allowed access to the seven steps of the shrine. In 1929, disturbances in the *Al-Haram Al-Sharif* in Jerusalem (qq.v.) erupted because the Palestinians feared that the Jews wanted to take over the Western Wall (q.v.), which they saw as an extension of *Al-Haram Al-Sharif*. Before long, the unrest spread to Hebron and 67 Jews were killed.

The situation changed on June 8, 1967, when the city came under Israeli control. The Jews claimed it as their own and demanded access so they could worship there. They pointed out specific references to it in Genesis, Chapter 23, where Abraham paid the Hittites 400 shekels for it.

"Abraham then buried Sarah, his wife, in the cave of the field of Machpela before Mamra. The same is true of Hebron in the land of Canaan."

The first time Jews were authorized to pray there was during Yom Kippur (Day of Atonement) in 1968, when they held Kol Nidre services. A bomb was thrown and 45 people were injured, 15 seriously. In April 1968, Rabbi Moshe Levinger rented a hotel for 70 people in the middle of the city, then refused to move out. Since then, approximately 450 Jewish settlers have taken up residence in the center of Hebron. On October 19, 1968, Jewish settlers began the construction of Kiryat Arba, a settlement (q.v.) on the outskirts of Hebron. In 1971, Jews brought a Torah scroll and placed it in Abraham Hall. Later, the scroll was desecrated. In September 1976, both Jewish and Moslem holy books were desecrated. The Likud government in 1979 gave permission to Jewish worshipers to hold services in Issac Hall, which is considered important because it has two entrances to the cave where the tombs of the Patriarchs are located.

It is in this hall that on February 25, 1994, an Israeli doctor, Baruch Goldstein, a resident of the settlement of Kiryat Arba in Hebron, killed 29 Palestinians and injured hundreds of Muslim worshipers in the mosque during the Muslim holy month of Ramadan. The site was immediately closed by the Israelis. The United Nations (q.v.) condemned the massacre and issued Resolution 904 on March 18, 1994, and stationed the "temporary international observers" in Hebron.

The site was reopened in November 1994, with new arrangements for Jewish and Muslim worshipers. The Muslims were given Issac Hall and the Jalawiya Mosque. The Jews were given Abraham Hall, Jacobs Hall, a corridor for circumcision, and a partly covered courtyard. Moreover, the new arrangements specified that there would be two entrances and different times of prayers for each group. For 10 days a year, each religious group has exclusive access to the site. The new arrangements stipulate that the *Ibrahimi* Mosque is closed to Jews during Muslim prayers, and closed Friday to Jews until sunset. Jews may hold one minyan or prayer quorum in Issac Hall, but as individuals, they may pray all day and at any time. Similar arrangements had been made in August 1975.

According to the Oslo Two Agreement (q.v.), the status quo at the Cave of Machpela is to continue as it is. However, when the Israeli army redeploys from Hebron, special arrangements have been agreed upon whereby the Palestinian police will be responsible for the protection of Israelis visiting the site.

IMAM. For the Sunni Muslims, a Muslim religious leader who conducts sermons, leads prayers, and is in charge of the overall affairs of the mosque. The Shi'ites consider the *Imam* the leader of the Muslim community, or *umma,* who has supernatural qualilties and is a descendant of the Prophet Mohammad's family.

IN'ASH AL-USRA. Society for the Rehabilitation of the Family established by Samiha Khalil (q.v.) to train women in sewing, weaving, secretarial, and other vocations, to help them earn an income and contribute to their families' budgets. The organization today has an annual budget of $500,000, and employs 5,000 women at its headquarters in al-Bireh (q.v.) and throughout the villages of the West Bank (q.v.). The society has five vocational centers, a kindergarten, a day care, and a home for underpriviledged girls. The organization was ordered closed for two years by an Israeli military order in June 1988, because of anti-Israeli literature found there. However, the order was successfully overturned in court. See SAMIHA KHALIL.

INDUSTRY. Palestinian industry can be characterized as stagnant and undeveloped, and has been hampered by Israel's (q.v.) economic policies since its occupation of the West Bank and the Gaza Strip (qq.v.)

in 1967. Israel has heavily taxed raw products imported by Palestinians. It has levied customs on machinery and equipment, and kept them in ports for long periods of time. Israel also has restricted and controlled the marketing of Palestinian products. Israeli businessmen were encouraged to engage in business in the territories through subcontracting small plants and factories, and to employ Palestinian laborers cheaply. Israeli products flooded the markets of the West Bank and the Gaza Strip, which became an important export market for Israel. Palestinians, themselves were apprehensive about investing in industrial projects because of the unstable political climate.

Traditionally, Palestinian industry has included stone-quarrying, which has been concentrated in Jerusalem (q.v.), Hebron (q.v.), and Nablus (q.v.). Manufacturing has included stone-cutting and preparation, foods, beverages, pharmaceuticals, textiles, clothing, and footwear, mainly subcontracting for Israeli firms. There also has been some metal-processing, as well as production of plastics and chemicals. Industrial zones are found in most major cities in the West Bank (q.v.). Factories are mainly small workshops that employ family members or a limited number of workers.

After the signing of the Declaration of Principles (q.v.), the Palestinians hoped that the area would experience rapid industrial development, particularly in the autonomous areas (q.v.). The PNA and Israel agreed to establish nine industrial zones in the autonomous areas (q.v.): three in Gaza and six in the West Bank. Each individual park would be built on 500 dunums (125 acres) and would cost between $70 million and $100 million. The industrial parks would be financed by the U.S., Japan, the European Union, and the World Bank. Altogether, the industrial parks would provide work for 30,000 laborers.

There has been a construction boom. In Gaza (q.v.) in 1994, for instance, $540 million was spent on the construction of 166 new buildings, gas stations, restaurants, and hotels. However, all other indicators show that economically the situation has not improved. Unemployment figures for 1994–1995 in Gaza is 40 percent. Approximately 350 small textile workshops in the Gaza Strip have been forced to close since the PNA (q.v.) took over, and 5,000 workers have been laid off. This is because of the constant closure of the borders by Israel and irregular deliveries. Israel allows 25 trucks for the textile industry to cross into Israel from Gaza per day. In the past, it allowed 45 trucks.

Obstacles to industrial development include the constant closure of the borders with the West Bank and the Gaza Strip. The Tripatrite Agreement signed in Paris on April 29, 1994 between the Palestine National Authority (q.v.), Israel (q.v.), and donor countries grants Israel the right to close the West Bank (q.v.) and the borders of the autonomous areas (q.v.) with Jordan and Egypt (qq.v.) if security matters warrant. Israel also regulates the transfer of goods and the import of raw material, and monitors the crossing points to the autonomous areas. This makes the Palestinian economy (q.v.) vulnerable to Israeli security measures and economic policies.

Other problems facing industrial development of the area include financial assistance pledged by the donor countries that has not yet been disbursed because the donor countries insist on a transparent accounting system. Moreover, potential investors are wary of investing capital in an unstable political environment. See ECONOMY and AGRICULTURE.

INSTITUTE OF PALESTINE STUDIES. Founded in Beirut, Lebanon (q.v.), in 1960. The institute is affiliated with the University of Kuwait (q.v.), and publishes a quarterly called the *Journal of Palestine Studies*, which deals with political, social, and economic issues in Palestinian society.

INTIFADA. The popular uprising or "shaking off" in the Occupied Territories (q.v.) began in December 1987. During the Israeli occupation, the Palestinians experienced every conceivable violation of human rights. They had seen their land confiscated and Israeli settlements (q.v.) built on it; their sons and relatives killed, imprisoned, or deported; their homes demolished; and collective punishments, such as the closures of schools and curfews (q.v.) imposed on entire communities. The Palestinians, frustrated and unhappy under an occupation that deprived them of their rights and subjected them to continuous harrassment and humilation, took matters into their own hands and rebelled.

The Intifada was directly preceded by a series of events that are said to have kindled the uprising. On Sunday, December 6, 1987, an Israeli plastics salesman, Shlomo Sakal, was stabbed to death in Gaza (q.v.). On December 8, 1987, four Arabs were killed and others wounded when an Israeli ran into two vans that were taking Arab workers home to Gaza. Residents of the Jabalya Refugee Camp, where the workers resided, suspected that the killings were intentional. They demonstrated and burned tires. On December 9, 1987, there were more demonstrations, and three youths were killed by Israeli soldiers. The uprising soon spread to all the Occupied Territories (q.v.). Demonstrations, strikes, a boycott of Israeli goods, and general unrest lasted from 1987 to 1993. The Israelis responded with harsher measures: travel restrictions were imposed, limitations were placed on the money that could be brought into the Occupied Territories, schools and universities were closed, there were mass arrests, and the shooting on sight of anyone who was suspect.

The Intifada was directed by an underground leadership, the Unified National Leadership of the Uprising (q.v.), which issued leaflets (q.v.) that provided information and direction to the people. Contact also was maintained with the PLO (q.v.) in Tunis. The objectives of the Intifada were to end the Israeli occupation and establish Palestinian independence. However, the toll was heavy: 40,000 Palestinians arrested; more than a thousand dead; the economy in shambles, as workers observed strike days and were confined to their homes during curfews; and unemployment which reached between 30 percent to 50 percent in the Occupied Territories. There was a decline in gross national product and in per capita income (in Gaza, from $1,700 to $1,200). Remittances no longer flowed in. Kuwait (q.v.) and the other Gulf countries no longer funneled assistance to the PLO or to the Occupied Territories, particularly after the Gulf War (q.v.). Moreover, exports and subcontracting stopped. The local Palestinian leadership began to exert pressure on the PLO to engage in peace talks with Israel, to advocate a two-state solution, and to renounce terrorism.

The Israelis, who had predicted that the Intifada would end the month that it began, also suffered. Forests were burned, cars were torched, kidnapping and killings increased, and, economically, Israel suffered from a decrease in exports to the Occupied Territories, and the burden of an increased military presence in the West Bank and the Gaza Strip (qq.v.). Yitzhak Rabin (q.v.), then defense minister, ordered the "breaking of bones," and any measure necessary to end the Intifada. Israel's image was tarnished as never before.

Altogether, the Intifada reaffirmed Palestinian in the pursuit of their nationalism, and led to fundamental changes in all sectors of Palestinian society. Popular committees for economy, health, and social welfare flourished. See HEALTH.

IRAQ, THE REPUBLIC OF. An Arab country bordered by Iran to the east, Kuwait (q.v.) to the south, Turkey to the northeast, Syria (q.v.) to the west, and Jordan and Saudi Arabia (qq.v.) to the southwest. The area of Iraq is 434,924 square kilometers (167,295 square miles). In the 1980s, Iraq was supported by western countries as it waged war against Iran and acquired an impressive arsenal of weapons. On August 2, 1990, Saddam Hussein, the president of Iraq, invaded Kuwait, claiming that two oil rich-islands on their joint borders belonged to Iraq. An impressive U.S.-sponsored alliance attacked Iraq, and forced it to withdraw from Kuwait in 1991. A total embargo was placed on Iraq. During the Gulf War (q.v.), Saddam Hussein sent a number of Scud missiles to Israel (q.v.), which caused considerable damage, but Israel did not get involved in the war at the request of the United States. The Palestinians, on the other hand, sided with Hussein, and Kuwait (q.v.) responded by expelling 300,000–400,000 Palestinians. Also, Kuwait discontinued its assistance to the PLO (q.v.) and to the Palestinians in the Occupied Territories (q.v.).

ISLAMIC FRONT FOR THE SALVATION OF PALESTINE. A new militant Islamic organization that has modeled itself on Algeria's Islamic Salvation Front. It issued its first leaflet in Gaza (q.v.) on March 25, 1995, threatening "every Jew on the land of Palestine," and launching an attack on the influence of the West as found in cinemas, alcohol, gambling, and prostitution.

ISLAMIC JIHAD. A militant Islamic faction that split from the Muslim Brotherhood (q.v.) in the 1980s. It was formed by Fathi Shiqaqi (q.v.) and Abd al-Aziz Oudeh in the Gaza Strip (q.v.). Islamic Jihad is considered to be more radical than HAMAS (q.v.). Its objectives are to liberate Palestine through armed struggle, and to establish an Islamic state that would replace Israel (q.v.). It participated actively in the Intifada (q.v.), and established relations with the Unified National Leadership of the Uprising (q.v). It has refused any political affiliation with the Palestine National Authority (q.v.), and completely rejects the Declaration of Principles (q.v.), signed between Israel and the PLO (q.v.). It has agreed to a ceasefire for three to six months with the PNA, provided that the following conditions are met: the immediate and permanent release of all prisoners; the dissolution of the special security courts (q.v.) that the Palestinian Authority (q.v) has set up to deal with its opponents; a guarantee of no future arrests; and no confiscation of weapons.

The organization's alleged activities have included the burning of the offices of the Palestinian Red Crescent Society (q.v.) in Gaza in 1980 to protest the politics of its president, Haidar Abd al-Shafi (q.v.). More recently, it has engaged in kamikaze-style tactics against Israeli targets. For instance, it has claimed responsibility for the suicidal bombing in Beit Led, near Netanya in Israel, on January 22, 1994, when 19 Israelis were killed and 60 injured. Support for the organization comes from Iran.

ISLAMIC NATIONAL AL-MASAR MOVEMENT. A new political party whose formation was announced in Gaza (q.v.) on August 13, 1995. It is composed of former HAMAS (q.v.) members, and financially supported by the Palestine National Authority (q.v.). It is led by Muhammad Abu Dan, a former member of Izzedin Al-Qassam (q.v.), who later joined the PNA intelligence.

ISLAMIC RESISTANCE MOVEMENT. see HAMAS.

ISLAMIC UNIVERSITY. Founded in Gaza (q.v.) in 1977 by Sheikh Muhammad Hassan Awad (q.v.), who raised funds from Saudi Arabia and Jordan (qq.v.) to establish the institution. The university plans to have eight colleges in the future, including the College of *Shari'a* (Islamic law), which had been started earlier. This college, which in the past had granted associate degrees, evolved into a teacher-training institute for English language and *Shari'a* instruction. The university in 1990 received accreditation from Al Imam al-Akbar of Egypt (q.v.), and its degree is equivalent to that given by Al-Azhar University in Cairo, Egypt. Three thousand students currently are enrolled at the university, which is said to be a HAMAS (q.v.) stronghold.

ISRAEL, THE REPUBLIC OF. The national home for Jews established by the U.N. Partition Plan of 1947 (q.v.). The state was declared in 1948 at a cost of 418 depopulated Arab villages and 700,000 Palestinian refugees (q.v.), who fled during the war of 1948 (q.v.). Israel's population today is 5.57 million.

Prior to 1967, Israel consisted of 8,000 square miles, bounded to the north by Lebanon (q.v.), to the northeast by Syria (q.v.), to the south by Egypt (q.v.), and to the east by Jordan (q.v.). After the war of 1967 (q.v.), Israel assumed control of the West Bank and the Gaza Strip (qq.v.), as well as the Egyptian Sinai Peninsula and the Syrian Golan Heights (qq.v.). It claimed that the Occupied Territories were part of Eretz Israel (the land of Israel), and began establishing facts on the ground to prevent the territories from being returned to the Arabs in the future. Exclusive Jewish settlements (q.v.) were built in the Occupied Territories (q.v.) and Jewish settlers resided there in contravention of the Fourth Geneva Convention (q.v.).

Israel has a parliament, called the Knesset, and elections are held every four years for political parties. The prime minister comes from the majority party, and is dismissed when his party loses. The president is in office for five years. Israel has no constitution.

Israel's dream of acceptance by its Arab neighbors became reality when it signed a peace treaty with Egypt on March 26, 1979, the Declaration of Principles (q.v.) with the Palestinians on September 13, 1993, and a peace treaty with Jordan on October 24, 1994. Negotiations for peace with Syria and Lebanon currently are underway.

ISRAELI-ARABS. The Palestinians who did not leave Palestine during the war of 1948 (q.v.), and who were eventually given Israeli citizenship. In 1948, the Arabs who remained in Palestine numbered 150,000. Today, their number is estimated to be 810,000, and they constitute 20 percent of Israel's (q.v.) population. They reside in the Galilee, north of Israel, in the Neqab Desert, and in the coastal plains. They also live in the cities of Haifa, Jaffa, Acre, and Nazareth. Theoretically, the Israeli-Arabs are equal to Israeli Jews, but in practice they are not. They do not serve in the army, although both the Druze and the bedouins do. They can, however, vote and run for election to the Israeli parliament, or Knesset.

ISTIQLAL (1). Arabic for "independence". A weekly newspaper that first appeared in Gaza (q.v.) in October 1994 and was licensed by the Palestine National Authority (q.v.). It is supported by Islamic Jihad (q.v.). One of its co-editors, Hani Abed (q.v.), was assassinated by a car bomb believed to have been placed by the Israeli secret service soon after the magazine was established. The other editor is Ali al-Saftawi, the son of As'ad al-Saftawi, a FATAH (q.v.) supporter who was assassinated in 1993 in the Gaza Strip.

ISTIQLAL (2). A party founded after World War I that supported Amir Faisal (q.v.) in Damascus, Syria (q.v.), when he wanted to unite the Arabs. Later, it became a group that advocated pan-Arab unity. On August 2, 1932, Awni Abd-al-Hadi and Izzat Darwazza (qq.v.) co-founded the first independent Palestinian political party, and called it *Istiqlal.* Its purpose was to organize resistance against British policies, and it comprised professionals and youths. It eventually became inactive, but re-emerged in the 1940s in opposition to the establishment of the Arab Party.

J

AL-JA'BARI, MOHAMMAD ALI, SHEIKH. Born and raised in Hebron (q.v.), he was elected mayor of that city in 1948 and held that post until 1976. He was the leader of the Jericho Conference, at which notables and mayors met on December 1, 1948, and approved King Abdallah's annexation of the West Bank (qq.v.). Known for his partiality to Jordan (q.v.), he was nominated to serve in the Jordanian government in the 1950s; he served three terms as cabinet minister for Jordan. A savvy politician, he also maintained good relations with Israel (q.v.), and was one of the first to advocate a political solution after the war of 1967 (q.v.) between a "Palestinian entity" and Israel based on the 1947 U.N. Partition Plan (qq.v.). He suggested a transitional period of five years during which the Israelis would redeploy their forces, and the Palestinians would have autonomy. Jordan rejected his plan, and called him a traitor for encouraging negotiations between Israel and the Palestinians. Relations between him and King Hussein (q.v.) soured in 1969. However, he continued to maintain close ties with Jordan. He died on May 29, 1980.

AL-JA'BARI, NABIL MOHAMMAD. President of the board of trustees of Hebron University (q.v.), a member of the Palestinian Red Crescent Society (q.v.), and founding member of the Society of the Friends of the Sick established in 1980. The son of Sheikh Mohammad Ali al-Ja'bari (q.v.), he was born in Hebron (q.v.) in 1945. Educated in England, he earned a B.S. in dental surgery from London University in 1973, and worked for two years in London hospitals. When he returned to the West Bank (q.v.), he worked in Ramallah Hospital for six months, then opened his own clinic in East Jerusalem (q.v.). In 1988, he was imprisoned for two months for political activities. Appointed a member of the Palestinian delegation to the Madrid Peace Conference (q.v.), he participated in two rounds of talks.

AL-JA'BARI, SULEIMAN, SHEIKH. The former *mufti* (q.v.) of Jerusalem (q.v.), born in Hebron (q.v.) in 1912. After completing his education at al-Azhar University in Cairo, Egypt (q.v.), he returned to Palestine and worked in the educational system in Jaffa, Lydd, and Hebron. He then worked in the *Shari'a* (q.v.) Courts in Jaffa, Saffad, and Lydd. During the British Mandate (q.v.) of Palestine (q.v.), he was appointed the deputy *mufti* of Jerusalem. Later, he was authorized by Jordan's Ministry of Education to work in Saudi Arabia and Qatar to jump-start the educational system there. After completing his assignment, he returned and served as a counselor for the Department of Education in Jerusalem, Hebron, al-Bireh, and Ramallah (qq.v.) until his retirement in 1975. Jordan appointed him the deputy *mufti* of Jerusalem and later *mufti* to the Jordanian army. He became the *mufti* of Jerusalem on March 20, 1993, and remained in that position until he died on October 11, 1994.

AL-JAM'IYYAH AL-FILASTINIYYA. Arabic for the "Palestinian Society". An organization established in Syria (q.v.) in 1919. The purpose of the society was to unite and coordinate Arab support for the Palestinian cause. Sheikh Abdel Qader al-Muthaffar and Izzat Darwazza (qq.v.) were among the founders of the orgaization.

AL-JAM'IYYAH AL-ISLAMIYYEH. Arabic for the " Islamic Society". An Arabic daily newspaper that was published in 1931 by Suleiman al-Farraj, a religious leader from the city of Ramleh, Palestine. It supported the Nashashibi (q.v.) clan politics. Publication of the newspaper was stopped when its owner died.

JARRAR, BASSAM. A leader of HAMAS (q.v.) in the West Bank. Born in 1951 to a landowning family in Jenin (q.v.). His great grandfather, Yousef, led the attack against Napoleon when the French invaded Palestine (q.v.), and his father worked as a customs official for the Jordanian government. Jarrar had his first religious experience when he called the prayer from the minaret of a mosque at the age of 12. His father tried to dissuade him from studying religion, wanting him instead to study law or medicine. Currently an instructor at Ramallah Teachers College, an UNRWA (q.v.) institution, he teaches international relations, economics, and Islamic culture. He also serves as the *imam* (religious leader) (q.v.) of the Ramallah Mosque, where he is known for his charisma, oratory skills, and powerful influence over youth. Also, Jarrar is a member of the Higher Islamic Council (q.v.). He has been interrogated and imprisoned by Jordan (q.v.), and placed under house arrest (q.v.) by Israel (q.v.). He also was one of the 415 Palestinians that Israel deported to Lebanon (q.v.) for a year in 1992.

JENIN. A city on the West Bank with a population of 21,840. It is bound to the north by the Israeli cities of Beisan, Nazareth, and Haifa; to the east by Beisan and Nablus (q.v.); to the south by Nablus and Tulkarm (q.v.); and to the west by Haifa and Tulkarm. It also is where the Arabs first resisted the British Mandate (q.v). The city is surrounded by fertile land, that yields wheat, olives, chick peas, corn, sesame seeds, watermelon, and grapes. The Israelis redeployed from the city in November 13, 1995, in accordance with the Oslo Two Agreement (q.v.). See also DISTRICTS.

JERICHO. The oldest city in the world, Jericho or—*Riha* (aroma), as it is called in Arabic, because of the fragrant blossoms of the citrus fruits grown there—is an agricultural center and winter resort, with a population of 13,774. It is 1,300 feet below sea level. The Canaanite city of the Old Testament was discovered in Jericho in 1907. Places of interest include the 8th century Hisham Palace, built by the Ummayyads, and Mount Temptation, where Jesus is said to have fasted 40 days and nights after his baptism.

According to the DOP (q.v.), signed between the Israelis and Palestinians, Jericho and Gaza (q.v.) became the first Palestinian autonomous areas (q.v.) under the Palestine National Authority (qq.v.) on May 17, 1994. See DISTRICTS.

JERUSALEM. *Al-Quds Al-Saharif* in Arabic. The holy city is sacred to Christians, Jews, and Muslims. The holy places for the Christians include the Church of the Holy Sepulchre; the traditional site of the crucifixion and the tomb of Jesus; the Via Dolorosa, with its stations of the cross; the Cenacle, or the room where the last supper is said to have taken place; the Mount of Olives; the Dormition Church, which, according to tradition, where Mary died; the Garden of Gethsemane; and the Church of the Ascension. The holy places for the Muslims include *Al-Haram Al-Sharif* (q.v.), with *Al-Aqsa* and the Dome of the Rock Mosques. For the Jews, there is the Wailing or Western Wall (q.v.), which borders the area of *Al-Haram Al-Sharif.*

The city also is at the heart of the Arab-Israeli conflict. Between 1920 to 1948, Jerusalem grew and eventually became the capital of Palestine (q.v.). The different religious groups began to build and develop their institutions in the city. Before long, Muslims clashed with Jews over the Western Wall, which the Muslims considered part of *Al-Haram Al-Sharif.*

There were more Jews than Arabs in the city. However, to appease the Arabs, British officials in Jerusalem appointed only Arab mayors: Mussa Qassem al-Husseini (q.v.) from 1918 to 1920; Ragheb al-Nashashibi (q.v.) from 1920 to 1934; Hussein al-Kahlidi (q.v.) from 1934 to 1937; and Mustafa al-Khalidi (q.v.) from 1937 to 1944. This, however did not stop the continuous Arab protests and disturbances against Jewish immigration and land acquisitions. Finally, exasperated by the situation, the British introduced a plan in 1937 that would partition Palestine into two parts, and place Jerusalem under British control. But it was unanimously rejected. In November 1947, the United Nations passed Resolution 181, calling for the partition of Palestine, into an Arab state and a Jewish state. Jerusalem would be internationalized and placed under a U.N. Trusteeship Council. Needless to say, this plan was rejected by both Jews and Arabs. On December 11, 1947, the U.N. General Assembly reiterated that Jerusalem was to be placed under U.N. auspices. The Arabs rejected the plan and entered into a war with the Jews.

When the fighting broke out, Jordan (q.v.) joined the war. King Abdallah of Jordan (q.v.) had earlier negotiated a secret pact with Jewish leaders; one of the conditions was that Abdallah would not fight them on territory given to them by the U.N. Partition Plan (q.v.). However, the agreement had not included the city of Jerusalem. The city and adjacent villages became the center of the war. Finally, on May 28, 1948, the Jews surrendered.

On December 1, 1948, Jordan took over the territory of the West Bank and East Jerusalem (qq.v.), with the exception of a small area on Mount Scopus, which included the Hebrew University and Hadassah Hospital. An Israeli-Jordanian Armistice Agreement signed on April 3, 1949, formalized the partition of Jerusalem into east and west sections. A committee was formed to arrange access to the holy places for all three religions. However, the committee was ineffective, and access to East Jerusalem (q.v.) was denied to the Jews, except for a small group that regularly went to Mount Scopus under U.N. protection. The Arabs could not enter West Jerusalem.

On three separate occasions—December 1948, December 1949, and in 1950—the U.N. General Assembly called for the internationalization of Jerusalem under the auspices of the United Nations. Both Jordan and Israel rejected these proposals. In 1950, Jordan annexed East Jerusalem. Israel had already moved its parliament, the Knesset, to West Jerusalem in 1949. On January 23, 1950, Israel declared Jerusalem its capital, and began to establish facts on the ground by setting up institutions and various government offices there. Most foreign embassies, however, kept their offices in Tel Aviv.

After the war of 1967 (q.v.), both the U.N. General Assembly (July 4 and 14, 1967, May 1968 and July 1969) and the Security Council (May 21, 1968, and July 3, 1969) passed a series of resolutions calling on Israel (q.v.) to stop its annexation of the eastern part of the city, and not to change the status of Jerusalem. To no avail. On June 29, 1967, Israel placed East Jerusalem (q.v.) under its jurisdiction, and on June 30, 1980, it completely annexed the city, and began uniting it to prevent its division in the future. Settlements (q.v.) were built in and around Jerusalem, and building permits were denied to the Arabs to ensure a Jewish demographic majority in the city. Hence, Jerusalem was physically united, but spiritually and ethnically divided. The international community did not recognize the annexation of Jerusalem.

Israel did, however, give the Palestinians in East Jerusalem (who according to the Israeli Central Bureau of Statistics in 1993, numbered 160,700 of the city's total population of 567,000) control over their holy places, in addition to the right to apply for Israeli citizenship and the right to vote in municipal elections.

The war for Jerusalem rages on. The Israelis unequivocally state that Jerusalem will never again be divided, and the Palestinians say it is the capital of their future Palestinian state. Various solutions to resolving the conflict have been proposed, ranging from the borough system to the internationalization of the city. In the Declaration of Principles (q.v.), both sides have agreed to address the issue of Jerusalem in the final stages of negotiations, which are to begin no later than May 1996. A Jerusalem committee, headed by Faisal al-Husseini (q.v.), has been set up by Arafat (q.v.) to oversee the affairs of East Jerusalem. Moreover, in June 1995, Arafat revitalized the 1967 East Jerusalem municipality that Israel had dissolved on June 29, 1967 and appointed Dr. Amin Majjaj (q.v.) as mayor of East Jerusalem. To counter the influence of the Palestine National Authority (q.v.) in East

Jerusalem, Israel, in turn, has banned the establishment of PNA offices there.

JERUSALEM REVIEW. A Palestinian journal published in 1932 that expressed the views of a group of Arab intellectuals who advocated Arab unity to resist the Zionist threat to Palestine (q.v.). The journal was banned and its publication stopped in 1936 by an order of the British Mandate (q.v.) authorities.

JERUSALEM TIMES. Also *Biladi* (My Country) Jerusalem Times. An English weekly that appeared in February 1994 and is published by Hanna Siniora (q.v.). See also AL-FAJR.

JIBRIL, AHMAD. The founder and leader of the PFLP-GC (q.v.). He was born in the village of Yazur, near Jaffa, Palestine, in 1936, but his family moved to Syria (q.v.) during the war of 1948 (q.v.) and became refugees (q.v.). Jibril eventually entered the Syrian Military Academy, where he majored in engineering. He became a member of the Palestinian underground in the early 1960s, when he served as an agent for Syrian military intelligence, and where he perfected his skills in military and operational planning. In 1961, he formed the Palestine Liberation Front (q.v.) which joined forces with the PFLP (q.v.). Differences over policy surfaced, and in 1969 Jibril broke away from the PFLP to form the PFLP-GC, a small faction within the PLO (q.v.) that was very much against Arafat's (q.v.) politics. Jibril is based in Damascus, Syria, and oppposes Arafat's peace initiative.

JIHAD AL-ISLAM. see ISLAMIC JIHAD.

JOINT JORDANIAN-PLO COMMITTEE. The Committee formed on November 15, 1978, at the ninth Arab Summit in Baghdad, Iraq, in opposition to the Camp David Accords (q.v.). It was to provide financial assistance to the Palestinians in the Occupied Territories (q.v.) and to strengthen their steadfastness, despite the many Israeli restrictions imposed on them that resulted in a lack of credit, housing shortages, and high unemployment. The committee also transferred funds to the West Bank and the Gaza Strip (qq.v.) to be used for the investments and economic development that eventually would lay the infrastructure for a Palestinian state. A special fund, *Sumud*, or the Steadfastness Aid Fund, was set up. In 1983, financial assistance also was extended to Israeli-Arabs (q.v.) to help them improve their conditions in Israel (q.v.).

JORDAN. The Hashemite Kingdom of Jordan is a constitutional monarchy ruled by King Hussein I (q.v.) of the Hashemite family, who trace their descendents back to the lineage of the Prophet Muhammad. Jordan is located in the southwestern part of Asia, at the northwestern edge of the Arabian Peninsula. It is surrounded to the west by Israel and the Occupied Territories (qq.v.); to the north by Syria (q.v.); and to the east by Iraq and Saudi Arabia (qq.v.). Its area is 91,740 square kilometers, or 35,468 square miles. Jordan annexed the West Bank and East Jerusalem (qq.v.), an area of 5,878 square kilometers, or 2,270 square miles, in 1950. Jordan was forced to renounce its claim to the West Bank at the Arab Summit in Rabat, Morocco, on October 28, 1974, after passage of a unanimous resolution declaring the Palestine Liberation Organization (q.v.) to be the sole legitimate representative of the Palestinian people. On July 31, 1988, Jordan cut all legal and administrative links with the West Bank. This caused a problem for the 50 percent to 60 percent of the population of Jordan who are Palestinians and who reside in Jordan. Jordan's overall population is about 4 million.

After the defeat of the Ottoman-Turks (q.v.) in World War I, the territory of Jordan was part of the Syrian Kingdom that was given to Faisal I (q.v.). The French, in defeating Faisal I in 1920, dissolved the union he had created and took over the administration of the territory. The territory of Transjordan was included in Britain's Mandate of Palestine, and Abdallah (q.v.), Faisal's brother, was given Transjordan rule in 1921. The British also gave him assurances that in return for his loyalty Transjordan would not be affected by the establishment of a Jewish state in Palestine. Abdallah agreed to go along with the British, and Transjordan was made a constitutional monarchy in 1928. A treaty signed on March 22, 1946, created the Hashemite Kingdom of Transjordan, which was changed to Jordan in 1949. Transjordan opposed the U.N. Partition of Palestine (q.v.), and joined the Arab countries fighting Israel in 1948. At the end of the war, Abdallah occupied the West Bank, the territory that had been given to the Palestinians under the U.N. Partition Plan (q.v.), and annexed it to his country in 1950. When King Abdallah was assassinated in Jerusalem in 1951, his son Talal ruled for a year, but was forced to abdicate because of illness. Talal's son, Hussein I (q.v.), came to the throne at the age of 17.

In the Six-Day War of June 1967 (q.v.), Israel defeated Jordan's forces and occupied the West Bank. Palestinian refugees flowed into Jordan. Palestinian commando groups established bases in Jordan, much to Israel's chagrin. Consequently, Israel made Jordan its adversary. In 1970, a civil war between Jordanian forces and the PLO (q.v.) resulted in the expulsion of the PLO from Jordan. It is estimated that several thousand Palestinians were killed in the confrontation. However, throughout the 28 years of occupation, Jordan has maintained an "open bridge policy" (q.v.) with Israel, allowing people and goods to enter its territory.

When Israel and Egypt signed a peace treaty in 1979, Jordan broke diplomatic ties with Egypt until 1984. Hussein and Arafat launched a peace effort in 1985, but their efforts failed in 1986 due to pressure from the various Palestinian organizations. In July 1988, Jordan formally severed its ties with the West Bank after harsh criticism by the Palestinians and the failed efforts at rapprochement. King Hussein began a policy of democratizing Jordan. He held legislative elections in 1989, abolished martial law, which had been imposed in 1967, and introduced a new national charter that removed a 1957 restriction on the formation of political parties.

Jordan refused to join the allies in the 1991 Persian Gulf War (q.v.), and was ostracized by the allies. However, Hussein was lauded for agreeing to form a delegation of Jordanian and non-PLO Palestinians to attend the U.S.-sponsored peace negotiations at the Madrid Peace Conference (q.v.). The negotiations eventually culminated in the signing of a Jordanian-Israeli peace treaty on October 26, 1994, ending decades of hostility between the two countries.

JUDEA AND SAMARIA The biblical term that Israel (q.v.) uses for the West Bank (q.v.).

K

KAFAITY, RT. REV. SAMIR. The Anglican bishop and the president-bishop of the Central Synod of the Episcopal Church in Jerusalem (q.v.) and the Middle East. The Right Reverend Samir Kafaity was born in Haifa in 1933. He received his education at the Friends Boys School in Ramallah (q.v.), and later studied at the American University of Beirut, Lebanon (q.v.), and at the Near East School of Theology. In 1957, he was ordained at St. George's Anglican Cathedral in Jerusalem. He became archdeacon in 1974, and in 1982 was made coadjutor bishop in Jerusalem. On January 6, 1984, he became the 12th Anglican bishop in Jerusalem. This placed the Diocese of Jerusalem, which includes the West Bank, Gaza, Israel, Jordan, Syria, and Lebanon (qq.v.), under his jurisdiction. Moreover, his election as president-bishop of the Central Synod of the Episcopal Church in Jerusalem and the Middle East has placed him in charge of three dioceses: the diocese of Egypt, which includes Egypt, Algeria, Libya, Tunisia, Ethiopia, and Somalia; the diocese of Cyprus and the Gulf, including Iraq, Saudi Arabia, and the Gulf states; and the diocese of Iran. This has extended his administration over the entire Christian community in Palestine and the Middle East, which is estimated at 12 million.

Active in ecumenical affairs, he has been the president of the Middle East Council of Churches since 1985 and also is the vice-moderator of the World Council of Churches Commission on Inter-Church Aid, Refugees, and World Service. Furthermore, he spearheaded the change of the Near East Council of Churches to the Middle East Council of Churches in 1974, and was elected one of the presidents in 1985. Bishop Kafaity has been honored with many awards and tributes. In 1985, he received the Doctor of Sacred Theology from Dickinson College in Pennsylvania and the Doctor of Divinity from the Virginia Theological Seminary, and was made Honorary Canon of the Cathedral Church of St. John the Divine, New York.

KAFFIYEH. The traditional black-and-white headdress worn by men that has become a symbol of Palestinian nationalism. It is worn by Arafat and members of FATAH (qq.v.). Arafat often would arrange it on his forehead, after putting on the *ekal* (the black headband to hold the *kaffiyeh* in place) in the shape of the map of Palestine (q.v.). A red-and-white *kaffiyeh* was worn during the Intifada (q.v.) by members of the leftist Palestinian factions. The *kaffiyeh* also was placed on the dashboards of cars belonging to Palestinians who are residents of East Jerusalem (q.v.) and whose cars have yellow license plates like the Israelis, to identify them as Palestinians. (West Bank (q.v.) residents have blue license plates.)

KAMAL, ZAHIRA. A prominent activist and a member of the executive committee of the Palestinian Federation of Women's Action Committees, formerly the Palestinian Union of the Women Works Committee (q.v.). She has been closely identified with the Democratic Front for the Liberation of Palestine (q.v.), Abed Rabbo's faction, and is a member of Fida (qq.v.).

Kamal was born in Jerusalem (q.v.) in 1945. She received a B.S. in natural science from 'Ain Shams University in Egypt (q.v.) in 1968, and a teaching diploma from the University of Jordan in 1977. After returning to the West Bank (q.v.), she taught physics at UNRAWA's (q.v.) Teacher Training Center For Women. She was placed under administrative detention (q.v.) in 1979, then town arrest (q.v.) from June 1984 to March 1986 because of alleged hostile activities against the state of Israel (q.v.). Amnesty International adopted her case and lobbied on her behalf. In 1988, together with other leaders of women's organizations, she helped establish the Higher Council of Women to ensure the protection and rights of women in a Palestinian state. She was one of 13 Palestinians who met with members of the

U.S. State Department Policy Planning staff, and with John Kelly, the U.S. assistant secretary of state, on August 3, 1989, to discuss Palestinian issues. Kamal also was a member of the steering committee for the Madrid Peace Conference (q.v.). She ran for an East Jerusalem seat in the PLC (q.v.) elections, but was not elected.

KANAFANI, GHASSAN. Political activist and author of short stories and novels, such as *Men in the Sun and Other Palestinian Stories* (London, 1978). He was born in Acre, Palestine, in 1936 and studied at the Friar College in Jaffa, Palestine. During the war of 1948 (q.v.), he went with his family to Lebanon and then to Damascus, Syria (qq.v.), where he completed his education. After working in Kuwait (q.v.) for some years, he returned to Beirut, Lebanon, and worked as a journalist and editor for several newspapers. He wrote novels, short stories, and poetry that dealt with Palestinian history and society. Politically active, he served as a member of the political bureau of the PFLP (q.v.) and as its spokesperson, and published the faction's paper, *Al-Hadaf (q*.v.). He was killed in Beirut on July 8, 1972, when his booby-trapped car exploded, allegedly the work of Israeli agents.

KAN'AN, SA'ID MISBAH. A prominent businessman and political activist, he was born in Nablus (q.v.) in 1940. He attended the American University of Beirut, Lebanon (q.v.), where he received a B.A. in economics in 1963. While at the university, he served as the secretary of the Union of Palestinian Students and supported the Arab Nationalist Movement (q.v.). He returned to Nablus and worked at the Jordan Vegetable Oil Company in 1966. He then went to work in Saudi Arabia, and headed the Popular Committee for the Assistance of the Families of Palestinian Martyrs. In 1973, he returned to Nablus and started an animal fodder plant. From 1978 to 1981, he was the representative of the Palestinian Red Crescent Society (q.v.) in Nablus and a member of the executive committee of the Palestinian Red Crescent Society. He also served as a member of the board of trustees of *Al-Fajr* (q.v.) newspaper and chaired An-Najah National University's (q.v) Friends Society. Kan'an was also one of the founders in 1973 of the West Bank National Front (q.v.), and is closely associated with FATAH (q.v.). Mahmoud Abbas (q.v.) claimed in his memoir in 1994 that Kan'an had met 20 times with Ephraim Sneh to help the Labor Party snare Arab-Israeli (q.v.) votes and win in the 1992 Israeli elections.

KARA'EEN, IBRAHIM MOHAMMAD. Journalist, co-founder of the Palestinian Press Services (q.v.), and editor of *Al-Awdah* (q.v.), a magazine that the P.P.S. publishes. He was born in Silwan, a suburb of Jerusalem, in 1947, and studied English literature at the Hebrew University in Jerusalem (q.v.). Kara'een taught high school from 1967 to 1977. He has been the president of the Palestine Council for Culture and Media since 1992.

AL-KARAMEH, THE BATTLE OF. The battle that took place on March 21, 1968 in the village of Karameh, east of the Jordan River, where Palestinian commandos (q.v.) had established a base. The battle between Israel, the Palestinian commandos, and the Jordanian army lasted 15 hours, and effectively blocked Israel from entering the East Bank. The battle is considered important to the Palestinians because, together with the Jordanians, they were able to hold their own with Israel. Moreover, it motivated a large number of volunteers to join the Palestinian *feda'yeen* organizations (q.v.).

AL-KARMIL. The first Palestinian nationalist newspaper. It was established in Haifa in 1908 by Najeb Nasser.

KHALAF, KARIM HANNA SAM'AN. Former mayor of Ramallah (q.v.) who was an ardent supporter of the Palestine Liberation Organization (q.v.). He was the leading figure in the Palestine National Front and the National Guidance Committee (qq.v.). Born in 1938, he came from a wealthy Greek Orthodox Christian family. He was educated at Cairo University Law School and worked from 1967 to 1972 as a criminal attorney in the Israeli military courts in the West Bank (q.v.). Soon after, he was appointed as attorney general of Ramallah and became a judge in Jericho (qq.v.). He resigned in 1976 to run on the nationalist PLO (q.v) platform for the municipal elections and was elected mayor of Ramallah. A bomb was planted in his car by Jewish underground organizations on June 2, 1980, that exploded and left him crippled. In March 1982, he was dismissed from his mayoral post by Ariel Sharon (q.v.), then Israeli Minister of Defense. He died from a heart attack in Jericho on March 30, 1985.

KHALAF, SALAH. Nom de guerre, Abu Iyyad. One of the founders of FATAH (q.v.) in the 1950s and chief of PLO (q.v.) security and counterintelligence. He was born in Jaffa, Palestine, in 1933, and left for Gaza (q.v.) in 1948. He attended the University of Cairo in Egypt (q.v.), where he became a close friend of Arafat (q.v.) and helped establish the General Union of Palestinian Students (q.v.) in Cairo in 1952. In 1956, Khalaf spent time in Kuwait (q.v.), where he taught high school. After the war of 1967 (q.v.), Khalaf left for Syria (q.v.). When fighting erupted between Palestinians and the Jordanian army in September 1970, he was arrested in Jordan (q.v.) and sentenced to death. The sentence was not carried out because of Arab and, particularly, Egyptian pressure. The experience understandably left him with a lot of anti-Jordanian hostilities, and Khalaf later helped establish the Black September Organization (q.v.). He was considered the number three man after Arafat and Khalil al-Wazir (q.v.) in the FATAH (q.v.) hierarchy. He was killed on March 14, 1991.

KHALED, LEILA. One of the first Palestinian women commandos to take part in an anti-Israeli attack. She participated in the abortive hijacking of an Israeli El-Al airplane, which failed because of the presence of Israeli security guards on the flight. She was captured, but released, and now lives in Syria (q.v.). Khaled is a member of the Palestine Front for the Liberation of Palestine (q.v.) and secretary-general of the General Union of Palestinian Women. She returned to the autonomous areas (q.v.) on April 18, 1996 to participate in the PNC (q.v.) meeting convened to amend the Palestinian charter (q.v.). An account of her experiences is in her book, *My People Shall Live: An Autobiography of a Revloutionary* (London, 1973).

AL-KHALIDI, AHMAD SAMEH. Prominent educator and brother of Hussein al-Kahlidi and father of Walid al-Khalidi (qq.v.). He was born in Jerusalem (q.v.) in 1896. Employed by the British in the Education Department, he became the principal of the Arab College of Jerusalem. In 1941, he was appointed deputy director of Education. He introduced many innovative educational methods in the Palestinian school system, and emphasized the importance of Arabizing the curriculum. He died in 1951.

AL-KHALIDI, HUSSEIN FAKHRI. He was born in 1894 and studied medicine at the American University of Beirut, Lebanon (q.v.). After completing his studies, he worked in Aleppo, Syria (q.v.). When he returned to Palestine (q.v.), he became mayor of Jerusalem from 1934 to 1937. Fakhri also established the Reform Party (*Hizb Al-Islah*) in 1935, and became its representative to the Arab Higher Committee (q.v.). He was exiled in 1937 to the Seychelles Islands along with other nationalists for inciting the rebellion and revolts in Palestine. After his release, he went to Lebanon (q.v.). Khalidi participated in the London Round Table Conference (q.v.) in 1939, where he objected to the British White Paper (q.v.). When he returned to Palestine in 1943, he was appointed to the new Arab Higher Committee formed by the Arab League (q.v.). After the war of 1948 (q.v.), he joined the "All-Palestine Government" (q.v.), but soon resigned and departed to Jordan (q.v.). In the 1950s, he was appointed a cabinet minister in the Jordanian government. He passed away on December 26, 1962.

AL-KHALIDI, GHALIB, SHEIKH. Prominent judge and founder of the Khalidiyeh Library in East Jerusalem (q.v.) in 1900, which has many collections of valuable books. He was born in 1866 and studied Islamic jurisprudence. He was appointed by the Ottoman-Turks (q.v.) as a member of the district court and of the Council of Education in the Jerusalem District. In 1920, during the British Mandate (q.v.), he was appointed a judge. Three years later, he became a member of the Central Court in Haifa and Jaffa. He retired in 1929.

AL-KHALIDI, WALID AHMAD. Prominent professor, leading authority on the Arab-Israeli conflict, and a PLO (q.v.) supporter. He was born in Jerusalem (q.v.) in 1925, where his father, Ahmad al-Khalidi (q.v.), had earlier served as mayor. Educated at Oxford, Walid began his career by working in the Arab Information Offices founded by Alami (q.v.). In 1960, he helped establish the Institute of Palestine Studies (q.v.) and served as its secretary-general. He also taught at the American University of Beirut in Lebanon. In 1970, Harvard University invited him to become a senior research fellow at the Center for Middle Eastern Studies. He has written several books and is renowned for his intellectual abilities. During the '80s, he was one of the few Palestinian-American professors whose name was proposed to serve as a representative in any future negotiations with Israel (q.v.). He also was a member of the Jordanian-Palestinian delegation to the peace talks with Israel.

KHALIFA, SAHAR. Activist and novelist. She wrote *Wild Thorns* and *The Sunflower*, describing the position of women and life under Israeli occupation. Born in Nablus (q.v.), she attended Birzeit University (q.v.) and worked in the public-relations office. Afterward, she left for the United States and received a Ph.D. from the University of Iowa. Upon her return to the West Bank (q.v.), she became the director of the Womens' Research Center in Nablus. Khalifa has always championed women's rights in the Palestinian community, and has been criticized because she writes of society's oppression of women.

KHALIL, SAMIHA SALAMEH. Um Khalil, as she is popularly called, is president and one of the founding members of In'ash al-Usra (the Society for the Rehabilitation of the Family) (q.v). She was born in 1923 to a landowning family in Anabta, Tulkarm (q.v.), where her father was mayor. They later moved to 'Asqalan, Palestine, in the 1940s. At the age of 17, she married Samir Khalil, who was a school principal, and moved with him to Gaza (q.v.) in 1948. They eventually found their way back to Anabta, and in 1952 finally settled in al-Bireh (q.v.), where she was one of the founders of the Women's

Union of al-Bireh. Samiha finished her high-school examinations with her son and went to Beirut, Lebanon, to study Arabic literature, leaving her mother in charge of her children. She first set up In'ash al-Usra in a garage in 1965, and started classes in sewing, weaving, embroidery, secretarial courses, and hairdressing to help women master a vocation, earn money, and contribute to their family income.

Samiha Khalil also is a member of the Council For Higher Education (q.v.) and on the coordinating Committtee of the Charitable Organizations of Jerusalem, Nablus, and Hebron (qq.v.). She has been a member of the Palestine National Council (q.v.) since 1965. She also is a member of the Union of Voluntary Women's Societies and the General Union of Palestinian Women (q.v).

Khalil was imprisoned for a month by the Israelis on alleged charges of incitement, and was banned from traveling from 1972 to 1978. In the '80s, she was placed under house arrest (q.v.) for two and a half years. On January 20, 1996, she ran in the election for the presidency of the PNA (q.v.), but lost to Arafat (q.v.).

AL-KHATIB, ANWAR. Former mayor of Jerusalem (q.v.) in the 1950s, Jordanian ambassador to Egypt (q.v.), and governor of Jerusalem. Born in Jerusalem to a landowning family, Al-Khatib was chosen mayor of Jerusalem in the 1950s. Loyalty to King Hussein (q.v.) of Jordan in the 1960s earned him the ambassadorial post to Cairo in 1963. He later became affiliated with the Arab Socialist Party. He passed away in Jerusalem on February 7, 1993.

AL-KHATIB, GHASSAN ABDULWAHAAB. Political activist and leading member of the Palestine People's Party (q.v.). He was born in 1954 in Nablus (q.v.). Immediately after graduating from high school was imprisoned by the Israelis for four years. After he was released, he enrolled at Birzeit University (q.v.) and graduated in 1982 with a B.A. in economics and business administration. Al-Khatib worked as an academic assistant at Birzeit University from 1982 to 1985. He continued his education in England, where he received an M.A. in 1986 from Manchester University in developmental economics. Afterward, he returned to the West Bank (q.v.), where he lectured at Birzeit University.

During the Intifada (q.v.), he established the Jerusalem Media and Communication Center to facilitate the work of journalists and interested groups on fact-finding missions who wanted to meet with Palestinians. Al-Khatib also served as the director of the United Agricultural Company, which provides agricultural know-how, marketing strategies, and interest-free loans to small farmers. In return for these services, the company receives agricultural produce that it sells to wholesale markets.

Al-Khatib was a member of the Palestinian delegation to the peace talks. He participated in many conferences, among them the NGO (q.v.) Conference held in 1988 in Geneva; the 1989 Symposium on Israeli-Arab Dialogue in Jerusalem (q.v.); and the February 1989 meeting with Israeli officials in the Notre Dame Hotel in Jerusalem (q.v.).

AL-KHATIB, RAWHI. A former mayor of East Jerusalem (q.v.) who was elected in 1963 and deported by the Israelis on March 7, 1968. He was born in Jerusalem in 1914, and studied at al-Rashidiyeh High School and at the English College in Jerusalem. His family, formerly known as al-Kanani, settled in Jerusalem in the 12th century and became preachers at *Al-Aqsa* Mosque (q.v.). Al-Khatib taught briefly at the Islamic Orphanage School in Jerusalem. He worked for the Department of Immigration in Palestine in 1931; for the Department of Labor Affairs from 1943 to 1945: and headed the Arab Office of Information that Alami (q.v.) established in Jerusalem from 1946 to 1948. After the war of 1948 (q.v.), he organized the Arab Hotels Incorporation, became chairman of the board and helped establish al-Zahra Hotel, the first Arab-owned hotel in Jerusalem. Al-Khatib also encouraged the Palestinians to organize the Jerusalem Electric Company in 1956. He became a member of the first municipal council of Jerusalem in 1951, and mayor as a Jordanian appointee in 1957. Israel (q.v.) deported him to Jordan (q.v.) in 1968. He was allowed to return in October 1993, one month after the signing of the DOP (q.v.).

KHAZMO, JAQUES YOUSEF. Publisher and editor of *Al-Bayader As-Siyyasia* (q.v.), a political weekly that supports the PLO (q.v.). He was born in Jerusalem (q.v.) in 1951, and went to the St. George School in Jerusalem. He attended the American University of Beirut, Lebanon (q.v.), and majored in chemistry. From 1977 to 1982, he was director of the Catholic Relief Services and Rural Development, a reporter for *Al-Fajr* (q.v.), and also a schoolteacher at the Lutheran Schools. He founded *Al-Bayader As-Siyassia*, and was the first to hire an Israeli correspondent to write a weekly column. *Al-Bayader* is also the name of the cultural and literary monthly that Khazmo publishes. He also established *Al-Bayader*, a publishing company. Khazmo is a member of the Association of Journalists, and serves as secretary-general of the Syriac Welfare Clinic in Bethlehem (q.v.).

KUWAIT. A constitutional monarchy, this small Arab country has become important because of the discovery of oil in its territory. Located at the northwestern end of the Persian Gulf, its area is about 17, 800 square kilometers or 6,500 square miles. In 1899, while still under the rule of the Ottoman-Turks (q.v.), Kuwait became a British protectorate. It declared its independence in 1961, and was governed by the Sabah family. The following year, a constitution was approved. In 1975, Kuwait nationalized all the oil companies and embarked on an ambitious development program that has transformed and modernized the country. With economic development, there came the need for a labor force, which had to be imported. Palestinians, Egyptians, Jordanians, and others flocked to the country. Kuwait also established the Fund for Economic Development, which has contributed significant amounts of money to neighboring Arab countries.

In August 1990, Iraq (q.v.) invaded Kuwait because of a territorial dispute over the two oil-rich islands of Bubiyan and Warba. This soon led to the Gulf War (q.v.) in 1991, when Iraq was attacked by a U.S.-led alliance.

Iraq had long had designs on Kuwait and claimed that it was part of its territory. Kuwait thereafter requested British protection. In 1963, Iraq finally recognized Kuwait's independence. However, it still demanded control of some territory on the borders and particularly the two islands. In the '70s, there were many confrontations over territory between Kuwait and Iraq. However, during Iraq's war with Iran in the '80s, Kuwait provided financial assistance to Iraq because it too felt threatened by Iran. Iraq's occupation of Kuwait in 1990 devastated the country's economy, particularly because its oil wells were set on fire. The PLO (q.v.) supported the Iraqis, and consequently some 300,000 to 400,000 Palestinians were expelled from Kuwait. Not only were these Palestinians deprived of their jobs, but Kuwait also stopped its considerable financial assistance to the Occupied Territories (q.v.) and the PLO.

L

LABOR. The Palestinian labor force is unskilled and does not possess technical know-how. Laborers are employed part-time and change jobs frequently. During the occupation, Palestinian laborers were forced into the Israeli labor market, which needed cheap, unskilled workers. Figures released in 1993 by the Democracy and Workers' Rights Center in the West Bank (q.v.) put the total number of workers at 339,000. Of these, 90,000 are in the West Bank, 60,000 in Gaza (q.v.) and 189,000 in Israel (q.v.). The latter figures were drastically reduced, given the recurring closure of Israel (q.v.) to workers from the Gaza Strip and the West Bank (qq.v.). In April 1995, Israel imported about 60,000 foreign workers from abroad and employed only 28,000 Palestinians. Consequently, the unemployment rate for Gaza jumped to 40 percent and for the West Bank, to about 30 percent. Recently, it has begun to decline due to the expansion of the construction sector in both the Occupied Territories and the autonomous areas (qq.v.). The PNA (q.v.) has created jobs for 68,000 people in the Palestinian territories.

LAND DAY. On March 30, 1976, Israeli-Arabs (q.v.) held a general strike to protest the confiscation of their land by Israel (q.v.). Six Arabs were killed and 70 injured when Israeli soldiers opened fire on demonstrators in Nazareth. The event, declared a national day, is commemorated annually on March 30 by Palestinians in both Israel and the Occupied Territories (q.v.).

LEAFLETS. Numbered bulletins and handbills that were distributed during the Intifada (q.v.). They informed and directed the Palestinians on how to resist the Israelis. At the beginning, the leaflets were anonymous. But in January 1988, they were signed by the Unified National Leadership of the Uprising (q.v.). The leaflets gave instructions on how to confront the Israelis, demanded that the Palestinian police force resign, ordered that all purchases of Israeli goods stop, encouraged the development of a domestic economy, and ordered the strike days. The leaflets were written by the UNLU and faxed to Tunis, where they were modified and approved by the PLO (q.v.) leadership. Then the *shabibeh* (q.v.) would distribute them during the night all over the Occupied Territories (q.v.).

Leaflets also were issued by HAMAS (q.v.), independent of the UNLU. A "war of leaflets," took place between the UNLU and HAMAS, but it quickly ended when it became apparent that the divisive leaflets were part of an Israeli ploy to cause strife among the Palestinian factions.

LEBANON, THE REPUBLIC OF. An Arab country known for its beautiful mountains and beaches. It is bounded to the south by Israel (q.v.), to the north by Turkey, to the east by Syria (q.v), and to the west by the Mediterranean Sea. Lebanon is a small country with an area of 4,015 square miles (approximately 130 miles long and 30 miles wide). The population of Lebanon is 3.5 million, composed of Muslims and Christians of various sects and denominations. In an agreement called the National Pact of 1943, the president of Lebanon was to be a Maronite Christian, the prime minister a Sunni Muslim, and the speaker of the assembly a Shi'ite Muslim. In 1944, Lebanon became independent and free from the French Mandate that had been in control since 1920. After the signing of the Cairo Agreement (q.v.), the PLO (q.v.) established Fatahland in the 'Arkoub area near the Golan Heights (q.v.). Supported by Lebanese Muslims, Druze, and Greek Orthodox Christians, they would often target Israel. In May 1973, the Lebanese army, in a futile attempt to restrict the PLO (q.v.) from assuming too much power in Lebanon, clashed with the organization.

In 1975, the Lebanese Civil War began. It devastated Lebanon and divided the people; Muslims against Christians, radicals against conservatives, Palestinians against Christian Phalangists. The war raged and an estimated 60,000 persons were killed, and the Lebanese economic infrastructure was destroyed. On August 12, 1976, Christian militia laid siege to Tal al-Za'tar, a Palestinian refugee camp, killing 3,000 Palestinians. Israel invaded South Lebanon in 1978, and placed a Christian Phalangist, Major Sa'ad Haddad, in control of the area. Syria also decided to enter Lebanon in an attempt to restore order. In 1981, Syria reached an agreement with Israel, whereby it would control the PLO in South Lebanon and stop the attacks on Israel. However, Israel soon took matters into its own hands and, in July 1981, conducted an air raid on Beirut, killing 300 civilians. In June 1982, Israel initiated "Operation Peace for Galilee" and invaded Lebanon. The Israeli army laid siege to Beirut for 79 days, ending it on August 30, 1982. The international community arranged for the safe evacuation of the PLO from Lebanon. A massacre occurred from September 16–18, 1982, when the Phalangists entered the Palestinian refugee camps of Sabra and Shatilla and slaughtered an estimated 2,000 men, women, and children. Israel, assisted by Lebanese Major Anton Lahad, who assumed control after Major Sa'ad Haddad's death, remains in control of Southern Lebanon.

Lebanon participated in the Madrid Peace Conference (q.v.), and is engaged in negotiations with Israel.

LITERARY CLUB. *Muntada al-Adabi* in Arabic. A nationalist movement founded in January 1919 by Hassan al-Dajani in Jerusalem (qq.v.). The movement was both anti-British and anti-Zionist, and it received the support of the French. The Literary Club advocated the idea of a Greater Syria united with an independent Palestinian state under the leadership of Faisal I (q.v.). Most of its members were young and came from the Nashashibi (q.v.) family. The Black Hand, an underground organization that planned and carried out resistance activities against the British in 1920, is said to have been under the control of the club.

LONDON CONFERENCES. A series of conferences held in London and attended by Palestinians, Arabs, and representatives of the British government to discuss Jewish immigration to Palestine and the problems arising from it. In 1920, a conference was held to protest the Balfour Declaration (q.v.). In 1930, another conference was convened to denounce Jewish mass immigration and land acquisitions, and to discuss establishment of a Palestinian government. In February-March 1939, the Round Table Conference was assembled at St. James's Palace. It was attended by British, Palestinian, Jewish, and Arab representatives, who attempted to reach an agreement that would be favorable to all parties in Palestine. However, they failed to reach a compromise.

M

MADRID PEACE CONFERENCE. The conference held in Madrid, Spain, from October 30 through November 1, 1991, under the auspices of the United States and the Russian Federation that launched the Middle East peace process. A number of events led to the convening of the conference: the collapse of the Soviet Union; the U.S.-led alliance that inflicted a humiliating defeat on Iraq (q.v.) in the Gulf War (q.v.) of 1991; and the reaffirmation of the U.S. position, after the Gulf War, as the only superpower in the world. The Palestinians, who supported Iraq, realized they had allowed too many opportunities to slip through their hands, and agreed to attend the conference as part of a joint Jordanian-non-PLO delegation.

The groundwork for the conference was arranged by U.S. Secretary of State James A. Baker III, in the administration of President George Bush. The framework for the negotiations were the following: comprehensive peace based on U.N. Security Council Resolution 242 and 338 (qq.v.); direct bilateral negotiations between Israel and the Arab countries of Jordan (q.v.), Syria (q.v.), and Lebanon (q.v.), and between the Palestinians and the Israelis; and the convening of multilateral negotiations on issues of regional importance, such as security, water, refugees, the environment, and economic development.

The Madrid Conference culminated in the signing of the Declaration of Principles (q.v.) between the Palestinians and Israelis, and the peace treaty between Jordan and Israel (q.v.).

MAJJAJ, AMIN. Medical doctor, former deputy mayor of the East Jerusalem (q.v.) municipality, and later mayor, when the Israelis deported Rawhi al-Khatib (q.v.) in 1967. Majjaj was born in 1921. After studying medicine, he returned to Jerusalem (q.v.), where he set up his practice. He was first elected to the Jerusalem city council in 1950. When Jordan (q.v.) appointed him as health minister in 1964, he resigned his post in the municipality. After the war of 1967 (q.v.), Israel (q.v.) abolished the East Jerusalem council. However, Majjaj continued to represent the city of Jerusalem in the Jordanian parliament until 1988, when Jordan severed its legal and administrative ties with the West Bank (q.v.).

PNA (q.v.) Chairman Yasser Arafat (q.v.) reactivated the pre-1967 East Jerusalem municipality with the surviving members of the 12-member city council in June 1995. Arafat reappointed Majjaj as mayor. The municipal members had included Rawhi al-Khatib, mayor (deceased); George Khader, deputy mayor (deceased); Amin Majjaj; Nihad Abu Gharbiyeh; Musa al-Bitar; Faeq Barakat; Subhi Ghosheh and Zaki al-Ghoul (the last two members are in Jordan). The appointment is symbolic, because the status of Jerusalem is to be discussed during the final stage of negotiations with Israel (q.v.), according to the DOP (q.v.). The Palestinians assert that this action was taken in accordance with a letter of assurances from Israeli Foreign Minister Shimon Peres (q.v.) and given to his Norwegian counterpart, Jorgen Holst (who has since died), in which the Israeli government promised to protect Palestinian institutions in the Holy City.

MAJLESIYOUN. Arabic for "councilmen". *Majlesiyoun* was the term used to designate supporters of the Husseinis (q.v.) who were mainly religious officials and the intelligentsia, and primarly resided in the urban areas in Palestine (q.v.).

AL-MALKI, RIYAD NAJIB. Political activist and former spokesman for the Popular Front for the Liberation of Palestine in the Occupied Territories (qq.v.). Although his family is from Kufur Malik, a village adjacent to Ramallah (q.v.), he was born in Bethlehem (q.v.) in 1955. After completing high school, he left for Austria, where he stayed for six months before leaving for Latin America. Malki received his B.A. from a university in Colombia in 1978. He later studied in the United States, and received his Ph.D. in civil engineering from the Polytechnic Institute of New York in 1986. Malki also was a professor of civil engineering at Birzeit University. He co-founded and is the director of the Center for the Dissemination of Alternative Information (Panorama), which has been active in setting up democracy workshops in the Occupied Territories (q.v.).

MANDATE SYSTEM. see BRITISH MANDATE.

MANDELA INSTITUTE FOR PALESTINIAN POLITICAL PRISONERS. A Palestinian human rights organization established in 1990. A non-profit and non-partisan institute, it was founded by a group of

Palestinian doctors, lawyers, and clergymen. The objectives of the institute include lobbying on behalf of Palestinian prisoners and their families; improving the living conditions of the detainees; ensuring their legal and human rights; and monitoring cases of illness and solitary confinement among the prisoners. The institute also keeps detailed, up-to-date accounts of prisoners. Mandela publishes *Samed: Palestinian Prison Voices,* a bi-monthly newsletter that provides information about political prisoners.

MANSOUR, SULIEMAN ANIS. An aspiring artist, born on July 27, 1947, in the village of Birzeit to a Christian family. In 1962, Sulieman won an award for a painting that he submitted to the U.N. Childrens' Paintings for Peace. He attended Betzalel Academy for Arts in Jerusalem from 1967 to 1970, but did not graduate. Mansour then taught at al-Tireh, the UNRWA's Women Training Center in Ramallah (qq.v.). In 1981, he joined Birzeit University (q.v.) and also began to do freelance work. He drew cartoons, illustrated books and conducted research on folklore for In'ash Al-Usra (q.v.). He has co-authored a book, with Nabil Anani, called *Palestinian Costumes* (1984) and another entitled *A Directory of the Art of Palestinian Embroidery* (Jerusalem, 1989)

The Intifada (q.v.) affected Mansour's work, and he began to experiment with local products and to mix mud with hay, painting it with whitewash mixed with colors, as the Palestinian peasants had done for years to their outdoor ovens. He translated politics into art, and played an important role in transmitting Palestinian ideas and culture, as well as developing Palestinian art. Exhibitions of his work have been held regularly. Together with other Palestinian artists, he has co-founded an art society, and opened a center in East Jerusalem called al-Wasiti, named after an Arab artist who lived in the 12th century.

AL-MASRI, HIKMAT. A longtime member of the municipal council of Nablus (q.v.), president of the deanship of An-Najah National College, and a successful businessman, president of the Vegetable Oil Company in Nablus. He was born in Nablus in 1906, and attended An-Najah National School. He studied economics at the American University of Beirut and graduated in 1929.

An ardent Palestinian nationalist, al-Masri served as the treasurer of the National Committee in Nablus in 1936, which helped coordinate the Arab-Palestinian revolt (q.v.) of 1936 in Palestine (q.v.). Consequently, the British imprisoned him for incitement with other Palestinians in Sarafand. Al-Masri was one of the founders of the PLO (q.v.) in 1964 and vice president of the first Palestinian National

Council (q.v.). Working for the Jordanian government bureaucracy, he became a military governor. Later, he served two terms as president of the Jordanian parliament, and was appointed minister of agriculture. Elected president of the Jordanian Senate, he held that position until 1988, when Jordan (q.v.) severed administrative and legal ties with the West Bank (q.v.). He also led the team that established An-Najah National University (q.v.) and was elected president of the board of trustees. He passed away on December 13, 1994.

Al-MASRI, MA'ZUZ. Born in Nablus (q.v.), he was first elected to the Nablus municipal council in 1945. He then became deputy mayor, then mayor until 1976. Al-Masri was appointed the deputy director of the first chamber of commerce in Nablus in 1935, and later became the director, a position he held until 1965. A successful entrepreneur, he established wheat mills and a match factory in Nablus. He was one of the founders in 1965 of the Jordanian Vegetable Oils Company, and became its chairman.

Al-Masri served on the board of trustees of numerous organizations, among them the *Shar'ia* (q.v.) College and the Society for Arab Orphans in Nablus. He was involved in philanthropic activities and contributed to many welfare and social organizations. He built two schools in Nablus—one named after him, the other after his wife, Rujda. He died in August 1994.

AL-MASRI, ZAFER. Former mayor of Nablus (q.v.) who was assassinated because of his political moderation. He was born in Nablus in 1942 to a wealthy and influential family. Educated in Nablus and then the American University in Beirut, he received a B.A. in business administration in 1963. A prominent businessman, he was elected the chairman of the Nablus Chamber of Commerce in 1973. In 1976, he became a council member in the Nablus municipality, and later the deputy mayor. He resigned from that post in 1981. However, Israeli authorities appointed him as the mayor of Nablus in November 26, 1985. He encouraged the PLO (q.v.) to engage in diplomacy to explain the Palestinian situation to the world public. He was assassinated on March 2, 1986, allegedly by a member of the PFLP (q.v.) for being too accommodating to the Israelis. Raghida al-Masri, Zafer's widow, was deported from the West Bank (q.v.) by the Israelis on June 9, 1988. She was accused of smuggling large sums of money into the West Bank to support the Intifada (q.v.).

AL-MATARI, MOHAMMAD ARAFAT DAOUD. Actor, whose stage name is Ghassan Matar. He was born in Jaffa in 1940, and left Palestine (q.v.) in 1948 for Lebanon (q.v.) with his family. He graduated from the College of Islamic Studies in Tripoli, Lebanon. At the age of 13, he distributed *Al-Thar* (the Revenge) newspaper, which was published by the Arab Nationalist Movement (q.v.). The Egyptian revolution, led by Gamal Abd al-Nasser (q.v.), affected him greatly. He was arrested once for reading a speech by Nasser to a group of illiterate men. The speech encouraged people to blow up oil pipes. One man took it literally, and blew up the pipes in Tripoli, Lebanon. Matar himself was accused of incitement and was imprisoned briefly for that offense. In 1956, he was in charge of the youth groups *Nahr al-Badya* and *al-Bidawi*, which were affiliated with the Arab Nationalist Movement. Currently residing in Cairo, he has served as the secretary-general of the Palestinian Artists Association, and is a member of both the PLO Central Committee and the PNC (qq.v.).

MEDIA. Palestinian newspapers published during the British Man-date (q.v.) include *Filastine* and *Al-Dif'a* (q.v.). After 1948, *Akhbar Filastine* circulated in the Gaza Strip (q.v.), and *A-Dif'a* merged with *Al-Jihad* to form *Al-Quds* in the West Bank. In 1965, *Al-Dustour* evolved from the merger of *Filastine* and *An-Nahar*. Two weeklies also were published: *Al-Masa* and the *Jerusalem Times* (q.v.) which appeared in English.

After the war of 1967 (q.v.), the newspaper business came to a halt. In November 1968, *Al-Quds* (q.v.) was permitted to resume publication. This was followed by a weekly, *Al-Fajr* (q.v.), in 1972, which became a daily in 1974. A weekly English edition called *Al-Fajr* was also published. *Al-Sha'b* and *An-Nahar* (qq.v.) soon followed.

Weeklies include *Gesher* (bridge), which appears in Hebrew and is published by Ziyad Abu Zayyad (q.v.); *Al-Tali'a* (q.v.); *Al-Usb'u al-Jadid* (The New Week); *Al-Bayader as-Siyasiya* (q.v.); and a women's magazine, *Abeer*. Journals included *Al-Kateb* and *Al-Raed al-Iqtissadi*, the latter dealing with economic issues. In the autonomous areas (q.v.), the Palestine National Authority publishes *Al-Aqsa* and *Al-Hayah Al-Jadidah* (The New Life). Faction papers with permission to publish include *Filastine* (independent); *Al-Watan* (The Nation), a HAMAS (qq.v.) publication, *Al-Istiqlal* (Independence), issued by the Islamic Jihad; and *Al-Thawra*, a FATAH (q.v.) supported publication. Two independent daily newspapers have recently appeared in the Palestinian territories: *Al-Ayyam* (The Days), founded in 1995 by Akram Haniyeh (q.v.) and *Al-Bilad* (The Country), established on December 13, 1995.

The Palestine Broadcasting Corporation headed by Radwan Abu Ayyash (q.v.) is responsible for the planning and administering of the Palestine Authority's (q.v.) radio and television broadcasts. The Voice of Palestine (q.v.) radio broadcast includes news, music, current events, and discussions about social problems. Palestinian television was launched in Jericho, Bethlehem, Jerusalem, and Ramallah on June 8, 1995. Since then, private television and radio stations also have begun operations.

MILHEM, MUHAMMAD. Abu 'Ala, as he is known, is an independent member of the PLO Executive Committee (q.v.) and the former mayor of Halhul, a city on the West Bank (q.v.). He was born in 1929 and studied in Jerusalem (q.v.) and at the University of Lebanon. Upon his return to the West Bank (q.v.), he taught school in Halhul until he became mayor. Elected on the PLO nationalist slate in 1976, he was very outspoken and forthright. He often met with foreign representatives and spoke out against Israel's (q.v.) oppressive policies in the Occupied Territories (q.v.). On May 2, 1980, together with Fahd al-Qawasmi (q.v.), the mayor of Hebron, he was deported by the Israelis to Lebanon (q.v.). After his deportation, he served as the head of the PLO Committee of the Occupied Homeland (West Bank and Gaza) and the PLO Higher Education Department.

MIRAT AL-SHARK. Arabic for "Mirror of the East". A daily newspaper that was published from 1919 to 1939. It was the mouthpiece of the National Party that was formed by the Nashashibis (q.v.) on November 9–10, 1923. The paper criticized both Hajj Amin al-Husseini (q.v.) and British policy in Palestine. However, it did call for cooperation with the British government to achieve Palestinian self-rule. *Mirat Al-Shark*'s office was burned in 1925, but it continued to be published.

AL-MITHAQ. Arabic for "covenant". A daily newspaper owned by Sufian and Mahmoud al-Khatib. It was regarded as the mouthpiece of the Palestinian Front for the Liberation of Palestine (q.v.). It was closed by the Israelis on August 12, 1986.

MU'ARIDIN. Arabic for the "opposition". Nashashibi (q.v.) supporters, who came from the villages and were mainly *fellaheen* (peasants). The group was organized to challenge and check the influence of the Husseinis (q.v.), who formed the *Majlesiyoun* (q.v.).

MUBARAK, MOHAMMAD HOSNI. Politician, military man, and the president of Egypt (q.v.) since October 1981. He was born in 1928 and educated in Egypt. He attended the Military College and the Air Force Academy from 1951 to 1961. He was appointed the commander-in-chief of the air force, and vice president in April 1975. When Anwar al-Sadat (q.v.) was assassinated in October 1981, Mubarak became the president of Egypt. He has continued with Sadat's policies, and maintains a cold peace with Israel (q.v.). He has played an important mediatory role in the peace talks between the Palestinians and the Israelis.

MUFTI. A Muslim theologian, who serves as the Muslim spiritual leader and issues formal legal opinions on matters of concern to the public in accordance with Islamic law. The government appoints the *mufti*, and the individual chosen usually supports governmental policies. See FATWA.

MUHSIN, ZUHAIR. Later changed his name to Issam al-Qadi. He was the secretary-general of al-Sa'iqa (q.v.) in 1971 and head of the PLO (q.v.) military department. Muhsin was born in Tulkarm (q.v.) in 1936, and later moved to Amman, Jordan (q.v.), with his family. He graduated from Amman's Teachers College with a degree in mathematics and for a few years taught school in Jordan. After several confrontations with Jordanian authorities and numerous arrests, he was finally expelled from Jordan in 1960. He then moved to Kuwait (q.v.), where he worked for eight years. In 1968, he moved to Damascus, Syria (q.v.), where he became closely affiliated with the Ba'th (q.v.) Party, and it was there that he joined al-Sa'iqa. He was assassinated in France.

AL-MUHTASIB, HILMI SHEIKH. Religious preacher, judge and member of the Higher Islamic Council (q.v.). Born in Hebron (q.v.) in 1910, he dedicated his entire life to religious study, guidance, and preaching. He served as a preacher in Beer al-Sab'e in 1943, and was later appointed a *qadi* (judge) (q.v.) in Acre, Jerusalem (q.v.), Irbid, Nablus, and Amman (q.v.). Al-Muhtasib was elected to the Higher Islamic Council. He passed away in 1982.

AL-MULTAQA AL-FIKRI AL-ARABI. Arabic for "Arab Thought Forum" (q.v.).

MURAGHA, SA'ID MUSSA, COLONEL. Nom de guerre, Abu Mussa. Leader of FATAH Provisional Command or FATAH Uprising (q.v.). He served as a military commander in Lebanon (q.v.), and in 1983 organized the National Salvation Front (q.v.) to overthrow Arafat. He is based in Syria (q.v.), and continues to receive support from that country.

MUSLIM BROTHERHOOD. In Arabic, *Ikhwan al-Muslimin*. A fundamentalist political-religious group that opposes the West and most ruling regimes in the Middle East. It was established in 1929 in Egypt (q.v.) by Sheikh Hassan al-Banna, a schoolteacher who preached the necessity of implementing Islamic laws in society. The movement quickly gained the support of the masses by providing a well-organized welfare system, building mosques, and establishing educational institutions. In 1947, when Egyptian minister Nuqrashi Pasha submitted a law to have the organization banned, he was subsequently killed. Al-Banna was assassinated in 1949, and many thought it had been done with the approval of the Egyptian government. The relationship between the Muslim Brotherhood and the Egyptian government has been strained ever since. The group allegedly conspired to assassinate President Gamal Abd al-Nasser (q.v.) in 1954. It has also been blamed for the assassination of Anwar al-Sadat (q.v.), the former president of Egypt, on October 6, 1981 for signing a peace treaty with Israel (q.v.).

Members of the Muslim Brotherhood are in Syria (q.v.), Iraq (q.v.), Jordan (q.v.), Saudi Arabia (q.v.), and other Arab countries. Relations between the group and the ruling regimes are strained. In Syria, for example, a confrontation took place in 1982 in which an estimated 20,000 Muslim Brotherhood members were killed by the Syrian regime.

The organization of the brotherhood has become fluid and fragmented; groups have splintered off, forming numerous factions, each with a leader. But the movement continues to be appealing to laymen because it emphasizes the Islamic origins of the society and has an anti-Western agenda. In Palestine, the movement's priority is the Islamization of society followed by the liberation of Palestine (q.v.). The brotherhood's official paper is *The Call.* See HAMAS.

MUSLIM-CHRISTIAN ASSOCIATION (MCA). An organization formed in November 1918 in Jaffa and Jerusalem (q.v.). The objective of the association was to unite the various Palestinian national Muslim and Christian groups for collective action against the British Mandate (q.v.) policies, and Zionist-Jewish immigration to Palestine (q.v.). The association was composed primarily of members of urban families. It dissolved in the 1930s, but later re-emerged as separate religious groups, such as the Young Men's Muslim Association.

AL-MUTHAFFAR, ABDEL QADER, SHEIKH. Prominent politician born in Jerusalem (q.v.). He was a supporter of the Ottoman-Turks (q.v.), but later became critical of them and was exiled to Damascus, Syria (q.v.). He was one of the founders of *Al-Jam'iyyah Al-Filastiniyya* (q.v.) in Syria in 1919. Al-Muthaffar served as a member and president of the Arab Club, and was involved with the Arab Executive (qq.v.). He encouraged the Palestinians to rebel against the British, and was incarcerated in 1933 for inciting demonstrations against Jewish immigration to Palestine. He suggested that the way to resolve the Palestinian-Israeli standoff was to cantonize the country. He passed away in Amman on June 11, 1949.

N

NABLUS. The largest city in the West Bank, with an estimated population of 101,743. It is located between two peaks, Mount Ebal and Mount Gerizim, where the Samaritans live. The major industries in Nablus since 1920 have been soap-making and olive-oil processing. Holy sites in Nablus include Joseph's tomb and Jacob's well, where, according to the biblical story, Jesus stopped to quench his thirst and a Samaritan woman drew water from the well for him.

Nablus has always been an important center of Palestinian nationalism, and has often competed with Jerusalem for that political status. During the Intifada (q.v.), it was called *Jabal Al-Nar* (the Mountain of Fire) and the "City of Fire" because of the Nabulsis' (people of Nablus) fierceness in resisting and confronting the Israeli soldiers.

NADI AL-ARAB. Arabic for "Arab club" (q.v.).

AN-NAHAR. Arabic for "the day". The second-largest Arabic daily newspaper, published in East Jerusalem (q.v.), and considered to be supportive of Jordan (q.v.) and its policies. It is owned and published by Osman al-Hallak (q.v.), who founded the paper in 1985. Distribution of the paper was banned for one month in August 1994 in the West Bank and the autonomous areas by the Palestine National Authority (qq.v.) because of its pro-Jordanian position, particularly regarding Jerusalem (q.v.). *An-Nahar* also runs a research center that conducts public opinion polls and does general research.

AN-NAJAH NATIONAL UNIVERSITY. The largest Palestinian university, with 5,300 students, is in the city of Nablus (q.v.). It began in 1918 as An-Najah Nabulsi School. In 1941, it became An-Najah College, and in 1963 it began to grant associate degrees. In 1977, An-Najah National University was admitted to the Union of Arab Universities, and in 1981 it became a member of the International Union of Universities. It offers bachelor of arts and science degrees and recently granted masters degrees in chemistry, Islamic studies, and education. At the beginning of the Intifada (q.v.) in 1988, as student unrest was gathering steam, the university was closed by an Israeli military order. It reopened in August 1991.

Al-NAJJAB, SULEIMAN. The leader of the Palestine Communist Party, which has been re-named the Palestine People's Party (q.v.). He also is the head of the PLO (q.v.) Social Affairs Department and a member of the PLO Executive Committee (q.v.). He served as minister of Agriculture in the first PNA (q.v.) government in 1994.

Al-NAJJAR, MUHAMMAD YOUSEF. Nom de guerre, Abu Yousef. Born in Gaza (q.v.) in 1929, he was one of the founders of FATAH (q.v.) in the 1950s, and a tireless fighter for the liberation of Palestine. In 1955, he was imprisoned for two years by the Egyptians for leading demonstrations protesting the settlement of Palestinian refugees (q.v.) in Rafah, the Gaza Strip (q.v.). He was apprehensive about settling the refugees, because it would lead to a change in their status, and they would be deprived of their right to return and of compensation for the property they left behind in Palestine (q.v.). After his release, he lived in Egypt for a while, but later left for Qatar and Saudi Arabia (q.v.), where he helped set up FATAH offices and eventually became a commander of the al-'Assifa (q.v.) forces. Appointed the head of FATAH's special unit for intelligence, he also became a member of the PLO Executive Committee (q.v.) in 1968. Stung by the PLO defeat in Jordan (q.v.) in 1970, he co-founded, with Arafat and Salah Khalaf (qq.v.), the Black September Organization (q.v.). He was killed during an Israeli raid on FATAH's headquarters in Beirut on April 10, 1973.

AL-NASHASHIBI. A Jerusalem (q.v.) clan that played an important role in Palestinian nationalism and politics in the 1920s and 1930s. They formed the *Mu'aridin* (q.v.) and opposed the Husseinis' (q.v.) politics. They established the National Party on November 9–10, 1923, and the Defense Party in 1934. They were politically moderate, maintained contact with the British and King Abdallah of Jordan (qq.v.), and were not averse to limited Jewish immigration to Palestine. They united with the Husseinis during the Palestinian revolts (q.v.) and disturbances in 1936, but the competition and rivalry between them was too great. They later established their own commando group, the Peace Gang. See individual entries AL-NASHASHIBI.

Al-NASHASHIBI, MOHAMMED ZUHDI. Appointed minister of Finance and acting minister of Agriculture in the Palestine National Authority (q.v.) in July 1994. A member of the well-known Nashashibi family, he was born in 1925 in Jerusalem. Nashashibi took a post-graduate course in economics and finance at Ruskin College, Oxford University in 1958. For many years, he was the manager, and then the regional general manager, of the Commercial Bank of Syria (q.v.). He has written extensively on economics. Active in the PLO (q.v.), he joined the Executive Committee (q.v.) in 1972. He was reappointed the PNA's (q.v.) minister of Finance in 1996.

Al-NASHASHIBI, NASSER AL-DIN. Renowned journalist and author. He was born in 1925 in Jerusalem (q.v.). In 1936, he enrolled at the National University in Lebanon (q.v.), and two years later transferred to the American University of Beirut, Lebanon (q.v.). Afterward, he worked as a journalist in London, Geneva, Jordan, and Palestine (q.v.). Working in the Arab Information Office established by Mussa al-Alami (q.v.) in 1946, he made many contacts, and in 1949 became King Abdallah's (q.v.) private advisor. He was later appointed the director-general of the Jordanian Broadcasting Service, and served as a roving editor for the Egyptian newspaper *Akhbar Al-Yawm* (Todays' News). In 1959, he became editor-in-chief for the Egyptian newspaper *Al-Jumhuriyya* (The Republic). The Arab League (q.v.) appointed him as ambassador-at-large in 1965. He has written several books, among them *Roving Ambassador* (Arabic, 1970), *An Arab in China, What Happened in the Middle East, The Talk of the Great, Women in the Middle East,* and *Who killed Abdallah.* He currently resides in Jerusalem.

AL-NASHASHIBI, RAGHEB. Palestinian leader and political activist. He was born in Jerusalem (q.v.) in 1881, and studied engineering in Istanbul, Turkey. After returning home, he worked as an engineer and became the representative of Jerusalem in the Turkish parliament. When the British took control of Palestine (q.v.) in 1918, he formed the Literary Club (q.v.), an organization that was supportive of Faisal I's (q.v.) dream of a Greater Syria. In 1920, he was appointed mayor of Jerusalem and remained in that office for the next four years. In 1923, he headed the National Party. Opposing the politics of the Husseinis (q.v.) in 1934, Nashashibi became the leader of the Defense Party (q.v.). He also represented the party to the Arab Higher Committee (q.v.). A moderate, he is said to have encouraged the Arabs to accept the British proposals regarding the partition of Palestine and Jewish immigration to the country. He also maintained close relations with Abdallah (q.v.) of Transjordan, and supported the Jordanian annexation of the West Bank and East Jerusalem (qq.v.). This loyalty to Jordan earned him an appointment as the governor-general of the

West Bank and the posts of minister of Agriculture and of Transportation. He died on April 10, 1951.

AL-NASSER, GAMAL ABED. Born on January 15, 1918, Nasser was the president of Egypt (q.v.) from 1957 to 1970. A military officer, he commanded a battalion that fought in the war of 1948 (q.v.). He was a member of the Revolutionary Command Council (the Free Officers), which led the Egyptian revolution that toppled King Farouq on July 23, 1952. He nationalized the Suez Canal on July 26, 1956, and introduced other measures that became known as Arab socialism. Nasser was the president of the United Arab Republic (q.v.) from February 1958 to September 1961. He also cultivated a close alliance with Russia. In 1967, Nasser blockaded the Straits of Tiran and demanded the withdrawal of the U.N. Emergency Force from Sinai, which had been stationed there since 1956. Nasser convinced Syria and Jordan (qq.v.) to join him in the confrontation with Israel (q.v.). After the debacle of the war of 1967, he submitted his resignation, but it was rejected. Nasser accepted U.N. Resolution 242 (q.v.), but he refused to recognize or to discuss peace with Israel. Through some manuvering on his part, Nasser helped establish Fatahland in Lebanon in 1969 by helping to negotiate the Cairo agreements (q.v.), which gave the PLO (q.v.) free rein in Lebanon. Nasser also mediated the PLO dispute with Jordan after the 1970 confrontation. He was greatly admired by the Arab people, and especially by the Palestinians. He died on September 28, 1970.

NASSER, ḤANNA. President of Birzeit University (q.v.). He was born in 1935 in Birzeit, a village north of Ramallah (q.v.). His father, Mussa, worked as an official in the British Mandate (q.v.) bureaucracy, served as minister of Foreign Affairs in Jordan, and later founded Birzeit College in the 1960s. Hanna became the president of Birzeit University in August 1971 upon the death of his father. In November 1974, he was deported to Jordan after widespread demonstrations erupted throughout the Occupied Territories (q.v.) in support of the decision taken at the Rabat Summit to make the PLO (q.v.) the sole legitimate representative of the Palestinian people. In exile, Nasser became a member of the PLO Executive Committee (q.v.) and, later, president of the Palestine National Fund (q.v.). He remained president of the university while in Jordan, and Gabi Baramki (q.v.) became acting president, conducting the day-to-day affairs of the university. In April 1993, Israel allowed him to return, along with 15 other post-1967 deportees.

NASSER, KAMAL. Born in Birzeit, a town north of Ramallah (q.v.), he studied at Birzeit University (q.v.) when it was still a junior college, and attended the American University of Beirut in Lebanon (q.v.), graduating in 1945. After the war of 1948 (q.v.), he published a Ba'th (q.v.) daily newspaper and magazine called *Al-Jeel Al-Jadid* (The New Generation). In 1949, the magazine was banned by Jordan. He left for Kuwait (q.v.), and in 1952 became an advisor to the leaders of Kuwait. Four years later, he returned to the West Bank (q.v.) and became a member of the Jordanian parliament, representing the Ba'th party for the district of Ramallah. In 1967, Israel (q.v.) deported him. Moving quickly up the PLO (q.v.) hierarchy, he was elected a member of the PLO Executive Committee (q.v.) in 1969. He also became the director of the PLO Information Office, and served as the spokesperson for the PLO. At one time, he also edited *Filistine Al-Thawra* (Palestine, the Revolution). He was killed in an Israeli raid on Beirut on April 10, 1973.

NASSER, KAMIL. Former secretary-general of the Young Mens' Christian Association (YMCA) in Jerusalem (q.v.) from 1980 to 1994. He was born in Jerusalem in 1948, and graduated from the American University of Beirut with a B.A. in business. He was a member of the following religious and social organizations: Princess Basma Society for the Handicapped, al-Ahli Hospital in Gaza (q.v.), the Bible Hospital in Nablus (q.v.), and the St. George School and College in Jerusalem. He also was a member of the General Committee for Palestinian Refugees (q.v.). During the Intifada (q.v.), he founded the Center for Rehabilitation of the Intifada Disabled, which provides physical therapy to Palestinians who were injured by the Israelis. The center also established an outreach program in different villages in the West Bank (q.v.). He passed away in 1994.

NATIONAL ALLIANCE. An anti-Arafat (q.v.) group formed in May 1984. It included Al-Sa'iqa (q.v.), FATAH (q.v.) rebels, the PFLP-GC (q.v.), the PSF (q.v.), and other smaller groups who wanted to overthrow Arafat because of his rapprochement with King Hussein (q.v.). The alliance later formed the Palestinian National Salvation Front (q.v.).

NATIONAL FRONT. A committee organized in the Occupied Territories (q.v.) for resistance activities against the Israelis after 1967.

NATIONAL SALVATION FRONT. see PALESTINIAN NATIONAL SALVATION FRONT.

NATSHEH, MUSTAFA ABD AL-NABI. Mayor of Hebron (q.v.) reinstated by the Palestine National Authority (q.v.) on April 1, 1994.

Natshe was born in Hebron on December 12, 1930, and studied chemical engineering at Cairo University in Egypt (q.v.), where he received his B.S. in 1956. Elected the deputy mayor of Hebron in 1976, he was appointed mayor when Fahd al-Qawasmi (q.v.) was deported in May 1980. However, in 1983, he was deposed from office, along with his council, when the Israeli Civil Administration (q.v.) was established.

Natsheh was a member of numerous organizations and institutions. Since 1980, he has been president of the *Al-Ibrahimi* Mosque (q.v.) Renovation Committee, a member of the Board of Trustees of An-Najah National University (q.v.), and a member of the Council for Higher Education (q.v.). Politically active, he is a moderate, and is closely affiliated with the PLO (q.v.). He has been detained several times by the Israelis and banned from traveling. He was a member of the negotiating team with Israel, but later resigned. A successful businessman, he has been the chairman of the Arab Cement Company since 1978.

NETANYAHU, BENYAMIN (BIBI). Israeli prime minister who won the May 29, 1996 elections and defeated Shimon Peres (q.v.) of the Labor Party. Netanyahu was born in Tel Aviv in 1949 and moved with his family to the United States in 1962. He was educated at the Massachusetts Institute of Technology, where he received his B.A. and M.A., in architecture and business administration. He later served in an elite Israel Defense Force unit and fought in the Six Day War (q.v.) in 1967. In 1982 Moshe Arens, then ambassador to Washington appointed him as his deputy. The following year, he was assigned as a member of the first delegation for strategic agreements talks with the Uniterd States. In 1984, he became Israel's ambassador to the U.N. He entered the Knesset (parliament) in 1988 and served as deputy foreign minister. During the Madrid Peace Conference (q.v.) in 1991, he served as Israel's spokesperson. In 1993, he was elected the Likud Party leader. Netanyahu wrote *Terrorism: How the West Can Win* in 1986, and established the Jonathan Institute to combat international terrorism to commemorate his brother, who was killed in the Entebbe rescue raid in 1976.

NETWORK OF EUROPEAN NON-GOVERNMENT ORGANIZATIONS IN THE OCCUPIED TERRITORIES (NENGOOT). The network, originally the brainchild of Europeans working for both European and Palestinian NGOs (q.v.), was established in Jerusalem (q.v.) in 1991. The purpose of the organization is to provide support and promote cooperation between European and Palestinian NGOs to ensure the development of more efficient social and economic programs. It also encourages the exchange of information and ideas between NGOs in order to prevent duplication of programs and services. Moreover, it monitors and encourages European support for Palestinian development and political self-determination.

NUSEIBEH, ANWAR. Politician and attorney. Nuseibeh was born in Jerusalem (q.v.) to an influential family. He served as a member of the All-Palestine Government (q.v.) in 1948. Elected in 1950 as the Palestinian representative to the Jordanian parliament, he also was appointed the Jordanian minister of Development and Reconstruction in 1952 and, a few years later, the minister of Defense and Education. King Hussein (q.v.) appointed him to the Jordanian Senate in 1962, and he later became Jordan's ambassador to England. Nuseibeh also was the director of the East Jerusalem Electric Company, and was able to solicit funds from Jordan (q.v.) to build housing projects for Palestinians in East Jerusalem (q.v.). He died on November 23, 1986, in Jerusalem.

NUSEIBEH, SARI. Political activist, professor of philosophy, and president of Al-Quds University (q.v). He was born in 1949, and is the son of Anwar Nuseibeh (q.v.). He received his education at Oxford University in England and later attended Harvard University, where he earned a Ph.D. in philosophy in 1978. He then taught at Birzeit University (q.v.) from 1978 to 1990, and directed the Jerusalem Center for Strategic Studies, a Palestinian think tank. Nuseibeh also was a visiting lecturer in Islamic Studies at the Hebrew University.

In 1979, Nuseibeh co-founded the Jerusalem Friends of the Sick Society, the Union of Faculty and Staff at Birzeit University (q.v.) in 1980, and the Federation of Employees in the Education Sector in the West Bank (q.v.) in 1981. In 1984, he co-founded the Arab Council for Public Affairs and later became the chief editor of *Al-Mawqif* (The Position), a newsletter issued by the council. Nuseibeh also co-founded the Committee Confronting the Israeli Iron Fist Policy, which was organized to resist Israeli policies in the Occupied Territories (q.v.). In 1986, he became a member of the board of the Jerusalem Center for Higher Islamic Research, and in 1987 co-founded the Palestinian Academic Society for the Study of International Affairs (q.v.), and established a news agency called The Holy Land Media Center, which distributed *The Monday Report*, a weekly that is no longer published. In May 1989, the Israelis closed the Media Center for two years. He has twice been detained by the Israelis—in 1981–1982 and 1988–1989.

Nuseibeh has participated extensively in Israeli-Palestinian dialogue. He was attacked by students on the Birzeit University campus in 1987 for his activities with the Israelis, and because of his suggestion that Palestinians should obtain Israeli citizenship and struggle against Israel from within.

O

OBEID, YASSER. Founder of the College of Nursing and the Arab Health Center in al-Bireh (q.v.), the West Bank (q.v.). He was born to a well-to-do Hebronite family; his father owned the National Bus Company. Educated at Bishop Gorbat, an Anglican school, and El-Uma College in Bethlehem (q.v.), he was awarded a Jordanian scholarship to the American University of Beirut in Lebanon (q.v.). After graduating, he attended Baylor University Southwestern Medical School in Texas. He worked at the Ramallah Government Hospital, where he became the deputy director. In 1978, Jordan (q.v.) appointed him as the top medical official in the West Bank and gave him a budget of $7 million. Obeid immediately established the Arab Health Center in al-Bireh, which provides low-cost medical care for Palestinians. He also lobbied for many years to open a Palestinian hospital in East Jerusalem (q.v.), but Israel (q.v.) adamantly refused to issue a building permit under the pretext that there were already too many hospitals in Israel. When Jordan severed its ties with the West Bank in July 1988, his positon was eliminated. On the night of September 28, 1986, Obeid was stabbed as he was entering his home; some assumed it was because of his pro-Jordanian stance. He met with Rabin (q.v.) in 1988, and it was interpreted by some as another Israeli attempt to create an alternative leadership to the PLO (q.v.).

OCCUPIED TERRITORIES. The areas that Israel (q.v.) occupied during the Six-Day War of 1967 (q.v.). They include the Golan Heights that belong to Syria (q.v.), the West Bank seized from Jordan (qq.v.), and the Gaza Strip and Sinai Peninsula taken from Egypt (qq.v.). This territory totaled more than 27,000 square miles.

Israel returned the Sinai Peninsula to Egypt after the signing of the peace treaty in 1979. It also has withdrawn from Jericho (q.v.) and the Gaza Strip, as was stipulated in the Declaration of Principles (q.v.), and from the major cities in the West Bank, in accordance with the Oslo Two Agreement (q.v.). However, Israel continues to occupy the rest of the West Bank, and the Golan Heights, which Syria insists must be returned if it is to make peace with Israel.

The Occupied Territories were governed by an Israeli Civil Administration (q.v.) under a system of British, Jordanian, and Israeli laws (Israel has introduced 1,365 military orders since the occupation).

ODEH, MOHAMMED SA'ADEH. Nom de guerre, Taysir Khaled. He is a member of the Democratic Front for the Liberation of Palestine (q.v.), the Palestine National Committee (1972), and the PLO Executive Committee (1991) (q.v.). He was born in Nablus (q.v.) in 1941. Educated in Germany, he majored in politics and international law. While there, he became active in the General Union of Palestinian Students (q.v.). He also was active in the Socialist Student Union in Germany, and helped establish the German Communist League. He worked in the broadcasting field in Kuwait (q.v.) from 1960 to 1963.

Odeh joined the Democratic Front for the Liberation of Palestine in 1969, and quickly moved up its ranks, becoming a member of the central committee and political bureau. Angered by the secret Oslo negotiations that led to the signing of the Declaration of Principles (q.v.), he suspended all of his political activities in September 1993.

OPEN BRIDGES. This refers to the border policy between Jordan and Israel (qq.v.). After the war of 1967 (q.v.), Israel and Jordan allowed the Palestinians from the Occupied Territories to export their agricultural goods and to cross into Jordan with permits, via the Allenby and Damia bridges. Visitors, particularly during the summer, also were permitted to cross into Israel from Jordan.

ORIENT HOUSE. A beautiful mansion in East Jerusalem built by Musa al-Husseini (q.v.) in 1897. Over the years, it became the place to host dignitaries. Between 1949 and 1950, the house was used as the headquarters of the Palestine Conciliation Committee and UNRWA (qq.v.). Later, it was converted into a hotel, known as the "The New Orient House," and was among the first hotels in East Jerusalem (q.v.) to be established after the withdrawal of the British Mandate (q.v.) from Palestine in 1948. After 1967, the owners closed the hotel and used it as a private residence. However, the upkeep was too expensive and the building was soon rented out. In 1983, the Arab Studies Society (q.v.) rented a section of the building, as well as the annex, and set up offices there. On July 28, 1988, the Israeli occupational forces broke into the building and closed it for security reasons. Faisal al-Husseini (q.v.) then rented the entire premise in 1991, and used it as the offices of the Palestinian delegation to the peace negotiations.

The Palestinians maintain that the Orient House should be off-limits to Israelis because it is where they keep their documents and official papers. Israel contends that the Oslo Accords (q.v.) prohibit the Palestine National Authority (q.v) from engaging in any activities outside the Palestinian autonomous areas (q.v.). Political activities carried out by Palestinians in East Jerusalem are seen as endangering Israel's sovereignty. On Monday, December 26, 1994, the Israeli government passed the "Orient House Law," which restricts political activity at the institution and prohibits the establishment of any institution by the PNA in East Jerusalem. The law allows the government to take action against the establishment of PNA offices at the Orient House and anywhere else in Jerusalem.

OSLO ACCORDS. Ahmad Qre'i and Mahmoud Abbas (qq.v.) in 1993 conducted secret negotiations with Israelis, mediated by Norwegians in Oslo, Norway. These negotiations were held simultaneously with public negotiations conducted in Washington and attended by a Palestinian delegation from the Occupied Territories (q.v.) led by Haidar Abd al-Shafi (q.v.). The Oslo negotiations culminated in the signing of the Declaration of Principles (q.v.), or the Oslo Accords, on September 13, 1993. See Oslo Two Agreement.

OSLO TWO AGREEMENT. An agreement signed in Washington, D.C., on September 28, 1995, between the Palestinians and Israelis, representing the second phase of the DOP (q.v.). It dealt with expanding Palestinian self-rule to other areas of the Occupied Territories (q.v.) and Israeli redeployment. The agreement contains the following principles: The West Bank is divided into three areas. Area A represent 3 percent of the West Bank and will be administered by the PNA (q.v.). It includes the seven heavily populated cities of Jenin (q.v.), Tulkarm (q.v.), Qalqilya (q.v.), Nablus (q.v.), Ramallah (q.v.), Bethlehem (q.v.), and Hebron (q.v.). Israel, however, is to maintain control of 15 percent of the city of Hebron, to protect the 450 Israeli settlers who live there. Area B, which comprises 27 percent of the West Bank and includes more than 450 small towns and villages will be under Palestinian administration, and Israeli security. Area C, or the remaining 70 percent, which includes Jewish settlements (q.v.) and Israeli military bases, will remain under Israeli control. Israel will redeploy its army by March 1996 from areas A and B, but it will remain in 15 percent of Hebron (q.v.) to protect the 450 Jewish residents in the city, and to control the security of the Machpela Cave or *Al-Ibrahimi* Mosque (q.v.) and the roads leading to and from the settlements (q.v.). Israel also agreed to a second phase of redeployment in the Occupied Territories, to take place in three stages, each six months apart. Elections for the 82-member Palestininan Legislative Council (q.v.) and a president will be held in 1996. Moreover, 25 Palestinian police stations manned by 12,000 Palestinian policemen would be established to maintain public order. Palestinian police movement on intercity roads will be coordinated with the Israelis. Palestinian prisoners in Israeli jails will be released in three stages: the first group will be released on September 28, 1995; the second group will be released just before the elections; and the third would be decided in future negotiations. Arafat (q.v.) also agreed that two months after the inauguration of the Palestinian Legislative Council, he would convene a meeting of the PNC (q.v.) to revoke all statements calling for the destruction of Israel from the Palestinian National Charter (q.v.).

OTTOMAN-TURKS. The rulers of the Ottoman Empire from 1250 to 1916. Their empire began to weaken at the beginning of the 19th century because of internal strife and rebellions. During World War I, they were defeated by the Allies. The empire was dissolved, and new nations were carved out. Attaturk, the Turkish reformer and leader, established modern Turkey in the 1920s.

P

PALESTINE. In the early 1900s, the term Palestine was used to refer to a geographical territory within the Ottoman Empire in western Asia.

The people who lived in this area, and were ruled by the Ottoman-Turks (q.v.), wanted to be part of the Greater Syrian dream of Faisal I (q.v.). Two Palestinian political organizations at the time supported this idea. They were *al-Muntada Al-Adabi* (The Literary Club) and *Al-Nadi Al-'Arabi* (The Arab Club) (qq.v.).

Palestine was used politically in 1918, when it was occupied by the Allied forces at the end of World War I. The Western countries then proceeded to carve up the Middle East and divide it among themselves. Palestine was bounded to the north by Lebanon and Syria (q.v.); to the east by Jordan (q.v.); to the west by the Mediterranean Sea; and to the south, by the Gulf of Aqaba and the Sinai Peninsula.

Palestinian nationalism emerged in response to the British Mandate (q.v.) over Palestine and the establishment of a national home for the Jews. The British established a Supreme Muslim Council (q.v.) in 1922, and wanted the Palestinians to elect a legislative council, form their own institutions, and run their affairs. The Palestinians, rejected this, however, and instead formed the Arab Executive (q.v.) in Haifa in December 1920 under the leadership of Mussa Qassem al-Husseini (q.v.) to champion the cause of the Palestinians and negotiate with the British. The Arab Executive sent delegations to London in 1921, 1922, and 1923. Very little was achieved, however, and the Arab Executive vanished when al-Husseini died in 1934.

Hajj Amin al-Husseini (q.v.) took charge of Palestinian nationalism in 1920. He was the *mufti* (q.v.) of Jerusalem and was supported by the *Majlisiyoun* (q.v.), who were opposed by the Nashashibi dominated *Mu'aridin* (q.v.).

In 1931, the total population of Palestine was 1,035,154. The Arabs constituted 83.10 percent of the population and the Jews, 16.9 percent. Nevertheless, the Zionists had long been arguing that Palestine was "a land without people, for a people without a land". To counter this, there followed a frenzy of political activity as the Palestinians organized themselves to oppose British policies and the number of Jewish immigrants burgeoned. Ragheb Nashashibi (q.v.) formed the National Defense Party; Jamal al-Husseini (q.v.) formed the Palestine Arab Party; and Awni Abd al-Hadi (q.v.) formed the *Istiqlal* (q.v.) Party. The Youth Congress was organized in 1932 by Ya'qub Ghussein; the Reform Party was established in 1935 by Dr. Hussein al-Khalidi (q.v.); and the National Bloc was organized by Abd al-Latif Saleh (q.v.) of Nablus. The Palestinian resistance between the two world wars was futile. U.N. Resolution 181 (q.v.) of November 1947 divided Palestine into a Jewish state and an Arab state. The war of 1948 (q.v.) began, and King Abdallah of Transjordan joined in the fighting. At the end of the war, the portion of Palestine allocated by the United Nations for the Palestinian Arabs was annexed by Jordan, while the rest was occupied by Israel (q.v.). Israel held control of 77 percent of Palestine, instead of the 56 percent apportioned by the U.N. Partition Plan (q.v.).

Palestine today refers to the state of Palestine that Palestinians hope to establish. Article I of the Palestinian Charter (q.v.) defines Palestine as "the homeland of the Arab people" and "an integral part of the great Arab homeland. . . ." According to the covenant, a Palestinian is anyone born to a Palestinian-Arab father after 1947. Article 5 of the covenant defines Palestinians as those "who were living permanently in Palestine until 1947, whether they were expelled from there or remained." In Article 6 Jews, too, are considered Palestinians if they were "living permanently in Palestine until the beginning of the Zionist invasion."

PALESTINE ARAB PARTY. The Husseini (q.v) clan party established in 1935 by Jamal al-Husseini (q.v.). The party's paper was called *Al-Liwa* (The District).

PALESTINE AUTHORITY'S SECURITY COURTS. Special courts set up by the Palestinian National Authority (q.v.) in February 1995 because of pressure exerted by the United States and Israel (q.v.) to control the opposition, primarily HAMAS and Islamic Jihad (qq.v.), and to serve as a deterrent to prevent them from engaging in militant attacks against Israel. Israel claimed that, since the signing of the DOP in September 1993, 124 Israelis had been killed by members of Islamic organizations. These groups rejected the DOP (q.v.), and refused to give up their weapons in spite of a May 11 deadline, which was extended to May 15, 1995.

Trials in these courts are held at midnight, and are said to last only a few minutes. There are no lawyers and no public announcements of the trial or the location. The courts were condemned by Amnesty International in its report of April 1995. Amnesty demanded that the courts be dismantled, because they violate basic legal standards of a right to a proper defense and the right to a fair and public trial. The PNA Attorney-General Khaled al-Qudwa has stated that the courts will be eliminated once the opposition joins the peace process, and either register their weapons or give them up. To date, defendants have received sentences that range from one to 25 years.

The conviction of HAMAS activist Sayed Abu Musameh on May 14, 1995, for incitement against the Palestinian police, and his imprisonment for two years by the security courts, caused outrage in the Gaza Strip (q.v.). It was the first sentence passed by the security courts against a senior HAMAS leader, and an indication that the PNA would not tolerate dissidents. Musameh was arrested a day before his conviction for writing an article comparing PNA police to Israeli soldiers, and PNA security practices, particularly in torturing suspects, to those used by the Israeli army. *Al-Watan* (the Nation), the HAMAS weekly that Abu Musameh edits, was ordered closed for three months for publishing allegedly seditious material libeling the PNA.

There are special revolutionary courts to try Palestinian police who commit crimes. On May 2, 1995, a policeman was sentenced to life for the murder of another policeman.

PALESTINE CENTRAL COUNCIL. Established in 1972 by the PLO Executive Committee (q.v.) to expedite the decision-making process of the Palestine National Council. In the PLO (q.v.) hierarchy, the council is the intermediate organization between the Executive Committee and the Palestine National Council (q.v.).

PALESTINE CONCILIATION COMMISSION (PCC). Established by the U.N. General Assembly in December 1948 to resolve the Arab-Israeli conflict. The members of the PCC were from the United States, Turkey, and France. In 1949, it issued the Protocol of Lausanne in which members made suggestions for a settlement, but it was ignored by the parties concerned. In 1951, they recommended a solution to the refugee problem, but again were ignored. In 1961, the commission sent an American, Dr. Joseph Johnson, to the Middle East, to report on the refugees, but his efforts was dismissed. The commission has not done anything since 1962.

PALESTINE COMMUNIST PARTY. see PALESTINE PEOPLE'S PARTY.

PALESTINE DEMOCRATIC UNION. Also known as FIDA. A political party that branched off from the Popular Democratic Front for the Liberation of Palestine (q.v.), it was established in February 1993. The party has a leftist ideology and advocates democratic pluralism. It supports the Declaration of Principles (q.v.) and participated in the PLC elections in 1996. Among its leaders are Yasser Abed-Rabbo and Zahira Kamal (qq.v.).

PALESTINE ECONOMIC COUNCIL FOR DEVELOPMENT AND RECONSTRUCTION (PECDAR). Established on November 4, 1993, to formulate economic policies, to select investment and technical projects, and coordinate financial assistance that the PNA (q.v.) receives. It was formed after the convening of the donor conference on October 1, 1993, in Washington, at which $2 billion were pledged to assist the Palestinians. PECDAR's board of governors is composed of 14 members, who are appointed by the Palestine National Authority, and it has 144 employees.

PALESTINE EXECUTIVE COMMITTEE (PEC). The highest decision-making body of the PLO (q.v.). It represents the Palestinians, directs the management of the PLO, administers the PLO institutions, and prepares the budget. It is composed of 15 members, nine of whom are independent, and all of whom are elected by the PNC (q.v.). The PEC is in charge of the following PLO departments or bureaus: foreign affairs, education, military, the Occupied Territories (q.v.), relations with the Arab states and the international community, culture, economy, health, information and national guidance, youth, and finance. Each of these departments is headed by a member of the Executive Committee. The following have served as members of the Executive Committee (see individual entries where indicated): Yasser Arafat (q.v.), chairman of the Executive Committee; Mahmoud Abbas (q.v.); Muhammad Abbas (q.v.); Ahmad Abd Al-Rahim; Suleiman Al-Najjab (q.v.); Jamal Al-Sourani (q.v.); Mustafa Az-Zibri; Mahmoud Darwish (q.v); Abadallah Hourani (q.v.); Farouq al-Qaddumi (q.v.); and Muhammad Milhem (q.v.).

PALESTINE LIBERATION ARMY (PLA). The first Palestinian National Congress (q.v.) in 1964 decreed the establishment of an independent army composed of 20,000 to 30,000 men, divided into four units. Each unit was to be led by a Palestinian commander. However, the independence of the PLA would be short-lived, because each brigade came under the auspices of the country it was located in, and was integrated into that country's army. For example, the 'Ain Jalut Brigade came under the Egyptian army; the Hittin and Yarmuk Brigade under the Syrians; the Qadisiyya Brigade and Battalion 421 came under the Iraqi army; and the al-Badr Brigade came under the Jordanians. The PLA was prohibited from assisting or supporting any Palestinian commando activities. After the signing of the DOP and the Cairo Agreement (qq.v.) on May 4, 1994, the PLA was deployed in the autonomous areas as the Palestine National Authority's (q.v.) police force.

PALESTINE LIBERATION FRONT (PLF). A radical faction that split off from the PFLP-GC (qq.v.) in 1977. It was led by Muhammad Abbas (q.v.), who was appalled because the PFLP-GC did not oppose Syrian support of the Phalangists against the PLO in Lebanon (q.v.). A split occurred in 1983, which led to the formation of two groups: an anti-Arafat group led by Tal'at Ya'qub and another faction led by Abbas.

The PLF is said to be based in Syria and Iraq (qq.v.) and also receives support from Libya. It claimed responsibility for the 1985 hijacking of the cruise ship the Achille Lauro (q.v.), and the unsuccessful May 30, 1990 attack on the beach in Tel Aviv.

PALESTINE LIBERATION ORGANIZATION (PLO). A political organization established in 1964 in Jerusalem by the Arab League (q.v.) to provide an umbrella for the various Palestinian factions that emerged as a result of the Palestinian-Israeli conflict. At the inaugural meeting, the Palestine National Council (q.v.), the Executive Committee, and the Palestine National Fund (qq.v.) were established. Moreover, a national charter, or *mithaq* (covenant) (q.v.), also was passed. Ahmad Shuqeiri (q.v.) became the first chairman of the PLO. Palestinian factions, such as FATAH (q.v.), Sa'iqa (q.v.), PDFLP (q.v.), and PFLP (q.v.), joined the organization.

In February 1969, Arafat was elected chairman of the organization, and launched a campaign to enhance the prestige of the PLO. On October 14, 1974, the U.N. General Assembly passed Resolution 3236 (q.v.) that recognized the PLO as the representative of the Palestinian people, and the organization was given observer status. Four years later, it was granted access to the U.N. Security Council. The PLO also ordered its factions to stop all militant activities. However, some groups ignored the order. Divisions surfaced in the organization. In 1983, Arafat was encouraged to accept Israel's right to exist and to accept U.N. Resolution 242 (q.v.), which the Palestinians had rejected because it does not specifically refer to Palestinians, but to "refugees."

PLO relations with Jordan, Syria, and Lebanon (qq.v.) were not productive. In the early 1970s, a violent confrontation between the Jordanian army and the PLO took place. It ended badly for the Palestinians, not only because of the casualties they suffered, but their hopes of establishing a territorial base from which to target Israel were destroyed when they were ousted from Jordan.

Arafat, hoping to bring an end to the enmity with Jordan, began rapprochement talks with King Hussein (q.v.) in 1982. The two agreed that a joint Jordanian-Palestinian delegation would participate in any negotiations of a settlement of the Palestinian-Israeli conflict. Furthermore, once a settlement was achieved, confederation between Palestine and Jordan would be established. In 1985, the Arafat-Hussein Agreement (q.v.) was signed. However, this agreement caused dissent among the PLO factions that did not approve it. The agreement was voided in 1986 by King Hussein, because of his displeasure with Arafat, who failed to honor it.

The PLO also was having problems in Lebanon (q.v.). It had successfully established a state-within-a-state structure there, but Israeli pressure on Syria and the Israeli invasion of Beirut disrupted this arrangement. The PLO, under international supervision, was forced to evacuate Lebanon between August and September 1982, and to relocate its soldiers outside of Lebanese territory. The Phalange militia entered the refugee camps of Sabra and Shatilla on September 17, 1982, and massacred 2,000 Palestinians. Arafat attempted to reestablish himself in Lebanon, but was stopped by the Syrians, who were assisted by a Palestinian rebel group, FATAH Uprising (qq.v.). In December 1983, Arafat was evacuated with his men under the aegis of the international community. He was allowed to set up headquarters in Tunis, but without his armed forces. Another attempt by Arafat's men to infiltrate Lebanon took place between 1985 and 1986. But it was thwarted by Amal militias and the forces of al-Sa'iqa (q.v.), PFLP-GC (q.v.), and FATAH Uprising.

The PLO also was plagued by internal strife. In November 1984, a number of PLO groups did not attend the National Council meeting in Amman, because of their displeasure with Arafat's rapprochement with Hussein. In May of that year, the groups organized themselves into two camps—the Democratic Alliance (q.v.), which wanted to reconcile with Arafat, and the National Alliance (q.v.), which wanted to topple Arafat. In March 1985, the two anti-Arafat groups joined to form the Palestine National Salvation Fronts (q.v.). The PFLP, the PDFLP, and the communists, however, refused to join the Front. Arafat's own faction, FATAH was not wholeheartedly behind him, and an opposition led by Salah Khalaf and Farouq al-Qaddumi (qq.v.) was formed. A reconciliation eventually took place in 1987, and Arafat, under intense pressure, breached the agreement he had made with Jordan and Egypt, and rejected U.N. Resolution 242 (q.v.). The Syrian-supported factions remained on the sidelines, however, and refused to reconcile with Arafat.

In December 1987, the Intifada (q.v.) began in the Occupied Territories (q.v.) and the PLO and the Palestinians were once again in the spotlight. On November 15, 1988, the PNC took a bold step and declared the establishment of a Palestinian state, and Arafat accepted a two-state solution. Arafat renounced terrorism, and in December 1988 affirmed Israel's right to exist. Israel had not yet recognized the PLO as the representative of the Palestinian people. On January 12, 1989, the U.N. Security Council granted the PLO the right to speak directly to the council as "Palestine", and with the same status as any member nation.

PLO relations with the United States deteriorated because of the PLF's (q.v.) aborted seaborne attack on Israel on May 30, 1990. The United States viewed the attack as a breach of Arafat's promise that terrorist activity would end. In July 1990, the United States ended its 17-month dialogue with the PLO.

The PLO's decision not to join the anti-Iraqi alliance during the Gulf War (q.v.) devastated the organization. It was ostracized, and the political clout it had gained as a result of the Intifada (q.v.) was undermined. In the aftermath of the Gulf War (q.v.), Arab leaders ignored both Arafat and the Palestinians. Financial assistance came to a halt. Angry Palestinians demanded that reforms be introduced in the organization and that the misuse of funds be examined. These reforms included the democratization of PLO institutions and changes in its representational system. On the verge of moral and financial bankruptcy, the PNC convened its 20th session in Algiers on September 23, 1991, and approved sending a Palestinian delegation from the Occupied Territories (q.v.) to the Madrid Peace Conference (q.v.). The demands for reforms were placed on hold, and the organization's status was slowly restored. In 1992, Egypt made overtures to the PLO that bolstered the organization's position vis-à-vis other Palestinian factions. On June 5, 1993, PLO members Mahmoud Abbas and Faisal Husseini (qq.v.) visited the United Arab Emirates to encourage a reconciliation. The Oslo Accords (q.v.) were signed on September 23, 1993, and on October 11, 1993, were ratified by the PLO Central Council (q.v.) in Tunis by a vote of 63-to-8, with 11 abstentions. Israel (q.v.) recognized the PLO. The status of the PLO was salvaged by international recognition that it would represent the Palestinians at any peace conference.

A split emerged within the PLO. Palestinian factions, such as the Iraqi-supported Arab Liberation Front (q.v.), the Palestine Liberation Front (q.v.), and independents, boycotted the PNC meeting in Tunis, which was called to ratify the treaty. Moreover, a group called the Palestinian Forces Alliance composed of 10 Palestinian factions was formed on January 19, 1994, to oppose the DOP (q.v.) and the peace process. The factions included the DFLP (q.v.), the PFLP (q.v.), the Palestine Liberation Front (Tal'at Yaqub faction), the Palestine Revolutionary Communist Party, the PFLP-GC (q.v.), FATAH Uprising (q.v.), Saiqa (q.v.), HAMAS, and Islamic Jihad (qq.v.).

The PNA (q.v.) moved to the autonomous areas (q.v.) in accordance with the DOP in July 1994. (The idea that a Palestinian Authority be established on any liberated area of Palestine had actually been the brainchild of the DFLP, and a resolution to this effect had been passed in 1974 by the Palestine National Council.) The PLO Executive Committee (q.v.) was to monitor and supervise the PNA. Also, it was revealed on October 31, 1995, that Arafat had asked Rabin (q.v.) to let all PNC members living abroad return to Gaza (q.v.) to amend the 1964 PLO Charter that calls for the destruction of Israel. According to the Oslo Two Agreement (q.v.), the PNC is to amend the charter within two months of the inauguration of the Palestinian Legislative Council (q.v.), elections for which would be held on January 20, 1996. On April 24, 1996, the PNC met in Gaza and by a majority of 504–54, with 14 abstentions, amended the statements calling for the destruction of Israel (q.v.).

PALESTINE MARTYRS' WORK SOCIETY. see SAMED.

PALESTINE NATIONAL AUTHORITY (PNA). The Palestinian government set up by Arafat (q.v.) in the autonomous regions of the Gaza Strip and Jericho (qq.v.) after the signing of the Declaration of Principles (q.v.). The PNA also assumed responsibility for tourism, education, health, taxes, and social welfare throughout the Occupied Territories (q.v.). On August 20, 1995, the PNA took over the administration of commerce and industry, agriculture, local government, gas and petrol, postal services, labor, insurance, and statistics. Moreover, negotiations were held throughout 1995 to discuss the remaining 25 spheres of authority. The ministers of the first Palestinian Authority are as follows (see individual entries where indicated):

President	Yasser Arafat (q.v.)
Ministers:	
Agriculture	Suleiman Al-Najjab

Economy and Trade	Ahmad Qre'i (q.v.)
Finance	Mohammed Nashashibi (q.v.)
Education	Yasser Amro (q.v.)
Culture and Information	Yasser Abed-Rabbo (q.v.)
Tourism and Antiquities	Elias Freij (q.v)
Health	Riad Za'noun (q.v.)
Planning and International Cooperation	Nabil Sha'ath (q.v.)
Post and Telecommunications	Abdel Hafiz Al-Ashab (q.v.)
Sports and Youth Affairs	Azmi Shu'eibi (q.v.)
Justice	Freih Abu Middeyan q.v.)
Housing and Public Works	Zakaria Ahga (q.v.)
Labor	Samir Ghosheh (q.v.)
Local Government and Municipal Affairs	Saeb 'Erekat (q.v.)
Transportation	Abdel Aziz Haj Ahmad (q.v.)
Social Affairs	Intisar Al-Wazir (q.v.)
Interior	Ahmad Said al-Tamimi
Religious Affairs	Hassan Tahboub (q.v.)
Secretary-General	Tayeb Abed Rahim (q.v.)
Jerusalem File	Faisal Al-Husseini (q.v.)

After elections for the PLC (q.v.) were held on January 20, 1996, a new Palestinian cabinet was appointed by Arafat in March–June 1996. The members are:

President	Yasser Arafat
Ministers:	
Agriculture	Abedel Jawad Saleh (q.v.)
Civil Affairs	Jamil Tarifi (q.v.)
Culture and Information	Yasser Abed-Rabbo (q.v.)
Economy and Trade	Maher Al-Masri
Education	Yasser Amro (q.v.)
Higher Education	Dr. Hanan Ashrawi (q.v.)
Finance	Muhammad Nashashibi (q.v.)
Health	Dr. Riad Za'noun (q.v.)
Health Ministry Advisor	Dr. A. Al-Aziz al-Haj Ahmad
Housing	Dr. Abdel Rahman Hamad
Industry	Bashir Barghouthi (q.v.)
Jerusalem File	Faisal Al-Husseini (q.v.)
Justice	Freih Abu Middeyan (q.v.)
Labor	Samir Ghosheh (q.v.)
Local Government	Dr. Saeb 'Erekat (q.v.)

Planning and International Relations	Nabil Sha'ath (q.v.)
Public Works	Azzam Al-Hamad
Refugee Affairs Advisor	Abdallah Hourani (q.v.)
Secretary-General of Cabinet	Ahmad Abd Al-Rahman (q.v.)
Secretary-General of Presidency	Tayeb Abed Rahim (q.v.)
Social Affairs	Intisar Al-Wazir (q.v.)
Supply	Abdel Aziz Shaheen
Telecommunication	Imad Falouji (q.v.)
Tourism	Elias Freij (q.v.)
Transportation	Ali al-Qawasmi
Waqf and Islamic Affairs	Hassan Tahboub (q.v.)

PALESTINE NATIONAL CHARTER (PNC-MITHAQ). The covenant (*al-mithaq*) was issued in 1964 and amended in Cairo, Egypt, in July 1968. The earlier 1964 version of the charter stated that the PLO had no sovereignty over the land annexed by Jordan. Due to intense lobbying efforts and pressure from the various factions in July 1968, the charter was amended to include the liberation of all the land of Palestine.

The charter is composed of 33 articles, which delineate the Palestinian situation and views on Zionism (q.v.). It states that the Palestinians have the right to their homeland, that all of Palestine should be liberated and that Israel should be eliminated. Article 19 states that the establishment of the state of Israel in 1947 is "null and void." Therefore, the charter denies Israel's right to exist, denies any association between the Palestinians and Jews, and rejects any solution that deals with coexistence. It asserts, however, that Jews living in Palestine before 1917 are Palestinians, and have the right to remain in Palestine. It maintains that armed struggle is the only means of liberating the country. Article 26 of the covenant states that the PLO is the representative of the Palestinian people, and responsible for the revolution to liberate the country.

One of the demands made by the Israelis during the peace negotiations was that changes should be made in the covenant, and that all statements hostile and damaging to Israel (q.v.) be removed. Specifically, one of the conditions in the Oslo Two Agreement (q.v.) is that, within two months of the inauguration of the Palestinian Legislative Council (q.v.), all statements calling for the destruction of Israel are to be removed. The covenant, however, can be amended only if two-thirds of all the members of the Palestine National Council (q.v) vote in favor of the change. On April 18, 1996, PNC members living abroad were allowed to return to the autonomous areas (q.v.) and participate in the meeting convened to change the charter. On April 24, 1996, by a majority of 504–54, with 14 abstentions, the PNC approved amending the articles calling for the destruction of Israel (q.v.).

PALESTINE NATIONAL CONGRESS. The Arab League (q.v.), encouraged by Egypt (q.v.) in September 1963, called for the liberation of Palestine and the establishment of a Palestinian entity to be led by Ahmad Shuqeiri (q.v.). Consequently, a meeting was held in May 1964 in East Jerusalem (q.v.), and a resolution was passed establishing the Palestine Liberation Organization (q.v.). A national covenant was adopted, the Palestinian National Fund was set up, and the Palestine National Council was organized (qq.v.). The meeting became known as the first Palestine National Congress.

PALESTINE NATIONAL COUNCIL (PNC). The Palestinian parliament-in-exile, the legislative body, and the decision-making authority of the Palestinians. It comprises representatives of professional associations, trade unions, women's organizations, and political factions from the Occupied Territories (q.v.) and the diaspora. The identity of the members from the Occupied Territories were, until recently, unknown because of the fear of Israeli reprisals. The PNC is composed of 452 members (1993 figures, though the number usually fluctuates), who serve two-to-three year terms. More than half of the representatives in the PNC are members of FATAH (q.v.). In the organizational hierarchy, the PNC is second to the Executive Committee (q.v.). However, the Palestine Central Council (q.v.) was formed to facilitate and implement decisions when the PNC is not in session. The PNC meets annually to elect the Executive Committee and to approve the policies and budget of the PLO (qq.v.).

Major decisions taken by the PNC include amending the *Mithaq* (Covenant) (q.v.) in 1968 to emphasize the liberation of all of Palestine. In the 1964 version, no reference had been made to the territory (the West Bank, including East Jerusalem) that was annexed by Jordan (qq.v.) in 1950. In 1974, the PNC decreed that it would establish a "national authority" in any part of Palestine that Israel would vacate; the PNC declared the establishment of an independent Palestinian State on November 15, 1988. Meeting in Gaza on April 24, 1996, the PNC, by a majority of 504–54, with 14 abstentions, approved amending the statements calling for the destruction of Israel. See PALESTINE NATIONAL CHARTER.

PALESTINE NATIONAL FRONT (PNF). The Palestine National Council (q.v.), in January 1973, secretly authorized the establishment of a committee that would collectively organize resistance against Israeli policies, and weaken Jordan's influence in the Occupied Territories (q.v.). The committee included representatives of Palestinian political factions who became very influential. In 1976, the front organized a group of candidates who ran for municipal elections, on pro-PLO platforms, and won most of the seats on the municipal councils in the Occupied Territories (q.v.).

The PLO was threatened by the popularity of the front leaders in the Occupied Territories, and demanded that all decisions made by the front be approved by the PLO before they were made public. Israel, too, made things difficult for the front by deporting many of its leaders. Jordan also played a role in fragmenting the front, which dissolved in 1977, just before Israel declared it illegal in October 1978. There was an attempt to revive the front after the Committee for National Guidance (q.v.) was established.

PALESTINE NATIONAL FUND (PNF). Established in May 1964 during the first Palestinian National Congress (q.v.) to finance the Palestine Liberation Organization (q.v.) and its activities. It also cooperates with other PLO institutions in the distribution of the fund's resources. Support for the fund comes from Qatar, Morocco, Saudi Arabia (q.v.), Oman, Sudan, Iran, Pakistan, and Tunisia. It also is funded by a 5 percent "liberation tax," that is deducted from the wages of Palestinian workers in the Gulf countries and transferred directly to the PLO. In 1977, a Steadfastness Fund, or *Sunduq Al-Sumud*, was set up to assist the Palestinians under occupation and discourage their emigration from the West Bank and the Gaza Strip (qq.v.). The money was used to support municipalities, medical facilities, education, and housing. During the Intifada (q.v.), it was used for welfare purposes, to support Palestinians who were unable to work and the families of prisoners and martyrs. There are no exact figures for the fund's budget, although it is rumored to be several hundred million dollars.

PALESTINE NATIONAL LIBERATION MOVEMENT. see FATAH.

PALESTINE NON-GOVERNMENT ORGANIZATIONS (PNGOS). The economic, health, social, and educational non-profit organizations that were created to meet the needs of the Palestinians in the absence of a national authority. These organizations provided financial assistance and services ranging from loans to low-cost health care to Palestinians in the Occupied Territories (q.v.). They continue to funtion under the PNA (q.v.).

Some institutions in the economic sector are: the Arab Development and Credit Company, the United Arab Agricultural Company, the Economic Development Group (q.v.), and the Technical Development Center. Organizations in the health sphere include: the Health Service Council, Patients Friends Societies, Zakaat Charitable Societies, Health Work Committees, and Medical Relief Committees.

PALESTINE PEOPLE'S PARTY (PPP). Formerly the Palestinian Communist Party formed in the Occupied Territories (q.v.) in February 1982 and led by Bashir al-Barghouthi (q.v.). The party discarded the ideology of Lenin in 1991 and renamed itself the Palestine People's Party. It does not engage in militant activities. The party has played an important role in the politics of the Occupied Territories. It helped establish the Palestine National Front (q.v.); it pioneered Palestinian-Israeli dialogue and advocated a two-state solution. It is considered pragmatic and supportive of the peace process, and active in professional organizations, municipalities, trade unions, and welfare associations. The PPP was the only organized party to run against FATAH (q.v.) in the January 20,1996 elections for the PLC (q.v.). No candidate from the PPP, however, was elected. Nevertheless, members of the party are actively participating in political activities (q.c.). Bashir al-Barghouthi has been appointed minister of Indusrty in the PNA (q.v.). The party publishes a weekly, *Al-Tali'a* (The Vanguard).

PALESTINE PRESS SERVICE (PPS). A pro-PLO wire service for newspapers located in East Jerusalem (q.v.) that was established by Raymonda Tawil (q.v.), Ibrahim Kara'een, and Radwan Abu Ayyash (qq.v.). It arranges meetings for journalists and politicians with Palestinian leaders. It also publishes a weekly magazine, *Al-Awdah* (q.v.). During the Intifada (q.v.), the Palestine Press Service was closed by Israeli military authorities.

PALESTINE THEOLOGICAL SOCIETY (PTS). The highest decision-making body within HAMAS (q.v.). It is headed by Ahmad Bitawi (q.v.).

PALESTINE UNION OF WOMEN WORKS COMMITTEES (PUWWC). Renamed the Palestine Federation of Women's Action Committees in June 1987. It is affiliated with the Democratic Front for the Liberation of Palestine (q.v.).

PALESTINE WOMEN'S COMMITTEE. The committee is affiliated with the Popular Front for the Liberation of Palestine (q.v.), and works to improve the status of women in the Occupied Territories (q.v.)

PALESTINIAN ACADEMIC SOCIETY FOR THE STUDY OF INTERNATIONAL AFFAIRS (PASSIA). A Palestinian think-tank established in March 1987 by Mahdi Abd al-Hadi (q.v.) and others, and located in East Jerusalem (q.v.). It publishes political, social, and economic studies on the Occupied Territories (q.v.). It also focuses on foreign policy and strategic studies, and provides training in diplomacy and international affairs. It holds conferences and round-table discussions with local and visiting scholars.

PALESTINIAN AUTHORITY. see PALESTINE NATIONAL AUTHORITY.

PALESTINIAN DEMOCRATIC CONSTRUCTION MOVEMENT. A movement established in Gaza (q.v.) by Haidar Abd Al-Shafi (q.v.) on June 9, 1994, to promote democracy and human rights.

PALESTINIAN FEDERATION. In Arabic, *Al-Tajamou' al-Filistini.* The faction was organized in February 1995 by Bassam al-Shak'a (q.v.), the former mayor of Nablus (q.v.). It is composed of political factions that rejected the Declaration of Principles (q.v.). It includes HAMAS (q.v.), Islamic Jihad (q.v.), the PFLP (q.v.), the DFLP (q.v.), and independents.

The Palestinian Federation believes the PNA (q.v.) is not representative of the Palestinian people, and that it has made too many concessions to Israel, which is not abiding by the agreement as it continues to confiscate Arab land and build new settlements in the Occupied Territories (q.v.).

PALESTINIAN FEDERATION OF WOMEN'S ACTION COMMITTEES (PFWAC). The federation was established in 1978 to increase the participation of women in Palestinian national life. It also works to raise the consciousness of women and to stop oppression and violence against them. It encourages programs that foster the economic independence of women and assists in setting up projects and sponsoring lectures and workshops.

PALESTINIAN INTERIM SELF-GOVERNING AUTHORITY (PISGA). The model for the Palestinian political entity that the Palestinian delegation presented to the Israelis on January 14, 1992. PISGA would be composed of Palestinian representatives chosen by the people in free elections (universal suffrage and secret ballot) under international supervision that would be held in the West Bank and Gaza Strip (qq.v.). Israel would then transfer authority in the

Occupied Territories (q.v.), including East Jerusalem (q.v.), to the Palestinians.

PISGA, or the self-governing authority, would be part of an interim agreement. It would have legislative and executive power, a strong police force, and a judiciary. It also would represent the Palestinians in any future negotiations with Israel (q.v.).

PALESTINIAN LEGISLATIVE COUNCIL (PLC). The Oslo Two Agreement (q.v.) stipulated that after Israel redeploys from the major cities in the West Bank (q.v.), elections for the president of the PNA (q.v.) and an 82-member legislative council would take place. The elections took place on January 20, 1996. Between November 12 and December 12, 1995 (later extended to January 8, 1996), 7,000 specially-trained Palestinian teachers registered a total of 1,013,235 voters in the West Bank, East Jerusalem (q.v.), and the Gaza Strip (q.v.). A Central Election Commission was established on December 22, 1995, and Mahmoud Abbas (q.v.) was appointed its chairman. Arafat (q.v.) increased the number of the legislative council seats with Israel's permission, from 82 to 88. A quota system was introduced which guaranteed Christians one seat in Gaza (q.v.), two seats in Jerusalem, two seats in Bethlehem (q.v.), and one seat in Ramallah (q.v.). The 400-member Samaritan community of Nablus (q.v.) also received one seat.

The West Bank, East Jerusalem, and the Gaza Strip were divided into 16 electoral districts (q.v.)—5 districts in Gaza and 11 in the West Bank. A total of 676 candidates registered to run for the 88-member legislative council. FATAH (q.v.), Arafat's party presented more candidates than any other party or faction. The PPP (q.v.) was the only organized party that ran against FATAH in the elections, thus no real ideological debate took place in the elections. HAMAS (q.v.), the PFLP (q.v.), the DFLP (q.v.), and Islamic Jihad (q.v.) boycotted the elections.

FATAH won 52 seats (61 percent of the votes), FATAH independents (rebels and activists) garnered 12 seats (14 percent of the votes), Independents won 16 seats (18 percent of the votes), candidates affiliated with small parties (Fida (q.v.), etc.) won two seats, and independent candidates (Islamists) won 4 seats or 5 percent of the votes. Five women were elected, 28 ran as candidates in the elections. One seat is held by Arafat, the elected president of the PNA and another seat, by the Samaritans.

PALESTINIAN NATIONAL SALVATION FRONT (PNSF). An anti-Arafat (q.v.), Syrian-supported alliance of factions formed on March 25, 1985, to oppose the Arafat-Hussein Agreement (q.v.) of February

11, 1985. It included FATAH Uprising (q.v.), PNF (q.v.), PFLP (q.v.), PFLP-GC (q.v.), PPSF (q.v.), PLF-Ya'koub faction and al-Sa'iqa (qq.v.). It was led by Khalid al-Fahum (q.v.). The factions had earlier boycotted the Palestine National Council (q.v.) meeting held from November 22–29, 1984. At that PNC meeting, a decision had been made to dismiss the speaker, Khalid al-Fahum, and replace him with Abd al-Hamid al-Sayyeh (q.v.).

PALESTINIAN PREVENTIVE SECURITY SERVICE. The security service was set up by the PNA (q.v.) in 1994, and it answers directly to Arafat (q.v.). It is one of nine similar bodies that serve as part of the policing forces for the PNA. Members of the preventive security service are local activists who were members of FATAH's *shabibeh* (q.v.), which was formed in the 1980s, and those who joined FATAH's underground organization before or during the Intifada (q.v.). The Israelis have restricted the operational services of the Preventive Security in the Occupied Territories, and allow it to function only in the areas where there has been redeployment of Israeli soldiers. The head of the Preventive Security Service in Jericho is Jibril Rajoub (qq.v.), a close assistant to Arafat (q.v.).

PALESTINIAN RED CRESCENT SOCIETY (PRCS). Also known as *Hilal*, Arabic for crescent. The Palestinian society was established in Jordan in 1969 by Fathi Arafat (q.v.) to provide low-cost medical assistance to the Palestinians. Since then, it has evolved into an intricate organization that has branches in many Arab countries and in the West Bank and the Gaza Strip (qq.v.). It has built medical facilities, such as clinics, laboratories, and blood banks. It also has opened nursing schools and a center for the production of artificial limbs. Furthermore, it provides social services for the Palestinians. During the Intifada (q.v.), the Palestinian Red Crescent was very active in supporting the families of the prisoners by sending food, such as olive oil (a breakfast stable), clothes, and other items allowed by the Israelis to Palestinian prisoners. The Palestinian Red Crescent also arranged for buses to transport families to visit their relatives in prisons. The Palestinian Red Crescent has observer status at the International Red Cross. Currently, the president of the Red Crescent Society is its founder, Dr. Fathi Arafat (q.v.).

PALESTINIAN SOCIALIST BA'TH PARTY. A Palestinian political party that is closely aligned with the Iraqi Ba'th (q.v.) ideology. It is part of the Palestinian national movement and is supportive of Arafat (q.v.), the Palestine National Authority, and the peace process (q.v.). It is also called the Palestinian-Arab Socialist Ba'th Party.

PALESTINIAN WOMEN'S UNION (PWU). The union was established on July 15, 1965, in Gaza (q.v.) to improve the status of women and to encourage their greater participation in and contribution to Palestinian national life.

PECDAR. see PALESTINIAN ECONOMIC COUNCIL FOR DEVELOPMENT AND RECONSTRUCTION.

PEEL COMMISSION. The British government, in the aftermath of the Arab revolt (q.v.) and the rebellions of 1936 sent Lord Earl Peel, as the head of a royal commission, to investigate the situation in Palestine (q.v.). The commission recommended that Palestine be partitioned into two states, a Jewish state and a Palestinian state that would include Transjordan. Both the Arabs and the Jews rejected this compromise. Consequently, the proposals were discarded by the Palestine Partition Commission in 1938. To assuage the Arabs, the British White Paper (q.v.) was proposed in 1939, which limited Jewish immigration to Palestine to 75,000 for the period between 1939 and 1944.

PERES, SHIMON. Born in Poland in 1923, he emigrated with his family to Palestine (q.v.) in 1934. Peres became active in the paramilitary youth movement at an early age. He joined the Haganah, the Jewish underground movement, in 1947. In 1952, he became the director-general and later helped form the Israeli Labor Party. Peres was appointed to several ministerial positions; minister of Immigrant Absorption (1969), minister of Transport and Communication (1972), and minister of Information (1974). When Yitzhak Rabin (q.v.) resigned, Peres became the prime minister on April 7, 1977. When the National Unity government was formed on September 13, 1984, it stipulated that Peres would be prime minister for two years, then Yitzhak Shamir (q.v.) would hold the post for two years. In 1992, Rabin appointed him as foreign minister. He remained in that position until November 5, 1995, when Rabin was assassinated and he was appointed acting Prime Minister.

Peres supported the establishment of peace with the Palestinians and participated in the secret negotiations in Oslo that eventually led to the signing of the DOP (q.v.) with the Palestinians. He also encouraged the peace process with Jordan (q.v.), which led to the signing of a peace treaty on October 24, 1994. Peres was a co-winner of the Nobel Peace Prize in December 1994 with Arafat (q.v.) and Rabin.

POPULAR DEMOCRATIC FRONT FOR THE LIBERATION OF PALESTINE (PDFLP). see DEMOCRATIC FRONT FOR THE LIBERATION OF PALESTINE (DFLP).

POPULAR FRONT FOR THE LIBERATION OF PALESTINE (PFLP). A political Marxist faction formed on December 11, 1967, by George Habash (q.v.). It is an independent faction, and although its headquarters are in Syria (q.v.), it has no affiliation with the ideology of the Syrian Ba'th (q.v.). Many PFLP supporters and members are recruited from refugee camps in Lebanon (q.v.), Syria, and Jordan (q.v.).

The PFLP has engaged in militant activities. In 1970, it hijacked three airplanes and forced them to land in Zarqa, Jordan, then proceeded to blow them up. That same year, the PFLP also was involved in an attempt to overthrow King Hussein (q.v.). In 1972, members of the PFLP and a Japanese "Red Army" guerrilla group attacked Ben-Gurion Airport in Israel (q.v.) in "Operation Deir Yassin," a reference to the village of Deir Yassin (q.v.), where 245 Palestinians had been killed.

During the Intifada (q.v.), it joined the Unified National Leadership of the Uprising (q.v.). Its military wing is called the Red Eagle Squads (q.v.). The Popular Front for the Liberation of Palestine split twice. In 1968, the Palestine Liberation Front withdrew and re-named itself the PFLP-GC (q.v.). In 1969, the Democratic Front for the Liberation of Palestine (q.v.) seceded and went off on its own.

The PFLP is against the mainstream policy of the PLO (q.v.), particularly with regard to any political settlement with Israel, as well as the Declaration of Principles and the Oslo Two Agreement (qq.v.). In 1974, the faction disagreed with the PNC's (q.v.) decision to establish a state anywhere in Palestine. It boycotted the PLO Executive Committee and the Central Council (qq.v.) from 1974 to 1981, and again from 1983 to 1987. Moreover, it refused to participate in the elections for the PLC (q.v.) on January 20, 1996.

POPULAR FRONT FOR THE LIBERATION OF PALESTINE-GENERAL COMMAND (PFLP-GC). The PFLP-GC seceded from the PFLP (q.v.) in 1969 under the leadership of Ahmad Jibril (q.v.), who was then an officer in the Syrian army. Composed of secret cells, the faction is based in Syria (q.v.), and it adheres closely to the Ba'th (q.v.) ideology. It also is supported by Libya. In 1983, it joined the anti-Arafat (q.v.) camp, but did not participate in the reconciliation that took place with him in 1987. It uses extreme tactics and is allegedly to blame for the bombing of Pan American flight 103 over Lockerbie, Scotland, and other subversive activities. Moreover, it rejects any negotiations with Israel (q.v.) and did not participate in the PLC (q.v.) elections held on January 20, 1996. See also DEMOCRATIC ALLIANCE and NATIONAL SALVATION FRONT.

POPULAR STRUGGLE FRONT (PSF). A leftist PLO faction that adheres to the Ba'th (q.v.) ideology and is based in Syria (q.v.). In 1969, the Popular Struggle Front seceded from FATAH (q.v.) under the leadership of Samir Ghosheh (q.v.), Subhi Gosheh, and Bahjat Abu Gahrbiyyeh (q.v.). The front joined the 1984 National Alliance (q.v.), and later the National Salvation Front (q.v.).

POPULATION. In 1995, the Palestinian population was estimated to be about 6,882,000. A report by the Palestinian Planning and Research Center estimates the population of the West Bank (q.v.) to be 1,250,000 and that of the Gaza Strip (q.v) to be 880,000—for a total of 2,130,000 The Palestinians in the diaspora, according to a report by UNRWA (q.v.), number 3,942,000. They are distributed as follows: Jordan, 2,170,000; Lebanon, 395,000; Syria, 360,000; other Arab countries, 517,000; and the rest of the world, 500,000. Israel has 810,000 Palestinians or Israeli-Arabs (q.v.).

PRESS. After the war of 1967 (q.v.), the Palestinian press was subjected to strict censorship regulations. Everything that was to be printed had to be submitted to the Israeli censor. Often, newspapers would appear with empty columns, except for the words "we apologize," because that material had been removed by the censors.

New press laws were announced by the Palestine National Authority's (q.v.) minister of Culture and Information, Yasser Abed-Rabbo, in the Gaza Strip (qq.v.). The laws consist of 51 articles that were approved by Arafat and the PNC (qq.v.) and became effective on July 25, 1995. They replaced the Press Law of 1933 that had been introduced by the British Mandate (q.v.) and included an array of Egyptian, British, and Israeli military laws dealing with the press.

The new press law imposes restrictions on the press concerning the activities of the PNA police and the national guards, as well as information concerning arms, location of military bases, movement of police, or any report that would threaten national security or those that jeopardize the national currency. It bans reports that incite violence or racism. All papers that lack permits or receive aid and financial instruction from foreign governments are prohibited from publication (Article 37).

The law permits the Ministry of Culture and Information to ask for retractions and corrections, and to impose $750 fines or one-month prison sentences if the law is disregarded. The courts also are allowed to impose penalties, such as fines, prison terms, and the suspension of publication for up to three months. Although the law does not permit restraining the press prior to publication (although it can be done later by court actions), it does allow for a one-day confiscation of the paper, and gives the publisher the right to petition the courts.

Unlike Israeli practices, journalists cannot be interrogated by government officials, but they can be taken to court. They do not have to submit their stories to government officials prior to publication, nor do they have to reveal their sources, unless the courts order them to do so. On the other hand, books and other publications must be submitted to the ministry before publication. See also MEDIA.

Q

AL-QADDUMI, FAROUQ. Nom de guerre, Abu Lutf. Secretary-General of FATAH (q.v.), PLO (q.v.) Executive Committee (q.v.) member, and head of the PLO Political Department. Regarded as the PLO's foreign minister, al-Qaddumi worked tirelessly to encourage contacts in order to win recognition for the PLO, and to open representational offices in these countries. He is known for his diplomatic skills and extensive contacts in the Middle East and the international community.

Born in Nablus (q.v.) in 1931, his early years were spent in Haifa, Palestine. After the war of 1948 (q.v.), his family moved back to Nablus (q.v.). Educated at the American University of Cairo, he majored in economics and became affiliated with the Ba'th (q.v.) Party. He worked in Libya, Saudi Arabia, and Kuwait (qq.v.). In 1965, he left for Syria (q.v.), where he became active in organizing FATAH. At one time, he was imprisoned and sentenced to death by Jordan (q.v.). He has not joined the Palestine National Authority in the autonomous areas (qq.v.), but remains active on behalf of the PLO in Tunis.

QADI. A Muslim religious judge in the Islamic judicial system who administers justice in accordance with the *Shari'a* (Islamic law), and who decides on civil and criminal matters. Among his tasks are officiating at contracts-of-marriage-signing ceremonies, adjudicating divorce and child custody cases, and resolving disputes over inheritance rights.

QALQILYA. A town in the northern part of the West Bank (q.v.), with a population of 9,780. It is an agricultural area known for its citrus fruits and vegetables.

AL-QAQ, ANIS. Deputy minister of Planning and International Coordination in the Palestine National Authority (q.v.), and secretary-general of the Health Services Council, which provides primary, curative, and rehabilitative care to needy Palestinians. Since 1986, the council has supervised the establishment of 88 health-care centers, and it cooperates with the Palestinian Red Crescent Society (q.v.) and the Patients Friends Society.

Al-Qaq was born in Silwan, a village adjacent to Jerusalem (q.v.). Excelling in school, he received a scholarship to study dentistry in Iraq. While there, he became active in the General Union of Palestinian Students (q.v.). He graduated with a B.S. in dentistry and returned to Jerusalem to open a private clinic. Since 1984, al-Qaq has been the chairman of the board of trustees of the National Palestinian Theater; president of the Palestinian Swedish Friendship Society, which he has headed since 1989; and an executive member of the Council for Higher Education (q.v.). He also served as the head of the Professional Unions (a union comprising representatives of a number of professional unions) from 1986 to 1990, and was chairman of the Dental Association in the West Bank (q.v.). In 1991, he was a board member of the International Coordinating Committee on the Question of Palestine.

AL-QASSAM, IZZEDIN. A Syrian, he was born in Jabala in 1882, and was sent to Al-Azhar University in Cairo to study religion when he was 14 years old. He returned to Syria (q.v.) in 1903, but left for Turkey to study *Shari'a* (q.v.). He moved to Haifa, Palestine (q.v.), in 1925. A charismatic Muslim preacher and religious teacher, he was closely affiliated with the Muslim Brotherhood (q.v.). He preached against the presence of the British and the Jews in Palestine, and was able to recruit many supporters from the rural areas and the lower classes. Taking matters into his own hands, he organized and led a commando group against the British on November 11, 1934 and was subsequently killed in that first attack. He is buried in the Muslim cemetery in Nesher near Haifa. The special military wing of HAMAS (q.v.) is named after him.

AL-QAUQJI, FAWZI. A supporter of pan-Arabism, he came to Palestine (q.v.) in 1936 with 200 volunteer fighters from Syria and Iraq (qq.v.) to join forces with the Palestinian-Arabs in fighting the British and Zionists. He was born in Syria and trained by the French military. In 1925, he led an unsuccessful revolt against the French in Syria. Afterward, he gathered a unit of fighters and headed for Palestine, where he was eventually expelled by the British for his activities.

AL-QAWASMI, FAHD. Political activist and former mayor of Hebron (q.v.), he was born in Hebron (q.v.) on April 13, 1939. From 1962 to 1968, he taught at UNRWA schools in the West Bank (qq.v.). Later, he worked as an engineer in the agricultural department for the Israeli military government, and was promoted to supervisor of Research and Guidance in the Civil Administration (q.v.). Qawasmi ran successfully on the pro-PLO (q.v.) nationalist platform in the 1976 municipal elections, after Sheikh Mohammad al-Ja'bari (q.v.) refused to declare his candidacy. He was thought to harbor pro-Jordanian sentiments, and was criticized and denounced several times by *Falastine Al-Thawra* (Palestine, the Revolution). He helped establish the Council for Higher Education (q.v.), and was a member of the Committee for National Guidance (q.v.). Israeli authorities deported Qawasmi, together with Muhammad Milhem (q.v.), to Lebanon (q.v.) on May 2, 1980. Qawasmi was assassinated in Jordan (q.v.) on December 29, 1985.

QRE'I, AHMAD. Nom de guerre, Abu 'Ala. He is a PLC (q.v.) member for East Jerusalem (q.v.) and the council's spokesman. Qrei' returned to the West Bank (q.v.) on July 14, 1994 and was appointed minister of Economy, Trade, and Industry in the first PNA (q.v.) government. Qrei' is considered the Palestinian architect, together with Mahmoud Abbas, of the Oslo Accords (qq.v.). He was born in the village of Abu Dis near Jerusalem (q.v.). Deported by the Israelis in 1970, he went to Lebanon (q.v.). In Beirut in the early 1970s, he founded SAMED (q.v.), now a multimillion-dollar investment firm, and also headed the PLO (q.v.) Economic Department in Tunis. In the late 1980s, he became a leading member of FATAH and Arafat's (q.v.) confidant. He has been a member of the FATAH Central Committee since 1989, and a member of the Palestine National Council (q.v.). He currently serves as the secretary-general of the Palestinian Economic Council for Development and Reconstruction (q.v.) in the Occupied Territories (q.v).

AL-QUDS. Arabic for "Jerusalem" (q.v.). A Palestinian Arabic daily newspaper that is published by Mahmoud Abu Zuluf (q.v.) in East Jerusalem (q.v.). The newspaper started as *Al-Jihad* (The Struggle or Holy War), which Abu Zuluf founded with two partners in 1951. After the 1967 war (q.v.), the newspaper was renamed *Al-Quds* and published in East Jerusalem. Since then, it has played a pivotal role in formulating public opinion in the West Bank and the Gaza Strip (qq.v.), and has reflected various political ideologies. It has a circulation of 50,000, and was the first in the Occupied Territories (q.v.) to introduce the Web-Offset printing press, as well as full-color printing facilities for newspapers and advertising.

AL-QUDS AL-SHARIF. Arabic for "Jerusalem (q.v.), the noble".

AL-QUDS UNIVERSITY. The first Arab university in East Jerusalem (q.v.). It was established in 1984 to incorporate four colleges: the College of Science and Technology (est. in 1979) in Abu Dis, a suburb of Jerusalem the Arab College for Medical Professions (est. in 1979) in al-Bireh (q.v.); the College of Religious Studies and Jurisprudence (est. in 1978) in Beit Hanina, another suburb of Jerusalem; and the College of Arts for Women (est. in 1980) in East Jerusalem. It also has two institutes: the Higher Institute for Islamic Archeology (est. in 1992) in Jerusalem, which offers a master's degree in Islamic archeology, and the Islamic Research Center (est. in 1988). Altogether, student enrollment is about 2,000. The current president of Al-Quds University is Sari Nuseibeh (q.v.).

R

RABAH, KHALIL. An architect and artist born in Ramallah (q.v.) in 1961. Rabah left for the United States in 1980 to study art and architecture. He returned to Ramallah in 1992 and established an architectural consulting center.

Rabah has held a one-person show in Florida, Michigan, Texas, and East Jerusalem (q.v.). He also has participated in group exhibitions in Jordan (q.v.) at the Shoman Foundation Gallery and in Saint Nazaire, France.

RABAT SUMMIT RESOLUTION. The resolution passed on October 28, 1974 at the Arab Summit Conference in Rabat, Morocco. It stated that the Palestinians had the right to self-determination and to return to their homeland. It also decreed that the Palestine Liberation Organization (q.v.) is the sole legitimate representative of the Palestinian people. The Arab states attending the summit pledged to support the Palestinians and not to interfere in their internal affairs. King Hussein of Jordan (qq.v.) was furious at the passage of this resolution because it minimized his role in the West Bank (q.v.), and gave the PLO (q.v.) responsibilities for Palestinian affairs in the Occupied Territories (q.v.). Hussein had no choice, however, but to go along with the summit's decision.

RABIN, YITZHAK. Israeli army general, Labor Party leader, defense minister, and two-term Israeli prime minister—from 1974–1977 and from 1992 until November 4, 1995. He also is a co-winner of the 1994 Nobel Peace Prize, along with Shimon Peres (q.v.), the Israeli foreign minister, and Yasser Arafat (q.v.) for their efforts in bringing peace to their people.

Rabin was born on March 1, 1922, in Jerusalem and studied at the Kadourie Agricultural School. He joined the Haganah, the Jewish resistance organization, that was active during the British Mandate (q.v.), and participated in the Palmah's operation in Syria (q.v.) in 1941. In 1946, he was arrested by the British and sent to the British detention camp in Rafah, Gaza (q.v.), for six months. Rabin also participated in the 1948 war, particularly in the battles in Lydd and Ramleh, and was chief of operations in the Neqab and Eilat. He also was a member of the Israeli delegation that signed the armstice agreements with the Arabs in 1949.

Rabin steadily moved up the hierarchy of the Israeli Defense Force, as his military prowess became apparent. After graduating from Staff College in Britain in 1953, he was appointed head of the General Staff Branch. On January 1, 1964, he was appointed Israel's seventh chief-of-staff. He became a war hero in the aftermath of the war of 1967 (q.v.) Rabin was appointed Israel's (q.v.) ambassador to the United States from 1968 to 1973. On December 31, 1973, he was elected to the Israeli Knesset, or parliament. He became the labor minister in March 1974 in Golda Meir's government. At the age of 52, he became Israel's fifth prime minister. Rabin met with King Hussein in 1976 to resolve their differences, but Hussein rejected the return of the West Bank (q.v.) when the Israelis insisted on maintaining a defense line along the Jordan River. When it was later revealed that his wife Leah had a U.S. bank account (illegal for Israelis), he was forced to resign the premiership on April 7, 1977. However, he remained prominent in the Labor Party and became defense minister in a coalition formed in 1981. In 1987, when the Intifada (q.v.) broke out, he introduced the "iron fist policy" against the Palestinians. In 1992, he was re-elected prime minister.

As a member of Israel's Labor Party and as prime minister, Rabin commited himself to establishing peace for Israel with its Arab neighbors. He encouraged the secret negotiations in Oslo, Norway, and signed the DOP (q.v.) in Washington. In September 1995, he oversaw the negotiations for the Oslo Two Agreement (q.v.). Rabin also encouraged the establishment of peace with Jordan, which culminated in the signing of a peace treaty on October 26, 1994. Moreover, under Rabin's leadership, Israel drew closer to negotiating a peace with Syria and Lebanon (qq.v.).

Rabin was assassinated by an Israeli, Yigal Amir, a 25-year-old law student who allegedly was a member of an extreme right-wing organization opposed to the peace process, after the prime minister had appeared at a peace rally in Tel Aviv on November 4, 1995.

RAHIM, TAYEB ABED. Secretary-general in the Palestine National Authority in the Gaza Strip (qq.v.) in 1994, and secretary-general of the Palestinian presidency in 1996. He was born in the West Bank (q.v.) village of Anabta, near Nablus (q.v.), in 1943. He grew up in Nazareth and stayed there until his father, Abed al-Rahim, was killed in the battle of al-Shajara in the war of 1948 (q.v.). Afterward, the family returned to Anabta. Continuing his education in Egypt (q.v.), Tayeb studied at al-Azhar University. After joining FATAH (q.v.), he served as the vice-director, and then director of FATAH's broadcasting station, al-'Asifa (Thunderstorm) (q.v.), from 1973 until 1978. Abed Rahim was a member of the Palestine National Council (q.v.) in 1977, a member of the FATAH Revolutionary Council (q.v.) in 1980, and a member of the PLO Central Council (q.v.) in 1983. He was appointed the PLO representative to China, and also served as the deputy commander of political affairs for the Palestinian forces. He later was assigned as the PLO representative to Egypt, Yugoslavia, the non-aligned nations, and Jordan. He returned to the Gaza Strip with Arafat (qq.v.), in 1994.

RAJOUB, JIBRIL. The chief of the Palestine National Authority's Preventive Security Services (qq.v.). He was born in 1953 in Dura, a village near Hebron (q.v.). After the war of 1967 (q.v.), he joined FATAH (q.v.) and became an active member. In 1968, he was caught throwing a grenade at an Israeli bus south of Hebron. Although no one was injured, he was sentenced to 18 years in prison. During his tenure in jail, he became a FATAH leader and organized strikes inside the prison. In 1985, Israel and the PLO (q.v.) brokered an agreement whereby 1,150 Palestinian prisoners were exchanged for three Israeli prisoners of war. Of the freed Palestinians, 600 were allowed to return to their homes. Rajoub was one of those who returned. He became the deputy editor of the women's magazine *Abeer*. His covert activities included organizing shock troops or strike forces during the Intifada (q.v.) against Palestinians who collaborated with Israel (q.v.). He was arrested, placed in administrative detention (q.v.), and finally deported in 1988. Arafat (q.v.) took him to Tunis, when Jordan (q.v.), Lebanon, and Egypt (qq.v.) refused to give him asylum. Rajoub was put in charge of the distribution of funds to the Intifada leaders, a task that gave him a great deal of influence and power in the Occupied Territories (q.v.). He currently is headquartered in Jericho (q.v.).

RAMALLAH. A commercial city in the heart of the West Bank (qq.v.) that provides economic, health, and educational services to the surrounding villages and towns. It currently is experiencing a construction boom because of the signing of the Declaration of Principles (q.v.), and the Israeli law that prohibits the Palestine National Authority (q.v.) from opening offices in East Jerusalem (q.v.). Prior to the Israeli occupation of 1967, with its cool weather, natural fountains, and rose gardens, it was considered a summer resort by many who flocked to it from the Gulf countries to escape the heat. Ramallah has a population of 28,103. See DISTRICTS.

RANTISI, ABD AL-AZIZ. One of the leaders of HAMAS (q.v.), he assumed control of the movement in 1989. He was born in 1947 in Yebna (Jibna), a village adjacent to Ashdud and Jaffa, Palestine (q.v.). During the war of 1948 (q.v.), he fled to Khan Younis in the Gaza Strip (q.v.). He continued his education in Egypt (q.v.), and in 1971 received an M.S. in medicine and, five years later, an M.S. in pediatrics, from the University of Alexandria. During his stay in Egypt, he became affiliated with the Muslim Brotherhood (q.v.). When he returned to the Gaza Strip, he worked from 1976 to 1986 as chief pediatrician at the Government Hospital in Khan Younis. In 1983, he was fired by the Israelis, who were in charge of the hospital, because of his political activities. He then worked as a general practitioner in Rafah, in the Gaza Strip, until he joined the Nursing College at the Islamic University (q.v.) in 1985. But the Israelis soon closed the college, and Rantisi was transferred to the university's faculty of science. During the Intifada (q.v.), he spent four years in prison, including two terms in administrative detention (q.v.). He was released in December 1991. On December 15, 1992, he was expelled to Marj Al-Zuhur in Lebanon (q.v.) with 415 other Palestinians alleged by Israel (q.v.) to be members of Islamic organizations, after the killing of an Israeli border policeman, Nissim Toledano. The deportees remained in Lebanon until September 1993, when Israel permitted them to return. Rantisi, however, was imprisoned by the Israelis in December 1993 and charged with membership in HAMAS, which Israel declared an illegal organization. On August 23, 1995, he was sentenced by the Israeli military court to 42 months in prison for membership in HAMAS and for the recruiting of members.

AL-RAYYES, ZUHEIR. A member of the PLO (q.v.) who co-wrote the Palestinian National Charter (q.v.). He was born in 1943 in Nazareth, Palestine, but grew up in Gaza (q.v.). In 1954, he received his LL.B. from Cairo University in Egypt (q.v.). He returned to Gaza and practiced law. In 1956, he co-founded the Union of Arab lawyers and the Union of Arab Journalists, and remained its deputy secretary-general until 1967. Changing careers, al-Rayyes published a newspaper called *Al-Tahrir* (The Liberation) from 1957 to 1960, and *Akhbar Filistine* (News of Palestine) from 1963 to 1967. The PLO later took over the paper, and he became an associate editor with Muhammad al-Radwan. Because of his strong pan-Arab sentiments, he was a great supporter of Arab unity under President Nasser of Egypt (qq.v.), and served as a member of the legislative council of the National Union when Egypt was in control of the Gaza Strip from 1962 to 1965. He later became secretary of the Palestinian Council of Operations Solidarity, an affiliate of the PLO (q.v.), and secretary-general of the Palestinian Council for World Peace. In 1975, he founded a local magazine, *Ulum* (Sciences), that continued to be published until 1987, when it was closed because of financial problems. From 1976 to 1979, he was a member and chairman of the editorial board of *Al-Fajr* (Dawn) (q.v.). He also published a newspaper, *Al-Mawqif* (The Position). In 1988, he received a Ph.D. from the University of California for advanced studies.

RED EAGLE SQUADS. The military wing of the Popular Front for the Liberation of Palestine (q.v.) that carried out sabotage activities against Israeli targets, particularly during the Intifada (q.v.).

REFUGEES. A refugee is defined as any one who left his home or land during wars or disasters. UNRWA (q.v.) defines a Palestinian refugee as any Palestinian who was "shut out of his homeland and stripped of his money and property." The right of return for the refugees is recognized internationally by U.N. Resolution 194 (q.v.) of December 1948. In 1947–48, the population of Palestine was 1.3 million. During the war of 1948 (q.v.), 700,000 left their homes. Approximately 100,000 to 150,000 remained in what became the state of Israel (q.v.).

There are 20 refugee camps in the West Bank (q.v.) and eight in the Gaza Strip (q.v.). Most of these camps were established between 1948 and 1953. The exception is Shu'fat camp, which was established in East Jerusalem (q.v.) in 1965. The refugees from the Old City of Jerusalem were relocated to Shu'fat camp, in order to expand the Jewish quarter. Refugees who originally came from Palestine (q.v.) cities of Jaffa, Haifa, and Acre settled in West Bank (q.v.) cities of Jenin (q.v.), Nablus and Tulkarm (qq.v.). Most of the refugees who settled in Gaza came from the coastal and southern parts of Palestine. In 1946, the population of the Gaza Strip (q.v.) was approximately 75,000. It is estimated that approximately 150,000 Palestinian refugees moved to the Gaza Strip after the war of 1948.

In the aftermath of the Six-Day War of 1967 (q.v.), 300,000 to 400,000 Palestinian Arabs were uprooted from the West Bank, the Gaza Strip, and the Syrian Golan Heights (q.v.), many of them for the second time. The refugees settled in Jordan, Syria, Lebanon, Kuwait (qq.v.), and the Gulf countries. Those who went to Jordan were granted citizenship.

According to UNRWA (q.v.) figures of July 1994, there are a total of 3,172,641 Palestinian refugees distributed as follows: Jordan, 1,288,197; the West Bank, 517,412; the Gaza Strip, 683,560; Lebanon, 346,164; and Syria, 337,308. Not all these refugees are camp dwellers. Those who are registered inside the camps total 1,044,822, distributed as follows: 252,089 in 10 refugee camps in Jordan (Amman, Irbid, Zarqa); 132,508 in the West Bank (20 camps); 379,778 in the Gaza Strip (eight camps); 185,581 in Lebanon (13 refugee camps); and 94,866 in Syria (10 camps).

UNRWA provides services and assistance to the refugees who are registered and live in or outside refugee camps.

The Palestine National Authority (q.v.) is demanding the return to the West Bank and the Gaza Strip of 800,000 to 1 million refugees—including dependents—more than 700,000 of whom are Jordanian citizens, and another 100,000 of whom are in Egypt. The Palestinians define "displaced persons" as those who left during the wars; those residents who were outside the country on June 4, 1967, and could not return; and the thousands who left in the months following the war. Israel, however, insists on allowing only 200,000 Palestinians and "natural growth" (current growth is 3 percent to 3.5 percent).

REJECTIONIST FRONT. The Palestinian factions who oppose any compromise with Israel. They include the PFLP, PFLP-GC, PSF, and PLF (qq.v.). They are supported by Iraq (q.v.), Libya, Algeria, and South Yemen, the hard-line states that refused to acknowledge the existence of Israel (q.v.).

On September 26, 1974, George Habash (q.v.), leader of the PFLP, resigned from the PLO Executive Committee (q.v.), and together with the leaders of the Popular Front for the Liberation of Palestine-General Command and the Arab Liberation Front (q.v.), established the Rejectionist Front to protest Palestinian participation in a Geneva Peace Conference. On October 1, 1977, rejectionist members established a front to oppose Sadat's peace initiative.

RELIGION. Islam is the religion of 97 percent of the Palestinian population in the West Bank and 99 percent of those in the Gaza Strip (qq.v.). The remaining percentages are Christian. The Muslims belong to the mainstream orthodox Sunni sect. The Christians are divided among many different denominations, including Greek Orthodox, Latins, Greek Catholics, and Anglicans. Most of the Christian community is concentrated in Ramallah, Jerusalem, and Bethlehem (qq.v.). There is a Samaritan community of 400 people in Nablus (q.v.).

The majority of Muslims in the West Bank and the Gaza Strip strictly observe the Islamic rituals of prayer, fasting, *zakat* (tithing), and the *hajj* or pilgrimage (q.v.) to Mecca, Saudi Arabia (q.v.). The rest are secular, non-practicing Muslims. Political views among the Muslims range from those who are apolitical, secularists (affiliated with FATAH (q.v.), PFLP (q.v.), DFLP (q.v.), etc.), and those who are members of HAMAS (q.v.), Islamic Jihad (q.v.); and the Muslim Brotherhood (q.v.).

Women who are religious and/or whose families are conservative don the Islamic dress or the *djalabeh* (the long coatdress) and the headscarf.

RISHMAWI, MONA. A lawyer who specializes in human rights and international law. She was born in Gaza (q.v.) in 1958, and received an LL.B. from 'Ain Shams University in Egypt (q.v.). She then returned to the West Bank (q.v.) in 1981, where she practiced law in the Israeli military and civil courts, defending Palestinians until 1988. Rishmawi was a member of the executive committee of Al-Haq (q.v.) in 1985, and became its director in 1989. She also received an LL.M. from Columbia University in New York in 1989.

S

SABA, FUAD. A successful accountant who founded the firm Saba and Company in 1920 in Haifa, Palestine. In 1930, he helped establish an organization that later would evolve into the Palestinian National Fund (q.v.) to support land acquisitions and modernize methods of farming in Palestinian rural areas. He also lobbied incessantly to discourage the sale of land to Jews. He was a supporter of the Husseinis (q.v.), and served as the secretary of the Arab Higher Committee (q.v.) in 1936. He was among the Palestinian leaders who were deported by the British to the Seychelles Islands in 1937, after being accused of inciting anti-British sentiment. Saba participated in the delegation to the London Conference (q.v.) in 1939, and rejected the British White Paper (q.v.) proposal. After 1948, he left Palestine (q.v.) and established branches of his company in several Middle Eastern countries.

SABAH, MICHAEL, HIS BEATITUDE MONSIGNOR. The first Palestinian Latin patriarch of Jerusalem (q.v.), consecrated by Pope John Paul II in St. Peter's Cathedral in Rome on January 6, 1988. He was born on March 1, 1933 in Nazareth, Palestine, and received his elementary education at the Freres des Ecoles Chretiennes in Nazareth. Afterward, his family sent him to the Junior Latin Patriarchal Seminary in Beit Jala, near Bethlehem (q.v.). He received his Ph.D. in philology of the Arabic language from the University of the Sorbonne in France. After he was ordained a priest on June 6, 1955, he served a mission in Djibouti, and at Christ the King Parish in Amman, Jordan. On March 24, 1975, he was appointed as the principal of the National Secondary College in Amman, and five years later became president of Bethlehem University (q.v.). In 1985, Patriarch Sabah was appointed Canon of the Holy Sepulchre (Patriarchal Council). He also is the president of the Episcopal Conference for the Latin Bishops of the Arab Countries, president of the Catholic Bishops Assembly of the Holy Land, and, since 1994, the elected president of the Catholic Family in the Middle East Council of Churches.

SABRI, EKRAMEH, SHEIKH. Appointed by Yasser Arafat (q.v.) in October 1994 as the Grand *Mufti* of Jerusalem (q.v.) and the Palestinian lands, he succeeded Suleiman al-Ja'bari (q.v.). He was born in Qalqilya (q.v.) in 1939 and graduated from the *Shari'a* (Islamic Law) College in Baghdad, Iraq (q.v.), in 1963. After teaching for several years at the *Al-Aqsa Shari'a* Secondary School in Jerusalem, he became the headmaster. In 1973, he became the *imam* (q.v.) of *Al-Aqsa* Mosque (q.v.) in Jerusalem, and provided religious guidance for more than 20 years. He also is a distinguished member of the Jerusalem *Zakat* (tithing) Committee, which oversees the *Al-Aqsa* Nursery School.

AL-SADAT, ANWAR. A member of the Free Officers, who, along with Gamal Abd al-Nasser (q.v.), carried out the coup against the Egyptian monarchy in 1952. When Nasser died on September 28, 1970, Sadat became the president of Egypt (q.v.). Unlike his predecessor, he brought an end to his country's dependence on Russia in September 1981. Undertaking a bold and aggressive step toward establishing peace with Israel, he visited Jerusalem (q.v.) on November 20, 1977, breaking decades of hostility and psychological barriers. He signed a peace treaty with Israel (q.v.) in 1979, regaining the Sinai Peninsula (q.v.) for Egypt. Ostracized by the Arab countries, he nevertheless was firm in his convictions. Sadat, however, was assassinated by a member of an Islamic group who gunned him down on October 6, 1981, as he was reviewing his armed forces in commemoration of the war of 1973 (q.v.). On December 10, 1979, Sadat and Israel's Prime Minister Menachem Begin (q.v.) received the Nobel Peace Prize for their efforts in establishing peace in the Middle East.

SA'ED, SHAHER ABD AL-KARIM. Trade unionist born in Nablus (q.v.) in 1957. He received an associate degree in engineering from UNRWA's (q.v.) Kalandia Training Center in 1976. After working several years in the engineering department of the Nablus municipality, he became the technical supervisor of buildings at An-Najah National University (q.v.) in 1979. During that period, Sa'ed became involved in union activities, and quickly moved up the ranks: in 1978, he was elected to the Construction Workers Union; in 1980, he became the secretary of the Technical Workers' Union; in 1983, the General Federation of Palestinian Trade Unions (q.v.) elected him a member of the executive committee; in 1985, he served as the treasurer of the General Federation of Unions in the West Bank (q.v.); and in 1990, he was elected secretary-general of the Labor Unions in the West Bank. Sa'ed represents the Palestinian trade unions abroad and at international labor organizations. His activities and affiliation with unions have cost him several terms of administrative detentions (q.v.) in Israeli jails. He also is a representative of the Center for Vocational Rehabilitation of the Handicapped and a member of the Palestinian-French Friendship Society.

SAID, EDWARD. Prominent professor and author born in Jerusalem (q.v.) in 1935. He completed his elementary and secondary education in both Jerusalem and Cairo. In 1957, he received his B.A. from Princeton University and a Ph.D. from Harvard in 1963. A member of the Palestine National Council (q.v.), he became a leading PLO (q.v.) spokesman in the United States. Said often was mentioned in the 1980s as a possible negotiator for the Palestinians in peace talks with the Israelis. He currently holds a chair in English literature at Columbia University, and is a leading U.S. academic. He has published widely; among his most influential books are *Orientalism; After the Last Sky: Palestinian Lives; Blaming the Victim;* and *Culture and Imperialism.*

AL-SA'IQA. Arabic for "lightning". A Palestinian faction, al-Sai'iqa is the acronym in Arabic for Vanguard of the Popular War of Liberation. It was founded in 1968 under the aegis of the Syrians as a military unit, and it strictly adheres to the Ba'th (q.v.) ideology. It advocates the liberation of all of Palestine (q.v.) within a framework of pan-Arabism. Based in Syria (q.v.), it also is active in Lebanon (q.v.). Its leaders, who have included Zuheir Muhsen (q.v.) and Muhammad al-Mu'aita, both of whom have been assassinated, change intermittently. Al-Sa'iqa was one of the factions that withdrew from the PLO (q.v.) in 1983, because of disagreements with Arafat's (q.v.) policies.

AL-SAKAKINI, KHALIL. Leading nationalist, educator, and founder of al-Nahda College in Jerusalem (q.v.). He was born in 1878 to a Christian family from Jerusalem, and educated at an English missionary school in the city. In 1908, he opened a night school in Jerusalem, where he taught Arabic. He became renowned for his introduction of innovative educational methods; in 1923, he became the principal of the Teacher's Training School in Jerusalem. Two years later, he was appointed an inspector of education. In 1936, he turned down the position of director of the Palestine Broadcasting Station, and founded al-Nahda College, which he administered until 1948. He also participated in the Arab Executive (q.v.) that met in Jaffa in 1923. He died on August 13, 1953, in Cairo, Egypt.

SALAMEH, ALI HASSAN. FATAH (q.v.) member, former head of its Bureau of Security Operations and former commander of Force 17 (q.v.), Arafat's (q.v.) elite security unit. He was born in Iraq in 1942, but grew up in Beirut and Cairo. His father, Sheikh Hassan Salameh, led the *Jihad Al-Muqaddas* (The Holy War Squads) in 1934, and was a commander in the war of 1948 (q.v.). Sheikh Hassan was killed by an underground Zionist organization in a battle near Ramleh, after his headquarters were blown up. After Ali joined FATAH (q.v.), he specialized in intelligence, and became the head of the Jihaz al-Razd (the PLO counterintelligence) before assuming his assignment as the head of Force 17. Prior to that, he was thought to have masterminded subversive attacks in Europe. After the 1970 confrontation with Jordan (q.v.), he moved to Lebanon (q.v.), then settled in Syria (q.v.). He was killed in a car bombing on January 22, 1979.

SALEH, ABD AL-JAWAD. Former mayor of al-Bireh (q.v.) who was deported by Israel (q.v.) in 1973. Between 1974 and 1981, he was a member of the PLO Executive Committee (q.v.) and the head of the Office for the Affairs of the Occupied Territories (q.v.). He also was a co-founder of the Palestine National Front (q.v.). Saleh was permitted to return to the West Bank (q.v.) in 1994. He ran for the PLC (q.v.) elections in January 1996 as an independent and won a seat for the Ramallah-al-Bireh district (qq.v.). Arafat (q.v.) appointed him minister of Agriculture in his cabinet, in June 1996.

SAMED. Arabic for "steadfast". The acronym for the Society of the Sons of the Palestinian Martyrs established in 1969 by Ahmad Qre'i (q.v.) to provide work opportunities and financial assistance to families whose breadwinners had been killed fighting for the Palestinian cause. It started with simple projects of embroidery and crafts, and later expanded to factories producing furniture, textiles, machinery, toys, and films. SAMED also became involved in farming and agricultural productivity in African countries (bananas in Somalia). Many of its products are sold in the Middle East and Europe. This once-small economic venture has evolved into a successful investment institution that is owned by FATAH (q.v.), and comes under the aegis of the Palestine National Fund (q.v.). Future plans include investment ventures in the Palestinian autonomous areas (q.v.). SAMED is a member of the International Workers' Conference and the Food and Agricultural Organization.

SAMED: PALESTINIAN PRISON VOICES. A bimonthly newsletter that is published by the Mandela Institute for Political Prisoners (q.v.). It provides information about prisoners in the Occupied Territories (q.v.).

SARTAWI, ISSAM. Cardiologist and PLO (q.v.) member. He was born in Acre, Palestine, and educated in Baghdad. In 1970, he joined the Palestine Liberation Organization (q.v.). For some time, he was closely affiliated with the Egyptian government under Nasser (q.v.), and established his own commando group, the Arab Command for the Liberation of Palestine (q.v.). After dissolving his commando group in the mid-1970s, Sartwi became one of Arafat's (q.v.) closest advisors. He also served as the PLO's ambassador without portfolio in Westen Europe, and it was in that capacity that he headed a delegation to talks with moderate Israelis in 1976. Sartawi won the Kreisky Peace Prize in Paris in 1980, together with Israeli peace advocate Lova Eliav, for their efforts in encouraging Israeli-Arab dialogue. Sartawi was assassinated in Lisbon, Portugal while attending a meeting of the Socialist International (an umbrella organization representing the Socialist Democratic Parties of Europe) on April 10, 1983.

SAUDI ARABIA. An oil-rich Arab country in the Arabian Peninsula. A monarchy ruled by the House of Sa'ud, it also is the center of pilgrimage, or *hajj* (q.v.) for Muslims who travel from all over the world to visit the holy cities of Mecca and Medina. Most of its inhabitants are Sunni Muslims from the Wahhabi school. Its population is 13.5 million, 5 million of whom are expatriates.

The kingdom of Saudi Arabia was declared on September 18, 1932 and became a member of the United Nations in 1945. Inhabited by bedouins, peasants who farmed around oases, and fishermen, Saudi Arabia began to modernize in 1940 with the production of oil. When King Faisal ascended the throne on November 2, 1964, he introduced a major development plan that has transformed Saudi Arabia into a modern country. He built schools, hospitals, a university, and roads.

Faisal was assassinated in March 1975. His brother Khaled ruled the country until he died in 1982. The real power, however, was another brother, Fahd, who eventually became king.

Saudi Arabia has supported the PLO (q.v.) and the Palestinians with large infusions of cash. It is estimated that, together with other Gulf states, it has provided $10 billion for the Palestinians. During the first year of the Intifada (q.v.) alone, Saudi Arabia, Qatar, Kuwait (q.v.), and the United Arab Emirates provided $118 million for the Palestinians. Moreover, they pledged $150 million annually to the PLO-Jordanian Joint Committee (q.v.) at the Algiers summit in 1988, a continuation of the annual pledge that had begun in 1978 at the Baghdad summit. Hence, the Palestinians received a total of $368 million for the first year of the Intifada from the Gulf countries, including Saudi Arabia.

After the Gulf War (q.v.), Saudi Arabia stopped assisting the Occupied Territories because the Palestinians supported Iraq (qq.v.) in the war. In early 1992, however, Saudi Arabia did offer to send $9 million through the United Nations for the renovation of the Dome of the Rock at *Al-Haram Al-Sharif* in Jerusalem (qq.v.). But it was rejected by King Hussein (q.v.), who financed the renovations himself.

Palestinian leaders visited Saudi Arabia many times and tried to reconciliate. However, their overtures were not accepted until April 1992, when Saudi Arabia exerted its influence and persuaded Arafat (q.v.) to return to the negotiating table with the Israelis, and promised $200 million for Palestinian institutions if he did so. After the signing of the Oslo Accords (q.v.), Saudi Arabia channeled $100 million for the Palestinians through an international fund for projects slated in the Occupied Territories.

AL-SAYYEH, ABD AL-HAMID, SHEIKH. A Muslim *qadi* (q.v.) and the head of the Supreme Higher Muslim Council (q.v.), which was established after the war of 1967 (q.v.) to manage Muslim affairs in Jerusalem and the West Bank (qq.v.). Sheikh Sayyeh was deported to Jordan (qq.v.) on September 23, 1967, when the council protested the annexation of East Jerusalem by Israel (qq.v.). A FATAH member (q.v.), he was appointed as the speaker of the Palestine National Council (q.v.) in November 1984, and held that post until he resigned in May 1993, in disagreement with the Declaration of Principles (q.v.) signed earlier that year.

SETTLEMENTS. Jewish residential areas built in the Occupied Territories (q.v.) to establish irreversible facts on the ground and to assert that the entire land is Eretz Israel, or the land of Israel. Settlements have been built on the periphery of Palestinian communities and are located on hills, adjacent to populated areas, on both public (state domain) and expropriated land. There are a total of 194 settlements: 144 in the West Bank (q.v.), 17 in the Gaza Strip (q.v.), and 28 in Jerusalem (q.v.). There are approximately 140,000 settlers in the West Bank, 160,000 in East Jerusalem (q.v.), and 5,000 in the Gaza Strip.

The settlements are subsidized by the Israeli government to encourage Israelis to settle in the Occupied Territories (q.v.); they nevertheless remain underpopulated. For example, more than a hundred settlements have a few hundred people living in them. The most populated settlement is Benjamin, which has 20,430 settlers and is located in the district of Jerusalem; it is followed by Ma'ale Adumin, near Jericho (q.v.), with a population of 19,870; Ariel, near Nablus (q.v.), with 12,900; and Givat Ze'ev, near Ramallah (q.v.), with 7,200 persons.

Settlers who live in the West Bank and the Gaza Strip, often have taken the law into their hands, and caused extensive damage to Palestinian property and lives. The Palestinians, particularly during the Intifada (q.v.), waged an all-out war on the settlers by smashing the windshields of Israeli cars, throwing molotov bombs, and ambushing and killing settlers. The issue of the settlements, according to the DOP (q.v.), is to be negotiated in the final phase—along with the question of Jerusalem—which is to commence no later than May 1996, and to be completed by May 1999. In the meantime, Israel continues with settlement building, to the consternation of the Palestinians.

During the summer of 1995, the settlers began a campaign to protest Israeli redeployment from the Occupied Territories (q.v.) and to bring attention to the plight of settlers and settlements during the Palestinian-Israeli negotiations. According to the Taba Agreement (q.v.), negotiated in August 1995, settlers do not have to evacuate even if there is agreement on the final status of the territories in May 1999.

SHA'ATH, NABIL. Appointed as the Palestinian minister of Planning and International Relations in March 1996 and also served as the minister of Planning and International Coordination in 1994, in the first PNA (q.v.) government. He is a PLC (q.v.) member for Gaza and a member of PECDAR's (q.v.) board of directors. Sha'ath was born in Safed, in the Galilee. He became a member of the Palestine National Committee in 1969. The following year, he assumed the chairmanship of the PLO (q.v.) political committee and joined the PLO Central Committee. For the next decade, he directed the PLO Planning Center in Lebanon (q.v.). He also served as chairman of FATAH's General Congress and was a member of the FATAH Revolutionary Council (qq.v.). Since 1982, Sha'ath has advised Arafat (q.v.) on international relations. He also served as the director of the coordinating committee for the Palestinian delegation to the peace talks.

AL-SHA'B. Arabic for "the masses". A pro-PLO (q.v.) Arabic daily that is the third-largest newspaper in the West Bank and Gaza (qq.v.). It stopped publication in February 1993 because of financial difficulties, but reappeared as a weekly in January 1995.

SHABIBEH. Arabic for "youth". Another name for the Youth Committee for Social Work, which is a pro-PLO FATAH (q.v.) youth group established in the early 1980s. Its objective was to render community services. It assumed a political role when it began to provide support for Palestinians whose land was confiscated by the Israelis for settlement (q.v.) purposes, and for those whose homes were demolished because a family member had been accused of committing a security offense against Israel (q.v.). It also played a prominent role during the Intifada (q.v.), organizing resistance groups to confront the Israeli occupational forces and providing financial assistance to families whose breadwinners were confined to Israeli jails.

AL-SHAFI, HAIDAR ABD. PLC (q.v.) member for the district (q.v.) of Gaza. Born in 1919 in the Gaza Strip (q.v.), which at the time was under the British Mandate (q.v.). His father, Sheikh Muhyidin, was the wealthy director of the *Waqf* (Islamic endowment) in Gaza (qq.v.). In 1925, Shafi's father was transferred to Hebron (q.v.), and the family resided in a building across the hall from a Jewish family. In 1927, the family returned to Gaza and, because there was no high school, Haidar was sent to the Arab College in Jerusalem (q.v.). In 1937, Haidar went to the American University of Beirut to study medicine and, while there, became a member of the Arab Nationalist Movement (q.v.). After graduating in 1943, Haidar joined the British army for a brief stint, but in 1945 decided to go into private practice. After witnessing how the war of 1948 (q.v.) devastated the Palestinians, Haidar left for the United States to study surgery at Miami Valley Hospital in Dayton, Ohio. He came back in 1954 and worked for the Egyptians at Tal Zahur Hospital. He served as the director of health services in Gaza from 1957 until 1967.

Upon the convening of the Palestinian National Congress (q.v.) in May 1964 in Jerusalem and the establishment of the Palestine Liberation Organization (q.v.), Haidar was appointed with 15 others to its executive committee. He also was the first deputy speaker and a founding member of the Palestine National Council (q.v.). After the war of 1967 (q.v.), he was expelled to the Sinai Peninsula (q.v.) by Moshe Dayan, the Israeli defense minister. He was charged by the

Israelis with encouraging protests. In 1970, Haidar was once again deported with six others to Lebanon (q.v.), but returned three months later. In 1972, he became the head of the Gaza branch of the Palestinian Red Crescent Society (q.v.). In 1976, he became a member of the al-Maqassed Islamic Charitable Hospital Board, and was appointed as a member of the board of trustees of Birzeit University (q.v.). In 1990, he was chosen to be the leader and chief negotiator of the Palestinian delegation to the Madrid Peace Conference (q.v.), and participated in the negotiations in Washington. He was surprised by the PLO's secret negotiations in Oslo, Norway, that led to the signing of the DOP (q.v.).

Al-Shafi believes that the Palestinians should suspend the peace negotiations until the Israelis stop building settlements (q.v.). In Gaza on June 9, 1994, he officially announced the establishment of a new political group called "The Palestinian Democratic Construction Movement." It is not a political party, but rather an organization whose objectives are to promote and educate people on the ideals and principles of democracy, and to raise Palestinian consciousness to create a pluralistic society. It also emphasizes legality and human rights. The movement is supported by the Palestine People's Party (q.v.), but not by FATAH (q.v.).

AL-SHAK'A, BASSAM AHMAD HASSAN. Former mayor of Nablus (q.v.) and the founder of *Al-Tajamo'u al-Filistini* (Palestine Federation) in 1995. He was born in Nablus (q.v.) in 1930 to a wealthy family, and only finished the 10th grade of school. His involvement in politics began at an early age. He joined the Syrian Ba'th Party (q.v.), and became a senior member and leader of the party in the West Bank (q.v.). Persecuted by Jordan (q.v.), he fled to Syria (q.v.) in 1958, and afterward to Egypt (q.v.). He remained there until 1965, when Jordan issued a general amnesty, and he was able to return to Nablus. In 1976, he ran for muncipal elections on the pro-PLO (q.v.) slate, and was elected mayor of Nablus. He was also one of the three mayors in the West Bank (Karim Khalaf and Ibrahim al-Tawil (qq.v.) were the other two) who were targeted by the Jewish underground in 1980. He lost his legs as a result of a car bomb that exploded as he turned on the ignition. In March 1982, he was dismissed from office by the Israelis. He was the leader of the Committee for National Guidance (q.v.), established in October 1978 following the Palestinian rejection of the Camp David Accords (q.v.). In 1980, he won the peace prize awarded by the Committee for Human Rights, and also the Medal of Omayya awarded by Syria.

In 1995, Shak'a was unhappy with the Oslo Accords and the Cairo Agreement (qq.v.), because they did not specify the Palestinian right of return to their land, nor the dismantlement of the settlements. Moreover, he thought the agreements would not lead to the establishment of a Palestinian state. Consequently, he and the representatives of the PFLP (q.v.), PFLP-GC (q.v.), DFLP (q.v.), Islamic Jihad, and FATAH Uprising (qq.v.), who were also dissatisfied with the agreements, formed *Al-Tajamo'u al-Filistini.*

SHAK'A, GHASSAN. A lawyer by profession, and appointed as the mayor of Nablus (q.v.) by the Palestine National Authority (q.v.) in 1994. He was born in Nablus in 1943, and later studied law at Beirut University in Lebanon (q.v.), where he graduated in 1971. He is a member of the Council for Higher Education (q.v.), and was elected the head of the Lawyers Bar Association in the West Bank (q.v.) in 1990.

SHALAH, RAMADAN ABDALLAH. A member of the Islamic Jihad (q.v.), who was chosen on October 27, 1995, to succeed Fathi Shiqaqi (q.v.), who was assassinated by the Mossad, Israeli Secret Service, on October 26, 1995.

Shalah was born in 1958 in the Gaza Strip (q.v.) and received his education in Egypt (q.v.), where he befriended Shiqaqi. Shalah returned to Gaza after completing his education and worked at Al-Azhar University. He helped establish Islamic Jihad in the Occupied Territories (q.v.). In 1984, he left for Egypt (q.v.), and later the United States, where he studied political science and economics. In 1986, he moved to England, where he received a doctorate in economics. During this time, he was active on behalf of Islamic Jihad in Europe. In 1991, he moved to the United States and became the director of the World Islamic Exploration Center in Tampa, Florida. He now resides in Lebanon and Syria (qq.v.).

SHAMIR, YITZHAK. Born in Poland in 1915, he received his education at Warsaw University and graduated in 1934. The following year, he immigrated to Palestine (q.v.) and joined the Irgun, an underground Jewish organization that fought the Arabs and the British Mandate (q.v.) in 1937. He was imprisoned by the British in 1941 and 1946. Later, he studied law at the Hebrew University in Jerusalem (q.v.).

Shamir joined the Mossad, the Israeli secret service, and was quickly promoted to a senior position. He joined the Israeli political party, Herut, in 1970, became a Knesset member in 1974 and the speaker of the Knesset (parliament). In 1980, as minister for Foreign Affairs, he played an important role after peace was established with Egypt (q.v.). On October 10, 1983, he became Israel's prime minister after Begin (q.v.) resigned. When Peres (q.v.) formed the National Government in 1984, Shamir served as the deputy prime minister, and in 1986 became the Prime Minister.

AL-SHANTI, IBRAHIM. A journalist by profession, he was born in Jaffa, Palestine, in 1910. He completed his schooling at the American University of Beirut in Lebanon (q.v.). A member of the Palestinian *Istiqlal* Party (q.v.), he began publishing *Al-Dif'a* (q.v.) newspaper in Jaffa in February 1934. In 1948, he left for Egypt (q.v.), but returned two years later to Jerusalem (q.v.), where he resumed publication of his newspaper until the war of 1967 (q.v.) broke out. Afterward, he left for Jordan (q.v.) and published his paper there until 1971, when the Jordanian government ordered it closed. He died in Amman, Jordan, on April 15, 1979.

SHARABI, HISHAM. Prominent professor and leading Palestinian intellectual. He was born in 1927 in Jaffa, Palestine, and received his education at the Friends Quaker School in Ramallah (q.v.). He later continued his education at the American University of Beirut and the University of Chicago, which he attended from 1949 to 1953. Sharabi currently teaches history at Georgetown University in Washington, D.C., and edits the *Journal of Palestine Studies* (q.v.). For a time, he was affiliated with the Syrian Nationalist Party. He currently is the director of the Jerusalem Fund, which distributes financial assistance to Palestinians, and also is the director of the Center for Policy Analysis on Palestine, a think-tank based in Washington, D.C. In the '80s, he was one of the few Palestinian-American professors mentioned as a possible negotiator with Israel (q.v).

SHARI'A. The Islamic judicial code based on the Koran (the Muslim holy book), the *hadith* (sayings) of the Prophet Muhammad, the *ijm'a* (consensus), *qiyas* (intention), and *maslaha* or public good, which can be altered.

The *Shari'a* provides direction, guidance, and penalties should transgression occur, for every aspect of life for a Muslim. This includes marriage, divorce, child custody, inheritance, and adultery. *Shari'a* laws are administered by a *qadi* (q.v.) in a *Shari'a* court. There are civil courts, however, that try cases of murder, theft, and other criminal violations. Israeli military courts in the Occupied Territories (q.v.) adjudicate security-related cases.

In addition to *Shari'a* laws, there is the *'urf*, or customary laws, which govern social relationships in which people utilize the *sulha* (q.v.), or ritual reconciliation, to resolve their differences. Both the Occupied Territories and the autonomous areas (qq.v.) are ruled by a mix of Ottoman-Turkish, British, Egyptian, and Jordanian laws, in addition to over 1,365 Israeli military orders that still remain on record. During the Intifada (q.v.), the Palestinians boycotted the courts and resorted to the traditional *sulha* as often as possible to resolve their problems.

SHARON, ARIEL. Also Arik. Born in 1928, he was educated at the Hebrew University in Jerusalem and Camberley Staff College in Great Britain, and later attended law school in Tel Aviv. An illustrious Israeli military commander, he fought in the war of 1956 (q.v.) and the war of 1967 (q.v.), and destroyed Palestinian resistance in the Gaza Strip (q.v.) in 1971. He was one of the commanders of the Yom Kippur (Day of Atonement) War in 1973 (q.v.). In June 1973, he was elected to the Israeli Knesset (parliament), and publicly stated that he would negotiate with the PLO (q.v.), if the framework for negotiations was based on the premise that "Jordan is Palestine."

Sharon was appointed Prime Minister Rabin's (q.v.) advisor in 1975. He later established his own political party, Shlomzion, which won two seats in the Knesset in 1977. Shlomzion disappeared when Sharon joined the Herut, an extreme-right party. Sharon also served as minister of Agriculture and the chairman of the Ministerial Committee for Settlements. He formulated the Sharon Plan, which called for the annexation of the West Bank to Israel (qq.v.), but excluded the populated areas of Nablus (q.v.), Ramallah (q.v.), Tulkarm (q.v.), and Qalqilya (q.v.). Sharon also encouraged Menachem Begin (q.v.) to establish peace with Egypt (q.v.) and became minister of Defense in 1981. He was appointed minister of Industry and Trade in the National Unity Government in 1984. In June 1996, he was appointed minister of Infrastructure by Netanyahu (q.v.), in the Likud government.

Problems arose for Sharon when Israel invaded Lebanon (q.v.), and because of the massacre of Sabra and Shatilla, which took place on September 16, 1982. Several thousand Palestinians were murdered by Lebanese Phalangists that day. Sharon later resigned and sued Time Magazine for libel, because it claimed that the Kahan Commission, which had investigated the massacre, had documents implicating Sharon in the massacre. The court found that no proof existed for such a claim.

SHAW COMMISSION. Named after Sir Walter Shaw, who, together with Sir John-Hope Simpson, was sent by the British government to Palestine in 1929 to investigate the Arab-Palestinian revolts (q.v.) and rebellions that had erupted in Jerusalem and Hebron (qq.v.). The Jews demanded that the regulations concerning access to the Western Wall (q.v.), which is adjacent to the *Al-Haram Al-Sharif* (qq.v.), be changed. The commission concluded its mission by suggesting that Jews and Arabs would never be able to share a state. Their observations led to restricting the number of Jewish immigrants to Palestine.

SHAWWA, MANSOUR. The son of Rashad al-Shawwa (q.v.), he was born in Gaza (q.v.) and attended Filistine Secondary School. After graduating, he majored in mechanical engineering at Oxford University in England and aeronautical engineering at London University. In 1970, he returned to Gaza and worked in the family business of exporting citrus fruits. Since September 1990, he has been the chairman of the Benevolent Society, which his father, Rashad, established. In December 1993, he was asked by the Palestine National Authority (q.v.) to form a municipal council in Gaza City. Mansour proposed a council of 21 members representing all the Palestinian political factions. The proposal was rejected.

AL-SHAWWA, RASHAD. Entrepreneur, nationalist, and philanthropist, he was born in the Gaza Strip (q.v.) in 1909. He was educated at the al-Rawda School in Jerusalem (q.v.) and attended the American University of Beirut and the American University of Cairo. Politically active, he participated in the Arab-Palestinian revolts of 1936 in Palestine (qq.v.). The British accused him of procuring arms for the Palestinian rebels, and summarily fired him as governor of Haifa and deported him. In the 1950s, he cooperated with the Egyptian administration. Shawwa also served two terms as mayor of Gaza under the Israelis, but was dismissed from office both times. In 1970, he established the Benevolent Society of the Gaza Strip and the Shawwa Cultural Center, where conferences and exhibits are held. He died on September 27, 1988.

SHAWWA, RAWIYA. PLC (q.v.) member for the district of Gaza (q.v.). She also is a popular columnist and writer who is a member of the Council for Higher Education (q.v.), the Arab Thought Forum (q.v.), and the Independent Group for Elections. Rawiya is also the president of the Gaza Cultural Group. She was born in Gaza (q.v.), where she received her education. After she married, she left for Saudi Arabia (q.v.) and stayed there until 1974. When she returned to Gaza, she was the first woman to open a commercial enterprise (designing and selling tailored clothing) and an agricultural venture.

SHEHADEH, 'AZIZ. A prominent lawyer and politician born in Bethlehem (q.v.) in 1912. His father was a poet, a journalist, and editor of the weekly newspaper *Mirat Al-Shark* (q.v.). His mother died when he was still young, and the family moved to Jerusalem (q.v.), where he grew up. Shehadeh studied law at the Jerusalem Law Classes and moved to Jaffa to practice. During the disturbances and the Arab-Palestinian revolts (q.v.) in the 1930s, he defended Palestinian activists. When the war of 1948 (q.v.) broke out, he and other Palestinians were forced out of Jaffa, and he settled with his family in Ramallah (q.v.).

Shehadeh was a delegate to the Refugee Council at the peace talks held in Lausanne. He also defended one of the men who was accused of the murder of King Abadallah (q.v.). During the Jordanian regime of the West Bank (q.v.), he publicly declared the necessity of establishing Palestinian autonomy. As early as 1968, he proposed a two-state solution to Cyrus Vance, then U.S.-secretary of state, to resolve the Palestinian-Israeli conflict. He wrote, "As a first step toward the implementation of the Palestinian people's inalienable right to self-determination, it is imperative that both Israel and the Arab states recognize the basic rights of the Palestinian Arabs to set up a state of their own. For the interim period, a Peace Promoting Force, acceptable to both Israelis and Palestinians, might be needed. I am confident that a prosperous, independent Palestinian state will be a bridge toward lasting peace and cooperation between the Arab nations and Israel. I suggest separate municipalities to be established for Israeli and the Palestinian areas of Jerusalem, with a joint commission to control and coordinate public services. A just and generous settlement for the refugees, either by return to their old homes or by direct compensation to them, should be worked out. I am convinced that such an approach would solve our basic conflict, lay the foundation for a stable peace in this region, and be to the benefit of both nations."

Shehadeh was ahead of his time. His ideas were not received well by the PLO (q.v.) or the Jordanians. On December 2, 1985, Shehadeh was stabbed to death outside his home in Ramallah (q.v.) by an unknown assailant. No accused was brought to trial by the Israeli security apparatus that investigated the case.

SHEHADEH, RAJA AZIZ. Son of Aziz Shehadeh (q.v.), prominent lawyer and co-founder of al-Haq (q.v.), a human-rights organization that monitors Israeli infringement on Palestinian rights. He was born in 1951 and educated at the Friends Quakers Schools in Ramallah (q.v.). He received his B.A. in literature and philosophy at the American University of Beirut in 1973, and later went to England for advanced study. In 1976, he was called to the English Bar and became a member of Lincoln's Inn. He then returned to practice law in Ramallah. A human-rights activist, he became a member of the advisory board of the Dutch Council on Human Rights in 1983, and also is a member of the World Council of Churches Committee on Human Rights. In 1986, he was awarded the Rothko Chapel award for commitment to truth and freedom.

Shehadeh has written several books, among them *Samed, A Journal of Life in the West Bank; The West Bank and the Rule of Law* (with Jonathan Kuttab); *Occupier Law: Israel and the West Bank;* and *The Sealed Room: Selections From the Diary of a Palestinian Living Under Israeli Occupation, September 1990–August 1991.*

SHIQAQI, FATHI. Born in the Gaza Strip (q.v.) in 1951, he studied medicine in Egypt (q.v.) at the Islamic University of Zagazig in the 1970s. While he was a student there, he was influenced by the ideology of Iranian groups, and joined the Muslim Brotherhood (q.v.). He returned to the Gaza Strip in 1981 and founded Islamic Jihad (q.v.), which gained notoriety by undertaking suicidal attacks against Israeli targets in Israel and the Occupied Territories (qq.v.). For instance, the Beit Led bombing, in which 20 soldiers were killed and 40 were injured in February 1995, is alleged to have been carried out by members of Islamic Jihad. Shiqaqi was deported by Israel in 1988 and resided in the Yarmouk Refugee Camp in Damascus, Syria (q.v.), from where he directed the activities of his organization. In June 1995, disagreements broke out between him and Abd al-Aziz Oudeh, the co-founder of Islamic Jihad, over funding and organizational policy, particularly the use of violence in the struggle against Israel. Shiqaqi was assassinated in Malta on October 26, 1995, while on his way from Libya, where he had been mediating on behalf of Palestinians expelled from that country. The assassination is alleged to have been carried out by the Israeli Secret Service, the Mossad. He is buried at the Martyr's Cemetery in the Yarmouk Refugee Camp in Damascus, Syria.

SHOMAN, ABDUL-HAMID. A banker, he established the Arab Bank in 1930, which opened branches in Jaffa, Haifa, Amman, Damascus, Baghdad, and Cairo. In 1933, he founded the Arab Agricultural Bank, which offered loans to Palestinians to prevent them from borrowing from Jewish sources and going into debt and consequently losing their land. The Arab Agricultural Bank later became the Bank of the Arab Nation.

Shoman was born in 1891 in the suburb of Beit Hanina, near Jerusalem (q.v.). He went to the United States in 1911, where he was involved in business for many years. He was a close friend and supporter of Hajj Amin al-Husseini (q.v.), and often was harassed by the British during the 1939 resistance. His son, Abdul-Majeed, became chairman of the Palestine National Fund (q.v.) and the director of the Arab Bank, Ltd.

SHQEIR, MAHMOUD. Short-story writer, editor-in-chief of *Al-Tali'a* (The Vanguard), the paper published by the Palestine Peoples' Party (q.v.), and a member of the General Union of Palestinian Writers. He was born in Sawahreh, a village adjacent to Jerusalem (q.v.), in 1941. In 1961, he published some of his early writing, in an East Jerusalem magazine, *Al-Ufuq* (The Horizon). He attended Damascus University in Syria, earning a degree in philosophy and sociology in 1965. After returning to the West Bank (q.v.), he began writing short stories, and in 1975 published his first collection, *The Bread of Others*. That same year, he was deported by the Israelis from the Occupied Territories (q.v.). He continued to write in the diaspora and published numerous works that have been translated into many languages. Shqeir's stories are very short and condensed; some are only a few lines, with extremely intense ideas. His collection *The Rituals of the Wretched Woman* particularly reflects this style.

For his innovativeness, Shqeir received the Jordanian Writers Association award for 1990. After the signing of the DOP (q.v.) in 1993, he was able to return to his home after 18 years in exile.

SHU'EIBI, AZMI. Palestine National Authority's (q.v.) first minister of Sports and Youth Affairs, appointed in July 1994. He is a member of the PLC (q.v.) for the Ramallah-al-Bireh district (qq.v.). He was born in Jerusalem in 1947, and attended schools in Ramallah and al-Bireh (qq.v.). After studying dentistry at Alexandria University in 1972, he returned home and opened a private clinic. In 1976, he was elected a member of the al-Bireh Municipal Council and continued to serve in that capacity until it was dissolved by the Israeli military government in 1982, after the Civil Administration (q.v.) was established. Shu'eibi also co-founded the Committee for National Guidance (q.v.). On October 28, 1985, he was deported by Israel (q.v.), after being accused of subversive political activities and membership in the Democratic Front for the Liberation of Palestine (q.v.). In exile, he became a member of the Palestine National Council (q.v.) and the Higher Committee of the Intifada (q.v.) Leadership. He also was appointed to the steering committee for the peace negotiations with Israel. A member of the DFLP, he co-founded Fida (q.v.). He was allowed to return in 1993, after the signing of the DOP (q.v.).

SHUQEIRI, AHMAD. Appointed in June 1964 as the first chairman of the PLO (q.v.), he held that position until 1967. He was born in 1908 in Tabuin, South Lebanon. In 1916, he moved to Tulkarm (q.v.), then to Acre, Palestine, and finally completed high school in Jerusalem (q.v.). He began studying law at the American University of Beirut, but was expelled by the French Mandate government then in control of Lebanon (q.v.) because of his political activities. Upon his return to Jerusalem, he became a member of the *Istiqlal* (q.v.) Party and worked in the Arab Information Offices in Jerusalem that had been established by Mussa Al-Alami (q.v.). He also was a member of the Arab Higher Committee (q.v.) in 1946; a member of the Syrian delegation to the United Nations in 1949, and the head of Saudi Arabia's U.N. delegation from 1957 to 1962. In 1963, he was appointed the Palestinian representative to the Arab League (q.v.). He passed away in 1980. His experiences are chronicled in his autobiography, *Forty Years of Arab and International Life*.

SINAI PENINSULA. Egyptian territory occupied by Israel (q.v.) in 1967. It is located in northeast Africa, and is bounded on the north by both the Red Sea and the Mediterranean. Israel returned the Sinai to Egypt (q.v.) when the two countries signed a peace treaty in 1979. The Israeli withdrawal from the Sinai was finalized in April 1982.

SINIORA, HANNA. A successful businessman, former editor of the Arabic and English edition of *Al-Fajr* (q.v.) and publisher of *Al-Usb'u Al-Jadid* (The New Week), an Arabic weekly. He currently is the publisher and editor of *Biladi Jerusalem Times* (q.v.), an English-language weekly. He also is a member of the Arab Council for Public Affairs, and since 1989 has been a board member of the Palestine Pharmaceutical Company and the United Nations Development Center.

Siniora was born in Jerusalem (q.v.) in 1937 and is a pharmacist by training, having earned his B.S. in pharmacy from India. In 1985, he and Gaza (q.v.) lawyer Fayez Abu Rahmah (q.v.) were chosen to represent the PLO (q.v.) on a Jordanian-Palestinian negotiating team with Israel (q.v.). A moderate, he very early supported the idea that Palestinians should run for city council elections in East Jerusalem (q.v.), and said he would run on a platform that rejected Israel's annexation of East Jerusalem. He also encouraged the Palestinians to run for elections in the Israeli Knesset.

Long a champion of Palestinian-Israeli dialogue, Siniora advocated mutual recognition in return for the establishment of an independent Palestinian state. He met with Abba Eban, the former Labor Party leader, and together they signed a statement that Israel and Palestine should respect each others' self-determination. On March 25, 1987, they announced their support for the convening of an international conference, with each party selecting its own representatives. The

Palestinians, however, criticized Siniora because there was no specific mention of the PLO, and the move was seen as de facto acceptance of Israel's control of the area. Siniora, together with Fayez Abu-Rahmah, presented George Shultz, then secretary of state in Washington, with a 14-point proposal outlining the Palestinian position and calling for an international conference to settle the Palestinian-Israeli conflict, Palestinian self-determination, and the establishment of an independent state with the PLO as the representative of the Palestinian people. A meeting with Schultz and some Palestinian representatives was arranged in February 1988 at the American Colony Hotel (q.v.), but the Palestinians failed to show.

Siniora, at the beginning of the Intifada (q.v.), along with other Palestinians, called for an economic boycott of Israeli goods during the Intifada and for the revival of the East Jerusalem Municipal Council, which had been inactive since the Israeli occupation of the city in 1967. The Palestinians opposed this idea, however, because they were apprehensive that Israel would then give Jordan (q.v.) the opportunity to extend its jurisdiction over the city. In June 1995, Arafat (q.v.) revitalized the council and asked it to resume its activities, however symbolic, given the continued occupation of the city.

SIRSAWI, FAYEZ. An artist born in Gaza (q.v.) in 1961. He studied in Istanbul, Turkey, at the Academy of Fine Arts, a prestigious arts school, under the Turkish artist Thamar Oglo. He received an M.A. in art in 1986, and one of his works, an abstract sculpture of a woman, was prominently displayed in front of the academy. He has exhibited both nationally and internationally, and has received honorable mentions for his pieces. He also has done sculptures of the Intifada (q.v.). One of his most interesting works, "The Hand," symbolizes the power and steadfastness of young men confronting the Israelis with stones. Another is of three fists, side-by-side, symbolizing the Palestinian struggle for their land.

SIX-DAY WAR OF JUNE 1967. The war fought between Israel (q.v.) and the Arab countries of Egypt (q.v.), Syria (q.v.), and Jordan (q.v.), that began on June 5, 1967 and lasted only six days. At the end of the war, Egypt had lost the Sinai Peninsula (q.v.), Jordan, the West Bank and East Jerusalem (qq.v.); and Syria (q.v.), the Golan Heights (q.v.). Israel imposed a military occupation on the inhabitants of the lands that it occupied. See WARS.

SOCIETY FOR THE REHABILITATION OF THE FAMILY. see IN'ASH AL-USRA.

SOCIETY OF THE SONS OF THE PALESTINIAN MARTYRS. see SAMED.

AL-SOURANI, JAMAL. Independent member of the PLO (q.v.), director of the Administrative Affairs Department and secretary-general of the PLO Executive Committee (q.v.). He also served as the head of the PLO Organization Department.

SOURANI, RAJI KHADER. A leading human rights lawyer who was fired from his job at the Gaza Center for Rights and Law by the Palestine National Authority (q.v.) the week of April 5, 1995. Sourani had been arrested on February 15, 1995, for a day, because he had criticized the PNA for establishing security courts (q.v.), which he viewed as a violation of the PNA's commitment to uphold the law and protect human rights.

Sourani was born in Gaza (q.v.) on December 31, 1953, and attended schools in Gaza and Bethlehem (q.v.). He then went to London for a year, and afterward attended the Faculty of Law at Beirut Arab University in Lebanon (q.v.). When fighting broke out in Lebanon in the 1970s, he left for Egypt (q.v.), where he studied law and received his LL.B. degree—from Alexandria University in 1977. After returning to the Gaza Strip, he practiced law until 1979, when he was imprisoned by the Israelis for three years. They alleged that he was a member of the PFLP (q.v.). Released in 1982, he began to defend Palestinian youths accused of security offenses against Israel (q.v.). He was repeatedly imprisoned, and finally placed under administrative detention (q.v.) in 1985. When he was freed, he was denied the right to defend cases in Israeli military courts. In 1988, he was again placed in administrative detention after the Israelis accused him of organizing the lawyers' strike in Gaza. His case was adopted by the New York-based Lawyers Committe for Human Rights, Middle East Watch, Amnesty International, and the American Bar Association.

Sourani has been a board member of the Committee for the Defense of the Child and the Palestine Human Rights Information Center. He also was a visiting scholar at the Center for the Study of Human Rights at New York's Columbia University in 1990. Since 1991, he has served as the director of the Gaza Center for Rights and Law. He has received numerous awards for his contributions. In 1991, he was the co-recipient of the Robert F. Kennedy Human Rights Award.

SULHA. The ritual reconciliation or traditional litigation system whereby community conflicts are resolved between two feuding parties through the mediation of neutral clan members. Meetings are held on neutral territory, where the feuding parties are encouraged to air their grievances. During these meetings, compensation and penalties are also agreed upon, although in many cases, out of deference to the mediating clan members and Islamic tradition, no money actually exchanges hands. After a reconciliation takes place, the men share a communal meal, and a report of the reconciliation is placed in the local newspapers. The *sulha* is preferred to modern litigation, because it collectively resolves problems among the clans, and restores harmony to the entire community.

SUPREME HIGHER MUSLIM COUNCIL (SHMC). see HIGHER ISLAMIC COUNCIL.

SUPREME MUSLIM COUNCIL (SMC). A five-member council created by a British Mandate (q.v.) decree in December 1922 to manage Muslim religious affairs. The council members were elected, and Hajj Amin al-Husseini (q.v.) was chosen president. The two major functions of the council were supervision of *Waqf* (q.v.) property and income to see that it was properly used, and the appointment of Muslim religious staff and officials. The council also assumed a political role. It was supported by the Husseinis (q.v.) and opposed by the Nashashibis (q.v.). The British dissolved the council in 1937, accusing it of encouraging the Arab-Palestinian revolt (q.v.) and the disturbances of 1936–37. Under Jordanian rule, the council became obsolete, and its responsibilities were transferred to the *Waqf* (Islamic endowment). It was revitalized after the Israeli occupation in 1967, becoming an influential religious and political body. It administers the *Waqf* and the *Shari'a* (q.v.) Courts. The chairman of the council is Hassan Tahboub (q.v.).

SYRIAN ARAB REPUBLIC. Syria is an Arab country, located at the east end of the Mediterranean. It is bound by Turkey to the north, Jordan (q.v.) to the south, Iraq (q.v.) to the east, and Lebanon and Palestine/Israel (qq.v.) to the southwest. A country of 13 million people, it is 71,498 square miles.

The territory of Syria was part of the Ottoman-Turkish Empire (in 1516). During World War I, this territory was promised to Sharif Hussein (q.v.), the Arab leader who led the Arab Revolt against the Turks, in return for fighting with the Allies. In October 1918, Syria was given to Faisal I (q.v.), Sharif Hussein's son. He immediately declared it the kingdom of Syria, which also included the territory of Lebanon and Palestine. However, this entity had a short life span. Faisal was soon forced out, and the French took control of this territory in July 1922. France did not officially withdraw from Syria until April 1946.

In February 1958, Egypt and Syria formed the United Arab Republic (q.v.), which lasted until September 1961. The Ba'th Party (q.v.) took over the government and emerged as the ruling power. During the war of 1967, Israel occupied the Syrian Golan Heights (q.v.). Though Syria accepted a ceasefire with Israel, it refused to negotiate a settlement. Between 1969 and 1970, Hafez al-Assad emerged as the leader of Syria, and is the president to this day. Syria is currently engaged in negotiations with Israel for peace.

T

TABA AGREEMENT. see OSLO TWO AGREEMENT.

TAHBOUB, HASSAN. Appointed the minister of *Waqf* (q.v.) and Islamic Affairs in Arafat's (q.v.) cabinet in March 1996, and the chairman of the Supreme Muslim Council (q.v.). In 1993, he also served as minister of *Waqf* and Religious Affairs in the first PNA (q.v.) government. Tahboub was born in Hebron (q.v.) in 1927 and studied in Jerusalem (q.v.). In 1960, he was appointed director of the *Waqf* (religious endowment) of Jerusalem (q.v.) and retained that position until 1967. His appointment as PNA minister came after September 27, 1994, when Jordan severed its relations with the *Waqf* in the West Bank (q.v.). Jordan (q.v.) maintained that the decision had already been made in July 1988, when it broke its administrative and legal ties with the West Bank. Jordan insisted, however, that it would still control the *Waqf* in Jerusalem because of spiritual, religious, and historical ties to the city, and that it would continue to be the guardian of the holy shrines. In the agreement signed between Jordan and Israel (q.v.) on October 26, 1994, Jordan's special relationship to the holy places in Jerusalem was emphasized.

TAMARI, VERA. An artist, a ceramist and co-founder of al-Wasiti, an art and cultural center in East Jerusalem (q.v.). She was born in Jerusalem in 1945. Tamari studied at Beirut College for Women in Lebanon (q.v.), and returned to teach at UNRAWA's (q.v.) Women's Training Center in al-Tireh, Ramallah (q.v.). She continued her higher education in Oxford, England, after which she returned to the West Bank (q.v.) to teach Islamic Art at Birzeit University (q.v.), and to work in her studio producing ceramics.

Tamari has exhibited her work both nationally and internationally. One-person exhibits of Tamari's works were held in Jerusalem in

1974 and in Ramallah in 1981. She also has participated in shows held by the League of Palestinian Artists in the Occupied Territories (q.v.), Jordan (q.v.), England, and the United States. Her work also appeared in the "Third World Artists Exhibition" held in London in 1981; in "Women Arab Artists" in Baghdad in 1980; and in "Tallat" in 1986 (this was the first Palestinian women's art exhibition to be held in Jerusalem). Between 1989 and 1992, Tamari's sculptural ceramics were featured in "New Visions," an exhibition featuring four other leading Palestinian artists from the Occupied Territories that was held in Jerusalem, Jordan, Italy, and Germany. In 1992, she took part in the exhibition "Seven Artists from the Occupied Territories," sponsored by the Shouman Foundation in Amman, Jordan (q.v.). In 1993, Tamari presented a ceramic sculptural piece in "Forces of Change: Women Artists from the Arab World," an exhibition held in Washington and now on tour throughout the United States.

Themes of Palestinian lives and demolished houses and villages dominate Tamari's ceramic tiles and three-dimensional sculptures. Tamari also has co-authored a book, *The Palestinian Village House*, with Su'ad Amiry (q.v.), a publication of the British Museum in London.

TANNOUS, IZZAT. Medical doctor, political activist, and a staunch supporter of the Husseinis (q.v.). He was born to a Christian family, and served as the Palestinian representative to the Arab Higher Committee (q.v.) at the United Nations during the British Mandate (q.v.). He adamantly opposed the U.N. Partition Plan (q.v.).

TARIFI, JAMIL. PLC (q.v.) member for the Ramallah-al-Bireh district (qq.v.). Appointed minister of Civil Affairs in Arafat's (q.v.) government in March 1996. He also served as coordinator of the Civil Affairs Liaison Committee in the Palestine National Authority (q.v.) in 1994. Tarifi was born in 1947 in Deir Tarif, a village close to Ramallah (q.v.), and comes from a prominent clan. After studying at 'Ain Shams University in Egypt (q.v.), he returned to practice law in the West Bank (q.v.), and became a prominent businessman. From 1976 to 1982, he served as deputy mayor of al-Bireh (q.v.). He was dismissed by the Israelis in 1982, when the Civil Administration (q.v.) was established and the Israelis wanted to begin implementing the Camp David Accords (q.v.).

Tarifi is said to have met in 1989 with Yitzhak Shamir (q.v.), Israel's (q.v.) prime minister, to discuss Shamir's peace initiative. At the time, Tarifi said that the initiative was an attempt to stop the Intifada (q.v.). Tarifi also was involved in the negotiations for the peace process.

TAWIL, IBRAHIM. Former mayor of al-Bireh (q.v.). He was born in 1943, and attended Alexandria University in Egypt (q.v.), where he received a degree in pharmacology in 1970. Afterward, he taught for a year at al-Riyad University in Saudi Arabia. Returning to the West Bank (q.v.), he eventually ran for mayor in al-Bireh on the pro-PLO (q.v.) nationalist platform in 1976 and won. He also was a member of the Committee for National Guidance (q.v), an organization that directed the resistance in the Occupied Territories (q.v.). In 1980, he escaped an assassination attempt, when he and two other mayors, Karim Khalaf and Bassam al-Shak'a (qq.v.), were targeted by the Jewish underground. Unlike Khalaf and al-Shak'a, he was warned before opening his garage door, and an Israeli bomb expert was blinded when the bomb exploded in his face as he opened the door of the garage. Tawil remained in office until 1982, at which time he was dismissed by the Israelis after the establishment of the Civil Administration (q.v.).

AL-TAWIL, RAYMONDA HAWWA. Journalist, political activist, and founder of Palestine Press Services (q.v.), a news service in East Jerusalem (q.v.). Imprisoned several times, she also was placed under house arrest (q.v.) in 1980. She has written an autobiography, *My Home My Prison* (Tel Aviv, 1979), about her experiences as a Palestinian woman under the Israeli military occupation. Al-Tawil is the mother of Suha Arafat, the wife of Yasser Arafat (q.v.).

TAWFIQ, HAMMAD AL-HAJ. Mayor of Nablus (q.v.) prior to the outbreak of World War I. He was a supporter of the Ottoman-Turkish (q.v.) empire. In 1919, he established a branch of the Muslim-Christian Association (q.v.) in Nablus, and was active in stirring up nationalistic fervor against the British and Zionist presence in Palestine (q.v.). He was a member and then vice-president of the Syrian-Palestine Congress in September 1921, vice-president of the Arab Committtee that negotiated with the British, and a member of the delegation to the London Conference (q.v.) in 1923.

TOUQAN, FADWA ABD AL-FATAH. Poet and member of the board of trustees of An-Najah National University (q.v.). She was born in 1917 in Nablus (q.v.), where she finished high school, and later spent two years in Oxford, England. Touqan received numerous awards for her work. In 1978, she was given the international award for poetry in Palermo, Italy; in 1983, she received the poetry award from the Jordanian Writers' Association; and in 1990, she received the Jerusalem Award for Culture and Art.

TOUQAN, SULEIMAN. Mayor of Nablus (q.v.) in the 1940s and a political activist. Born and raised in Nablus, he was a staunch nationalist and advocated Palestinian participation in the armstice negotiations in Rhodes after the war of 1948 (q.v.). Later, he closely aligned himself with the Jordanian government. Recognized for his loyalty, he was appointed as Jordan's minister of Agriculture, and in the 1950s as minister of Defense. He also served a term as governor of a Jordanian province. He was killed in Iraq (q.v.) in 1958.

TOWN ARREST. A measure used by Israel (q.v.) to confine Palestinians to their immediate towns and villages to curtail their mobility. It often is used in conjunction with house arrest (q.v.).

TRADE UNIONS. The trade union movement in the Occupied Territories (q.v.) is weak, politicized, and riddled with division. The morale of the 393,000 workers is extremely low, and concern about the Israeli occupation and nationalism have consumed concern for unity and the conditions of the workers. Participation in trade unions is minuscule. Moreover, the trade unions and the three general trade-union federations are controlled by the various Palestinian political factions. Israel (q.v.) has constantly interfered in the activities of the unions, and has imprisoned and deported union activists.

After the signing of the Declaration of Principles (q.v.), the federations were to hold elections on the basis of proportional representation and choose their representatives. The trade unions also were to receive several million dollars deducted from the wages of Palestinian workers from the Histadrut, the Israeli Trade Union, in accordance with the Palestinian-Israeli Economic Agreement of April 1994. The elections have not been held, and only $1.3 million, to be paid in two installments in September and December 1995, has been designated for transfer to the Palestinian trade unions.

TULKARM. A West Bank (q.v.) city and a commercial center. It has a population of 28,253, and its size is 333 square kilometers. Tulkarm is located 15 kilometers from the Mediterranean Sea, between the Nablus mountains to the east and the sea to the west. Tulkarm is surrounded by fertile land, on which agricultural produce, such as melons, watermelon, olives, almonds, chick peas, and lentils, are grown and distributed throughout the Occupied Territories (q.v.). See DISTRICTS.

U

'UDWAN, KAMAL. Co-founder of the Black September Organization and director of FATAH (qq.v.) intelligence. Born in Gaza (q.v.) in

1925, he received his education in Cairo, Egypt (q.v.). He returned to Gaza, which had come under Egyptian control, and became active in organizing Palestinian resistance cells. Before long, he was arrested by the Egyptians. After he was released, he went to Jordan (q.v.), where he took part in the Palestinian-Jordanian confrontation of 1970. 'Udwan was assassinated by Israeli commandos in Beirut, Lebanon (q.v.), in 1973.

UNIFIED NATIONAL COMMAND OF THE UPRISING. see UNIFIED NATIONAL LEADERSHIP OF THE UPRISING (UNLU).

UNIFIED NATIONAL LEADERSHIP OF THE UPRISING (UNLU). The underground leadership comprising PLO (q.v.) factions that united at the beginning of the Intifada (q.v.) in order to coordinate their activities against the Israelis. It was composed of FATAH (q.v.), the Popular Front for the Liberation of Palestine (q.v.), the Democratic Front for the Liberation of Palestine, and the Palestine People's Party (qq.v.). HAMAS (q.v.) did not join the UNLU, but worked independently during the Intifada. The UNLU controlled the Occupied Territories (q.v.) and maintained direct contact with the PLO in Tunis. See INTIFADA and LEAFLETS.

UNION OF PALESTINIAN MEDICAL RELIEF COMMITTEES (UPMRC). An independent Palestinian grassroots health organization established by Mustafa Barghouthi (q.v.) and others in 1979, because of the deteriorating medical and health conditions in the Occupied Territories (q.v.). Its main objective is to make health care available to people in rural areas and those of low socioeconomic status. It provides primary medical care, emphasizing both preventive and curative health services and the utilization of local resources. Its policy also is to encourage people to participate in their health care. Therefore, health education is of vital importance. The organization has a training center where village women can be trained as community health workers. The organization serves 182 localities and runs 32 clinics throughout the West Bank and Gaza (qq.v.) It also runs a number of mobile clinics, in addition to the regular health clinics, which are staffed by volunteer medical professionals. See HEALTH.

UNION OF PALESTINIAN WOMEN'S WORKS COMMITTEES (UPWWC). The Union was established on March 8, 1981, when 55 representatives of women's groups met and agreed to coordinate their activities and to work collectively to improve the social, economic, and political conditions of women. The union regularly coordinates training sessions and educational lectures.

UNION OF WOMEN'S COMMITTEES FOR UNIFIED WORK (UWCUW). Established in 1989, in Ramallah (q.v.), the purpose of the union is to coordinate the social, political, and economic activities of women's committees to enhance the position of Palestinian women. The union also conducts activities to increase women's awareness of their conditions, to facilitate social and economic improvement in their lives, and to increase their participation in national life.

UNITED ARAB KINGDOM PLAN. A proposal suggested by King Hussein of Jordan (qq.v.) on March 15, 1972 to establish a kingdom that would be a confederation or a federation between the country of Jordan and a Palestine in the West Bank (qq.v.). Amman would be the capital of Jordan (q.v.) and Jerusalem (q.v.) would be the capital of the Palestinian state. An executive power would govern each region, and the king would be the head of this entity. There also would be a single armed force, with the king as commander-in-chief. The idea was not received well by Palestinians at the time, because they were furious with the king for the 1970 Palestinian-Jordanian confrontation, when several thousand Palestinians were killed and the PLO (q.v.) was evicted from Jordan (q.v.).

UNITED ARAB REPUBLIC. The union formed between Syria and Egypt (qq.v.) in 1958 under the leadership of Gamal Abd al-Nasser (q.v.), then president of Egypt (q.v.). The union lasted until September 1961. The Syrians, supported by the Ba'th (q.v.) Party, were disenchanted with Egypt's socialism and increasing domination of Syria.

UNITED NATIONS PARTITION PLAN. The division of Palestine into a Jewish state and a Palestinian state, with Jerusalem (q.v.) placed under the supervision of the United Nations, in accordance with U.N. General Assembly Resolution 181 (q.v.) of November 29, 1947. The Jews were granted 56 percent of Palestine at a time when they owned 7 percent of the land and represented only a third of the population. The partition plan, which was adopted by the General Assembly but not ratified by the Security Council, caused anger and resentment among the Palestinians, and served as the spark that ignited the war of 1948 (q.v.). At the end of the war, when Israel declared statehood on May 14, 1948, it was in control of more than three-quarters of Palestine, including the coastal areas. See UNITED NATIONS RESOLUTIONS.

UNITED NATIONS RELIEF AND WORKS AGENCY FOR PALESTINIAN REFUGEES IN THE NEAR EAST (UNRWA). The organization established to assist the Palestinians after the war of 1948 (q.v). The United Nations Economic Survey Mission, or the Clapp Commission, proposed setting up the organization temporarily to assist the 700,000 Palestinian refugees (q.v.) who fled their homes during the 1948 war. The U.N. General Assembly Resolution 302 of December 8, 1949, established the United Nations Relief and Works Agency for Palestinian Refugees, and funded it for three years with a budget of $250 million. The organization began its work on May 1, 1950.

UNRWA provides housing, food rations, medical services, education, and vocational training to 2 million Palestinian refugees in Jordan (q.v.), Lebanon (q.v.), Syria (q.v.), the West Bank (q.v.), and the Gaza Strip (q.v.). Altogether, UNRWA provides services to 61 refugee camps, in addition to services that are available to refugees who reside outside the camps. To be identified a refugee, the individual or his family must have lived at least two years in Palestine before the outbreak of the 1948 Arab-Israeli conflict. See REFUGEES.

UNITED NATIONS RESOLUTIONS ON PALESTINE. The United Nations (q.v.) issued numerous resolutions on the question of Palestine. The most important of these are the following:

U.N. General Assembly Resolution 181 (II) of November 29, 1947. The General Assembly, with a vote of 33 to 13 and 10 abstentions, approved the partition of Palestine into a Jewish and an Arab state, with Jerusalem and Bethlehem (qq.v.), being corpus separatum and placed under a U.N. Trusteeship Council. The resolution not only affirmed the establishment of a national home for the Jews, but also laid the basis for establishing a state of Palestine and the right of the Palestinians to self-determination and statehood.

U.N. General Assembly Resolution 194 (III) of December 11, 1948. The resolution recognized the right of return of Palestinian refugees (q.v.) and provided for their immediate return, to live in peace, after the war of 1948 (q.v.). The resolution also stated that refugees who did not want to return should be compensated for the property they left behind. The resolution also established the Palestine Conciliation Commission (q.v.).

U.N. General Assembly Resolution 303 of December 9, 1949. The city of Jerusalem was corpus separatum, to be placed under a special U.N. international administration. The mandate also included Bethlehem and the suburbs of East Jerusalem, which are Abu Dis, Ein Karim, and Shu'fat.

U.N. Security Council Resolution 242 of November 22, 1967. The resolution was passed after the war of 1967 (q.v.), and maintained the inadmissibility of territory by war. It stated that Israel (q.v.) must withdraw from the territories it had occupied during the war in return for peace with its Arab neighbors. It went on to declare that all states in the area had the right to live in peace, and that respect for each other's sovereignty and territorial integrity must be observed and maintained. The resolution also guarantees the right for all states to navigate through international waters, and calls for a just solution to the refugee problem.

U.N. Security Council Resolution 298 of September 25, 1971, on Jerusalem. The resolution declared that the changes Israel had made in Jerusalem were invalid, and that Israel should rescind them.

U.N. Security Resolution 338 of October 21–22, 1973. The resolution was issued during the War of 1973 (q.v.), and it called on all parties involved in the Arab-Israeli conflict to stop fighting and to implement U.N. Resolution 242 through negotiations, and with the assistance of an appropriate third party, in order to establish a just and lasting peace in the Middle East.

U.N. Resolutions (3236 and 3237) of October 14, 1974. The resolutions acknowledged that the PLO (q.v.) is the representative of the Palestinian people, and that the Palestinians have the right to self-determination and statehood. The PLO (q.v.) was granted the status of observer at the United Nations.

U.N. Resolution 446 of March 1979. The resolution stated that settlements (q.v.) are illegal and constitute an obstacle to peace.

U.N. General Assembly Resolution 38/58 of December 13, 1983. The resolution reaffirmed the Fourth Geneva Convention (q.v.) and its applicability to the Occupied Territories (q.v.), including Jerusalem (q.v.). Moreover, it called for a halt to settlement (q.v.) construction by Israel and the reversal of all past settlement building.

UNIVERSITIES. The major universities in the West Bank and the Gaza Strip (see individual entries where indicated): Birzeit University (q.v.), established in 1975; Al-Quds University (q.v.), established in 1984; An-Najah National University (q.v.), established in 1977; Bethlehem University (q.v.), established in 1973; Hebron University (q.v.), established in 1971; and Gaza Islamic University (q.v.), established in 1977.

UPRISING. see INTIFADA.

V

VENICE DECLARATION (JUNE 13, 1980). The European Economic Community, comprising nine member states, convened a two-day summit in Venice. They issued a declaration stating that all the states in the region, including Israel (q.v.) and the Palestinians, have the right to live in peace within secure borders. It maintained that the Palestinians had a right to self-determination; that a just solution had to be found for the Palestinian people and not only the "refugees" (q.v.); and that the PLO (q.v.) was to represent the Palestinians in any future settlement of the conflict. Moreover, it called on Israel to stop building settlements (q.v.), to end the military occupation of the West Bank and Gaza Strip (qq.v.), and to stop claiming exclusive control over Jerusalem (qq.v).

VILLAGE LEAGUES. The formation of village organizations in the rural areas was initiated and encouraged by Israel (q.v.) in its quest to create an alternative leadership to PLO (q.v.) municipalities and village councils in the Occupied Territories (q.v.), particularly after the Palestinians rejected the Camp David Accords (q.v.).

The Israeli occupational forces asked a village leader, Mustafa Dudin (q.v.) from Dura, Hebron (q.v.), to organize the leagues. Leagues were then established in Bethlehem (q.v.), Ramallah (q.v.), Nablus (q.v.), Jenin (q.v.), Qabatiya, and the village of Habla. To enhance the position of the village leagues, Israel in 1982 dismissed nine mayors, among them the mayors of al-Bireh (q.v.), Ramallah, and Nablus. The other municipalities and village councils in the Occupied Territories, with the exception of Bethlehem, went on strike and stopped all municipal services to protest the dismissals.

Palestinians' reactions to the leagues were hostile: Members were labeled collaborators, and people were warned not to have anything to do with them. On November 18, 1981, Yousuf al-Khatib, the head of the Ramallah League, was killed. On March 9, 1982, the Jordanian government considered membership and activity in these leagues to be high treason, punishable by death and the confiscation of property. The village leagues consequently proved ineffective; the Palestinians would not approach them for assistance, and Israeli support for them declined in 1984.

VOICE OF PALESTINE (VOP). Palestinian program that began broadcasting from Cairo, Egypt (q.v.). The Voice of the Arabs, an Egyptian radio station in Cairo, expanded its programs and established a "Palestine Corner" on October 29, 1960. The name was later changed to the Voice of Palestine. The VOP also has broadcasted from Syria (q.v.), Iraq, and Lebanon (qq.v.). After the signing of the DOP (q.v.), the Voice of Palestine began broadcasting from Ramallah (q.v.).

W

WAFA. Acronym in Arabic for *Wikalat Al-Anba Al-Filastiniyya Al-Arabiyya* (The Palestinian-Arab News Agency). It is the official PLO (q.v.) news agency. After the DOP (q.v.) was signed, WAFA moved its offices to the Gaza Strip (q.v.). Its headquarters, however, was moved to Ramallah (q.v.) when the Israelis redeployed from that city in 1995.

WAQF. Arabic for the Muslim religious endowment or trust. It is the institution to which Muslims bequeath land and property for distribution to the poor, and in support of mosques, educational institutions, and charitable organizations and activities. This is known as *Waqf Kheiri* or charitable trust, where any income generated from the trust is used for the welfare and development of the Muslim community. It is distinguished from *Waqf Ahli* or family trust, where the income derived from the endowed property is used by the family of the person who has made the bequest. This *Waqf* is subject to *Shari'a* (q.v.) laws, and an executor is assigned to administer it for the family.

In Israel, *Waqf Kheiri* is under the auspices of a Muslim board of trustees. In the autonomous areas (q.v.), *Waqf* property is administered by the PNA (q.v.). Hassan Tahboub (q.v.) is the director. In East Jerusalem (q.v.), the *Waqf* is administered by the Jordanian Ministry of Religious Affairs. Currently, the head of the *Waqf* in East Jerusalem is Adnan al-Husseini (q.v.).

WARS. (1) War of 1948. The war took place as a result of the U.N. Partition Plan (q.v.), which proposed internationalization of the city of Jerusalem (q.v.) and by the declaration of independence of the Jewish state on May 15, 1948. The Arab army, comprising 20,000 soldiers from Iraq (q.v.), Lebanon (q.v.), Saudi Arabia (q.v.), Transjordan, Syria (q.v.), and Egypt (q.v.), faced a strong Jewish force of some 130,000 men that also included members of the Jewish underground groups, the Haganah, Irgun, and Stern. The Arabs were defeated; refugees fled their homes, either to neighboring Arab countries or to the West Bank and the Gaza Strip (qq.v.). The Palestinians who remained became a minority in the Jewish state, and were subsequently given Israeli citizenship. In 1949, Israel (q.v.) signed armstice agreements with Egypt (February 24), Jordan (April 3), Lebanon (March 23), and Syria (July 20). Israel consequently was able to expand its territory, and gained more land than it had been previously allotted under the U.N. Partition Plan. The Partition Plan had given 56 percent of Palestine to the Jews, when they had owned less than 7 percent. After the war, Israel controlled 77 percent of the land of Palestine (q.v.). Transjordan assumed control of the West Bank and East Jerusalem (q.v.), and Egypt administered the Gaza Strip (q.v.).

(2) War of 1956. President Nasser of Egypt (qq.v.), who came to power in the coup of 1952 that deposed the monarchy in Egypt, na-

tionalized the Suez Canal in July 1956. Consequently, Britian, France, and Israel attacked Egypt. Both the United Nations and the United States expressed displeasure, and they pressured Israel to withdraw from the territory it occupied. A U.N. emergency peacekeeping force was stationed in the Sinai in 1956.

(3) Six-Day War (q.v.) or the war of 1967. Israel had acquired the port of Eilat on the Gulf of Aqaba, giving it access to the Indian Ocean and the Red Sea. Nevertheless, Israeli ships had to pass through the Straits of Tiran, Egyptian territory. On May 16, 1967, President Nasser of Egypt (qq.v.) demanded the withdrawal of the U.N. emergency peacekeeping force that had been stationed in the Sinai since 1956. The Straits of Tiran were closed to Israeli shipping on May 22, 1967. Tension mounted in the region, as Iraq (q.v.), Syria (q.v.), and Jordan (q.v.) mobilized their forces. Israel attacked the Egyptian air force while it was on the ground and completely destroyed it. It then occupied the Sinai and reached the Suez Canal. It also took the West Bank, the Gaza Strip, and the Syrian Golan Heights (qq.v.). On June 10, 1967, the war was over. The U.N. General Assembly in November 1967 passed Resolution 242 (q.v.).

(4) War of 1973. The war took place on October 6, 1973, when Syrian and Egyptian forces attacked Israel during Ramadan, the Muslim month of fasting, and the Jewish Yom Kippur (Day of Atonement). Egypt launched its attack, crossed the Israeli Bar-lev line of defense and moved forward from the Suez Canal. Syria marched on the Golan Heights (qq.v.), taking the Israelis by surprise. Israel (q.v.) quickly recovered, invaded Egypt and surrounded the Egyptian army. Russia and the United States intervened to stop the war. The war lasted three weeks, and a cease-fire was mediated by Henry Kissinger, then U.S. secretary of state. Israel accepted the Disengagement Agreement of January 1974. Egyptian soldiers were placed in the Sinai with a United Nations force in the buffer zone. The Suez Canal was reopened in June 1975, and Israeli cargo was allowed to pass, but the agreement stipulated that it had to be carried in non-Israeli ships. Under an interim agreement signed on September 1, 1975, between Egypt and Israel, the Egyptian and the U.N. forces in the Sinai Peninsula (q.v.) were increased, and the oil installations on the Gulf of the Suez were returned to Egypt. In the peace treaty signed between Egypt and Israel on March 26, 1979, Israel agreed to withdraw from the Suez Canal and the Sinai, and to normalize relations. The withdrawal from Egyptian territory was completed by April 1982.

(5) War of 1982. Israel planned "Operation Peace for the Galilee" in January 1982 because of the presence of the PLO (q.v.) in south Lebanon, and the continuous shelling of Israeli settlements in the northern part of the country. Israel invaded Lebanon on June 5, 1982,

and laid siege to Beirut for 79 days. When the siege ended, the PLO had to evacuate Beirut on August 30, 1982. Moreover, Israel took control of a strip, or "security zone," in southern Lebanon, and installed a Lebanese Maronite, General Sa'ad Haddad, who was sympathetic to Israel, to run the area. On September 16, 1982, the Phalangists entered the refugee camps of Sabra and Shatilla and massacred thousands of Palestinians. It was alleged that the Phalangists had been encouraged by the Israelis. See SHARON.

WATER. One of the most controversial issues in the Arab-Israeli conflict has been water. Israel (q.v.) insists that it must have total control of the water resources in the West Bank (q.v.), in order to maintain its hydrological system. During the past 28 years of the occupation, Israel has restricted the Palestinians from using their water sources. It has prohibited the digging of new wells, placed meters on existing wells, rationed water, and increased the cost for Palestinians, while subsidizing it for Israelis.

Approximately 30 percent of Israel's water supply comes from water that runs through underground West Bank (q.v.) aquifers. The western and northern aquifers flow under the hills of Samaria in the West Bank and produce 600 million cubic meters a year. From this source, Israel draws 490 million cubic meters and the Palestinians 110 million cubic meters. Another source, the Yarkon-Taninim Aquifer, which flows under Qalqilya and Tulkarm (qq.v.), produces 920 million cubic meters and provides Jerusalem and the coastal plains with a large portion of their water supply. The eastern aquifer, which has the capacity for 130 million cubic meters—of which only 90 million cubic meters are utilized—flows from mountain springs through Wadi Kelt and Wadi Ouja to the Jordan Valley.

The Palestinians claim that Israel has been unfair in the distribution of water, given the fact that only 20 percent of the water flows under the Green Line (q.v.). The Palestinians strongly believe that water is a natural resource, and insist on maintaining control of their resources. This, they believe is necessary given the future economic development of the area and the influx of Palestinian refugees (q.v.) to the territories, which will increase their per capita need for water.

The DOP (q.v.) established a Palestinian Water Authority, and the Palestinians are permitted to dig wells in the autonomous areas of Gaza and Jericho (qq.v.). The Palestinians want 80 million cubic meters from the eastern aquifer that runs through the Jordan Valley. They also want control of at least 500 million of the 920 million cubic meters of water from the Yarkon-Taninim. The Oslo Accords (q.v.) stipulated the establishment of a Joint Water Monitoring Commission. Joint control would be for the western aquifer, the Jordan River, and the Ein Gidi system, from which Israel takes 500 million cubic meters and the Palestinians receive 130 million cubic meters. In the Oslo Two Agreement (q.v.), which was signed on September 28, 1995, Israel agreed to increase the Palestinians' share of water by 28 million cubic meters.

The subject of water understandably remains a controversial issue in the Palestinian-Israeli negotiations. Both sides agree on the need to protect the existing water supply and reserves, to conduct full-scale treatment of sewage for fear of pollution of the underground water reservoirs, and to restrict overpumping to prevent the water table from reaching sea level.

AL-WAZIR, INTISAR. Nom de guerre, Um Jihad. She was appointed Minister of Social Affairs by the Palestine National Authority (q.v.) in July 1994, and again in June 1996. Um Jihad was born in 1941 in the Bedee neighborhood in Gaza (q.v.), and graduated from Zahra Secondary School in 1960. She joined FATAH (q.v.) in 1959, when it was a fledgling organization made up of a few resistance cells. In 1962, she married her cousin, Khalil al-Wazir (q.v.). The following year, they left Gaza to help organize the resistance abroad. She was very active on behalf of Palestinian children whose fathers were killed in the Arab-Israeli conflict. In 1966, she became the head of the Martyr's Society, an organization that provided assistance to the families whose breadwinners had died fighting for the Palestinian cause, and also took care of the families of prisoners. In 1974, she became a member of the Palestine National Council (q.v.). During this time, she continued her education and graduated from Damascus University in 1978. She has gradually moved up the FATAH hierarchy, and was elected a member of the Central Council of FATAH in August 1989.

AL-WAZIR, KHALIL. Nom de guerre, Abu Jihad. Co-founder of FATAH (q.v.), and Arafat's (q.v.) former deputy and head of military operations in the Occupied Territories (q.v.). Abu Jihad was born on October 10, 1935, in Ramleh, Palestine. During the war of 1948 (q.v.), his family fled to Gaza (q.v.). He studied in Egypt (q.v.), where he met Arafat in 1954. In 1957, they established the first Palestinian resistance group. During that time, al-Wazir was carrying out sabotage attacks against Israel (q.v.) from Egypt. In 1958, he became a founding member of FATAH (q.v.) and a member of the FATAH Central Committee. A tireless organizer and a skilled military tactician, he became the deputy commander-in-chief of the PLO (q.v.) forces, and headed the first FATAH office in Algeria in 1963. He also was the first editor of *Filastinu* (q.v.), the publication issued by FATAH in Lebanon (q.v.) in 1959. Politically astute, he maintained good relations with the leaders of the Arab states, and with the Palestinians in the Occupied Territories (q.v.), particularly the various youth groups.

Al-Wazir was assassinated in his home by an Israeli commando group in Tunis on April 16, 1988. He was very popular, and his death shocked many Palestinians, who draped black flags over their homes in mourning. A military unit of FATAH, or a "strike force," was named after him, and carried out resistance activities against the Israelis during the Intifada (q.v.).

WEST BANK. Part of the area allotted by the U.N. Partition Plan (q.v.) of 1947 for the Palestinian Arabs. It was annexed by Jordan (q.v.) in 1950. The term "West Bank" was used after the annexation, when it referred to the country of Jordan (q.v.), west of the river, and after the term "Palestine" was banned from official use by Jordan.

The West Bank is 5,900 square kilometers (3,700 square miles). It is bordered on the west by the 1949 armstice or green line (q.v.), and on the east by the Jordan River. It is divided into two main regions: the south, dominated by Hebron (q.v.), and the north, dominated by Nablus (q.v.). There are approximately 450 villages and towns in the West Bank. See DISTRICTS.

WEST BANK PALESTINE NATIONAL FRONT (WBPNF). see PALESTINE NATIONAL FRONT (PNF).

WESTERN WALL. Also called the Wailing Wall by Jewish worshipers. The wall, which borders *Al-Haram al-Sharif* (q.v.), is considered sacred by the Jews because they believe it is part of the Second Temple that was destroyed in 70 CE (Common Era). The Palestinians were disturbed by Jewish worshipers praying there in the 1920s and 1930s, and they believed the Jews wanted to take over the entire area of *Al-Haram al-Sharif*. This led to many protests and riots by the Palestinians. See ARAB-PALESTINIAN REVOLTS.

WHITE PAPERS. see BRITISH WHITE PAPERS.

WOMEN. Palestinian women have been active politically, socially, and economically in their society. They have worked in the house and in the fields, which were often viewed as an extension of the house. In the urban areas, Palestinian women formed social and charitable organizations, composed of upper-and middle-class women. Not only did they engage in tasks of a charitable nature, but they also were active politically. They participated in the Arab Palestinian revolts (q.v.) in the 1920s and 1930s, and protested British policies and Jewish immigration into Palestine (q.v.). Moreover, a number of women's organizations united and formed the Arab Women's Association in 1929 and the Arab Women's Union in 1938. Their activities included demonstrations, fund-raising and sending delegations to express grievances to British authorities. More recently, Palestinian women were active participants in the Intifada (q.v.). They saw their sons and husbands imprisoned and their brothers killed, but still they resisted and persevered. Some women, including Hanan Ashrawi (q.v.), Zahira Kamal (q.v.), and Samiha Khalil (q.v.), gained international prominence for their contributions to Palestinian society. Intisar al-Wazir (q.v.) was appointed as the PNA's (q.v.) minister of Social Affairs.

Palestinian women have been burdened by social and economic factors. For instance, illiteracy rates are higher among women (28.5 percent) than men (7.4 percent) in the Occupied Territories and the autonomous areas (qq.v.). They also are higher among women between the ages of 14 and 44, than in any other age group. Women's overall participation in education (q.v.) is high in the elementary and preparatory stages (44 percent and 38 percent, respectively) and declines in the secondary stage (34 percent). Although women now marry later (17–19 years in 1992, up from 15–17 years in 1987), families still prefer to marry their daughters off at an early age, given the emphasis that is still placed on virginity. Women start bearing children immediately after marriage, so that the fertility rate for Palestinian women is 5.6 children—meaning the population will probably double in 17 years. Women's participation in the labor force has ranged from 8 percent to 15.2 percent. This is due to the lack of employment opportunities open to women and social and cultural conditions that impede their entry into the labor force.

A great deal must be done to improve the overall status of Palestinian women in the Occupied Territories and the autonomous areas (qq.v.). The Palestinian Declaration of Independence (q.v.) states that "governance will be based on principles of social justice, equality, and non-discrimination in public rights of men and women . . . under the aegis of a constitution which ensures the rule of law under an independent judiciary system". Moreover, a Higher Council for Women's Rights has been formed and is involved in writing the Palestinian constitution.

WOMEN'S CENTER FOR LEGAL AID AND COUNSELING. A non-profit organization established in 1991 to serve and assist women in legal matters and to provide personal counseling.

WOMEN'S INTERNATIONAL LEAGUE FOR PEACE AND FREEDOM. The league was born in 1988 and advocates the peaceful establishment of a Palestinian state. Its objectives include training women in political skills to enable them to participate more effectively in the political processes of their state.

WOMEN'S TRAINING AND RESEARCH SOCIETY. Also called the Women's Studies Center. It was established in 1989 to empower women to bring about social change and improvements in their lives. The society also conducts social research programs for women, rather than research about women.

Y

YAHYA, ABDUL RAZAK. Alias Abu Anas. Member of the PLO Executive Committee (q.v.) and senior PLO (q.v.) representative stationed in Jordan. He served as the head of the PLO Economic Department. Yahya returned to the Gaza Strip (q.v.) after the signing of the DOP (q.v.), and was a member of the Palestinian committee that negotiated redeployment and the withdrawal of the Israeli army from the Occupied Territories (q.v.).

YA'ISH, MAHMOUD ALI. Journalist and publisher. He was born in Nablus (q.v.) in 1904, and studied at An-Najah College in Nablus. He then worked for the *Al-Jam'iyyah Al-Islamiyyeh* (The Islamic Society) (q.v.) newspaper, which was published in Jaffa, Palestine. In 1934, he published *Al-Dif'a* (q.v.), *Al-Jihad* (The Holy War) and the *Jerusalem Times* newspapers. He also published *Al-Massa* (The Evening) for three years, after which he founded *Al-Sha'b* (q.v.) newspaper.

YASSIN, AHMAD, SHEIKH. A religious leader, founder of the Islamic Center in Gaza (1973), and a leader of HAMAS (q.v.). He was born in 1937 in 'Asqalan, a city now in Israel (q.v.), and fled to Gaza (q.v.) during the war of 1948 (q.v.). A quadriplegic who has been confined to a wheelchair since an accident that occurred in his youth, he was first arrested by the Israelis in 1984 and sentenced to 13 years in jail for possession of arms. However, he was released in the 1985 prison exchange, in which 1,400 Palestinian prisoners were freed in return for three Israeli soldiers. He was arrested again in May 1989, and sentenced to 15 years in prison for directing HAMAS activities that included the kidnapping of Israeli soldiers. On October 16, 1991, Yassin was sentenced to life in prison. Yassin believes that an Islamic state should be established in Palestine, and that no one has the right to negotiate any part of Palestine and hand it over to non-Muslims.

During the Intifada (q.v.), Sheikh Yassin allowed nationalist symbols and language to be incorporated into HAMAS' ideology.

AL-YAZAJI, AHMAD TEWFIQ HUSNI. Medical doctor and political activist, he was born in the Gaza Strip (q.v.) on June 10, 1947. He studied medicine at Cairo University, then at Alexandria University in Egypt (q.v.), graduating in 1979. He worked at Al-Shifa Hospital in Gaza until 1989, when he was fired by the Israelis during the Intifada (q.v). Afterward, he did volunteer work for the Palestinian Medical Relief Services and worked at Al Ahli Al-Arabi Hospital.

Al-Yazaji is a member of many organizations, among them the Palestinian Red Crescent Society (q.v.), the Gaza Central Blood Bank, the Senior Citizens Society, the Health Services Council of Jerusalem, and the Sports Federation Club. He also was a board member of the Arab Medical Association from 1981 until 1991. He was banned from traveling by the Israelis for many years. Al-Yazaji was a member of the Palestinian advisory delegation to the peace talks.

Z

AL-ZABARI, MUSTAF. Alias Abu Ali Mustafa. He is a member of the Popular Front for the Liberation of Palestine (q.v.) and head of the Department of Palestinian Refugees (q.v.). He has also been a member of the PLO Executive Committee (q.v.).

AL-ZAHHAR, MAHMOUD. Born in 1945, he trained as a surgeon and lectures at the Islamic University in Gaza (qq.v.). He was a member of the Council for Higher Education (q.v.), and in 1990 became the elected chairman of the Arab Medical Association in Gaza.

Zahhar is a senior leader in HAMAS' (q.v.) political wing and the faction's spokesperson. He has negotiated on several occasions with the Palestine National Authority (q.v.) to reach a modus vivendi regarding HAMAS' participation in the elections for the Palestinian government, and to reach a compromise regarding their opposition to the peace process.

ZA'NOUN, RIAD DEEB. The Palestine National Authority's (q.v.) minister of Health, appointed in July 1994, and again in June 1996. He was elected a member of the PLC (q.v.) for the district of Gaza (q.v.). Za'noun was born in Gaza in 1937 and studied medicine at Cairo University in Egypt (q.v.). After graduating in 1960, he returned to work at Gaza's Shifa Hospital, where he was appointed chief of internal medicine. Za'noun then worked in Kuwait (q.v.) and

Qatar for more than 20 years before returning to Gaza. In 1993, he was appointed the director of the Palestinian Council of Health in the Gaza Strip.

ZA'NOUN, SALIM. Nom de guerre, Abu Adib. Chief representative of the PLO (q.v.) in the Arab Gulf states, and a member of FATAH's (q.v.) Central Committee. He also was the deputy chairman of the Palestine National Council (q.v.).

ZIONISM. A national Jewish movement that led to the establishment of Israel (q.v.). It was initiated by Theodor Herzl, who, in his book, *Der Judenstaat* (The Jewish State), called for a national home for the Jews that would provide them with a refuge from anti-Semitism and the injustices of the world. In 1897, a Zionist Congress was convened in Basel, Switzerland, to discuss this venture, and ways of acquiring land in Palestine (q.v.), encouraging and fostering Jewish immigration, and establishing kibbutzim (collective communes) to help Jews adjust to life in Palestine (q.v.). Waves of Jewish immigrants soon arrived in Palestine—a land that the Palestinian Arabs, who were living there, insisted was necessary to fulfill their own national aspiration. By 1948, when the state of Israel was declared, there were 625,000 Jews in Palestine; by 1951, their number had reached 1.5 million.

On November 10, 1975, the U.N. General Assembly passed Resolution 3379, characterizing Zionism as a "form of racism and racial discrimination." On December 16, 1991, the General Assembly repealed this resolution.

Bibliography

Introduction

Many sources have been included in the bibliography, but for a more thorough list, the reader should refer to Walid Khalidi and Jill Khadduri (eds.), *Palestine and the Arab-Israeli Conflict: An Annotated Bibliography,* published by the Institute of Palestine Studies: Beirut (1974); H. I. Hussaini (ed.), *The Palestine Problem: An Annotated Bibliography, 1967–1980*, Palestine Information Office: Washington (1980); and Issa Nakhleh, *Encyclopedia of the Palestine Problem,* Intercontinental Books: New York (1991).

An excellent collection of essays on the Palestinian-Israeli conflict may be found in a reader edited by Walid Khalidi and published in 1971, *From Haven to Conquest: Readings in Zionism and the Palestine Problem Until 1948*, and Ibrahim Abu Lughod (ed.), *The Transformation of Palestine: Essays on the Origin and Development of the Arab-Israeli Conflict,* published in 1987.

A good diary is Robert John and Sami Hadawi, *The Palestine Diary, Volume I, 1914–1945*, and *Volume II, 1945–1948,* published in 1970. Two useful sources on Palestinian refugees are Nafez Nazzal's *Palestinian Exodus From the Galilee, 1948* (1978), and Benny Morris' *The Birth of the Palestinian Refugee Problem, 1947–1949,* published in 1987. A general history of the West Bank can be found in Don Peretz, *The West Bank: History, Politics, Society and Economy* (1986). A collection of articles written by Palestinians about different aspects of the Israeli occupation is in Emile Nakhleh's (ed.), *A Palestinian Agenda for the West Bank and Gaza* (1980). A discussion of the social, political and economic dimensions of the Intifada, or uprising, is found in Jamal Nasser and Roger Heacock (eds.), *Intifada: Palestine at the Crossroads* (1990).

An excellent handbook on the Palestinians is Khalil Nakhleh and Elia Zureik (eds.), *The Sociology of the Palestinians* (1988). An informative source on Palestinians in the diaspora is Lauri Brand, *Palestinians in the Arab World: Institution Building and the Search for State* (1988). The economy of the West Bank is thoroughly analyzed in George Abed's (ed.), *The Palestinian Economy: Studies in Development Under Prolonged Occupation* (1988). Two organizations, Al-Haq (Law in the

Service of Man) and B'Tselem (Israeli Information Center for Human Rights in the Occupied Territories) have thoroughly documented violations of Palestinians' human rights in the Occupied Territories and regularly publish their findings.

English language publications that frequently write about Palestine are: *Journal of Palestine Studies, Middle East Policy, British Journal of Middle Eastern Studies,* the Jerusalem-based *Palestine-Israel Journal*, the *Middle East Journal, American-Arab Affairs, Arab Studies Quarterly, The Jerusalem Quarterly, Middle East Review, Middle East International*, and *Middle East Report.* English newspaper coverage of the Palestinians and the conflict include *The Jerusalem Times,* and *The Jerusalem Report.*

Arabic words, titles, and names appear as they are spelled by their authors. At times, the spelling of the author's name differs from source to source. The definite articles, such as *al* or *el* are ignored, and it is the second word that determines the alphabetization order. Whether the *a* in *al* is capitalized depends on how it is used by the authors.

The bibliography has been divided into subject categories, with subheadings for each category. Hence, for information on settlements, check the subject category Political, and its sub-heading Israeli Policies and Settlements.

Bibliography: Contents

6. POLITICAL

Bibliography

1. GENERAL

Bibliographies and Yearbooks

Badr, Ahmed M. *Education of the Palestinians: An Annotated Bibliography.* Detroit: Association of Arab American University Graduates, 1977.

el-Khalidi, Walid and Jill Khadduri, eds. *Palestine and the Arab-Israeli Conflict: An Annotated Bibliography.* Beirut: Institute for Palestine Studies, 1974.

McNeill, Graham and Mahmoud Hawari. *A Bibliography of Modern Jerusalem.* Jerusalem: Arab Thought Forum, 1992.

Nakhleh, Issa. *Encyclopedia of the Palestine Problem.* New York: Intercontinental Books, 1991.

United Nations, Dag Hammarskjold Library. *Palestine Question: A Selected Bibliography.* New York: United Nations, 1976.

General Information and Interdisciplinary Studies

Arab Office (London). *The Future of Palestine.* Westport, Conn: Hyperion Press, 1976.

Azar, George Baramki. *Palestine: A Photographic Journey.* Berkeley: University of California Press, 1991.

Benvenisti, Meron. *1986 Report: Demographic, Economic, Legal, Social, and Political Developments in the West Bank.* Jerusalem: West Bank Data Project, 1986.

———. *1987 Report: Demographic, Economic, Legal, Social, and Political Developments in the West Bank.* Jerusalem: West Bank Data Project, 1987.

Boullata, Kamal. *Palestine Today.* Washington, D.C.: Palestinian Center for the Study of Non-Violence, 1990.

Cohen, Amnon. *Population and Revenue in the Towns of Palestine in the Sixteenth Century.* Princeton: Princeton University Press, 1978.

Dimbleby, J. and D. McCullin. *The Palestinians.* London: Quartet Books, 1980.

Duncan, Alistair. *The Noble Sanctuary: Portrait of a Holy Place in Arab Jerusalem.* London: Longman Group Limited, 1972.

Jones, Christina. *The Untempered Wind: Forty Years in Palestine.* London: Longman, 1975.

Luke, Harry Charles Joseph, ed. *The Handbook of Palestine and Trans-Jordan.* London: Macmillan, 1930.

Ritter, Karl. *The Comparative Geography of Palestine and the Sinaitic Peninsula.* New York: Greenwood Press, 1968.

Roof, M. K. and K. G. Kinsella. *Palestinian Arab Population: 1950–1984*. Washington: Center for International Research, U.S. Bureau of the Census, 1987.

Sinai, Anne and Allen Pollacks, eds. *The Hashemite Kingdom of Jordan and the West Bank*. New York: American Association for Peace in the Middle East, 1977.

Guides, Travel and Description

Benvenisti, Meron and Shlomo Khayat. *The West Bank and Gaza Atlas*. Boulder, Colo.: Westview Press, 1988.

Hoade, Eugene. *Guide to the Holy Land.* Jerusalem: Franciscan Printing Press, 1974.

Hollis, Christopher and Ronald Brownrigg. *Holy Places: Christian and Muslim Monuments in the Holy Land.* Princeton: Princeton University Press, 1991.

Luke, Harry Charles Joseph, ed. *The Traveller's Handbook for Palestine and Syria.* London: Simpkin, Marshall, Hamilton, Kent, 1924.

Peale, Norman Vincent. *Adventures in the Holy Land.* Englewood, N.J.: Prentice-Hall, 1963.

Petrozzi, Maria Teresa. *Bethlehem.* Jerusalem: Franciscan Press, 1971.

Storme, Albert. *Bethany.* Jerusalem: Franciscan Press, 1973.

Statistical Abstracts and Surveys

Abdeen, Ziad and Hasan Abu Libdeh. *Palestinian Population Handbook: The West Bank and Gaza Strip.* Jerusalem: Planning and Research Center, 1993.

Abu Libdeh, Hassan, Salim Tamari, and Rita Giacaman, et al. *Survey of the Occupied Territories.* Oslo: Norwegian Institute of Social Sciences, 1993.

Arab Thought Forum and Agricultural Relief Committees. *Preliminary Report on Population Agglomerations Survey in the West Bank and Gaza Strip*. Jerusalem: Agricultural Data Base Reports, 1992.

Awartani, H. *A Survey of Industry in the West Bank and the Gaza Strip*. Birzeit, West Bank: Birzeit University Research Center, 1979.

Barron, J. B. *Report and General Abstracts of the Census of 1922.* Jerusalem: Palestine Census Office, 1922.

Center for Policy Analysis on Palestine. *Facts and Figures about the Palestinians.* Washington: Center for Policy Analysis on Palestine, 1992.

Conder, Claude Reignier. *The Survey of Western Palestine.* Jerusalem: Palestine Exploration Fund, 1970.

Hadawi, Sami. *Village Statistics 1945: A Classification of Land and Area Ownership in Palestine.* Beirut: Palestine Liberation Organization Research Center, 1970.

Institute for Palestine Studies. *A Survey of Palestine.* Washington: Institute for Palestine Studies, 1991

Israel, Ministry of Defence. *Judea, Samaria and the Gaza District: An Eighteen Year Survey.* Tel Aviv: Ministry of Defence, 1985.

Jaber, Faiez. *List of the 394 Palestinian Villages and Towns Obliterated and Their Lands Stolen by the Zionist Jews Since 1948.* Amman: Royal Commission for Jerusalem Affairs, 1988.

McCarthy, Justin. *The Population of Palestine: Population Statistics of the Late Ottoman Period and the Mandate Period.* New York: Columbia University Press, 1990.

McDowall, David. "A Profile of the Population of the West Bank and Gaza Strip." *Journal of Refugee Studies* 1, No. 1 (1989): 20–25.

Nour, Amar. *Coming Home: A Survey of the Socio-Economic Conditions of the West Bank and Gaza Strip Returnees after the 1991 Gulf War.* Jerusalem: Palestine Human Rights Information Center, 1993.

Palestinian Liberation Organization. *Agricultural Statistical Bulletin for the West Bank and Gaza Strip, 1981.* Damascus: PLO Central Bureau of Statistics, 1981.

———. *Agricultural Statistical Bulletin for the West Bank and Gaza Strip 1984–1985.* Damascus: PLO Central Bureau of Statistics, 1987.

———. *Educational Statistical Bulletin for the West Bank and Gaza Strip and Pre–1967 Occupied Territories.* Damascus: PLO Central Bureau of Statistics, 1982.

———. *Educational Statistical Bulletin for the West Bank, Gaza Strip and Pre–1967 Occupied Palestine.* Damascus: PLO Central Bureau of Statistics, 1988.

———. *Industrial Statistical Bulletin for the West Bank and Gaza Strip, 1983.* Damascus: PLO Central Bureau of Statistics, 1983.

———. *Industrial Statistical Bulletin for the West Bank and Gaza Strip 1988.* Damascus: PLO Central Bureau of Statistics, 1988.

Palestinian Bureau of Statistics. *Small Area Population in the West Bank and Gaza Strip.* Ramallah, West Bank: Palestinian Bureau of Statistics, 1994

Roy, Sara M. *The Gaza Strip Survey.* Jerusalem: The West Bank Data Base Project, 1986.

———. *The Gaza Strip: A Demograhpic, Economic, Social and Legal Survey.* Boulder, Colo.: Westview Press. 1986.

Sabatello, E. *Population of the Administered Territories: Some Demo-*

graphic Trends and Implications. Jerusalem: West Bank Data Base Project, 1983.

Warren, Charles. *The Survey of Western Palestine.* Jerusalem: Kedem Publishing Company, 1970.

2. CULTURAL

General

Divine, D. "Islamic Culture and Political Practice in British Mandate Palestine, 1918–1948." *The Review of Politics* 45, No. 1 (January 1983): 71–93.

Haddad, Yousef. *Society and Folklore in Palestine: A Study.* Acre, Israel: Dar el-Aswar, 1987.

Lees, George Robinson. *Village Life in Palestine: A Description of the Religion, Home, Life, Manners, Customs, Characteristics, and Superstitions of the Peasants of the Holy Land with Reference to the Bible.* London: Longmans, Green, 1905.

El-Najjar, Hassan. "Planned Emigration: The Palestinian Case." *International Migration Review* 27, No. 1 (Spring 1993): 34–50.

Qleibo, Ali H. *Before the Mountains Disappear: An Ethnographic Chronicle of the Modern Palestinians.* Cairo: Al-Ahram Press, 1992.

Winternitz, Helen. *A Season of Stones: Living in a Palestinian Village.* New York: The Atlantic Monthly Press, 1991.

Archaeology

Abu-Omar, Abdul al-Samih. *Traditional Palestinian Embroidery and Jewelry.* London: Al-Sharq, 1986.

Albright, William Foxwell. *The Archaeology of Palestine.* Harmondsworth, Middlesex: Penguin Books, 1949.

Archaeological Institute of America. *Archaeological Discoveries in the Holy Land.* New York: Crowell, 1967.

Glock, Albert. "Archaeology as Cultural Survival: The Future of the Palestinian Past." *Journal of Palestine Studies* 91, No. 3 (Spring 1994): 70–84.

———. "Cultural Bias in the Archaeology of Palestine." *Journal of Palestine Studies* 94, No. 2 (Winter 1995): 48–59.

Kenyon, Kathleen M. *Archaeology in the Holy Land.* New York: Praeger, 1960.

———. *Digging Up Jericho.* London: Ernest Benn, 1974.

Kenyon, Kathleen, et. al. *Excavations at Jericho.* London: British School of Archaeology in Jerusalem, 1965.

Macalister, Robert A. *A Century of Excavation in Palestine.* New York: Arno Press, 1977.

Negev, Avraham, ed. *Archaeological Encyclopedia of the Holy Land.* New York: Putnam, 1972.

Art and Architecture

Amiry, Suad and Vera Tamari. *The Palestinian Village.* London: British Museum, 1989.

Audeh, I. "Palestinian Posters: Art Serving a Cause." *Arab Perspective* 6 (April 1985): 16–23.

Avi-Yonah, Michael. *Art in Ancient Palestine.* Jerusalem: Magnes Press, 1981.

Baramki, Dimitri C. *The Art and Architecture of Ancient Palestine.* Beirut: Palestine Research Center, 1969.

Conder, Claude R. *Tent Work in Palestine: A Record of Discovery and Adventure,* vol. 1. London: R. Bentley, 1895.

Rajab, Jehan. *Palestinian Costume.* London: KPI, 1989.

———. *Palestinian Folk Custom.* New York: Kegan Paul International, 1989.

Seger, Karen, ed. *Portrait of a Palestinian Village: The Photographs of Hilma Granqvist.* London: Third World Center for Research and Publishing, 1981.

Stillman, Yedida Kalfon. *Palestinian Costume and Jewelry.* Albuquerque: University of New Mexico Press, 1979.

Weir, Shelagh. *Palestinian Embroidery: A Village Arab Craft.* London: British Museum, 1970.

———. *Palestinian Embroidery: Cross-Stitch Patterns from the Traditional Costumes of the Village Women of Palestine.* London: British Museum, 1988.

———. *Palestinian Costume.* Austin: University of Texas Press, 1989.

Linguistics and Literature

Adonis, Ali Ahmad Said, Mahmoud Darwish, and Samih al-Qasim. *Victims of a Map: A Bilingual Anthology of Arabic Poetry.* Edited and translated by Abdullah al-Udhari. London: Al-Saqi Books, 1984.

Al-Messiri, Abdul Waheb (ed.). *A Lover From Palestine and Other Poems.* Washington: Free Palestine Press, 1970.

Altoma, Salih Jawad. *Palestinian Themes in Modern Arabic Literature,* 1917–1970. Cairo: Anglo-Egyptian Bookship, 1972.

Aruri, Nasser and Edmund Gareeb. *Enemy of the Sun.* Washington: Drum and Spear Press, 1970.

Ashrawi, Hanan Mikhail. "The Contemporary Palestinian Poetry of Occupation." *Journal of Palestine Studies* 27, No. 3 (Spring 1978): 77–101.

El-Asmar, Fouzi. *Poems From an Israeli Prison.* New York: Know Books, 1973.

Barakat, Halim. *Days of Dust.* Wilmette, Ill.: Medina University Press, 1974.

Boullata, Issa J., ed. *Modern Arab Poets 1950–1975.* Washington: Three Continents Press, 1976.

Busailah, Reja-e. *We Are Human Too: Poems on the Palestinian Condition.* Wilmette, Ill.: Medina Press, 1970.

Darwish, Mahmoud. *Sand and Other Poems.* Selected and translated by Rena Kabani. London: KPI, 1986.

Elmessiri, A. M., trans. *The Palestinian Wedding: A Bilingual Anthology of Contemporary Palestinian Resistance Poetry.* Washington: Three Continents Press, 1982.

Ghazzawi, Izzat. *Point of Departure—Letters from Prison.* Jerusalem: Arab Center for Contemporary Studies, 1993.

Jayyusi, Salma Khadra, ed. *Anthology of Modern Palestinian Literature.* New York: Columbia University Press, 1992.

Kanafani, Ghassan. *Men in the Sun, and Other Palestinian Stories.* Washington: Three Continents Press, 1983.

Khalifa, Sahar. *Wild Thorns.* Translated by Trevor LeGassiek and Elizabeth Fernau. Atlantic Highlands, N.J.: Al Saqi Books, 1985.

McGuire, Edward. *Songs of the Fedayeen.* London: Bellman Bookshop, 1970.

Muhawi, Ibrahim and Sharif Kanaana. *Speak, Bird, Speak Again: Palestinian Arab Folktales.* Berkeley, CA: University of California Press, 1989.

Siddig, Mohammad. "The Fiction of Saher Khalifah: Between Defiance and Deliverance." *Arab Studies Quarterly* 8, No. 2 (Spring 1986): 143–160.

Slyomovics, Susan. "To Put One's Fingers in the Bleeding Wound: Palestinian Theatre Under Israeli Censorship." *TDR* 35 (Summer 1991): 18–38.

Sulaiman, Khalid A. *Palestine and Modern Arabic Poetry.* London: Zed Books, 1984.

Tuqan, Fadwa. *A Mountainous Journey: The Life of Palestine's Outstanding Woman Poet.* London: The Women's Press, 1990.

3. SOCIETY

General

Abdo, Nahla. "Women of the Intifada: Gender, Class and National Liberation." *Race and Class* 32, No. 4 (April–June 1991): 19–34.

Abu-Libdeh, H., C. Smith, K. Nabris, and M. Shahin. *Infant Mortality*

Survey in the West Bank and Gaza Strip. Interim Report. Jerusalem: UNICEF, 1992

Abu-Lughod, Janet. "Palestinians: Exiles at Home and Abroad." *Current Sociology* 36, No. 2 (1988): 61–69.

Alterman, Eric. "Report From the Occupied Territories: Palestinians Speak." *World Policy Journal* 5, No. 3 (Summer 1988): 519–542.

Avlas, M. "The Daily Life of Palestinians." *Arab Studies Quarterly* 6, No. 3 (Summer 1984) 228–231.

Ayoub, S. *Class Structure of the Palestinians.* Beirut: Arab University Press, 1977.

Ben Porath, Yoram and Emmanuel Marx. *Some Sociological and Economic Aspects of Refugee Camps in the West Bank.* Santa Monica, Calif.: Rand Corporation, 1971.

Ben-Meir, Alon. "Israelis and Palestinians: Harsh Demographic Reality and Peace." *Middle East Policy* 2, No. 2 (1993): 74–86.

Cervenak, Christine M. "Promoting Inequality: Gender-Based Discrimination in UNRWA's Approach to Palestine Refugee Status." *Human Rights Quarterly* 16, No. 2 (May 1994): 300–347.

Graff, James A., ed. *Palestine and the Palestinians.* Toronto: The Near East Cultural and Educational Foundation of Canada, 1989.

Graham-Brown, Sarah. *Palestinians and their Society, 1880–1946: A Photographic Essay*. New York: Quartet Books, 1980.

Heiberg, Marianne and Geir Ovensen, eds. *Palestinian Society in Gaza, West Bank and Arab Jerusalem: A Survey of Living Conditions*. Oslo: FAFO, 1993.

Jerusalem Media and Communication Center. *Reporting Harassment: Israeli Restrictions of Press Freedom in the West Bank and Gaza Strip*. Jerusalem: JMCC, 1989.

Khaled, Leila. *My People Shall Live: Autobiography of a Revolutionary*. London: Hodder and Stoughton, 1973.

Khawaja, M. "Repression and Popular Collective Action: Evidence from the West Bank." *Sociological Forum* 8, No. 1 (1993): 47–71.

Kimmerling, Baruch. "Sociology, Ideology, and Nation-Building: The Palestinians and Their Meaning in Israeli Sociology." *American Sociological Review* 57 (August 1992): 446–460.

Migdal, J. S., ed. *Palestinian Society and Politics.* Princeton, N.J.: Princeton University Press, 1980.

Nakhleh, Khalil and Elia Zureik, eds. *The Sociology of the Palestinians.* London: Croom Helm, 1980.

Sayigh, Rosemary. *Too Many Enemies: The Palestinian Experience in Lebanon.* London: Zed Books, 1994.

Senker, Cath. *Defiance: Palestinian Women in the Uprising.* London: Israel Mirror Publications, 1989.

Shinar, Dov and Danny Rubinstein. *Palestinian Press in the West Bank: The Political Dimension.* Boulder, Colo.: Westview Press, 1988.

Sirhan, Bassem. "Palestinian Refugee Camp Life in Lebanon." *Journal of Palestine Studies* 14, No. 2 (Winter 1975): 91–107.

Swedenburg, T. "The Palestinian Peasant as National Signifier." *Anthropological Quarterly* 63 (January 1990): 18–30.

Szulc, Tad. "Who Are the Palestinians?" *National Geographic* 181, No. 6 (June 1992): 84–113.

Tack, Deane A. *The Palestinian.* Battleboro, Vt.: Amana Books, 1986.

Taraki, Lisa, ed. *Palestinian Society in the West Bank and the Gaza Strip.* Acre, Israel: Dar Al-Aswar, 1990.

Zahlan, A. B. and Edward Hagopian. "Palestine's Arab Population: The Demography of the Palestinian." *Journal of Palestine Studies* 12, No. 4 (Summer 1974): 32–73.

Education

Abdel, Shafi, S. *The Socio-Economic Role of Vocational Training Centers in the Gaza Strip*. Jerusalem: Arab Thought Forum, 1992.

Abu-Lughod, Ibrahim. "Educating a Community in Exile: The Palestinian Experience." *Journal of Palestine Studies* 3, No. 3 (Spring 1973): 94–111.

Abu-Ghazaleh, H. *The Role of the Palestinian Universities in Adult Education and Community Development.* Birzeit, West Bank: Birzeit University Research Center, 1989.

Al Haq/Law in the Service of Man. *Israel's War Against Education in the Occupied West Bank: A Penalty for the Future*. Ramallah, West Bank: November 1988.

Anabtawi, Samir N. *Palestinian Higher Education in the West Bank and Gaza.* New York: Routledge and Kegan Paul, 1986.

Awad, Munir A. *A Statistical Bulletin About Education in the West Bank and Gaza Strip.* Jerusalem: Arab Studies Society, 1983.

Badran, Nabil A. "The Means of Survival: Education and the Palestinian Community, 1948–1967." *Journal of Palestine Studies* 36, No. 4 (Summer 1980): 44–74.

Baramki, Gabi. "Aspects of Palestinian Life Under Military Control: With a Special Focus on Education and Development." *British Journal of Middle Eastern Studies* 19 (1992): 125–132.

———. "Building Palestinian Universities Under Occupation." *Journal of Palestine Studies* 65, No. 1 (Autumn 1987): 12–20.

Davis, Philip E. "The Educated West Bank Palestinians." *Journal of Palestine Studies* 31, No. 3 (Spring 1979): 65–80.

Dickerson, George. "Education for the Palestine Refugees: the UNRWA/UNESCO." *Journal of Palestine Studies* 11, No. 3 (Spring 1974): 122–130.

Graham-Brown, Sarah. *Education, Repression and Liberation: Palestinians.* London: World University Service, 1984.

Hallaj, Muhammad. "The Mission of Palestinian Higher Education." *Journal of Palestine Studies* 36, No. 4 (Summer 1980): 75–95.

Jerusalem Media and Communication Center. *Palestinian Education: A Threat to Israel's Security?* Jerusalem: JMCC, 1989.

Johnson, Penny. "Palestinian Universities Under Occupation, 15 August–15 November 1988." *Journal of Palestine Studies* 70, No. 2 (Winter 1989): 92–100.

Mahshi, Khalil and K. Bush. "The Palestinian Uprising and Education for the Future." *Harvard Educational Review* 59, No. 4 (1989): 470–483.

Nasru, Fathiya. *West Bank Education in Government Schools, 1967–1977.* Birzeit, West Bank: Birzeit University Research Center, 1977.

———. *Education in the West Bank Government Schools: 1968/69–1977.* Birzeit, West Bank: Birzeit University Research Center, 1977.

———. *Preliminary Vision of a Palestinian Education System.* Birzeit, West Bank: Birzeit University Research Center, 1993.

O'Brien, Lee. "Palestinian Universities Under Occupation, 15 May–15 August 1988." *Journal of Palestine Studies* 18, No. 1 (Autumn 1988): 191–197.

Rigby, Andrew. *The Intifada: The Struggle over Education.* Jerusalem: Palestinian Academic Society for the Study of International Affairs, 1989.

Roberts, Adam. *Academic Freedom Under Israeli Military Occupation.* London: World University Service and the International Commission of Jurists, 1984.

Shaath, Nabil. "Palestinian High Level Manpower." *Journal of Palestine Studies* 1, No. 2 (Winter 1972): 80–95.

Steinbaum, S. and Y. Bargur. *Academic Manpower in the West Bank and the Gaza Strip.* Tel Aviv: Tel Aviv University, 1991.

Sullivan, Antony T. *Palestinian Universities under Occupation.* Cairo: The American University Press, 1988.

———. "Palestinian Universities in the West Bank and Gaza Strip." *Minerva* 29 (Autumn 1991): 249–268.

———. "Palestinian Universities in the West Bank and Gaza Strip." *The Muslim World* 83, No. 1–2 (January–April 1994): 168–188.

Tahir, Jamil. "An Assessment of Palestinian Human Resources: Higher Education and Manpower." *Journal of Palestine Studies* 55, No. 3 (Spring 1985): 32–53.

Tibawi, A. L. *Arab Education in Mandatory Palestine. A Study of Three Decades of British Administration.* London: Luzac, 1956.

Yusuf, Muhsin D. "The Potential Impact of Palestinian Education on a

Palestinian State." *Journal of Palestine Studies* 32, No. 4 (Summer 1979): 70–93.

Zahlan, Antoine and Rosemari Zahlan. "The Palestinian Future: Education and Manpower." *Journal of Palestine Studies* 24, No. 4 (Summer 1977): 103–122.

Zahlan, Antoine. "The Science and Technology Gap in the Arab–Israeli Conflict." *Journal of Palestine Studies* 1, No.3 (Spring 1972): 17–36.

Family

Aburish, Said K. *Children of Bethany: The Story of a Palestinian Family.* Bloomington: Indiana University Press, 1988.

Al-Aqtum, Musa T. "Smoking in the West Bank: Habits, Symptoms and Opinions." *Bethlehem University Journal* 10 (1991): 25–39.

Al-Haj, Majid. *Social Change and Family Processes: Arab Communities in Shefa 'Amr.* Boulder, Colo.: Westview Press, 1987.

Ata, Ibrahim Wade. "The West Bank Palestinian Family After 1967 and the Political Socio-Economic Structure." *Arab Perspective* 6 (1985): 31–46.

———. *The West Bank Palestinian Family.* New York: KPI, 1986.

Baker, Ahmad M. "Gender, Urban-Rural-Camp, and Regional Differences Among Self-Esteem Scores of Palestinian Children." *Journal of Psychology* 126 (March 1992): 207–209.

Boullata, Kamal. *Faithful Witness: Palestinian Children Recreate their World.* New York: Olive Branch Press, 1991.

Caradon, Lord and Muhammed El-Farra. *Children of Palestine: Eyewitness Evidence of International Photographers.* New York: Morris International, 1983.

Ghabra, Shafeeq N. *Palestinians in Kuwait: The Family and the Politics of Survival.* Boulder, Colo.: Westview Press, 1987.

Gorkin, Michael. *Days of Honey, Days of Onion: The Story of a Palestinian Family in Israel.* Boston: Beacon Press, 1991.

Granqvist, H. *Marriage Conditions in a Palestinian Village.* Helsinki: Societas Scientiarum Fennica, 1931–35.

Kanafani, Ghassan. *Palestine's Children.* Translated by Barbara Harlow. Washington: Three Continents Press, 1984.

Monsour, Sylvie. "The Sense of Identity Among Palestinian Youth: Male and Female Differentials." *Journal of Palestine Studies* 24, No. 4 (Summer 1977): 71–89.

Rogers, Mary Eliza. *Domestic Life in Palestine.* London: Kegan Paul International, 1989.

White, Patrick. *Children of Bethlehem: Witnessing the Intifada.* Leominster, Hereford, England: Fowler Wright Books, 1989.

Health

Baker, Ahmad M. "The Psychological Impact of the Intifada on Palestinian Children in the Occupied West Bank and Gaza—An Exploratory Study." *American Journal of Orthopsychiatry Study* 60, No. 4 (October 1990): 496–505.

Barghouthi, Mustafa. "Palestinian Health: Toward a Healthy Development Strategy in the West Bank and Gaza Strip." Jerusalem: Union of Palestinian Medical Relief Committees (1993): 1–14.

Bellisari, Anna. "Public Health and the Water Crisis in the Occupied Palestinian Territories." *Journal of Palestine Studies* 90, No. 2 (Winter 1994): 52–63.

Ellis, Marc H. "An Epidemic of Violence: Medical Rights Abuses in the West Bank and Gaza Strip." *Health/PAC Bulletin* 19 (Fall 1989): 1–34.

Gerner, Deborah. "Israeli Restrictions on the Palestinian Universities in the Occupied West Bank and Gaza." *Journal of Arab Affairs* 8, No. 1 (Spring 1989): 74–123.

Giacaman, Rita. *Life and Health in Three Palestinian Villages.* Birzeit, West Bank: Birzeit University Research Center, 1986.

Union of Palestinian Medical Relief Committees. *Health For All: Objectives, Organisation and Activities, 1979–1990.* Jerusalem: UPMRC, 1990.

Women

Al-Wahaidi, Maysoon. *Palestinian Women in the Occupied Territories.* Tunis: League of Arab States, 1985.

Antonius, Soraya. "Fighting on Two Fronts: Conversations With Palestinian Women." *Journal of Palestine Studies* 31, No. 3 (Spring 1979): 28–45.

———. "Prisoners for Palestine. A List of Women Political Prisoners." *Journal of Palestine Studies* 35, No. 3 (Spring 1980): 27–80.

Arab Women's Information Committee. *Facts about the Palestine Problem: Women's Resistance.* Beirut: Arab Women's Information Committee, 1970.

Augustin, Ebba, ed. *Palestinian Women: Identity and Experience.* London: Zed Books, 1993.

Baumann, Pari. *Annotated Bibliography on Palestinian Women.* Jerusalem: Arab Thought Forum, 1989.

Bendt, Ingela and James Downing. *We Shall Return: Women of Palestine.* London: Zed Press, 1982.

Fahum, Siba, ed. *Palestinian Political Women Prisoners and Detainees in Israeli Prisons.* Beirut: Women's International League for Peace and Freedom, 1975.

Falah, Ghazi. *The Role of the British Administration in the Sedentarization of the Bedouin Tribes in Northern Palestine, 1918–1948.* Durham, England: University of Durham Centre for Middle Eastern and Islamic Studies, 1983.

Fernea, Elizabeth, ed. *Women and Family in the Middle East: New Voices of Change.* Austin: University of Texas Press, 1985.

Finn, E. A. *The Palestinian Peasantry: Notes on their Clans, Customs, Religions and Wars.* London: Marshall, 1923.

Fitch, Florence. *The Daughter of Abd Salam: The Life of a Palestinian Peasant Woman.* Boston: B. Humphries, 1934.

Giacaman, Rita. *Palestinian Women in the Uprising: From Followers to Leaders.* Birzeit, West Bank: Birzeit University Research Center, 1988.

———. "Palestinian Women, the Intifada and the State of Independence." *Race and Class* 34, No. 3 (1993): 31–43.

Haj, Samira. "Palestinian Women and Patriarchal Relations." *Signs* 17 (Summer 1992): 761–778.

Hijab, Nadia. *Womanpower: The Arab Debate on Women and Work.* Cambridge: Cambridge University Press, 1988.

Hilterman, Joost. "The Woman's Movement During the Uprising." *Journal of Palestine Studies* 79, No. 3 (Spring 1991): 48–57.

———. *Behind the Intifada: Labour in Women's Movements in the Occupied Territories.* Princeton, NJ: Princeton University Press, 1992.

Holt, Maria. *Half the People: Women, History and the Palestinian Intifada.* Jerusalem: PASSIA Publication, 1992.

Jabbour, Hala Deeb. *A Woman of Nazareth.* New York: Olive Branch Press, 1986.

Lipman, Beata. *Israel: The Embattled Land: Jewish and Palestinian Women Talk About Their Lives.* London: Pandora Press, 1988.

Mogannam, Matiel E. T. *The Arab Woman and the Palestine Problem.* Westport, Conn.: Hyperion Press, 1976.

Najjar, Orayb Aref and Kitty Warnock. *Portraits of Palestinian Women.* Salt Lake City: University of Utah Press, 1992.

Peteet, Julie Marie. *Gender in Crisis: Women and the Palestinian Resistance Movement.* New York: Columbia University Press, 1991.

Ridd, Rosemary and Helen Calaway, eds. *Caught Up in Conflict: Women's Responses to Political Strife.* London: Macmillan Education Ltd., 1986.

Sabbagh, Suha, ed. *Gender in the Intifada.* Bloomington: Indiana University Press, 1995.

Sabbagh, Suha and Ghada Talhemi, eds. *Images and Reality: Palestinian Women Under Occupation and in the Diaspora.* Washington: The Institute for Arab Women's Studies, 1990.

Sayegh, May. *The Arab Palestinian Women: Reality and Impediments.* Beirut: General Union of Palestinian Women, 1980.

Sayigh, Rosemary. "Encounters With Palestinian Women Under Occupation." *Journal of Palestine Studies* 40, No. 4 (Summer 1981): 3–26.

Shultz, J. "The Political Transformation of Palestinian Women." *Journal of Third World Studies,* 10, No. 1 (1993): 225–251.

Strum, Philippa. *The Women are Marching: The Second Sex and the Palestinian Revolution.* New York: Lawrence Hill Books, 1992.

Tawil, Raymonda Hawa. *My Home, My Prison.* New York: Holt, Rinehart and Winston, 1980.

Toubia, N., ed. *Women of the Arab World: The Coming Challenges.* London: Zed Books, 1988.

Tucker, Judith. *Arab Women: Old Boundaries New Frontiers.* Bloomington: Indiana University Press, 1993.

Warnock, Kitty. *Land Before Honor: Palestinian Women in the Occupied Territories.* New York: Monthly Review Press, 1990.

Wing, Adrien Katherine. "Custom, Religion, and Rights: The Future Legal Status of Palestinian Women." *Harvard International Law Journal* 35, No. 1 (Winter 1994): 149–200.

Young, Elise G. *Keepers of the History: Women and the Israeli-Palestinian Conflict.* New York: Teachers College Press, 1992.

4. ECONOMIC

General

Abed, George T., ed. *The Palestinian Economy: Studies in Development Under Prolonged Occupation.* London: Routledge, 1988.

———. *The Economic Viability of a Palestinian State.* Washington: Institute for Palestine Studies, 1990.

———. "Developing the Palestinian Economy." *Journal of Palestine Studies* 92, No. 4 (Summer 1994): 41–51.

Abu Kishk, Bakir. *Human Settlements: Problems and Social Dimensions in the West Bank and Gaza Strip.* Birzeit, West Bank: Birzeit University Research Center, 1981.

———. *The Industrial and Economic Trends in the West Bank and Gaza Strip.* New York: United Nations Economic Commission for Western Asia, 1981.

———. *The Current Economic Situation of the Occupied Territories and the Prospects for the Future.* Birzeit, West Bank: Birzeit University Research Center, 1982.

Ahiram, Ephraim. *Economic Issues Within Alternative Political Accords Between Israel and the West Bank and Gaza Strip.* Tel Aviv: Tel Aviv University, 1988.

Arkadie, Bryan Van. *Benefits and Burdens: A Report on the West Bank and Gaza Strip Economies Since 1967.* New York: Carnegie Endowment for International Peace, 1971.

———. "The Impact of Israeli Occupation on the Economies of the West Bank and the Gaza Strip." *Journal of Palestine Studies* 22, No. 2 (Winter 1977): 103–129.

Awartani, Hisham. *The Occupied Territories' Economy.* Jerusalem: Arab Thought Forum, 1989.

Bahiri, Simcha. *Alternative Economic Scenarios for the West Bank and Gaza Strip.* Tel Aviv: Tel Aviv University, Middle East Economic Cooperation Project, 1983.

———. *Peaceful Separation or Enforced Unity: Economic Consequences for Israel and the West Bank/Gaza Strip Area.* Tel Aviv: International Center for Peace in the Middle East, 1984.

———. *Construction and Housing in the West Bank and Gaza.* Boulder, Colo.: Westview Press, 1990.

———. "Gaza and Jericho First: The Economic Angle." *Palestine-Israel Journal* 1 (Winter 1994): 58–64.

Bahiri Simcha, Samir Huleileh, and Daniel Gavron. *Palestinians, Israelis and the Regional Economy.* Jerusalem: Israel/Palestine Center for Research and Information, 1993.

Baidoun, Amin. *The Role of Health in Economic Development in the West Bank.* Jerusalem: Arab Thought Forum, 1981.

Bainerman, Joel. "The Long Road to Palestinian Economic Independence." *Middle East Focus* 11 (Winter/Spring 1990): 2–5, 22.

Baums, Ron. *The Econometric Model of the West Bank.* Tel Aviv: Armand Hammer Fund for Economic Cooperation in the Middle East, Tel Aviv University, 1989.

Baxendale, Sidney J. "Taxation of Income in Israel and the West Bank: A Comparative Study." *Journal of Palestine Studies* 71, No. 3 (Spring 1989): 134–141.

Ben Shahar, Haim and Abba Lerner. *The Economics of Efficiency and Growth. Lessons from Israel and the West Bank.* Cambridge: Ballinger Publishing Company, 1975.

Clawson, Patrick and Howard Rosen. *The Economic Consequences of Peace for Israel, the Palestinians and Jordan.* Washington : Washington Institute for Near East Policy, 1991.

Drury, Richard T. and Robert C. Winn. *Plowshares and Swords: The Economies of the Occupation in the West Bank.* Boston: Beacon Press, 1992.

Economic Department of the Royal Scientific Society of Jordan. "Israel and the Resources of the West Bank." *Journal of Palestine Studies* 32, No. 4 (Summer 1979): 94–104.

Efrat, Elisha. "Settlement Pattern and Economic Changes of the Gaza Strip." *Middle East Journal* 31, No. 3 (Summer 1977): 349–358.

Elmusa, Sharif S. and Mahmud El-Jaafari. "Power and Trade: The Israeli-Palestinian Economic Protocol." *Journal of Palestine Studies* 94, No. 2 (Winter 1995): 14–32.

Feiler, Gil. "Palestinian Employment Prospects." *Middle East Journal* 47, No. 4 (Autumn 1993): 635–651.

Fischer, Stanley. "Building Palestinian Prosperity." *Foreign Policy*, No. 93 (Winter 1993–1994): 60–75.

———. "Economic Transition in the Occupied Territories." *Journal of Palestine Studies* 92, No. 4 (Summer 1994): 52–61.

Fried, Jerome F. *The West Bank-Gaza Economy: Problems and Prospects, Report.* Washington: U.S. Government Printing Office, 1980.

Gabrial, Judith. "The Economic Side of the Intifada." *Journal of Palestine Studies 69,* No. 1 (Autumn 1988): 198–213.

Gharaibeh, Fawzi A. *The Economies of the West Bank and Gaza Strip.* Boulder, Colo.: Westview Press, 1985.

Grace, Anne. "The Tax Resistance at Bayt Sahur." *Journal of Palestine Studies* 74, No. 2 (Winter 1990): 99–107.

Gross, Nachum T. *The Economic Policy of the Mandatory Government in Palestine.* Jerusalem: The Maurice Falk Institute for Economic Research, 1982.

Hazboun, Samir. *General Transport in the West Bank and Gaza Strip: Problems and Solutions.* Birzeit, West Bank: Birzeit University, 1991.

Hilal, Jamil. *The West Bank: Its Social and Economic Structure, 1948–1973.* Beirut: Palestinian Liberation Organization Research Center, 1975.

Himadeh, Said, ed. *Economic Organization of Palestine*. Beirut: American Press, 1938.

Israel/Palestine Center for Research and Information. *Economic Aspects of the Closure of the West Bank and Gaza*. Jerusalem: IPCFRI, 1993.

Jerusalem Media and Communication Center. *Israeli Obstacles to Economic Development in the Occupied Palestinian Territories*. Jerusalem: JMCC, 1992.

Kanovsky, Eliyahu. *The Economic Impact of the Six-Day War.* New York: Praeger, 1970.

Khameyseh, Rasem Muhyiddin. *Israeli Planning and House Demolishing Policy in the West Bank.* Jerusalem: Palestinian Academic Society for the Study of International Affairs, 1989.

Kleiman, Ephraim. *The Future of Palestinian-Arab and Israel Economic Relations.* Jerusalem: The Harry S. Truman Institute, Hebrew University, 1991.

Hebrew University, Kressel, Gideon M. "The Cultural-Economic Variable in the Use of Disposable Personal Income: Patterns of Consumption of the West Bank and in the Gaza Strip, 1967–1977." *Asian and African Studies* 20, No. 3 (November 1986): 281–308.

Kubursi, Atif. *The Economic Consequences of the Camp David Agreements*. Beirut: Institute for Palestine Studies, 1981.

Laufer, Leopold Yehuda. *Western Europe and the Palestinians: The Socio-Economic Dimension.* Jerusalem: The Leonard Davis Institute for International Relations, Hebrew University, 1990.

Lesch, Ann Mosley. *Israel's Occupation of the West Bank: The First Two Years.* Santa Monica, Calif.: The Rand Corporation, 1970.

Litvin, Uri. *The Economy of the Administered Areas, 1976–1977*. Jerusalem: Bank of Israel Research Department, 1980.

Loftus, P. J. *National Income of Palestine, 1945*. Jerusalem: Government of Palestine Press, 1947.

Lowdermilk, Walter Clay. *Palestine, Land of Promise.* New York: Harper and Brothers, 1944.

Mansour, Antoine. "Monetary Dualism: The Case of the West Bank Under Occupation." *Journal of Palestine Studies* 43, No. 3 (Spring 1982): 103–116.

Maron, Stanley. "The West Bank and Gaza: Population, Education, Economy." *New Outlook* 31, No. 8 (August 1988): 12–15.

Metzer, Jacob. *Technology, Labor and Growth in a Dual Economy's Traditional Sector: Mandatory Palestine, 1921–1936*. Jerusalem: The Maurice Falk Institute for Economic Research in Israel, 1982.

———. "What Kind of Growth? A Comparative Look at the Arab Economies in the Mandatory Palestine and in the Administered Territories." *Economic Development and Cultural Change* 40 (July 1992): 843–865.

Michaelis, D. "One Hundred Years of Banking and Currency in Palestine." *Research in Economic History* 19 (1986): 155–197.

Nabulsi, Muhammad S. "The Palestine Problem and its Relation to Arab Oil and Financial Resources." *Arab Perspective* 2 (February 1982): 46–58.

Owen, Roger, ed. *Studies in the Economic and Social History of Palestine in the Nineteenth and Twentieth Centuries.* Edwardsville: Southern Illinois University Press, 1982.

Rauhana, Kate. *Directory of Arab Municipalities in the West Bank and Gaza.* Jerusalem: Arab Council for Public Affairs, 1987.

Roy, Sara. "The Political Economy of Despair: Changing Political and Economic Realities in the Gaza Strip." *Journal of Palestine Studies* 79, No. 3 (Spring 1991): 58–69.

———. "Separation or Integration: Closure and the Economic Future of the Gaza Strip Revisited." *Middle East Journal* 48, No. 1 (Winter 1994); 11–30.

Royal Scientific Society. *Financial and Banking Situation in the Occupied West Bank and Gaza Strip.* Amman, Jordan: Royal Scientific Society, 1985.

Rubenberg, Cheryl. "Twenty Years of Israeli Economic Policies in the West Bank and Gaza: Prologue to the Intifada." *Journal of Arab Affairs* 8, No. 1 (Spring 1989): 28–73.

Ryan, Sheila. "Israeli Economic Policy in the Occupied Areas." *MERIP Report* 24 (January 1974): 3–24.

———. *The Colonial Exploitation of Occupied Palestine.* London: Croom Helm, 1979.

Sabri, Nidal Rashid. "Budget Analysis of the Palestinian Family." *Arab Studies Quarterly* 14, No. 1 (Winter 1992): 35–44.

Saggnuie, E., J. Sheinin and M. Fedelman. *The Palestinian Economy and Its Economic Relations With Israel.* Tel Aviv: Tel Aviv University, 1992.

Sayigh, Rosemary. "The Struggle for Survival: The Economic Conditions of Palestinian Refugees in Lebanon." *Journal of Palestine Studies* 26, No. 2 (Winter 1978): 101–119.

Sayigh, Yusif A. "The Palestinian Economy Under Occupation: Dependency and Pauperization." *Journal of Palestine Studies* 60, No. 4 (Summer 1986): 46–67.

Shinar, D. *Palestinian Voices: Communication and Nation Building in the West Bank.* Boulder, Colo.: Lynne Rienner, 1987.

Shunnar, Hazem I. and Samir Huleileh. *Impact of the Gulf Crisis on the Occupied Territories.* Ramallah, West Bank: Bisan Center for Research and Development, 1990.

Smith, Barbara J. *The Roots of Separatism in Palestine: British Economic Policy, 1920–1929.* Syracuse, N.Y.: Syracuse University Press, 1993.

Stephens, Marc. *Taxation in the Occupied West Bank, 1967–1989.* Ramallah, West Bank: Al-Haq/Law in the Service of Man, 1990.

Tuma, Elias H. and Haim Darin-Drabkin. *The Economic Case for Palestine.* London: Croom Helm, 1978.

Tuma, Elias. "The Economic Viability of a Palestinian State." *Journal of Palestine Studies* 27, No. 3 (Spring 1978): 102–124.

———. *Economics of a Palestinian State—A Two State Solution.* Davis, Calif.: University of California, 1990.

United Nations Relief and Works Agency. *Economic Conditions in Gaza Following the Gulf War.* Vienna: United Nations Relief and Works Agency, 1991.

Wharton Middle East Economic Service. *Survey of the Economy of the West Bank.* Washington: Wharton ME Economic Service, 1983.

Agricultural

Agricultural Coordinating Committee and ANERA. *Report on the Agricultural Extension Workshop—Status and Needs in the West Bank and Gaza Strip.* Birzeit, West Bank: Birzeit University Research Center, 1993.

Agricultural Coordinating Committee. *The Effects of the Prolonged Curfew on the Agricultural Sector in the Occupied Territories.* Jerusalem: ACC, 1991.

Arab Thought Forum. *Agricultural Relief Committees, Final Report on Population Agglomerations Survey in the West Bank and Gaza Strip.* Jerusalem: ATF, 1992.

Assadi, Fawzi. "How Viable Will the Agricultural Economy be in the New State of Palestine." *Geo* 21 (August 1990): 375–383.

Assaf, Samir, et al. *West Bank Olive Oil: Effect on Methods of Extraction or its Physico-Chemical Properties.* Ramallah/El-Bireh, West Bank: Arab Scientific Institution for Research and Transfer of Technology, 1983.

Awad, Munir A. *Marketing Problems of the Olive Oil in the West Bank.* Nablus, West Bank: An-Najah National University, 1984.

Awartani, Hisham. "West Bank Agriculture: A New Outlook." Nablus, West Bank: An-Najah National University, 1978.

———. *Grape Production in the West Bank—An Analytical Outlook.* Nablus, West Bank: An-Najah National University, 1984.

———. *European Market: New Prospects for Palestinian Farmers.* Jerusalem: Economic Development Group, 1987.

Awartani, Hisham and Shaker Judeh. *Irrigation Agriculture in the Occupied Palestinian Territories.* Nablus: Rural Research Centre, An-Najah National University, 1991.

Buheiry, Marwan R. "The Agricultural Exports of Southern Palestine, 1885–1914." *Journal of Palestine Studies* 40, No. 4 (Summer 1981): 61–81.

Firestone, Yaakov. "Crop-Sharing in Mandatory Palestine." *Middle Eastern Studies* 2, No. 1 (January 1975): 3–23.

Gavoret, L. and E. Grange. *Dairy Sector in the West Bank and Gaza Strip.* Jerusalem: Consulate General of France in Jerusalem, Cultural Section, 1992.

El-Jafari, Mahmoud. "Non-Tariff Trade Barriers: The Case of the West Bank and Gaza Strip Agricultural Exports." *Journal of World Trade* 25 (June 1991): 15–32.

Jerusalem Media and Communication Center. *The Siege of Agriculture: Examples of Israeli Sanctions against Agriculture in the Occupied Territories during the Palestinian Uprising.* Jerusalem: JMCC, 1988.

———. *Bitter Harvest. Israeli Sanctions Against Palestinian Agriculture During the Uprising.* Jerusalem: JMCC, 1989.

Judah, Shaker. *The Agricultural Sector in the West Bank.* Jerusalem: Agriculture Engineers Association, 1991.

Kahan, David. *Agriculture and Water Resources in the West Bank and Gaza,* 1967–1987. Boulder, Colo.: Westview Press, 1988.

Kamen, Charles S. *Little Common Ground: Arab Agriculture and Jewish Settlement in Palestine, 1920–1948.* Pittsburgh: University of Pittsburgh Press, 1991.

Palestine Agricultural Relief Committee. *Marketing of Agricultural Produce in the West Bank and Gaza.* Jerusalem: PARC, 1988.

Powell, Alison. *Food Resources and Food Systems in Two West Bank Villages.* Jerusalem: Arab Thought Forum, 1986.

Rahan David. *Agriculture and Water Resources in the West Bank and Gaza, 1967–1987.* Jerusalem: West Bank Data Base Project, 1987.

Sawalha, Feras. *Citrus Orchards in the Gaza Strip.* Nablus, West Bank: An-Najah National University, 1983.

———. *Nurseries of Fruit Trees in the West Bank.* Nablus, West Bank: An-Najah National University, 1986.

Shawwa, Aoun. *Feasibility of Vegetable Exports from Gaza Strip to the EEC: Evaluation and Recommendations.* Jerusalem: Cooperative Development Program, 1990.

Stein, Kenneth W. "Palestine Rural Economy, 1917–1939." *Studies in Zionism* 8, No. 1 (Spring 1987): 25–49.

Tamari, Salim and R. Giacaman. *The Social Impact of Drip Irrigation on a Palestinian Peasant Community in the Jordan Valley.* Birzeit: Birzeit University Community Health Unit, 1980.

Development

Abdul Razig, Omar. *Waste Management: A Proposal for the Establishment of a Scrap Steel Recycling Project in the Occupied Palestinian Territories.* Nablus, West Bank: An-Najah National University, 1989.

Abu Ayyash, A. "Israeli Regional Planning Policy in the Occupied Territories." *Journal of Palestine Studies* 19/20, Nos. 3/4 (Spring–Summer 1976): 83–108.

———. "Israeli Planning Policy in the Occupied Territories." *Journal of Palestine Studies* 41, No. 1 (Autumn 1981): 111–123.

Abu-Shukor, Abdel Fattah, Samir Abdallah Saleh, and Atef Kamal Alawneh. *Industrialization in the West Bank.* Nablus, West Bank: An-Najah National University, 1992.

Ben Shahar, Haim. *Economic Structure and Development Prospects of the West Bank and Gaza Strip.* Santa Monica, Calif.: Rand Report, 1971.

Benvenisti, Meron. *U.S. Government Funded Projects in the West Bank and Gaza Strip, 1977–1983.* Jerusalem: West Bank Data Base Project, 1984.

Bouhabib, Abdallah. "The World Bank and International Aid to Palestine [Interview]." *Journal of Palestine Studies* 23, No. 2 (Winter 1994): 64–74.

Bull, Vivian. *The West Bank—Is it Viable?* Lexington, Mass.: Lexington Books, 1975.

Coles, Roberta L. "Economic Development in the Occupied Territories." *American-Arab Affairs 25* (Summer 1988): 113–125.

Coon, Anthony. *The Urban Planning in the West Bank Under Military Occupation.* Ramallah, West Bank: Al-Haq/ Man in the Service of Law, 1991.

Escribano, Maria and Nazmi el-Joubeh. "Migration and Change in the West Bank Village: The Case of Deir Dibwan." *Journal of Palestine Studies* 41, No.1 (Autumn 1981): 150–160.

Giacaman, Rita. *Palestinian Women and Development in the Occupied West Bank.* Birzeit, West Bank: Birzeit University Research Center, 1984.

Graham-Brown, Sara. "The West Bank and Gaza Strip: The Structural Impact of Israeli Colonisation." *MERIP Report* 9, No. 74 (January 1979): 9–20.

Gubser, Peter. *West Bank and Gaza Economic and Social Development: Now and the Future.* Washington,: Middle East Institute, 1979.

Haselkorn, A., M. Kurz, and A. R. Wagner. *Trade and Economic Links in the Transition Phase: The West Bank and Gaza Strip.* Marina del Rey, Calif.: Analytical Assessments Corporation, 1978.

Hazboun, Samir. "Needed: A Modern Infrastructure." *Palestine-Israel Journal* 1 (Winter 1994): 77–88.

Hirsch, Zeev, Shanli Katzelson and David Sassoon. *A Free Economic Zone and Post for the Gaza Region.* Tel Aviv: Armand Hammer Fund for Economic Cooperation in the Middle East, Israel Institute of Business Research, and Leon Recanati Graduate School of Business Administration, 1991.

Hochstein, Annette. *Metropolitan Links Between Israel and the West Bank.* Jerusalem: West Bank Data Project, 1989.

Hyman, B. et al. *Jerusalem in Transition: Urban Growth and Change, 1970–1980.* Jerusalem: The Jerusalem Institute for Israel Studies, 1985.

Iskander, Marwan. "Economic Consequences of Peace between Israel and its Neighbors." *Middle East Insight* 2, No. 2 (January–February 1993): 38–44.

Jabr, Hisham. *The Financial and the Banking Policies in the Occupied West Bank.* Nablus, West Bank: An-Najah National University, 1993.

Khalidi, Raji "The Arab Economy in Israel: Dependency or Development?" *Journal of Palestine Studies* 51, No. 3 (Spring 1984): 63–86.

———. *The Arab Economy in Israel: The Dynamics of a Region's Development.* London: Croom Helm, 1988.

Laufer, Leopold Yehuda. *U.S. Aid to the West Bank and Gaza: Policy Dilemmas.* Jerusalem: Hebrew University, The Leonard Davis Institute for International Relations, 1985.

McNeill, Graham. *An Unsettling Affair: Housing Conditions, Tenancy Regulations and the Coming of the Messiah in the Old City of Jerusalem.* Birzeit: Birzeit University Research Center, 1991.

Meron, Raphael. *Economic Development in Judea-Samaria and the Gaza District 1967–1980: Economic Growth and Structural Change.* Jerusalem: Bank of Israel, Research Department, 1982.

Nakhleh, Khalil. "Non-Governmental Organizations and Palestine: The Policies of Money." *Journal of Refugee Studies* 2 (1989): 113–124.

———. *Indigenous Organizations in Palestine: Toward a Purposeful Societal Development.* Jerusalem: Arab Thought Forum, 1991.

Palestine Studies Project. *Masterplanning the State of Palestine: Suggested Guidelines for Comprehensive Development.* Ramallah: Center for Engineering and Planning, 1992.

Al-Qutub, Ishaq Y. "The Challenge for Urban Development Policies: The Case of Refugee Camp-Cities in the Middle East." *Journal of Arab Affairs* 8 (Fall 1989): 207–228.

Robinson, Glenn E. "The Role of the Professional Middle Class in the Mobilization of Palestinian Society: The Medical and Agricultural Committees." *International Journal of Middle East Studies* 25, No. 2 (May 1993): 301–326.

Roy, Sara. *The Gaza Strip: The Political Economy of De-Development.* Washington: Institute for Palestine Studies, 1995.

Sahliyeh, Emile. "West Bank Industrial and Agricultural Development: The Basic Problem." *Journal of Palestine Studies* 42, No. 2 (Winter 1982): 55–69.

Saleh, Abdul Jawad. *Israel's Policy of De-Institutionalisation: A Case Study of Palestinian Local Governments.* London: Jerusalem Center for Development Studies, 1987.

Samara, Adel. *The Political Economy of the West Bank 1967–1987: From Peripherization to Development.* London: Khamsin Journal in Cooperation with Al-Mashrik for Economic and Development Studies, Jerusalem, 1988.

Sayigh, Yousif A. *Priorities and Needs: The Palestinian Position.* Paris: UNESCO, 1993.

Scholch, Alexander. *Palestine 1865–1882: Studies in Economic, Social and Political Transformation.* Washington: Institute for Palestine Studies, 1991.

Spector, B. I. R., S. Kayvan, F. Keynon, and W. Harvey. *Economic Im-*

plications of a Middle East Peace Settlement: Economic Development Model for West Bank and Gaza. Purcerville, Vt.: CACI, Inc., 1978.

Starr, Joyce R. *Development Diplomacy: U.S. Economic Assistance to the West Bank and Gaza.* Washington: Washington Institute for Near East Policy, 1989.

———. *Economic Development in the West Bank and Gaza Strip: Illusion or Vision.* Tel Aviv: Tel Aviv University, Armand Hammer Fund for Economic Cooperation in the Middle East, 1990.

The World Bank. *Developing the Occupied Territories—An Investment in Peace. vol. 1: Overview.* Washington: A World Bank Publication, 1993.

———. *Developing the Occupied Territories—An Investment in Peace. vol. 2: The Economy.* Washington: A World Bank Publication, 1993.

———. *Developing the Occupied Territories—An Investment in Peace. vol. 3: Private Sector Development.* Washington: A World Bank Publication, 1993.

———. *Developing the Occupied Territories—An Investment in Peace. vol. 4: Agriculture.* Washington: A World Bank Publication, 1993.

———. *Developing the Occupied Territories—An Investment in Peace. vol. 5: Infrastructure.* Washington: A World Bank Publication, 1993.

———. *Developing the Occupied Territories—An Investment in Peace. vol. 6: Human Resources and Social Policy.* Washington: A World Bank Publication, 1993.

Wooton, Len B. *Consultancy Report: Marketing, Education, Training and Market Development in the West Bank.* Washington: Agricultural Cooperative Development International Aid, 1987.

Younis, Mona. *Community Development Versus Personal Prosperity: Israel's Pacification Policy in the Occupied West Bank and Gaza Strip.* Amman, Jordan: Yarmouk University, Center for Hebraic Studies, 1987.

Zu'bi, Nahla. "The Development of Capitalism in Palestine: The Expropriation of the Palestinian Direct Producers." *Journal of Palestine Studies* 52, No. 4 (Summer 1984): 88–109.

Industry

Abu-Shukor, Abdel Fattah, Samir Abdallah Saleh, and Atef Kamal Alawneh. *Industrialization in the West Bank.* Nablus, West Bank: An-Najah National University, 1992.

Ahiram, Ephraim. *Strategy for the Development of Industry in the West Bank and Gaza Strip: A General Framework.* Jerusalem: The Harry S. Truman Institute, Hebrew University, 1991.

Awad, Munir A. *Fishing Resources in Gaza Strip.* Nablus, West Bank: An-Najah National University, 1987.

Awartani, Hisham. *A Survey of Industries in the West Bank and the Gaza Strip.* Birzeit, West Bank: Birzeit University Research Center, 1979.

Bahiri, Simcha. *Industrialization in the West Bank and Gaza.* Boulder, Colo.: Westview Press, 1987.

Frisch, Hillel. *Stagnation and Frontier: Arab and Jewish Industry in the West Bank.* Jerusalem: West Bank Data Project, 1983.

Hazboun, Samir. *Services in the Palestinian Economy.* Birzeit, West Bank: Birzeit University Research Center, 1992.

Kuttab, S. and R. Sansur. *A Study of the Pharmaceutical Industry in the West Bank and Gaza Strip.* Birzeit, West Bank: Birzeit University Research Center, 1983.

Salman, Hind K. *Manufacturing in Bethlehem Area: Survey of Manufacturing Industries in Bethlehem, Beit Jala and Beit Sahur.* Jerusalem: Arab Thought Forum, 1990.

Samara, Adel. *Industrialization in the West Bank.* Jerusalem: Al-Mashriq, 1992.

Smith, Barbara J. "British Mandatory Policy Towards Industry in Palestine, 1920–29." *The Muslim World* 83, Nos. 1–2 (January–April 1994): 36–59.

Tuma, Elias. *Industrialization in the Occupied Territories.* Jerusalem: The Harry S. Truman Institute, Hebrew University, 1991.

Labor

Angrist, Joshua D. *Wages and Employment in the West Bank and Gaza Strip, 1981–1990.* Jerusalem: The Maurice Falk Institute for Economic Research in Israel, 1992.

Farris, Amin, Gideon Fishelson, Raymond Jubran, and Roby Nathanson. *The Labor Market in the Territories.* Tel Aviv: Histradut, General Federation of Labor in Israel, 1993.

Hilal, Jamil "Class Transformation in the West Bank and Gaza." *MERIP Report* 53 (December 1976): 10–15.

Hilterman, Joost. "Mass Mobilization Under Occupation: The Emerging Trade Union Movement in the West Bank." *MERIP Report* 15 (October-December 1985): 26–31.

———. "Workers' Rights During the Uprising." *Journal of Palestine Studies* 73, No. 1 (Autumn 1989): 83–91.

Kleiman, Ephraim. *The Flow of Labor Services from the West Bank and Gaza.* Jerusalem: Hebrew University, 1992.

Lang, Erica and Itimad Mohanna. *A Study of Women and Work in "Shatti" Refugee Camp in the Gaza Strip.* Jerusalem: Arab Thought Forum, 1991.

Qaimari, Mohammad Suleiman. *Implications of the Palestinian Labour Movement.* Amman, Jordan: Palestine Labour Union, 1990.

Rockwell, Susan. "Palestinian Women Workers in the Israeli-Occupied Gaza Strip." *Journal of Palestine Studies* 54, No. 2 (Winter 1985): 114–136.

Shalev, Michael. *Labor and Political Economy in Palestine.* Oxford: Oxford University Press, 1992.

Al-Qutub, Ishaq Y. "The Challenge for Urban Development Policies: The Case of Refugee Camp-Cities in the Middle East." *Journal of Arab Affairs* 8 (Fall 1989): 207–228.

Siniora, Randa G. *Palestinian Labour in a Dependent Economy: Women Workers in the West Bank Clothing Industry.* Cairo: American University Press, 1989.

Taggart, Simon. *Workers in Struggle: Palestinian Trade Unions in the Occupied West Bank.* London: Editpride, 1985.

Tamari, Salim. "Building Other People's Homes: Palestinian Peasant's Household and Work in Israel." *Journal of Palestine Studies* 41, No. 1 (Autumn 1981): 31–66.

Wazwaz, Adel. *Israeli Harassments of the Palestinian Working Class and its Union Movement.* Ramallah, West Bank: Labor Studies Center, 1990.

Land

Abboushi, Suhail. "Impact of Individual Variables on the Work Values of Palestinian Arabs." *International Studies of Management and Organization* 20, No. 3 (Fall 1990); 53–68.

Abu Kishk, Bakir. "Arab Land and Israeli Policy." *Journal of Palestine Studies* 41, No. 1 (Autumn 1981): 124–135.

Granott, A. *The Land System in Palestine.* London: Eyre and Spottiswoode, 1952.

Granovsky, Abraham. *Land Policy in Palestine*. New York: Bloch Publishing Company, 1940.

Grossman, David and A. Derman. *The Impact of Regional Road Construction on Land Use in the West Bank.* Jerusalem: West Bank Data Project, 1989.

Halabi, Usama, Aron Turner, and Meron Benvenisti. *Land Alienation in the West Bank: A Legal Spatial Analysis.* Jerusalem: West Bank Data Base Project, 1985.

Rishmawi, Mona. "Land Use Planning as a Strategy for Judaization." *Journal of Palestine Studies* 62, No. 2 (Winter 1987): 105–116.

Shafir, Gershon. *Land, Labor, and the Origins of the Israeli-Palestinian Conflict, 1882–1914*. Cambridge: Cambridge University Press, 1989.

Shehadeh, Aziz, et al. *Israeli Proposed Road Plan for the West Bank.* New York: United Nations, 1985.

Shehadeh, Raja. "The Land Law of Palestine: An Analysis of the Defi-

nition of State Land." *Journal of Palestine Studies* 42, No. 2 (Winter 1982): 82–99.
———. *The Law of the Land: Settlements and Land Issues Under Israeli Military Occupation.* Jerusalem: PASSIA Publication, 1993.
Stein, Kenneth W. *The Land Question in Palestine, 1917–1939.* Chapel Hill, N.C.: University of North Carolina Press, 1984.

Water

Abdulhadi, Rami S. "Land Use Planning in the Occupied Palestinian Territories." *Journal of Palestine Studies* 76, No. 4 (Summer 1990): 46–63.
Abu Mayli, Yusuf. *An Introduction to the Water Problem in the Gaza Strip.* Gaza: Islamic University, 1990.
Awartani, Hisham. *A Projection of the Demand for Water in the West Bank and Gaza Strip, 1990–2000.* Nablus, West Bank: An-Najah National University, 1991.
———. *The Artesian Wells in the Occupied Palestinian Territories: Reality and Ambition.* Nablus, West Bank: An-Najah National University, 1991.
Baskin, Gershon (ed.). *Water: Conflict or Cooperation.* Jerusalem: Israel/Palestine Center for Research and Information, 1993.
Baskin, Gershon. "The West Bank and Israel's Water Crisis." *Palestine-Israel Journal* 2, No. 2 (March 1993): 1–11.
Davis, Uri Antonia Maks and John Richardson. "Israel's Water Policies." *Journal of Palestine Studies* 34, No. 2 (Winter 1980): 3–31.
Dillman, Jeffrey D. "Water Rights in the Occupied Territories." *Journal of Palestine Studies* 19, No. 1 (Autumn 1989): 46–71.
Elmusa, Sharif S. *The Water Issue and the Palestinian-Israeli Conflict.* Washington: Center for Policy Analysis on Palestine, 1993.
———. "Dividing the Common Palestinian—Israeli Waters: An International Water Law Approach." *Journal of Palestine Studies* 87, No. 3 (Spring 1993): 57–77.
———. "The Israeli-Palestinian Water Dispute Can be Resolved." *Palestine-Israel Journal* No. 3 (Summer 1994): 18–26.
Haddad, Marwan and Samir Abu 'Aysha. *Consumption of Water in the West Bank: Past, Present and Future.* Nablus, West Bank: An-Najah National University, 1992.
Jaradat, Mohammed. *The Water Crisis in the Southern West Bank.* Jerusalem: Alternative Information Center, 1993.
Kahaleh, Subhi. *The Water Problem in Israel and its Repercussions on the Arab-Israeli Conflict.* Beirut, Lebanon: Institute for Palestine Studies, 1981.
Kally, Elisha. *Water Supply to the West Bank and Gaza Strip: Interim*

Report. Tel Aviv: Tel Aviv University, Armand Hammer Fund for Economic Cooperation in the Middle East, 1986.

———. *Options for Solving the Palestinian Water Problem in the Context of Regional Peace.* Jerusalem: The Harry S. Truman Institute, Hebrew University, 1991/92.

Al-Khatib, Nader. "Palestinian Water Rights." *Israel/Palestine: Issues in Conflict-Issues for Cooperation* 2, No. 2 (March 1993): 13–36.

Lowi, Miriam R. "Bridging the Divide: Transboundary Resource Disputes and the Case of West Bank Water." *International Security* 18, No. 1 (Summer 1993): 113–138.

Rowley, Gwyn. "The West Bank: Native Water-Resource System and Competition." *Political Geography Quarterly* 9, No. 1 (January 1990): 29–52.

Schmida, Leslie C. *Keys to Control: Israel's Pursuit of Arab Water Resources.* Washington: American Educational Trust, 1983.

Shuval, Hillel I. "Approaches to Finding an Equitable Solution to the Water Resources Problem Shared by Israeli and Palestinians Over the Use of the Mountain Aquifer." *Palestine-Israel Journal* 2, No. 2 (March 1993): 37–84.

5. HISTORIC

General

Abboushi, W. F. *The Angry Arabs.* Philadelphia: The Westminister Press, 1974.

———. *The Unmaking of Palestine.* Boulder, Colo.: Lynne Rienner Publishers, 1985.

Abcarius, Michael F. *Palestine Through the Fog of Propaganda.* London: Hutchinson, 1946.

Abu Iyad, with Eric Rouleau. *My Home, My Land: A Narrative of Palestinian Struggle.* New York: Times Books, 1981.

Abu-Lughod, Ibrahim, ed. *The Transformation of Palestine: Essay on the Origin and Development of the Arab-Israeli Conflict.* Evanston, Ill.: Northwestern University Press, 1987.

Al-Abid, Ibrahim, ed. *Selected Essays on the Palestine Question.* Beirut: Palestine Research Center, 1969.

Al-Abid, Ibrahim. *A Handbook to the Palestine Question.* Beirut: Palestine Research Center, 1969.

Arab-Women's Information Committee. *The ABC of the Palestine Problem, Part I: 1896–1949; Part II: 1949–1967.* Beirut: AWIC, 1974.

El-Aref, Aref. *The Tragedy of Palestine.* Sidon, Lebanon: Modern Library, 1962.

Aronsfeld, C. C. "The Historical Boundaries of Palestine." *Jewish Frontier* 45, No. 3 (March 1978): 23–28.

Babour, Nevill. *Nisi Dominus: A Survey of the Palestine Controversy.* Beirut: Institute for Palestine Studies, 1969.

Ben-Dor, Gabriel, ed. *The Palestinians and the Middle East Conflict: Studies in their History, Sociology and Politics.* Ramat-Gan, Israel: Turtledove, 1979.

Berger, Elmer. *Letters and Non-Letters.* Beirut: Institute for Palestine Studies, 1972.

Boullata, Kamal, ed. *Palestine Today.* Washington,: Palestine Center for the Study of Nonviolence, 1990.

Cattan, Henry. *The Palestine Question.* New York: Croom Helm, 1988.

Chiha, Michel. *Palestine.* Beirut: Trident Publications, 1969.

Curtis, Michael, et. al., eds. *The Palestinians: People, History, Politics.* New Brunswick, N.J.: Transaction Books, 1975.

Darwaza, Al-Hakam. *The Palestine Question: A Brief Analysis.* Beirut: Palestine Research Center, 1973.

Davis, John H. *The Evasive Peace.* New York: New World Press, 1968.

Elpeleg, Z. *The Grand Mufti: Haj Amin al-Hussaini, Founder of the Palestinian National Movement.* London: Frank Cass, 1993.

Flapan, Simha. *Zionism and the Palestinians.* New York: Barnes and Noble, 1979.

Forrest, A. C. *The Unholy Land.* Toronto: McClelland and Stewart Limited, 1971.

Geddes, Charles L., ed. *A Documentary History of the Arab-Israeli Conflict.* New York: Praeger Publishers, 1991.

Genet, Jean. "The Palestinians." *Journal of Palestine Studies* 9, No. 1 (Autumn 1973): 3–34.

George, Alan. "Making the Desert Bloom: A Myth Examined." *Journal of Palestine Studies* 30, No. 2 (Winter 1979): 88–100.

Gerner, Deborah J. *One Land, Two Peoples: The Conflict Over Palestine.* Boulder, Colo.: Westview Press, 1991.

Gil, Moshe. *A History of Palestine, 634–1099.* Cambridge: Cambridge University Press, 1992.

Gilmour, David. *Dispossessed: The Ordeal of the Palestinians, 1917–1980.* London: Sidgwick and Jackson, 1980.

Glubb, John Bagot. *The Middle East Crisis.* London: Hodder and Stoughton, 1967.

Goodman, Hirsch and Seth W. Carns. *The Future Battlefield of the Arab-Israeli Conflict.* New Brunswick, N.J.: Transaction Publishers, 1990.

Hadawi, Sami. *Palestine: Loss of Heritage.* San Antonio, Texas: The Naylor Company, 1963.

Hong, Christopher C. *To Whom the Land of Palestine Belongs.* Hicksville, N.Y.: Exposition Press, 1979.

Hurewitz, J. C. *The Struggle for Palestine*. New York: Schocken Books, 1976.

Jastrow, Morris. *Zionist and the Future of Palestine: The Fallacies and Dangers of Political Zionism*. New York: Macmillan, 1919.

Jeffries, Joseph M. N. *Palestine: The Reality*. London: Longmans, Green, 1939.

John, Robert. *Behind the Balfour Declaration*. Costa Mesa, Calif.: Institute for Historical Review, 1988.

Kayyali, Abdul al-Wahhab. *Palestine: A Modern History*. London: Croom Helm, 1978.

Kerr, Malcolm H. *The Middle East Conflict*. New York: Foreign Policy Association, 1968.

Khalidi, Walid, ed. *From Haven to Conquest: Readings in Zionism and the Palestine Problem Until 1948*. Beirut: Institute for Palestine Studies, 1971.

Khalidi, Walid. *Before Their Diaspora: A Photographic History of the Palestinians, 1876–1948*. Washington: Institute for Palestine Studies, 1984.

———. *Palestine Reborn*. London: I. B. Tauris, 1992.

Khouri, Fred J. *The Arab-Israeli Dilemma*. Syracuse, N.Y.: Syracuse University Press, 1985.

Kimmerling, Baruch and Joel Migdal. *Palestinians: The Making of a People*. New York: Free Press, 1993.

Kishtainy, Khalid. *Whither Israel? A Study of Zionist Expansionism*. Beirut: Palestine Research Center, 1970.

———. *Palestine in Perspective: On the Image and Reality of Palestine Throughout the Ages*. Beirut: Palestine Liberation Organization Research Center, 1971.

Laqueur, Walter and Barry Rubin, eds. *The Israel-Arab Reader: A Documentary History of the Middle East Conflict*. New York: Penguin Books, 1984.

Lowdermilk, Walter C. *Palestine, Land of Promise*. London: Gollancz, 1947.

Lukacs, Yehuda and Abdallah Battah, eds. *The Arab-Israeli Conflict: Two Decades of Change*. Boulder, Colo.: Westview Press, 1988.

Main, Ernest. *Palestine at the Crossroads*. London: George Allen and Unwin, 1973.

Marks, J. H. "The Problem of Palestine." *Muslim World* 60, No. 1 (January 1970): 25–46.

McDowall, David. *The Palestinians*. London: Minority Rights Group, 1990.

Mehdi, M. R. *A Palestine Chronicle*. London: Alpha Associates, 1973.

O'Mahony, Anthony. "Christianity in the Holy Land: The Historical Background." *Month* 254, No. 1512 (December 1993): 469–476.

Parkes, James William. *Whose Land? A History of the People of Palestine.* Baltimore : Penguin Books, 1970.

Peretz, Don. *Israel and the Palestine Arabs.* Washington: Middle East Institute, 1958.

Rizk, Edward, trans. *The Palestine Question.* Beirut: Institute for Palestine Studies, 1968.

Robnett, George W. *Conquest Through Immigration: How Zionism Turned Palestine into a Jewish State.* Pasadena: California Institute for Special Research, 1968.

Shaheen, Azeez. *Ramallah: Its History and its Genealogies.* Birzeit, West Bank: Birzeit University Press, 1982.

Smith, Charles D. *Palestine and the Arab-Israeli Conflict.* New York: St. Martin's Press, 1988.

Smith, Pamela Ann. *Palestine and the Palestinians, 1876–1983.* New York: St. Martin's Press, 1984.

Strange, Guy Le. *Palestine Under the Moslems: A Description of Syria and the Holy Land from A. D. 650 to 1500.* Beirut: Khayats, 1965.

Tsimhoni, Daphne. "Demographic Trends of the Christian Populations in Jerusalem and the West Bank, 1948–1978." *Middle East Journal* 37, No. 1 (Winter 1983): 54–64.

Turki, Fawaz. "Meaning of Palestinian History: Text and Context." *Arab Studies Quarterly* 3, No. 4 (Fall 1981): 371–383.

———. *Soul in Exile: Lives of a Palestinian Revolutionary.* New York: Monthly Review Press, 1988.

Wright, Clifford A. *Facts and Fables: The Arab-Israeli Conflict.* New York: Routledge, Chapman and Hall, 1989.

Zogby, James. *Palestinians: The Invisible Victims.* Washington: American-Arab Anti-Discrimination Committee, 1981.

Zu'iter, Akram. *The Palestine Question.* Damascus, Syria: Palestine Arab Refugee Institution, 1958.

THE OTTOMAN EMPIRE

Aaronsohn, Ran. "Baron Rothschild and the Initial Stages of Jewish Settlement in Palestine (1882–1980): A Different Type of Colonization?" *Journal of Historical Geography* 19, No. 2 (April 1993): 142–156.

Avneri, Arieh L. *The Claim of Dispossession: Jewish Land Settlement and the Arabs 1878– 1948.* New Brunswick, N.J.: Transaction Books, 1984.

Cohen, Amnon. *Palestine in the 18th Century: Pattern of Government and Administration.* Jerusalem: Magnes Press, 1973.

Divine, Donna Robinson. *Politics and Society in Ottoman Palestine: The Arab Struggle for Survival and Power.* Boulder, Colo.: Lynne Rienner Publishers, 1994.

Doumani, Beshara B. "The Political Economy of Population Counts in Ottoman Palestine: Nablus, Circa 1850." *International Journal of Middle East Studies* 26, No. 1 (February 1994): 1–17.

Friedman, Isaiah. *The Questions of Palestine, 1914–1918: British-Jewish-Arab Relations.* New Brunswick, N.J.: Transaction Publishers, 1992.

Gilbar, Gad G., ed. *Ottoman Palestine 1800–1914: Studies in Economic and Social History.* Leiden, Holland: E.J. Brill, 1990.

Jamoos, W. "The Balfour Declaration." *Arab Palestinian Resistance* 10, No. 8 (August 1978): 23–31.

Katz, Yossi. "The Palestinian Mountain Region and Zionist Settlement Policy, 1882–1948." *Middle Eastern Studies* 30, No. 2 (April 1994): 304–329.

Landes, D. "Palestine Before the Zionists." *Commentary* 61, No. 2 (February 1976): 47–56.

Ma'oz, Moshe. *Ottoman Reform in Syria and Palestine, 1840–1861: The Impact of the Tanzimat on Politics and Society.* Oxford, England: Oxford University Press, 1968.

Ma'oz, Moshe, ed. *Studies on Palestine During the Ottoman Period.* Jerusalem: Magnes Press, Hebrew University, 1975.

Manna', Adel. "Eighteenth and Nineteenth-Century Rebellions in Palestine." *Journal of Palestine Studies* 93, No. 1 (Autumn 1994): 51–66.

Parfitt, Tudor. *The Jews in Palestine, 1800–1882*. Woodbridge, Suffolk: Boydell Press for the Royal Historical Society, 1987.

Rosen, Jacob. "Captain Reginald Hall and the Balfour Declaration." *Middle Eastern Studies* 24, No. 1 (January 1988): 56–67.

Sanders, Ronald. *The High Walls of Jerusalem: A History of the Balfour Declaration. The Birth of the British Mandate for Palestine.* New York: Holt, Rinehart and Winston, 1984.

Sayegh, Fayez. *Zionist Colonization of Palestine.* Beirut: Palestine Research Center, 1965.

Verete, Mayir. *From Palmerston to Balfour: Collected Essays of Mayir Verete.* London: Frank Cass, 1992.

Wilson, Robert. *Palestine 1917* [A Diary]. Tunbridge Wells, Kent, England: Costello, 1989.

Yusef, Muhsin D. "The Zionists and the Process of Defining the Borders of Palestine, 1915–1923." *Journal of South Asian and Middle Eastern Studies* 15, No.1 (Fall 1991): 18–39.

The British Mandate in Palestine

Abu-Ghazaleh, Adnan Mohammad. *Arab Cultural Nationalism in Palestine During the British Mandate.* Beirut: Institute for Palestine Studies, 1973.

Ahmad, H. "From the Balfour Declaration to World War II: The U. S. Stand on Palestinian Self-Determination." *Arab Studies Quarterly* 12, Nos. 1–2 (Winter/Spring 1990): 9– 41.

Beloff, Max. *The Role of the Palestine Mandate in the Period of Britain's Imperial Decline.* Haifa, Israel: University of Haifa, 1981.

Bethell, Nicholas. *The Palestine Triangle: The Struggle for the Holy Land, 1935–48.* New York: G.P. Putnam's Sons, 1979.

Bowden, T. "The Politics of the Arab Rebellion in Palestine 1936–39." *Middle East Studies* 11, No. 2 (March 1975): 147–174.

Budeiri, Musa. *The Palestine Communist Party 1919–1948: Arab and Jew in the Struggle for Internationalism.* London: Ithaca Press, 1979.

Bullock, David L. *Allenby's War: The Palestine-Arabian Campaigns, 1916–1918.* London: Blandford Press, 1988.

Caplan, Neil. *Palestine Jewry and the Arab Question, 1917–1925.* London: Frank Cass, 1978.

———. "Zionist Visions of Palestine, 1917–1936." *The Muslim World* 83, No. 1–2 (January-April 1994): 19–35.

Cohen, Michael J. *Palestine to Israel: From Mandate to Independence.* London: Frank Cass, 1988.

Cohen, Stuart A. "Imperial Policing Against Illegal Immigration: The Royal Navy and Palestine, 1945–48." *Journal of Imperial and Commonwealth History* 22, No. 2 (May 1993): 275–293.

Davis, Ronald W. "Jewish Military Recruitment in Palestine, 1940–1943." *Journal of Palestine Studies* 30, No. 2 (Winter 1979): 55–76.

ESCO Foundation for Palestine. *Palestine: A Study of Jewish, Arab and British Policies.* 2 vols. New Haven: Yale University Press, 1947.

Eisenman, Robert H. *Islamic Law in Palestine and Israel: A History of the Survival of Tanzimat and Shari'a in the British Mandate and the Jewish State.* Leiden, Holland: E. J. Brill, 1978.

Friedman, Thomas. *From Beirut to Jerusalem.* New York: Farrar Straus Giroux, 1989.

Frischwasser-Ra'anan, H. F. *The Frontiers of a Nation: A Re-examination of the Forces Which Created the Palestine Mandate.* Westport, Conn.: Hyperion Press, 1975.

Gelber, Sylva M. *No Balm in Gilead: A Personal Retrospective of Mandate Days in Palestine.* Ottawa, Canada: Carleton University Press, 1989.

Hadari, Ze'ev Venia. *Second Exodus: The Full Story of Jewish Illegal Immigration to Palestine, 1945–1948.* London: Valentine Mitchell, 1991.

Haim, Yehoyada. *Abandonment of Illusions: Zionist Political Attitudes Towards Palestinian Arab Nationalism, 1936–1939.* Boulder, Colo.: Westview Press, 1983.

Haymson, Albery H. *Palestine Under the Mandate.* Westport, Conn.: Greenwood Press, 1976.

Ingrams, Doreen. *Palestine Papers, 1917–1922: Seeds of Conflict.* New York: G. Braziller, 1973.

Jbara, Taysir. *Palestinian Leader Hajj Amin Al-Husayni, Mufti of Jerusalem.* Princeton, N.J.: Kingston Press, 1985.

Jones, Philip. *Britain and Palestine, 1914–1948: Archival Sources for the History of the British Mandate.* Oxford, England: Oxford University Press, 1979.

Louis, Wm. Roger and Robert W. Stookey, eds. *The End of the Palestine Mandate.* Austin: University of Texas Press, 1989.

Kolinsky, Martin. *Law, Order, and Riots in Mandatory Palestine, 1928–35.* New York: St. Martin's Press, 1993.

Marlowe, John. *The Seat of Pilate: An Account of the Palestine Mandate.* London: Cresset Press, 1959.

Mattar, Philip. *The Mufti of Jerusalem: al-Hajj Amin al-Husayni and the Palestinian National Movement.* New York: Columbia University Press, 1988.

Mossek, M. *Palestine Immigration Policy Under Sir Herbert Samuel: British Zionist and Arab Attitudes.* London: Frank Cass, 1978.

Nashashibi, Nasser Eddine. *Jerusalem's Other Voice: Raghib Nashashibi and Moderation in Palestinian Politics, 1920–1948.* Exeter, England: Ithaca Press, 1990.

Newton, Frances Emily. *Fifty Years in Palestine.* London: Coldharbour Press, 1948.

Sakran, Frank Charles. *Palestine Dilemma: Arab Rights Versus Zionist Aspirations.* Washington: Public Affairs Press, 1948.

Sela, Avraham. "The Wailing Wall Riots (1929) as a Watershed in the Palestine Conflict." *The Muslim World* 83, No. 1–2 (January–April 1994): 60–94.

Stein, Leonard. *The Balfour Declaration.* London: Valentine Mitchell, 1961.

Stevens, Richard P. *Zionism and Palestine Before the Mandate: A Phase of Western Imperialism.* Beirut: Institute for Palestine Studies, 1972.

Tannus, Izzat. *The Palestinians: A Detailed Documented Eyewitness History of Palestine Under British Mandate.* New York: I. G. T. Company, 1988.

Taylor, Alan R. *Prelude to Israel, 1897–1947.* Beirut: Institute for Palestine Studies, 1970.

Wilson, Evan M. "The Palestine Papers, 1943–47." *Journal of Palestine Studies* 4, No. 4 (Summer 1973): 33–54.

The War of 1948 and the Jordanian Era

Abdullah of Jordan, King. *My Memories Completed "Al Takmilah."* Translated by Harold W. Glidden. New York: Longman, 1978.

Alami, Musa. "The Lesson of Palestine." *The Middle East Journal* 3 (October 1949): 373– 405.

Bailey, Clinton. *Jordan's Palestinian Challenge, 1948–1983: A Political History.* Boulder, Colo.: Westview Press, 1984.

Bickerton, Ian J. and Carla L. Klausner. *A Concise History of the Arab-Israeli Conflict.* Englewood Cliffs, N.J.: Prentice Hall, 1991.

Binur, Yoram. *My Enemy, My Self.* New York: Doubleday, 1989.

Busailah, Reja-e. "The Fall of Lydda, 1948: Impressions and Reminiscences." *Arab Studies Quarterly* 2 (Spring 1981): 123–141.

Carrol, Raymond. *The Palestine Question.* New York: F. Watts, 1983.

Dupuy, Trevor N. *Elusive Victory: The Arab-Israeli Wars, 1947–1974.* New York: Harper and Row, 1978.

El-Shazly, Lt. General Saad. *The Crossing of the Suez.* San Francisco: American Mideast Research, 1980.

Furlonge, Geoffrey Warren, Sir. *Palestine is My Country: The Story of Musa Alami.* London: Murray, 1969.

Hadawi, Sami. *Crime And No Punishment.* Beirut: Palestine Research Center, 1972.

———. *Palestinian Rights and Losses in 1948: A Comparative Study.* London: Saqi, 1988.

———. *Bitter Harvest: A Modern History of Palestine.* New York: Olive Branch Press, 1991.

Ilan, Amitzur. *Bernadotte in Palestine, 1948.* London: Macmillan Press, 1990.

Institute for Palestine Studies. *All That Remains: The Palestinian Villages Occupied and Depopulated by Israel in 1948.* Washington: Institute for Palestine Studies, 1992.

Jiryis, Sabri. "Forty Years Since the Seizure of Palestine." *Journal of Palestine Studies* 69, No. 1 (Autumn 1988): 83–95.

John, Robert and Sami Hadawi. *The Palestine Diary.* New York: New World Press, 1970.

Karmi, Ghada. "The 1948 Exodus: A Family Story." *Journal of Palestine Studies* 90, No. 2 (Winter 1994): 31–40.

Khalidi, Rashid. "Revisionist Views of the Modern History of Palestine: 1948." *Arab Studies Quarterly* 10, No. 4 (Fall 1988): 427–32.

Khalidi, Walid. "Plan Dalet: Master Plan for the Conquest of Palestine." *Journal of Palestine Studies* 69, No. 1 (Autumn 1988): 3–70.

Love, Kennett. *Suez: The Twice Fought War.* New York: McGraw-Hill Company, 1969.

Morris, Benny. *1948 and After: Israel and the Palestinians.* Oxford, England: Oxford University Press, 1994.

Murphy, Jay, ed. *For Palestine.* New York: Writers and Readers Publishing, 1993.

Nazzal, Nafez. "The Zionist Occupation of Western Galilee, 1948." *Journal of Palestine Studies* 11, No. 3 (Spring 1974): 58–76.

Nutting, Anthony. *No End of a Lesson: The Story of Suez.* New York: Clarkson Potter, 1967.

Pappe, Ilan. *The Making of the Arab-Israeli Conflict 1947–1951.* London: I. B. Tauris, 1992.

Peled, Alisa Rubin. "The Crystallization of an Israeli Policy Towards Muslim and Christian Holy Places, 1948–1955." *The Muslim World* 83, No. 1–2 (January-April 1994): 95–126.

Polk, William Roe. *Backdrop to Tragedy: The Struggle of Palestine.* Boston: Beacon Press, 1957.

Pryce-Jones, David. *The Face of Defeat.* New York: Holt, Rinehart and Winston, 1973.

al-Qawugji, Fauzi, "Memoirs, 1948, Part I." *Journal of Palestine Studies* 1, No. 4 (Summer 1972): 27–58.

———. "Memoirs, 1948, Part II." *Journal of Palestine Studies* 2, No. 1 (Autumn 1972): 3–33.

Rihani, Amin. *The Fate of Palestine.* Beirut: Rihani Printing and Publishing House, 1967.

Rowley, Gwyn. *Israel into Palestine.* New York: Mansell Publishing, 1984.

Sayigh, Rosemary. *Palestinians: From Peasants to Revolutionaries.* London: Zed Books, 1979.

Sheffer, Gabriel, ed. *Dynamics of Conflict: A Re-examination of the Arab Israeli Conflict.* Atlantic Highlands, N.J.: Humanities Press, 1975.

Stewart, Desmond. *The Palestinians: Victims of Expediency.* London: Quartet, 1982.

Toroen, S. Ilan. "The Price of Partition, 1948: The Dissolution of the Palestine Potash Company." *Journal of Israeli History* 15, No. 1 (Spring 1994): 53–81.

Turki, Fawaz. *The Disinherited: Journal of a Palestinian Exile.* New York: Monthly Review Press, 1972.

Kurzman, Dan. *Genesis 1948: The First Arab-Israeli War.* New York: The World Publishing Company, 1970.

The 1967 War: Palestine Under Israeli Occupation

Abdul Rahman, As'ad. *Memoirs of a Prisoner.* Beirut: Palestine Research Center, 1969.

Abu-Lughod, Ibrahim, ed. *The Arab-Israeli Confrontation of June 1967: An Arab Perspective.* Evanston, Ill.: Northwestern University Press, 1970.

Abu-Lughod, Ibrahim. *Altered Relations: The Palestinians Since 1967.*

North Dartmouth, Mass.: Arab-American University Graduates, 1972.

Adams, Michael. "Revisiting Palestine." *Journal of Palestine Studies* 56, No. 4 (Summer 1985): 58–67.

Aker, Frank. *October 1973: The Arab-Israeli War.* Hamden, Conn.: Archon Books, The Shoe String Press, 1985.

Aruri, Naseer H. *Middle East Crucible: Studies on the Arab-Israeli War of 1973.* Evanston, Ill.: Medina University Press, 1975.

El-Ayonty, Y. "The Palestinians and the Fourth Arab-Israeli War." *Current History* 66, No. 390 (February 1974): 74–78.

Basisu, Mu'in. *Descent into the Water: Palestinian Notes from Arab Exile.* Translated by Saleh Omar. Wilmette, Ill.: Medina Press, 1980.

Cattan, Henry. *The Dimensions of the Palestine Problem, 1967.* Beirut: Institute for Palestine Studies, 1967.

Cohen, Richard I., ed. *Vision and Conflict in the Holy Land.* New York: St. Martin's Press, 1985.

El-Khalidi, Ahmad Samih. *The Arab-Israeli War 1967.* Beirut: Arab Women's Information Committee, 1969.

Elpeleg, Zvi. "West Bank Story." *Middle East Review* 18, No. 4 (Summer 1986): 7–16.

Epp, Frank H. *Palestinians: Portrait of a People in Conflict.* Toronto: McClelland and Stewart, 1976.

Graham-Brown, Sara. *The Palestinian Situation.* Oxford, England: University of Oxford, Refugee Studies Programme, 1989.

Halabi, Rafik. *The West Bank Story.* Translated by Ina Friedman. New York: Harcourt Brace Jovanovich, 1981.

Harkabi, Y. *Palestinians and Israel.* New York: Halsted Press, 1974.

Haykal, Muhammed Hussayn. *The Road to Ramadan.* London: William Collins and Sons, 1975.

Jones, Christina. *The Untempered Wind: Forty Years in Palestine.* London: Longman, 1975.

Khalidi, Ahmad S. "The Palestinians: Current Dilemmas, Future Challenges." *Journal of Palestine Studies* 94, No. 2 (Winter 1995): 5–14.

Khalidi, Walid. "The Palestinian Problem: An Overview." *Journal of Palestine Studies* 81, No. 1 (Autumn 1991): 5–16.

Lukacs, Yehuda, ed. *The Israeli-Palestinian Conflict: A Documentary Record, 1967–1990.* Cambridge: Cambridge University Press, 1992.

Miller, Aaron David. "The Arab-Israeli Conflict, 1967–1987: A Retrospective." *The Middle East Journal* 41, No. 3 (Summer 1987): 349–360.

———. "The Palestinians: Past as Prologue." *Current History* 87 (February 1988): 73–76, 83–85.

Murray, Nancy. *Palestinians: Life Under Occupation.* Cambridge, Mass.: The Middle East Justice Network, 1992.

Nakhleh, Emile A. "The West Bank and Gaza: Twenty Years Later." *Middle East Journal* 42, No. 2 (Spring 1988): 209–226.

Oz, Amos. "The Israeli-Palestinian Conflict: A Storyteller's Point of View." *Michigan Quarterly Review* 32, No. 2 (Spring 1992): 156–177.

Palestine Book Project. *Our Roots are Still Alive*. San Francisco: Peoples Press, 1977.

Palumbo, Michael. "What Happened to Palestine? The Revisionists Revisited." *The Link* 23, (September/October 1990): 1–12.

———. *Imperial Israel: The History of the Occupation of the West Bank and Gaza*. London: Bloomsburg Press, 1992.

Parker, R. "The June 1967 War: Some Mysteries Explored." *Middle East Journal* 46, No. 2 (Spring 1992): 177–197.

Peretz, Don. *The West Bank: History, Politics, Society, and Economy*. Boulder, Colo.: Westview Press, 1986.

Perry, Glenn E., ed. *Palestine: Continuing Dispossession*. Belmont, Mass.: Association of Arab-American University Graduates, 1986.

Reich, Walter. *A Stranger in My House: Jews and Arabs in the West Bank*. New York: Holt, Rinehart and Winston, 1984.

Roth, S. J., S. Avineri, and I. Rabinovich, eds. *The Impact of the Six-Day War: A Twenty Year Assessment*. Basingstoke: Macmillan, 1988.

Said, Edward W. *The Question of Palestine*. New York: Times Books, 1980.

———. *After the Last Sky: Palestinian Lives*. New York: Pantheon Books, 1986.

———. "The Challenge of Palestine." *Journal of Refugee Studies* 2, No. 1 (1989): 170–178.

———. "Reflection on Twenty Years of Palestinian History." *Journal of Palestine Studies* 80, No. 4 (Summer 1991): 5–22.

Said, Edward W. and Christopher Hitchens, et. al. *Blaming the Victims: Spurious Scholarships and the Palestinian Question*. New York: Verso, 1987.

Samara, Adel, et al. *Palestine: Profile of an Occupation*. London: Zed Books Ltd., 1989.

Samo, Elias, ed. *The June 1967 Arab-Israeli War*. Wilmette, Ill.: Medina University Press, 1971.

Sharabi, Hisham. *Palestine and Israel: The Lethal Dilemma*. New York: Pegasus, 1969.

Siniora, Hanna S. "Twenty Four Years of Occupation." *Mediterranean Quarterly* 2 (Summer 1991): 55–70.

Stone, I. F. *Underground to Palestine*. New York: Pantheon Books, 1978.

Tordai, J. C. and Harvey Morris. *Into the Promised Land*. Manchester: Cornerhouse, 1991.

Venn-Brown, Janet, ed. *For a Palestinian: A Memorial to Wael Zuaiter.* Boston: Kegan Paul International, 1984.

Watkins, David. *Palestine: An Inescapable Duty*. London: Alhani International Books, 1992.

Woolfson, Marion. *Bassam Shak'a- Portrait of a Palestinian.* London: Third World Centre, 1981.

The Intifada

Abed Rabbo, Samir and Doris Safi, eds. *The Palestinian Uprising.* Belmont, Mass.: Association of Arab-American University Graduates, 1990.

Abu-Amr, Ziad. "The Palestinian Uprising in the West Bank and Gaza Strip." *Arab Studies Quarterly* 10 (1988): 384–405.

———. *The Intifada: Causes and Factors of Continuity*. Jerusalem: PASSIA Publication, 1989.

Ateek, N.S., M. H. Ellis, and R. R. Ruether, eds. *Faith and the Intifada: Palestinian Christian Voices.* Maryknoll, N.Y.: Orbis Books, 1992.

Aruri, N. *The Intifada.* Brattleboro, Vt.: Amana Books, 1989.

Bassiouni, M. Cherif and Louise Cainkar, eds. *The Palestinian Intifada—December 9, 1987–December 8, 1988: A Record of Israeli Repression.* Chicago: Data Base Project on Palestinian Human Rights, 1989.

Baumann, Melissa. "Gaza Diary." *Middle East Report* 18, No. 3 (May-June 1988): 13–17.

Bennis, Phyllis and Neal Cassidy. *From Stones to Statehood: The Palestinian Uprising*. London: Zed Books, 1990.

Emerson, Gloria J. *Gaza: A Year in the Intifada—A Personal Account From an Occupied Land.* New York: The Atlantic Monthly Press, 1991.

Emery, Michael. "Press Coverage of the Palestinian Intifada." *Journal of Arab Affairs* 7 (Fall 1988): 199–205.

Freedman, Robert O., ed. *The Intifada: Its Impact on Israel, the Arab World and the Superpowers.* Miami: Florida International University Press, 1991.

Goldberg, Giora, et al. *The Impact of Intercommunal Conflict: The Intifada and Israeli Public Opinion.* Jerusalem: Davis Institute for International Relations, Hebrew University, 1991.

Hilterman, Joost. "Israel's Strategy to Break the Uprising." *Journal of Palestine Studies* 74, No. 2 (Winter 1990): 87–98.

Holt, Maria. *Half the People: Women, History and the Palestinian Intifada.* Jerusalem: PASSIA Publication, 1992.

Hunter, Robert. *The Palestinian Uprising: A War by Other Means.* Los Angeles: University of California Press, 1991.

Jerusalem Media and Communication Center. *The Stone and the Olive Branch: Four Years of the Intifada-From Jabalia to Madrid*. Jerusalem: JMCC, 1991.

Khalidi, Rashid I. "The Uprising and the Palestine Question." *World Policy Journal* 5, No. 3 (Summer 1988): 497–518.

Langer, Felicia. *Age of Stone*. London: Quartet Books, 1988.

Lederman, Jim. "Dateline West Bank: Interpreting the Intifada." *Foreign Policy* 72 (Fall 1988): 230–246.

Lesch, Ann M. "Uprising for Palestine: Editorial Comment." *Journal of South Asian and Middle Eastern Studies* 9 (Summer 1988): 3–20.

———. "Prelude to the Uprising in the Gaza Strip." *Journal of Palestine Studies* 77, No. 1 (Autumn 1990): 1–23.

Levitt, Wendy. *Intifada: The Palestinians' Popular Uprising*. London: Kegan Paul International, 1989.

Litvak, Meir. "Palestinian Leadership in the Territories During the Intifada 1987–1992." *Orient* 34, No. 2 (June 1993): 199–220.

Lockman, Zachary and Joel Beinin, eds. *Intifada: The Palestinian Uprising Against Israeli Occupation.* Boston: South End Press, 1989.

Lustick, Ian S. "Writing the Intifada: Collective Action in the Occupied Territories." *World Politics* 45, No. 4 (July 93): 560–94.

Maksoud, Clovis. "The Implications of the Palestinian Uprising-Where From Here?" *American-Arab Affairs* 26 (Fall 1988): 50–55.

Mandel, Neville J. *The Arabs and Zionism Before World War I.* Berkeley: University of California Press, 1976.

Mandelbaum, Michael. *Israel and the Occupied Territories: A Personal Report on the Uprising.* New York: Council on Foreign Relations, 1988.

Marshall, Phil. *Intifada. Zionism, Imperialism, and the Palestinian Resistance*. Chicago: Bookmarks, 1989.

McDowall, David. *Palestine and Israel: The Uprising and Beyond.* Berkeley: University of California Press, 1989.

Melman, Y. and D. Raviv. *Behind the Uprising: Israelis, Jordanians, and Palestinians*. New York: Greenwood Press, 1989.

Miller, David A. "Palestinians and the Intifada: One Year Later." *Current History* 88 (February 1989): 73–76, 106–107.

Mishal, Shaul. "Paper War-Words Behind Stories: The Intifada Leaflets." *The Jerusalem Quarterly* 51 (Summer 1989): 71–94.

Nassar, Jamal R. and Roger Heacock, eds. *Intifada: Palestine at the Crossroads.* New York: Praeger, 1990.

Noble, Allen G. and E. Efrat. "Geography of the Intifada." *Geography Review* 80 (July 1990): 288–307.

Perry, Mark. *Counting: Impressions of the Palestinian Intifada*. Washington: Roots and Friends of Palestinian Prisoners, 1989.

Peteet, Julie M. "The Graffiti of the Intifada." *The Muslim World* 83, No. 1–2 (January-April 1994): 155–167.

Pressberg, Gail. "The Uprising: Causes and Consequences." *Journal of Palestine Studies* 17, No. 3 (Spring 1988): 38–50.

Quandt, William. "The Uprising: Breaking a Ten-Year Deadlock." *American-Arab Affairs* 27 (Winter 1988–1989): 18–28.

Rigby, Andrew. *Economic Aspects of the Intifada*. Jerusalem: PASSIA Publication, 1988.

Rouhana, Nadim. "The Intifada and the Palestinians of Israel: Resurrecting the Green Line." *Journal of Palestine Studies* 75, No. 3 (Spring 1990): 58–75.

Roy, Sara. "From Hardship to Hunger: The Economic Impact of the Intifada on the Gaza Strip." *American-Arab Affairs* 3 (1990): 109–132.

Rubenstein, Danny. "The Political and Social Impact of the Intifada on Palestinian Arab Society." *The Jerusalem Quarterly* 52 (Autumn 1989): 3–17.

Saleh, Abdul Jawad. *Implications of the Duties of the Next State: Methods for Public Support of the Intifada*. London: Jerusalem Center for Development Studies, 1990.

Schiff, Ze'ev and Ehud Ya'ari. *Intifada: The Palestinian Uprising—Israel's Third Front*. New York: Simon and Schuster, 1990.

Shaben, Carol. "Six Months in Palestine." *Arab Studies Quarterly* 11, Nos. 2–3 (Spring-Summer 1989): 181–192.

Shindler, Colin. *Ploughshares into Swords? Israelis and Jews in the Shadow of the Intifada*. London: I. B. Tauris, 1991.

Siniora, Hanna. "An Analysis of the Current Revolt." *Journal of Palestine Studies* 17, No. 3 (Spring 1988): 3–13.

Sosebee, Stephen J. "The Palestinian Women's Movement and the Intifada." *American-Arab Affairs,* No. 32 (Spring 1990): 81–91.

Stein, Kenneth W. "The Palestinian Uprising and the Shultz Initiative." *Middle East Review* 21 (Winter 1988–1989): 13–20.

———. "The Intifada and the 1936–39 Uprising: A Comparison." *Journal of Palestine Studies* 76, No. 4 (Summer 1990): 64–85.

Steinberg, Matti. "The Palestinian Uprising and the Shultz Initiative." *Middle East Review* 21 (Winter 1988–1989): 37–54.

Steinberg, Paul and A.M. Oliver. *The Graffiti of the Intifada: A Brief Survey*. Jerusalem: PASSIA Publication, 1990.

Stockton, Ronald R. "Intifada Deaths." *Journal of Palestine Studies* 70, No. 2 (Winter 1989): 101–108.

Suleiman, Michael. "Intifada—The Latest Uprising for Palestinian Independence." *Journal of Arab Affairs* 8, No. 1 (Spring 1989): 1–9.

Tamari, Salim. "What the Uprising Means." *Middle East Report* 18, No. 3 (May-June 1988): 24–30.

Vitullo, Anita. "Uprising in Gaza." *Middle East Report* 18, No. 3 (May-June 1988): 18–23.

White, Patrick. *Let Us Be Free; A Narrative Before and During the Intifada.* Clifton, N.J.: Kingston Press, Inc., 1989.

Younes, Fayez and Jamileh Saad. *The Uprising*. Nicosia: Beisan Press, 1988.

6. POLITICAL

General

Abdel Hamid, [Princess] Dina. *Duet for Freedom.* New York: Quartet Books, 1988.

Adams, Michael. *Chaos or Rebirth: The Arab Outlook.* London: British Broadcasting Corporation, 1968.

Anabtawi, S.N. "The Palestinians as a Political Entity." *The Muslim World* 60, No. 1 (January 1970): 47–58.

El-Asmar, Fouzi, et. al., eds. *Debate on Palestine*. London: Ithaca Press, 1981.

Avineri, Shlomo, ed. *Israel and the Palestinians.* New York: St. Martin's Press, 1971.

Awwad, Tawfiq Yusif. *Death in Beirut: A Novel.* Translated by Leslie McLoughlin. Washington: Three Continents Press, 1976.

Bar-Illan, David. "Palestinian Nationalism—Unguided Missile." *Global Affairs* 3 (Fall 1988): 87–98.

Bard, Mitchell G. and Joel Himelfarb. *Myths and Facts: A Concise Record of the Arab-Israeli Conflict.* Washington: Near East Report, 1992.

Benvenisti, Meron, Ziad Abu Zayad, and Danny Rubinstein. *The West Bank Handbook: A Political Lexicon.* Jerusalem: West Bank Data Base Project, 1986.

Beres, Louis-Rene. "The Question of Palestine and Israel's Nuclear Strategy." *Political Quarterly* 62 (October–December 1991): 451–60.

Brown, Alison, Roger Heacock, and Franco La Torre, eds. *The Proceedings of the ECCP-NENGOOT Conference Brussels September 28–October 1, 1992.* Jerusalem: The Network of European Non-Governmental Organizations in the Occupied Territories, 1992.

Brown, L. Dean. *The Land of Palestine: West Bank not East Bank.* Washington: Middle East Institute, 1982.

Brownlee, William Hugh. *Rights and Wrongs in Palestine.* Claremont, Calif.: Claremont Graduate School, 1972.

Buch, Peter. *Burning Issues of the Middle East Crisis.* New York: Pathfinder Press, 1967.

Cohen, Amnon. *Palestine in the 18th Century: Patterns of Government and Administration.* Jerusalem: Magnes Press, Hebrew University, 1973.

Davis, Uri. *The State of Palestine.* Reading, England: Ithaca Press, 1991.

Dossa, S. "Mastering Palestinians: Hegel and Revisionist Zionism." *Arab Studies Quarterly* 6, No. 4 (Fall 1984): 296–303.

Elpeleg, Zvi. "Why was 'Independent Palestine' never created in 1948?" *The Jerusalem Quarterly* 50 (Spring 1989): 3–22.

Ferguson, Pamela. *The Palestine Problem.* London: Martin, Brian and O'Keefe, 1973.

Gans, Jonathan B. "Journey to the West Bank." *Journal of Palestine Studies* 32, No. 4 (Summer 1979): 57–69.

Goldstein, Yaacov. "David Ben-Gurion and the Bi-National Idea in Palestine." *Middle Eastern Studies* 24, No. 4 (October 1988): 460–72.

Goodman, Hirsh and W. Seth Carns. *The Future Battlefield and the Arab-Israeli Conflict.* New Brunswick, N.J.: Transaction Publishers, 1990.

Grollenberg, Lucas. *Palestine Comes First.* London: SCM Press Ltd., 1980.

Hassan Bin Talal, H.R.H. Crown Prince. *Palestinian Self-Determination: A Study of the West Bank and Gaza Strip.* New York: Quartet Books, 1981.

Jammal, L. "Contribution by Palestinian Women to the Struggle for Liberation During the British Mandate." *Palestine Bulletin* 7, No. 13 (July 15–August 15, 1981): 30–34.

Kadduri, Majdia D., ed. *The Arab-Israeli Impasse.* Washington: Robert B. Luce, 1968.

Kuroda, Alice K. and Yasumas Kuroda. *Palestinians Without Palestine: A Study of Political Socialization Among Palestinian Youths.* Washington: University Press of America, 1978.

Lalor, Paul. *Toward a Palestinian Entity.* London: Royal Institute of International Affairs, 1989.

Ma'oz, Moshe, ed. *Palestinian Arab Politics.* Jerusalem: Academic Press, 1975.

Ma'oz, Moshe. *Palestinian Leadership on the West Bank: The Changing Role of the Mayors Under Jordan and Israel.* London: Frank Cass, 1984.

Mendes-Flohr, Paul R., ed. *A Land of Two Peoples: Martin Buber on Jews and Arabs.* New York: Oxford University Press, 1983.

Miller, A. "The Future of Palestinian Nationalism." *Middle East Insight* 3, No. 5 (July-August 1984): 23–29.

Miller, Ylana N. *Government and Society in Rural Palestine, 1920–1948.* Austin: University of Texas Press, 1984.

Monre, E. "The West Bank: Palestinian or Israeli?" *The Middle East Journal* 31, No. 4 (Autumn 1977): 397–412.

Muslih, Muhammad Y. *The Origins of Palestinian Nationalism.* New York: Columbia University Press, 1988.

Nakhleh, Emile, ed. *A Palestinian Agenda for the West Bank and Gaza.* Washington: American Enterprise Institute, 1980.

Nijim, Basheer K. and Bishara Muammar. *Toward the De-Arabization of Palestine / Israel*, 1945–1977. Madison, Wis.: Kendall-Hunt, 1984.

Ovendale, Ritchie. *The Origins of the Arab-Israeli Wars.* New York: Longman, 1992.

Oz, Amos. "The Making of a Homeland." *New Outlook* 31, No. 1 (January 1988): 19–25.

Peretz, D. "Arab Palestine: Phoenix or Phantom?" *Foreign Affairs* 48, No. 2 (January 1970): 322–333.

Peretz, Don, et. al. *A Palestine Entity?* Washington: Middle East Institute, 1970.

Porath, Yehoshua. *The Emergence of the Palestinian National Movement, 1918–1929.* London: Frank Cass, 1973.

———. *The Palestinian Arab National Movement: From Riots to Rebellion, Volume Two, 1929–1939.* London: Frank Cass, 1977.

Quandt, William B. *Palestinian Nationalism: Its Political and Military Dimension.* Santa Monica, Calif.: Rand Corporation, 1971.

Quandt, William B., Fuad Jabber and Ann Mosely Lesch. *The Politics of Palestinian Nationalism.* Berkeley: University of California Press, 1973.

Richardson, John P. *The West Bank: A Portrait*. Washington: The Middle East Institute, 1984.

Rodinson, Maxime. *Israel and the Arabs.* New York: Pantheon Books, 1968.

Sahliyeh, Emile. *In Search of Leadership: West Bank Politics Since 1967.* Washington: Brookings Institution, 1988.

Said, Edward W. "Identity, Negation, and Violence." *The New Left Review* 171 (September/October 1988): 46–62.

———. *The Politics of Dispossession: The Struggle for Palestinian Self-Determination 1969–1994*. London: Chatto and Windus, 1994.

Sandler, Shmuel and Hillel Frisch. *Israel, the Palestinians, and the West Bank.* Lexington, Mass.: Lexington Books, 1984.

Shalev, Aryeh. *The West Bank: Line of Defence.* New York: Praeger Publishers, 1985.

Shinar, Dov and Danny Rubinstein. *Palestinian Press in the West Bank: The Political Dimension.* Boulder, Colo.: Westview Press, 1987.

Shinar, Dov. *Palestinian Voices: Communications and Nation Building in the West Bank.* Boulder, Colo.: Lynne Rienner Publishers, 1987.

Shipler, David K. *Arab and Jew: Wounded Spirits in a Promised Land.* New York: Penguin Books, 1987.

Shlaim, Avi. "The Rise and Fall of the All-Palestine Government in Gaza." *Journal of Palestine Studies* 77, No. 1 (Autumn 1990): 37–53.

Slapikoff, Saul A. *Consider and Hear Me: Voices From Palestine and Israel.* Philadelphia: Temple University Press, 1993.

Slater, Jerome. "A Palestinian State and Israeli Security." *Political Science Quarterly* 106 (Fall 1991): 411–429.

Stetler, Russell, ed. *Palestine—The Arab Israeli Conflict.* San Francisco: Ramparts Press, 1972.

Tahtinen, Dale R. *The Arab-Israeli Military Balance Today.* Washington: American Enterprise Institute, 1973.

Taylor, Alan and Richard N. Tetlie, eds. *Palestine: A Search for Truth: Approaches to the Arab-Israeli Conflict.* Washington: Public Affairs Press, 1970.

Terry, J. "The Arab-Israeli Conflict in Popular Literature." *American-Arab Affairs*, No. 2 (Fall 1982): 97–104.

Teveth, Shabtai. *Ben Gurion and the Palestinian Arabs: From Peace to War.* Oxford, England: Oxford University Press, 1985.

The Institute for Palestine Studies. *Christians, Zionism and Palestine: A Selection of Articles and Statements on the Religious Aspects of the Palestine Problem.* Beirut: Institute of Palestine Studies, 1970.

Vatikiotis, P.J. *Conflict in The Middle East.* London: George Allen and Unwin, 1971.

Waines, David. *The Unholy War. Israel And Palestine 1897–1971.* Montreal: Chateau Books, 1971.

Human Rights

Al-Abid, Ibrahim. *Human Rights in the Occupied Territories.* Beirut: Palestine Research Center, 1970.

Abu-Lughod, Ibrahim, ed. *Palestinian Rights: Affirmation and Denial.* Willmette, Ill.: Medina Press, 1982.

Amad, Adnan. *Israeli League for Human and Civil Rights.* Beirut: Near East Ecumenical Bureau for Information and Interpretation, 1973.

Amnesty International. *Report on the Treatment of Certain Prisoners Under Interrogation in Israel.* London: 1970.

Ateek, Naim Stifan. *Justice and Only Justice: A Palestinian Theology of Liberation.* Maryknoll, N.Y.: Orbis Books, 1989.

Bassiouni, M. Cherif. *The Palestinian's Right of Self-Determination and National Independence.* Detroit: Association of Arab-American University Graduates, 1978.

Be'er, Yizhar and 'Abdel-Jawad Saleh. *Collaborators in the Occupied Territories: Human Rights Abuses and Violations.* Jerusalem: B'T-selem (The Israeli Information Center for Human Rights in the Occupied Territories), 1994.

Bisharat, George Emile. *Palestinian Lawyers and Israeli Rule: Law and Disorder in the West Bank.* Austin: University of Texas Press, 1990.

Cleveland, Ray L. *Palestine and Israel: The Civil Rights Configuration.* Beirut: Palestine Research Center, 1974.

Cohen, Esther R. *Human Rights in the Israeli-Occupied Territories 1967–82.* Manchester, England: Manchester University Press, 1986.

Collins, Frank. *Non-Violence and Death at Bir Zeit University: An Investigative Report.* Jerusalem: The Palestinian Human Rights Information Center, 1989.

Cossali, Paul and Clive Robson. *Stateless in Gaza.* London: Zed Books, 1986.

Dib, George and Fuad Jabber. *Israel's Violation of Human Rights in the Occupied Territories.* Beirut: Institute for Palestine Studies, 1968.

Dobbing, Herbert. *Cause for Concern: A Quaker's View of the Palestine Problem.* Beirut: Institute for Palestine Studies, 1970.

Falk, Richard A. and Burns H. Weston. "The Relevance of International Law to Palestinian Rights in the West Bank and Gaza: In Legal Defense of the Intifada." *Harvard International Law Journal* 32, No. 1 (Winter 1991): 129–157.

Galtung, Johan. *Nonviolence and Israel/Palestine.* Honolulu: University of Hawaii, 1989.

Golan, Daphna. "Detained Without Trial: Administrative Detention in the Occupied Territories Since the Beginning of the Intifada." *B'Tselem* (October 1992): 1–69.

Al Haq/ Law in the Service of Man. *Punishing a Nation: Human Rights Violations During the Palestinian Uprising, December 1987–December 1988.* Ramallah, West Bank: 1988.

———. *Twenty Years of Israel's Occupation of the West Bank and Gaza.* Ramallah, West Bank: 1987.

Israeli League for Human and Civil Rights. *Report on the Violations of Human Rights in the Territories During the Uprising.* Tel Aviv: The Israeli League for Human and Civil Rights, 1988.

Karp Report. *An Israeli Government Inquiry into Settler Violence against Palestinians on the West Bank.* Washington: Institute for Palestine Studies, 1963.

Lerner, Michael. "End the Occupation and Show Respect for the Palestinian People." *Judaism* 37, No. 4 (Fall 1988): 434–441.

Ott, David H. *Palestine in Perspective: Politics, Human Rights and the West Bank.* London: Quartet Books, 1981.

Prior, Michael. "Palestinian Christians and the Liberation of Theology." *Month* 254, No. 1512 (December 1993): 482–490.

Quigley, John. *Palestine and Israel: A Challenge to Justice.* Durham, N.C.: Duke University Press, 1990.

Rishmawi, Mona. "What Palestinians Want: Let Our People Go." *The Nation* 246, 19 (March 1988): 368–370.

Shehadeh, Raja and Jonathan Kuttab. *The West Bank and the Rule of Law.* Geneva: The International Commission of Jurists and Law in the Service of Man, 1980.

Zucker, David, et al. *Research of Human Rights in the Occupied Territories 1979–1983.* Tel Aviv: International Center for Peace in the Middle East, 1983.

Israeli Policies and Settlements

Abdul Hadi, Mahdi. *Notes on Palestinian-Israeli Meetings in the Occupied Territories.* Jerusalem: PASSIA Publication, 1987.

Abu Harb, Qasem. *Israeli Settlements in the West Bank and Gaza Strip 1967–1987.* Jerusalem: Arab Studies Society, 1987.

Abu-Lughod, Janet. "Israeli Settlements in the Occupied Arab Land: Conquest to Colony." *Journal of Palestine Studies* 42, No. 2 (Winter 1982): 16–54.

Abu Shakrah, Jan, D. Betz, and D. Wagner. *Israeli Settler Violence in the Occupied Territories, 1980–1984.* Chicago: Palestine Human Rights Campaign, 1985.

Alpher, Joseph. *Settlements and Borders.* Tel Aviv: Tel Aviv University, Jaffee Center for Strategic Studies, 1994.

Amnesty International. *Israel and the Occupied Territories: Amnesty International Concerns in 1988.* New York, 1989.

Arian, Asher, et. al. "Public Opinion and Political Change: Israel and the Intifadah." *Comparative Politics* 24, No. 3 (April 1992): 317–334.

Aronson, Geoffrey. "Israel and the Occupied Territories: Can Israel's Occupation of the West Bank Ever Be Reversed?" *Journal of Defense and Diplomacy* 3, No. 1 (January 1985): 38–43.

———. *Israel, Palestinians and the Intifada: Creating Facts on the West Bank.* New York: Kegan Paul International, 1990.

Aruri, Naseer. *The Palestinian Resistance to Israeli Occupation.* Wilmette, Ill.: Medina University Press International, 1970.

Aruri, Naseer, ed. *Occupation: Israel Over Palestine.* Belmont, Mass.: Association of Arab-American University Graduates, 1989.

B'tselem. *The Military Judicial System in the West Bank.* Jerusalem: Israeli Information Center for Human Rights in the Occupied Territories, 1989.

Bard, Mitchell and David Bar-Illan. "Can Israel Withdraw." *Commentary* 85, No. 4 (April 1988): 27–38.

Benvenisti, Meron. *The West Bank Data Project: A Study of Israel's Policies.* Washington: American Enterprise Institute, 1984.

Bishara, Azmi. "Israel Faces the Uprising: A Preliminary Assessment." *Middle East Report* 157 (March-April 1989): 6–14.

Brynen, Rex, ed. *Echoes of the Intifada: Regional Repercussions of the Palestinian-Israeli Conflict.* Boulder, Colo.: Westview Press, 1991.

Cohen, Esther Rosalind. *International Criticism of Israeli-Security Measures in the Occupied Territories.* Jerusalem: The Magnes Press, 1984.

Dahlan, Ahmad Said. "Housing Demolition and Refugee Resettlement Schemes in the Gaza Strip." *Geo* 21 (August 1990): 385–395.

David Uri, et. al., eds. *Israel and the Palestinians.* London: Ithaca Press, 1975.

Davies, Rhoua and Peter Johnson. *The Uzi and the Stone.* Calgary: Detseling Enterprises, 1991.

Dayanim, Bahnam. "The Israeli Supreme Court and the Deportations of Palestinians: Interaction of Law and Legitimacy." *Stanford Journal of International Law* 30, No. 1 (Winter 1994): 115–186.

Dehter, Aaron. *How Expensive Are the West Bank Settlements? A Comparative Analysis of the Financing of Social Services.* Boulder, Colo.: Westview Press, 1987.

diGiovanni, Janine. *Against the Stranger: Lives in Occupied Territory.* London: Penguin Books, 1994.

Elazer, Daniel J., ed. *Judea, Samaria and Gaza: Views on the Present and Future.* Washington: American Enterprise Institute, 1982.

Falloon, Virgil. *Excessive Secrecy, Lack of Guidelines: A Report on Military Censorship in the West Bank.* Ramallah, West Bank: Law in the Service of Man/Al Haq, 1985.

Farer, Tom. "Israel's Unlawful Occupation." *Foreign Policy,* No. 82 (Spring 1991): 37–58.

Foda, Ezzeldin. *Israeli Belligerent Occupation and Armed Palestinian Resistance in International Law.* Beirut: Palestine Research Center, 1970.

Gaff, Angela. *An Illusion of Legality: A Legal Analysis of Israel's Mass Deportation of Palestinians on 17 December 1992.* Ramallah, West Bank: Al-Haq Occasional Paper, 1993.

George, Donald E. *Israeli Occupation: International Law and Policies.* Hicksville, N.Y.: Exposition Press, 1980.

Grossman, David. *Jewish and Arab Settlements in the Tulkarm Sub District.* Jerusalem: West Bank Data Base project, 1986.

Hallaj, Muhammad. "Zionist Violence Against Palestinians." *The Link* 21 (September 1988): 1–14.

Harris, William Wilson. *Taking Roots: Israeli Settlements in the West Bank, the Golan and Gaza-Sinai, 1967–1980.* Letchworth, England: John Wiley and Sons, 1980.

Hillier, Bill. *Israel and Palestine.* London: Housmans, 1968.

Hudson, Brian. "Hysteria by Law: The Palestinian Deportation Case and the INS Contingency Plan." *Without Prejudice* 2, No. 1 (1989): 40–60.

Jarbawi, Ali and Roger Heacock. "The Deportations and the Palestinian-Israeli Negotiations." *Journal of Palestine Studies* 87, No. 3 (Spring 1993): 32–45.

Jerusalem Media and Communication Center. *No Exit, Israel's Curfew Policy in the Occupied Palestinian Territories.* Jerusalem: JMCC, 1991.

Keller, Adam. "Israel and Palestinians." *New Politics* 2, No. 1 (Summer 1988): 41–54.

Khameyseh, Rasem. *Israeli Planning and House Demolishing Policy in the West Bank.* Jerusalem: PASSIA Publication, 1989.

Khamsin Group. *Palestine: Profile of an Occupation.* London: Zed Books, 1989.

Kieval, Gershan R. *Party Politics in Israel and the Occupied Territories.* Westport, Colo.: Greenwood Press, 1983.

Krough, Peter F. and Mary C. McDavid, eds. *Palestinians Under Occupation: Prospects for the Future.* Washington: Center for Contempory Arab Studies, Georgetown University, 1989.

Kupferschmidt, Uri M. *The Supreme Muslim Council: Islam Under the British Mandate for Palestine.* Leiden, Holland: E.J. Brill, 1987.

Kuttab, Jonathan and Raja Shehadeh. *Civilian Administration in the Occupied West Bank: Analysis of Israeli Military Government Order No. 947.* Ramallah: West Bank: Al Haq/Law in the Service of Man, 1982.

Langer, Felicia. *With My Own Eyes.* London: Ithaca Press, 1975.

Langfur, Stephen. *Confession from a Jericho Jail: What Happened When I Refused to Fight the Palestinians.* New York: Grove Weidenfeld, 1992.

Lesch, Ann. "Israeli Settlements in the Occupied Territories." *Journal of Palestine Studies* 8, No. 1 (Autumn 1978): 100–119.

——— "Israeli Deportation of Palestinians from the West Bank and Gaza Strip, 1967–1978 (part II)." *Journal of Palestine Studies* 31, No. 3 (Spring 1979): 81–112.

———. "Israeli Deportation of Palestinians from the West Bank and Gaza Strip, 1967–1978," *Journal of Palestine Studies* 30, No. 2 (Winter 1979): 100–131.

Lesch, Ann and Mark Tessler. "The West Bank and Gaza: Political and Ideological Responses to Occupation. *The Muslim World* 77, Nos. 3–4 (July–October 1987): 229–249.

Locke, Richard and Antony Stewart. *Bantustan Gaza.* London: Zed Books, 1985.

Mallison, Sally V. and Thomas W. Mallison. *Settlements and the Law:*

A Judicial Analysis of the Israeli Settlements in the Occupied Territories. Washington: American Educational Trust, 1982.

Mansour, Antoine S. "Monetary Dualism: The Case of the West Bank Under Occupation." *Journal of Palestine Studies* 43, No. 3 (Spring 1982): 103–116.

Masalha, Nur. *Expulsion of the Palestinians: The Concept of "Transfer" in Zionist Political Thought, 1882–1948.* Washington: Institute for Palestine Studies, 1992.

Matar, Ibrahim. "Israeli Settlements in the West Bank and Gaza Strip." *Journal of Palestine Studies* 41, No. 1 (Autumn 1981): 93–110.

Metzger, Jan. *This Land is Our Land: The West Bank Under Israeli Occupation.* London: Zed Books, 1983.

Milson, Menahem. *Israel's Policy in the West Bank and Gaza Strip.* Washington: Wilson Center, 1986.

Moughrabi, Fouad. "Israeli Control and Palestinian Resistance." *Social Justice* 19, No. 3 (1992): 46–62.

Nairn, Allan. "The Occupation: Israel Lost its Grip on the West Bank." *Village Voice* 23, No. 1 (March 1988): 25–26, 28–32.

Nakhleh, Khalil. *Palestinian Struggle Under Occupation.* Belmont, Mass.: Association of Arab-American University Graduates, 1980.

Nazzal, Nafez. "Policies of the Israeli Occupation in the West Bank." (Working Papers No. 46) Washington: Woodrow Wilson Center, 1983.

Newman, David. *Jewish Settlements in the West Bank: The Role of Gush Emumin.* Durham: Centre for Middle Eastern Studies, University of Durham, 1982.

——— *Population, Settlement and Conflict: Israel and the West Bank.* Cambridge: Cambridge University Press, 1991.

Newman, D., ed. *The Impact of Gush Emunim: Politics and Settlement in the West Bank.* London: Croom Helm, 1985.

Nisan, Mordechai. *Israel and the Territories: A Study in Control 1967–1977.* Ramat Gan, Israel: Turtledove Publishing, 1978.

O'Brien, William. *Law and Morality in Israel's War with the PLO.* London: Routledge, 1991.

Playfair, E. *The Demolition and Sealing of Houses: A Punitive Measure in the Israeli Occupied West Bank.* London: Ithaca Press, 1987.

Playfair, Emma, ed. *International Law and the Administered Occupied Territories. Two Decades of Israeli Occupation of the West Bank and Gaza Strip.* Oxford, England: Clarendon Press, 1992.

Portugali, Juval. "Jewish Settlement in the Occupied Territories: Israel's Settlement Structure and the Palestinians." *Political Geography Quarterly* 10, No. 1 (January 1991): 26–53.

Quigley, John. "Family Reunion and the Right to Return to Occupied

Territory." *Georgetown Immigration Law Journal* 6, No. 2 (June 1992): 223–251.

Rabah, Jamil and Natasha Fairweather, eds. *Israeli Military Orders in the Occupied Palestinian West Bank: 1967–1992*. Jerusalem: Jerusalem Media and Communication Center, 1993.

Romann, Michael. *Jewish Kiryat Arba Versus Arab Hebron*. Jerusalem: West Bank Data Project, 1986.

Roy, Sara M. "The Gaza Strip: Critical Effects of the Occupation." *Arab Studies Quarterly* 10, No. 1 (Winter 1988): 59–103.

———. "Gaza: New Dynamics of Civic Disintegration." *Journal of Palestine Studies* 22, No. 4 (Summer 1993): 20–31.

——— "The Seed of Chaos, and of Night: The Gaza Strip After the Agreement." *Journal of Palestine Studies* 91, No. 3 (Spring 1994): 85–98.

Ryan, Sheila. *The Colonial Exploitation of Occupied Palestine*. London: Croom Helm, 1979.

Schnall, D. J. *Beyond the Green Line: Israeli Settlements West of the Jordan.* New York: Praeger, 1984.

Shehadeh, Raja. *The Third Way: A Journal of Life in the West Bank.* London: Quartet Books, 1982.

———. "Occupier's Law and the Uprising." *Journal of Palestine Studies* 17, No. 3 (Spring 1988): 24–37.

———. *Occupiers's Law: Israel and the West Bank.* Washington: Institute of Palestine Studies, 1989.

———. *The Sealed Room: Selections from the Diary of a Palestinian Living Under Israeli Occupation, September 1990–August 1991.* London: Quartet Books, 1992

——— The Law of the Land: Settlements and Land Issues Under Israeli Military Occupation. Jerusalem: PASSIA Publication, 1993

Sellick, Patricia. "The Old City of Hebron: Can It Be Saved?" *Journal of Palestine Studies* 92, No. 4 (Summer 1994): 69–82.

Shahak, Israel. "Israel Apartheid and the Intifada." *Race and Class* 30, No. 1 (July-September 1988): 1–12.

Singer, Joel. *The Establishment of a Civilian Administration in the Areas Administered By Israel.* Tel Aviv: Tel Aviv University/Faculty of Law, 1971.

Siniora, Hanna. "On the Palestinian Struggle." *World Policy Journal* 3, No. 4 (Fall 1986): 723–38.

Sullivan, Antony Thrall. *Palestinian Universities Under Occupation.* Cairo: American University of Cairo Press, 1988.

Thorpe, Merle, Jr. *Prescription for Conflict: Israel's West Bank Settlement Policy*. Washington: Foundation for Middle East Peace, 1984.

Thornhill, Theresa. *Making Women Talk: The Interrogation of Palestin-*

ian Women Detainees by the Israeli General Security Services. London: Lawyers for Palestinian Human Rights, 1992.

Tillman, Seth. "The West Bank Hearings: Israel's Colonization of Occupied Territories." *Journal of Palestine Studies* 26, No. 2 (Winter 1978): 71–87.

United States Senate Committee on the Judiciary. *The Colonization of the West Bank Territories by Israel.* Washington: Hearings before the Subcommittee on Immigration and Naturalization, October 17–18, 1977.

Vitullo, Anita. *Israel's War by Bureaucracy: "We'll Blow Your House Down".* Chicago: Human Rights Research and Education Foundation, 1988.

Wallach, John and Janet. *Still Small Voices: The Untold Human Stories Behind the Violence on the West Bank and Gaza.* New York: Harcourt Brace Jovanovich, 1989.

Yahav, David, ed. *Israel, the "Intifada" and the Rule of Law.* Tel Aviv: Israel Ministry of Defense Publications, 1993.

Yitzhaki, Ahiya. "Milson's Year on the West Bank." *Middle East Review* 18, No. 2 (Winter 1985/86): 37–48.

Zureik, Elia. "Crime, Justice, and Underdevelopment: The Palestinians Under Israeli Control." *International Journal of Middle East Studies* 20, No. 4 (November 1988): 411–42.

Palestine and the Arab States

Abed, George T. "The Palestinians and the Gulf Crisis." *Journal of Palestine Studies* 78, No. 2 (Winter 1991): 29–42.

Abu-Lughod, Ibrahim and Ahmad Eqbal, eds. *The Invasion of Lebanon.* Washington: Institute for Policy Studies, 1983.

Avi-Ran, Reuvan. "The Syrian-Palestinian Conflict in Lebanon." *The Jerusalem Quarterly* 42 (Spring 1987): 57–82.

Bailey, C. "Changing Attitudes Towards Jordan in the West Bank." *The Middle East Journal* 32, No. 2 (Spring 1978): 155–66.

Bishara, Ghassan. "Impotence in the Face of Adversity: Arab Regimes and the Palestine Question." *Arab Studies Quarterly* 2, Nos. 2–31 (Spring/Summer 1989): 303–314.

Brand, Laurie A. *Palestinians in the Arab World: Insitution Building and the Search for State.* New York: Columbia University Press, 1988.

——— "Palestinians in Syria: The Politics of Integration." *Middle East Journal* 42, No. 4 (Autumn 1988): 621–638.

Dajani, Maha Ahmad. *The Institutionalization of Palestinian Identity in Egypt.* Cairo: The American University Press, 1986.

Eppel, Michael. *The Palestine Conflict in the History of Modern Iraq.* London: Frank Cass, 1994.

Finkelstein, Norman. "Reflections on Palestinian Attitudes during the Gulf War." *Journal of Palestine Studies* 83, No. 3 (Spring 1992): 54–70.

Garfinkle, Adam. *Israel and Jordan in the Shadow of War.* New York: St. Martin's Press, 1992.

Genet, Jean. "Four Hours in Shatila." *Journal of Palestine Studies* 12, No. 3 (Spring 1983): 3–22.

Hallaj, Muhammad. "The Palestinians After the Gulf War." *American-Arab Affairs*, No. 35 (Winter 1990–91): 117–25.

———. "Taking Sides: Palestinians and the Gulf Crisis." *Journal of Palestine Studies* 79, No. 3 (Spring 1991): 41–47.

Hudson, Michael. "The Palestinian Factor in the Lebanese Civil War." *The Middle East Journal* 32, No. 3 (Summer 1978): 261–78.

Israel, Raphael. *Palestinians Between Israel and Jordan: Squaring the Triangle*. New York: Praeger, 1991.

Jansen, Michael E. *The United States and the Palestinian People.* Beirut: Institute for Palestine Studies, 1970.

———. *The Three Basic American Decisions on Palestine.* Beirut: Palestine Research Center, 1971.

Kadi, Leila S. *Arab Summit Conferences and the Palestinian Problem, 1936–50 and 1964–66.* Beirut: PLO Research Center, 1966.

Kazziha, Walid. *Palestine in the Arab Dilemma.* New York: Barnes and Noble, 1979.

Khalidi, R. "The Palestinians in Lebanon: Social Repercussions of Israel's Invasion." *Middle East Journal* 38, No. 2 (Spring 1984): 255–266.

Khalidi, Rashid and Camille Mansour, eds. *Palestine and the Gulf.* Beirut: Institute for Palestine Studies, 1982.

King Hussein. "The Jordanian-Palestinian Initiative: Mutual Recognition and Territory for Peace." *Journal of Palestine Studies* 56, No. 4 (Summer 1985): 11–22.

Lesch, Ann Mosely. *Arab Politics in Palestine, 1917–1936: The Frustration of a Nationalist Movement.* Ithaca, N.Y.: Cornell University Press, 1979.

———. "Palestinians in Kuwait." *Journal of Palestine Studies* 80, No. 4 (Summer 1991): 42–54.

Lesch, Ann Mosley and Mark Tessler. *Israel, Egypt and the Palestinians: From Camp David to Intifada.* Bloomington: Indiana University Press, 1989.

Mattar, Philip. "The PLO and the Gulf Crisis." *Middle East Journal* 48, No. 1 (Winter 1994): 31–46.

Mayer, Thomas. *Egypt and the Palestine Question, 1936–1945.* Berlin: K. Schwars, 1983.

———. "Egypt and the Arab Revolt in Palestine." *Journal of Contemporary History* 19, No. 2 (April 1984): 275–287.

Miller, Aaron David. *The Arab States and the Palestine Question: Between Ideology and Self-Interest.* New York: Praeger, 1986.

Monshipouri, Mahmood and Wallace L. Rigsbee. "Intifada: Prospects and Obstacles in the Aftermath of the Gulf Crisis." *Journal of South Asian and Middle Eastern Studies* 15, No. 2 (Winter 1991): 46–67.

Mishal, Saul. *West Bank, East Bank: The Palestinians in Jordan, 1949–1967.* New Haven, Conn.: Yale University Press, 1976.

Mousa, S. "A Matter of Principle: King Hussein of the Hijaz and the Arabs of Palestine." *International Journal of Middle East Studies* 9, No. 2 (May 1978): 183–94.

Peteet, Julie. "Socio-Political Integration and Conflict Resolution in the Palestinian Camps in Lebanon." *Journal of Palestine Studies* 62, No. 2 (Winter 1987): 29–44.

El-Sayed, Mustapha K. "Egyptian Popular Attitudes Toward the Palestinians Since 1977." *Journal of Palestine Studies* 18, No. 4 (Summer 1989): 37–51.

Sayigh, Anis. *Palestine and Arab Nationalism.* Beirut: PLO Research Center, 1970.

Sayigh, Rosemary. *Too Many Enemies: The Palestinian Experience in Lebanon.* London: Zed Books, 1994.

Sayigh, Yezid. "Reconstructing the Paradox: The Arab Nationalist Movement, Armed Struggle, and Palestine, 1951–1966." *Middle East Journal* 45, No. 4 (Autumn 1991): 608–629.

Shemesh, Moshe. *The Palestinian Entity 1959–1974: Arab Politics and the PLO.* Totowa, N.J.: Frank Cass, 1988.

Shlaim, Avi. *Collusion Across the Jordan: King Abdullah, the Zionist Movement, and the Partition of Palestine.* New York: Columbia University Press, 1988.

———. *The Politics of Partition: King Abdullah, the Zionists, and Palestine, 1921–1951.* New York: Columbia University Press, 1990.

Talhami, Ghada Hashem. *Palestine and Egyptian National Identity.* New York: Praeger, 1992.

Tibawi, Abdul Latif. *Anglo-Arab Relations and the Question of Palestine, 1914–1921.* London: Luzac, 1977.

Palestine in World Affairs

Abu-Lughod, Ibrahim and Edward W. Said. *Two Studies on the Palestinians Today and American Policy.* Detroit: Association of Arab-American University Graduates, 1976.

Adler, Stephen. "The United States and the Jerusalem Issue." *Middle East Review* 17, No. 4 (1985): 45–53.

Arakie, Margaret. *The Broken Sword of Justice: America, Israel and the Palestine Tragedy.* London: Quartet Books, 1973.

Aruri, Naseer H. Fouad Moughrabi and Joe Stork. *Reagan and the Middle East.* Belmont, Mass.: Association of Arab-American University Graduates, 1984.

Aruri, Naseer. "The United States and Palestine: Reagan's Legacy to Bush." *Journal of Palestine Studies* 71, No. 3 (Spring 1989): 3–21.

Avineri, Shlomo. "The Impact of Changes in the Soviet Union and Eastern Europe on the Arab-Israeli Conflict." *Mediterranean Quarterly* 2, No. 1 (Winter 1991): 45–57.

Ben Zvi, Abraham. *The United States and the Palestinians: The Carter Era.* Tel Aviv: Center for Strategic Studies, 1981.

Bethel, Nicholas William and Baron Bethel. *The Palestinian Triangle: The Struggle Between the British, the Jews and the Arabs, 1935–48.* London: A. Deutsch, 1979.

Buheiry, Marwan. "The Sanders Document." *Journal of Palestine Studies* 29, No. 1 (Autumn 1978): 28–40.

Cattan, Henry. *Palestine and International Law: The Legal Aspects of the Arab-Israeli Conflict.* New York: Longman, 1976.

Cheal, Beryle. "Refugees in the Gaza Strip, December 1948–May 1950." *Journal of Palestine Studies* 69, No. 1 (Autumn 1988): 138–157.

Chomsky, Noam. *The Fateful Triangle: The U.S., Israel and the Palestinians.* Boston: South End Press, 1984.

Christison, Kathleen. "The American Experience: Palestinians in the U.S." *Journal of Palestine Studies* 18, No. 4 (Summer 1989): 18–36.

———. "Splitting the Difference: The Palestinian Israeli Policy of James Baker." *Journal of Palestine Studies* 93, No. 1 (Autumn 1994): 39–50.

Cohen, Michael J. *Palestine: Retreat from the Mandate: The Making of British Policy, 1936–1945.* New York: Holmes and Meier, 1978.

———. *Palestine and the Great Powers, 1945–1948.* Princeton, N.J.: Princeton University Press, 1982.

———. "William A. Eddy, the Oil Lobby and the Palestine Problem." *Middle Eastern Studies* 30, No. 1 (January 1994): 167–180.

Cohen, Naomi W. *The Year After the Riots. American Responses to Palestine Crisis of 1929–1930* . Detroit: Wayne State University Press, 1988.

Davidson, Lawrence. "Historical Ignorance and Popular Perception: The Case of U.S. Perceptions of Palestine, 1917." *Middle East Policy* 3, No. 2 (1994): 125–148.

Dessouki, Ali. *Canadian Foreign Policy and the Palestine Problem.* Ottawa: Middle East Research Centre, 1969.

Ellis, Marc H. and Rosemary, Radford Renther, eds. *Beyond Occupa-*

tion: American Jewish, Christian, and Palestinian Voices for Peace. Boston: Beacon Press, 1990.

Farsoun, S. "The Palestinians, the PLO, and U.S. Foreign Policy." *American-Arab Affairs*, No. 1 (Summer 1982): 81–95.

Feintuch, Yossi. *U. S. Policy on Jerusalem.* Westport, Conn.: Greenwood Press, 1987.

Friedlander, Melvin A. "Ronald Reagan's Flirtation With the West Bank, 1982–88." *American-Arab Affairs* 25 (Summer 1988): 16–29.

Gerson, Allan. *Israel, the West Bank and International Law.* London: Frank Cass, 1978.

Gil-Har, Yitzhak. "British Commitments to the Arabs and their Applications to the Palestine-Trans-Jordan Boundary: The Issue of the Semakh Triangle." *Middle East Studies* 29, No. 4 (October 1993): 690–701.

Glick, Edward. *Latin America and the Palestine Problem.* New York: The Theodor Herzl Foundation, 1958.

Golan, Galia. *The Soviet Union and the Palestine Liberation Organizatin: An Uneasy Alliance.* New York: Praeger, 1980.

Gruen, George E. "Turkey's Relations with Israel and Its Neighbors." *Middle East Review* 17, No. 3 (Spring 1985): 33–43.

Hanna, Paul L. *British Policy in Palestine.* Washington: American Council on Public Affairs, 1942.

Harris, L. "China's Relations with the PLO." *Journal of Palestine Studies 7*, No. 1 (Autumn 1977): 123–53.

Hoffman, Bruce. *The Failure of British Military Strategy Within Palestine, 1939–1947.* Ramat Gan, Israel: Bar-Ilan University Press, 1983.

Jasse, Richard L. "Great Britian and Abdullah's Plan to Partition Palestine: A Natural Sorting Out?" *Middle Eastern Studies* 22, No. 4 (October 1986): 505–521.

——— "Great Britain and Palestine Toward the United Nations, 1947." *Middle Eastern Studies* 30, No. 3 (July 1994): 558–578.

Jones, Martin. *Failure in Palestine: British and United States Policy after the Second World War.* New York: Mansell, 1986.

Khalidi, R. I. *British Policy Toward Syria and Palestine 1906–1914.* London: Ithaca Press, 1980.

Kay, Zachariah. *Canada and Palestine: The Politics of Noncommitment.* Jerusalem: Israel Universities Press, 1978.

Khalidi, Rashid. *British Policy Towards Syria and Palestine, 1906–1914: A Study of the Antecedents of the Hussein-McMahon Correspondence, the Sykes-Picot Agreement, and the Balfour Declaration.* London: Ithaca Press, 1980.

Khalidi, Walid. *At a Critical Juncture: The United States and the Palestinian People.* Washington: Center for Comparative Arab Studies, 1989.

Kirisci, Kemal. *The PLO and World Politics: A Study of the Mobilization of Support for the Palestinian Cause*. New York: St. Martin's Press, 1986.

Kreutz, Andrej. "The Vatican and the Palestine Question." *Social Campus* 37, No. 3 (June 1990): 239–54.

———. *Vatican Policy on the Palestinian-Israeli Conflict: The Struggle for the Holy Land.* Westport, Conn.: Greenwood Press, 1990.

Kuniholm, Bruce R. and Michael Rubner. *The Palestinian Problem and United States Policy: A Guide to Issues and References.* Claremont, Calif.: Regina Books, 1986.

Landman, Samuel. *Great Britain, the Jews and Palestine.* London: New Zionist Press, 1936.

Mallison, W. Thomas and Sally V. Mallison. *The Palestine Problem in International Law and World Order.* Harlow, Essex: Longman, 1983.

McTague, John J. *British Policy in Palestine, 1917–1922.* Washington: University Press of America, 1983.

Mossek, M. *Palestine Immigration Policy Under Sir Herbert Samuel: British, Zionist and Arab Attitudes.* London: Frank Cass, 1978.

Nakhleh, Khalil and Clifford A. Wright. *After the Palestine-Israeli War: Limits to U.S. and Israeli Policy.* Belmont, Mass.: Institute of Arab Studies, 1983.

Neff, Donald. "U. S. Policy and the Palestinian Refugees." *Journal of Palestine Studies* 69, No. 1 (Autumn 1988): 96–11.

———. *Fallen Pillars: US Policy Towards Palestine and Israel, 1947–1994*. Washington: Institute for Palestine Studies, 1995.

Ovendale, Ritchie. *Britain, the United States, and the End of the Palestinian Mandate, 1942–1948.* Woodbridge, Suffolk: Royal Historical Society/Boydell Press, 1989.

Peck, Juliana S. *The Reagan Administration and the Palestinian Question: The First Thousand Days.* Washington: Institute for Palestine Studies, 1984.

Pranger, Robert J. *American Policy for Peace in The Middle East, 1969–1971.* Washington: American Enterprise Institute, 1971.

Quandt, William B. *The United States Policy in the Middle East: Constraints And Choices.* Santa Monica, Calif.: Rand Corporation, 1970.

———. *Decades Of Decisions: American Policy Toward the Arab-Israeli Conflict, 1967–1976.* Berkeley: University of California Press, 1977.

———. "After the Israeli-PLO Breakthrough: Next Steps for the United States." *Brookings Review* 12, No. 1 (Winter 1994): 28–35.

Quigley, John. "The Palestinian Question in International Law: A Historical Perspective." *Arab Studies Quarterly* 10, No. 1 (Winter 1988): 44–58.

Ray, Zachariah. *Canada and Palestine: The Politics of Noncommitment.* Jerusalem: Israel Universities Press, 1978.

Rolach, Livia. *The Catholic Church and the Question of Palestine.* Atlantic Highlands, N.J.: Saqi Books, 1987.

Rubenberg, Cheryl. "U. S. Policy Toward the Palestinians: A Twenty Years Assessment." *Arab Studies Quarterly* 10, No. 1 (Winter 1988): 1–43.

Said, Edward W. *The Palestine Question and the American Context.* Beirut: Institute for Palestine Studies, 1979.

Shepherd, Naomi. *The Zealous Intruders: The Western Rediscovery of Palestine.* San Francisco: Harper and Row, 1990.

Simons, Chaim. *International Proposals to Transfer Arabs from Palestine, 1895–1947: A Historical Survey.* Hoboken, N.J.: Ktav Publishing House, 1988.

Terry, Janice J. *Attitudes of United States Congressmen Toward Aid to the Palestinians and Arms to Israel.* Beirut: Palestine Research Center, 1973.

Tibawi, A. L. *British Interests in Palestine 1800–1901: A Study of Religions and Educational Enterprise.* Oxford, England: Oxford University Press, 1961.

Wasserstein, Bernard. *The British in Palestine: The Mandatory Government and the Arab-Jewish Conflict 1917–1929.* Cambridge, Mass.: B. Blackwell, 1991.

Weiler, Joseph. *Israel and the Creation of a Palestinian State—A European Perspective*. London: Croom Helm, 1985.

Wilson, Evan M. *Decision on Palestine: How the U.S. Came to Recognize Israel.* Stanford, Calif.: Hoover Institution Press, 1979.

Zweig, Ronald W. *Britain and Palestine during the Second World War.* Woodbridge, England: Boydell Press, 1986.

Palestinian Refugees

Abu-Lughod, Janet. "Palestinians: Exiles at Home and Abroad." *Current Sociology* 36, No. 2 (1988): 61–69.

Barakat, Halim. "The Palestinian Refugees: An Uprooted Community Seeking Repatriation." *International Migration Review* 7 (Summer 1973): 147–161.

Ben Porath, Yoram and Emmanuel Marx. *Some Sociological and Economic Aspects of Refugee Camps in the West Bank.* Santa Monica, Calif.: Rand Corporation, 1971.

Cossali, Paul and Clive Robson. *Stateless in Gaza*. London: Zed Press, 1986.

Dodd, Peter and Halim Barakat. *River Without Bridges: A Study of the Exodus of the 1967 Palestinian Arab Refugees.* Beirut: Institute for Palestine Studies, 1969.

Flapan, Simha. "The Palestinian Exodus, 1948." *Journal of Palestine Studies* 64, No. 4 (Summer 1987): 3–26.

Friedman, Robert I. "The Palestinian Refugees." *New York Review of Books* 37, (March 29 1990): 36–44.

Institute for Palestine Studies. *The Palestinian Refugees: A Collection of United Nations Documents:* Beirut: IPS, 1970.

Jabr, Hisham. "Housing Conditions in the Refugee Camps of the West Bank." *Journal of Refugee Studies* 2, No. 1 (1989): 75–87.

Journal of Refugee Studies. *Palestinian Refugees and Non-Refugees in the West Bank and Gaza Strip.* Oxford, England: Oxford University Press, 1989.

Kapelionk, Amnon. "New Light on the Arab-Israeli Conflict and Refugee Problems and Its Origin." *Journal of Palestine Studies* 63, No. 3 (Spring 1987): 16–24.

Lawrence, Dina and Kameel Nasr. *Children of Palestinian Refugees vs. the Israeli Military: Personal Accounts of Arrest, Detention, and Torture*. Lafayette, Calif.: BIP Publications, 1987.

Mallison, W. Thomas and Sally V. Mallison. "The Right of Return." *Journal of Palestine Studies* 35, No. 3 (Spring 1980): 125–136.

Marx, Emanuel. *Changes in Arab Refugee Camps*. Jerusalem: The Harry S. Truman Institute, Hebrew University, 1978.

———. "Palestinian Refugee Camps in the West Bank and the Gaza Strip." *Middle Eastern Studies* 28, No. 2 (April 1992): 281–294.

Morris, Benny. "Operation Dani and the Palestinian Exodus from Lydda and Ramle in 1948." *Middle East Journal* 40, No. 1 (Winter 1986): 82–110.

———. "Haifa's Arabs: Displacement and Concentration, July 1948." *Middle East Journal* 42, No. 2 (Spring 1988): 241–259.

———. *The Birth of the Palestinian Refugee Problem, 1947–1949.* Cambridge, Mass.: Cambridge University Press, 1988.

Nazzal, Nafez. *The Palestinian Exodus From Galilee, 1948.* Beirut: Institute for Palestine Studies, 1978.

Palumbo, Michael. *The Palestinian Catastrophe: The 1948 Expulsion of a People from Their Homeland.* London: Faber and Faber, 1987.

Peretz, Don. *The Palestine Arab Refugee Problem.* Santa Monica, Calif.: Rand, 1969.

———. *Palestinian Refugees and the Middle East Peace Process.* Washington: U.S. Institute of Peace, 1993.

Plascov, Avi. *The Palestinian Refugees in Jordan, 1948–1957.* London: Frank Cass, 1981.

Pryce-Jones, David. *The Face of Defeat: Palestinian Refugees and Guerrillas.* New York: Holt, Rinehart and Winston, 1972.

Sayigh, Rosemary. "The Palestinian Identity Among Camp Residents." *Journal of Palestine Studies* 23, No. 3 (Spring 1977): 3–22.

Smith, Pamela Ann "The Palestinian Diaspora, 1948–1985." *Journal of Palestine Studies* 59, No. 3 (Spring 1986): 90–108.

———. "The Exile Bourgeoisie of Palestine." *MERIP Reports* No. 142 (September–October 1986): 23–9.

Tomeh, George J. *Legal Status of Arab Refugees.* Beirut: Institute for Palestine Studies, 1969.

Turki, Fawaz. *Tel Zaatar was the Hill of Thyme.* Washington: Free Palestine Press, 1978.

Waines, David. *A Sentence of Exile: the Palestine/Israel Conflict, 1897–1977.* Wilmette, Ill: Medina Press, 1977.

Zureik, Elia. "Palestinian Refugees and Peace." *Journal of Palestine Studies* 93, No. 1 (Autumn 1994): 5–17.

The Peace Process

Abed, George T. "The Palestinians in the Peace Process: The Risks and the Opportunities." *Journal of Palestine Studies* 85, No. 1 (Autumn 1992): 5–17.

Abu Amr, Ziad. *Emerging Trends in Palestinian Strategic Political Thinking and Practice.* Jerusalem: PASSIA Publication, 1992.

———. "The View from Palestine: In the Wake of the Agreement." *Journal of Palestinian Studies* 90, No. 2 (Winter 1994): 75–83.

Al-Haj, Majid, Elihu Katz, and Samuel Shye. "Arab and Jewish Attitudes Toward a Palestinian State. *Journal of Conflict Resolution* 37, No. 4 (December 1993): 619–632.

Alin, Erika G. "West Bank and Gaza Palestinians and the Peace Process." *Critique,* No. 3 (Fall 1993): 13–34.

Alpher, Joseph and Shai Feldman, eds. *The West Bank and Gaza: Israel's Options for Peace.* Tel Aviv: The Jaffee Center for Strategic Studies, Tel Aviv University, 1989.

American Friends Service Committee, ed. *Search for Peace in the Middle East: A Report Prepared for the American Friends Service Committee.* New York: Hill and Wang, 1970.

American Friends Service Committee. *A Compassionate Peace: A Future for the Middle East—A Report Prepared for the American Friends Service Committee.* New York: Hill and Wang, 1982.

Amery, H. M. "The PLO-Israel Agreement: Implications and Opportunities." *Middle Eastern Times* 1, No. 3 (October 1993): 4–14.

Amit, Daniel J. "Strategies for Struggle, Strategies for Peace." *Journal of Palestine Studies* 47, No. 3 (Spring 1983): 23–30.

El-Asmar, Fouzi, et. al., eds. *Towards a Socialist Republic of Palestine.* London: Ithaca Press, 1978.

Aruri, Naseer H. "Early Empowerment: The Burden Not the Responsibility." *Journal of Palestine Studies* 94, No. 2 (Winter 1995): 33–39.

Avnery, Uri. *My Friend, the Enemy.* London: Zed Books, 1986.

Bailey, Sydney. *Four Arab-Israeli Wars and the Peace Process.* London: Macmillan, 1990.

Bar-Ilan, David. "Why a Palestinian State is Still a Mortal Threat." *Commentary* 96, No. 5 (November 1993): 27–31.

Bar-Siman-Tov, Yaacov. "The Arab-Israeli Conflict: Learning Conflict Resolution." *Journal of Peace Research* 1 (February 1994): 75–92.

Bargal, David. "Conflict Management Workshops for Arab Palestinians and Jewish Youth: A Framework for Planning, Intervention, and Evaluation." *Social Work With Groups* 15, No. 1 (1992): 51–68.

Benvenisti, Meron. "The Peace Process and Intercommunal Strife." *Journal of Palestine Studies* 65, No. 1 (Autumn 1987): 3–11.

———. *Intifadah, The Gulf War, The Peace Process.* Jerusalem: Keter Publishing Limited, 1992.

Berger, Elmer. *Peace for Palestine: First Lost Opportunity.* Gainesville: University Press of Florida, 1993.

Birkland, Carol. *Unified in Hope: Arabs and Jews Talk About Peace.* New York: Friendship Press, 1988.

Boyle, Francis A. "Create the State of Palestine!" *American-Arab Affairs* 25 (Summer 1988): 86–105.

Brookings Study Group on Arab-Israeli Peace. *Toward Arab-Israeli Peace: Report of a Study Group.* Washington: Brookings Institution, 1988.

Carter, Jimmy. *The Blood of Abraham.* Boston: Houghton Mifflin, 1985.

Center for Palestine Research and Studies. "The Declaration of Principles: What's in it for the Palestinians." *Palestine-Israel Journal of Politics, Economics and Culture* 1 (Winter 1994): 39–55.

Chomsky, Noam. "The Israel-Arafat Agreement." *Z Magazine* 6, No. 10 (October 1993): 19–24.

Collins, Frank. "The Post-Handshake Landscape." *Link* 27, No. 3 (July/August 1994): 1–13.

Corbin, Jane. *Gaza First: The Secret Norway Channel to Peace Between Israel and the PLO.* London: Bloomsbury Press, 1994.

Curtis, Michael. "The Uprising's Impact on the Options for Peace." *Middle East Review* 21, No. 2 (Winter 1988/89): 3–12.

Dajani, Burhan. "The September 1993 Israeli-PLO Document: A Textual Analysis." *Journal of Palestine Studies* 91, No. 3 (Spring 1994): 5–23.

Elazar, Daniel, ed. *From Autonomy to Shared Rule: Options for Judea, Samaria and Gaza.* Jerusalem: Jerusalem Center for Public Affairs, 1983.

Ellis, Marc H. "The Occupation is Over: Creating a Theological Framework for Peace." *American-Arab Affairs* 25 (Summer 1988): 113–125.

Falk, Gloria H. "Israeli Public Opinion: Looking Toward a Palestinian Solution." *Middle East Journal,* 39, No. 3 (Summer 1985): 247–769.

Fernea, Elizabeth Warnock and Mary Evelyn Hocking, eds. *The Struggle for Peace: Israelis and Palestinians.* Austin: University of Texas Press, 1992.

Fisher, Roger. *Dear Israelis, Dear Arabs.* New York: Harper and Row Publishers, 1972.

Flapan, Simha, ed. *When Enemies Dare to Talk: An Israeli-Palestinian Debate.* London: Croom Helm, 1979.

Foster, Charles. "Now What? The Brand New Palestine That Never Was." *Contemporary Review* 264, No. 1536 (January 1994): 1–8.

Fuller, Graham E. *The West Bank of Israel: Point of No Return?* Santa Monica, Calif.: The Rand Corporation, 1989.

Garfinkle, Adam. "Israeli and Palestinian Proposals for the West Bank." *Orbis* 36, No. 3 (Summer 1992): 429–442.

Glubb, John Bagot. *Peace in the Holy Land.* London: Hodder and Stoughton, 1971.

Gordon, Haim and Gorden Rivca, eds. *Israel/Palestine: The Quest for Dialogue.* Maryknoll, N.Y.: Orbis Books, 1991.

Grossman, David. *The Yellow Wind.* New York: Farrar, Straus and Giroux, 1988.

Hadar, Leon. "The Real Lesson of the Oslo Accord: Localize the Arab-Israeli Conflict." *Foreign Policy Briefing* 31, No. 9 (May 1994): 1–15.

Hammami, S. "A Palestinian Strategy for Peaceful Coexistence." *New Outlook* 18, No. 3 (March–April 1975): 56–61.

Hareven, Alouph, ed. *Can the Palestinian Problem Be Solved? Israeli Positions.* Jerusalem: The Van Leer Foundation, 1983.

Harkabi, Yehoshafat. "Choosing Between Bad and Worse." *Journal of Palestine Studies* 16, No. 3 (Spring 1987): 43–52.

———. *Israel's Fateful Hour.* Translated by Nenn Schramm. New York: Harper and Row, 1988.

Hassassian, Manuel. "From Armed Struggle to Negotiation." *Palestine-Israel Journal* 1 (Winter 1994): 15–22.

Heller, Mark and Sari Nusseibeh. *No Trumpets, No Drums: A Two State Settlement of the Israel-Palestinian Conflict.* New York: Hill and Wang, 1991.

Heller, Mark. *A Palestinian State: The Implications for Israel.* Cambridge, Mass.: Harvard University Press, 1983.

———. *The Israeli-PLO Agreement: What if it Fails? How Will We Know?* Tel Aviv: Tel Aviv University, Jaffee Center for Strategic Studies, 1994.

Honig-Parnass, T. "Palestinian-Israeli Agreement: A Defeat for Palestinian People." *New Politics* 4, No. 4 (Winter 1994): 20–33.

Hudson, Michael, ed. *Alternative Approaches to the Arab-Israeli Conflict: A Comparative Analysis of the Principal Actors.* Washington: Center for Contemporary Arab Studies, Georgetown University, 1984.

———. *The Palestinians: New Directions.* Washington: Center for Contemporary Arab Studies, Georgetown University, 1990.

Hurwitz, Deena, ed. *Walking the Red Line: Israelis in Search of Justice for Palestine.* Philadelphia: New Society Publishers, 1992.

Hussaini, H. I., ed. *Toward Peace in Palestine.* Washington: Palestine Information Office, 1978.

Inbar, Michael and Ephraim Yuchtman-Yaar. "The People's Image of Conflict Resolution: Israelis and Palestinians." *Journal of Conflict Resolution* 33, No. 1 (March 1989): 37–66.

Jaffee Center for Strategic Studies, Study Group. *Israel, the West Bank and Gaza: Toward a Solution.* Tel Aviv: Tel Aviv University, Jaffee Center for Strategic Studies, 1989.

———. *The West Bank and Gaza: Israel's Options for Peace.* Tel Aviv: Tel Aviv University, Jaffee Center for Strategic Studies, 1989.

Kadi, Leila S. *The Arab-Israeli Conflict: The Peaceful Proposals.* Beirut: Palestine Research Center, 1973.

Kaufman, Edy, Shukri B. Abed, and Robert L. Rothstein, eds. *Democracy, Peace and the Israeli-Palestinian Conflict.* Boulder, Colo.: Lynne Rienner Publishers, 1991.

Kelman, Herbert C. *Creating the Conditions for Israeli-Palestinian Negotiations.* Washington: The Wilson Center, 1981.

———. "The Palestinianization of the Arab-Israeli Conflict." *The Jerusalem Quarterly* 46 (Spring 1988): 3–15.

Khalidi, Rashid. "A Palestinian View of the Accord With Israel." *Current History* 93, No. 580 (February 1994): 67–71.

Khalidi, Walid. "Thinking the Unthinkable: A Sovereign Palestinian State." *Foreign Affairs* 59, (July 1978): 695–713.

———. "Toward Peace in the Holy Land." *Foreign Affairs* 66, No. 4 (Spring 1988): 771–789.

Laqueur, W. "Is Peace Still Possible in the Middle East? The View from Tel Aviv." *Commentary* 66, No. 1 (July 1978): 29–36.

Lesch, Ann Mosely. *Transition to Palestinian Self-Government: Practical Steps Toward Israeli-Palestinian Peace.* Bloomington: Indiana University Press, 1992.

———. "Transition to Palestinian Self-Government." *Journal of Palestine Studies* 87, No. 3 (Spring 1993): 46–56.

Mansur, Camille. "The Palestinian-Israeli Peace Negotiations: An Overview and Assessment." *Journal of Palestine Studies* 87, No. 3 (Spring 1993): 5–31.

Marantz, Paul and Janice Gross Stein, eds. *Peace-Making in the Middle East: Problems and Prospects.* Totowa, N.J.: Barnes and Noble Books, 1985.

Mehdi, M. T. *Peace In The Middle East.* New York: New World Press, 1967.

Mendelsohn, Everett. *A Compassionate Peace: A Future for Israel, Palestine, and the Middle East.* New York: Hill and Wang, 1989.

Mikhail-Ashrawi, Hanan. *From Intifada to Independence.* The Hague: The Palestine Information Office and the Arab League, 1989.

Monsour, Camille. "The Palestinian-Israeli Peace Negotiations: An Overview and Assessment." *Journal of Palestine Studies* 87, No. 3 (Spring 1993): 5–31.

Moughrabi, Fouad, et. al. "Palestinians and the Peace Process." *Journal of Palestine Studies* 21, No. 1 (Autumn 1991): 36–53.

Muslih, Muhammad. *Towards Coexistence: An Analysis of the Resolutions of the Palestine National Council.* Washington: Institute for Palestine Studies, 1990.

———. "The Shift in Palestinian Thinking." *Current History* 91, No. 561 (January 1992): 22–28.

———. "Jericho and its Meaning: A New Strategy for the Palestinians." *Current History* 93, No. 580 (February 1994): 72–77.

Nakhleh, Emile A. *The West Bank and Gaza: Toward the Making of a Palestinian State.* Washington: American Enterprise Institute, 1979.

———. "The Palestinians and the Future: Peace through Realism." *Journal of Palestine Studies* 70, No. 2 (Winter 1989): 3–15.

———. "Palestinians and Israelis: Options for Coexistence." *Journal of Palestine Studies* 22, No. 2 (Winter 1993): 5–16.

Nusseibah, Sari and Yaron Ezrahi. "Breaking the Deadlock: A Palestinian View; An Israeli View." *New York Times Magazine*, 21 (February 1988): 6–28, 30, 82, 84.

Orange, Wendy. "Dimensions of Dialogue." *Tikkun* 8, No. 6 (November/December 1993): 62–70.

Pennar, Margaret, ed. *The Middle East: Five Perspectives.* North Dartmouth, Mass.: A.A.U.G Publications, 1973.

Plascov, Avi. "A Palestinian State? Examining the Alternative." *Adelphi Papers: No. 163.* London: International Institute for Strategic Studies, 1981.

Rabinovich, Itamar. *The Road Not Taken: Early Arab-Israeli Negotiations.* New York: Oxford University Press, 1991.

Rasheed, Mohammad. *Towards a Democratic State in Palestine.* Beirut: Palestine Liberation Organization Research Center, 1970.

Reddaway, John. *"Seek Peace, and Ensure It": Selected Papers on Palestine and the Search for Peace.* London: Aldrige Print Group, 1980.

Rice, Michael. *False Inheritances: Israel in Palestine and the Search for a Solution.* London: Kegan Paul International, 1994.

Rosenwasser, Penny. *Voices from a "Promised Land": Palestinian and Israeli Peace Activists Speak Their Hearts.* Willimantic, Conn.: Curbstone Press, 1992.

Rothman, Jay. "The Human Dimension in Israeli–Palestinian Negotiations." *Jerusalem Journal of International Relations* 14, No. 3 (September 1992): 69–81.

Saunders, H. H. "An Israeli-Palestinian Peace." *Foreign Affairs* 61, No. 1 (Fall 1982): 100–121.

Sayegh, Fayez A. *Palestine, Israel and Peace.* Beirut: Palestine Research Center, 1970.

———. *Camp David and Palestine: a Preliminary Analysis.* New York: Americans for Middle East Understanding, 1978.

———. "The Camp David Agreement and the Palestinians." *Journal of Palestine Studies* 30, No. 2 (Winter 1979): 3–54.

Sayegh, Fayez A. and Sohair Soukkary. *Palestine: Concordance of United Nations Resolutions 1967–1971.* New York: New World Press, 1971.

Schiff, Ze'ev. *Security for Peace: Israel's Minimal Security Requirements in Negotiations With the Palestinians.* Washington: Washington Institute for Near East Policy, 1989.

Schnell, Izhak. "Israeli Palestinian Territorial Perceptions." *Environment and Behavior* 25 (July 1993): 419–456.

Segal, Jerome M. "A Foreign Policy for the State of Palestine." *Journal of Palestine Studies* 18, No. 2 (Winter 1989): 16–28.

———. *Creating the Palestinian State: A Strategy for Peace.* Chicago: Lawrence Hill Book, 1989.

———. *Notes on Palestinian Declaration of Independence.* Jerusalem: PASSIA Publication, 1989.

Sha'ath, Nabil. *Palestine of Tomorrow for Jews, Christians, and Muslims.* Birmingham, Ala.: Committee for Better American Relations in the Middle East, 1971.

———. "Challenges of 1992: The Palestinian Situation." *Middle East Policy* 1, No. 1 (1992): 39–45.

Shehadeh, Raja. "Negotiating Self-Government Arrangements." *Journal of Palestine Studies* 84, No. 4 (Summer 1992): 22–31.

———. "Questions of Jurisdiction: A Legal Analysis of the Gaza-Jericho Agreement." *Journal of Palestine Studies* 92, No. 4 (Summer 1994): 18–25.

Shlaim, Avi. "The Oslo Accords." *Journal of Palestine Studies* 91, No. 3 (Spring 1994): 24–40.

———. "Prelude to the Accord: Likud, Labor, and the Palestinians." *Journal of Palestine Studies* 90, No. 2 (Winter 1994): 5–19.

Shukairy, Ahmed. *Liberation-Not Negotiation.* Beirut: PLO Research Center, 1966.

Sicherman, Harvey. *Palestinian Self-Government (Autonomy): Its Past and Its Future.* Washington: Washington Institute for Near East Policy, 1991.

———. *Palestinian Autonomy, Self Government, and Peace.* Boulder, Colo.: Westview Press, 1993.

Spiegel, Steven L., ed. *The Arab-Israeli Search for Peace.* Boulder, Colo.: Lynne Rienner Publishers, 1992.

Stanly, Bruce. "Raising the Flag Over Jerusalem: The Search for a Palestinian Government." *American-Arab Affairs* 26 (Fall 1988): 9–27.

Stebbing, John. *A Structure of Peace: The Arab-Israeli Conflict.* Oxford, England: New Cherwell Press, 1993.

Ward, Richard, Don Peretz, and Evan M. Wilson. *The Palestine State: A Rational Approach.* New York: Kennikat Press, 1977.

Yorke, Valerie. "Imagining a Palestinian State: An International Security Plan." *International Affairs* (London) 66 (January 1990): 115–136.

Palestine Liberation Organization (PLO)

Alexander, Yonah and Joshua Sinai. *Terrorism: PLO Connection.* Bristol, Pa.: Crane Russak, 1989.

Amos, John W. *Palestinian Resistance: Organization of a Nationalist Movement.* New York: Pergamon Press, 1980.

Andoni, Lamis. "The PLO at the Crossroad." *Journal of Palestine Studies* 81, No. 1 (Autumn 1991): 54–65.

Aruri, Naseer H. and John J. Carroll. "A New Palestinian Charter." *Journal of Palestine Studies* 92, No. 4 (Summer 1994): 5–17.

Baum, Phil and Raphael Danziger. "A Regenerated PLO? The Palestine National Council's 1988 Resolutions and Their Repercussions." *Middle East Review* 22, No. 1 (Fall 1989): 17–25.

Becker, Jillian. *The PLO: The Rise and Fall of the Palestine Liberation Organization.* New York: St. Martin's Press, 1984.

Ben Rafael, Eliezer. *Israel–Palestine: A Guerrilla Conflict in International Politics.* New York: Greenwood Press, 1987.

Brynen, Rex. "PLO Policy in Lebanon: Legacies and Lessons." *Journal of Palestine Studies* 70, No. 2 (Winter 1989): 48–70.

———. *Sanctuary and Survival: The PLO in Lebanon.* Boulder, Colo.: Westview Press, 1990.

Chaliand, Gerard. *The Palestinian Resistance.* Baltimore: Penguin Books, 1972.

Cobban, Helena. *The Palestinian Liberation Organization: People, Power, and Politics.* New York: Columbia University Press, 1984.

———. "The PLO and the Intifada." *Middle East Journal* 44, No. 2 (Spring 1990): 207–233.

Cooley, John K. *Green March, Black September: The Story of the Palestinian Arab.* London: Frank Cass, 1973.

Crowers, Andrew and Tony Walker. *Behind the Myth: Yassir Arafat and the Palestinian Revolution.* Brooklyn, N.Y.: Olive Branch Press, 1991.

Dobson, Christopher. *Black September; Its Short, Violent History.* New York: Macmillan, 1974.

El-Rayyes, Riad and Dunia Nahas. *Guerrillas for Palestine.* London: Croom Helm, 1976.

Eytan, Z. "The Palestinian Armed Forces After Beirut." *The Jerusalem Quarterly* 32 (Summer 1984): 131–139.

Frangi, Abdallah. *The PLO and Palestine.* London: Zed Books, 1983.

Frankel, Norman. "Abu Za'im: Alternative to Yasir Arafat." *Terrorism* 11, No. 2 (1988): 151–164.

Frisch, Hillel. "The Palestinian Movement in the Territories: The Middle Command." *Middle Eastern Studies* 29, No. 2 (April 1993): 254–274.

Gabriel, Richard A. *Operation Peace for Galilee: The Israeli-PLO War in Lebanon.* New York: Hall and Wang, 1984.

Gaspard, J. "Palestine: Who's Who Among the Guerrillas." *New Middle East* 18 (March 1970): 12–17.

Gowers, Andrew and Tony Walker. *Behind the Myth: Yasir Arafat and the Palestinian Revolution.* London: Corgi, 1992.

———. *Arafat: The Biography.* London: Virgin Publishing, 1994.

Gresh, Alain. *The PLO: The Struggle Within: Towards an Independent Palestinian State.* London: Zed Books, 1988.

Harkabi, Yehoshafat. "Fedayeen Action and Arab Strategy." *Adelphi Papers 53* (1968).

———. *The Palestinian Covenant and Its Meaning.* London: Valentine Mitchell, 1981.

Hart, Alan. *Arafat: Terrorist or Peacemaker?* London: Sidgwick and Jackson, 1984.

Heradstveit, Daniel. "A Profile of the Palestine Guerrillas." *Cooperation and Conflict 7* (1972): 13–36.

Hilal, Jamil. "PLO Institutions: The Challenge Ahead." *Journal of Palestine Studies* 89, No. 1 (Autumn 1993): 46–60.

Hilleh, Frisch. "The Palestinian Movement in the Territories: The Middle Command." *Middle Eastern Studies* 29, No. 2 (April 1993): 254–274.

Hirst, David. *The Gun and the Olive Branch: The Roots of Violence in the Middle East.* New York: Harcourt Brace Jovanovich, 1977.

Hussain, Mehmood. *The Palestinian Liberation Organization*. Dehli: University Publishers, 1975.

Israeli, Raphael, ed. *PLO in Lebanon: Selected Documents.* New York: St. Martin's Press, 1983.

Jureidini, Paul A. and William E. Hazen. *The Palestinian Movement in Politics.* Lexington, Mass.: Lexington Books, 1976.

Jureidini, Paul A. *The Palestinian Revolution: Its Organizations, Ideologies, and Dynamics.* Washington: The American University, 1970.

Kadi, Leila S., ed. *Basic Political Documents of the Armed Palestinian Resistance Movement.* Beirut: Palestine Research Center, 1969.

Kamin, J. "The PLO in the Aftermath of Rebellion." *SAIS Review,* vol. 5, No. 1 (Winter–Spring 1985): 91–105.

Kelman, Herbert. *Understanding Arafat.* Tel Aviv: The International Center for Peace in the Middle East, 1983.

Khalidi, Rashid. *Under Siege: PLO Decision Making During the 1982 War.* New York: Columbia University Press, 1986.

Kiernan, Thomas. *Arafat, the Man the Myth.* New York: W. W. Norton, 1976.

Kuroda, Y. "Young Palestinian Commandos in Political Socialization Perspective." *The Middle East Journal* 26, No. 3 (Summer 1972): 253–270.

Lehn, Walter. *The Development of Palestinian Resistance.* North Dartmouth, Mass.: Association of Arab-American Graduates, 1974.

Livingstone, Neil C. and David Halevy. *Inside the PLO: Convert Units, Secret Funds, and the War Against Israel and the United States.* New York: William Morrow and Co., 1990.

Merhav, Meir, et al. *Facing the PLO Question*. Washington: Foundations for Middle East Peace, 1985.

Miller, Aaron David. *The PLO and the Politics of Survival.* New York: Praeger Publications with The Center for Strategic and International Studies, Georgetown University, 1983.

———. "The PLO and the Peace Process: The Organizational Imperative." *SAIS Review* 7, No. 1 (Winter–Spring 1987): 95–109.

Mishal, Saul. *The PLO Under Arafat: Between Gun and Olive Branch.* New Haven, Conn.: Yale University Press, 1986.

Musallem, Sami. *The Palestine Liberation Organization: Its Structure and Function.* Brattleboro, Vt.: Amana Books, 1988.

Muslih, Muhammad Y. "Moderates and Rejectionists Within the Palestine Liberation Organization." *Middle East Journal* 30, No. 2 (Spring 1976): 127–140.

Nakhleh, E. "The Anatomy of Violence: Theoretical Reflections on Palestinian Resistance." *Middle East Journal* 25, No. 2 (Spring 1971): 180–200.

Nasser, Jamal R. *The Palestine Liberation Organization: From Armed*

Struggle to the Declaration of Independence. London: Eurospan, 1992.

Norton, Augustus Richard and Martin H Greenberg, eds. *The International Relations of the Palestine Liberation Organization.* Carbondale, Ill.: Southern Illinois University Press, 1989.

O'Neill, Brad E. *Armed Struggle in Palestine: A Political-Military Analysis.* Boulder, Colo.: Westview Press, 1978.

Pipes, Daniel. "Declaring Statehood: Israel and the PLO." *Orbis* 33, No. 2 (Spring 1989): 247–259.

Price, D. "Jordan and Palestinians: The PLO's Prospects." *Conflict Studies*, No. 66 (December 1975): 525–556.

Reische, Diana L. *Arafat and the Palestine Liberation Organization.* New York: F. Watts, 1991.

Rubenberg, Cheryl A. *The Palestine Liberation Organization: Its Institutional Infrastructure.* Belmont, Mass.: Institute for Arab Studies, 1982.

Rubin, Barry M. *The Arab States and the Palestine Conflict.* Syracuse, N.Y.: Syracuse University Press, 1981

———. "The PLO's Intractable Foreign Policy." *Policy Papers 3.* Washington: Washington Institute for Near East Policy, 1985.

———. *The PLO's New Policy: Evolution Until Victory?* Washington: Washington Institute for Near East Policy, 1989.

Rubinstein, Danny. *The Mystery of Arafat.* Translated by Dan Leon. South Royalton, Vt.: Steerforth Press, 1995.

Sahliyeh, Emile. *The PLO After the Lebanon War.* Boulder, Colo.: Westview Press, 1986.

Sayigh, Rosemary. *Palestinians: From Peasants to Revolutionaries.* London: Zed Press, 1979.

Sayigh, Yezid. "Palestinian Military Performance in the 1982 War." *Journal of Palestine Studies* 48, No. 4 (Summer 1983): 3–24.

———. "Palestinian Armed Struggle: Means and Ends." *Journal of Palestine Studies* 61, No. 1 (Autumn 1986): 95–112.

———. "Struggle Within, Struggle Without: The Transformation of PLO Politics Since 1982." *International Affairs* 65, No. 2 (Spring 1989): 247–72.

———. "Turning Defeat into Opportunity: The Palestinian Guerrillas after the June 1967 War." *Middle East Journal* 46, No. 2 (Spring 1992): 244–265.

Schenker, Hillel, ed. *After Lebanon: The Israeli-Palestinian Connection.* New York: The Pilgrim Press, 1983.

———. "Deciding Not to Decide?" *New Outlook* 31, No. 2 (February 1988): 17–20.

Schiff, Zeev and Raphael Rothstein. *Fedayeen: The Story of the Palestinian Guerrillas.* London: Valentine Mitchell, 1973.

Sela, Abraham, "The PLO, the West Bank and the Gaza Strip." *Jerusalem Quarterly*, No. 8 (Summer 1978): 66–77.

Sharabi, Hisham. *Palestine Guerrillas: Their Credibility and Effectiveness.* Beirut: Institute for Palestine Studies, 1970.

Stanley, Bruce. "Fragmentation and the National Liberation Movements: The PLO." *Orbis 22* (Winter 1979): 1033–1055.

Steinberg, Matti. "The Pragmatic Stream of Thought Within the PLO According to Khalid Al-Hasen." *Jerusalem Journal of International Relations* 11, No. 1 (March 1989): 37–57.

———. "The Demographic Dimension of the Struggle With Israel—As Seen by the PLO." *Jerusalem Journal of International Relations* 11, No. 4 (December 1989): 27–51.

Wallach, Janet and John Wallach. *Arafat: In the Eyes of the Beholder.* New York: Carol Publishing Group, 1990.

Yaniv, Avner. *P.L.O.: A Profile.* Jerusalem: Israel Universities Study Group for Middle Eastern Affairs, 1974.

Yodfat, Aryeh. *PLO Strategy and Politics.* New York: St. Martin's Press, 1981.

Political Factions

Abu-Amr, Ziad. "Hamas: A Historical and Political Background." *Journal of Palestine Studies* 88, No. 4 (Summer 1993): 5–19.

———. *Islamic Fundamentalism in the West Bank and Gaza: Muslim Brotherhood and Islamic Jihad.* Bloomington: Indiana University Press, 1994.

Ahmad, Hisham H. *From Religious Salvation to Political Transformation: The Rise of Hamas in Palestinian Society.* Jerusalem: PASSIA Publication, 1994.

al-Hout, Bayan Nuweihid. "The Palestinian Political Elite During the Mandate Period." *Journal of Palestine Studies* 33, No. 1 (Autumn 1979): 85–111.

al-Jarbawi, Ali. The Position of Palestinian Islamists on the Palestine-Israel Accord." *The Muslim World* 83, Nos. 1–2 (January–April 1994): 127–154.

Bailey, Clinton. *Hamas: The Fundamentalist Challenge to the PLO.* Washington: Institute for Near East Policy Research, 1992.

Barghouti, Iyad. "Palestinian Islamists and the Middle East Peace Conference." *The International Spectator* 28, Nos. 1–2 (January–March 1993): 61–73.

Beinen, J. "The Palestine Communist Party, 1919–1948." *MERIP Reports,* No. 55 (March 1977): 3–15.

Browne, D. "The Voices of Palestine: A Broadcasting House Divided." *Middle East Journal* 29, No. 2 (Spring 1975): 133–150.

Budeiri, Musa. *The Palestine Communist Party, 1919–48: Arab and Jew in the Struggle for Internationalism.* London: Ithaca Press, 1979.

Cohen, Amnon. *Political Parties in the West Bank Under the Jordanian Regime, 1949–1967.* Ithaca: Cornell University Press, 1982.

Gershoni, I. "The Muslim Brothers and the Arab Revolt in Palestine, 1936–39." *Middle Eastern Studies* 22, No. 3 (July 1986): 367–97.

Hassassian, Manuel. *Palestine Factionalism in the National Movement, 1919–1939.* Jerusalem: PASSIA Publication, 1990.

Hentov, Jacob. *Communism and Zionism in Palestine.* Cambridge, Mass.: Schenkman Publishing Company, 1974.

Johnson, Nels. *Islam and the Politics of Meaning in Palestinian Nationalism.* London: Kegan Paul International, 1982.

Jubran, Michael and Laura Drake. "The Islamic Fundamentalist Movement in the West Bank and Gaza Strip." *Middle East Policy* 2, No. 2 (1993): 1–15.

Karmi, H. "How Holy is Palestine to the Muslims?" *Islamic Quarterly* 14, No. 2 (April–June 1970): 63–90.

Khalaf, Issa. *Politics in Palestine: Arab Factionalism and Social Disintegration, 1939–1948.* Albany: State University of New York Press, 1991.

Lesch, Ann Mosley. *Political Perceptions of the Palestinians on the West Bank and the Gaza Strip.* Washington: The Middle East Institute, 1980.

Ma'oz, Moshe. *Palestinian Leadership on the West Bank.* London: Frank Cass, 1984.

Masad, J. "Palestinians and the Limits of Radicalized Discourse." *Social Text,* No. 34 (1993): 94–114.

Miller, Sondra. *The Communist Movement in Palestine and Israel, 1919–1984.* Boulder, Colo.: Westview Press, 1986.

Milton-Edwards, Beverley. "The Concept of Jihad and the Palestinian Islamic Movement: A Comparison of Ideas and Techniques." *British Journal of Middle Eastern Studies* 19, No. 1 (1993): 48–53.

Nakhleh, Emile A. "The West Bank and Gaza: People, Perceptions and Policies." *American-Arab Affairs*, No. l (Summer 1982): 95–103.

Nakhleh, Khalil. *Indigenous Organisations in Palestine: Towards a Purposeful Societal Development.* Jerusalem: Arab Thought Forum, 1991.

Peretz, Don. "Palestinian Social Stratification: The Political Implication." *Journal of Palestine Studies* 25, No. 1 (Autumn 1977): 48–74.

———. *Intifada: The Palestinian Uprising.* Boulder, Colo.: Westview Press, 1990.

Robinson, Glenn E. "The Role of the Professional Middle Class in the Mobilization of Palestinian Society: The Medical and Agricultural

Committees." *International Journal of Middle East Studies* 25, No. 2 (May 1993): 301–326.

Rubenstein, Sondra Miller. *The Communist Movement in Palestine and Israel 1919–1984.* Boulder, Colo.: Westview Press, 1985.

Sahliyeh, Emile. "The West Bank Pragmatic Elite: The Uncertain Future." *Journal of Palestine Studies* 60, No. 4 (Summer 1986): 34–45.

———. *In Search of a Leadership: West Bank Politics Since 1967.* Washington: The Brookings Institution, 1988.

Satloff, Robert. "Islam in the Palestinian Uprising." *Orbis* 33, No. 3 (Summer 1989): 389–402.

Shadid, Mohammad K. "The Muslim Brotherhood Movement in the West Bank and Gaza." *Third World Quarterly* 10, No. 2 (April 1988): 658–682.

Shadid, Mohammad and Rick Seltzer. "Trends in Palestinian Nationalism: Moderate, Radical, and Religious Alternatives." *Journal of South Asian and Middle Eastern Studies* 9 (Summer 1988): 54–69.

———. "Political Attitudes of Palestinians in the West Bank and Gaza Strip." *Middle East Journal* 42, No. 1 (Winter 1988): 16–32.

———. "Growth in Islamic Fundamentalism: The Case of Palestine." *Sociological Analysis* 50, No. 3 (1989): 291–298.

———. "Student-Youth Differences Among Palestinians in the West Bank." *Youth and Society* 20, No. 4 (1989): 445–60.

Shemesh, M. "The West Bank: Rise and Decline of Traditional Leadership, June 1967 to October 1973." *Middle Eastern Studies* 20, No. 3 (July 1984): 290–323.

Talhami, Ghada. "Islamic Fundamentalism and the Palestinians." *The Muslim World* 78, No. 3–4 (July-October 1988): 173–188.

Tessler, M. "Secularism in the Middle East? Reflections on Recent Palestinian Proposals." *Ethnicity* 2, No. 2 (January 1975): 178–203.

The Palestinian Arabs in Israel

Amun, Hasan, et. al. *Palestinian Arabs in Israel: The Two Case Studies.* London: Ithaca Press, 1977.

El-Asmar, Fouzi. *To Be an Arab in Israel.* Beirut: Institute for Palestine Studies, 1978.

Bertelsen, Judy. *The Palestinian Arabs, A Non-State Nation System Analysis*. Beverly Hills, Calif.: Sage Publications, 1976.

Chacour, Elias and Mary E. Jensen. *We Belong to the Land: The Story of a Palestinian Israeli Who Lives for Peace and Reconciliation.* San Francisco: Harper Collins, 1990.

Douglas-Home, Charles. *The Arabs and Israel.* London: The Bodley Head, 1968.

Eliachar, Elie. *Israeli Jews and Palestinian Arabs: Key to Arab-Jewish Co-existence.* Jerusalem: Council of the Sephardi Community, 1970.

Falah, Ghazi. "Israelization of Palestine Human Geography." *Progress in Human Geography* 13, No. 4 (December 1989): 535–550.

Grossman, David. *Sleeping on a Wire: Conversations with Palestinians in Israel.* New York: Farrar, Straus and Giroux, 1993.

Hofman, J. E., et al. *Arab-Jewish Relations in Israel: A Quest in Human Understanding.* Bristol, Ind.: Wyndham Press, 1988.

Jiryis, Sabri. *The Arabs In Israel.* Beirut: Institute for Palestine Studies, 1969.

Lustick, Ian. *Arabs in the Jewish State: Israel's Control of a National Minority.* Austin: University of Texas Press, 1980.

Marks, Shannee. *Where is Palestine? The Arabs in Israel.* London: Pluto Press, 1984.

Masalha, Nur. (trans. and ed.). *The Palestinians in Israel: Is Israel the State of All Its Citizens and "Absentees"?* Haifa: Galilee Center for Social Research, 1993.

Nakhleh, K. *Palestinian Dilemma: Nationalist Consciousness and University Education in Israel.* Belmont, Mass.: Association of Arab-American University Graduates, 1979.

Rekess, E. "Israeli Arabs and the Arabs of the West Bank and Gaza: Political Affinity and National Solidarity." *Asian and African Studies* 23, Nos. 2–3 (1989): 119–154.

Rouhana, Nadim. "The Political Transformation of the Palestinians in Israel." *Journal of Palestine Studies* 18, No. 3 (Spring 1989): 38–59.

Scholch, Alexander, ed. *Palestinian Over the Green Line: Studies on Relations Between Palestinians on Both Sides of the 1949 Armistice Line Since 1967.* London: Ithaca Press, 1983.

Shahak, Israel, ed. *The Non-Jew in the Jewish State. A Collection of Documents.* Jerusalem, 1975.

Smooha, Sammy. *The Orientation and Politicization of the Arab Minority in Israel.* Haifa: University of Haifa, 1978.

Zureik, Elias. *The Palestinians in Israel: A Study in Internal Colonialism.* London: Routledge and Kegan Paul, 1979.

United Nations and Palestine

Beker, Avi. "UN North-South Politics and the Arab-Israeli Conflict." *The Jerusalem Journal of International Relations* 10, No. 1 (March 1988): 44–59.

Bite, Vita. *The United Nations and Jerusalem.* Washington: Foreign Affairs and National Defense Division, 1984.

Buehrig, Edward H. *The U.N. and the Palestinian Refugees: A Study in Non-Territorial Administration.* Bloomington: Indiana University Press, 1971.

———. "The U.N., the U.S. and Palestine." *Middle East Journal* 33, No. 4 (Autumn 1979): 435–444.

Gordenker, Leon, "The United Nations as a Third Party in Israeli-Arab Conflicts." The *Jerusalem Journal of International Relations* 10, No. 1 (March 1988): 60–76.

Hadawi, Sami, ed. *United Nations Resolutions on Palestine, 1947–1965.* Beirut: Institute for Palestine Studies, 1965.

Howley, Dennis C. *United Nations and Palestine.* New York: Exposition Press, 1975.

Institute for Palestine Studies. *Jerusalem: A Collection of United Nations Documents.* Beirut: Institute for Palestine Studies, 1970.

———. *United Nations Resolutions on Palestine and the Arab-Israeli Conflict.* Washington: Institute for Palestine Studies, 1987.

Magnes, Judah Leon. *Palestine—Divided or United?: The Case for a Bi-National Palestine Before the United Nations.* Westport, Colo.: Greenwood Press, 1983.

Musallam, Sami. *United Nations Resolutions on Palestine, 1947–1972.* Beirut: Institute for Palestine Studies, 1973.

Nuseibeh, Hazem Zaki. *Palestine and the United Nations.* New York: Quartet Books, 1981.

Pelcovits, Nathan A. "Uses of U.N. Peacekeeping on Arab-Israeli Fronts: Will Changing Power Relations Improve the Prospects." *The Jerusalem Journal of International Relations* 10, No. 1 (March 1988): 77–113.

———. *The Long Armistice: U.N. Peacekeeping and the Arab-Israeli Conflict, 1948–1960.* Boulder, Colo.: Westview Press, 1993.

Rivlin, Benjamin. "Changing Perspectives on Internationalism at the United Nations: The Impact of the Ideological Factor on the Arab-Israeli Dispute." *The Jerusalem Journal of Internal Relations* 10, No. 1 (March 1988): 1–11.

Sayegh, Fayez A. and Sohair Soukkary. *Palestine: Concordance of United Nations Resolutions 1967–1971.* New York: New World Press, 1971.

Schiff, Benjamin N. "Between Occupier and Occupied: UNRWA in the West Bank and the Gaza Strip." *Journal of Palestine Studies* 71, No. 3 (Spring 1989): 38–59.

Schoenberg, Harris O. *A Mandate for Terror: The U.N. and the PLO.* New York: Shapolsky Publishers, 1987.

Tomeh, George J., ed. *United Nations Resolutions on Palestine and the Arab-Israeli Conflict, 1943–1974.* Beirut: Institute for Palestine Studies, 1974.

United Nations. *The Origins and Evolution of the Palestine Problem.* New York: United Nations, 1984.

United Nations Department of Public Information. *Prospects for Peace in the Middle East: An Israeli-Palestinian Dialogue.* New York: United Nations Department of Public Information, 1992.

Viorst, Milton. *Reaching for the Olive Branch: UNRWA and Peace in the Middle East.* Bloomington: Indiana University Press, 1989.

Jerusalem

Abdul Hadi, Mahdi. *Thoughts on Israel's Policies and Practices in Jerusalem.* Cambridge, Mass.: Harvard University Press, 1985.

Albin, Cecilia. *The Conflict Over Jerusalem: Some Palestinian Responses to Concepts of Dispute Resolution.* Jerusalem: PASSIA Publication, 1990.

———. "Negotiating Indivisible Goods: The Case of Jerusalem." *The Jerusalem Journal of International Relations* 13, No. 1 (1991): 45–76.

Amirav, Moshe and Hanna Siniora. "Jerusalem: Resolving the Unresolvable." *International Spectator* 27, No. 3 (July–September 1992): 3–24.

Asali, Kamel J., ed. *Jerusalem in History.* London: Scorpion Publishing, 1989.

Ashkenasi, Abraham. *Opinion Trends Among Jerusalem Palestinians.* Jerusalem: Leonard Davis Institute, Hebrew University, 1990.

Barzilai, Yousef. "Jerusalem, August 1929 (A Memoir)". *The Jerusalem Quarterly* , No. 46 (Spring 1988): 16–32.

Benvenisti, Meron. *Jerusalem: The Torn City*. Minneapolis: The University of Minnesota Press, 1976.

———. "Some Guidelines for Positive Thinking on Jerusalem." *Middle East Review* 13, Nos. 3–4 (Spring/Summer 1981): 35–40.

———. *Jerusalem: A Study of a Polarised Community*. Jerusalem: West Bank Data Base Project, 1983.

———. "Two Generations: Growing Up in Jerusalem." *The New York Times Magazine* 16 (October 1988): 35–36, 66–72.

Bovis, H. Eugene. *The Jerusalem Question, 1917–1968.* Stanford, Calif.: Hoover Institution Press, 1971.

Brecher, M. "Jerusalem: Israel's Political Decisions, 1947–1977." *The Middle East Journal* 32, No. 1 (Winter 1978): 13–34.

Brown, A. and J. de Jong. *Recreating East Jerusalem*. Jerusalem: Palestine Human Rights Information Center, 1992.

Cattan, Henry. *Jerusalem.* New York: St. Martin's Press, 1981.

———."The Status of Jerusalem Under International Law and United Nations Resolutions." *Journal of Palestine Studies* 39, No. 3 (Spring 1981): 3–15.

Cohen, Shaul Ephraim. "Jerusalem: A Geopolitical Imperative." *Midstream* 21, No. 5 (May 1975): 18–32.

———. *The Politics of Planting: Israeli-Palestinian Competition for Control of Land in the Jerusalem Periphery.* Chicago: The University of Chicago Press, 1993.

Cohen, Yona. *Jerusalem Under Siege*. Los Angeles: Ridgefield Publishing Company, 1982.

Dumper, Michael. "Israeli Settlement in the Old City of Jerusalem." *Journal of Palestine Studies* 21, No. 4 (Summer 1992): 32–53.

———. "Jerusalem's Infrastructure: Is Annexation Irreversible?" *Journal of Palestine Studies* 87, No. 3 (Spring 1993): 78–95.

Elon, Amos. *Jerusalem: City of Mirrors.* London: George Weidenfeld and Nicolson, 1989.

Ferrari, Silvio. "The Holy See and the Postwar Palestine Issue: The Internationalization of Jerusalem and the Protection of the Holy Places." *International Affairs* 60, No. 2 (Spring 1984): 261–283.

———. "The Vatican, Israel and the Jerusalem Question, 1943–1984." *Middle East Journal* 39, No. 2 (Spring 1985): 316–322.

Gray, John. *A History of Jerusalem.* New York: Praeger, 1969.

Husseini, Hassan Jamal. *Return to Jerusalem.* London: Quartet Books, 1989.

Hyman, B., et al. *Jerusalem in Transition-Urban Growth and Change, 1970s–1980.* Jerusalem: The Jerusalem Institute for Israel Studies, 1985.

Ingram, O. Kelly, ed. *Jerusalem: Key to Peace in the Middle East*. Durham, N.C.: Triangle Friends of the Middle East, 1978.

Kark, Ruth. *Jerusalem Neighborhoods: Planning and By-Laws, 1855–1930.* Jerusalem: Magnes Press, 1991.

———. "A Communication: Ottoman Policy and U.S. Attitudes Regarding Land Purchase and Settlement by American Jews in Palestine." *Studies in Zionism* 14, No. 2 (August 1993): 211–218.

Khalidi, Rashid. "The Future of Arab Jerusalem." *British Journal of Middle Eastern Studies* 19, No. 2 (1992): 133–43.

———. "Ottoman Notables in Jerusalem: Nationalism and Other Options." *The Muslim World* 83, Nos. 1–2 (January–April 1994): 1–18.

Khatib, Khaled A. *The Conservation of Jerusalem*. Jerusalem: PASSIA Publication, 1993.

Kimhi, I., S. Reichmann and J. Schwaid. *Metropolitan Area of Jerusalem: The Urban Development of Metropolitan Jerusalem.* Jerusalem: The Jerusalem Institute for Israel Studies, 1984.

———. *Arab Settlement in the Metropolitan Area of Jerusalem.* Jerusalem: The Jerusalem Institute for Israel Studies, 1986.

Kollek, Teddy. "Jerusalem." *Foreign Affairs* 55, No. 4 (July 1977): 701–716.

———. "Jerusalem: Present and Future." *Foreign Affairs* 59, No. 5 (1981): 1040–1049.

———. "Sharing United Jerusalem." *Foreign Affairs* 67, No. 7 (1988): 156–168.

———. *One Man's Jerusalem.* London: Weidenfeld and Nicholson, 1990.

Kraemer, J. L., ed. *Jerusalem: Problems and Prospects.* New York: Praeger, 1980.

Kutcher, Arthur. *The New Jerusalem—Planning and Politics.* London: Thomas and Hudson, 1973.

Lapp, John A. *The View from East Jerusalem.* Scottsdale, Pa.: Herald Press, 1980.

Littke, Grant. "The Jerusalem Dispute: Settlement Proposals and Prospects." *Middle East Focus* 10, No. 4 (1988): 11–26.

Levin, Harry. *Jerusalem Enthralled: A Diary of a City Under Siege.* London: Victor Gollancz, Ltd., 1950.

Litwin, Howard. "Neighborhood Self-Management in Jerusalem: Planning Issues and Implementation Dilemmas." *Administration and Society* 25, No. 3 (November 1993): 335–352.

Lustick, Ian S. "Reinventing Jerusalem." *Foreign Policy* 93 (Winter 1993–1994): 41–59.

Maguire, Kate. *The Israelisation of Jerusalem.* London: Arab Research Center, 1981.

Mansour, Atallah and Ernest Stock. "Arab Jerusalem After Annexation." *New Outlook* 14, No. 1 (January 1971): 22–36.

Mattar, Ibrahim. "From Palestinian to Israeli: Jerusalem 1948–1982." *Journal of Palestine Studies* 48, No. 4 (Summer 1983): 57–63.

Medzizi, Meron. "The International Relations of Jerusalem." *The Center Magazine* 18 (January-February 1985): 41–50.

Moskin, Robert J. *Among Lions: The Battle for Jerusalem, June 5–7, 1967.* New York: Arbor House, 1982.

Neff, Donald. *Warriors for Jerusalem: Six Days That Changed the Middle East.* Brattleboro, Vt.: Amana Press, 1988.

———. "Struggle Over Jerusalem." *American-Arab Affairs*, No. 23 (Winter 1987–88): 15–23.

Pfaff, Richard H. *Jerusalem: Keystone of an Arab-Israeli Settlement.* Washington: American Enterprise for Public Policy Research, 1969.

Rabinovich, Abraham. *The Battle for Jerusalem, June 5–7, 1967.* Philadelphia: The Jewish Publication Society, 1987.

Romann, Michael and Alex Weingrad. *Living Together Separately, Arabs and Jews in Contemporary Jerusalem.* Princeton, N.J.: Princeton University Press, 1991.

Rose, John H. Melkon. *Armenians of Jerusalem: Memories of Life in Palestine.* London: Radcliffe, 1993.

Schleifer, Abdullah. *The Fall Of Jerusalem.* New York: Monthly Review Press, 1972.

Soffer, N. "The Political Status of Jerusalem in the Hashemite Kingdom of Jordan, 1948–1967." *Middle Eastern Studies* 12, No. 1 (January 1976): 73–94.

Tibawi, Abdul Latif. *Jerusalem: Its Place in Islam and Arab History.* Beirut: Institute for Palestine Studies, 1969.

———. "Special Report: The Destruction of an Islamic Heritage in Jerusalem." *Arab Studies Quarterly* 2, No. 2 (Spring 1980): 180–201.

Tomeh, George J. *Jerusalem at the United Nations.* Beirut: Palestine Research Center, 1974.

Tsimhoni, Daphne. "Demographic Trends of the Christian Population in Jerusalem and the West Bank, 1948–1978." *Middle East Journal* 37, No. 1 (Winter 1983): 54–64.

Wilson, Evan M. *Jerusalem: Key To Peace.* Washington: Middle East Institute, 1970.

———. "The Question of Jerusalem." *American Arab Affairs,* No. 1 (Summer 1982): 111–119.

Appendix A
Declaration of Palestinian Independence

In the name of God, the Compassionate, the Merciful.

Palestine, the Land of the three monotheistic faiths, is where the Palestinian Arab People were born, on which it grew, developed and excelled. The Palestinian people were never separated from or diminished in its integral bond with Palestine. Thus, the Palestinian Arab People ensured for itself an everlasting union between itself, its land and its history.

Resolute throughout that history, the Palestinian Arab people forged its national identity, rising even to unimagined levels in its defense, as invasion, the design of others, and the special appeal of Palestine's ancient and luminous place on that eminence where powers and civilizations are joined—all this intervened thereby to deprive the people of its political independence. Yet the undying connection between Palestine and its people, secured for the land its character, and for the people its national spirit.

Nourished by an unfolding series of civilizations and cultures, inspired by a heritage rich in variety and kind, the Palestinian Arab People added to its stature by consolidating a union between itself and its patrimonial land. The call went out from Temple, Church and Mosque that to praise the Creator, to celebrate compassion and peace, was indeed the message of Palestine. And in generation after generation, the Palestinian Arab people gave of itself unsparingly in the valiant battle for liberation and homeland. For what has been the unbroken chain of our people's rebellion but the heroic embodiment of our will for national independence? And so the people was sustained in the struggle to stay and to prevail.

When in the course of modern times a new order of values was declared with norms and values fair for all, it was the Palestinian Arab people that had been excluded from the destiny of all other peoples by a hostile array of local and foreign powers. Yet again had unaided justice been revealed as insufficient to drive the world's history along its preferred course.

And it was the Palestinian people, already wounded in its body, that was submitted to yet another type of occupation over which floated the falsehood that "Palestine was a land without a people." This notion was foisted upon some in the world, whereas in Article 22 of the Covenant of the League of Nations (1919) and in the Treaty of Lausanne (1923) the community of nations had recognized that all the Arab territories, including Palestine, of the formerly Ottoman provinces were to have granted to them their freedom as provisionally independent nations.

Despite the historical injustice inflicted on the Palestinian Arab people resulting in their dispersion and depriving them of their right to self-determination, following upon U.N. General Assembly Resolution 181 (1947), which partitioned Palestine into two states, one Arab, one Jewish, yet it is this resolution that still provides those conditions of international legitimacy that ensure the right of the Palestinian Arab people to sovereignty and national independence.

By stages, the occupation of Palestine and parts of other Arab territories by Israeli forces, the willed dispossession and expulsion from their ancestral homes of the majority of Palestine's civilian inhabitants was achieved by organized terror; those Palestinians who remained, as a vestige subjugated in its homeland, were persecuted and forced to endure the destruction of their national life.

Thus were principles of international legitimacy violated. Thus were the Charter of the United Nations and its resolutions disfigured, for they had recognized the Palestinian Arab people's national rights, including the right of return, the right of independence, the right to sovereignty over territory and homeland.

In Palestine and on its perimeters, in exile distant and near, the Palestinian Arab people never faltered and never abandoned its conviction in its right of return and independence. Occupation, massacres, and dispersion achieved no gain in the unabated Palestinian consciousness of self and political identity, as Palestinians went forward with their destiny, undeterred and unbowed. And from out of the long years of trial in ever-mounting struggle, the Palestinian political identity emerged further consolidated and confirmed. And the collective Palestinian national will forge for itself a political embodiment, the Palestine Liberation Organization, its sole, legitimate representative recognized by the world community as a whole, as well as by related regional and international institutions. Standing on the very rock of conviction in the Palestinian people's inalienable rights, and on the ground of Arab national consensus, and of international legitimacy, the PLO led the campaigns of its great people, moulded into unity and powerful resolve, one and indivisible in its triumphs, even as it suffered massacres and confinement within and without its home. And so Palestinian resistance was clarified and raised into the forefront of Arab and world awareness, as the struggle of the Palestinian Arab people achieved unique prominence among the world's liberation movements in the modern era.

The massive national uprising, the Intifada, now intensifying in cumulative scope and power on occupied Palestinian territories, as well as the unflinching resistance of the refugee camps outside the homeland, have elevated consciousness of the Palestinian truth and right into still higher realms of comprehension and actuality. Now, at last, the curtain has been dropped around a whole epoch of prevarication and negation.

The Intifada has set siege to the mind of official Israel, which has for too long relied exclusively upon myth and terror to deny Palestinian existence altogether. Because of the Intifada and its revolutionary irreversible impulse, the history of Palestine has therefore arrived at a decisive juncture.

Whereas the Palestinian people reaffirms most definitely its inalienable rights in the land of its patrimony:

Now by virtue of natural right, and the exercise of those rights historical and legal, and the sacrifice of successive generations who gave of themselves in defense of the freedom and independence of their homeland;

In pursuance of resolutions adopted by the Arab Summit Conferences and relying on the authority bestowed by international legitimacy as embodied in the resolutions of the United Nations Organization since 1947;

And in exercise by the Palestinian Arab people of its right to self-determination, political independence, and sovereignty over its territory.

The Palestine National Council, in the name of God, and in the name of the Palestinian Arab People, hereby proclaims the establishment of the State of Palestine on our Palestinian territory with its capital Jerusalem (Al-Quds Ash-Sharif).

The State of Palestine is the state of Palestinians wherever they may be. The state is for them to enjoy in it their collective national and cultural identity, theirs to pursue in it a complete equality of rights. In it will be safeguarded their political and religious convictions and their human dignity by means of a parliamentary democratic system of governance, itself based on freedom of expression and the freedom to form parties. The rights of minorities will duly be respected by the majority, as minorities must abide by decisions of the majority. Governance will be based on principles of social justice, equality and non-discrimination in public rights, on grounds of race, religion, color, or sex under the aegis of a constitution which ensures the rule of law and an independent judiciary. Thus shall these principles allow no departure from Palestine's age-old spiritual and civilizational heritage of religious tolerance and coexistence.

The State of Palestine is an Arab state, an integral and indivisible part of the Arab nation, at one with that nation in heritage and civilization, with it also in its aspiration for liberation, progress, democracy and unity. The State of Palestine affirms its obligation to abide by the Charter of the League of Arab States, whereby the coordination of the Arab state with each other shall be strengthened. It calls upon Arab compatriots to consolidate and enhance the emergence in reality of our state, to mobilize potential and to intensify efforts whose goal is to end Israeli occupation.

The State of Palestine proclaims its commitment to the principles and purposes of the United Nations and to the Universal Declaration of Human Rights. It proclaims its commitment as well to the principles and policies of the Non-Aligned Movement.

It further announces itself to be a peace-loving state, in adherence to the principles of peaceful coexistence. It will join with all states and peoples in order to assure a permanent peace based upon justice and the respect of rights so that humanity's potential for well-being may be assured, an earnest competition for excellence maintained, and in which confidence in the future will eliminate fear for those who are just and for whom justice is the only recourse.

In the context of its struggle for peace in the Land of Love and Peace, the State of Palestine calls upon the United Nations to bear special responsibility for the Palestinian Arab people and its homeland. It calls upon all peace-and-freedom loving peoples and states to assist it in the attainment of its objectives, to provide it with security, to alleviate the tragedy of its people, and to help it terminate Israel's occupation of the Palestinian territories.

The State of Palestine herewith declares that it believes in the settlement of regional and international disputes by peaceful means, in accordance with the United Nations Charter and resolutions. Without prejudice to its natural right to defend its territorial integrity and independence, it therefore rejects the threat of use of force, violence, and terrorism against its territorial integrity, or political independence, as it also rejects their use against the territorial integrity of other states.

Therefore, on this day unlike all others, November 15, 1988, as we stand at the threshold of a new dawn, in all honor and modesty we humbly bow to the sacred spirits of our fallen ones, Palestinian and Arab, by the purity of whose sacrifice for the homeland our sky has been illuminated and our land given life. Our hearts are lifted up and irradiated by the light emanating from the much-blessed Intifada, from those who have endured and have fought the fight of the camps, of dispersion, of exile, from those who have borne the standard of freedom, our children, our aged, our youths, our prisoners, detainees, and wounded, all those whose ties to our sacred soil are confirmed in camp, village, and town. We render special tribute to that brave Palestinian woman, guardian of sustenance and life, keeper of our people's perennial flame. To the souls of our sainted martyrs, to the whole of our Palestinian Arab People, to all free and honorable peoples everywhere, we pledge that our struggle shall be continued until the occupation ends, and the foundation of our sovereignty and independence shall be fortified accordingly.

Therefore, we call upon our great people to rally to the banner of Palestine, to cherish and defend it, so that it may forever be the symbol of our freedom and dignity in that homeland, which is the homeland for the free, now and always.

In the name of God, the Compassionate, the Merciful, say: "O God, Master of the Kingdom,

Thou givest the Kingdom, To whom Thou wilt and seizes the Kingdom from whom Thou wilt. Thou exaltest whom Thou wilt and Thou abasest whom Thou wilt; in Thy hand is the good; Thou art powerful over everything."

Sadaqa Alahu Al-Azim. (God the almighty speak the truth).

Appendix B
Declaration of Principles

The Government of the State of Israel and the PLO team (in the Jordanian-Palestinian delegation to the Middle East Peace Conference) (the "Palestinian Delegation"), representing the Palestinian people, agree that it is time to put an end to decades of confrontation and conflict, recognize their mutual legitimate and political rights, and strive to live in peaceful coexistence and mutual dignity and security and achieve a just, lasting, and comprehensive peace settlement and historic reconciliation through the agreed political process. Accordingly, the two sides agree to the following principles:

ARTICLE I
AIM OF THE NEGOTIATIONS

The aim of the Israeli-Palestinian negotiations within the current Middle East peace process is, among other things, to establish a Palestinian Interim Self-Governing Authority, the elected Council (the "Council"), for the Palestinian people in the West Bank and the Gaza Strip, for a transitional period not exceeding five years, leading to a permanent settlement based on Security Council Resolutions 242 and 238.

It is understood that the interim arrangements are an integral part of the whole peace process and that the negotiations on the permanent status will lead to the implementation of Security Council Resolutions 242 and 338.

ARTICLE II
FRAMEWORK FOR THE INTERIM PERIOD

The agreed framework for the interim period is set forth in this Declaration of Principles.

ARTICLE III
ELECTIONS

1. In order that the Palestinian people in the West Bank and Gaza Strip may govern themselves according to democratic principles, direct,

free, and general political elections will be held for the Council under agreed supervision and international observation, while the Palestinian police will ensure public order.

2. An agreement will be concluded on the exact mode and conditions of the elections in accordance with the protocol attached as Annex I, with the goal of holding the elections not later than nine months after the entry into force of this Declaration of Principles.

3. These elections will constitute a significant interim preparatory step toward the realization of the legitimate rights of the Palestinian people and their just requirements.

ARTICLE IV
JURISDICTION

Jurisdiction of the Council will cover West Bank and Gaza Strip territory, except for issues that will be negotiated in the permanent status negotiations. The two sides view the West Bank and the Gaza Strip as a single territorial unit, whose integrity will be preserved during the interim period.

ARTICLE V
TRANSITIONAL PERIOD AND PERMANENT STATUS NEGOTIATIONS

1. The five-year transitional period will begin upon the withdrawal from the Gaza Strip and Jericho area.

2. Permanent status negotiations will commence as soon as possible, but no later than the beginning of the third year of the interim period, between the Government of Israel and the Palestinian people representatives.

3. It is understood that these negotiations shall cover remaining issues, including: Jerusalem, refugees, settlements, security arrangements, borders, relations, and cooperation with other neighbors, and other issues of common interest.

4. The two parties agree that the outcome of the permanent status negotiations should not be prejudiced or preempted by agreements reached for the interim period.

ARTICLE VI
PREPARATORY TRANSFER OF POWERS AND RESPONSIBILITIES

1. Upon the entry into force of this Declaration of Principles and the withdrawal from the Gaza Strip and the Jericho area, a transfer of authority from the Israeli military government and its Civil Administration

to the authorized Palestinians for this task, as detailed herein, will commence. This transfer of authority will be of a preparatory nature until the inauguration of the Council.

2. Immediately after the entry into force of this Declaration of Principles and the withdrawal from the Gaza Strip and Jericho area, with the view to promoting economic development in the West Bank and Gaza Strip, authority will be transferred to the Palestinians on the following spheres: education and culture, health, social welfare, direct taxation, and tourism. The Palestinian side will commence in building the Palestinian police force, as agreed upon. Pending the inauguration of the Council, the two parties may negotiate the transfer of additional powers and responsibilities, as agreed upon.

ARTICLE VII
INTERIM AGREEMENT

1. The Israeli and Palestinian delegations will negotiate an agreement on the interim period (the "Interim Agreement").

2. The Interim Agreement shall specify, among other things, the structure of the Council, the number of its members, and the transfer of powers and responsibilities from the Israeli military government and its Civil Administration to the Council. The Interim Agreement shall also specify the Council's executive authority, legislative authority in accordance with Article IX below, and the independent Palestinian judicial organs.

3. The Interim Agreement shall include the arrangements, to be implemented upon the inauguration of the Council, for the assumption by the Council of all the powers and responsibilities transferred previously in accordance with Article VI above.

4. In order to enable the Council to promote economic growth, upon its inauguration, the Council will establish, among other things, a Palestinian Electricity Authority, a Gaza Sea Port Authority, a Palestinian Development Bank, a Palestinian Export Promotion Board, a Palestinian Environmental Authority, a Palestinian Land Authority and a Palestinian Water Administration Authority, and any other Authorities agreed upon, in accordance with the Interim Agreement that will specify their powers and responsibilities.

5. After the inauguration of the Council, the Civil Administration will be dissolved, and the Israeli military government will be withdrawn.

ARTICLE VIII
PUBLIC ORDER AND SECURITY

In order to guarantee public order and internal security for the Palestinans of the West Bank and the Gaza Strip, the Council will establish a strong police force, while Israel will continue to carry the responsibility for defending against external threats, as well as the responsibility for overall security of Israelis for the purpose of safeguarding their internal security and public order.

ARTICLE IX
LAW AND MILITARY ORDERS

1. The Council will be empowered to legislate in accordance with the Interim Agreement, within all authorities transferred to it.
2. Both parties will review jointly laws and military orders presently in force in remaining spheres.

ARTICLE X
JOINT ISRAELI-PALESTINIAN LIAISON COMMITTEE

In order to provide for a smooth implementation of this Declaration of Principles and any subsequent agreements pertaining to the interim period, upon the entry into force of this Declaration of Principles, a joint Israeli-Palestinian Liaison Committee will be established in order to deal with issues requiring coordination, other issues of common interest, and disputes.

ARTICLE XI
ISRAELI-PALESTINIAN COOPERATION IN ECONOMIC FIELDS

Recognizing the mutual benefit of cooperation in promoting the development of the West Bank, the Gaza Strip, and Israel, upon the entry into force of this Declaration of Principles, an Israeli-Palestinian Economic Cooperation Committee will be established in order to develop and implement in a cooperative manner the programs identified in the protocols attached as Annex III and Annex IV.

ARTICLE XII
LIAISON AND COOPERATION WITH JORDAN AND EGYPT

The two parties will invite the Government of Jordan and Egypt to participate in establishing further liaison and cooperation arrangements between the Government of Israel and the Palestinian representatives, on the one hand, and the Governments of Jordan and Egypt, on the other hand, to promote cooperation between them. These arrangements will include the constitution of a Continuing Committee that will decide by agreement on the modalities of admission of persons displaced from the West Bank and Gaza Strip in 1967, together with necessary measures to prevent disruption and disorder. Other matters of common concern will be dealt with by this Committee.

ARTICLE XIII
REDEPLOYMENT OF ISRAELI FORCES

1. After the entry into force of this Declaration of Principles, and not later than the eve of elections for the Council, a redeployment of Israeli military forces in the West Bank and the Gaza Strip will take place, in addition to withdrawal of Israeli forces carried out in accordance with Article XIV.

2. In redeploying its military forces, Israel will be guided by the principle that its military forces should be redeployed ouside populated areas.

3. Further redeployments to specified locations will be gradually implemented commensurate with the assumption of responsibility for public order and internal security by the Palestinian police force pursuant to Article VIII above.

ARTICLE XIV
ISRAELI WITHDRAWAL FROM THE GAZA STRIP AND JERICHO

Israel will withdraw from the Gaza Strip and Jericho area, as detailed in the protocol attached as Annex II.

ARTICLE XV
RESOLUTIONS OF DISPUTES

1. Disputes arising out of the application or interpretation of this Declaration of Principles, or any subsequent agreements pertaining to the interim period, shall be resolved by negotiations through the Joint Liaison Committee to be established pursuant to Article X above.

2. Disputes which cannot be settled by negotiations may be resolved by a mechanism of conciliation to be agreed upon by the parties.

3. The parties may agree to submit to arbitration disputes relating to the interim period, which cannot be settled through conciliation. To this end, upon the agreement of both parties, the parties will establish an Arbitration Committee.

ARTICLE XVI
ISRAELI-PALESTINIAN COOPERATION CONCERNING REGIONAL PROGRAMS

Both parties view the multilateral working groups as an appropriate instrument for promoting a "Marshall Plan," the regional programs and other programs, including special programs for the West Bank and the Gaza Strip, as indicated in the protocol attached as Annex IV.

ARTICLE XVII
MISCELLANEOUS PROVISIONS

1. This Declaration of Principles will enter into force one month after its signing.

2. All protocols annexed to this Declaration of Principles and Agreed Minutes pertaining thereto shall be regarded as an integral part hereof.

The Declaration of Principles also includes four Annexes and an addendum of explanations for the articles: Annex I is the protocol on the mode and conditions of elections. Annex II is on the protocol of the withdrawal of Israeli forces from the Gaza Strip and the Jericho area. Annex III is the protocol on Israeli-Palestinian cooperation in economic and development programs. Annex IV is the protocol on Israeli-Palestinian cooperation concerning regional development programs.

About the Authors

Nafez Nazzal was born in Palestine. He received his B.A. from the State University of New York, Albany, in 1967, and an M.A. from SUNY in political science in 1969. He received a Ph.D. in Middle East History from Georgetown University in 1974.

While a student, Nazzal was a research assistant for the New York State Senate. After completing his master's degree, he joined the faculty of York College of Pennsylvania and remained there until 1971. After he received his Ph.D., he joined the faculty of the University of Benghazi, the Libyan Arab Republic. In 1975, he taught at Birzeit University in the West Bank, where he was appointed the chairman of the Middle East Studies Department. Currently, Professor Nazzal teaches at Brigham Young University, Jerusalem Center for Near Eastern Studies.

Dr. Nazzal has been a visiting professor at the University of Pennsylvania, the University of California in Los Angeles, and the University of Southern California. He also has been a fellow at Harvard University's Center for International Affairs, the Aspen Institute for Humanistic Studies, the Institute for East-West Security Studies, the Middle East Research Institute of the University of Pennsylvania, the International Security Studies Program of the Woodrow Wilson Center, and the Salzburg Seminar. Professor Nazzal is the author of *The Palestinian Exodus from the Galilee, 1948.* He has had articles published in many books and periodicals and has contributed papers at various conferences.

Laila Ahed Nazzal was born in Palestine. She studied at the Quaker Friends School in Ramallah, and attended Birzeit University for a year before leaving to the United States to study at the University of Tennessee at Knoxville, where she received her B.A. and M.A. in sociology. After completing her master's degree, she returned to the West Bank in 1976, and joined the faculty of Birzeit University. In 1982, she attended the University of Pennsylvania and was awarded her Ph.D. in sociology in 1986. Currently, she teaches at Brigham Young University, Jerusalem Center for Near Eastern Studies.

Professor Nazzal has been a visiting professor at the University of

California in Los Angeles and the Tantur Ecumenical Institute for Theological Studies in Jerusalem, and has been a fellow at the Aspen Institute for Humanistic Studies and the Salzburg Seminar. She has contributed many papers at various conferences, and has lectured at several universities.